ACADIAN
AWAKENINGS

William D. Gerrior

Routes & Roots • International Links • An Acadian Family in Exile

Port Royal
Publishing Limited

Copyright © 2003
All rights reserved. Except for the quotation of short passages for review purposes, no part of this publication may be reproduced in any form without prior permission of the author.

Layout and Design: Richard Rogers, Brenda Conroy
Editing: Michèle Raymond

Cover Design: Min Landry, Wink Design: paintings on left of cover: Nelson Surette, Yarmouth Nova Scotia: "Lay Waste" and "The Return"; painting on right of cover: L. Dunham, France, courtesy of Michèle Touret, Présidente de l'Association de La Maison de L'Acadie et de L'Association de l'Acadie, naissance d'un Peuple. Photo of 15th century church at la Chaussée by Suzanne (Gerrior) Williams, daughter of the author.
Cover of the New Brunswick book shown on back cover: Design by Min Landry, Wink Design: Sculpture, "Awakenings" by Marie Hélène Allain, Girouard descendant, Ste-Marie-de-Kent, New Brunswick.
Cover of Louisiana book shown on back cover: Design by Min Landry Wink Design, Painting: "Crawfishing on the Bayou" by Ida Belle (Girouard) Pesson, Broussard, Louisiana.

Spine Logo: Awakenings sculpture icon identifying each book in the series of Acadian Awakenings: sculptured by Marie Hélène Allain.

National Library of Canada Cataloguing in Publication
Gerrior, William D. (William Dawson), 1944-
    Acadian Awakenings: Roots & Routes, International connections / William D. Gerrior.

Includes bibliographical references.
Contents: v. 1. France & Port Royal — v. 2. Nova Scotia and
    Prince Edward Island — v. 3. New Brunswick — v. 4. Québec —
    v. 5. Louisiana.
ISBN 0-9730781-6-2 (set).—ISBN 0-9730781-1-1 (v. 1).—
ISBN 0-9730781-2-X (v. 2).—ISBN 0-9730781-3-8 (v. 3).—
ISBN 0-9730781-4-6 (v. 4).—ISBN 0-9730781-5-4 (v. 5)

    1. Acadians—History. 2. Acadians—Biography. 3. Girouard family. 4. Acadians—Migrations—History. I. Title.

FC2042.A1G47 2002   971.5'004114   C2002-905370-6
F1036.8.G47 2002

Acknowledgements

First and foremost, to my wife, Audrey and my children Suzanne and Steve-thank you for the unselfish sacrifice of your time in allowing me to work through my long obsession while still growing in our love as a family through many rich experiences, with each new acquaintance in this exciting world of family ancestry and Acadian culture. Also a special thanks to all my cousins and friends in Larry's River, Charlos Cove, Lundy and Port Felix, N. S. for their constant support in many ways throughout the many years of research and reunion events.

This work has been the result of twenty years of research and sharing with descendants, related interest groups, organizations, historians and genealogists, resulting in rich cultural experiences, locally and on an international scale. This sharing included: host families during my research; correspondents (via letters and surveys); reunion committees in Louisiana, New Brunswick, Québec, France, and Nova Scotia; participants at many international family reunions; financial support via patrons who are listed in the appendix; numerous descendants who shared genealogy, stories and photos; many family genealogists, numerous descendants who were interviewed; all of my own family and their great support throughout the years, especially at family reunion gatherings, providing excellent music with our musician friends: Tom Rusinak; Marcel and Sharon Aucoin, Mike Gillis; Rhythm 'N' Roots; Harmony; The River Band; the constant support of very close family friends; dance troupe under the direction of my sister, Marie Nugent and many other family entertainers;   the French group, *Heritage* and the French Department of the Halifax Regional School Board; the support of various writing groups in this board linked with Masters' programs in writing at Mount St. Vincent University, Halifax; the encouragement of a national group of writers from England and their counterpart from Canada of which I was a member. Madame Michèle Touret, France former Directrice of the Syndicate d'Initiative (Tourist Bureau in Loudun, France) for all her assistance, and the warm hospitality of both she and her husband, Jean Touret who was recently elected Mayor of Loudun; Baudouin de la Bouillerie, and his wife Marie (Giroire) Bouillerie, France, owners of la Château Bonnetièrre on the cover of this book, Guy Secq for his organization of the Giroir(e) family in France soon after my visits; Gaston Giroire, France, for his genealogy work and correspondence; Centre d'études acadiennes, Université de Moncton, New Brunswick , in particular, the support of Stephen A White, Professional Genealogist, for his personal interest and professional assistance; Ronald-Gilles LeBlanc, archivist, New Brunswick for his kind assistance; Régis Brun, archivist/author, for kindly sharing part of his research; Paul Surette, Dieppe, New Brunswick, historian/author, for his personal and professional assistance and encouragement, Dr. Sally Ross, Tantallon, Nova Scotia, for her keen observations and helpful suggestions in the final stages and for of her writing of the forward of this book; Dr. Neil Boucher, Vice President, Université Sainte-Anne, region of Clare, Nova Scotia, and fellow member of the Board of Directors of the CMA2004, for sharing a part of his research and his encouragement and assistance; Léopold Lanctôt, Ottawa, author, for sharing a part of his research and his encouragement and assistance; web page entrepreneurs, and specialists, Michael Girouard and Pierre Girouard. Steven Williams, Robert Currie; Nova Scotia Museum, in particular David Christianson, Curator of Archaeology, and Scott Robinson, Curator, Collection Management; Environment Canada Parks Service in particular Wayne Kerr, Interpretation Specialists and Regan Oliver, Resource Technician; Tupperville (Giroir Vill/Girouard Village) School Museum Committee in the Annapolis River region near Port Royal under the direction of chairperson, Marion Inglis; Donna Doucet, Directrice of the Grand Pré National Historic Site and her assistant, Joycelyn Comeau for their constant support and encouragement over many years and in particular, during my workshops presentations held on this historic site during their annual Acadian Day celebrations; Dr. Barbara LeBlanc, professor /author, Université Sainte-Anne for her continuous support, interest and encouragement; Marc Veilleux, President of EdiConseil, Inc. et Editions du Libre-Echange, Québec, and William Trueman of the same company for their kind assistance; James Boxall, Head Curator Map and Geospatial Information Collection, Killam Library, Dalhousie University; Gary Shutlak, Senior Archivist, Provincial Archives of Nova Scotia; Novacadie Tours, under the direction of Richard Laurin for his direct involvement and support in the recent Port Royal research; Jonathan Fowler for his archaeology interest and support at Tupperville (Giroir Vill/Girouard Village in the 1600s and early 1700s) and his keen initiative regarding this project; Teacher, Ron Robichaud for initiating and directing a student map project for Giroir Vill/Girouard Village at Tupperville via Marcel Gilinas a senior student at Nova Scotia Community College (Centre of Geographic Sciences); Port Royal 1605-2005 Organization, under the direction of David Kern, President, for his interest and support; many artists, Nelson Surette, Claude Picard, Louis Parker, Azor Vienneau, Margaretha van Gurp, and Evelyn Oakley, Janie (Inglis) Barkhouse as well as video production entrepreneurs, CBC television documentary producers under the direction of Paul-Émile Comeau; Julia and Nelson Surette,Yarmouth County for Nelson's beautiful paintings on the cover of this book; and Daniel Comeau for his constant belief and encouragement throughout many years of my research; Pauline d'Entrement, West Pubnico, for her kind hospitality and support during a series of workshops which I presented for families in this region, and also presentations for the families in Yarmouth County area, under the direction of Cyrille LeBlanc; the *Courrier*, the only French newspaper in Nova Scotia, under the direction of Denise Comeau-Desautels, for carrying many stories concerning my research and related work. A special thanks to Dr. Henri Dominique Paratte, Editions of Grand Pré, who during the first seven years of the publishing process gave his valuable time, expertise and advice. Also special thanks to Richard Rogers, Glen Margaret Publishing, and the technology expertise of Brenda Conroy as well as the helpful suggestions and editing in the pre publishing stage, by Michèle, H. Raymond preparing for final layout and editing, Paul McCormick for map drawings; Min Landry, Wink Design, for the beautiful covers of all five books in this series–all under the direction of Richard Rogers whose experience, skill, expertise and team work are largely responsible for the actual realization of this project; descendants who assisted with editing and/or translations in the first draft of the pre-publishing editing stage: Paul Girouard, the late, Brad Pellerin, Rita (Girouard) Kay, Bernice Campbell, Carol (Gerrior) Finch, Anne Marie Long, Christine (Morin) Oderkirk, Jean Le Jeune, Fr. Conrad P. Giroir, all of the Maritime provinces; teacher colleagues, Monique Arsenault and Rima Majaess for their assistance with translations in earlier stages of the book; C. J. Malton, computer consultant and her assistance with charts; Craig Brigley, cartographer, for a number of maps throughout all books in the series, Brad Comeau for original master chart and committee photo layout and design, in collaboration with Arnold Hughes photography services- all under the direction of Bill Gerrior, Port Royal Publishing Limited; Mary Jane Siracusa of Louisiana for her initiative, hospitality, genealogy work, chairperson of the Louisiana Reunions; to Maurice Girouard, Fernand Girouard, president and Vice President of the New Brunswick Girouard, Giroir, Gerrior…Family Association, as well as Joanne Godin and all her Girouard committee in Néguac, New Brunswick, and Paul Girouard Vice President of the Gerrior, Girouard…Family Organization of Nova Scotia- to all committee members of these organizations and all other associations promoting family history, heritage and culture in North America and France, with whom I have been in contact; Cécile, Amand, Amande Girouard and their French-Canadian reunion committee members as well as Judge Jean Girouard; Gabriel Girouard and Richard Ste-Marie-all with roots in the province of Québec; the Federation of Acadians Nova Scotia (of Nouvelle Ecosse), (FANE) for their constant support; the Congrès mondial acadien 2004 (the World Congress of Acadians 2004) and all the board of Directors with whom I have the pleasure of working, and whose high ideals concerning the culture and history of all Acadians, are promoted in this book.

To all of the Girouard, Giroir, and Giroire descendants in France, from both the Acadian and the French Canadian branches and the Belgium branches in Québec, and all the other Acadian and Cajun branches of Girouards, Giroir(e)… in North America who shared this dream with me. To all my cousins near and far-thank you for sharing, making this book a reality and an indispensable part of our international heritage, history and culture. We certainly can feel proud of sharing this among ourselves and other Acadian families, other interested readers, and with many generations to come. Vive la Vie! (To Life!) Laissez les bons temps rouler! (Let the good times roll! - a Cajun Louisiana favorite expression).

Credits

Margaretha van Gurp

Margaretha (Margaret) van Gurp is the principle artist for sketches throughout all five books in this series. She was born in Delft, Holland and began her art studies as a young girl. In 1953 she came to Canada. Margaretha, resides in Halifax, Nova Scotia. She has a family of six children. She paints, draws and sculpts, specializing in portraiture for which she has studied at the Art Student's League in New York. The artist has participated in many juried group exhibitions. She taught Pottery at the Halifax School of Pottery and at Holland College, P.E.I. She also gives workshops to art associations and artists groups. Her work can be found in many private and corporate collections, including a permanent collection at the Art Gallery in Nova Scotia. A special thanks to Margaretha van Gurp for her wonderful talent.

Maps: Maps on page 250 and 286 reproduced and designed by Craig Brigley. All other maps, unless otherwise indicated were reproduced and designed by Paul Mc Cormick. Research and concept of all maps unless otherwise indicated are by Bill Gerrior, the author.

Paintings: Lewis Parker, Claude Picard, Azor Vienneau, Nelson Surette, Terry MacDonald. Sketches: Margaretha van Gurp, Evelyn (Gerrior) Oakley, Janie (Inglis)Barkhouse.

Forward

Bill Gerrior is a modest, soft-spoken and extremely likeable man who, over the past twenty years, has been relentlessly pursuing the threads that connect the countless individuals of the huge Gerrior-Girroir-Giroir(e)-Girouard family. He has developed a unique system of master charts to link internationally the 12 generations of this Acadian family that first settled in Port-Royal. He has travelled, met relatives, made friends and done research in Nova Scotia, New Brunswick, Prince Edward Island, Québec, Louisiana and France. He was instrumental in bringing together hundreds of members of this family at the first Maritime Provinces Reunion in 1985 and at the first International Reunion in 1990. Through his tireless efforts, Bill Gerrior has given innumerable people a sense of belonging not only to a family, but to history.

Acadian Awakenings is, as the subtitle "Roots and Routes" suggests, a personal and collective journey in time and space. The structure of this book is based on the interweaving of three main storylines: the development of a passion, the piecing together of the Gerrior-Girroir-Giroir(e)-Girouard mosaic, and the history of a people. The first story takes the form of a diary that chronicles the author's increasingly consuming passion for genealogical research. It provides wonderful, and often very moving, descriptions of his travels in search of his roots. With each new discovery or fruitful encounter, the author is energized and his quest becomes more meaningful. As a reader, I could not help but share in the excitement of his first meeting with Madame Michèle Touret, Director of the Tourist Bureau in Loudun, France. Thanks to her enthusiasm and generosity, Bill made all sorts of interesting connections. Part of the excitement, of course, was due to the fact that François Girouard – the patriarch of the Gerrior-Girroir-Giroir(e)-Girouard family in Acadie – probably originated from the Loudun area. Although the exact date and circumstances of his departure from France are not known, it is thought that he arrived in Port-Royal around 1640. Did he arrive with his wife Jeanne Aucoin? Or did they marry on this side of the Atlantic? Whatever the answer, Bill has nevertheless walked on the piece of land on which they built their homestead. He has also traced, to the present day, descendants from each of their five children and most of their descendants.

Using George Mitchell's map and other documents, he was also able to locate the site of the homestead of Jacques Girouard, the eldest son François Girouard and Jeanne Aucoin. Like many other second generation Acadians, Jacques moved away from his parents' home in Port-Royal. He founded the settlement that came to be known as Girouard Ville (Girouard Village) – now called Tupperville, situated about 10 miles east of present-day Annapolis Royal. In 1984, Bill and his son, Stephen, visited the farm that occupies the land once owned by their ancestors. That they were welcomed to explore the farm is a true testimony of Bill Gerrior's special gift for making connections. It is also a reflection of the openness of Mrs. Marion Inglis whose family owned the farm since 1777. The pages in which Bill describes his visit to this farm are very thought-provoking. We can but hope that archeological digs will some day reveal more about the material culture of this pre-

Deportation Girouard settlement.

As one might expect, the settlement patterns and the voluntary and forced migrations of the Girouard family mirror those of other Acadian families. By the early 1750s, like other Acadians, a number of Girouards had moved out of mainland Nova Scotia. Thanks to Sieur de la Roque's detailed census of 1752, we learn, for example, that Louis-Paul Girouard and his wife Marie Thibodeau were living near Malpèque on what is known today as Prince Edward Island. They escaped deportation and, like many other families, took refuge along the Bay of Chaleurs. After the hostilities were over, they eventually were able to make their way south to settle in Bouctouche, New Brunswick. It is interesting to note that one of Louis-Paul Girouard's descendants established the " Girouard" branch in Louisiana.

Although Grand-Pré has come to symbolize the Deportation, the removal of Acadians actually began at Fort Beauséjour. The list of prisoners at Fort Beauséjour includes Jean-Baptiste Girouard, the direct ancestor of all the Gerriors/Girroirs in Antigonish and Guysborough Counties. Two of Jean-Baptiste Girouard's brothers were among the Acadian Girouard branches established in Québec.

Descendants of François Girouard and Jeanne Aucoin living in mainland Nova Scotia were loaded onto transport ships and deported to various colonies along the eastern seaboard. Some found themselves in more far flung destinations like the West Indies and France. For over twenty years, Bill Gerrior has dedicated himself to the daunting task of bringing together, not only in charts but in reality, all the pieces of this family, shattered and dispersed during the Deportation years. *Acadian Awakenings* is a very visual and tangible celebration of a family that was part of history and that has contributed to history. Bill Gerrior has succeeded in sharing his passion and validating the importance of family connections.

Sally Ross, co-author of *The Acadians of Nova Scotia, Past and Present* and author of *Les écoles acadiennes de la Nouvelle-Écosse, 1758-2000*.

Dedications

To my wife and children

Neither the family reunions nor this book, and the four others to follow would have been possible without my wife's constant support and unselfish sharing of precious family time. To my wife, Audrey, and our children, Stephen and Suzanne, who also share my dream, a deep, heartfelt thank you. Also thank you, on behalf of all descendants and readers around the world, whom this work may reach.

Back: Steve, Bill, and Suzanne   Front: Audrey

To my parents and grandparents

The author's parents:
Mary Beatrice Fougère of Poulamon, near D'Escousse, Isle Madame, NS
John S. Gerrior, b. Larry's River, Guysborough County, NS

The author's paternal grandmother and grandfather: Annie Fougère and Jeffrey Gerrior, both of Larry's River, Guysborough County, NS

The author's maternal grandmother: Laura Doiron, Port Royal, Isle Madame, NS
The author's maternal grandfather: Wilfred Fougère, Poulamon, near D'Escousse, Isle Madame, NS

To my paternal great-grandparents

The author's paternal great-grandmother: Sophie Pellerin, Larry's River, NS, and great-grandfather: William A. Gerrior, Justice of the Peace, Larry's River, NS.

Heredity
By Oliver Wendell Holmes (1809-1894)
Chief Justice, U.S. Supreme Court

What is called my character, or nature, is made up of infinite particles of inherited tendencies from my ancestors—those whose blood runs in my veins. A little seed of laziness comes from one grandparent and of prodigality from the other one. One of them may have been a moody person and a pessimist, while another was a jovial nature who always saw the sunny side of every event. One may have had a most satisfactory life as a philosopher; while another ambitious one never was content with actual conditions whatever they were. Some remote grandmother, perhaps has stamped me with a fear of dogs and love of horses. There may be in me a bit of outlawry from some pirate forefather and a dash of piety from one who was a Saint.

My so-called peculiarities: my gestures, my eyes and my mannerisms, I borrowed from all without any exception. So everything in me passes on through my children. I am sewn between ancestry and posterity. I am a drop of water in the flowing river of time; a molecule in the mountain; a cell in a great family tree.

As we enter life we find all these fears and fancies; likes and dislikes, dispositions and temperament already made in the human beehive, and crawl into them so that they become a part of our true fibre, part of our personal texture, part of our frame and body.

This is our birthmark; this is our heritage.

To all our ancestors and cousins near and far, as represented by the following poem

THE GIROUARDS, NOS ANCETRES
　 __ Author unknown
Ils sont venus du vieux pays de France
En cette terre nouvelle et indomptée.
Ils ont buché, labouré, irrigué,
Au bords des fleuves, ils se sont implantés.
Ils ont vaincu la foret et la neige.
Les Girouards, nos ancêtres.

Il y a trois siècles en sol de Nouvelle-France
Malgré le froid, le vent, la giboulée
Ils ont construit, combattu, défriché.
À leurs enfants, ils ont su inculquer
Le grand amour de ce pays immense.
Les Girouards, nos ancêtres

Comme de beaux arbes, aux racines profondes,
Ils ont grandi, se sont développé,
Et de leurs troncs solides, équilibrés
Leurs descendants se sont multipliés.
Ils ont peuplé ces blancs arpents de neige.
Les Girouards, nos ancêtres.

Ces pionniers, en terre de Nouvelle-France
Par trop souvent, on les a oublié.
En ignorant hommes et femmes du passé
On croyait bien pouvoir s'émanciper,
Mais ils inspirent nos rêves, nos espérances.
Les Girouard , nos ancêtres.
—*Author unknown. The copy which I originally received in French was provided by Girouard descendant Emilie Perkinson, New Brunswick.*

THE GIROUARDS, OUR ANCESTORS

They came from the old country of France
To this new and untamed land.
They hewed, laboured, irrigated,
They settled by the riverside.
They conquered the forest and the snow,
The Girouards, our ancestors.

Three centuries ago, on the soil of New France
In spite of the cold, the wind, the downpours,
They struggled, cleared, constructed.
In their children they knew how to instill
A great love for this vast country.
The Girouards our ancestors.

Like beautiful trees, with deep roots,
They grew, they developed,
And from their solid stable trunks
Their descendants multiplied.
They populated these white acres of snow.
The Girouards, our ancestors.

Too often, we have forgotten them
These pioneers, in the land of New France.
By ignoring the men and women of old
We thought we could be liberated,
But they inspired our dreams, our hopes.
The Girouards, our ancestors.
    —*Trans. Rita (Girouard) Kay*
—*Author unknown*

This poem, while dedicated to the Girouards, could also apply to all Acadians with a slight change to the last lines:

"The Acadians, our ancestors"

Contents

PREFACE 16
Background leading up to the writing of this book-the process! 16

INTRODUCTION 31
MASTER CHARTS and HOW TO USE THEM 34

FAMILY NAME 47
Girouard, Giroir, Giroire, Gerrior: How many spellings? 47
A Germanic origin, from the north of Europe? 48
A Latin origin, from the south of Europe? 48
An occupational origin? 48
Which is the most likely? 49

COAT OF ARMS 49
Did the Girouards have a coat of arms? 49
What do coats of arms mean? 50
The First Girouard Coat of Arms 50
The second Girouard coat of arms 51
The third coat of arms 51
Central and Western France 52

I FRANCE 53
Roots & Routes 53
1989 - Second Trip to France 122

II PORT ROYAL AND OLD ACADIE 149
THE SETTLEMENT AT PORT ROYAL 149
The First Generation: François Girouard and Jeanne Aucoin Port Royal 182
The Second Generation: Extended Family, and the Aucoin link Port Royal,
    Grand Pré and Beaubassin 186
Third Generation of the Acadian Master Chart 209
The Fourth Generation of the Acadian Master Chart 224
The Deportation 247
(1755-1763) 247
Deportation from Ile St-Jean (second phase of Deportation) 264
1758 264

DEPORTATION DESTINATIONS 269
From the Past: The Acadians 270
Banished from Canada in 1755, they looked to Connecticut for succor. They
    didn't find much! 270

EPILOGUE 309
Giroir Vill/Girouard Village 309
 (Tupperville) Today 309
Conclusion: 340
International Family Reunion 1990 342
Preface Endnotes 365
Introduction Endnotes 365
Family Endnotes 365
France Endnotes 365
Port Royal and old Acadie Endnotes 367
Endnotes for Port Royal Captions 376

Appendix 1 Patrons ********With special thanks 379
Appendix 2 Subchart # Cross Reference to Master Chart Block 386
Appendix 3 Reference for each Block of the Acadian Master Chart 387
Appendix 4 Placide Gaudets Notes for Port Royal Map 1733 410
Appendix 5 Sample Subcharts- Early generations refer to Ancestors in 417
Port Royal and Old Acadie as indicated in the text. 417
Appendix 6 Girouard/Girroir/Gerrior etc. Names and Locations 441
Appendix 7 Letters, Surveys and Newsclips in Preparation For 443
7A- The First Maritime Provinces Family Reunion,1985 443
7B- The First International Family Reunion, 1990 443
Appendix 8 Alphabetical Index for All Charts 468

Preface

Background leading up to the writing of this book-the process!

February, 1981, Brookside, Nova Scotia. As a mathematics and social studies teacher, I was working as a teaching Principal at Shatford Memorial School in Hubbards, Nova Scotia. To allow my grade six students to become more familiar with ways to discover the past, I arranged a trip to the Provincial Archives of Nova Scotia in Halifax. As students were looking up their family name in the card index file, I happened to see an article written by my own kin, "the Gerriors" by a descendant, Mary Weekes.

Little did I know then that her article would start me on a trail that would keep me busy, while still teaching and working as a school administrator, for the next 20 years. I am sure the research and data collected would be more than enough for a thesis in Acadian and Canadian history, although academics might not grant such. I had an obsession with genealogy and its relation to present day, and spent my time organizing family reunions and contributing to permanent links between all those members of interconnected families named Girouard, Girroir(e), Gerrior..., and many other spellings. I also did not forget to include the many Girouard women descendants who often obtained and passed on other names through marriage, because of our patrilineal structures over the last few centuries.

Since then, while exploring ceaselessly the maze of genealogy, learning to be an author, to be edited and published, I've also made an important discovery: those "Girouard" roots that my "Gerrior" routes led me to, were also, first and foremost for me, *Acadian* roots, *des racines acadiennes*. I was not only a North American, a citizen of Canada, a Nova Scotian by birth and heritage: I also had deeper roots, going back to France, and reshaped on this continent into a unique culture, cut short in its development in the 1750s, but still very much alive. Without knowing it, I was embarking with Mary Weekes on a journey similar to Monique LeBlanc with her film *The Acadian link, Le lien acadien* (released in 1995), discovering not only my own roots, but also those of many other descendants in North America, in Europe, and the world over. We all had a link to that Girouard, Giroir(e)... original thread, although the name could be spelled in so many different ways, including the version which was mine, "Gerrior". Before 1981, I had heard many stories passed on through oral tradition, but seeing Mary Weekes' article represented the first time I had actually seen something significant in print with respect to the Gerrior family heritage and culture.

Mary Weekes, I have since learned, was the daughter of David John Gerrior and Liza Reddy of Tracadie (N.S.) She's a descendant of Joseph Nicholas Girroir [AMC Block E-5]. We shared a common ancestor in Tracadie: Jean Baptiste Gerrior, father of Joseph-Nicholas on the master chart, although I did not know this at the time. In an article from the *Dalhousie Review*, published in Halifax, she described the Gerriors/Girroirs as "superb horsemen", noted for their fine breed of horses, trotter and carriage horses. As an old resident put it:

Preface

> "The Gerriors were born on the saddle and cut their teeth on the stirrups". She went on to define those Gerriors/Girroirs, especially the men, as "a hardy, ruthless breed, intolerant of restraint", with "a toughness of character, a strength of purpose, and intelligent ability that even the constant dilution of the strain with milder blood could not weaken".

For the first time, I discovered how those stalwart young Gerriors, my ancestors and cousins, began migrating to the States, some to sail out of ports like Gloucester, Salem and Marblehead, some to accept, for the first time, to work for other masters than themselves in factories and lumber camps. Those Girroir/Gerrior men and women though had retained some of the indomitable spirit of independence that had marked Acadian culture in the 17th and 18th centuries, and made it so different from life in feudal Europe at the time. Like others of French-Canadian or Acadian origin moving in great numbers to the New England states to earn a better living for themselves and their families, they were not completely absorbed into the "melting pot".

The more I read Mary Weekes' prose, the more it confirmed what oral tradition in my direct line had taught me. She writes in the same article for example:

> With hard-earned American money secure in the pockets of their flannel shirts, the Gerrior men would return in the summer to their own loved land — so tenacious was the breed — to cut and store their hay (in their absence, the women and the children cared for the stock and cultivated gardens) and in the winter, the fishing men would come back for wood-cutting.

Needless to say, even though many had retained their abilities as farmers, from the old Acadian tradition they had in Poitou, France and later in what is now the Annapolis Valley, Nova Scotia, the tradition of many of the Gerriors was the sea. Perhaps some were seafaring ancestors in the Poitou region as well. "The salt sea was in their blood", wrote my guide into this Gerrior world, which I now had to discover. From the same source Mary Weekes writes:

> Never did the Gerrior men forsake the sea completely or give up laying keel for a vessel...Their calling was ships, which they laid and finished and sailed into open seas. Twenty-one was the common age for a man to have built his own ship and to captain and sail it. It is on record that a young Gerrior, at the age of 16, cut timbers for a vessel, built it and steered it into different ports.

Being a Gerrior, how could so many remarks fail to catch my immediate attention? Unaware, I had caught the bug. Luckily, my family did not know it or they might have tried to cure it immediately! Retracing your ancestors and long-forgotten family ties can get the best of you. Was it really the need for seafaring adventure in my genes? I was about to embark on a long voyage, without knowing then where it would lead me. When you sail for uncharted lands in genealogy, you're not only looking for yourself — you are searching for your own identity, but that identity only becomes defined through others and ironically you become totally absorbed in this quest of others while searching for your own identity.

I had brought my students to the archives... and now I had the bug myself! From that point on, I spent all my summers at the archives searching through microfilm, censuses, court records, crown land grants, for clues to the Girouard connections back to Port Royal in Acadie. For me, at the time, it felt like looking for a needle in the haystack. Starting from the earliest records, whenever I observed a Girouard, Giroir name, I just recorded its reference and copied the data in my three ring binder, having no idea how any of those loose, small pieces would fit together. This is not the recommended approach for a direct line research but I was interested in both the direct line and all its offshoots. I just kept gathering reams and reams of data, studying and analyzing them each night. Then, pieces started to fit together and gradually, a broader picture started to take shape. Academics would probably never grant me such a title, but I began to feel like a "real" historian. I was not only following well-known paths, I was orienteering through the genealogical jungle with my partially completed master chart to keep me on course. I was therefore following many unknown paths and making connections for the first time in history resulting in new historical facts and new information for all of us to share — I was recreating history! Very often I would find myself slipping into the past and imagining myself being right there, in those early pioneer days, with no engines and no roads, neither electric lights nor fridges, without any TVs or even radios, deprived of the computer that had become such a part of my life.

Simultaneously, I was off by myself, with my hardtop trailer and three-ring binder interviewing relatives, visiting Gerrior families throughout Nova Scotia, gathering as many facts as I could from the present day, back as far as I could go. This process also included research of church records in Nova Scotia communities of Larry's River, Charles Cove, Port Felix (records at Canso), Tracadie, and West Arichat, as well as records in Prince Edward Island. Leaving few stones unturned, I was scouring all the cemeteries in these areas where the Gerriors had settled. I now had a full-fledged case of what my family and many genealogists refer to as the "Genealogy pox". Symptoms were clear. I continually complained as to my need for other dates and new places. With a blank expression, somewhat deaf to spouse and children, I had no more taste for work of any kind except looking through records at libraries, churches, court houses, writing letters, frequenting strange places such as cemeteries, ruins, and remote desolate areas, and making secret long distance phone calls. I would start to swear at the mailman for never bringing the mail I needed (no e-mail then), I would hide phone bills from my spouse. Mumbling to myself, somewhat oblivious to things around me, I was suddenly living in another dimension. Attending genealogy workshops,

Bill working in his quiet corner in the den (portable lunch box computer dates photo)

subscribing to genealogy magazines, discovering even the most humble Acadian bulletins containing scraps of information about long-lost Girroir cousins in the United States, and later electronically searching via the Net. I was given a quiet corner in the house to hoard all my information and genealogical thoughts.

Little did I know when I started, how much many members of that galaxy called Girouard, Giroir, Gerrior, Girroir, and many other spellings, were really keen to know who they really were. Little did I know then that my research would prove useful not only to me, but to all those who wanted a broader picture of Acadian heritage and its importance in today's world. Little did I know that I would also become very interested in the French-Canadian Girouard branches, as well as the Acadian branches and their history, similarities and differences. The only thing I knew then was an urge to discover, to gather information before it was too late, and to share it, not only with my own family and friends, not only with all other Giroirs/Gerriors that I knew, but also with the whole world, made possible via the publishing of this book and other electronic media. From 1981, as diagnosed by my sisters Evelyn and Verna, my condition became more and more serious. I would soon learn that, however serious it was, I was not a lone case. Gerrior descendant Mary Weekes had obviously been affected by the bug herself. Also Edward Lavin Girroir Jr. and Lloyd Boucher, both Girroir descendants with roots in the Tracadie region, had the bug. Dr. Edgar Girouard, of Moncton, New Brunswick, had carried the virus himself for many years, and still was infected when I met him in July 1985 at the First Girouard Maritime Province Reunion. Actually, my condition progressively worsened, by June 1990, when the First International Reunion took place. I was not aware, when I began, that besides the research itself, there would be so much to organize, to put together, so that the "live" Girouard connections of today would add to the importance of knowing the Girouard connections of yesterday. I was keenly aware, though, that however interesting genealogy charts may be for the specialists, there was a lot more to be told. These families, in all corners of at least two continents, had played an important part in the broader history of their communities and countries and while doing so had created the yet unfolded and untold story of the Girouards.

Looking back today, I don't know if I would ever have started had I known how much work was in store for me. I was interviewing and taking notes at every opportunity. Just as one good idea usually leads to another, so also one interview led to another and I had no idea then how far I would have to go to complete my project which itself kept growing larger. My galaxy, at the time, included all those regions of Nova Scotia where I knew, by oral tradition and family history, that the Girroirs were present. My own origins were in Guysborough County, and during that summer of 1981, I started interviewing members of my immediate family: my late dad, my uncles, Ernie Pellerin, Brad Pellerin, and my uncle, Tom Gerrior as well as my aunts, Martina and Clara–all unfortunately passed away. Little did I know then that, as in any research to cover a number of years, many would not be with us to read and share the results of my work: not only those previously mentioned, but also Laguit Pellerin, Cecilia Pitts, Benjamin P. Gerrior, among many other descendants in the Maritime Provinces, to all of whom this book would, in the end, pay tribute. I interviewed the three Murphy sisters of Larry's River: Nina,

Visiting our cousin, Laguit Pellerin, d/o Benjamin A. Girouard [AMC Block H-8] Larry's River with my Dad. Laguit had a keen mind at 102 years of age.

Ethel, Margaret Murphy, Phonso Pitts, John Delorey, Gus Avery, Rita Louis, George Gerrior, Abraham Gerrior of Charles Cove and his relatives, Cora Mae Gerrior-Lundy, Barbara and Russell Gerrior, Debbie Lambert, Jean Robertson, the Delorey family–all descendants of Guysborough County, Nova Scotia Gerriors. I moved to Antigonish County, Nova Scotia and talked to Ben Gerrior and his wife Ann at Auld's Cove; to Marjorie Cunningham, Pat Cunningham, Mrs. Tremble, Tina Gerrior, Mary Fougère, Councillor Robert Girroir, Lloyd J. Boucher, all of Tracadie and surrounding area.

I then travelled to Ile Madame in Richmond County to learn all I could from Father Conrad P. Girroir and his brother, the late Raymond Girroir. I had interviews with Leonard Girroir, and Viola Paon. Brian Gerrior and Christine Morin told me all they knew about the Prince Edward Island Gerrior branches. I was not only charting the paths of my own genealogy, I was now tracing many branches and their numerous links and connections to each other, as well as many communities, all of Acadian origin. Meanwhile, I was discovering friends and relatives that I had never met before and enjoying the process of meeting all of them.

After my discovery of Mary Weekes, the second key encounter was definitely Dr. Edgar Girouard, one of the first key Girouard family genealogist in Moncton, New Brunswick. I talked then to Emilie Perkinson, Rita (Girouard) Kay, Lorraine (Allain) Robitaille, another key figure in the promotion of the Girouard family, all with Girouard roots in New Brunswick. The more information I gathered, the more valuable it seemed, and the more interesting and informative with regard to both the Maritime provinces history and the genealogy of our family.

Some humble advice for teachers: – Unless you want to spend fifteen years of your life working through the past and travelling miles and miles to obtain information about obscure genealogical data, heed my suggestion: When taking your grade six students to the provincial archives – or their equivalent where you live, be aware that a chance encounter may lead you to discover a lot more than you ever thought possible!

Let me continue with my background information. After two years of research I was still missing one important generation to link the earlier records and census of Port Royal and Grand Pré and other regions of old Acadie in the archives, with the more recent records collected from my family in Larry's River and Tracadie and the Church records in Nova Scotia. The late Laguit Pellerin, 102 years old at the time, put me onto our Tracadie roots in Monastery, Nova Scotia. I then researched the Tracadie church records, and was able to make a link to the Tracadie Girroirs and this established two more earlier generations. However, there was still another gap of one generation between Tracadie records and the archives research I had completed.

The answer to this gap came to me unexpectedly in the summer of 1984, while in the library, re-reading some of Bona Arsenault's work. All of a sudden there, in front of me, was the generation I had been searching for – Jean-Baptiste Girouard m. Madeleine LeBlanc and their children Marie, Joseph Nicholas and Marie Madeleine and Anastasie – all of the 4th and 5th generations of the master chart. The gap was solved although later I learned that the information had to be slightly altered because of other documents I found.

I couldn't believe my eyes! I felt like jumping up on the table and screaming: "I did it, I did it!..... Look here -me- back to François around 1641 at Port Royal who was from France and likely the Loudun region! "

Of course I didn't want to make a scene in the library so I had to just keep screaming these words inside, to myself. I packed everything up hurriedly and couldn't wait until I got home and finally yelled out loud to my wife and children while doing a little dance around the living room table. What a feeling! The puzzle was finally solved. It was too good to be true!

The mystery of my own direct line had been solved but to add to the excitement and joy, I realized that I also had the genealogy of literally hundreds of other branches of Girouard Girroir(e)…s who all tied in with my direct line. Using my Girouard Acadian Master Chart and a series of subcharts linking to the Acadian Master Chart, I became interested in the larger picture which would eventually tell us more about the Girouard, Giroir story, movement, heritage and history.

Convinced of the mysteriously attractive power of genealogy I wanted to find ways to share this information I had researched. After the first two years of part-time research, I decided not to let this seemingly endless task drag on more than another year. Well, was I naive to think that it would all end there!

That's when the idea occurred to bring it all together. I needed a purpose, to make these old, dusty manuscripts, and records come to life. I needed to refine and condense all my information to share it with others. The solution was simple —a reunion — with real, live descendants, which would bring all this research and new identity to life. In other words, I needed an appreciative audience for all this work to be displayed and shared – something we teach our children in school as part of the process of writing when thinking of the their final draft or product.

This would compel me to focus intensely for one year to confirm my facts and make further corrections and refinements which where needed and find some way of presenting all this genealogy information to a lot of people.

First, to obtain confirmation of what my research had shown, I visited the Acadian archives, at the Centre d'études acadiennes at the Université de Moncton, New Brunswick, where I met with Stephen A. White, a very well known, highly respected Acadian genealogist. His knowledge and record sources are extensive, giving the most accurate, detailed account of the first four generations where documentation is available, of all Acadian families. His two-volume Dictionnaire Généalogique des Familles Acadiennes, which is in high demand today, was not published at the time but he had quick access to all its contents. One change was made with respect to my archives research: François was chosen instead of his brother Pierre for [AMC Block F-3b]. This change differed from the opinions of some other genealogists, but there was good reason to differ based on supporting information, particularly an interview of a French historian, Rameau de Saint-Père, France, with Joseph Girroir of Tracadie, Nova Scotia in 1860. He was hired by the government of France to investigate, study, analyse and record the situation of the Acadians in the Maritime provinces, after deportation. This one change to my Acadian Master Chart was further supported by relations given by church dispensations that Stephen White had worked out from marriage and birth documents of other family members. All my archives research before the Deportation and a generation after matched with Stephen Whites' records and knowledge of the early generations. The rest of my research on later generations, I had found directly in old Church records and I certainly could attest to their validity.

Having confirmed the direct line, I now felt confident in linking all the other branches.

I then visited Dr. Edgar Girouard while in Moncton. Dr. Edgar Girouard had completed large charts of the Girouard genealogy in New Brunswick and, as we compared notes, it was amazing to see how two independent researchers came up with the same story. — We all descend from the first François Girouard in Port Royal, Nova Scotia, even though we spell our surname differently and live in different regions of the Maritimes. — Dr. Edgar Girouard allowed me to copy his charts in the grid format of my master chart system, so that his research could also be shared at the reunion.

At this point I was convinced that the best format to use to share my information would be a master chart system that I had developed, in order to organize the data I had collected in my earlier research. This system answered the important need to keep so many branches straight. It was also perfect to share with a lot of descendants because it was portable and extendable through the use of subcharts- Everyone would receive the master chart, then each family would receive a subchart or subcharts which would extend this master chart to their family by linking them to one of the blocks of the master chart, all leading back to the first François Girouard and Jeanne Aucoin. So this master chart-subchart format fulfilled my original purposes:

1) To link all branches of Gerriors, Girouards in the Maritimes in addition to showing my own direct line.

2) To be able to share this information with everyone so that everyone would feel a common identity and would participate and share information in its development. This would be accomplished through the use of two key charts. I refer to one of these charts in the text, as the Acadian Master Chart [AMC] for the Acadian descendants and the other chart as the 1French Canadian Master Chart [FCMC] for the Girouard descendants of the French Canadian branches.

Now I was ready to organize for the First Maritime Provinces Reunion.

Preface

The First Maritime Provinces Family Reunion, 1985, Antigonish, NS,

By the summer of 1984 I had a suspicion that every Gerrior in Nova Scotia, Prince Edward Island, New Brunswick, Louisiana, Québec and other provinces of Canada, as well as the United States (i.e. the descendants in North America), were all related and could be linked to the same family tree, and I wanted to try to prove that fact. But at that time I had only enough solid research completed and contacts made to document the genealogical links of all the Maritime provinces Girouard, Girroir, Gerrior, Giroir, Girrior,... families. This would be a big project in itself for the first reunion.

The First Maritime Provinces Reunion Organizing Committee L to r: Back Row: Brad Pellerin, Daniel Stewart, Fr. Conrad Girroir, Brian Gerrior
Anne Marie (Comeau) Schroeder, Bill Gerrior (Chairman), Mary Fougère

So I made sure I carefully filed all my telephone directory data on Québec and Louisiana for a later date and concentrated on the Maritime Provinces data collection, happy to know that the Acadian Girouard, Giroir families existed in these more distant areas as a result of the Deportation and would be part of the next phase of my research. Also I became aware that the Canadian Girouards established in Québec in close proximity to the Acadian Girouards, about 83 years after the arrival of the first Acadian Girouard, François, approximately 1640. I would also make contact with all of these branches in my next project. I was beginning to feel a real sense of identity with all of these branches from the limited genealogy and information that I presently had, indicating some definite connections and some definite similarities both physically and intellectually between the Canadian Girouards branches — the genealogical connection yet to be documented. This would be another challenge for a later time-after the First Maritime Provinces Reunion.

I then began in earnest to contact all Maritime provinces Girouard Girroir, Gerrior ... descendants by mailing out a survey questionnaire and cover letter (the first mail out) to families listed in the telephone directories of all areas of the provinces of Nova Scotia, Prince Edward Island, and New Brunswick, known collectively as the Maritime Provinces, (including a number of families unlisted in the directory).

A Maritime provinces committee was formed with representation from all three provinces, to help organize the reunion, contact their own branches and help obtain survey information. (See survey form and cover letter-first mail out

September, 1984 in Appendix 7)

I was able to link most of the families appearing on the survey returns to the master chart. Thus a second mailing to 600 families (including new addresses from the first survey letter to family descendants no longer carrying the family surname because of marriage) was mailed to thank those who had responded and to introduce the reunion idea and pre-registration for the First Maritime Reunion 1985. (see letter of second mailing–approx. March, 1985 in Appendix 7)

An agenda was confirmed for the First Maritime Provinces Reunion and the numbers were predicted accurately to be about 600 descendants. The third mailing listed final arrangements and directions: (see the third mail out in Appendix 7).

In summary, it was a huge success! What could we do next, to match this great event of the First Maritime Province Reunion, 1985? Remember I still had data to follow up concerning the Québec and Louisiana branches, but I was too tired and drained emotionally and mentally by the time we reached the closing of the 1985 family reunion. We all needed a break, after operating on the emotional highs of the family reunion weekend with cousins near and far. However the break was not that long. Some events soon followed which would ignite the embers again, leading to the First International Family reunion, 1990, in Antigonish and Tracadie, Nova Scotia.

The First International Family Reunion 1990

As mentioned, after the great success of our first reunion, being pretty much exhausted, I took a little rest from genealogy for a few months. But other things began to happen which caused me to rejuvenate very quickly: three trips to Québec, two trips to France, and one trip to Louisiana, an invitation to give a speech in French at the annual meeting of the Federation of Acadians of Nova Scotia (F.A.N.E.) on "Assimilation" – the first French speech ever for me. All of these experiences managed to get me hooked again, and caused me to take a bigger bite of the genealogy pie – the plan for the First International Reunion of the Girouard, Giroir (e)...s.

On the road again researching

Preface

As with the first Maritime Provinces Reunion, pre-planning for the First International Reunion involved three mail-outs, achieving the same results. To save space and time, the third mail out letter regarding this international reunion plan, tells the story in detail regarding background and organisation for the First International Reunion. (see Appendix 7) I will briefly summarise it here:

After our first Maritime Provinces Reunion in 1985 (600 in attendance), I received many letters from descendants who wanted to have another reunion.

Since that time, I had been able to extend my research via surveys and personal contacts to Louisiana and other southern states and to Québec.

This research went beyond the families who still have roots in the Maritime Provinces, to many other branches in Québec, Canada, Louisiana and many other states of the U.S. These Girouard/Giroir(e)… branches no longer had relatives living in the Maritime Provinces because they were part of the Deportation and Migrations begun in 1755, and had established themselves up to present day, in the areas where they were deported. Nevertheless, we still have accurate records (churches, censuses, family) to confirm that all of them descend from the same François Girouard who landed here in Acadie around 1640.

During both my visits to France, I found great interest in Loudun and surrounding area with respect to the Giroire, Giroir Girouard, Acadian heritage and our probable origins in La Chaussée. Madame Michèle Touret, Director of the Tourist Bureau in Loudun, France and her husband, Jean, were extremely helpful in assisting me with the Girouard Giroir(e)…research in France, by arranging for me to visit many Girroire families during my stay. It was an experience of a lifetime and very emotional for myself as well as for the Girroire, Girouard families I visited. More detail of my visits will be presented in the France chapter.

Since the First Maritime Provinces Reunion,1985, I had visited the province of Québec twice. During my first trip I visited Québec City, Montreal, and surrounding areas, as well as many of the communities along the St. Lawrence between these two cities where the Girouards settled. I researched our Girouard branches in Québec, at the archives at Laval University. I was able to link most of these families to the Girouard Acadian Master Chart [AMC] or to the French-Canadian Master Chart [FCMC], which I was beginning to construct.

The returns of surveys sent to over 1000 Girouards in the province of Québec, along with the research mentioned above, allowed me to positively, genealogically trace four more large Acadian, Québec Girouard family branches descending from our master chart. These branches were established in the province of Québec before, during and after the Deportation and definitely descend from our same family tree. Some of these branches descend from the brothers of the first Gerrior (Jean-Baptiste), who established himself in Tracadie, Nova Scotia, and from whom I descend.

The surveys, as mentioned, also allowed me to begin tracing the French Canadian Girouard branches because I did receive a number of responses from interested French-Canadian Girouard branches. It was a wonderful feeling to realize again that so many other Girouard branches have been linked. Judge Jean Girouard of St-Lambert, PQ, from the French-Canadian Girouard branch, was very instrumental in keeping the Canadian /Acadian Girouard connection alive via his interests, genealogical data, and attendance and participation at the International Reunion in 1990.

While in Québec and Montreal, I had interviews and meetings with many Girouard descendants.

In addition, I attended an International Language Arts Conference in New Orleans in April, 1989, involving workshops that were given by a writers' organization from Nova Scotia, to which I belonged. My days were extremely busy with the conference schedule but my lunch breaks and evenings were free time, so I filled them entirely, meeting Girouard, Giroir cousins, establishing more Cajun / Acadian links.

Three weeks prior to this visit to Louisiana in April 1989, I had sent another 1000 letters and survey forms to all Girouards Giroirs in Louisiana and other states of the U.S. As well, some letters and surveys were sent to the western provinces of Canada, (using the data from my telephone directory research which I had filed away back in 1984). I also added a note in the Louisiana survey letter that I would like to meet any Girouards, Giroirs who had a special interest in my project and their own genealogy. The response to this invitation to meet was so great that I could not meet everyone in separate meetings in the short time that I was in Louisiana. So, after a few individual meetings, we all agreed all to meet as one large group at my hotel conference room where I showed slides of Girouards, Giroires and Giroirs in France from my trip the previous year, 1988 and we shared genealogy notes with each other. They were very interested in my slide presentation of France and were inspired by the warm reception I received throughout my trip. Many of this group in Louisiana had completed their genealogy research of their own family line and had attended local Giroir reunions in Louisiana. So the spirit here, of their culture and heritage, was alive and well.

After my trip to Louisiana, I received much valuable feedback and information via letters, personal genealogies, and completed survey forms, from many other Girouards, Giroirs in Louisiana. Also I received the same from many other southern States of the U.S. and western provinces of Canada (all from the same survey mail-out referred to above) — all with the same story when all the pieces were finally fitted together with the early genealogical research– amazingly all descendants of François Girouard!

Therefore, I could now positively trace all these Girouards and Giroir family branches in Louisiana to our same Acadian Master Chart since they all descend from the first François Girouard in Port Royal, Nova Scotia, like ourselves in the Maritime Provinces.

Again just as in France and Québec, it was a feeling of warmth and pride beyond expression, to meet all of these Girouards, Giroirs, knowing that we all stem from the same root.

Consequently, with everyone's help and contacts made, I was able to supply all these mentioned Girouards (Québec and Louisiana and other parts of Canada and the USA), the Acadian Master Chart and the appropriate subchart which tied into the master chart, tracing each family's genealogy in North America, back to approximately 1640 in Port Royal, just as we were able to previously do for our own Maritime Provinces descendants.

I was also similarly able to trace many French-Canadian branches who descend from Antoine Girouard, thanks to the many French-Canadian Girouards who responded to my surveys with much information.

So we have made major leaps in our genealogy research and I was as close as ever to the completion of my search for representatives of all our branches stemming from each block on the master charts — my original objective.

We can say, with a certain amount of pride, that we may be the first Acadian family to have accomplished this international genealogical network in such detail, thanks to all your help, interest, and willingness to share our collective information with each other to pass down to our own children.

All this led to the planning of the First International Reunion of the Girouard, Girroir, Gerrior, Giroir, and Giroire etc. families which was held in Antigonish, and Tracadie, Nova Scotia, 1990 and the establishing of an international committee consisting of an Organizing Committee and a Committee at Large to help set

The organizing committee for the First International Reunion, July 1990)
l to r: Back Row: Rita (Girouard) Kay, Daniel Stewart, Mary Fougère, Evelyn(Gerrior) Oakley, Brad Comeau, Estelle (Avery) McMaster, Brad Pellerin, Jean Le Jeune, Blanche (Comeau) Hughes, Christine (Morin) Oderkirk, Ruth Nardocchio, Verna (Gerrior) Gionet.
Front Row: Paul Girouard, Clare (Pellerin) Hagen, Bill Gerrior (Chairman), Anne Marie (Comeau) Schroeder (Secretary), Fr. Conrad Girroir.

Next two pages: The composite committee photos of the Maritime Organizing committee and the Committee at Large

I will present other Girouard Committees, which have been formed outside of Nova Scotia, in the appropriate books, which follow in this five book series.

Preface

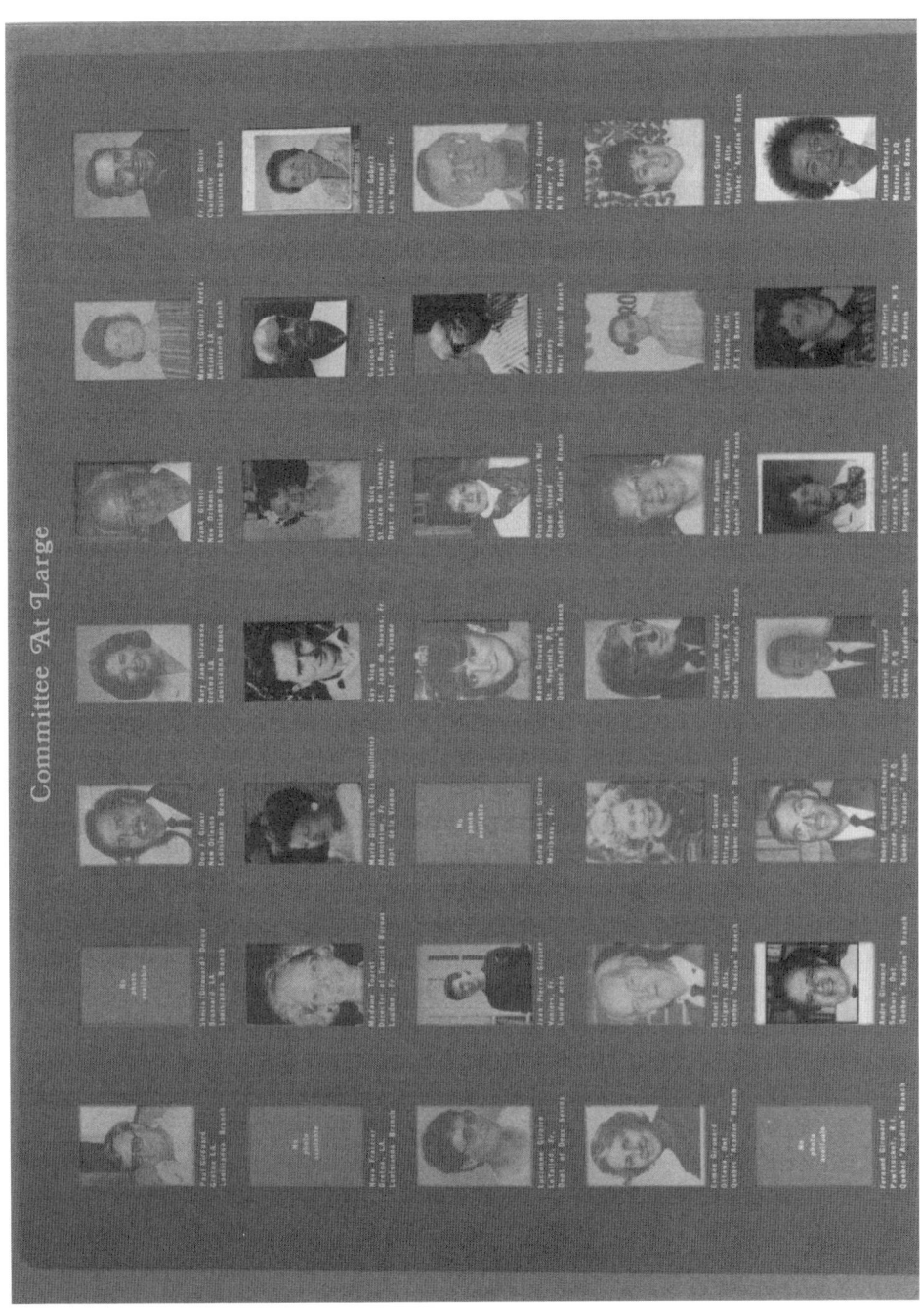

up the international network needed.

I am now ready to tell you the story of the Girouards, beginning in France, discovering the early history and routes of some of the Girouards, Giroir (e)… and other families, following the footsteps of Acadians who were deported back to France, or to England then France, as well as roots of the Québec French-Canadian branches, in France. We will then move to Port Royal, Acadie and follow the progress and trials and tribulations of the Acadian Girouard, Giroir (e)… before, during and after the Deportation of 1755. In the process we will also be including other Acadian families and presenting Acadian history common to many Acadain families. In particular with regard to the Girouards, I can tell you something of their travels and how the branches all divided during the Deportation; I can tell you where a great majority of the branches originally established after the deportation and migrations; I can tell you where, in North America, many of them are located today, and how we have come back together and how we have created our identity, heritage and pride as a family. I can tell you how we have grown since the Deportation and how many of our ancestors have been sea captains and sailed many ships to numerous far-away ports; how some of them have taken part in the government of their respective provinces and/or states and in particular at the federal (national) level of Canada's development as a country. You will realize the great contribution of some of our Acadian Girouard/Giroir(e) ancestors to the Acadian culture, language, identity, education, and rebirth of the Acadians in general. Our greatest triumph may be that seeing the vitality of the Acadian community in the Maritimes today, Charles Lawrence would realize the folly and the useless cruelty of his 1755 decision.

I can also share with you some of the history, heritage, genealogy and proud accomplishments of our French- Canadian branches of Girouards in the province of Québec.

We have much to be proud of in our ancestors and in our heritage, to pass on to our children. Let us begin our trip with France, our mother country, and follow our footsteps from there.

Introduction

April 21, 1991, a peaceful Saturday night at my Nova Scotia home in Brookside, near Halifax. A very ordinary spring evening was about to become a very special evening for me. It marked the beginning of the writing of this book.

Did I know, at that time, how many hours, how many years would pass before its conclusion? All I knew is that I was finally ready, and anxious to share with you the many stories and connections that constitute our family's heritage, its place in history, and its genealogy. As a reader, you may be one of the thousands of members of one of the branches of the Girouard family around the world, but also with you are the many readers interested in Acadian, French-Canadian, European and American history.

The arrival of François Girouard and his wife, Jeanne Aucoin, at Port Royal around 1640 marked the beginning of a long family odyssey, one which would see the couple's descendants spread across the North American continent, after being driven into hiding, imprisoned, some deported to England, the Channel Islands and France, finally returning to the New World. All would eventually settle in communities from the Maritime Provinces to Louisiana, Québec and California and many places in between. A great part of this story is told, in detail, beginning with this book as part of a five book series which is a culmination of twenty years of research, tracing the routes of this family, scattered in the wind.

A few explanations are in order, however. Firstly, you will discover that there are several different spellings of the family surname used throughout the book, In France there are, today, three commonly used surnames: Girouard, Giroir and Giroire. Sometimes, I have discovered, in my research, different old documents in France, referring to the same family, in which the spellings Girouard, Giroir or Giroire were all used interchangeably. This likely occurred because, phonetically, these spellings are close in sound.

In North America, our first Acadian ancestor was recorded as François "Girouard" in the first census of Nova Scotia, at Port Royal in 1671. Since that time the following seven variants were used and still are today for descendants of the same Francois Girouard: In Nova Scotia and Prince Edward Island, we find Girroir, Girrior, Gerroir, Gerrior, and Gerrier. In New Brunswick and Québec, Girouard only is used. In Louisiana we find both Girouard and Giroir. There exist other minor variations, but all are descendants of the same Francois Girouard and Jeanne Aucoin!

Periodically, to save space and repetition, wherever I intend to refer to all branches of the family, I will use the three surnames originally found in France, followed by three dots. "Girouard/Girroir(e). . ." to refer to all spellings of this family surname..

Some readers may be confused by the distinction between 'Acadian' and 'French-Canadian' in this book.

The Acadian branches of the family, which can be found not only in the Maritime provinces of Canada, but also in Québec and Louisiana and many parts of North America, descend from François Girouard and Jeanne Aucoin, who came from France to the French territory of Acadia (present-day Nova Scotia), and whose descendants were deported from their new country, imprisoned or went into hiding during *Le Grand Dérangement*, (the Deportation or Expulsion of the Acadians by the British) from 1755-1763.

The French-Canadian branches, on the other hand, are made up of Girouard descendants who did not settle in Acadia, but came directly from Europe to Québec. There are two French-Canadian branches of the family, respectively descending either from Antoine Girouard and Anne-Marie Barré of Montluçon, France, who arrived at Montreal, Canada (later Lower Canada) and married in the same place in 1723 or from Pierre Réalh Girouard and Marguerite Dupuis, who came from Waremme near Liège in Wallonie, (today part of Belgium), to settle at Ste-Foy, Québec, where they were married in 1726.

Descendants of both French-Canadian branches can be found throughout North America today. Not having lived in Nova Scotia, Prince Edward Island or New Brunswick (the Maritme Provinces) during the 18th century, they were not part of the Deportation.

Needless to say, all of these branches still have numerous cousins in Europe, where all these families originate.

Some of the leading Acadian Girouard/Girroir(e) . . . s of their time, were: In Nova Scotia: Father Hubert Girroir (1825-1864) a staunch nationalist and spirited leader in French education, religion and Acadian culture; Monsignor Edouard LeBlanc (1870-1935) also a Girouard descendant, became the first Acadian Bishop in 1912; Edward Lavin Girroir (1871-1932) the second Acadian Senator for Nova Scotia. Also, in Isle Madame we have many noted boat builders and captains of vessels such as Benjamin Gerroir (1799-1859) and Dominique Girouard (Girroir) (1818-1878) who were among the most famous Acadian names associated with the shipping business, to mention only a few. In addition there are war heroes such as the Gerrior brothers of Somerville, Mass. U.S.A, who died in action in France, 1917. Gerrior Square in Sommerville was erected in their honour.

From the descendants of Prince Edward Island: Richard (Rick) Joseph Gerrior, has been very much involved with the preservation of the music of our ancestors, having served as both Vice-president and President of the Maritime Fiddlers Association. Music, and in particular fiddle music, became part of the Acadian, as well as the Cajun, heritage and culture. Also from the Prince Edward Island descendants we have many prominent sea captains, who have voyaged worldwide, such as Captain Jack (John) Gerrior who lived to 105 years of age.

In New Brunswick: Honourable Gilbert Girouard (1846-1885) was the first Acadian Member of the Legislative Assembly (MLA) for New Brunswick; Edward Girouard was the first Acadian lawyer of Moncton, New Brunswick; Antoine Girouard was the first Acadian Deputy of Kent County, New Brunswick. Many other notable Girouard/Girroir(e) . . . descendants are also presented in the New Brunswick book, reflecting their participation at the National Convention held in Québec in 1880. This was the first time that the Acadians in the Maritimes were officially recognized and invited to celebrate their French culture with other Francophones, since they were tragically ripped from their roots in Acadie during

Introduction

the Deportation, 1755. The Acadian delegates at this convention, among them a number of Girouards from New Brunswick, can be counted among the founders of modern-day Acadie, establishing an important collective Acadian identity which exists to present day. The Honourable Gilbert Girouard, Bouctouche, New Brunswick with roots in Ste-Marie de Kent, N.B. was instrumental in helping to organize the first National Acadian Convention in Memramcook in 1881.

In Québec, Acadian lawyer and politician Jean-Joseph Girouard (1795-1855) was one of the well-known and respected leaders of the Patriot movement. Another renowned Acadian ancestor in Québec is the lawyer, and politician, Hon. Joseph ÉNA Girouard (1855-1937), a close family friend and political colleague of Prime Minister Wilfred Laurier during this period in history. As well, there is the well-known Acadian descendant, René de la Bruère Girouard (1882-1941) of Québec whose brilliant military and civil career accomplishments are described in the Québec book of this five book series. He was a prominent political leader in the Québec government of his day. I will also mention Louis Girouard, b. 1844, father of Dr. Joseph Arthur Girouard, Rhode Island descendant of the Québec branch, who was referenced in the book *L'Album de la Famille Girouard*, 1906 by Honourable Désiré Girouard.

Also in Québec, among prominent members of the French-Canadian branch, we can count the above mentioned Honourable Désiré Girouard (1836-1879), a Judge of the Supreme Court of Canada and historian. His descendants have also made their mark in history, especially Sir Percy Girouard (1867-1932), a war hero in military engineering for the British Government as it applied to the railway system in Africa, who in the process also became Governor of Kenya, Mark Girouard, grandson of Sir Percy Girouard, residing in England, is referred to as one of Britain's leading architectural historians today.

In Louisiana, Joseph O. Girouard (1839-1916) of Broussard was a prominent citizen, businessman, and landowner, as well as a key figure in developing the town of Broussard. Also among those preserving the highly distinctive Cajun culture today, is Alex Giroir of Pierre Part, Louisiana, whose works (construction of pirogues) are displayed at the Smithsonian Institute and which were exhibited at the World's Fair in 1984.

In conclusion, concerning this section on Acadian and French-Canadian Girouard Giroir(e)…leaders and prominent individuals, I have merely scratched the surface of what is to come in the four books which follow in this series. Many similarly distinguished descendants of the family not only survived pioneer life in North America (both in Canada and in the United States) but also contributed greatly to the growth of the New World, regionally and nationally. The Acadian branches have also provided leadership in the battle to protect their native French language and education. Some of them have been prominent as mentioned in the early renaissance of the Acadians as a proud race, with a distinctive culture and heritage.

The study of our family tree and its many branches, as well as the history of our ancestors in North America and France, has unveiled many treasures, such as the Girouard poem provided by a newly discovered cousin, Emilie Perkinson. As a result of all this research, the first Maritime Provinces Reunion in July, 1985, with 600 participants, the first International Reunion in July, 1990 with 800 participants, and the family reunions during the 1994 Congrès mondial acadien, in New Brunswick and the 1999 Congrès mondial acadien in Louisiana, can probably best be described as once-in-a-lifetime experiences.

In 1990, for the first time in the nearly 250 years since the tragic Deportation of the Acadians from their Nova Scotia homeland, Girouard/Giroir(e) . . . families who had been scattered all over North America and France were assembled in the same spot in Nova Scotia. They represented all the branches. We shared our history, heritage, pride and love, through music, slides, displays, genealogy workshops, stories, conversation and dance. What a wonderful feeling! It was like a dream, except that it really happened. These reunions are documented in detail, as well as being recorded in video format.

MASTER CHARTS and HOW TO USE THEM

Presenting genealogy in a clean, understandable format is not easy when dealing with several generations and many family branches. I designed the system of master charts to help me identify, and efficiently share all the genealogical and historical information gathered on the Girouard/Giroir(e) . . . heritage, internationally, concerning both the Acadian and French-Canadian branches. I will present the Acadian Master Chart here and one French-Canadian master chart. The other French-Canadian master chart, representing the first ancestor coming from Belgium, I will present in the Québec book. With their blocks and related subcharts, they constitute the basic structure of the genealogy and links for all the information presented in this book and the books to follow.

The reader should read these master charts and their explanations before going any further, to get a better understanding of all the connections. I refer to the master charts and their subcharts constantly throughout the book. A good understanding of the master charts and how they work will give you more of an appreciation of all the links, internationally and locally, in this huge network of Girouard/Giroir(e). . . family and of how various descendants are related.

Acadian Master Chart
The blocks of the Acadian Master Chart (AMC) are part of a grid reference system, which represents all twelve generations of the Girouard/Giroir(e). . . family in North America, from Port Royal around 1640 to the present day. If you are an Acadian Girouard/Giroir (e) anywhere in North America, then you are connected to one of these blocks (branches) on the AMC via a related subchart or genealogical block information section in the text, connecting to this block of the AMC.

I have, in most cases, traced family lines for each block of the Girouard Acadian Master Chart (AMC) to the present day. You will find this information both in the subcharts for each block of the Acadian Master Chart and in the corresponding sections of text in each of the books.

Introduction

Quite a number of subcharts for New Brunswick are based on the work of Dr. Edgar Girouard of Moncton, New Brunswick. With his permission, I have reorganized them into my grid chart format. Using his basic structure I have since provided further detailed research, numerous visits and interviews with various Girouard descendants in New Brunswick. Stephen White, professional genealogist at the Université de Moncton, NB, specializing in Acadian families, has also been extremely helpful with his exact and detailed data references relating to the early generations of these branches.

For the Louisiana subcharts of my Acadian Master Chart, I was fortunate to be able to rely on the genealogy work and the help of Mary-Jane Siracusa, Louis Giroir, Paul Girouard and Sheila Decou Girouard, as well as information and correspondence gathered from surveys and correspondence from many descendants.

In Nova Scotia, the work of Edward Lavin Girroir was a base for work on some of the branches in Tracadie, and certainly Father Conrad P. Girroir of Arichat was a great help concerning the Isle Madame Girroirs, as, again, were Stephen White's records and correspondence.

With respect to the PEI branches, Brian Gerrior and Christine Morin Oderkirk have been extremely helpful in sharing their research. This is also true for Gloria Hazard and Vernon Myers.

Jeanne Décarie, Dr. Paul Girouard, Gabriel Girouard, Richard Ste-Marie, Esmé and Désirée Girouard were very helpful in gathering information concerning particular Acadian branches in the province of Québec.

French-Canadian Master Chart [FCMC]
I have created Master Charts to organize the information on the two French-Canadian branches. The first details the descendants of Antoine Girouard, who emigrated directly from Montluçon, France, to Québec where he married in 1723. This French-Canadian master chart [FCMC] can be found in the French-Canadian chapter of the Québec book soon to be published. The second French-Canadian master chart with a Belgium connection was created and named the Belgium Master Chart [BMC], detailing the branches descending from the Pierre Réalh Girouard of Wallonie, (Belgium), whose descendants can also be found in Québec. This Belgium master chart [BMC] is also presented in the Québec book but their connection to the other French-Canadian branch descending from Antoine is not known at this time and is the subject for future research.

I have been able to create this French-Canadian Master chart using the data of Hon. Désiré Girouard, Dorval, P.Q., the genealogies and survey forms I have received from many French-Canadian branches in the province of Québec and my own research. In addition, my visits and work with Judge Jean Girouard of St-Lambert, have been very helpful in this regard.

ACADIAN MASTER CHART [AMC] OF ALL GIROUARDS* (GIROIRS)... OF NORTH AMERICA
By William D. (Bill) Gerrior (son of John S. Gerrior, Larry's River, Guys. Co., NS)

	A	B	C	D	E	F	G	H	I	J	K
1]		Note 1: This chart is a master chart for all Acadian Gerrior, Girouard, Giroir, Girouir, Girouard descendants, etc. in North America whose first ancestor originated in France. See text for explanation of how to read chart. Basically, the direct line descent of Bill Gerrior, the author, is shown in the centre column and the first name in all blocks to the right and left of the centre column, represent, brothers and sisters of the person in the centre columns for each generation. Chart updated, 2002. See Appendix for references for each block. Note 2: AMC is abbreviation of "ACADIAN MASTER CHART". Note 3: Surveys, interviews and research of William D. Gerrior, Acadian Awakenings, 2002.				ca. 1621 - 1693 François Jacques m. 1647 Jeanne Aucoin				Note 4: François Girouard, dit La Varenne, arrived at Port Royal approximately 1640, originating from the central-western section of France, likely from La Chaussée, France, Department of Vienne, in the region of Loudun, according to researcher Geneviève Massignon in her book, *Les Parlers Français D'Acadie*. Note 5. François is recorded as ancestor of Cardinal Villeneuve, Québec (ref: *Dictionnaire National des Canadiens Français*, Institut Drouin, P.Q.). Note 6: Marie [AMC Block C-3a] is the granddaughter of Charles Latour, first governor of Acadie; A. Petipas [AMC Block D-3a] is the daughter of Claude Sieur LaFleur, Secretary for the King at P.R. (Reference: research of Edward Lavin Girroir) Note 7: All children of François and Jeanne Aucoin were born in Port Royal, (row 2). Also all children of his son Jacques dit Jacob m.1699 Marguerite Gaudrot were also born in Port Royal (rows 3a and 3b). Marie Bourgeois [AMC Block D-2] is the daughter of Jacques Bourgeois, surgeon at Port Royal, who was later one of the prosperous landowners at Beaubassin (Amherst, Nova Scotia, near border to New Brunswick). Note 8: * Girouard is spelled several ways, as given in the "Chart explanation section" which should be referred to before using this master chart. (See text)
						Port Royal					
2]		1650 - (m. ca. 1669) Marie Jacques Blou Port Royal Beaubassin	1654 - Marie Madeleine (m. ca. 1668) Thomas Cormier Port Royal Beaubassin	1656 - 1693 Germain m. 1680 Marie Bourgeois Port Royal Beaubassin & Québec Cen.	1660 - 1742 Anne Charlotte (m. ca. 1675) Julien Lord dit LaMontagne	1648 - 1703 Jacques dit Jacob m.1699 Marguerite Gaudrot	1678 - Marie (m. ca. 1700) Jacques Granger Port Royal Grand Pré	1682 - Marguerite (m. ca. 1702) Louis Doucet Port Royal Maryland B.B.	1684 - 1738 Claude m. 1709 Elisabeth Blanchard (their son was dep. to Mass., then Que.) P.R., S.C. & Que.	1686 -1757 Guillaume (m. ca.1713) Marie Bernard (Renochet) Mck 1752 Québec & N.B. & P.R.	
		Port Royal Beaubassin	Port Royal Beaubassin	Port Royal	Port Royal	Port Royal					
3a]			1671 - 1744 Alexandre (m. ca. 1694) Marie Le Borgne P.R. (Son Pierre dep. to Phil.) P.Q.	1674 - 1741 Jacques m1.1704 A. Petipas m2. 1725 J. Amireau Port Royal Beaubassin P.Q. L.A.	1676 - Jean	←					
						Port Royal					
3b]		1688 - 1709 Denis m. 1709 Marguerite Barrieau at Grand Pré died at Port Royal Port Royal	1689 - 1742 Charles m1. 1713 P.R. Anne Bastarache m2. 1744 Marie J. Pitre N.B., Mck. W.Indies	1691 - 1760 Germain m. ca. 1710 Marie Doucet Port Royal Beaubassin Restigouche, N.B., Qué.		1680 - 1752 François m1. 1708 Anne Bourgeois m2. 1737 Marie Guilbeau Port Royal Mck	1698 - Anne Marie	1695 - 1742 Marie Magdeleine m. 1712 Pierre Richard Bel en Mer statements "La Varenne" Port Royal			
4m2]					1740 - Marie Josèphe	↔	1743 - Nathalie m. Amable Blanchard 1764 S.C.			Note 9: Names in this row are children from the second marriage of François. For information on the children from his first marriage see row (4m1) showing ten children from this marriage. Note 10: Nathalie [AMC Block G-4m2], Marie [AMC G-3a], Anne-Hélène [AMC H-4m1] are referenced by Janet Jehn, *Acadian Exiles in the Colonies*.	
4m1]		1708 - 1720 François Born Christmas Night at P.R. Port Royal	1721 - 1763 Pierre m1. 1743 at P.R., Marie Josèphe Forest m2. 1760 M. Douect Mck, C'ck & Que. 1758	1714 - 1716 Charles 1719 - Charles (named after deceased brother) Port Royal	1716 - 1805 Marie Madeleine m. Charles LeBlanc 1735 Port Royal St. Bernard, NS	1725 - 1808 Jean Baptiste m. 1751 Madeleine LeBlanc ca. 1751 Port Royal Mck. C'ck. & Tracadie	1733 - Marguerite Ref.:2118-3 Placide Gaudet	1728 - Anne-Hélène m. Claude H. Benoît, 1746 At.Mass., 1755 Grand Pré Memramcook St. Ours., P.Q. 1767	1731 - ca. 1792 Joseph m1. 1752 Françoise Blanchard m2. 1758 Marie Arseneau Port Royal & Que.	1719 - Charles	
5]	1711 - Marie Madeleine			1751 - 1811 Marie m. 1770 Basile Gouthro Halifax, Tracadie, NS	ca.1755 - 1789 Joseph m. 1776 Angélique Petitpas Tracadie, NS	1753 - 1841 François m. 1785 Marguerite Petitpas Tracadie, NS	1770 - Anastasie m. 1791 Jean Marc Romard Halifax, C'ck & C'pn, NS	1763 - Marie Madeleine (m. ca. 17778) Cyprien Duon Placide 2/05 France			

Introduction

ACADIAN MASTER CHART [AMC]

6]	Note11: Jacquet is also known as Deslauriers, Delorey, Delorie, etc.				1799 - 1865 Marie-Sophie m-1816 Moyse Jacquet Tracadie & Larry's River, NS	1786 - 1868 Luc (m. ca 1800) Ann Jacquet Tracadie & Larry's River. NS	1785 - Juliette (m.) Alex Petitpas Tracadie & Larry's River, NS	1791 - 1848 Marie Marguerite (m. ca. 1815) Paul M. Jacquet TR. & L.R.		1815 - Henrietta
7]		1805 - Francis m.1829 Julienne Bourke Tracadie, NS	1821 - 1823 Marcelline 1828 - 1830 Pierre		1819 - Isidore m1. Marguerite Pellerin m2. 1866 Caroline George Charlos Cove	1817 - 1895 Abraham (m. ca. 1842) Lavina (Devine) Fouere Tracadie Larry's River.	1823 - Joseph Simon m1.1847 Adele Belfontaine m2. C. Avery m3. C. McGillivray Lundy, NS	1808 - 1873 Maximin m. Helen (Nelly) MacDonald Tracadie, NS and USA	1811 - 1873 Jean Baptiste m. 1833 Sophie Pôte Tracadie, NS	1812 - 1834 Marguerite m. 1834 Joseph Doiron	
8]				1855 - 1945 Dennis A. m1. 1878 Ellen Delorey m2. 1930 Rebecca Bowman Larry's River, NS, Stellarton & U.S.A.	1848 - 1925 Luke A. m. Til Hushard Halifax & Canso, NS	1847 - 1942 William A. (Justice of the Peace) m. 1868 Sophie Pellerin Larry's River. NS	1843 - 1918 Michel A. m1. 1871 Julie Manette (m2.) Brigitte Haley,1884 Larry's River, Lundy, Guys.,NS	1852 - 1908 Benjamin A. m1. Helen (Ellen) (Lacatune) Pellerin Larry's River, NS	1862 - Julie m. Dan Driscoll Larry's River, NS & USA	1853 -1929 Delia m. Philip Bourgeois Larry's River, NS & U.S.A.	1858 - 1929 Adele m. Gus Benette N.H. Larry's River and N.H., U.S.A.
9]	1826 - 1860 Frédéric m. 1848 Nancy Gillis Larry's River, NS	1816 - ca. 1933 Vénérande m. 1836 Dennis Linden Tracadie, NS Charlos Cove NS	1878 - 1878 William (d) 1868 Jeffrey (d) 1868 1871 Jeffrey (d) 1871 1873 Jeffrey (d) William (d) Larry's River, NS	1888 - Adélina (Lena) Flora m. Archie Butler Larry's River, NS & USA	1884 - 1945 Simon m1. Angel Pellerin m2. Susan Jane Pellerin m3. Madeleine Surette Larry's River, NS & USA	1872 - 1964 Jeffrey m1. 1900 Anne Fouère m2. 1924 Louise Conway Larry's River. NS	1873 - Allan m1. Catherine Pellerin m2. Lissie Pellerin Larry's River & Sydney	1869 - Agnès m1. Wilbur Harding m2. Frank Williams Larry's River, NS & USA	1874 - Tom (d) young age given as seven in 1881 census. Larry's River, NS & USA	1885 - Geneva n.m. Larry's River, NS & USA	1880 - Sophia *Ref. Guys. Census, 1891*
10]	*Ref. Guys. Census, 1891*	1886 - Marguerite	1918 - Hubert (d) in infancy Larry's River, NS	1904 - 1990 Helen m. 1931 Frank Lally Larry's River, NS & USA	1906 - 1931 William Augustine (d) at 25 years old Larry's River, NS & USA	1913 - 1996 John Sylvester m. 1942 Beatrice Fouere Larry's River Sydney Halifax	1903 - 1991 Thomas Daniel m. Ella Muise Larry's River, NS & USA	1901 - 1989 Cecelia m. 1921 Bert Avery Larry's River, NS & Halifax	1908 - 1995 Clara m. 1934 Ernest Pellerin Larry's River, NS	1912 - 1996 Anna m. 1937 Basil Doucette Larry's River, NS	
11]			1951 - 1951 Thomas Gerard Olivet Mt. Cemetary, Halifax, NS	1955 - Theresa b. 24/02/55 m. Don Adams Halifax, NS	1949 - Herman b. 07/04/49 m. Avis Bona Halifax Truro	1943 - Reginald (reg) b. 28/03/43 m1. Elvira Kirk m2. Barbara Freer Halifax	1944 - William D. (Bill) b. 06/08/44 m. Audrey Gray, 1969 Halifax Co. Author	1946 - Delores b. 24/04/46 m. Mike de Repentigny Halifax & BC	1952 - Tom b. 04/07/52 m. Stella Herring Halifax	1947 - Verna b. 19/04/47 m. Alcide Gionet Halifax	1956 - Evelyn b. 03/11/56 m. Mike Oakley Halifax	1958 - Marie b. 12/11/58 m. Joe Nugent Sydney
12]						1971 - Stephen (Steve) 25/11/71 Halifax	1973 - Suzanne m. Steven Williams 1997 04/04/73 Halifax, NS				

© *Acadian Awakenings Girouard/Giroir... Routes and Roots*

37

Master Chart of William D. Gerrior (Son of John S. Gerrior, Larry's River, Guysborough Co., N.S)

Key to blocks on this chart:

Birth date	-	Death date

Gerrior first name

m1. 1st spouse/mate &date
m2. 2nd spouse/mate &date
m3. 3rd spouse/mate &date

Place names where born and /or where descendants established.

This chart has two main purposes:

I. To show the direct descent of William D. (Bill) Gerrior, and close relatives back to 1621. (François Girouard, La Chaussée, near Loudun, Dept. of Vienne, France)

2. To indicate how various other branches of Gerriors (in Canada & United States) are related to François of France (above).

How to read the chart:

1. Read the chart from the bottom up in the centre column or direct line of this chart.
2. The first name in each block of this chart is always a Gerrior (to save space the last name is not used).
3. The chart is divided into vertical columns lettered A to K, and horizontal rows, numbered 1 to 12, representing twelve generations of Gerrior descendants.

The, middle column 'F' (shaded on this chart) indicates the direct descent of Bill Gerrior. There is no direct descent in any of the other columns, however each block in each row on the chart is a brother or sister of the person in the centre column and is a branch in itself, having many descendants which are traced using other subcharts that link into the appropriate block of the master chart. In this way, every branch in Canada or United States links into one of these blocks on the Acadian Master Chart [AMC] via its corresponding subchart.

Example: Begin with Bill Gerrior at column 'F' row '11'. Bill's father 'John' is at column 'F' row '10', his grandfather 'Jeffery' is at column 'F' row '9', and his great grandfather 'William A. is at column 'F' row '8', and so on back to François at column 'F' row '1', in the year 1621- the first Girourah in North America from France.

4. Each row represents a generation of brothers and sisters of the Gerrior name shown in column ' F' of that row. i.e., In row 10 (tenth generation), Helen, Martina, Tom, Cecilia, Clara, Anna, etc., are all sisters or brothers of Bill's father John S. Gerrior in the centre of this row., at [AMC Block F-10].

5. The pattern is the same for each row of children on the chart, with the following exceptions:

a) Row 3a and 3b -It was necessary to use two rows here, to show all 14 children of Jacques Girouard and Marguerite Gautrot: (The arrow above François '1680' indicates that the parents of all these children is Jacques and Marguerite).

b) Row 4M1 and 4M2 -It was necessary to use two rows here, to show the children from the first and second marriage of François '1680'. (The arrow above Jean-Baptiste '1725' indicates that François was the father of these children in row 4M1 and 4M2 -see note on chart).

Various branches of Gerriors shown on this chart:

Introduction

[Block E-3b] Pierre Girouard has many descendants in New Brunswick, Prince Edward Island, & Louisiana.

Many branches from West Arichat, Prince Edward Island and New Brunswick, descend from the sons of Pierre. Research notes of Brian Gerrior and Fr. Conrad P. Gerrior have been very helpful in tracing some of the branches in P.E.I. and West Arichat, respectively. Dr. Edgar Girouard has completed extensive research of many of the branches in New Brunswick, descending from the same Pierre. Also the Louisiana branches descend from the same Pierre Girouard. One of Pierre's sons, Honoré "Giroir" was deported back to France and later returned to Louisiana, spelling his family name as "Girouard". In addition, Pierre's son " Firmin", established in Louisiana, after deportation and migrations, spelling his family name as "Girouard".

[Block C-3b] is another Girouard branch in New Brunswick. Some branches of this block of the master chart descend from Charles' son, Joseph (Biset) Girouard who was one of the original settlers in Bouctouche, New Brunswick. Other sons and daughters of Charles were deported to South Carolina.

[Block C-3a] Alexander's son 'Pierre' was deported to Philadelphia in 1755.

[Block E-5] & [Block F-5] Descendants from these blocks established in Nova Scotia in Antigonish Co. and Guysborough Co respectively. Many Gerriors in Antigonish Co., N.S. descends from Joseph [Block E-5]. Edward Lavin Gerroir, son of Senator Edward Lavin Gerroir, the second Acadian Senator of Nova Scotia, had done extensive research of his related branches in the Tracadie area. My research as shown that all Gerriors in Guysborough Co., descend from Joseph's brother 'François [Block F-5]. However there is one other branch of Gerriors who stayed in the Antigonish Co. who actually descend from the Guysborough François via his grandson, Francis [Block C-7].

Blocks [C-4m1], [H-4m1], and [J-4M] are Quebec branches- Pierre, Anne-Hélène and Joseph Girouard, brothers and sister of Jean Baptiste Girouard [Block F-4m1], who first settled in Tracadie, N.S., established in various parts of Québec, just after the deportation of 1755.

[Block J -3a], & [Block I -3a], are Quebec branches- Guilliame's [Block J-3a] son, 'Guilliame', settled in Lotbinière and Claude's [Block I-3a] son, Joseph, was deported to Massachusetts and later to St. Ours, Quebec in 1767.

[Block D-2] is a Quebec branch

Germain's descendants settled in Quebec at Deux Montagnes.

Abbreviations:

Hfx,–Halifax;
BB–Beaubassin is now known as Amherst, N.S.

S.C. -South Carolina
B.C. -British Columbia

L.R. -Larry's River
TR. –Tracadie

C'CP –Chéticamp
C'CK- Chezzetcook

M'CK –Memramcook
U.S.-United States

G.P. -Grand Pré
P.R. -Port Royal

Spelling: Spelling of the Gerrior names vary, since many documents spelled the name in different ways. Original spellings (from France) -Girouard, Giroire, Giroir. Other variations -Gerrior, Gerroir, Gerriore, Gernier, Geroire, Giroir, Jerrior etc.

Research references. Government census; N.S. Archives; personal interviews with many descendants; survey responses from many descendants in Canada and United States; Placide Gaudet`s genealogy on the Girouards, National Archives of Ottawa; correspondence and conversations with Steven White and Bona Arsenault; and notes from France Historian, Edmée Rameau; Information from Rameau's interview with Captain Joseph Girroir (son of Joseph Girroir [AMC Block E-5] together with an interview with Stephen White concerning his research on the Girouard genealogy, confirm that the father of Jean Baptiste Gerrior of Tracadie is François rather than his brother, Pierre from Grand Pré, as was the erroneous belief of some other genealogists.

Genealogy Research and Master chart designed by:

William D. (Bill) Gerrior,
15 Angela Dr., Hatchet Lake, N.S.
B3T1S2, Canada
Ph (902) 852-3926;
e-mail: bgerrior@ns.sympatico.ca.

Author of the work *Acadian Awakenings, Routes and Roots*. a major study of Acadian history via the Gerrior, Girouard... family genealogy, history and Heritage, Internationally. ©

39

MASTER CHART FOR ALL FRENCH CANADIAN GIROUARDS IN NORTH AMERICA DESCENDING FROM ANTOINE FROM MONTLUÇON, BOURBONNAIS, FRANCE

	L	M	N	O	P	Q	R	S	T	U	V
1]	Notes: 1. Research of William D. Gerrior, *Awakenings*, 2002. 2. Surveys, correspondence and interviews with Judge Jean Girouard of St-Lambert. Information supplied via the genealogical research records of Judge Jean Girouard of the ninth generation of this chart. References: The three works of Honorable Désiré Girouard: *L'Album De La Famille Girouard*, 1906; *La Famille Girouard*, 1884; *La Famille Girouard en France*, 1902. Genealogy cards of Judge Jean Girouard, Moncton, N.B.; Loiselle Lake genealogy notes, Université de Laval, PQ. My genealogical chart was checked and confirmed by Judge Jean Girouard of St-Lambert, PQ and André Girouard, with reference to their own research and related genealogy referring to each block of my master chart.						1651 - 1721 Jean Edmé Georgeon Counsellor to the King of France.	**CANADIAN MASTER CHART-ANTOINE** 6 Jean Edmé Girouard, father of Antoine Girouard, was Counsellor to the King of France and Comptroller of the Depot at Roni in Auvergne, France. He was from the parish of St-Eusache, in Paris. He married Pétronille Georgeon from Montluçon, France. (See France Chapter for more detail of the origins of this family in France.) Their son, Antoine, born in Montluçon, Bourbonnais (now Allier), France, came to Canada establishing the first Canadian Girouard Branch. He arrived at Montréal and married Marie-Anne Barré 1723, residing in Côte Ste-Marie, later at Faubourg Ste-Marie, parish of Montréal, just outside the city walls.			
2]				1705 - 1786 François du Buchet m. Catherine Marie Lucile Chambaud Montluçon	1693 Pierre m. Marie Burel, 1720 m2. Françoise Pérler, 1735 FR.	1696 - 1767 **Antoine** m. **Anne Marie Barré** Montréal N.D.-	Marie-Madeleine m. Pierre Ste-Martine Terjat, FR, 1726	6 Refer to the France Chapter for the genealogy of Antoine's two brothers: François, and Pierre and his sister Marie Madeleine.			
3]		1725 - 1815 Marie Anne m1 Julien Tavernier Montréal, 1749 m2. Gabriel Chèvrefils Montréal, 1767	1727 - 1727 Angélique	1729 - 1762 **Antoine** m. Marguerite Chaperon 1759 Son, Antoine, is Founder of St-Hyacinthe College, 1823	1735 - 1796 Louis Pascal m. Marie Anne Lamoureux Boucherville 1761	1733 - 1798 Henry m. Marie Josephte Cousineau St-Laurent,PQ 1758	1723 -1723 Antoine	1737 - 1830 JoachimAmable m. Marie Appoline Cousineau 1768 St-Laurent	1730 - 1799 Geneviève Marguerite m. Nicolas Gaudry, dit Bourbonnière 1760 Montréal		
4]	1776 - 1776 Marie Josephte St-Laurent 1783 - 1784 Catherine St-Laurent	1767 - 1778 Henry Jean St-Laurent 1765 - 1788 Michel, killed by an ox.	1775 - 1823 Rosalie m. François Allard 1796	1772 - 1836 **Joseph** m. Josephte Bleau 1799 Rivière Des Prairies	1759 - 1800 Louis Pascal m. Madeleine Robert dit Lamouche 1784 no children	1779 - 1865 Julien m. Marie-Clémence Lavoie 1801 St-Martin Isle Jesus Farmer at St-Laurent and St-Timothée	1762 - 1828 Antoine m. Marie-Louise Arel 1793 St-Vincent-de-Paul	1771 - 1828 Scholastique m. Alexis Danis 1791	1760 - 1826 Geneviève m. André Barron 1780	1763-1843 Marie Anne m. Pierre Barsalou 1784 St-Laurent	1769 - 1847 Gertrude m. Toussaint Martin dit Ladouceur November, 1788
5a]		1815 - 1893 Clémence m. Charles Quevillon 1832 St-Timothée,PQ 1832	1810 - 1874 **Jean Baptiste** m. **Brigitte Montpetit** 1833 at St-Clément de Beauharnois	1806 - 1806 Infant	1802 - 1831 Julien m. Françoise Beauharnois 1827	1811 - 1875 Jérémie m. Hippolyte Picard 1834 at Lachine (Dorval) St-Timothée,PQ	1804 - 1831 Desanges m. Antoine St-Germain 1825 St-Laurent PQ	1805 - 1805 Siméon	1808 - 1856 Sophie m. François Dugas dit La Brèche 1832. St-Laurent	1813-1905 Rose Antoine Quevillon 1829 St-Timothée, PQ	1817 - 1817 Antoine Germain St-Laurent, PQ
5b]			1827 - Rachel m. Joseph Laberge 1845	1822 - Flavie died at a young age	1820 - 1902 Marie m1. Louis Laurent Fortier 1842, St-Timothée m2. Benjamin Viau 1849	↔	1817 - 1817 Marie Louise, St-Laurent PQ	1823 - Eléonore m. Gésippe Cousineau 1844 St-Timothée Beauharnois PQ	1825 - Henriette m. Moïse Wattier 1846 St-Timothée PQ	1830 -1830 Henry Sulpice	1819 - Marie Nathalie m. Gilbert Mompetit 1835 St-Timothée PQ

Introduction

6]		1838 - 1882 Caroline m. Gédéon Fifre 1861	1835 - 1835 Infant born and died on the same day June 29.	1846 - 1846 Infant born and died on same day.	1842 - 1842 Infant born and died on the same day, December 28.	1836 - 1879 Hon. Désiré m1. Mathilda Pratt 1862 Montréal m2. Essie Cramwill 1865 Montréal m3. Edith Beatty 1881 Ottawa	1844 -1846 Julie	1839 - 1866 Constance died in Religious Home of Grey Nuns of Montréal	1843 - Alphonse m. Maria Le Chêne 1876 Indianapolis, Indiana, USA	
7]	Eléonore from m3. of Hon. Désiré m._____ Baskerville	1865 - Essie Augusta (Gussie) son of m2._____ m. Henry-John Skynner Brandon, Mass., USA	1882 - 1951 Ernest Chanteloup from m3. m. Pauline Parent	1879 - Anna (Nannie) from m2. m. Lawrence Russel	1869 - Désiré H. from m2. m. Virginia Chambliss Lawyer	1867 - 1932 Sir Édouard Percy from m2. m. Mary Gwendolyn Solomon, 1903 Governor of Kenya, Africa	1864 - 1864 Samuel	1877 - Mabel from m2. student at Convent of Sillery m. Omer Côté from Ottawa	1884 - 1939 Hector Henry from m3. Dorval Studied at Sorbonne, Paris	1862-1894 Emile from m1. Paris-Canada Journalist m. Louise Clément 1887
8]						1905 - 1989 Richard Désiré m. Lady Blanche Berisford				
9]						Marie Josepha m1. John Cresswell Turner 1961 London, G.B. 2. Peter D. Durlauzer 1985 London, G.B.	Lady Teresa m. Sir Kenneth Canning 1953 London, G.B.			
						Mark m. Dorothy Dorf 1970 One of Britain's leading Architectural Historians				MASTER CHART FOR ANTOINE GIROUARD FRENCH CANADIAN BRANCH (FCMC)

© *Awakenings Girouard/Giroir... Routes and Roots*

41

BLOCK GENEALOGY TEXT

I have coined this term to refer to genealogy information given in paragraph form in the text, which is used to extend any particular block on the master charts, or you may find these family lines traced on one of the subcharts.

Numbering system

The numbering system used in the block genealogy text sections was designed by the author to extend the genealogy of any particular block by first listing in numerical order the children (and their spouse) of a particular block. To save space the children of these numerically listed children are often given in parenthesis without numbering, which is a process the author refers to as nesting. (see Example I)

Example I
No numbering required (nesting): for Joe Smith, the first of ten children of the parents in any given block on the charts. No further information has been given for follow-up, so the children are nested within the parentheses with no numbering system required because the information is not complex.

Child # 1 Joe Smith m. Mary Brown (four children: John, Robert m. Sylvia Lancaster, Susan and Bill)

However, if there is to be further follow-up, the author will indicate that he is going to extend the genealogy further by indenting the entire block genealogy of text containing these children. He will then number the children for whom there will be some follow-up using the following number system. Consequently, if the reader sees any block of genealogy that is indented, he can expect to see follow-up of this text. (see Example II)

Example II
Where more information is given and therefore further follow-up is necessary, requiring a numbering system to keep information clear:

> Child # 1 Joe Smith m. Mary Brown: Four children: 1. John m. Catherine LeBlanc; 2. Robert m Sylvia Lancaster; 3. Susan; 4. Bill
>
> Child # (1-1) John m. Catherine LeBlanc. Three children: 1. Tom; 2. Fay; 3. Gary
>
> Child # (1-2) Robert m. Sylvia Lancaster. Two children: 1. Weldon; 2. Cathy.
>
> Child # (1-3) Susan m. Norman Hill. One child: 1. Joseph
>
> Child # (1-4) Bill m. Jacqueline Landry. Four children: 1. Wanda m. Wayne Fougère; 2. Joeseph m. Pearl LeBlanc; 3. Sharon m. Marcel White; Lynn m. John Spicer.

Introduction

> Child (1-4)-1 Wanda m. Wayne Fougère: three children: 1. Robin; 2. Carol; 4. Jim m. Donna Holt.
> Child (1-4-1)-4 Jim m. Donna Holt : Two children: 1. Sarah; 2. Michelle

This numbering system seems obvious and requires little explanation. However when the numbers in the parentheses get beyond two numbers, it is important for the reader to note that there is an easy pattern in tracing back to the original person in the block. The pattern consists of simply observing the numbers in the parenthesis and referring back to these numbers and only these numbers in the preceding paragraphs (regardless of the parenthesis arrangement of these numbers in the paragraphs). Here you will find the person you are looking for. Repeat this process until you get back to the original person in the block genealogy text.

NAMES
Depending on the source, the spellings of one person's name may vary. This is especially true in the spelling of some French names, where the accents have been dropped and in other cases retained. I have tried to retain the accents where appropriate, but the result remains inconsistent because in many cases the names have been anglicised in some documents or may otherwise vary in different sources. Hyphenated names often appear without hyphens on the charts, and in the appendices, for maximum efficient use of the limited space.

In addition, the reader may often see nicknames used. Since there were relatively few different Christian names being used in the early days, many people might have the same name. Nicknames, often based on place of origin or some personal characteristic, were an important way to distinguish between several people bearing the same name, e.g. François Girouard *dit* la Varenne or Julian Lord *dit* La Montagne. The word French word *dit* means "called " or "also called", which would actually be a more meaningful free translation.

DATES
Particularly in the early days, official records were few and far between. Important events, such as births, baptisms, marriages and deaths, might not be recorded until some time after they had occurred. Thus, exact dates and ages were sometimes forgotten, and may appear differently in various records.

BIRTH DATES
Generally, birth dates beyond 1920 have not been recorded unless specifically requested.

ADOPTIONS
It has always been the tradition in Girouard, Giroir, Giroire families to consider an adopted child a full member of the family in all respects of belonging, proudly carrying the family name and sharing the full richness of the culture and heritage. Therefore, adoptions are not specifically referred to as such in this work, unless they were recorded quite far in the past.

ABBREVIATIONS
b.   born
bap.   baptized
m.   "was or is married to", or, "is or was a mate of"
d.   died
bur.   buried
n.c.   no children
nm.   not married
vve.   *veuve* (widow)
ca.   approximately
Fr.   Father (priest)
AMC   Acadian Master Chart
FCMC   French-Canadian master chart
BMC   Belgian master chart
C.E.A. Centre d'études Acadiennes at Université de Moncton, NB
{sic } Reproduced as found in document

The letter *à* between names of persons is an Acadian way of showing a person's direct lineage. For example: Bill à Sylvester à Jeffrey à William à Abraham means Bill, son of Jeffrey who is son of William who is son of Abraham Gerrior. This chain can be as long as necessary to indicate the direct line. Normally, it is used to show the male line, as carrying the family surname, but in some cases, a women's name would appear in the lineage if she was widowed early in her marriage, because her husband's name, quite some time later would not be known by the people in the community and so her name would appear. in place of her husband as the last person in that lineage chain. Thus I have heard people in Larry's River, for example speak of William à Francis à Nancy. (we know Nancy was a widow from other records)

OLD UNITS OF MEASUREMENT
Distance
1 arpent=191.833 ft.
1 league= 3 miles
1 mile = 5 280 ft, or 1.6 km

Area
1 arpent square= .84628 acres
1 acre =1.1834 square arpents

SOURCES *used in the charts:*
I make reference to four major sources throughout the books and in the charts:
Loiselle Notes: Any reference number beginning with "00" always refers to page numbers in the Loiselle Notes, which refer to the work of the genealogist Rev. Loiselle. His work is found on microfiche at the National Archives of Québec. He

transcribed records from many parishes in the Province of Québec.

Moncton Cards: Any reference to "Moncton cards", refers to genealogical information on the Québec Girouards, contained on index cards, which were passed on to Dr. Edgar Girouard of Moncton, NB, who in turn, passed them to me for analysis and inclusion in my records. The original source is not known.

Placide Gaudet: Any reference using a series of four digits, sometimes followed by a dash and another number (i.e. 2187 or 2187-2), refers to page numbers in the genealogical research of the Girouards by a very early Acadian genealogist, Placide Gaudet, on microfilm at the National Archives (PAC call number C-2239).

Bergeron: Any reference to "Bergeron" refers to the genealogy work of Adrien Bergeron in *Le Grand Arrangement des Acadiens au Québec (1625-1925)*, Volume 4 in particular for Girouard genealogies.

CONTACT INFORMATION

It has been the author's desire to document the history and genealogy of the Girouard/Giroir(e). . . family as accurately as possible. Although the main framework is accurately supported by documentation available at present, with such a large project, small errors, omissions or discrepancies are bound to occur, especially with names, which have alternate spellings or dates, which sometimes appear differently in various documents. Any person researching their own family tree should also check with primary documentation in their local area.

If there is information here that you consider inaccurate, or if there is any additional information you can provide, you can send it directly to the author either through e-mail or by regular mail.

Contact: Bill Gerrior
Port Royal Publishing Ltd.
15 Angela Drive
Hatchet Lake, N.S. B3T 1S2
Phone /Fax (902) 852-3926
Web site: *acadianawakwenings.com*
Email: *gerriorb@ hfx.eastlink.ca*
          bgerrior@ns.sympatico.ca

Hon. Juge Girouard, de la Cour Suprême du Canada
(Reproduit du *Lake Saint-Louis*)

Family Name

Girouard, Giroir, Giroire, Gerrior: How many spellings?

Girouard is a French name in its pronunciation and a name with a long history in France. Many in North America confuse Girard with Girouard. However Girard is not part of the spellings connected to the family Girouard, Giroir(e) in North America. However, one might find a few exceptions; for example, one of the descendants from Nova Scotia moved to Western Canada and changed the spelling of his family surname name to Girard. But generally speaking, Girard is a family with a separate history in North America. The surname of Girouard, through the centuries, has been recorded as Giroüard, Giroird, Girrerd, Girouard, Giloir, Giloire, Gilloire, Giroire, Giroir, Geriore, Girroire, Gerriore Geroire, Gerroir, Gerrior, Girrior, Girroir, Giroir, Giroire, Girrier, Gerrier, Jerrior, Jerrier, Jerwa but also, Girouar, Girouer, Giroüer, Giroüard. We also have Girouart, Giroard, and Girouas, which seem to fix the last syllable to harmonize with the Anglo Saxon word Ger-Ward, which according to Mgr. Tanguay in his Dict.I, (xx and xxvii) means "garde-lance".[1] Finally, there is Girouere, probably pronounced Jeerwear, as in *Girouère*, a common French pronunciation in the 17th century still found in some parts of French Canada. Is it related to "Gérouard"? Possibly. In old documents from the Vendée region in France, the name Géroardi appears in 1042, Girardi in 1190 and Giroardo in 1332, with the same endings — closer to Italian or Spanish than modern French — being present in Girouardo in 1533. We also find Giruart in the 14th century and Giernard in 1648. In 1120 the spelling Giroare appears. Some historians even suggest an early connection with the family name Girard: the builder of the first chapel in the village of Le Girouard, in Vendée, was named Girard — or Giraud. Documents held at the town hall of Le Girouard, Vendée, France, state that the name Girouard possibly comes from *Capella Giroldi*, la Chapelle des Girauds (the Girauds' chapel).[2] There is documented evidence that in 1199, the Knight, Pierre Giroire, owned land in the Atlantic part of the Loire region of France.

In early French documents, Giroire and Giroir were frequently interchanged for Girouard, which is also found in Liège, Belgium. This is likely because these names sound similar phonetically. In North America we can find other variations of the name, the spelling of which was probably rarely fixed in writing until the end of the 19th century anyway, as was the case with many surnames.

The most common spellings existing today in France are Girouard, Giroir and Giroire. The most common spellings existing today in North America, in particular the descendants of the Nova Scotia and Prince Edward Island branches are: Girroir, Girrior, Gerrior and Gerroir, Girrier; the spelling Girouard is used by the New Brunswick and Québec descendants; and Girouard and Giroir are the two common spellings of the Louisiana branches. There are a small number of other variations of course.

What is the common origin, if any, of all these? Three routes/roots are open to us: a Germanic one, a Latin one, and an occupational one.

A Germanic origin, from the north of Europe?

This French surname may have a Germanic origin. A derivative of "Gari-wulf-hard", it has become Gerward or Gérowad, Giroward or Gerouward, G(e)iroüard, then Girouard. The origin refers to fighting abilities: "gari" means spear, "wulf" means wolf (a common surname for fierce fighters) and "hard" is an obvious reference to toughness. It would appear that war and hunting played a major part in the lives of our ancestors! The existence of the family surname in France goes back more than 15 centuries to the time in the 500s when France started to be built around invaders from eastern and northern Europe. They gradually mingled with Celts from the north and the Latins from the south. The fusion of all those ethnic and linguistic backgrounds gave France its identity.

We can follow the trail of our family name even further north. The spelling Gerrior may have originated in Scandinavia. It is found as the feminine form "Geirrior" among Old Norse names.[3] The corresponding masculine form, "Geirhildr", is closer to the formation of the word of Girouard. Could it be that Gerrior, rather than being an anglicized form of Girouard, is the feminine form, having survived through the ages? Also according to modern philologists, "hildr" means "war", thus one might assume that Geirhildr and its feminine form, Geirrior, mean warrior, which harmonizes with the Germanic origin suggested above.

A Latin origin, from the south of Europe?

A Latin origin should not be discounted. The village of Le Girouard, in Vendée, as mentioned previously, was called Capella Giroardi, the Gir(o)ard's chapel — or Capella Giroaldi, the Giraud's chapel.

The first syllables of the Girouard family name sounds like the first syllables of the French word *girouette*. For most people today, *girouette* means weather-vane, a spearhead which points in the direction of the wind, which is easy to connect with the old-fashioned French verbs *girer* (meaning "to turn", from the ancient Latin verb *girare* with the same meaning) and *rouer*, "to turn around". Both verbs possibly were mixed with a Scandinavian word from Normandy, "wire-witte", giving *girouette* its distinctive sound.

Girouette, however, also had another meaning in the Middle Ages. It meant "a banner", and such banners were granted to people of local or regional nobility by their *suzerains*, their feudal lords and protectors. The right to display such a banner was called *droit de girouette*. We can find on a Girouard coat of arms three banners proudly displayed in such a fashion. It is likely that some of those local noblemen were in fact referred to as "Girouards", with the use of the ending *ard*. Girouard could then be a collective name for all who displayed their *girouettes* so proudly.[4]

An occupational origin?

For a long time, family names, or surnames (from the French *surnom*, or nickname) were usually given to people as a way to describe where they came from, what they looked like, or what they did. On one coat of arms, Girouard means millstone grinder — hardly surprising for a family with a number of famous French and French-Acadian sculptors. Jean Girouard, one of a number of famous Girouard sculptors of Poitiers, France, for example, carved Louis IV, and today, from Ste-Marie-de-Kent, New Brunswick, we are very proud of renowned sculptor, a Girouard descendant, Marie–Hélène Allain, who sculpted many beautiful pieces, including one, very appropriately called *Awakenings*.

Which is the most likely?

Of course, over 10 centuries, a family name may change. It is likely that all the origins mentioned have some truth in them. Any Germanic origins may have been blended with Latin spellings. Nicknames may have been added to an existing root.

Looking at the whole picture, however, it appears that our family name comes originally from northern Europe. Long ago, our ancestors made their way to the more pleasant climates of France, south of the Loire River in particular — in Poitou, Charentes, Vendée. It could be that many of the Girouards found in Beauce (south of Paris) and in Paris itself, stayed there after the *Francs* started moving south, or possibly moved back to Paris to find work over the centuries (migrating back to larger centres for employment is a common pattern for many families). The name was brought to North America by our ancestors who wanted to meet new challenges. Such a desire to push to new frontiers may, after all, have been a genetic trait, going back to those Northern warriors who finally settled in milder surroundings.

Coat of Arms

Did the Girouards have a coat of arms?

The Honorable Désiré Girouard, a Supreme Court Judge of Canada , made reference to a coat of arms which he discovered during his research in France during the early 1900's. Up to this point I am not aware of the French-Canadian branch of Girouards in the province of Québec having carried any coats of arms to North America. Similarly, the Acadian Girouards also did not carry a coat of arms to North America, to my knowledge. However, from the well-documented information regarding the Giroire and Girouard ancestors; horsemen, knights, lawyers, in feudal times during the Middle Ages of Europe and the research of the coat arms by our French Canadian Supreme Court Judge Désiré Girouard in France, we are now certain that some of the Girouards carried their own coat of arms.

Due to the many variations in spelling of our family name, and the various localities where we find the Giroires, Giroirs, and Girouards, one can expect to see more than one coat of arms. In fact, I have seen three coats of arms related to our family names.

What do coats of arms mean?

Wars were almost a continual occurrence during the Middle Ages, and so more and more armour was added to a knight's battle uniform until he was finally protected from head to toe. It was virtually impossible to tell one knight from another without some visible means to identify each knight. Consequently, to prevent any knight from spearing his friend on the battlefield, they initially painted colorful patterns on their battle shields. These patterns were eventually woven into cloth surcoats which they wore over their suit of armour. In fact surcoats with the same pattern were worn by their horses. There must have been a Girouard in mediaeval armour to have been granted a coat of arms with its blazon. This colorful identification probably became as important to this Girouard as the Girouard name, and certainly the Girouard coat of arms would have been displayed with pride. As more designs were created, it became necessary to register or copyright them, to prevent two knights from using the same insignia. In many cases, records were kept, then compiled, listing the family name and an exact description of its coat of arms. These are called "armourials" or "blazons". The word "heraldry" is associated with coats of arms. Tournaments (or jousting contests) were common during the days of knighthood, and as each soldier was presented at a tournament, a herald sounded the trumpet, proclaimed the knight's achievements, and described his arms. We do have on record the knight Pierre Geroir (1199), St-Hilare, France; Guillaume (William) Geroire (1255), Talmont, France; and Giroir of Loudun (1030)1, all of nobility in their time.

The First Girouard Coat of Arms

In the first Girouard coat of arms, the blazon reads as follows: *"De gueules à trois girouettes, deux d'or en chef et une d'argent en pointe."* "The mouth of three weather vanes, two in gold and the leading one at the point, in silver." Documentation for this Girouard coat of arms can be found in the Grand Memorial book by Hossier, which was researched by the Honorable Désiré Girouard, in the early 1900's, when he visited France. A similar one is found on Michael Girouard's website, *http://www.girouard.org/index.html*. Désiré Girouard wrote the following concerning his research on the coat of arms.

On my return to Paris, I went to examine the coat of arms of the Girouard family which I had seen the first time, in 1882, at the National Library. Upon opening the *Grand Armorial* book by Hossier (drawings) Volume 39, page 917, I found there the coat of arms of Pierre and François Girouard, horsemen, probably the sons of Jean. On page 939, we discover that the "Girouard of Mayet" (Mayet is a few leagues from Montluçon) have the same design. We know that during that period, they write the name Girouard, indifferently, with the *tréma* [two dots

Names and Coats of Arms

over the "U" to pronounce the "U" distinctly in French, giving three syllables to the pronunciation rather than two] and without the *tréma* and that the name was written also as Girouas, Girouar, Girouer, Giroire. The regular spelling often seen in the civil acts of the state and other places is "Girouard". Antoine Girouard and his children used the *tréma* but his grandchildren, among others Antoine Girouard (priest and founder of the college at St. Hyacinthe, Québec) and all other descendants have omitted it as do the Girouards in other parts of France.[5]

The second Girouard coat of arms

Historically different creatures of nature denoted certain characteristics, and various inanimate shapes implied certain traits, historical factors or aspirations. For example, the chevron symbolized protection, and has often been placed on arms to tell others that the bearer had achieved some notable feat. This Girouard coats of arms is showing two lions facing each other on a chevron, described in the blazon as follows: "D'azur au chevron d'or, acc. en chef de deux lions de même rampons et affrontés et en pointe d'un coeur enflammé aussi d'or." When translated the arms description is: "A gold Chevron between two gold crawling lions facing each other in the top third, in the bottom a flaming heart of gold." (documentation for this Girouard coat of arms can be found in *Armorial Général de Mosseisiq*). This information was published by Sovereign, 583 Boundary Road, Cornwallis, Ontario.[6]

The third coat of arms

The Certificate of Authenticity states the following:
This is to certify that the Coat of Arms described hereon has been used in centuries past by a person of the family name of Gerrior or an onomatological variant thereof, judged to be associated with this name.
Arms description: "Gules a saltire ermine, within a bordure azure, charged with eight estoiles in saltire argent" [sic] Reference Source: Les Planches de l'Armorial General by J.B. Rietstap.
Manuscript / 300866-24
Confirmed by the presiding officer of Sanson Institute of Heraldry.[7]
I have been unable to contact the Sanson Institute.

Central and Western France
some places of interest

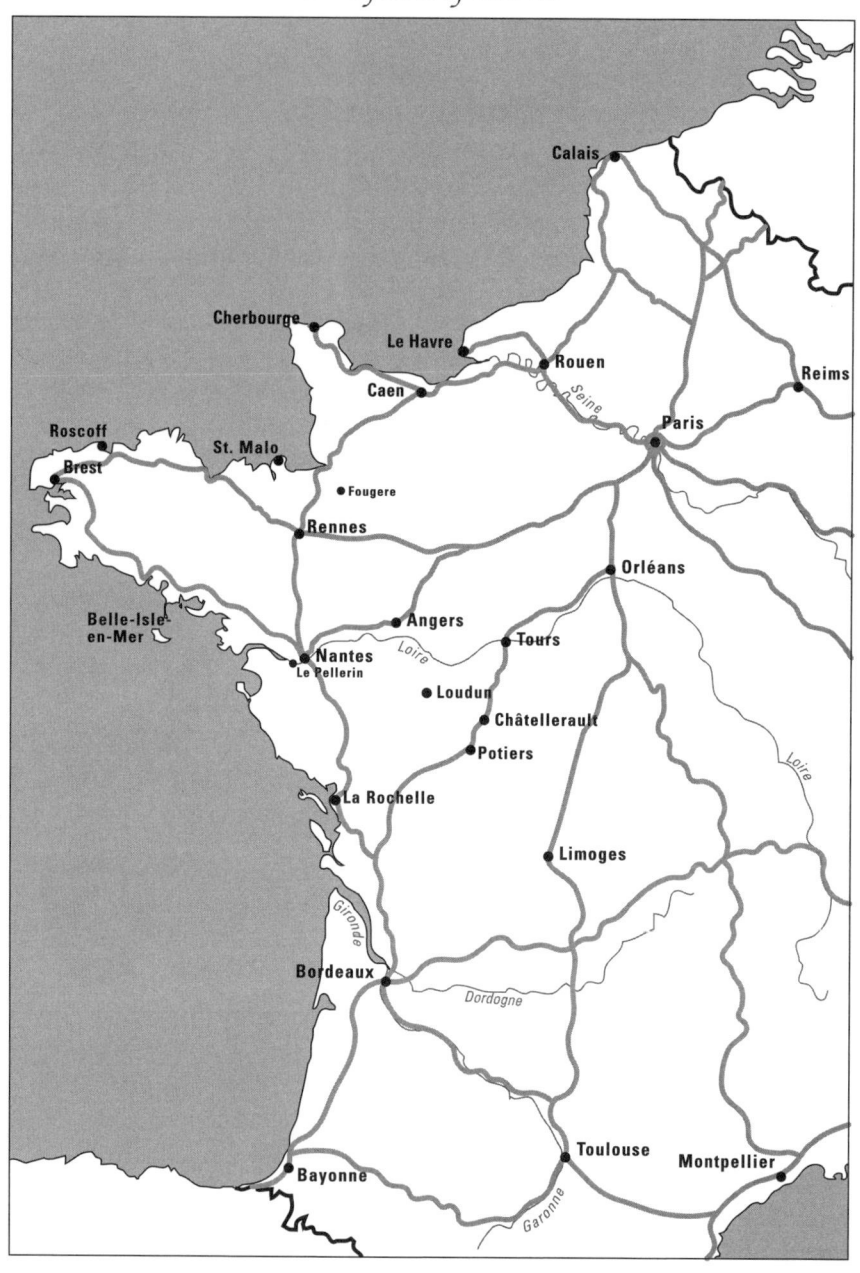

France
Roots & Routes

The Departments of France (Administrative Units)

SUNDAY: *Roscoff*

I arrived in Roscoff, in the Brittany region, for the first time, in August 1988. I had just completed a Master's course in writing, at the University of Exeter, southwest of London, with a group of colleagues from Canada and England.

In this short five-week period, we became one large extended family, studying, writing, sharing cultures and various writing skills, helping each other, collaborating in group projects, visiting schools and touring countryside, absorbing as much as we could of both the recent and ancient history of this country. I would soon be using some of the writing skills learned at this institute, in the process of my own research for this book.

Writing group at Exeter University (second from left in the front row is Exeter University, School of Education professor, Clive Carre, who worked with Professor Andy Manning of Mount St. Vincent University, Halifax, to arrange this Anglo-Canadian institute). Left to right: 1. Brenda Condran; 2. Clive Carre; 3. Connie White; 4. Sue Adams; 5. Pamela Crouse; 6. Cindy Haley; 7. Bill Urwin; 8. Janet Luke; 9. Bill Gerrior; 10. Jo Fawcett; 11. Carol Craft; 12. Carol Chipman; 13. Ali Cass; 14 Lorne Pidgeon; 15. Jo Stone; 16. Phyllis Porter; 17. Maisie Foster; 18. James Heald; 19. Rosa Parsloe; 20. Gerry Carty; 21. Lesly Brown; 22. Mary Davey; 23. Gordon Mason; 24. Bill Wagstaff.

After completion of the course, I crossed the English Channel to France by way of Plymouth. I was now travelling alone, for the first time that summer, without the company of my colleagues who had dispersed in many different directions. At first I felt isolated, but the feeling quickly left me, replaced by the challenge of this solo adventure. I was at last going to explore my roots in France.

My map-reading skills, as well as my French language skills, were finally going to be used for real purposes. The map-reading skills were no problem, but I had run out of time to prepare for speaking French. Knowing French as I know it now, still far from fluently, but well enough to understand many conversations, I realize how little I knew then! All of a sudden, on that first trip to France, I realized I urgently needed to study the language and brush up on my rusty high-school knowledge of French.

This would be my first time ever trying to speak French to a unilingual French person, since in Nova Scotia, Francophones are almost always bilingual. "It's now or never!" I said to myself on the crossing to Roscoff. Would the French understand me? Would I understand them?

These were my thoughts as I crossed the English Channel, frantically studying my verb book and dictionary, and heading to the land of my ancestors for the first time.

When the ferry reached Roscoff, it was getting dark but I could see that it was a picturesque seaport. Since I could see little else, I took a taxi to the Hotel Triton to rest up for the next day.

At the hotel, I walked up to the desk and said timidly, *"Je voudrais avoir une chambre, s'il vous plait."* (I would like to have a room please.)

The man looked at me for what I felt was an eternity before asking, *"Êtes-vous seul?"*

I paused for a moment to let his words register in my head, just catching the last word *"seul"* (alone) and answered, *"Oui, je suis seul."*

"Combien de jours?"

My daughter Suzanne at the same location in Roscoff, with her friend Henry Guiterrez, a professional soccer player in Brest, during her first visit to France, January, 1993.

First night in France: Hotel Triton

North and south views from the window of the hotel.

Just catching the word *"jours"* (days) I replied, *"Je voudrais avoir une chambre pour un jour, s'il vous plait."* (I would like a room for one day, please). He passed me the key and pointed upstairs.

Then it struck me. "Gee, we really understood each other!" I felt great. Immediately, though, thinking I was fluent in French, the desk clerk started rattling off a whole lot of things rapidly. I learned right then to rely on one valuable phrase in France: *"Si vous parlez lentement, je comprendrai."* (If you speak slowly, I will understand.) That phrase got me through the toughest spots during my entire stay in France because I certainly could understand if they spoke slowly. I picked up the keys to my room, unpacked, and fell asleep instantly—exhausted.

In the morning I had my first view of France through the dormer window of the roof, which extended from my room, overlooking beautiful stone courtyards, buildings and a tall church steeple. All the yards were fenced in with high stonewalls. It was beautiful, old and rustic!

Bright and early in the morning, I was off on my personal walking tour of the town, using my town map (not shown here). This quiet town looked quaint to North American eyes. I was amazed by the stone construction of almost everything. After a couple of hours, becoming more of a risk-taker, I thought I would see if I could order a meal in French at a seaside restaurant. I went in, took some time to look at the menu and ordered. To my great delight, the waitress under-

Roscoff

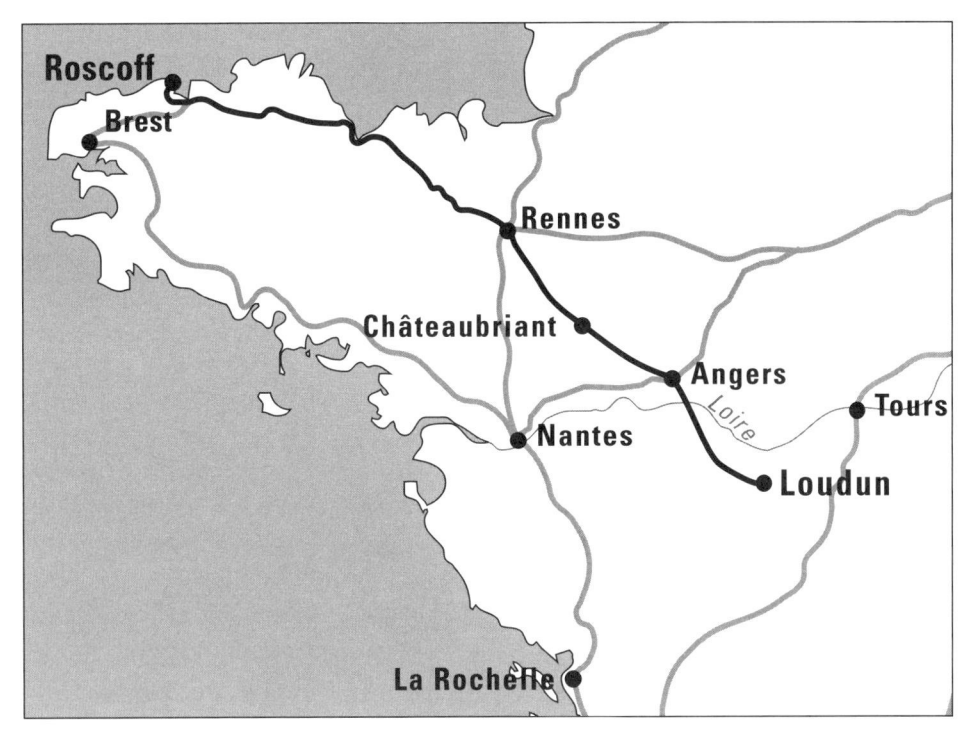

Route from Roscoff to Loudun

stood my order, and I even tried my taste buds on a few beers. It was all very lovely. I was beginning to feel more comfortable and confident, knowing that in at least two different French environments, the hotel, and now the waterfront restaurant, I could make myself understood and could also understand the French, if they spoke slowly. What a relief and good feeling that was!

MONDAY: Roscoff to Loudun

The next morning, I headed for the Roscoff *syndicat d'initiative* (tourist bureau), and asked where I could rent a car which I could return at Calais, in the northern part of France, where I would cross back to Britain (there was no Eurotunnel back then!) a week later, before heading home. I was able to rent a little red Renault. I drove up to my hotel and got out the map to plan my trip to Loudun (see preceding map).

Why Loudun? I had read an article at home in a monthly journal called *Acadian Réveil*,[1] which has over 300 subscribers among families of Acadian origin in North America. This journal promotes sharing our Acadian heritage. In one particular article, I read about an Acadian family who had visited the *syndicat d'initiative* in Loudun and had received a very warm welcome from the *directrice*, Madame Touret, so I thought this would be a good starting point for me.

I also knew from my research that many of the first families to come to Acadia were from western France and in particular, the Loudun area. While it had been a major recruiting area for the first settlers, many Girouard, Giroir, and Giroire families probably still lived in the surrounding area.

Last but not least, François Girouard, the first of the family to emigrate to North America, was referred to as *"dit la Varenne"* in his descendants' sworn statements at Belle-Ile-en-Mer, on the coast of Brittany, after the Deportation. There is at least one place named La Varenne near Loudun and many more in the surrounding area. I wanted to find out more about each of these locations. Geneviève Massignon, in her work *Les Parlers Français d'Acadie*, indicates a belief that François Girouard was originally from the La Chaussée region, not far from Loudun, although no precise records are available to prove or disprove her theory.

The following quote from an interesting article concerning the 11th century does, however, establish that the Giroir name was prominent in Loudun during this early period in the history of France. (Translation with the assistance of Paul Girouard).

GIROIR FAMILY OF LOUDUN[2]

We now come to the feudal records where we find the name of Loudun, where this family appears on several occasions, in the *cartulaire* of Noyers, as 'Giroir of Loudun'.

We also find him in the records of Saint-Florent de Saumer; he is designated in the act which dates around 1030 as 'Knight of Loudun' being husband of Witburge and father of Gaultier et Raoul. He is certainly a highly esteemed and rich noble. He gave to St-Florent de Véziers, the church and the site of Saint-Citroine.

The marriage of his son Gaultier [Giroir] would unite this family to a powerful dynasty of Anjou, the seigneur of Blou. They not only possessed the fief of Anjou but also for many generations possessed the seigniory of Champigny-sur-Veude, which would pass down eventually to the House of Bouay, following the marriage of Emma de Blou to Guy de Bauay.

Gauslin de Blou, who lived towards the end of the XI century, had at least two children. His son Robert who was an important feudal noble was part of the entourage of five barons who in 1128 accompanied Geoffrey, son of the Count d'Anjou to Rouen, where he was to marry the daughter of the Emperor Henri V.

The daughter of Gauslin was Eufémie; she married Gaultier [Giroir] of Loudun and gave him, as a dowry, the church of Parts. This sanctuary, on the left bank of the Vienne River, near a frequently used route joining this river to the old Paris to Bordeaux road, had the misfortune of being located in an area of Touraine where there were numerous scignieurs, and private wars were frequent. By the year 1096, the church was so deteriorated that it became impossible to hold church services there. Consequently, Gaultier became very disturbed because he had the responsibilities for its maintenance, and feeling guilty and being fearful of sinning, he donated the Church to the Noyers Monastery with all the surrounding land that would be necessary to form a hamlet and build homes for the monks.

This donation was confirmed by the son of Gaultier, who was named Giroir like his grandfather, Giroir of Loudun.

Let us also add that recently, important repair and renovation work was undertaken in this church. It is during this work that much evidence on the site was found of pre-Roman occupation of this same site.

Was Giroir of Loudun related to the famous Alléaume de Loudun, patron of this City and of Burgos, of whose origin we know very little? The late historian of the Loudun region, Charbonneay-Lassey, thought so.

So my first destination was Loudun, hopefully to share my information and genealogy from the Maritime Provinces Reunion with Madame Michèle Touret, Directrice of the syndicat d'initiative (Tourist Bureau) of Loudun and to visit La Chaussée, la Varenne and other areas of Acadian interest in the surrounding region. With luck, I would be able to find some Girouard/Girroir(e) families who might be interested in genealogy or the reunion project. I wanted to find out if any genealogy in France had been completed and how far back this research extended.

I had another exciting destination, which was the town of Le Girouard near the Atlantic coast in the department of Vendée. My mind was racing with all these thoughts as I left Roscoff for Loudun, enjoying the manual stick shift and relieved to drive on the right side of the road again, after driving in England for a month. How would I accomplish all I wanted to do in a week? Distances in France cannot be compared to distances in North America, yet I had a lot of places to visit.

It took me most of the day but as I approached signs showing directions to Loudun, my heartbeat began to race a little faster along with a heavier foot on the accelerator. Only seven kilometres (about 4.6 miles) to go. It seemed like a long way to go, but finally there it was!

I had a map and brief description of Loudun, which I had read some time previously. Now was the time to refresh my memory, so I pulled over the side of the road to study the map and brief history of the town. There was a peripheral road around the town, making all points in the town quite accessible from the various exits.

Loudun is in the *department* (an administrative unit) of Vienne. This small town, (whose mayor at the time was Renée Monory, also the president of the French Senate, and therefore the second-highest ranking official in the French Republic), is located 55 kilometers (34 miles) north of Poitiers, the largest town in the Poitou-Charentes region. The ancient country of Loudunais derives its name from the Celtic god Lug to whom a fortified hill (*'dun'*) was consecrated. "Lugdunum" later became Loudun.

Typical road through some villages and towns in France.

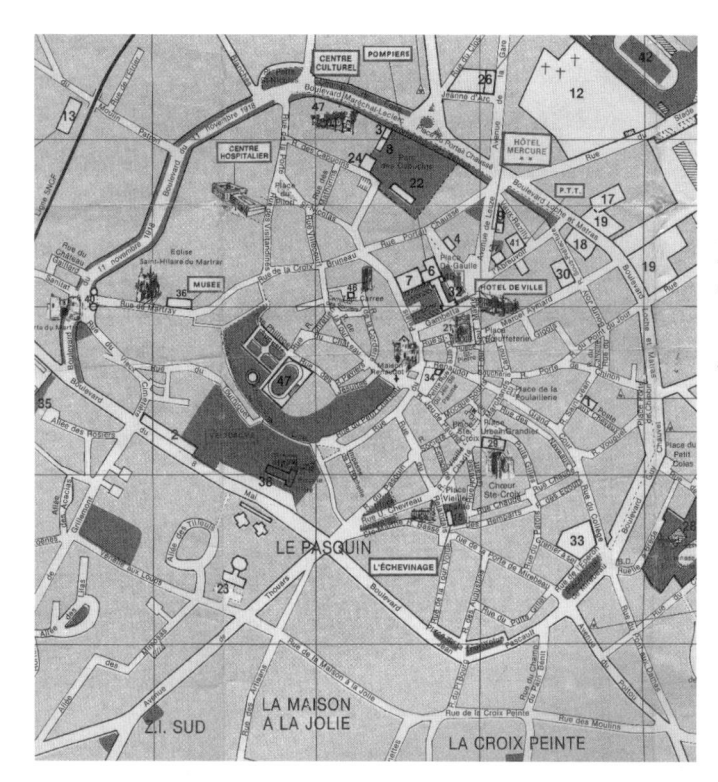

Loudun, two aerial views
courtesy of Syndicat d'Initiative

Opposite: Loudun sign

In the 17th century, when François Girouard emigrated, there were approximately 20,000 people in Loudun. Several of these people became well known, but many died anonymous, like the three thousand people killed by the plague in 1632.

Isaac de Razilly, with Menou d'Aulnay, was one of the founders of l'Acadie (Acadia). Théophraste Renaudot, a pioneer in journalism and medicine (whose birthplace is kept as a museum), operated the first printing press in France. His *Gazette*, the first printed newspaper, recounts among other news, the emigration of people of Poitiers to Acadia, signalling the departure for New France of "300 elite men."

Ismael Bouilleau was an astronomer, a lawyer and a theologian. Jean II Armagnac, governor of the city, was also Valet of the King's Chambers. Scévole, poet from Sainte Marthe, created a literary salon. Guy Chauvet founded a college. Notable for other reasons is Urbain Grandier, a priest whom the Ursuline sisters accused of witchcraft, who was burned alive in Loudun on the 18th of August 1634, after a memorable trial that was made into several movies in our century.

For the first settlers of Acadia who left this region, Loudun was the big town where fairs and festivities would have been held. The town is situated on a rounded hill surrounded by boulevards, following the line of the ancient walls, demolished by order of Richelieu, the first Prime Minister of King Louis XIII, who unified France politically and militarily. One huge main entrance door in the middle of the remaining walls around the town indicates that Loudun was an important fortified place.

As I began to drive into the town of Loudun, I experienced an eerie feeling, thinking and saying to myself: "If my ancestors could only see me or if those old castles and towers and ramparts could only talk — surely I would find that François!" I knew that other researchers had not found François' birth or marriage records. Also, I had no hope of finding anything in a week but if I could only start the fire burning here, someone else in France, maybe a Girouard, Giroir(e)... descendant, might have the time to continue the research.

That evening, I found a place to stay not far from the *syndicat d'initiative* in Loudun. It was about 10 p.m. I read a bit and found it difficult to sleep because it was incredibly humid.

TUESDAY: Loudun, and Aulnay, Martaizé and La Chaussée
In the morning, I arrived at the Loudun *syndicat d'initiative*. The place was buzzing with tourists, so I just looked around at pamphlets and listened to the French

Top: The gate entrance to the old part of the town of Loudun, which was encircled by a fortified wall.
Bottom: Chuck Gerrior, a West Arichat (Nova Scotia) descendant, standing by old wall of the town.

Courtesy of Chuck Gerrior

conversations, trying to understand what was being said, but most of it was too fast for me!

I sat down, pretending to read the pamphlets, the entire time saying to myself: "How am I going to explain the big Maritime Reunion of the Girroirs, Girouards, in French?" The story is so long and detailed. It wouldn't be as simple as asking for directions or using one-liners in conversation. I decided I had better write out my thoughts in French first, and then use this as a guide to explain my visit. I had much more experience and knowledge in writing French than speaking it. I wanted to wait for a quieter time anyway. No one noticed me writing, because the *syndicat* was still so busy.

After about fifteen minutes, I was ready. I walked up to the desk and in my best French accent, introduced myself. I told the receptionist that I was an Acadian from Nova Scotia, Canada, and talked about my research of the Girouards, Giroires, Giroirs, Gerriors, in Canada and about the 1985 reunion of over 600 descendants of the Maritime Province Girouards, Gerriors, Girroirs, Gerroirs. I also had some photos of the reunion to show. Immediately the room was full of excitement as the girl at the desk, called enthusiastically to the director of the *syndicat*, Madame Michèle Touret: *"Madame! Monsieur Giroire, du Canada!"*

Madame Touret, herself a descendant of Charles de Menou d'Aulnay, one of

Older part of Loudun. The square Tour de Guet, built in 1040 by the Count of Anjou Foulques Nerra, is located at Loudun (Vienne) cross roads to Anjou-Touraine-Poitou. It was spared demolition in the XVII century when the fortress was demolished.

Loudun town shopping area, tower, street photos with bars and restaurants, Acadian statue, City Hall, old city wall, residential street, old street, syndicat d'initiative.

Chuck Gerrior on the weekly market day, monument dedicated to Acadians in Loudun
both photos courtesy of Chuck Gerrior

France

the founding figures of Acadia, greeted me very graciously. She welcomed me to Loudun, and showed immediate interest in my project. She was very familiar with the Girouard, Giroire, and Giroir name in the Loudun region of France. We talked for a while and she offered to take me on a tour that afternoon. Meanwhile, we looked in the telephone directory and within five minutes Jacques Giroir of Loudun came up to meet me. He walked in the *syndicat d'initiative* door and in an emotional moment for both of us, I met my first Giroir of France, and he met his first Gerrior from Canada!

I arranged to meet Madame Touret in the afternoon and Jacques and I headed for the bar across the street to have a few cool ones—a universal language—and chatted in French about each other's families and the Gerrior families in France and Canada in general. What a great way to start my day! The time spent with Jacques was very enjoyable and informative but before long I realized it was time to meet Madame Touret for our tour. Jacques had another commitment, so I thanked him and told him that I looked forward to seeing him again before I left.

At 1 p.m., we headed out of town along the route to Aulnay, Martaizé, and La Chaussée. On our way, I noticed a sign which interested me, and I stopped to take photos; it displayed the three neighbouring villages which made up the lands or *seigniories* of d'Aulnay, the noble landowner for whom some of the Girouards, Giroires, Giroirs worked.

Aulnay, Martaizé, and La Chaussée, in the Départment of Vienne, are approximately 15 kilometers (10 miles) south of Loudun. From these villages, which in the 17th century were dependent on the Poitiers seignieury of Charles d'Aulnay (cousin and successor of Razilly) came the first settlers d'Aulnay brought to Acadia. The first few trips to Acadia included men only. Later, the other members of the

Madame Touret and Freddy Mouchard (destined to become a film maker), helping me to locate some Giroire, Giroir Girouard families in the telephone directory.

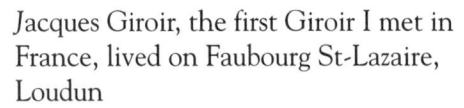

Jacques Giroir, the first Giroir I met in France, lived on Faubourg St-Lazaire, Loudun

France

Top: *Bar across the
street from the
syndicat d'initiative*

Middle: *Directional sign to
villages of St-Jean-de-Sauves,
Mirebeau, Moncontour*

Bottom: *Seigneurie D'Aulnay,
cradle of Acadie*

The following photos give an idea of the lay of the land in this area where our ancestors lived.

photo of the landscape

hay in barn and ladder

This page and opposite:
Farming in vicinity of La Chaussée
Farmhouse in La Chaussée
Hay storage area.
Typical landscape in Départment of Vienne

France

Acadian Awakenings: An Acadian Family In Exile

Opposite: Various methods of baling hay in Department of Vienne
I took particular note of this sign near Loudun since the first François was referred to as 'François dit la Varenne', according to the sworn statements on Belle-Isle-en-Mer

families were transported. Today the telephone directory of Moncton, NB, lists numerous surnames of the families recruited by Charles d'Aulnay for Acadia: Gautreau, Landry, LeBlanc, Blanchard, Girouard. In the quiet village of Aulnay, the castle marks the property of Charles d'Aulnay. The old stone church at La Chaussée, topped with a high steeple, still keeps the appearance it had in the 15th century.[3]

Madame Touret's involvement with the museum and her interests in the origins of Acadians from La Chaussée and surrounding area are summarized very well in the translation from an article which appeared in the American-based Acadian publication entitled *"Le Réveil"*, which had also appeared in France.

From the high esteem and recognition attributed to Michèle Touret of Loudun so obvious in this article, one can easily see why I had chosen to make Loudun my first destination in France to meet Madame Touret. True to her reputation, Madame Touret was now taking the time from her very busy schedule to escort me by car to La Chaussée, the village where some of the first Acadians likely originated, among them, we believe, François Girouard.

It is believed that some of first Acadian settlers were recruited between 1636-1644 from the lands belonging to Charles de Menou d'Aulnay, then Governor of Acadia. The little village of La Chaussée was probably the centre for recruitment because it was the home of Martin Le Godelier, a notary and the Governor's recruiter and overseer of lands.

Le Godelier's little chateau, the Manoir de Godelier, still stands, and is still inhabited. My school history was suddenly coming to life. For the first time, history, which was my worst school subject, was really meaningful to me. The reason, more than likely, was that my heritage and culture were being reflected here, and it was actually the "real thing" that authors write about in our history books. This was exciting!

We then visited the Maison de l'Acadie Museum. It is attached to Notre Dame Church in La Chaussée, the 13th-century church, seating about 50 people, where French farmers and other adventure-seeking souls

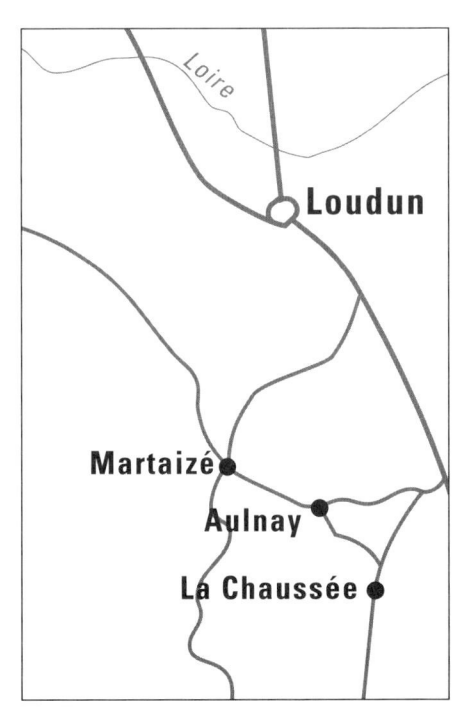

map of route from Loudun to LaChausée

Acadian Awakenings: An Acadian Family In Exile

Le Réveil Acadien
THE ACADIAN AWAKENING

Acadian Cultural Society
Société Culturelle Acadienne

MAISON DE L'ACADIE A LA CHAUSSEE (près de Loudun)
(A "Maison de l'Acadie," in La Chaussee - near Loudun)
An article which appeared in "Les Amitiés Acadiennes"
Translation by Jeannine Caissie

In a previous issue, we talked about the wonderful initiative, that of the creation of a "Maison de l'Acadie", under the chairmanship of Mme Michèle Touret.

So as to reply to several questions, we felt we should explain more precisely that the house is not a reconstitution, nor a copy of a Canadian house. This old house, so ravaged by time, was able to be saved, and restored, due to the generosity of the "Syndicat Intercommunal de Solidarité du Loudunais", which charged the "Maison de l'Acadie Association" with the task of reviving and bringing it to life.

The realization of this enterprise was accomplished, due to the collaboration of devoted volunteers and those interested by the project, and who gave their good support.

The mission of the Association is to administer this house, to promote Acadian history, study the genealogy of the Acadian families who originated Loudunais, to assure cultural exchanges between young french and young canadians, to welcome visitors to permit them to feel the Acadian presence in this region.

In the "Salle des Traditions Populaires", one can discover the different objects and furnishings which depict the life of our Poitou ancestors, and admire an Acadian costume, which was donated to the "Maison de l'Acadie" by the Historical Museum of Acadia in Caraquet.

One can also discover the Library, called "Salle Geneviève Massignon", in honor of this great ethnologue, too soon passed on, and great friend of the Acadians.

On the first floor, there is a great reunion hall, which is used to show films and to receive groups of visitors.

After having briefly responded to questions, we want, at this time, to renew our very sincere congratulations for this wonderful project, due to Mme Touret and her collaborators. The Amitiés Acadiennes vows to see the creation in France other "Maisons de l'Acadie", based on this one, where other Acadian Museums such as the one at Chatellerault, because they help in the "Renaissance Acadienne".

were probably gathered before leaving for the shores of North America, where they would give birth to the Acadian people.

Some of the first Acadians leaving this area for Nova Scotia would probably have been baptized here. Certainly, being very religious, the families of Landry, Martin, Girouard, Gouthro, Robichaud, Belliveau, and many others, would have come here to pray before their departure.

The museum (Maison de l'Acadie), which is attached to the church, contains ancient artefacts, books, maps, genealogy trees, and charts, and the Evangeline Room upstairs for films and meetings. Now, there is also on display a gold plaque of the Acadian Master Chart of all the Acadian Girouard/Girroir/Gerriors in North America.

One of the key figures involved in the plan to populate Acadie from this region of La Chaussée was Isaac De Razilly.

Top left: Entering La Chaussée, Berceau de l'Acadie (cradle of the Acadians).
Top right: Maison Le Godelier
Bottom: Maison de l'Acadie Museum

Acadian Awakenings: An Acadian Family In Exile

Notre Dame Church in La Chaussée.
This is the church where Acadians from this region would likely have gathered to pray before their departure.
Interior views of Notre Dame church
Arial Photo of the church and surrounding area of La Chausée
photo credit: V. Aguillon, Communauté de Communes du Pays Loudunais (CCPL)

ISAAC DE RAZILLY AND ACADIA
1632 - 1636

Acadia returned to France by the Treaty of St-Germain-en Laye on the 29th of March 1632, interested Richelieu, then Prime Minister of Louis XIII. Colonial developments would help France and boost its trade exchanges. He organized two companies, one for *la Nouvelle France* (New France, today Québec and some parts of Ontario), the other for Acadia. The trade monopoly and the consequent obligation to colonize constituted the two basic elements of the French colonization policy. Richelieu entrusted the company for Acadia to his cousin, Isaac de Razilly, naming him Lieutenant General of all the country of New France, called Canada. He was also named Governor of l'Acadie (Acadia). One of the principal associates of Isaac de Razilly was Charles d'Aulnay, 36, who then called upon the people of his lands, especially the young, to colonize this marvellous Acadia. François Girouard would have been around 19 years old at this time. De Razilly died in 1636 and was replaced by Charles D'Aulnay as Governor of Acadia.

To provide an overview of some of the other key players and history of the Loudun region in France including a number of Acadian names in this area, I have translated the following excerpts from information which Michèle Touret shared with me.[4]

It was during the period beginning in 1632 that the region of Loudun is directly implicated in the history of Acadia…In 1635, Claude de Launay-Razilly created a society for the settling of Acadia which Richelieu himself was associated, then carried on his brother's work with his successor, Charles Menou d'Aulnay.

In 1636, the first families in Acadia arrived aboard the *Saint-Jean*, some of them returning immediately the following year, some of them staying. The ship's roster—the list of passengers—contains the names Martin and Trahant among others, natives of Bourgueil (departement of Indre & Loire), as well as the Motins, among whom was the daughter of an associate of the de Razillys, who would marry their cousin, Charles Menou d'Aulnay.

Charles Menou d'Aulnay (1605-1650)
He was the son of René de Menou and of Nicole de Jousserand, a native of Aulnay, a neighbouring village of La Chaussée. As Isaac de Razilly's cousin, he was his companion in Acadia as early as 1632, then his successor as Governor of Acadia (1635-1650). It is under his governorship that the first families of settlers arrived, most of whom had been recruited from the lands of the Seigniory of Charles Menou d'Aulnay. He is well known for having been involved in a nasty civil war with Charles De La Tour, who also had legitimate claims to be the Governor of Acadia. Some consider him a haughty and unpleasant aristocrat; others feel he has been maligned by historians favourable to La Tour.

Martin Le Godelier (1595-1642)
Widower of Madeleine Sanglier, of the family of the lords of Bois-Rogue, near Loudun, he remarried in 1638 to Marie Mathieu. Squire of the Borough at La Chaussée, he was the man placed by Charles d'Aulnay in charge of recruiting volunteers among the farm tenants of Loudun. Kinsman and creditor to the Governor d'Aulnay, he followed him to Acadia with the

Vincent Landry
From a noble family attached to the Jousserand, he was an archer at the *maréchaussée* de Loudun [equivalent of a modern-day police force]. It is as a notary at La Chaussée that he lent his support to M. Le Godelier to the point of continuing with the recruiting after the death of the latter, till that of d'Aulnay, while promoting the emigration of members of his own family.

Michèle Touret continues in this booklet to describe the recruiting process as follows:

> The work of settling Acadia as an agricultural colony effectively made the south of Loudun the cradle of Acadia.
> In 1642, Claude de Launay-Razilly deeded his rights to his cousin d'Aulnay, Governor of Acadia, who recruited settlers on lands belonging to his mother, between La Chaussée and Martaizé. Nicole de Jousserand's *L'aveu au Roi*, [a sort of inventory and sworn report to the king of his estate at Martaizé], shows that, in 1634, no less than nine families of his farm tenants held names that are listed in the first French census of Acadia in 1671. It is in May 1642, wrote Mr. Caillebeau, that we can imagine the gathering of a dozen or so wagons before the church at La Chaussée, carrying the young couples of Loudun. The notary, Vincent Landry, was present as well as the squire of the Borough, M. Le Godelier, who was going to conduct the emigrants to Acadia. His home still exists today at La Chaussée, facing the Chateau de la Bonnetiere.

First Acadian Families from the region of Loudun
From Aulnay:
    BABIN
    DUPUIS
    GIROUARD
    DOUSSET
    POIRIER
From La Chaussée:
    BELLIVEAU
    BOURG
    BRAULT
    LANDRY
    ROBICHAUD
From Martaizé:
    BLANCHARD
    GAUDET
    GAUTREAU
    LEBLANC
    SAVOIE
    THERIAULT

Richelieu
1644   France

In 1644, despite the deaths of Richelieu and le Godelier, Menou d'Aulnay continued to recruit prospective settlers in Loudunais, with the help of Vincent Landry. A memoire of that year stipulates: "that there were 20 french couples who passed through this place to begin the population of the countries and D'Aulnay would have taken more if there were more families who met the criteria"....

That process was abruptly interrupted in 1650 by the death of d'Aulnay and a show of British military power in Acadia in 1654. From that point on, the people wanting to immigrate to New France, did so on an individual basis, heading toward the St. Lawrence River valley in what is now Québec, and was then Canada (as distinct from Acadia). They first had to go to La Rochelle to hire themselves out to a master in a legal contract for a period of about three years. The master would provide food and lodging and help them. After their term expired, several returned to France, but a few, with their wives, established themselves in New France

At the Maison d'Acadie one can also read the classic work of Geneviève Massignon, one of the earliest researchers to have analysed Acadian speech in *Les Parlers Français D'Acadie*. She also offers some insight into documents about the future Acadians and their genealogy in the Poitou regions of France. These volumes are also available in many university libraries in North America. I have translated two excerpts as follows:

The colonists recruited by Charles d'Aulnay (1635-1650)[5]-Massignon

I proceeded to examine the parish registers of Angliers to late 1692, also of d'Aulnay to late 1672, and of La Chaussée 1626 where are found (1626-1650) half the family names among 53 names of families in the census of 1671 in Acadia: Babin, Belliveau, Bertrand, Bour, Brault or Braude (feminine form), Brin, Dugast, Dupuy, Gaudet or Gaudette (feminine form), Giroire, Joffriau, Landry, LeBlanc, Morin, Poirier, Raimbault, Robichau, Savoie, Thibodeau. In addition, the names of Chébrat, Gauthier, Guion, and Mercier—carried by the women of the colonies of 1671—fall, in my view, in the same category. Here the records permitted positive identification of two families (extracts from the parish registers of La Chaussée, Vienne): January 24, baptism of Madeleine, daughter of Vincent Brun and Vincende Braude, godfather Vincent Brault, and the 21st of August baptism of Andrea, daughter of Vincent Brin and Renée Braude, residing at Grand Chaussée.

In the census of Port Royal (Acadia), in 1671 appears: Vincent Brun(farmer), age 60, his wife Renée Brode, age 55. Children: Madeleine, age 25, married to William Trahan; Andrée, age 24, married to Claude Terriau (5); Françoise, age 19, married to Bernard Bour, Bastion, age 15, and Marie, age 12. While the ages of the first two children of the Bruns coincide and since the acts of baptisms of the three younger do not appear in the registers of La Chaussée, one may fix the date of their departure (from La Chaussée) as between 1646-1650. Another observation suggests itself: the mother called herself Braude or Braud, and the godfather of the oldest, Vincent Brault: by another act taking place at La Chaussée one may find that he was of the same village of Grand Chaussée. We find him in Acadia in 1671, listed as Vincent Brot age 40 years, his wife Marie Bour age 26, farmer. It is probable that this

Vincent Brot was the young brother-in-law of Vincent Brun.

A third Act appears in the parish registers of La Chaussée, the baptism of Jeanne Chébra, February 5, 1627, which is to reappear in the census of 1671, where it is mentioned that Jeanne Chébrat, 45 years old, was married to Antoine Gougeon.

Of the numerous family ties existing between the first colonists of Acadia that we have found in the so important 1671 Port Royal census, here are the families said to have been allied before their arrival or establishment in Acadie:

The Terriot were related to the Dupuis through Perrine Terriot, wife of Martin Dupuis; both were dead in 1671.

There were two persons named René Landry, the older, 53, married to Perrine Bour, 45 years old, and the younger (omitted in the census of 1671, but recorded in the census of 1786, single, age 52. There is also Perrine Landry, 60 years, widow of Jacques Joiffriau (?), and Antoinette Landry, 53, married to Antoine Bourg, 62 years old.

The Aucoin were allied with the Girouard through Jeanne Aucoin, 40 years old, married to François Girouard, aged 50 years, and to the Boudrot by Michelle Aucoin, 53 years old, married to Michel Boudrot, 71 years old...

The Origins of today's Acadiens, according to their family names.[6]- Massignon:

The following 16 families appear to date back to the Seigniory of d'Aulnay [land and property belonging to Lord Aulnay], Governor of Acadia from 1632 to 1650, this seigniory having its seat at Aulnay (Loudunais) which included in its boundaries the three villages of Aulnay, La Chaussée and Martaizé (Département of Vienne): BABIN, BELLIVEAU, BLANCHARD, BOURQUE, BRAULT, DUPUIS, GAUDET, GAUTREAU, GIROUARD, HÉBERT, LANDRY, LEBLANC, POIRIER, ROBICHAUD, SAVOIE, THÉRIAULT....

Massignon continues to describe the roots of a number of other Acadian families, but more recent research shows that Acadian roots in France in general, are in fact, more diverse in origin than suspected at the time Massignon wrote her book.

On another note, while I was at the museum, looking at Massignon's work and talking to the receptionist, Isabelle Secq, a couple of wonderful coincidences occurred.

First, Isabelle herself told me she was a descendant of the Giroirs of France and was very interested in my project. As I later found out, her father Guy Secq was also very interested in the genealogy and research of the Girouard/Girroir(e) family in France and their connection to Canada and the USA. In fact, Guy would later be responsible for organizing a Giroir reunion in France.

Secondly, while Isabelle and I were talking, I noticed a lady, out of the corner of my eye, inching closer and closer, trying to hear our conversation better. At the time, I was explaining to Isabelle in my best French, that I was deeply involved with the research of the Girouards, Giroire, Giroir family history and genealogy.

Finally, the other woman, who was trying to hear our conversation, said:

"*Excusez moi, Monsieur, parlez-vous des Girouards?*" (Excuse me sir; are you talking about the Girouards).

"*Oui,*" I confirmed.

"*Je m'appelle Andrée Gombert,*" she said. "*Et voici mon mari, Yves. Nous habitons dans le midi de la France, à Chateauneuf, prés de Marseilles. Je suis une descendante de François Girouard et Jeanne Aucoin. Voici mes diagrammes de généalogie.*" (My name is Andrée Gombert and this is my husband Yves. We live in southern France, at Chateauneuf near Marseilles. I am a descendant of François Girouard and Jeanne Aucoin. Here are my genealogy charts).

As soon as I heard this, my mouth dropped in complete surprise. I immediately showed her my master chart and said, "*Mais c'est le méme François Girouard sur ma diagramme principale!*" (But this is the same François on my master chart!). We couldn't believe it! Shivers ran down my spine and legs and I am sure she also had similar feelings, by the look of excitement on her face, as we both realized our common ancestor was François, born approximately 1620 in France.

Let's face it: chances were a million to one that Andrée and I would ever meet under these circumstances—a Girouard descendant from Canada, and a Girouard descendant from southern France, both researching common roots, both arriving in La Chaussée at the same time, at that same particular minute, at that particular hour, and on that particular day, to make a connection via overhearing a conversation. It was a miracle! Or maybe an omen? That was certainly an emotional high for the trip, which I will always treasure. Someone very special must have arranged that meeting—God knows who it is! Anyway Andrée and I will never forget it, I am sure. We arranged other meetings that week to talk about our shared genealogy and the 1985 Maritime Gerrior Reunion.

Andrée Gombert descends in a number of ways from the second generation of Girouards at Port Royal:
1) via Madeleine Girouard, [AMC Block C-2], daughter of François Girouard and Jeanne Aucoin, married to Thomas Cormier. [AMC Block C-2] See also [Block P201-3 of subchart 201]

Michèle Touret then took me around to a number of Giroir, Giroire families living in the surrounding area.

Jean-Pierre Giroire greeted me at the hotel in Loudun and we visited his parents' home. His father was a very successful modern-day farmer, using all the new

Andrée, and I with her husband, Yves Gombert at la maison de l'Acadie

technologies available in the industry. We talked a great deal about the Girouards, Giroires, and looked at a very old family photo of their ancestors as well as at Jean-Pierre's computer, which called up all the names of Giroir, Giroire, and Girouards in the department of Vienne. Later, Jean-Pierre and his fiancée took me out to dinner in the town of Loudun. It was a very interesting and enjoyable visit. We also visited other Giroire families in the area.

Jean-Pierre Giroire of Véniers near Loudun and his father Guy Giroire during my visit in Aug. 1988 at his dad's home. Jean-Pierre Girouard was one of the city councillors of Loudun, at the time of my visit.

Home of Mr. and Mrs. Guy Giroire, living in le Monteil, Saint Jean de Sauvres. I loved this hug! Madame Touret is official photographer here as well as guide for my tour, August 1988.

France

Home of Mr.& Mrs. René Giroire in Martaizé, Vienne, France, May 1990 during Charles Gerrior's visit. Mr. & Mrs. René Giroire are the parents of Marie Giroire married to Baudouin de La Bouillerie. Charles Gerroir, who was stationed in Germany, descends from the Arichat Gerriors. See [Block T163-7m1 of subchart 163] in the Isle Madame chapter of the Nova Scotia volume. His grandfather is Benjamin Thomas, son of Abraham Gerrior and Emeline LeBlanc of Arichat.

Courtyard of Mr.and Mrs.René Giroire's home in "La Machinerie" in Martaizé, May 1990.

Barns and stables of René Giroire's horse breeding farm in Martaizé, (Vienne) France. Charles (Chuck) on left of photo and René on the right. My first sign in France of Giroire horsemanship and expertise.

Pierre Giroir and his father in courtyard at St-Jean-de-Sauves. Pierre's father and I having a cool one and comparing genealogy notes.

Pierre's lineage was given as follows, starting at present day to his oldest ancestors (à means son of).
Pierre Giroire m. Madeleine Sénécheau à (Marie-Thérèse Giroire m. -husband's name not available) à (Rudolphe Giroire (b.1900) m. Laurentin Odette) à (Benjamin Giroire (1862-1943) m. Elisa Coutreau) à (Pierre Giroire m.—Boinet) à (François Giroire m. Marie Dulac 1824) à (Pierre Giroire (St-Jean-de-Sauves) m. Marie-Madeleine Ravion).

This last, Pierre Giroire married to Marie-Madeleine Ravion, had two sisters: Marie, who m. Vincent Landry and Jeanne m. Jean Dulac. We know that Pierre, who married —— Boinet, had a brother François (not married). Also Benjamin Giroire m. Elisa Coutreau and had one brother Maximilien. This completes this branch to date.

Madame Touret and I then visited the town hall, the *mairie* (place where records are kept in villages and towns of France), in Roche Rigault, a village near La

France

Researching ancient documents at the mairie of La Roche Rigault and map of La Roche Rigault and surrounding area.

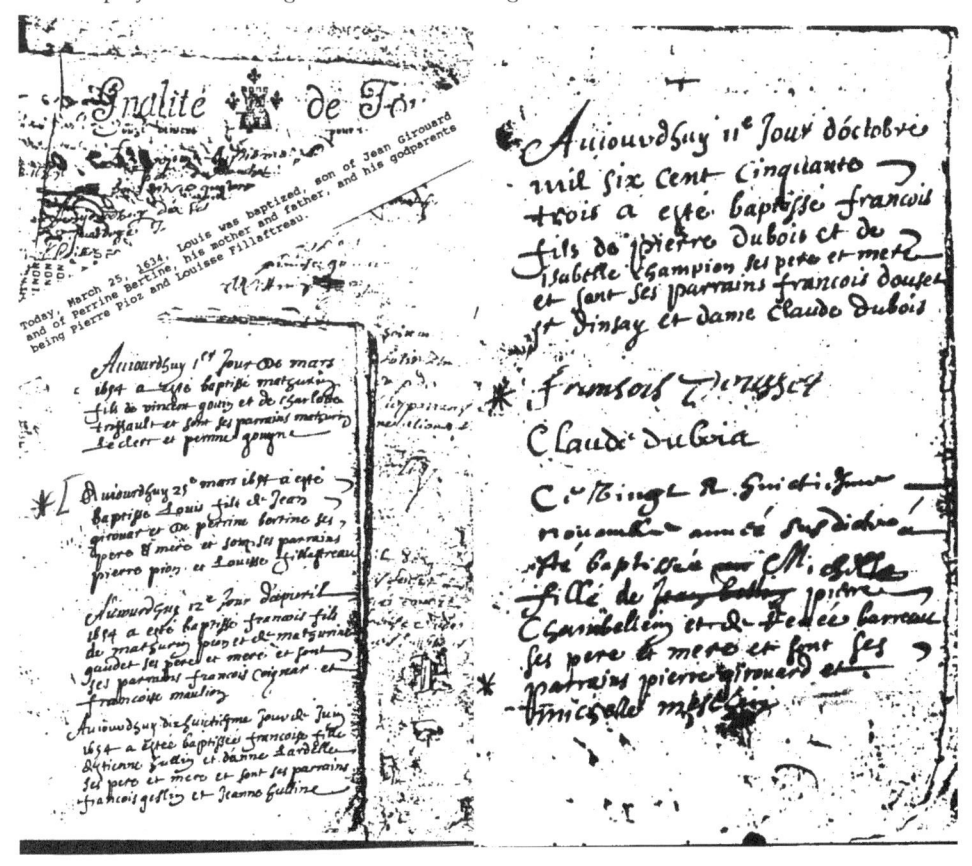

Record copy of this document showing Girouard families in 1600's supports Massignon's theory of François Girouard likely being from this locality.

Chaussée. In these records I found a very significant Girouard name indicating the existence of the family here during the period that François would have been in France. Note that in this particular early record in this region, the name is spelled Girouard. Could this be François's family or cousins?

WEDNESDAY: Castle of La Bonnetière

The next day, Madame Touret had arranged for me to meet Baudouin de la Bouillerie, owner of the castle and his wife Marie (Giroire). I was going to get a personal tour and visit a real castle, which dated back more than five hundred years. It now belonged to a family who, in part, descend from the Giroirs. This was an unexpected treat. Baudouin met me at the hotel. He greeted me warmly, and I followed him by car to the castle.

As I approached the castle, the sight was awe-inspiring: a long straight and narrow road, which set the castle in perspective, against the horizon, and focused my view directly upon the main gates between the two symmetrical towers.

View approaching castle.

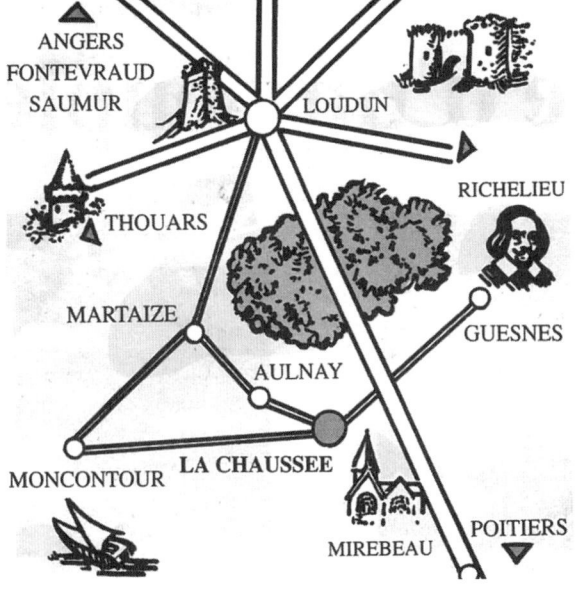

La Chaussée map.
Courtesy of Michèle Touret.

One could not help but think of the many things of great importance to the area that must have gone on in this castle. Perhaps great minds met here and discussed problems of concern to the community. How many knights would have lived here and how many celebrations must have taken place in this castle during special events and feast days? I pondered all these questions, saying to myself yet again, "If only these walls could talk."

Baudouin, married to Marie Giroire, was my personal guide at the castle.

This view and top of next page: views of the castle with photos by V. Agrieilon, CCPL for photography.

Courtesy of Baudouin de la Bouillerie.

Baudouin informed me that La Bonnetière was named for its good land. The original owners were powerful Lords, the Vaucelles family, who also owned much land in Poitou and Main. Baudouin mentioned that we should not be surprised to see family names like Landry, Robichaud and Giroire since these Acadian families lived in this region where this castle has stood for over 500 years.

About five years after my first trip to France in 1988, Freddy Mouchard of Poitou, a young filmmaker, returned to the Loudun region and, like myself, continued to be very impressed and moved with what he saw and experienced in La Chaussée and, in particular, at the Château de la Bonnetière. With the support of Baudouin de la Bouillerie, the owner of the castle, and Madame Touret, *directrice* of La Maison de l'Acadie, he produced a very successful film called *Acadie naissance d'un people*, (Acadia, Birth of a People), the place and setting being the Château de la Bonnetière. The film tells the story of the Acadians before their departure for New France. This castle has a great deal of history and certainly Baudouin de la Bouillerie and Madame Touret are promoting it by encouraging this work of Freddy Mouchard.

Since this time, the company called *Acadie, Naissance d'un Peuple*, has produced and presented a show called " La Grande Traversée" (the Big Crossing) for The World Francophonie Summit celebrations held in New Brunswick, Canada 1999.

After the tour of the castle, Baudouin invited me home for dinner that evening. Upon arriving at his home in Moncontour, I met his lovely wife, Marie (Giroire), who operates a pharmacy—their family business. We had the best of wine, made by Baudouin's ancestors. Throughout our meal we chatted about the Giroires of

Cover of Acadie naissance d'un Peuple, painting by L. Dunham
Courtesy of Michèle Touret.

France and Canada. We had a great evening. Their delightful children also dined with us. We talked slowly to understand each other and whenever we got stuck, we would pull out the dictionaries and have a great laugh each time we had to do so. However, we were able to understand each other quite clearly.

Marie shared her family tree, showing her Giroire direct descent beginning with her and going back to 1777 in France:

Baudouin and his wife Marie (Giroire) with their baby and their pet dog in the courtyard, Moncontour, August 1988

Below: Dining at the home of Baudouin and Marie (Giroir) de la Bouillerie and visiting Marie's mother who fondly recalls time spent in Canada in her youth. Moncontour, August, 1988

Marie-France Giroire m. Baudouin de la Bouillerie (Moncontour) à (René Giroire m. Héléne Royer) à (Lucien Giroire (1904-1982) m. Madeleine Perrot) à (Gustave Giroire (1873-1961) m. Zédonic Catin) à (Louis Giroire (1838-1922) m. Adélaide Turquais) à (Pierre Giroire (b. 1797) m. Moine Madeleine) à (Pierre Giroire b. 1777 m. Thérèse Tétreau)

Earlier I had obtained Pierre Giroire's genealogy (Puyrevault, St-Jean-de-Sauves, France), but there seemed to be no connection between the two families from the information we had collected thus far. However, I suspect the pattern is similar to all the Giroir, Gerriors in particular locations in Canada: when all the information is finally known, all of them will be related to common roots.

THURSDAY: Le Girouard, a village with our name!
Thursday, at daybreak, I headed west toward the coast of France, in the Vendée region, just above La Rochelle, to see the village of Le Girouard. Having observed this name on a map of France, I was curious as to its origin and connection to the present family of Girouards.

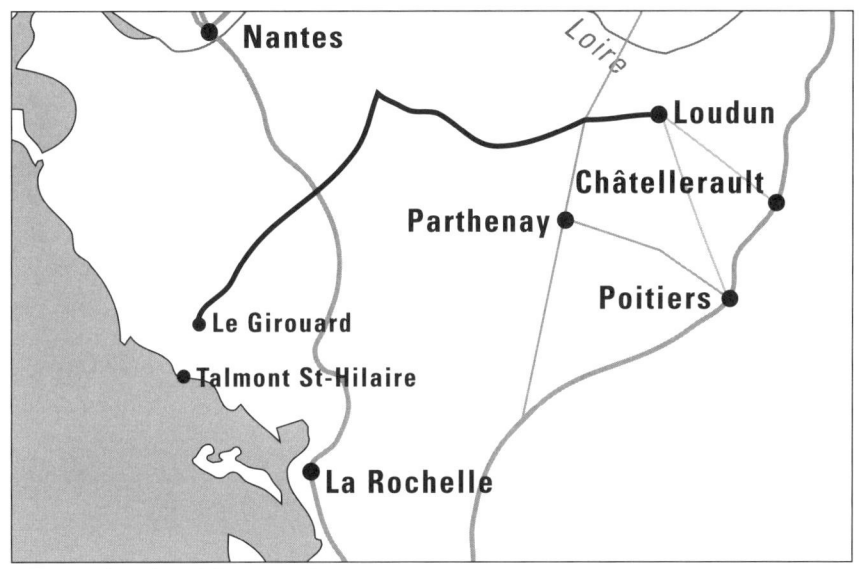

After a full non-stop, five- to six-hour drive, I finally found Le Girouard.

I talked to a few residents, all of whom told me there are no families of Girouards living here today. I visited the *mairie* and received some information on the origins of the village[7] (here is the translation).

Le Girouard, a *bourg* (large village), is situated in a green valley crossed by the Gilboule, a fast-running river, whose tributaries are the Chaon, la Minerie, le Gondeau, and la Mingerie. This site has been inhabited since the Stone Age: near this territory, axes of polished stone have been found. The name possibly comes from *Capella Giroldi*, la Chapelle des Girauds (the Girauds' chapel).

Lucienne Giroire Doussin and her husband, Gérard, of Parthenay, France who

Acadian Awakenings: An Acadian Family In Exile

attended our First International Girouard Giroir Giroire... Reunion in 1990, Antigonish, Nova Scotia, provided me with a number of Girouard genealogy notes

Le GIROUARD
(616 habitants)

Top right: The stone monument sign for le Girouard in the department of Vendée, my first clue, other than my map, that I was on the right track in finding this small village.

View of entrance into the town of Le Girouard
Ancient church in Le Girouard and the cross monument across the street, typical of many locations in France.
Mairie of Le Girouard.

90

containing *some* official document references in France of Giroire knights, landowners, and lawyers, one of which is appropriate to introduce here since we are talking about the town of Le Girouard. I have translated and footnoted this official document as follows:

> In 1225, William Giroire, Manager of the King's estate, born in Talmont (Vendée), left part of his property at the Abbey to build a hospital. This property later became known as the village of Girouard, near Talmont.[8]

I learned later, from correspondence with Gaston Giroir of La Boulonnière, Larçay, France, that there is another village named Girouard near Versailles, south of Paris; there were obviously many Girouards living in the Paris area. Gaston also told me that in the centre of France, southeast of Limoges, there is yet another location called Girouard. I believe today that this would be connected to the French-Canadian branch of Girouards from Montluçon and the surrounding area, because of its proximity. As shown on the maps discussing the various locations of Varennes below, there is yet another area named Girouard, just south of St-Jean-de-Sauves.[9] All of this is exciting information for future research.

FRIDAY/SATURDAY:
La Varenne, Varanne, La Varanne, Varanne, Varennes, Les Varennes

I concentrated my efforts on visiting places with names like "La Varenne", since François Girouard apparently carried the nickname "La Varenne", possibly from a place in France called "La Varenne". At the time when François would have come to Canada, family surnames alone were often not used except in official documents. This tradition was to become even more prevalent in Acadia, since Acadian families were often interconnected so closely that many people ended up with similar first and last names. Hence, nicknames were commonly used to distinguish people with similar names, based sometimes on profession/occupation, sometimes on physical appearance, sometimes on particular events in someone's life, sometimes on personal characteristics, and sometimes on regions of origin.

During the Deportation, however, many Acadian documents and family records disappeared. Some Acadians, who were first deported to England in 1756, were later brought to Belle-Ile-en-Mer, an island off the coast of France. While there, officials took a series of sworn statements from the displaced families, in an attempt to replace the lost records. It is in these affidavits that François Girouard appears as "La Varenne".

According to my research, there are only two places called "La Varenne" in France, but many places of similar spelling. I wanted to find out as much as I could about the location and history of each of these places. For this reason I need to digress to look at some documents in Belle-Île-en-Mer concerning the first appearance of this name (La Varenne) as it applies to our first François Girouard. Some of this documentation, which is held at the National Archives in Ottawa, contains very important information regarding our François, and his likely place of origin in France — La Varenne. The reference to La Varenne is clearly made in the document quoted at the end of this first article. I have a number of excerpts from this document and supplemented the information with a map of the region. The document is entitled: *The Acadians of Belle Isle (Belle Île) and the Lost Registers of Acadia*[10]

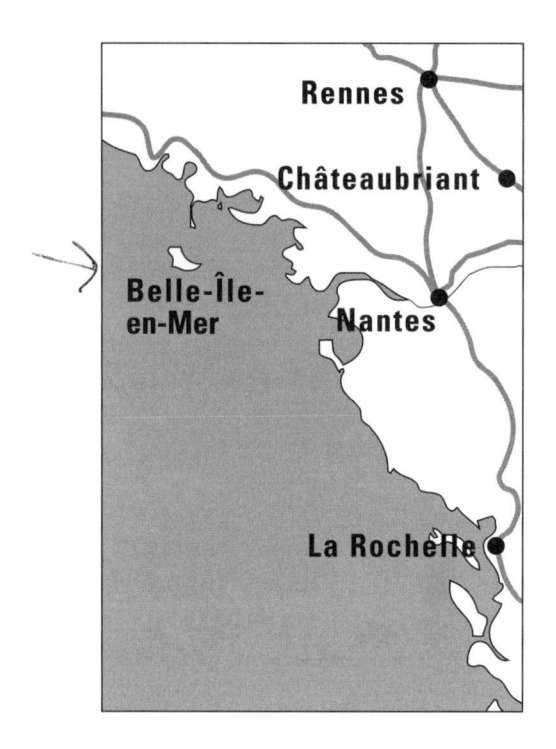

Map of relative location of Belle-Ile-En- Mer, departement of Morbihan, 502 km distance from Paris by ferry and road.

[The following is a report given the by Capt. C. E. Lart, which describes the situation at Belle Isle with some interesting details.]

After the Peace of Paris, as soon as it was possible, some of the Acadians were restored to France, and land and materials for resettlement in the land of their forefathers, were given them by the French Government.

One of these groups, consisting of seventy-eight families, was settled in Belle-Isle, off the coast of Southern Brittany, the Abbé le Loutre, "former Vicar-General of Québec", taking charge of it. Land was granted to them in the four parishes of Bangor, Locmaria, Sauzon and Le Palais on this island.

Seventy-eight houses were built for them, one per family, due to the initiative and representations of the Abbé le Loutre. The original inhabitants of the land already numbered 375 families, and the poor soil and wind-swept, treeless character of the island, held out small prospect of a successful outcome for the adventure.

France

In consequence of the loss of the original registers of the Acadian parishes, it was necessary to reconstruct them as far as possible, in order to establish the genealogies of the settlers, as proof of their Acadian and French descent. It was accordingly ordered that depositions should be taken before a committee in each parish, consisting of the Rector of the parish, the Abbé le Loutre and the Public Prosecutor of the King, with three witnesses, "all Acadians"; and that two copies of the registers so compiled should be made, one on stamp paper, and the other on common paper; and after being attested and signed, one kept by the rector, and the other deposited in the courthouse of Siège Royal Auray.

The report then goes on to describe the process of oaths or declarations taken by Acadians in more detail as follows:

COURT DECREE CONCERNING THE ACADIANS OF BELLE ISLE JANUARY 12, 1767

The declarations made by the heads of each family were checked, corrected or supplemented by the three Acadians present as witnesses, and afterwards read over in the presence of the Rector of the Parish or his Vicar, and the missionaries who accompanied the colonists from Canada. A declaration in French, made by the Abbé le Loutre, was appended to each register as follows (translation by the author)

"M. L'Abbé le Loutre, former Vicar General of the diocese of Québec in Canada, declared that the Acadians placed in this island were transported by the English, from Boston and other English colonies in the month of October, 1755, and from these English colonies they were transported to England and dispersed in various places in the kingdom in 1756. In 1763, after the Paris Peace Treaty, they were transported to France by the Cabarres of the King and placed in various seaports and then in 1765 in the middle of the month, they were sent to this Island by order of Mgr. le duc de Choiseul, Ministre de la Marine.
[Signed] M. le Loutre Missionary Priest, March 2, 1766"

The following map, based on a census taken at the time of their arrival and settlement of the 78 Acadian families, helps retrace their genealogies, and can be found in the city halls of the four counties shown on this map. Some family names appearing on the reference map on which the map was based, appear more than once accounting for the 78 stars on the map from a list of only 25 family names. However I will list family names appearing on the reference map, only once here, just to indicate all the surnames of Acadian families living on Belle Isle-en-Mer.

1. LEBLANC
2. DAIGRE
3. MELANÇON
4. RICHARD
5. TRAHAN
6. PITRE
7. AUCOIN
8. BOUDROT

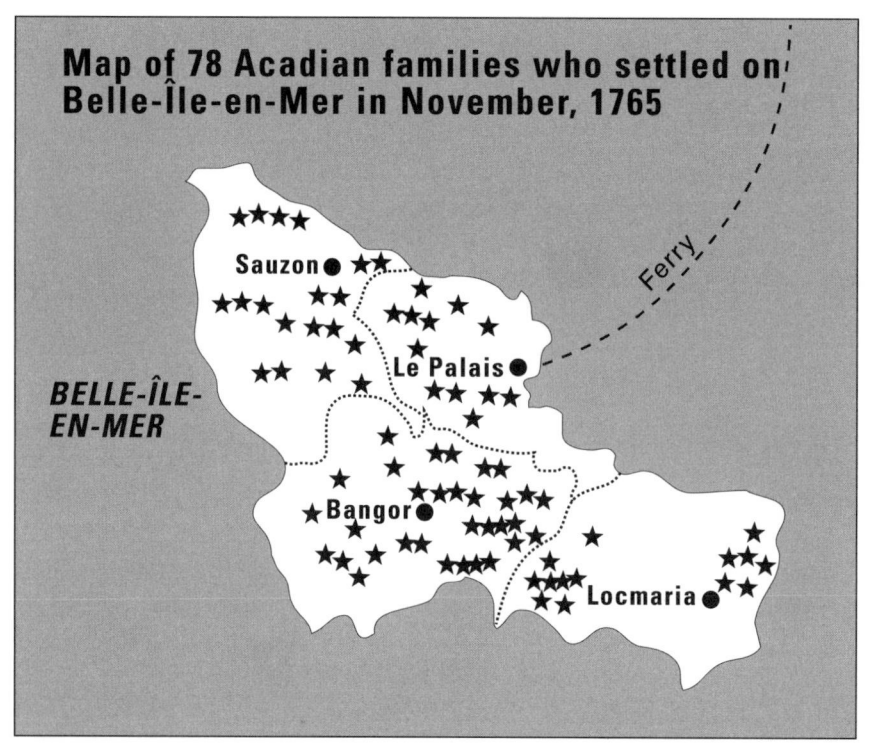

Map of 78 Acadian families who settled on Belle-Île-en-Mer in November, 1765

78 Acadian families at Belle-Isle-En-Mer, who settled on Belle Île-en-Mer, Nov. 1, 1765, information based on a map by Rene Daligaut, from the census of Receveur du Domaine and Sénehal de Belle Isle, François Le Bescond of Kamarquer Acadians (Family Archives), with a note stating that the declarations made by the Acadians in the month of February, 1767 are held by the Court of Bretagne (Community Archives). This reference map on which the above map is based was taken from the Acadians in Exile by Daniel Hébert

9. HEBERT
10. DUON
11. COURTIN
12. MONTET
13. DELINE
14. TERRIOT
15. DOURON
16. LANDRY
17. TIBAUDAULT
18. GAUTROT
19. MAUGER
20. GENDRE
21. POIRIER
22. SEGOILLOT
23. BILLERAY
24. TIERNAY
25. DOUCET

France

Also the map notes indicate the following other names:
Orphans carrying another name: VINCENT, HACHÉ, RIVET AND MARTIN
Spellings of names have been reproduced the same as they appeared on the reference map.

Continuing now with another excerpt of the report of Capt G.E. Lart called *The Acadians of Belle Isle and the Lost Registers of Acadie*, we discover how these families were distributed on Belle-île or Belle-Isle (both spellings are common and are found in various documents):

The families composing the colony, established in the four parishes of Belle-Isle as follows:
    1) In <u>Bangor</u>: LeBlanc, Richard, Thibodault, Trahan (t), Thérriot (Terriot), Tiernay, Hébert, Granger, Billeray, Deline, Montet, Landry, Daigre, Rivet, Duon, Aucoin, Gautrot, Boudet, Dupuis, Haché, Foret, Melançon (orig. English: Millenson), Pitre (of Flemish origin), Bourg, Moser (from Alsace).
    2) In <u>Le Palais</u>: LeBlanc, Daigre, Granger, Richard.
    3) In <u>Locmaria</u>: Trahant, Gautrot, Daigre, Granger, Hébert, Poirier, Gendre, Douaron, Ségoillot, Thériot (Terriot), Melançon.
    4) In <u>Sauzon</u>: Courtin, Pitre, Trahant, Granger, Daigre, Boudrot, LeBlanc, Babin, Dupuis, Doucet.

Capt Lart's report continues, giving more detailed information on the situation of the Acadians at Belle-Isle:

Because land in Belle-Isle was held in fief from the Marquis at Belle-Isle, manorial dues had to be paid by the colonists, but these were waived until 1769, when the first dues were to be paid, under pain of fine or expulsion, with the freedom from taxation to extend for five years from 1764 to 1768.
    In 1768, Oct. 30, the first year when payment was to commence, the colonists refused to pay their rents and dues, alleging that they were overcharged, and claiming a diminution. Some misunderstanding seems to have arisen, for the memoirs of 1787 states that the payments were not to begin until 1769.
    The colony however did not flourish. The island is open to the full fury of the Atlantic gales; the soil is rocky, and the seigniorial dues were evidently too heavy for the new habitants, who came from a patriarchal existence in a rich land, unburdened by seigniorial dues, taxes, and exactions and they found that the exchange was not for the better as far as the conditions of life went. It is very probable that the French Government found the Acadians more of a burden and made use of them to fill up waste and unprofitable land.
    In any event, partly owing to the government refusing any further help, and partly from the hostility of the original inhabitants of the island, the Acadians only remained for a few years before the bulk of them voluntarily returned to North America and a few migrated to Corsica.

From the booklet, Les Acadiens Pietons de l'Atlantique I learned that only sixteen families remained and are today absorbed in the original population. [Granger,

Térriot, Daigle]. This source also gives the following information regarding the Acadian houses:

A few original houses built by the Acadians still stand today, like that of Joseph-Simon Granger in Antoureau (Palais County), or that of Charles LeBlanc in Ker Ourdé (Bangor County).[11]

Let us look more closely now at a few of these sworn statements which are not part of Capt Lart's report but are of particular interest to the Girouard family and which mention François Girouard (Jacques) *dit* la Varenne. These documents concerning the genealogies of the Acadian families at Belle-Isle are also held by the National Archives collection, with the originals in the archives of the department of Morbihan, France.

These excerpts concerning the Girouards in Belle-Ile-En-Mer are taken from the actual sworn statements or declarations from the Acadian parishes of Locmaria, Sauzon, le Palais, and the parish of Bangor, all on the island of Belle Isle-en-Mer as shown on the map.[12]

Pierre Richard was one of the Acadians who gave a sworn statement at Belle Ile-En-Mer. You can find the parents of this Pierre on the Acadian Master Chart of William D. Gerrior. [AMC Block H-3b]. His parents are Pierre Richard married to Magdeleine Girouard who is the daughter of Jacques Girouard and Margarite Gauthrot, [AMC Block F-3b]. This Magdeleine, who is referred to in the following sworn statement, is therefore the granddaughter of François (or Jacques) *dit* la Varenne, the first Girouard arriving at Port Royal.

The following excerpts from the declarations previously mentioned were translated by the author (original French document on opposite page):

Testimony of Pierre Richard of the Village of Kerbellie, parish of Palais. February 9, 1767. There appeared before me Pierre Richard of the village of Kerbellie; witnesses Honoré LeBlanc, Joseph LeBlanc, Olivier Daigre, Laurent Babin, all Acadians, who declared he was born at Port Royal, capital of Acadia, November 15, 1710, son of Pierre Richard and Magdeleine Girouard. Pierre Richard, father of the declarant, died at Port Royal in 1726, son of René Richard and Magdeleine Landri [Landry], both of whom died in the said place.

The said René Richard issued from another René Richard, *dit* Sans Souci originally from France, married at the said place of Port Royal to Marie Blanchard. They both died there. The said Magdeleine Giroüard died at Port Royal 1752 being daughter of Jacques Giroüard and Anne Goudrot, and Jacques Giroüard himself being a son of another <u>Jacques Giroüard, *dit* "La Varenne"</u> originally from France with his wife, Jeanne Aucoin, and established at Port Royal, both having died in the said place. . .

The document goes on to say that Pierre Richard and Marie [Magdeleine] Girouard married at Port Royal in 1709, but we know that the marriage was actually January 26, 1712, from the Port Royal Register. So these statements, although very helpful in many cases, especially where records are missing, are sometimes inaccurate with regards to exact dates. Note also the use of the trema accent (two dots above the "u") in the family name during this period of history.

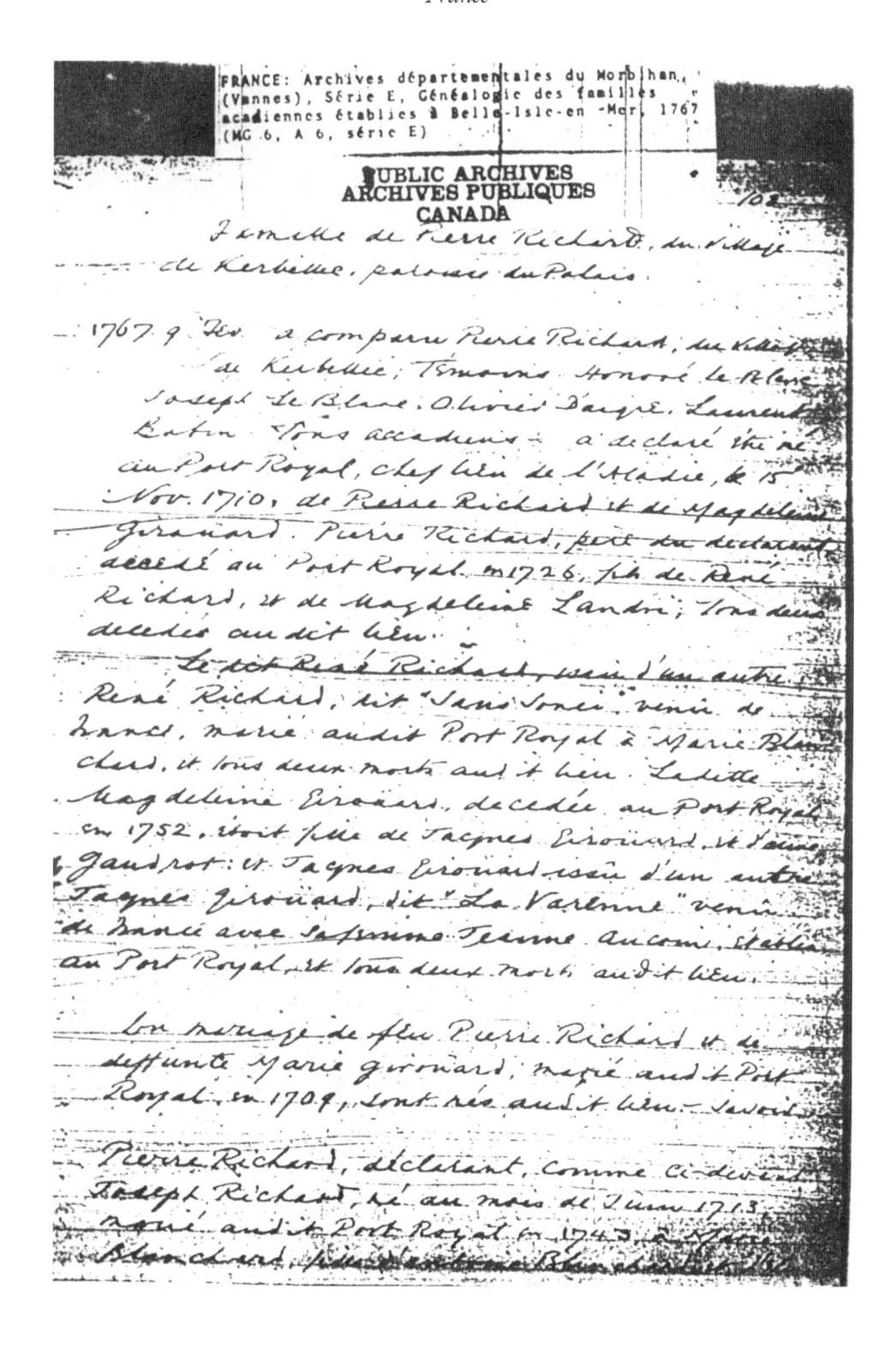

> FRANCE: Archives départementales du Morbihan, (Vannes), Série E, Généalogie des familles acadiennes établies à Belle-Isle-en-Mer, 1767 (MG 6, A 6, série E)
>
> PUBLIC ARCHIVES
> ARCHIVES PUBLIQUES
> CANADA

Famille de Pierre Richard, du village de Kerbellec, paroisse du Palais.

1767. 9 fev. a comparu Pierre Richard, du village de Kerbellec; Témoins Honoré Le Blanc, Joseph Le Blanc, Olivier Daigre, Laurent Babin. Tous acadiens – a déclaré être né au Port Royal, chef lieu de l'Acadie, le 15 Nov. 1710, de Pierre Richard et de Magdeleine Girouard. Pierre Richard, père du déclarant, décédé au Port Royal en 1726, fils de René Richard, et de Magdeleine Landri; Tous deux décédés au dit lieu.

Le dit René Richard, issu d'un autre René Richard, dit "Sans Souci", venu de France, marié audit Port Royal à Marie Blanchard, et tous deux morts au dit lieu. Ladite Magdeleine Girouard, décédée au Port Royal en 1752, était fille de Jacques Girouard et d'une Gaudrot: et Jacques Girouard issu d'un autre Jacques Girouard, dit "La Varenne" venu de France avec sa femme Jeanne du côté, établis au Port Royal, et tous deux morts audit lieu.

Du mariage de feu Pierre Richard et de défunte Marie Girouard, marié audit Port Royal, en 1709, sont nés audit lieu – savoir

Pierre Richard, déclarant, comme ci devant Joseph Richard, né au mois de Juin 1713 marié audit Port Royal en 1743 à Marie Blanchard

Declaration statement in French, regarding "La Varenne"

In addition to establishing La Varenne as the French dwelling place of the first Girouard in Port Royal, this document raises the question of how Jacques Girouard changed to François in the Port Royal census of 1671. For certain they are the same person, for we see his name on the census record of Port Royal, recorded as François Girouard, married, with wife Jeanne Aucoin. Perhaps his full name was François Jacques Girouard, known as Jacques to his friends, but officially recorded as François in the census at Port Royal. More importantly, this sworn statement confirms his place of origin in France as La Varenne. The way the document reads also suggests that the couple was married before arriving at Port Royal. In turn, this suggests that the marriage record could possibly be located in La Rochelle where the Aucoins originate. The Aucoins were also working on the seigniories of Aulnay. However, this interpretation has problems because we learn from Léopold Lanctôt in *Familles Acadiennes* that Jeanne Aucoin was born in 1631, making her only eight or nine years old in 1640 when the ships *Le Saint-Françoys* and *Le Saint-Jean* voyaged from France to Port Royal. The Aucoins were on one of these two ships. In fact, Lanctôt without qualification states that Jeanne Aucoin married François Girouard in 1647.

There is a second reference to "Jacques" Girouard and Jeanne Aucoin in the sworn statements at Belle-Île, regarding another granddaughter of Jacques *dit* la Varenne—Magdeleine Girouard who married Michel Martin.

Translation by the author (original document in French on opposite page:
Feb. 27, 1767
Louis Courtin living in the village of Arpens de Triboutons of Sauzon, witnessed by Simon Pierre Daigre, Joseph Babin, Jean-Baptiste LeBlanc and Amant Granger, all Acadians living on this Island, declaring to be born in this part, from St.-Nicholas de Fréteval Comté de Dunors, Evêché de Bloys. Marie-Joseph Martin was born at Port Royal in 1740 of Michel Martin and Magdeleine Girouard. Michel Martin is the son of Steven Martin and Marie Comeau and this Steven Martin is himself son of René Martin, originally from France and married to Marguerite Landry at Port Royal where both died.

    Magdeleine Girouard, born at the said Port Royal, daughter of Guillaume [William] Girouard who was son of Jacques Girouard and Anne Gautrot of Port Royal and this Jacques Girouard descended from another Jacques Girouard, coming from France with Jeanne Aucoin his wife, established herself and died at the said place of Port Royal........

The parents of this Magdeleine Girouard [William Girouard and Marie Bernard] can be found in [AMC Block J-3a] of the master chart of William D. Gerrior. More detail on her brothers and sisters can be found on subchart 208, of the Québec chapter. Magdeleine is found in [Block O 208-4 of subchart 208]

So, we are sure that François *dit* La Varenne lived in a place called La Varenne. I have found four places with that exact spelling. But I did not want to stop my research here because the name may have had various spellings over the years. So after this digression I will now turn to my search of places called la Varenne or places with similar spelling.

Second sworn declaration in French from the Genealogy of the Acadians established in the Parish of Sauzon at Belle-Ile-en-Mer

Friday and Saturday: In search of La Varanne

Friday morning, I went shopping at the stationery store in Loudun, looking for some detailed maps of the area showing small communities named La Varenne or a similar spelling. I found a series of *Cartes Topographiques* by l'Institut geographique national, which are topographic maps (1:25000), ideal for my purposes: I wanted to locate all the places called La Varenne or similar names and visit these places to see if I could find any traces of François Girouard or other Girouard, Giroire, Giroir names, (one such name I had already found, as mentioned, was in the community of Roche Rigault, near "Varanne." This is a strong possibility, since certainly some spellings changed over the years and I also discovered records of Girouards in this area in early 1600s.

I made a list of the places, which I found on these maps, and on Friday and Saturday I visited as many of these places as possible and made notes here for the benefit of other researchers. Otherwise, these places need to be investigated fur-

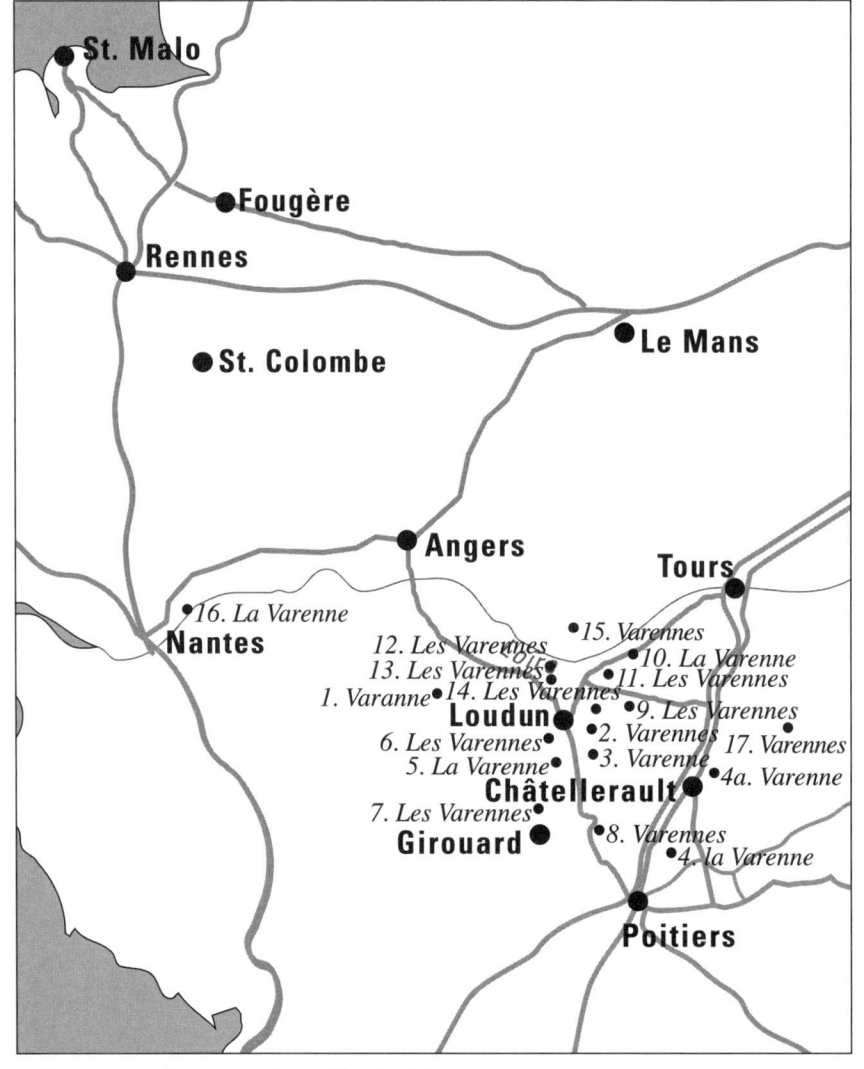

17 locations of various places like La Varenne.

ther for possible traces of François. If nothing is found after this thorough search, then at least we can say with more conviction and documentation that the likely location is La Varanne near La Chaussée, which over the years changed with just a slight variation to the "La Varenne" of the Belle-Isle-en-Mer sworn statement. For more detailed analysis, one can display all locations (#1- #17) below on the Michelin map #68 Niort, Poitiers, Chateroux (1:2000) by transposing some smaller locations from the following more detailed maps, onto the Michelin map 68 which itself shows some larger locations. Other maps used to achieve this result were:

1. Institut géographique national map, Carte topographique 1725 ouest, (1:20 000), L'encloiture ouest, Vienne area #86 and Michelin Map #68 to place the following locations (#5-#8)
2. A detailed reference map: Institut géographique national map (1:25000, Loudun Est, 1724) and Michelin map #68 to place (#9-#14).
3. Reference map: Recto Foldex map #3 Val de Loire: to place locations (#15-#17) below).

Locations which I discovered and recorded are as follows (these names can all be found on the map in italics on the preceding page with matching numbers):
1) Varanne, just northwest of Loudun between highway N147 and D938.
2) Varennes, south east of Loudun near highway D-14, north of Le Bouchet, about 15 km north of La Chaussée. In the Mairie of Roche Rigault, near La Chaussée I found a Girouard family recorded, dated 1664 (refer to earlier discussion of Roche Rigault).
3) Varenne, just north of Mont S. Guesnes. This same place appears on Carte Routière Michelin map No. 67, of Loudun (1:20 000) as "la Varenne". In the document Les Racines Françaises des Premières familles acadiennes, p. 20 by Nicole T. Bujold, and Maurice Caillebeau, Imprimerie l'Union Poitiers, 1979. Also appearing on the 18th-century map of La Chaussée area, (Carte de Cassini Archives, Département de Vienne) as "Varanne", (Bujold, p.21)
4) La Varenne, at the intersection of Highway D82 and D15 between Poitiers and Châtellerault.
4a) Varenne, just northeast of Châtellerault
5) La Varanne, about 12 km north of La Chaussée, the same side of the highway N147, just north of the intersection of 4-64 and D-52.
6) Les Varennes, just one km north of "La Varanne' in #5 above-map, represents a land area called les Varennes, where today there are no houses shown on map.
7) Les Varennes, one km south west of St-Jean-de-Sauves, represents a land area only, with no houses, which I visited. This area is located at the intersection of highways D-53 and D-57.
8) Varennes, approximately 20 km south of La Chaussée on Highway N147, south of Mirebeau. I searched here. No records of Girouard, Giroir, or Giroire in the Mairie but I am not sure I had access to all records because the person in charge of the Mairie was on vacation. There are Giroire families today in this vicinity.
9) Les Varennes, east of another place called La Chaussée, on the other side of

highway D-749.
10) La Varenne, just northwest of the city of Richelieu.
11) Les Varannes, just west of the above La Varenne, represents a land area which I visited, with no houses indicated on the map.
12) Les Varennes, approximately 20 km north of Loudun, located on the north side of highway D759, east of Verziers.
13) Les Varennes, approximately 5 km east of Loudun on the south side of highway D759.
14) Les Varennes, approximately 10 km northeast of Loudun, approximately 5 km east of Verniers
15) Varennes, north on highway 147, just across the Loire River on highway D85. I researched the Mairie records here without finding any trace of any Girouard, Giroire, and Giroir. Records here go back to 1500.
16) La Varenne, on the Loire River between Nantes and Champtoeaux. I phoned the archives here and was told that the old records had been burned in the Revolution. Also, because I am aware of many Pellerin families, some of whom are my close cousins in the small Acadian village of Larry's River, I took note of a place called "Le Pellerin" to the west of Nantes on the Loire River (also see map on first page of this chapter).
17) Varennes just past Descartes, approximately 130 km east of La Chaussée, southeast of Tours on highway D-31. I visited here and found no records of Girouards. Early records were also burned in the Revolution. See a detailed reference map: American Automobile Association map (France and Benelux) for locations # 18 and 19 below). (Alternatively, a map presented in this chapter showing the relative location of Loudun to Mountluçon, also shows these locations of Varennes)
18) Varannes-sur-Allier, near Montluçon, (where the French-Canadian Girouards established, after leaving Paris), just off highway A6. I have not checked this Varanne, since it is not located in the Acadian root areas.
19) Varanne-en-Argonnes, east of Paris, north of Verdun, by the border of Germany, off highway A4. I have not checked here for the same reason

In conclusion, I count only four spellings the same as that used to refer to François in the sworn statements at Belle-Ile-en-Mer. This spelling "La Varenne" is found
Near Mont Guesnes and Roche Rigault (see #3)
Between Poitiers and Châtellerault (see #4)
Near Richelieu (see #10)
Near Nantes on the Loire River (see #16)

There is still much research needed here. It was too time-consuming to be completed on a one-week visit to France, with so many other agendas to accomplish! However, a number of Giroire descendants in France are presently researching their ancestors and may have some opportunities to follow up on this part of the research.

France

SUNDAY: *"la Ligne Acadienne"*

On my last day in France, I drove to "la Ligne Acadienne" (the Acadian Line) at Archigny-La Puye-Vienne, about 25 km southeast of Châtellerault. Let me give you a brief history of this place.

Readers will remember that some of the Acadians were sent to England and then back to France, during the Deportation period, beginning in 1755. In most cases they had only what they could carry in their arms and the ragged clothes on their backs.

King Louis XV of France attempted to resettle some of them in the surrounding area of Châtellerault close to Archigny and La Puye along a strip of straight road which became known as the "la Ligne Acadienne," or "la Grande Ligne" (the Big Line) or just "la Ligne" (the Line), as it appears on some maps.

la Ligne Acadienne Road map showing la Ligne in relation to Loudun and also Leigné-le-bois)

103

The Acadian Colony in 1791

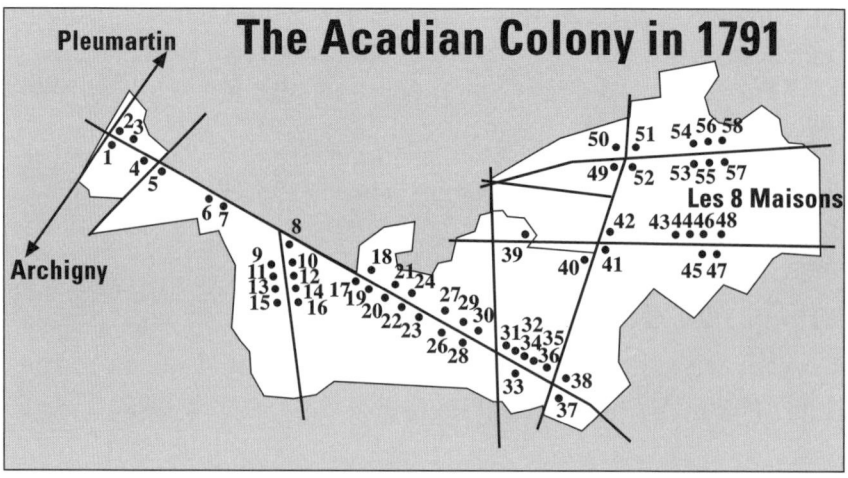

Map-la Ligne (Ferme Acadienne). The Acadian Colony in 1791 based on information from Association des Cousins acadiens, Mairie d'Archigny (reference map).

Plaque at la Ligne

Translation of the plaque at la Ligne Acadienne.

In 1773, by order of King Louis XV, the building of a large farming establishment, including 150 farms was undertaken, at the cost to the state, with the help of the competent and devoted Marquis de Perusse of Cars, Seignior of Monthoiron.

The general purpose of this project was to give exiled Acadians, wrecked by war and captivity, an opportunity to lead a new, peaceful and stable life, as farm owners, in their Mother country.

France

Names appearing on the reference map, on which this map is based, are as follows:

1. BEAULU
2. LANDRY
3. GAULTREAU
4. SEGNE
5. NO NAME GIVEN
6. FAULCON
7. DAIGLE F.
8. SAUVION
9. GUILLOT J.-B.
10. GUILLOT P.
11. GUILLOT D.
12. BIDAULT
13. DAIGLEM
14-16 NO NAMES GIVEN
17. LA TASCHE
18. NO NAME GIVEN
19. CHAREAUDEAU
20. NO NAME GIVEN
21. DAIGLER
22. NO NAME GIVEN
23. NO NAME GIVEN
24. MARTIN
25. not placed on map of reference
26. GUERIN
27. RICHARD
28. ARNAULT
29. BEAUDEAU
30. BARRAULT
31. ROUSSEAU
32. BOUDROT
33. PIOT
34. LAIDECK
35. NO NAME GIVEN
36. DOUSSET
37. THOMAS
38. DELACROIX
39. GUILLARD
40-45 NO NAMES GIVEN
46. ROUGER
47. DEBIÉN
48. MELANÇON
49-55 NO NAMES GIVEN
56. BRIONNE
56-58 NO NAMES GIVEN

There appear to be 25 family names missing and 33 family names given for a total of 58 locations as shown on the map and one location, # 25, not indicated on the reference map which this map is based. Family names are spelled as they appear on the reference map.

Acadian Awakenings: An Acadian Family In Exile

la Ligne, Archigny, France

France

A description of this historic site is given in *Les Acadiens Pietons d'Atlantique*[13] (The Acadians, Pedestrians of the Atlantic) from which I have translated the following:

> In the districts of Archigny, of la Puye, and of Saint-Pierre-de-Maillé, are grouped about forty houses, built in a totally different style from those of the region: long and low standing, with walls of clay, built in a line and not in a circle, they are a surprising sight in the countryside of Poitiers.
>
> The Line evokes the ambitious project, conceived by Louis XV and entrusted to the agronomist Pérusse des Cars, to create a model agricultural settlement where families of Acadian refugees would live. The plan proposed to give each family a new house, a barn, a stable, a well, two pair of oxen, two cows, a plough, a cart and 30 acres of land.
>
> But in reality, the settlement of the Acadian colony turned out to be much more complex than the theorists had anticipated. Faced with the requirement of the General Comptroller to build the farms in record time, Pérusse des Cars decided, in order to hasten the work, not to build with stone as in the rest of the country, but with *bousillis*, a mortar of soil mixed with branches. However, this clever idea and the desire to set up a remarkable agricultural establishment as quickly and as well as possible would meet with a certain passivity on the part of the Acadians. Trying to make these refugees model farmers was indeed to misjudge their personality: seamen, fishermen or breeders uprooted from a fertile coast, they proved to be poor land-clearers. Finally, the snail-paced administration was an additional brake on the efficiency of the project. The Acadians had to wait too long before obtaining a well-defined standing, bringing about distrust, discontent and deception on their part. The operation finally ended in a semi-failure, most of the Acadians preferring to sail once more and head for Louisiana which France had given up to the Spain in 1763.
>
> In 1776, there were 25 families left, who after the 1789 Revolution would become owners of their farms, without any obligation of seigniorial dues. Talking the same language as the people of Poitiers, the small colony was completely integrated. Today, for the Daigle, Baudrot, Thériot, whose parents lived in the low houses at a distance from the village, "la Ligne" is the symbol of their Acadian identity within the context of France. At the "Eight Houses" (huit Maisons), in one of the farms transformed into a small Acadian museum, the furniture and tools are preserved to evoke the daily life of the Acadians of Poitou during the 18th century. Several other houses have kept their original appearance.

Although no Girouard or Giroire names appear on the "la Ligne" lists, I am convinced that the Acadian Girouard, Giroir(e) families were actually there. I say this because of information contained in other documents listed below and because in my later correspondence with Gaston Giroir of France, he mentions a number of Acadian Giroire, Giroir, Girouards in a place called Cenan and other locations.[14] Cenan, as you can see from the map, is very close to "la Ligne." I have been able to link many of these Girouards in Cenan to my master chart, using various subcharts I had researched previously, and hence I can now link these Acadian Girouard/Giroir(e) families back to François Girouard and Jeanne Aucoin.

The following information describes these post-Deportation Girouard links with Cenan and Leigné-les-Bois, both very close to la Ligne (see map page 95).

Post-Deportation links to Cenan, Leigné-les-Bois, la Ligne and Châtellerault

[AMC Block D-3b] From correspondence of Gaston Giroir, we find a record of a Pierre Giroire, married to Marguerite Gaudet, who was registered on the third convoy for Nantes, December 1775 (Folio 110 of Gaston's notes), with their daughter Marie Théotiste Girouard (born 1757, and just recently married, Aug. 22, 1775, to Joseph Landry, in Cenan, Vienne, near la Ligne). Using my subcharts, previously researched, I was able to establish that this Pierre Girouard was the son of Germain II, who in turn was the son of Germain [AMC Block D-3b]. *Also see [Block T213-4 of subchart 213] in the Québec volume].* They had been in P.E.I. in 1752, and Miquelon in 1767, according to Bona Arsenault. Besides Marie Théotiste, her two brothers, Michel and Dominique (m. Agnes Broussard) were on the third convoy to Nantes, 1775.

All the children of Marie Théotiste Girouard and Joseph Landry (Joseph Clair, Marie Jeanne, Julien Roland, Agnes, Julie, Marguerite Sophie), were born in Ste-Martina de Chantenay, and Chantenaux, Nantes, France (Reference: Abbé Gallant pp. 5, 6, 9, 11, 14.)

Gaston Giroir also makes note of Anne Giroire married to Pierre Gaudet in 1740. I have been able to establish from the subcharts that Germain II had a daughter, Anne Giroire who married Pierre Gaudet, 1740 *[Block M213-4 of subchart 213] in the Acadian chapter of the Québec volume*. This is obviously the same person, since her brother Pierre Girouard m. Marguerite Gaudet [Block R213-4 of subchart 213] also appears in France.

In addition, the Acadian Marguerite Giroire m1. Jean Poujet 1750, m2. François Aucoin 1772, m3. Charles Tousalin 1776 (at Cenan), was living at Cenan. She had one son, Jean Poujet (1754-1781) m. Anne Marie Veulet and died at Cenan. Marguerite had three children, Jean (1783-1786); René (1778-1781) and Pierre (1784-1788) all born and died at Cenan. If the records of the children's birth are correct, Marguerite must have married a fourth time or the death date given for Jean Poujet (jr) was incorrect (according to information provided by Stephen White, Professional genealogist at Université de Moncton.)

[AMC Block C-3b] See Louisiana volume, on Acadians at St-Domingue, French West Indies.

[AMC Block E-3B] Among other Acadian names and links in France after the Deportation, we find the marriage record of Prospère Girouard, son of Honoré (subchart 162.1 of Louisiana volume), descending from Pierre [AMC Block E-3b] The family name is spelled Girouard in the marriage record of their parents, in St Coulomb, France. However the spelling changes in the birth of his daughter (Record in the *Acadian Exiles in Châtellerault* by Albert J. Robichaux Jr). In this record it is stated that Marie Giroire, daughter of Prosper-Honoré Giroire and Marie Dugast (St Coulomb, I et V), was born December 10, 1774 at Leigné-les-Bois, Vienne[15] which is not far from Cenan and la Ligne. (See map of this area in this chapter on page 95).

Since all of these families connect to one of the blocks of the Girouard Acadian Master Chart [AMC], they are therefore all descendants of François Girouard and Jeanne Aucoin, regardless of the different spellings that are recorded.

At Châtellerault, France, the same family is spelled "Giroire" in some documents, but as "Giroir" three years later on the passenger lists, when this family voyaged to Louisiana.[16] One must conclude from this example that the variations in spellings of the family name began early in France and simply continued in North America in the same way (see documents on the next two pages).

Prospère Honoré's sister, Hélène-Judith Giroire, daughter of Honoré Prospère Giroire was living in Leigné-les-bois, Vienne. Hélène married François Blanchard and one of her sons, Joseph François was born, 1775, at Ligné-les-Bois, Vienne, just northwest of la Ligne. Another daughter Marguerite was born in Nantes. The other children were born in Acadia (Françoise; Marie Edouage; and Rose Ann).

The children of Prospère Honoré Girouard were all born in Acadia except for their son Pierre, born in the region of Nantes. The family lived at St-Malo for a time before they departed for Nantes, March 13, 1776, in preparation for their voyage to Louisiana.

Also, Gaston Giroir mentions a Marguerite Giroire m. Basile Boudrot. This Marguerite Giroire is the Marguerite Giroire born 1723, daughter of Pierre Girouard [AMC Block E-3b] and m2. M. Doiron, who married a Basile Boudrot, *See [Block N163-4m2 of subchart 163] in Arichat section of the Nova Scotia volume.*

There is also record of a Charles Giroire[18] who, while in Acadia, married Michelle Potterie of St-Servan, and later living in St-Malo, France. They were on the third convoy for Nantes, December, 1775, heading to Louisiana. (Folio 863) of Gaston Giroir. *[See Louisiana volume for this connection, which I have been able to make via other documents—B.G.]*

Gaston Giroir mentions an Armand Giroire m. Margarete (Marguerite) Marie Daigle of whom I have no record, except possibly the Armand of [AMC Block C-3a] who is mentioned at the end of the Québec volume, or the Armand in the lists of prisoners at Fort Beauséjour and of whom I could find no more record in Canada.

[AMC Block H-5]
I have found a record of Marie-Madeleine Girouard m. Cyprien Duon. This family was recorded in St-Malo, France, coming from England, May 23, 1763 on the ship, *La Dorothy*. They resided in Plouer 1763-1772. The entire family went to England, 1773.

The above families were all descendants of François Girouard and were in Nova Scotia during the Expulsion. After 22 years back in France and 30 years after the deportation of 1755, some of these families voyaged to Louisiana to meet their cousin Firmin Girouard, and his family, finally establishing themselves in welcome territory, where their numerous descendants are found today. The entire branch spell their name as Giroir up to and including the present day.

Whether recorded as actually living in la Ligne Acadienne or in such close proximity to la Ligne, one would have to assume that either these Girouards were

France

ACADIANS IN CHATELLERAULT

married February 14, 1775 (Archigny, Vienne)
AGNES BROUSSARD
　　born about 1753
　　daughter of deceased Joseph BROUSSARD and
　　　deceased Ursule LEBLANC
　　resident of the parish of Archigny

Dominique Giroire (absent) and Agnes Broussard, his wife were in the Third Convoy leaving Chatellerault for Nantes on December 7, 1775.

83. PROSPER-HONORE GIROIRE
　　born about 1744
　　son of Honore GIROIRE and Marie-Joseph TERRIOT

married February 14, 1764 (St. Coulomb, I.-et-V.)
MARIE DUGAST
　　born about 1747
　　daughter of Paul DUGAST and Marie BOUDROT

Children: 1. Marie GIROIRE
　　　　　　born December 10, 1774
　　　　　　baptized December 10, 1774
　　　　　　　(Leigne-les-Bois, Vienne)
　　　　　　sponsors: Jean-Baptiste HEBERT and
　　　　　　　　Marie GIROIRE
　　　　　　died December 11, 1774
　　　　　　buried December 11, 1774
　　　　　　　(Leigne-les-Bois, Vienne)

Prosper Giroire, Marie Dugast, his wife and five children: Jean, Francois, Marie, Anne and Jeanne were in the Second Convoy leaving Chatellerault for Nantes on November 15, 1775.

ACADIANS IN CHATELLERAULT

daughter of Pierre DUGAST and Elizabeth BOURG
died at age of about 36 years
buried February 12, 1775
(St. Jean L'Evangeliste, Chatellerault, Vienne)

Charles Blanchard, widower of Marguerite-Josephe Dugast and his family of four persons were in the Fourth Convoy leaving Chatellerault for Nantes from March 6 to March 13, 1776.

23. FRANCOIS BLANCHARD
　　born about 1731 in the parish of St. Pierre and St.
　　　Paul of Cobequid in Acadie
　　son of Joseph BLANCHARD and Anne DUPUIS

married October 18, 1763 (Pleslin, C.-du-N.)
HELEN-JUDITH GIROIRE
　　born about 1742 in the parish of L'Assomption in
　　　Acadie
　　daughter of Honore GIROIRE and Marie-Josephe
　　　TERRIOT

Children: 1. Joseph-Francois BLANCHARD
　　　　　　baptized April 22, 1775
　　　　　　(Leigne-les-Bois, Vienne)
　　　　　　sponsors: Charles NAQUIN and
　　　　　　　　Francoise BLANCHARD

Francois Blanchard, Helen Giroire, his wife and family of 5 persons were in the Fourth Convoy leaving Chatellerault for Nantes from March 6 to March 13, 1776.

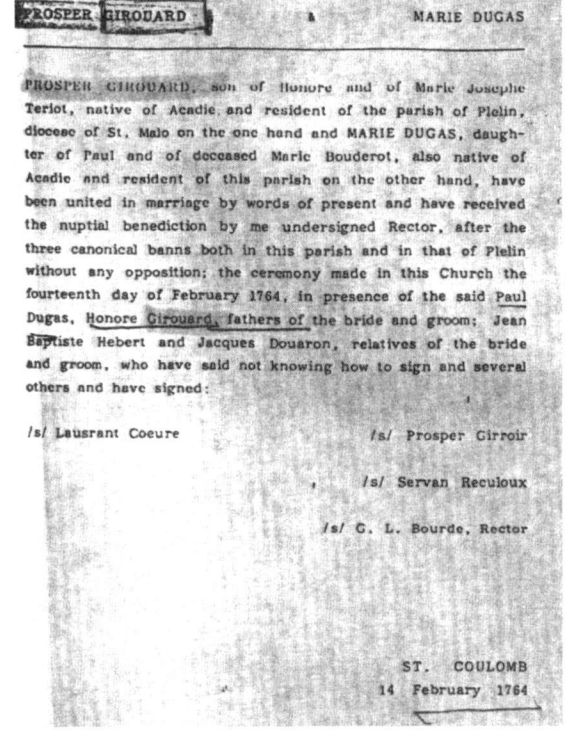

PROSPER GIROUARD　　　　　MARIE DUGAS

PROSPER GIROUARD, son of Honore and of Marie Josephe Teriot, native of Acadie and resident of the parish of Plelin, diocese of St. Malo on the one hand and MARIE DUGAS, daughter of Paul and of deceased Marie Bouderot, also native of Acadie and resident of this parish on the other hand, have been united in marriage by words of present and have received the nuptial benediction by me undersigned Rector, after the three canonical banns both in this parish and in that of Plelin without any opposition; the ceremony made in this Church the fourteenth day of February 1764, in presence of the said Paul Dugas, Honore Girouard, fathers of the bride and groom; Jean Baptiste Hebert and Jacques Douaron, relatives of the bride and groom, who have said not knowing how to sign and several others and have signed:

/s/ Laurant Coeure　　　　　　/s/ Prosper Cirroir

　　　　　　　　　　　　　/s/ Servan Reculoux

　　　　　　　　　　/s/ C. L. Bourde, Rector

　　　　　　　　　　　　ST. COULOMB
　　　　　　　　　　　　14 February 1764

Documents showing different spellings of the same family name.

List of Acadian names on the ship La Bergère going to New Orleans, Louisiana (note passenger #64 Prosper Giroir family).

Coutesy of Archives Department de Loire-Atlantique-Nantes[17]

part of Louis XV's plan of la Ligne awaiting placement, or else that they refused the plan because they were not happy with it and chose to live in proximity.

After returning from the day at la Ligne Acadienne, we had a little gathering at my hotel. It was my last day at Loudun, and almost time for me to leave France. It was a lovely evening, as we collected addresses and phone numbers, and said our last goodbyes.

Madame Touret and the Girouard, Giroir(e) descendants I met have caused me to look back on the land of my ancestors with great memories and pride, and to look with great optimism with regard to the continued research of the family in France.

MONDAY: *Journey to Paris*
I left Loudun feeling just great about my trip, my welcome, and my success in researching the Girouards and establishing other contacts. It was a fantastic visit, fulfilling more than my own expectations and dreams. I had accomplished a great deal. I headed straight for Paris. The driving was exciting to say the least, especially in the city of Paris itself. Modern highways, challenging drivers! The French are known to drive fast.

Madame Touret and her husband Jean joined us for dinner.

Just before I left for Paris some of the group posed for this last photo, holding up the master chart, hopefully a sign of continued interests and research on the part of the Girouard, Giroir, Giroire family and institutions like the syndicat d'initiative, promoting increased interest in the Acadian heritage, genealogy and history of the Loudunais area. l to r: Bill Gerrior, Yves Gombert, Andrée Gombert, John-Pierre Giroire and Michèle Touret.

Of course it didn't help my driving having to keep one eye on the map and the other on the road and street signs, while alternately watching out for all the traffic darting out in front of me and on all sides. The roads became like a jungle as I entered Paris, with a circle highway surrounding the entire city, the *Boulevard périphérique extérieur*. Somehow, I made it!

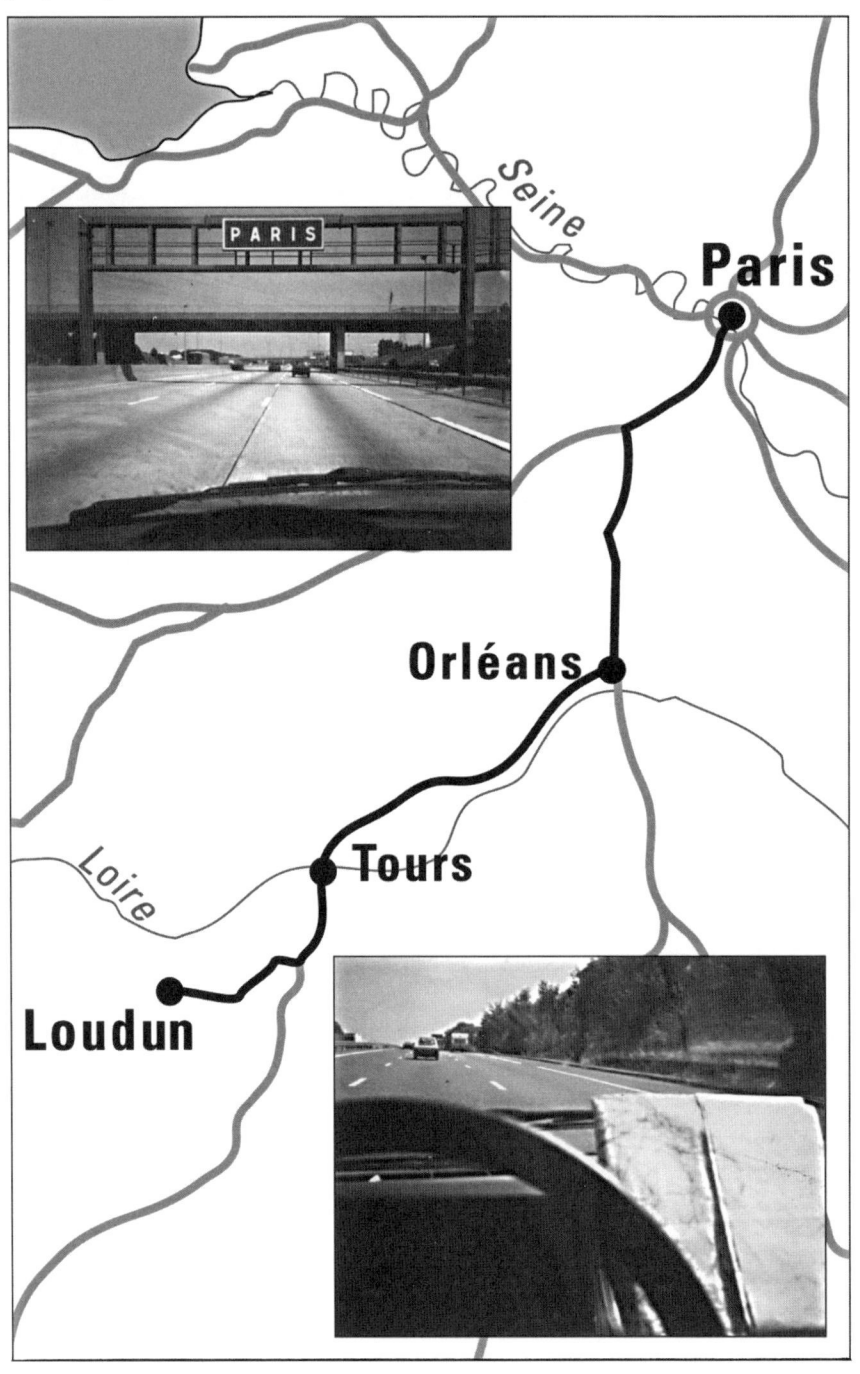

On my way to Paris.

France

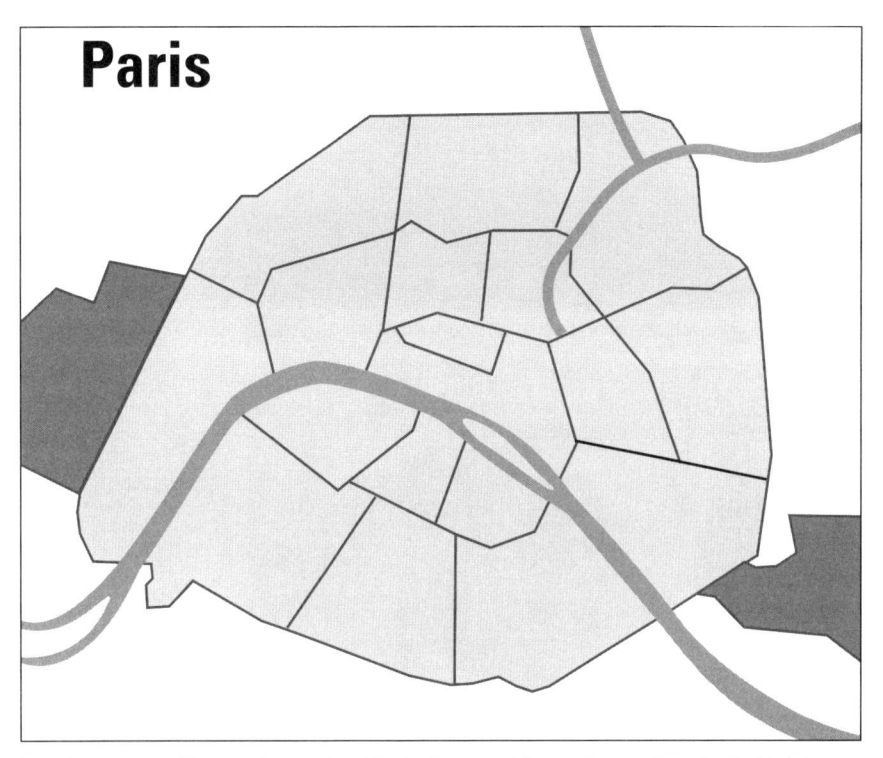

Roads surrounding and entering Paris (map with sections of Paris divided into numbered locations both inside the circle and outside in the peripheral areas of Paris).

To complicate matters more, while driving at about 120 km per hour, I was trying to take pictures for this book, with my camera through the front windshield of the car. That was crazy, and very dangerous when I think back. I don't recommend it to anyone. But I did survive and I did get some pictures. Here are a few.

Buildings and architecture in the heart of downtown Paris. Tour on the Seine River. The Eiffel Tower on the Seine River.

France

117

While in Paris I hoped to do some research at the Archives of Paris, since I was aware that some Girouards lived there in the 1600's, but there was just not enough time in my schedule before heading back home.

POSTSCRIPT: other locations of Acadian interest in France
There are other locations in France, which, although I did not have a chance to visit on this trip, played a part in the Acadian history of France. I learned of some of these locations from a publication called *Les Acadiens Pietons de L'Atlantique (Pedestrians of the Atlantique)* by Catherine Petit from which I have taken the following excerpts and translated: Châtellerault, Brouage, La Rochelle, Castle of Eeaux-Melles, and the community of Roiffé. I have added maps which show these regions in relation to other key areas that I have presented in this chapter and some photo visuals, which were provided to me as indicated in the credits.

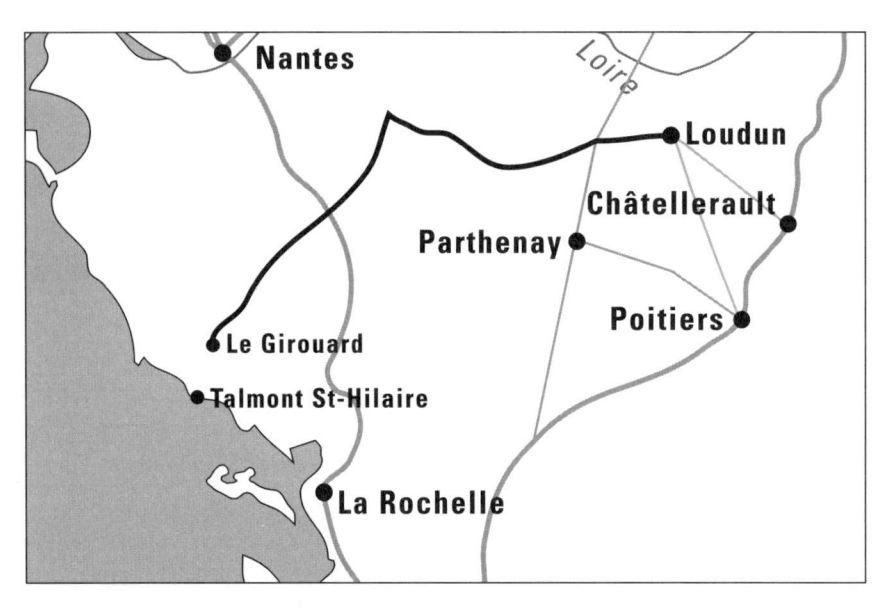

The actual dock in Châtellerault, near the Henry IV Bridge, where Acadians who were deported back to France, tied up their boats and disembarked. Photo by: Marie-Hélène Allain.

CHÂTELLERAULT, DÉPARTEMENT OF VIENNE, 33 km from Poitiers

…It was through Châtellerault that more than a thousand Acadians passed, expelled after the Great Deportation. Many of them rescued from English jails, they waited at Chateauneuf, a suburb of the city on the other side of the Henry VI bridge, to be given the plots of land

Plaque on Rue des Acadiens Photo by Marie-Hélène Allain.

promised by Louis XV, as part of la Ligne Acadienne project. The name "Rue des Acadiens" (Acadian Street) recalls this event in the history of repatriated Acadians.

The Hotel de Sully, 14 Sully Street, headquarters of the Association Châtellerault-Québec-Souvenir Acadien, incorporates the Acadian Museum. This small museum recounts, through various display panels, the history of the Acadians from the first expeditions of Champlain, and the settlement plan of the Acadians near Châtellerault, and displays genealogical documents donated by Acadians who have visited the museum. Among the many panels dedicated to Acadia, one evokes the considerable amount of work done in 1920 by Andrée Blanchard who undertook the first research on the genealogies of Acadian families…

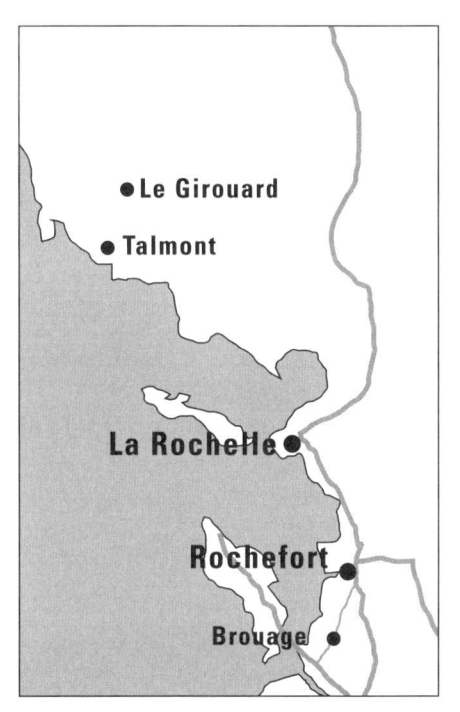

BROUAGE, DEPARTMENT OF CHARENTE-MARITIME

…It was Samuel de Champlain who created a sustained settlement in Acadia. After a first expedition, he returned in 1604, accompanied by Pierre du Gua de Monts. After passing the winter on Sainte-Croix Island, they settled in the spring on the other side of French Bay in Port Royal. The beginnings of the small colony were very harsh: however, the seeds were fruitful, and in 1605, the first habitation was built. Acadia was born. But in 1607, the merchant company founded by Pierre du Gua de Monts was dissolved, and his royal privilege was abolished. Champlain and de Monts were to abandon Acadia from now on and travel further north, to found Québec in 1608.

On Champlain Street, a monument in memory of the great navigator has been erected in a garden near the house where he was born. In the centre of the village, Saint-Pierre church (1608) holds a permanent exposition of documents concerning the foundation of the New France. A certain number of pioneers left Brouage for Canada in the 17th century. Recently the provincial government of New Brunswick gave a stained-glass window,

Samuel de Champlain,[19] founder of Québec City, was born here in 1567 Photo (engraving by Albert Décaires)

depicting the history of the Acadians.

Brouage, a 17th-century fortified city showing the channel to the sea. Today, at the foot of the citadel, the tight network of canals outlines the salt meadows used for breeding cattle.

…The Brouage Marsh, as well as the outer edge of the vast estuary of la Seudre, where saltworks were built during the Renaissance, relied on the commerce of salt. Later, the marshes of la Seudre were converted to "beds", breeding parks for oysters, but it was the salt merchants of the region who, with those of Aunis (hinterland of la Rochelle) and the Isles of Ré and Oloron, introduced in Acadia the technique for drying out the lowlands along the shore of the ocean…. Thanks to a complete system of dykes and canals with sluices, the Acadians were able to cultivate former marshes…

France

LA ROCHELLE, CHARANTE-MARITIME, *471 km from Paris, 335 km from Poitiers*

...A famous old port facing the Atlantic Ocean and guarded by its towers, La Rochelle was, for hundreds of settlers, the last image of France they took with them. During the 17th and 18th centuries, they embarked at this highly picturesque port. The city, where beautiful buildings and designs abound, remains greatly unchanged from that which the emigrants knew.

The 18th century was a great century for La Rochelle, marking the summit of maritime trade. Trade was established between Africa, the Caribbean and Canada, (where they obtained their furs), making the fortunes of powerful merchants and ship owners. The 18th-century *Hotel de la Chambre de Commerce* (Chamber of Commerce Hotel), Palais Street, symbolizes the prosperity of merchants of that era. In the yard, where the wings of the building are linked by elegant colonnades, emblems of maritime trade are placed side by side: the stems of ships and trophies of marine instruments. The Rue de L'Escale is still paved with rubble, pebbles of the Saint-Lawrence taken from the ballast of ships returning from Canada, too light in furs. Hotels dating back to the 17th and 18th centuries border the street.

CASTLE OF EAUX-MELLES, COMMUNE OF ROIFFÉ, DEPARTMENT OF VIENNE, *12 km north of Loudun*

Only the 16th-century wing of this house remains to evoke the appearance it must have had when in 1587, Isaac de Razilly was born here. Commander of the Order of Malta, he devoted his life to the Marine. After Acadia was formally returned to France by the Treaty of Sainte Germain-en Laye, March 29, 1632, Richelieu, Minister of Louis XIII, realised the importance of Acadia and Canada. That same year he named his cousin, de Razilly, as governor of Acadia. The tenure of the latter, even though decisive for the beginning of the real peopling of Acadia was brief. He died at la Hève in 1635. His colonization plan, adopted by Richelieu, provided for a rotation of ships to bring the settlers to Acadia and to bring them back after a certain time, in order to accomplish the clearing of the land.[20]

Map showing Roiffé, location of Castle Eaux-Melles

This concludes the postscript concerning my first trip to France in August 1988.

1989 - Second Trip to France

I returned to France a year later, in 1989, for another week, as part of a three-week vacation in the Majorca Islands off the coast of Spain. My wife, Audrey, and I boarded a plane to Amsterdam, rented a car there and drove to Loudun. We visited Jean Touret, husband of Michèle Touret, although she herself was away on business. We also revisited Jean Pierre Giroire of Verniers, and his wife Isabelle. In both cases we dined and chatted for the evening, about the research and various other topics of interests concerning life in France and Canada, including the question of assimilation, which is concerning France because of the American influence of television in France itself.

Audrey and I also went to visit Guy Secq and his family in St-Jean-de-Sauves. As you may recall, I had first met Guy Secq's daughter, Isabelle, at La Maison d'Acadie, where she was the receptionist. Guy was responsible for organizing the Giroire reunion in France after my first visit. This time we chatted with Guy and his wife, Nicole, over lunch, and again were very pleased to meet more interested Giroire descendants. Nicole gave us lovely home-baked goods to take with us when we left.

Guy Secq and Gaston Giroir have both been very active and interested in continuing the research of the family in France. Gaston supplied the following information regarding his grandfather Désiré Giroir, who would also be the great-uncle of Guy Secq. Although I did not meet Gaston Giroir during either of my visits to France, it was after my second trip, in correspondence, that I gathered more information regarding the Girouard families of France. We later met in Louisiana for the Second World Congress 1999.

Postcard photo: The family of the grandfather of Gaston-Désiré Giroir, 1915, great uncle of Guy Secq The family names are as follows: Désiré and wife Flavie (née Cognard). Children: Marcel, Irène, Flavien, Ismérie. Absent is Désiré born 1895, away at the time of the photo.

France

	L900	M900	N900	O900	P900	Q900	R900	S900	T900	U900	V900
1]	Research of William D. Gerrior, *Awakenings*, 2002.					Giroir (ca. 1700 to 1710)	Reference: This chart information on the genealogy of Gaston Giroir [Block Q900-9] was sent to me by Gaston Giroir (Larçay, France). I am using it as a master chart for the Vienne area, France descendants, to link other branches such as Guy Secq and other cousins to one of the blocks of this chart and later extending this chart to include other branches as more information becomes available. I have arbitrarily chosen #900 as a master chart number. This number series was not used in any other charts to date.				
2]					1732 - 1784 Magdeleine m. Jean Cousin (1727-)	1738 - 1805 Vincent Giroire m. Vincente Maison Scorbe, Clairveaux 1780	1746 - 1807 Louis m1. M. Bersil (-1778) m2. M. Berthault	Reference: Research sent by Gaston Giroir. Gaston and Guy Secq have been actively researching the Giroire, Girouard, Giroir branches and we have been sharing much information via correspondence, regarding their research in France and my own research in Canada and France. The dates in brackets at the bottom of the blocks refer to spouse's birth and death.			
3]						1771 - 1803 Vincent m. Anne Maison 13-04-1793					
4]				1794 - 1875 Anne m. Jean Ravion (1793-1832)	1796 - 1800 Vincente Marie	1801 - 1857 Vincent m. Marie Raguit 07-07-1828 at St. Genest	1800 - 1867 Marie m. Charles Phillipe (1798-)				
5]			1830 -1896 Marie m. Louis Maury	1832 - Louise m. Julien Barroux	1836 - 1897 Jean m. Marie Soreau who remarried to H.J.Benne	1844 - 1922 Frumence m. Marie Clément 05-07-1870	1840 - Delphine m. Léon Aurillard	1851 - Eugène m. Léonie Carcaillon	Note: There are law court records of name changes of some of the children of the 6th generation, recorded at Châtellerault in the "Mairie" of Scorbe-Clairveaux. The name change is to "Giloir" and also later to "Girouard". Ref: Gaston Giroir notes. The "Mairie" is the building where the town records,in France, are kept.		
6]			1872 - Emilien m. R. Marie Bascq.	1876 - 1953 Louis m. Anaise Pichereau	1879 - 1960 Athalie m. Elie Pelletier	1874 - 1937 Désiré m. Flavie Cognard 26-10-1896	1883 - 1971 Louise m. René Picard	1886 - 1963 Emilienne m. Adrien Redonnet	The descendants of Frumence Giroir held the first Giroire reunion in France, after my first visit.		
7]				Désiré m. Solange Berger	Irène m. Maurice Pinault	1904 - 1978 Flavien m. Denise Colas 26-04-1926	Marcel m. Germine Robin	Ismérie m. Emile Charles			
8]				France m. Jacqueline Chenault	1929 - 1969 Marc Micheline Monory (-1973)	Gaston m. Ginette Maillard 22-04-1950	Nadege m. Serge Aubugeau	Ginette m. Rémi Boyer			
9]				Dominique m. Yvon Gauthier	Claudine m. Patrick Vignot (-1992)	Gilles m. Martine Richard 19-01-1974	1956 - 1958 Martine	Catherine m. Malik Bouabdelli	Note: Down arrows at the bottom of this chart indicate children from the parents in the block above the arrow. Master chart Vienne.		
10]				9 Servine Cedric	9 Mathieu Jeremy	9 Sandrine Laetita	9 Maxime 20-06-85			FR. (Vienne) Giroir Subchart #900	

© *Awakenings* Girouard/Giroir... *Routes and Routes*

Back of postcard photo from Désiré to his father Frumence Giroir.

This page and next: Gaston Giroir and his extended family, children and grandchildren.

Gilles and Martine with children: Sandrine and Laetitia

Catherine and Malik Bouabdelli with son: Maxime

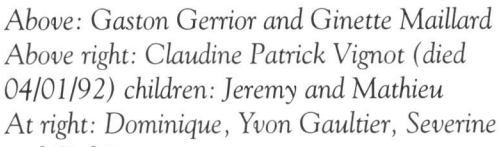

France

Above: Gaston Gerrior and Ginette Maillard
Above right: Claudine Patrick Vignot (died 04/01/92) children: Jeremy and Mathieu
At right: Dominique, Yvon Gaultier, Severine and Cedric

Since my second visit to France, I have requested and received the following information regarding Guy Secq's descent in the direct line beginning in St-Jean-de-Sauves, Dept.of Vienne, France near Loudun and La Chaussée: His genealogy ties into the France chart 900 at [Block R900-6].

[Block R900-6 of subchart 900] Louise Girouard (1883- 1971) m. René Picard (b. 1875). Louise Girouard *(Note that this family spells the name as Giroir on the rest of chart 900, yet 'Girouard' was used by Louise)* m. to René Picard had the following children: 1. Renée Picard, b. 1909, m. Raymond Secq (1909-); 2. Guy Secq m. Nicole Audet. Guy Secq and Nicole Audet have four

Left: Guy Secq

Top of next page:
The family of Guy Secq, descendants of the Girouard/Giroir(e)s, at meeting of Giroirs 1989, at St.-Jean-de-Sauves near La Chaussée.

125

L—r; Edmond (uncle of Guy Secq), Raymonde (sister of Guy), Guy, Nicole Audet Secq, Christian (brother of Guy), Jacqueline (sister-in-law of Guy), Sylvain (son of Guy), Isabelle (daughter of Guy).

Middle: Family of Christiane Giroire of Airvault, Deux-Sèvres, France. L—r: Nicholas, Marie Claire, Michel, Sylvie
Bottom: Frederic Jean-Marie and his wife Anne-Marie, Joseph, Laurent (husband of Christiane), Anne, Françoise, Oliver, Sandrine and Christiane in front of their home on the occasion of first Holy Communion of Oliver.

children: 1. Sylvain; 2. Isabelle; 3. Didier; 4. Angelina. *In some records we find Giroaurd also spelled Giroir.*[21]

Gaston has also supplied the descent of Frumence's brother Jean Giroire:
[Block P900-5 of subchart 900] **Jean Giroire** (1836-1897), m1. Marie Soreau (Two children: 1. Désiré, b. 1865; 2. Mélanie, b. 1868); m2 H.J. Benne (Four children: 3. J. Louis, b. 1870; 4. Emile, 1871-1871; 5. Célestin, 1873-1957; 6. Justine, 1874-1956)

Next we visited and met with Godu Giroir and the family of René Drault in Varannes near Mirebeau. We shared some lovely wine and talked about the Giroir history and family reunion in Canada. We had a wonderful afternoon. Hospitality was great, during this very short but enjoyable visit.

At this time, we also had an opportunity to spend some time with the mayor of La Chaussée, Mr. Gigon, and his family. Their hospitality was excellent: we enjoyed more wine and talk about La Chaussée and surrounding areas. In all these visits, the interest in Acadian history and genealogy was obviously genuine and very much appreciated. In later correspondence, I made contact with three more families from the Department of Deux-Sèvres, France: Christine Giroire, Mr. and Mrs. Perrault Michel, and Lucienne (Giroire) Doussin.

As mentioned, Lucienne (Giroire) Doussin also corresponded with me before the International Reunion. Lucienne (Giroire) and her husband Gérard Doussin attended First International Giroire, Girouard reunion in 1990 representing the Giroires of the department of Deux-Sèvres. Judge Jean Girouard and his wife Andrée of the Canadian branch of Girouards hosted them in St-Lambart near Montreal. In return, after Jean and his wife Andrée won the Air Canada return ticket for two to France at the International Reunion, Lucienne and Gérard returned the hospitality to them at their home in Bordeaux.

Lucienne resides in Parthenay, Department of Deux-Sèvres where many Giroire families live.

She supplied her genealogy as follows. I have converted her work to my chart format and arbitrarily selected a number series of 400 for the chart number for all Deux-Sèvres Giroires. It can serve as a master chart for all Giroires in this Department of France.

Left to right: Andrée, wife of Judge Jean Girouard, Lucienne (Giroire) Doussin, with Judge Jean Girouard and Gérard Doussin at the 1990 International Reunion at Tracadie, Antigonish County, Nova Scotia, Canada.

	L400	M400	N400	O400	P400	Q400	R400	S400	T400	U400	V400
1]	Reference: Genealogy sent to me by Lucienne (Giroire) Doussin. Parthenay is located on the route between Poitiers and Nantes. Le Tallud, where her father Lucien and Uncle Maurice live, is a suburb of Parthenay. Sculptures by Jean Girouard could be found at Église Saint-Laurent, Parthenay. Research of William B. Gerrior, Awakenings 2002. Surveys and correspondence with descendant Lucienne [Block Q400-11 of subchart 400].				Possible ? grandfather of Antoine Girouard of the French-Canadian Branch	1610 - ? Louis ? Beaulieu (Parthenay), father of Catherine	Possible father of François in Acadian Branch	Pompaire, where Mathurin lived is also a suburb of Parthenay. Pompaire and La Grippe are villages of Tallud. La Pignolerie, Cavenière, La Grace Vachée, and La Roullère are villages of Pompaire. Lucienne presently lives in Bordeaux, France, but is originally from Le Tallud near Parthenay (about 15,000 people). Lucienne attended first international reunion, 1990, Canada. Note: This chart is being used as a master chart for Deux Sèvres Girouir/Giroire descendants. I have made this choice because the chart extends back to 1610.			
2]				1742 died at 29 years old		1670 Mathurin Beaulieu or Parthenay Farmer at Cavenière	Catherine m. at Pompaire to be verified				
3]						1700 Joseph m. Louise Cassiou Farmer at Cavenière	1699 Mathurin Perrault 1730				
4]				Jean Baptiste	1742 - Joseph d. at 28 years of age m. Mattherine Rousselien	1738 - 1777 Jean m. Françoise né Conte died at La Grippe Farmer at Pignolière	1744 - Louise d. at 19 years of age.				
5]		1763 - 1763 Jean B.	1766 - 1785 Marie Louise	1773 Jean Baptiste d. at 34 years old at La Grace Vachée	1774 Françoise	1776 - 1837 Jean Louis son of Madeleine m. Jeanne Clisson Farmer at La Grippe, Tallud	1782 - Pierre	1783 - Joseph	1784 Marie Jeanne		
6]			François (1809-1959) is landowner and farmer in La Papinière Tallud.			1809 - 1859 François m. Rose Pélagie Guilbot Farm owner Tallud, Fr.					
7]				André	Raymond	1840 René Alexandre m. Joséphine Morin Blacksmith of Tallud, FR.	Joseph				
8]				Baptiste m. Eulalie Barreau	Radegonde Fergeau	1878 Moïse m. Juliette Souyreau Blacksmith	Radegonde d. at a young age				
9]					1910 Maurice	1905 Lucien m. Thérèse Fleury Blacksmith Le Tallud, FR.	1906 Marie m. Prudent Brechoire				
10]			Monique m. Pierre Poignant Parthenay, FR.	Jean Michel m. Bernadette Pédéhonta Bourdeaux, FR.	Maurice m. Theresa Rivière Le Tallud, FrR	Lucienne m. Gérard Doussin Bourdeaux, FR.	Jeanne m. Marcel Millérioux Parthenay			Deux Sèvres France Giroire Branches Subchart #400	

© Awakenings Girouard/Giroir... Routes and Roots

Top left: Lucien Giroire and his daughter, Lucienne (Giroire) Doussin.
Top right: Family of Lucienne and Gérard Doussin and their three children: Anne, Cécile and Christophe.
Left: Judge Jean Girouard of Montreal, Bernadette, Gerard, Lucien, Jean-Michel and Andrée Girouard, wife of Jean, at Bordeaux on the occasion of their trip to France, Sept 30, 1990.
Bottom: Marie Thérèse, Maurice, Lucienne, Lucien, Monique, Pierre, Jean Girouard (Montreal), Gérard with Alexandre in his arms. Photo taken at the Giroire family homestead of Lucien Giroire, Tallud, Parthenay, Deux-Sèvres, Oct 6, 1990.

Above left: Lucienne (Giroire) and her husband Gérard at Grand Falls, Canada.
Above right: Pascal Giroire and his uncle Gérard Doussin.

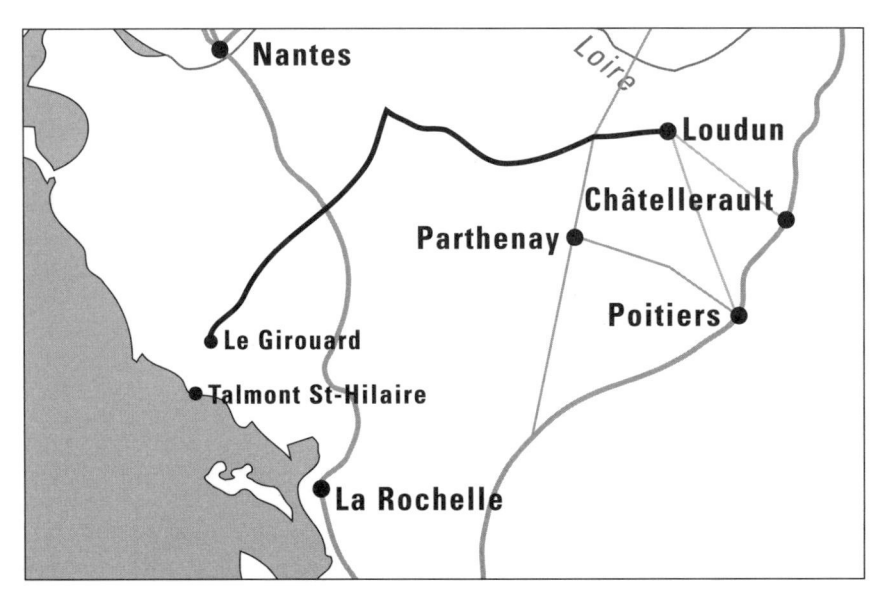

[Block P400-4 of subchart 400] Joseph Giroire, son of Joseph and Louise Cassiou b. 1742 m. Matherine Rosselin. Two children: 1. Andrée; 2. Marie b. 1763 d. 1765

[Block R400-6 of subchart 400] Jean-René Giroire, son of Jean-Louis (1776-1837) m.1 Madeleine Conte m.2 Victoire Vineau. One child: René, b. 1842, m. Marie Triboir, 1878).

[Block O 400- 8 of subchart 400] Baptiste Giroire, son of René Alexandre Giroire and Josephine Morin. m. Eulalie Barruau. Six children: 1. René; 2. Jeanne; 3. Germain; 4. Denise; 5. Lucie; 6. Danielle (three children: René, Jacques, Francette).

[Block R400-9 of subchart 400] Marie Giroire, daughter of Moïse Giroire and Juliette Rouvreau, m. to Prudent Brechoire. Four children: 1. Bernadette m. Reg Imbert (five children: Martine, Dennis, Claude, Valerie, Stéphane); 2. Jeanne-Marie m. Jacques Rambau (one son: Jean-Jacques); 3. Madeleine m. Jean Girard (four children: Laurent, Laure, Thomas, François); 4. Jacques (Priest at Poithier).

[Block Q400-10 of subchart 400] Lucienne Giroire, daughter of Lucien Giroire and Marie-Thérèse Fleury, m. Gérard Doussin. Three children: 1. Christophe; 2. Cécile; 3. Anne m. Bruno Dirks. Three children Simon, Martin, Thomas.

[Block R400-10 of subchart 400] Jeanne Giroire, daughter of Lucien Giroire and Marie-Thérèse Fleury, m. Marcel Millerioux. Four children: 1. Sophie; 2. Brigitte m. Jacques Bibard (one daughter: Pauline); 3. Antoine and 4. Françoise m. Gillet Guillet (two children: Sandrine and Damien).

[Block P400-10 of subchart 400] Maurice Giroire, son of Lucien Giroire and Marie-Thérèse Fleury, m. Teresa Rivière. One son: Alexandre Giroire.

[Block O 400-10 of subchart 400] Jean Michel Giroire, son of Lucien Giroire and Marie-Thérèse Fleury, m. Bernadette Pédéhonta. Two children: 1. Pascal; 2. Isabelle.

[Block N400-10 of subchart 400] Monique Giroire, daughter of Lucien Giroire and Marie-Thérèse Fleury, m. Pierre Poignant. Four children: 1. Philippe; 2 Xavier; 3. Oliver; 4. Veronique.

There is another interesting reference to L'Abbé Raoul Girouard of Parthenay in *L'Album de Famille Girouard* by Désiré Girouard. I wish he had gone one step further to name the grandfather and great-uncles, but it is another piece of the puzzle to help link the various Acadian branches in France. It certainly didn't take this Acadian family long to get back on its feet, considering the prestigious positions occupied by the grandfather and great-uncles. It should not be too difficult to trace the family in France with this information given by Désiré Girouard.

Wedding party at Deux-Sèvres, France 1912 Third row, from the bottom, the second couple from the right are Moïse Giroire and his wife Juiliette, grandparents of Lucienne. First row, first person from the left is Lucienne's father Lucien, 7 years old. photo supplied by Lucienne Giroir

L'Abbé Raoul Girouard, born at Parthenay . . . left three years ago, 1904, to become a Missionary Priest in Manitoba. He is the youngest of a family of eleven children. All the children married except a sister and a brother, also a Priest, and economist at the College of St.-Hilaire, Niort, and Deux-Sèvres, France. His parents also come from Parthenay, in the general area of their children and it is on his return from their Golden Wedding Anniversary that we had the pleasure of greeting him at the family reunion at "Quatre-Vents", Dorval, P.Q. Sept 14, 1907. In two letters that I received he writes: "My paternal grandfather was born at Tours approximately 110 years ago (ca. 1797), having two brothers, one a lawyer at Moulins and the other a Bridge Engineer at Chaussées of Riom. He came to establish at Parthenay as a manufacturer towards 1830. [Translation by BG]

L'Abbé Raoul Girouard, of Acadian origin, a missionary in Manitoba

Lucienne (Giroire) Doussin provided me

France

with copies of the following notes and manuscripts, found by Monique Giroire in Parthenay in the house of R (?) Giroire, a gardener, now deceased. His relation to Lucienne's branch is not yet established. Some of these well-documented references describe Giroire Knights of interest and Girouard, Giroir(e) noblemen. I have added the sketches and the description of Knights at the beginning to enrich the presentation of these authentic documents:

Knights on horses carrying coat of arms.
sketches by Margaretha van Gurp

" I dub you knight" were the words used when a squire (a young man in training to be a knight) earned the right to become a knight. The squires were knighted on the battlefield if they demonstrated great bravery and would receive their sword and other weapons from the king or from other elite men or women of the King's court. If a Knight felt he had been offended by another Knight, they would settle their differences in a duel tournament to protect their honour and reputation. They rode the best and most powerful horses and wore heavy armour and rode full speed at each other, trying to drive their lances into their opponents. Similar matches or jousts were arranged for sports, but in this case the wooden lances were blunted with the intention only to knock the opponent off his horse.

Girouard, Giroire and Giroir in Ancient Times in France
Notes of R. Giroire (translation of excerpts)

In 1199, it is recorded that Pierre Giroire, a knight, made an agreement with several others in their capacity as landlords, by which one Pierre Palastre gives up the wetlands and the salt marshes of Guillon, at Abbey of Buzay (interior of Loire) in exchange for the wetlands and the salt marshes of Fouchet-Gelet. (According to the formal letters submitted the following day at St Hilaire year of 1199, and according to the Trésor genealogy F. XLIII, National Library, 31926).

In 1255, Guillaume Giroire, Seneschal of the King, born near Talmont (Vendée), bequeaths a part of his property to the Abbey of Talmont to build a hospital. This property later became known as Girouard Village, near Talmont. (According to archives published by the Archaeological Society of Poitiers). [Seneschal is a manager of a nobleman's estate.]

In 1234, Maurice Giroire, Knight, gives up, by an act passed the day of the festival of St-Marthias, his future annual rent of 3000 anguilles, which was due to him by the religious of the Priory of Sallestaine, Vendée.

In 1428, Etienne Girouard, farmer of the Mill of The Priory of St-Romaine at Châtellerault, began Dec. 1, 1428, to build this mill, within a period of four years, at the end of the lock, which the Viscount of Châtellerault had recently constructed. (Archives of the Abbey of Cyprien, 1428).

Since the 14th century, the name of the family Giroire has taken different spellings. In Vendée and in Deux-Sèvres, this name is written generally as Giroire, but in Vienne and other locations of France and especially Canada, in the province of Québec (Girouard) in Acadia and Nouvelle Ecosse we often see the spellings of Giroire, sometimes Giroir, etc. *[In New Brunswick Girouard is mostly used, in Nova Scotia and PEI, we see Gerrior, Girroir, Gerroir and in Louisiana, we see Giroir and Girouard, while in Québec only Girouard is found.—B.G.]*

In 1488 mention is made in these notes of a Jeanne Girouard and her husband Philippe of Lande, landlord of Touchet.

In 1518, Pierre Giroire, licensed by law, (law of rights) attended compilation of Costumes of Loudunais (Loudun, Vienne).

In 1556, Marguerite Giroire, my ancestor, *[the direct ancestor of the unknown author of these notes- B.G.]* died at Parthenay, buried in the ancient cemetery of the rosary Chapel, Faubourg St-Paul, Parthenay where her tomb has been found by myself and my brother, Marcel, 1895.

In 1533, François Giroire, Lawyer, and his sister, Marguerite Lady of Golu and Plin(?) sold a house at Arcay (Vienne), October 1, 1533.

In 1568, it is recorded that Max Girouard is parish priest of St-Pierre de Martray (Loudun).

In 1644, Jean Girouard, descendant of the family of François Girouard, of Paris comes to Poitiers; he is a master sculptor, he lives in the parish of St-Porchaire, Poitiers. He is the creator of the famous entrance door of the Courthouse of Poitiers (1644-1648) and also the entrance doorway of the Church of Augustins (Poitiers) as well as numerous statues in churches of Poitiers. This Jean Girouard is buried in the same Church of St-Porchaire, Poitiers, Sept 13, 1676. From his marriage with Joachine Pastureau, he had ten children, all baptized at St-Porchaire, according to the registers of baptisms of this Church. Several of his sons were also renowned sculptors. (A part of their works used to be displayed at the Museum of Poitiers).

In 1644, Pierre Girouard, landlord of Villiers, baptized May 3, master Sculptor for the religious visitation, Poitiers. His wife is Marie de la Vergne. He is still living in 1706, at Poitiers, Rue de la Psallette, St-Hilaire.

In 1668, Joseph Girouard was baptized, February 1, at St-Porchaire, Poitiers, son of Jean Girouard. They attribute to him various sculptures for the Cistercian monks of the Abbey of Pin (Béruges, Vienne). He married Marguerite Gautron, according to the Church registers of St-Porchaire, Poitiers.

In 1669, Jacques Girouard was baptized at St-Porchaire, son of Jean Girouard and brother to Joseph. He married Louise Pain. He was also a sculptor, but his works are not mentioned.

Jean Girouard:
The Most Famous Sculptor

I have added a painting of Louis IV to enrich the presentation of these authentic documents:

The most famous of the Girouards from Poitou was Jean Girouard, son of Jean Girouard, baptised in 1661 at St-Porchaire, Poitiers. He spent part of his youth at Paris studying sculpture to become a master. Upon his return to Poitiers in 1686, he was charged with the task of making the statue of King Louis XIV, which was unveiled at Paris Aug. 25 1687, on the actual Place de la Concorde, but destroyed in 1793 by the Revolutionaries.

Jean Girouard is also the creator of statues of Sainte-Vierge, St.-Porchaire and St-Baptiste, above, of St-Rémi, Church of Verruyes (Deux-Sèvres) near Parthenay. He spent a part of his life in Brittany, where several of his descendants established themselves. In addition, he decorated the Churches of Ancenis, of Rennes, of Vannes, of Auray, etc. He died at the Abbey of Proères in Bretagne in 1720. He left unfinished the religious figure of an angel at his death, but his brother finished it for him so this statue can now be seen on the altar of the Abbey,

Louis IV at the founding of the Academy of sciences and the Observatory, 1667. Painting by Henri Testelin. Musée de Versailles.
Service de documentation photographique de la Réunion des musées nationaux.[22]

near the place where the readings are given. He was married to Marie Roy. A street in Poitiers carries his name, la Rue Girouard. Some of his sculptures were displayed at the museum of Poitiers. Two statues from the entrance door, of Prudence and of Justice used to be at the Museum of Fine Arts of Poitiers. He worked for the churches of Ancenis, Sainte Melanie de Rennes, and the Augustins of Rennes, les Carmes de Chaux de Vannes, and la Chartreuse d'Auray, among others.[23]

I have added the following visuals to enrich the presentation of this documentation. I will now summarize and conclude this section relating to the various Girouard sculptors with subchart 800 which I have created from the information presented in these documents:

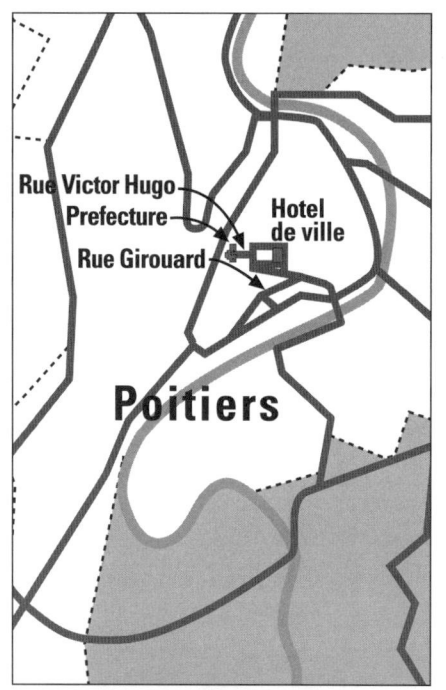

Map of Poitiers showing Girouard Street

Town Hall Poitiers: Photo of Place du Maréchal Leclerc in rentre-ville, Poitiers at the end of Victor Hugo Rd. Jean Girouard sculptured the columns below the flag, one on each side and above the central entrance way. Rue Girouard (Girouard street), named after this renowned sculptor, is located in walking distance from here.

Photo by Suzanne (Gerrior) Williams

Columns at main entrance door to Museum of Fine Arts, by Jean Girouard: This is the doorway that Jean Girouard designed & sculptured naming the columns on each side "Prudence and Justice". This is the entrance way to Musée Rupert-de-Chièvres on Victor Hugo Rd.

Photo by Suzanne (Gerrior) Williams

	L800	M800	N800	O800	P800	Q800	R800	S800	T800	U800	V800
1]						François Girouard of Paris m. (name not known)					
2]					1621- François ? Could François of Port Royal in Acadie b. ca. 1621, possibly be a brother to Jean Girouard ?	1611 - 1676 Jean Girouard (Sculptor) m. Joachine Pastureau	Research of William D. Gerrior, *Awakenings*, 2002 ◊ His family of Girouards were famous sculptors in St. Porchaire, Poitiers Area. Girouard Street in Poitiers is named after Jean Marie Girouard [Block Q800-3 of subchart 800], the most renowned sculptor of this family who was commissioned to make a sculpture of King Louis XIV, of France. Some of Jean Marie Girouard's sculptures can be found in and around Poitiers. He lived a great part of his life in Bretagne where some of his descendants are found today. (Future Research) Reference: Archive records France. [*French Biographical Dictionary* directed by Mrs. Provost at Romon d'Amat, Paris 1985, Volume 16, page 302. This reference was sent to me by Gaston Giroir confirming similar information found in R. Giroire's genealogical notes.]				
3]					1668 - Joseph Girouard (Sculptor) m. Marg. Gautron at St. Porchaire Poitiers	1661 - 1720 Jean Marie Girouard (most renowned Sculptor) m. Marie Roy at St. Porchaire, Poitiers	1669 - Jacques Girouard (Sculptor) m. Louise Pain	1644 - Pierre Seigneur de Villiers (Master Sculptor) m. Marie de la Vergne		Girouard Sculptors France Subchart #800	
	Reference: Archive records in France and documents and genealogy notes sent by Lucienne (Giroire) Doussin, handed down to her by Monique Giroire, written by R. Giroire, whose relation to Lucienne has not yet been established. This reference also states that Jean (1611-1676) had 10 children, all recorded at St. Porchaire, according to church records in the place. I only show four of the 10 children from my source (R. Giroire).					Descendants in Bretagne, France to be linked					

Names and Coats of Arms

	L420	M420	N420	O420	P420	Q420	R420	S420	T420	U420	V420
1]		Notes: 1. Research of William D. Gerrior, *Awakenings*, 2002. 2. Surveys and correspondence with descendants of the fifth generation. 3. Future research will 4.				Acadian ? Joseph m1 - m2. François Dupuy	Notes: Joseph Giroire [Block Q420-1 subchart 420] was a farmer. He died at 24, Germinal at Pougnes-Hérisson. He married Francoise Dupuy at Frécardière. Joseph Giroire [Block Q420-2 of Subchart 420] from Puy-Large de Moncoutant, was born in 1796 at Chattillon-sur-Thouet and died, 1867. The first marriage was ratified by the lower courts of Parthenay, 1/6/1824. Augustin Joseph Giroire, [Block Q420-3 of subchart 420] was a farmer and property owner at Champain de Fénéry, born at Moncoutant, 1849. He came to Theil commune of Saint-Aubin-le-Clou, and died around 1897. Ernest Giroire, [Block Q420-4 of subchart 420] was a railway agent, born 1883 at Champain de Fénéry, married at Paris, 1909, to Juliette Foucteau, died at Arçay, Vienne. Reference: The information for this chart was supplied to me via correspondence with Guy Giroire, Hérouville, St. Clair, France.				
2]						1796 - 1867 Joseph m1. Francois Boujiu m2. Marg. Brossard					
3]	1844 - two infants died at birth	1834 - René Clément	1830 - Louis Valentin	1828 - Louis Joseph	1839 - Louis Frédéric	1849 - 1897 Augustine Joseph m. Louise Pelletier, 1882	1850 - Henri Alexandre	1841 - Pierre Auguste	1829 - Marie Marguerite	1836 - Marie Florence	1845 - Marie Augustine
4]					Estelle	1883 - 1950 Ernest m. Juliette Foucteau					
5]	1918- Madeleine	1925 - 1973 Hélène	Marie	1920 - 1981 Robert	1909 - Marcel	1910 - Maurice m. Gisèle Perrault	1916 - 1979 Jean	1913 - 1996 Henriette	Isabelle	Yvette	
6]					Josette	Guy m. Nicole Laplaine					
7]					Sarah	Alex					
8]											France Giroire Branch Subchart #420

© *Awakenings/Girouard/Giroir... Routes and Roots*

Second Giroire Branch in Parthenay

Let us now look at another branch spelling their surname as Giroire, residing in the area of Parthenay. Likely some of these descendants, as well as those presented in charts 400 and 900 may have links to those ancient Knights that we have discussed earlier.

Guy Giroire of Hérouville, St Clair, France had corresponded with me, providing the following genealogy which I have converted to my chart system, arbitrarily assigning the number 420 to this chart. His father did the research, and the family reside in the Parthenay region close to the limit of Vienne and Deux-Sèvres, the main centre being a place called Fénery. The research goes back as far as 1791 at which time archive records disappeared, due to the wars in the region of Vendée. Perhaps a link will be found with those Giroire descendants in the 400 chart or to the Giroir branch in the 900 chart. All possibilities must remain open, considering the interchange ability of spelling of the surname that we have seen documented in some cases in France.

Although the links may have not yet been found between all these charts (chart #400, #420, # 900) it is important for all Families in France to find a medium to share all of their own research in the hopes of finding some common link at some point in the past history of France. Hopefully this sharing will, in the end, provide new information as that which has occurred with the international links in North America, after much sharing and research. This ideal would certainly enrich the full story of the families Girouard, Giroir(e).... .

Roots of the French-Canadian Girouard Branch, In France

I now turn my focus to the French-Canadian Branch of Girouards in Québec who have their roots in Montlucon, France, not that far from the Loudun region, as the reader may see in the following map.

The French-Canadian Girouard

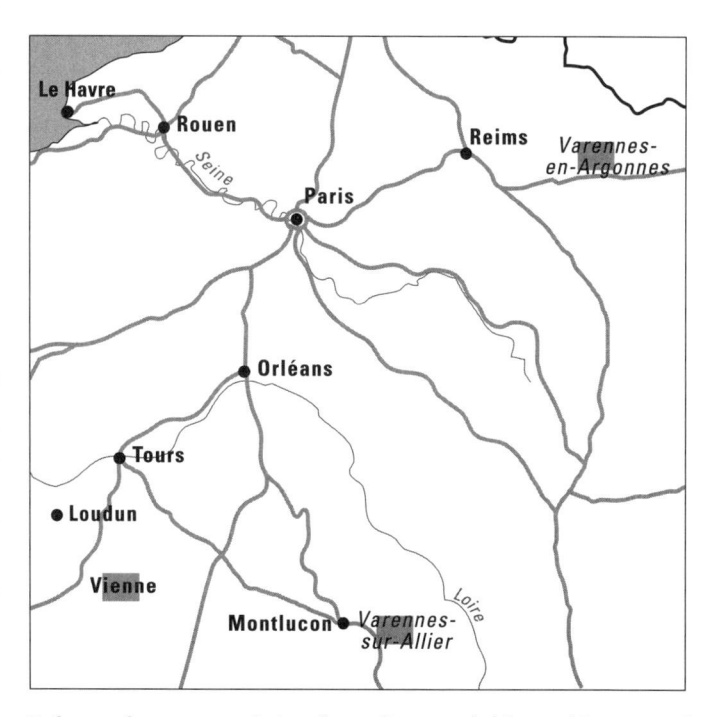

Relative locations of Acadian Girouards/Giroir/Giroire of Loudun, and of French-Canadian Branch to the east.

branches, originating in Montluçon to the southeast of Loudun, are documented in the research of Honorable Désiré Girouard[24] in the early 1900's, and further in my correspondence and visits with Judge Jean Girouard of St-Lambert, PQ, and other Canadian Girouard descendants via correspondence. The following excerpts from this work of Désiré Girouard were translated by the author and Brad Pellerin, his first cousin.

The French-Canadian Branch of Girouards in France
by Désiré Girouard

Official records from the city of Montluçon (Allier)[25]

Marriage of Jean Girouard
On November 23, the priest undersigned, upon the publication of the banns, engagement and other ceremonies and in the absence of Sieur de Cornosaille, Vicar of St-Eustache of Paris, under which, special permission from the diocese was given, by M. L'Official of Paris on the 24th day of October of the present year 1690. Signed by Cornosaille, Chervy and Mouissinot, opposition formed by Edmé Thibout from the city of Moulins against Jean Girouard, sentence was lifted by M. L'Official de Bourges on the 25th day of October. The undersigned received the nuptial blessing between Jean Esmé Girouard, Sieur of Boisrolin, and Petronville Marie Geongeon of my parish, and in the presence of the undersigned partisan agreement.

Signed ....

Baptism of Antoine Girouard
On May 20th, 1696, I, the undersigned and Deputy of the priest of the Church, and also the vicars, baptized Antoine Girouard, son of Jean Girouard born in Montluçon (parish of Notre-Dame). The mother is Marie Geongeon, wife of the said Girouard; the godfather was the noble Antoine Charton, seignior of Beaulieu, elected during the election of Montluçon and his godmother Miss Marie Catherine de la Grange, wife of the noble Messire Gilbert Berthet, Assessor in the election of Montluçon.
They have signed R. Charton, M.C.De la Grange and Charlut

Death of Jean Girouard
On May, 1721, Jean Girouard, Controller in the Dépôt at Riom in Auvergne died, leaving Mary of Petronville Geongeon, his wife about 70 years old, and was buried by myself the undersigned priest the 7th of this month and year, in the parish of Notre Dame, with all the ceremonies in the presence of (Signed) Girouard, Geongeon, Robert, Bonnaire, Depogniat, priest.

Notes from M. Des Gozis
(1) Seignior of Boisrolin, le Bouchet
(2) le Terray parish of Terjeat, Montrognon (parish of Echassière), Arginy (parish of Bizeneuille), Chez-Dandeau (parish of Montaigne-le-Combraille). Sources: Archives de l'Allier. Parish Registers of Montluçon de Montmaraud, etc. Titles in my collection.
Jean Girouard, Seignior of Boisrolin, King's Counsel, Controller in the salt depot of Riom, alive

in 1690, 1700, died 1721. He married Petronville Geongeon around 1690. He had at least four children.

Section I

1) Pierre (see the following section # II)

2) Marie-Madeleine Girouard de Boisrolin, who made a transaction with her brother François on July 26, 1726. She married, soon after, Pierre de Saint-Martin, Seignior of La Trimouille, controller of the King's rights. She died, leaving her husband widowed with two children before 1747.

3) Antoine Girouard, who departed for Canada where he left a small fortune.

4) François Girouard du Bouchet ? the posterity of his brother

Section II

Pierre Girouard, seignior de Boisrolin and Terray, *Greffier* (clerk of the court) of S.A.S. Mgr. Le Duc de Bourbon (1726) and clerk of the court of the chamber of Domaines de Bourbonnais at Moulins, born around 1693, died at 45 years old, April 6, 1738, at Montmaraud. He had bought the domain of Terray and Turret, in the Parish of Terjat, by land possession acts as early as June 16, 1726, January 17, 1733, etc.

Married twice, he married Marie Burel, around 1720: then a second marriage, by contract dated June, 1735, with Françoise Périer, daughter of Jacques, a bourgeois of Montmaraud, (Archives of Allier B 770). She survived him and remarried to Claude Guilbert Massonnet. In agreement with the children of the first [marriage] she came to an agreement with her brother-in-law, Françoise Girouard de Bouchet, on October 13, 1744 and admitted to owing him 800 pounds for a loan made to her husband who had since died.

From the first (marriage) we have the following four children:

1) François Girouard (who follows in section # III)

2) Catherine-Marguerite Girouard married June 20, 1741, to Paul Gilbert Alamargot, Clerk of the Court and head of the election of Montluçon, son of Paul Almargot, Sieur of the Grange Garreau, also clerk of the court, and of Marie-Jeanne Le Mercier. She became widow in 1747 or 1748, and was still living on Oct. 6, 1768.

From the second marriage:

3) Marie-Petronille Girouard de Boisrolin, born May 28, 1737, married February 10, 1755, to François Pailheret, solicitor at La Pérouze, son of François, also a solicitor, and of Marguerite Nivolon.

4) The other François Girouard of Boisrolin died long before Oct. 13, 1747, having his sister as heir.

Section III

François Girouard of Boisrolin, Sieur of Boisrolin, sometimes called François Alexandre Judge, Lord and *gruyer* of Marquisat de Bellenave, was chosen for this office on Oct. 1, 1750, replacing Simon Adécord (Archives of Allier, B 852). He lived in Montmaraud. On Oct. 25, 1778, he came to an agreement with his uncle in Paris, François Girouard of Bouchet. With this act, he recognized the fact that he owed his uncle 1388 livres, 15 sols and 4 deniers (cents). Later he received cancellation letters against this recognition, and then abstained from the benefit of these letters by signing, on March 2, 1784. In 1755, he was a farmer on the land of Chatel-Montagne, belonging to M. d'Envry, with his uncle François Girouard du Bouchet and his brother-in-law, Clause-Gilbert Massonnet. He married, according to contract of August 27, 1747, Antoinette-Barbe Bertin, daughter of the late Jacques, bourgeois of Paris, and of Marie Hychet. (Archives of Allier, B.767).

From this union were born at least two children:
1) Angelique-Françoise Girouard of Boisrolin, born June 30, 1749.
2) Gilbert Girouard of Boisrolin, born March 31, 1751.
I don't know what happened to these two children, who don't seem to have any descendants.

Du Bouchet branch
François Girouard of Bouchet, Sieur of Bouchet, (1) D'Arginy of Montrognon of Chez-Dandeau etc., youngest son of Jean and of Petronville Geongeon, born around 1705. The first clerk commissioned to the affairs of the king (1726), and farmer on the Bellenave's land and Marquisat's assistant (1735), he became as early as 1741, collector of the Chatellerie of Murat, and in 1744 became the King's prosecutor regarding matters of water and forestry at Montmaraud on June 10, 1741. He donated a house, located in Montmaraud, for the lodging of sickly poor people, but under the condition that the community could never take over. (Archives of Allier, B. 757). In July 18, 1754, he received, jointly with his wife, his daughter and his son-in-law, the land of d'Arginy, agreed in front of Hennequin, solicitor in Montmaraud, by Charles Lancel, bourgeois of Paris, and Marie-Marguerite-Judith Tirot al. Thiraud, his wife. This donation was later contested but it did not amount to anything. (Archives of Allier). On November 14, 1749, he bought the estate of Chez-Dandeau, Parish of Montaigne, from Andrée Boirat, Sieur of Pradelle, bourgeois of Excurolle, for 3000 pounds. On August 5, 1755 he bought from Gilbert Mallet of Vandègre and Gilbert of Salvert-Montrognon, his wife, three-quarters of the domain of Montrognon, in the Parish of Echassière. Towards the end of his life he sold his possessions to Jean-Baptiste of Montroquier, Marquis of Parazol, council member of Toulouse's Parliament, for the sum of 2,500 pounds, payable as a pension with provision that after his death the remaining money should be given to a person of age 30, that he would designate. He then moved to Paris. There he passed away on March 12, 1786. He was then living at the home of Sieur Dubois, wigmaker, Montoir Street, Parish of Saint-Jean-en-Grève. An inventory was made after his death by his grandfather on June 2, 1786. He had married around 1725-1728, Catherine Marie-Lucile of Chambaud, daughter of François of Chambaud, knight, Seignior de Tondière and of Gabrielle de Saint Martin. She was still living in July, 1754, giving him his only daughter.
1) Marie-Elizabeth of Bouchet, married on February 6, 1747, in Montmaraud, to Gilbert Cousin of Jeux, Sieur of Jeux and of Bare, Counsellor to the King, elected in Gannot, son of the late Mathieu Cousin, Sieur of Jeux and of Françoise Coindron. Of this marriage I know only the following: François Cousin living at Echassières in 1803.
Written at Montluçon, based on original documents and titles of my collection, July 22, 1902.

Désiré Girouard summarizes and concludes as follows:
Des Gozis (2)
There are still some Girouards in France, particularly in Paris, but the male branch of my ancestor Jean, outside of Canada has been wiped out, and the same is true of the family Geongeon. The last Girouard of Montluçon, François, brother of my ancestor Antoine, died in 1786 at Paris, whence his father came, leaving a daughter, and the last Geongeon (Antoine)

member of the Council of the Community of Montluçon in 1882, left no sons, only a daughter who is represented today by persons of high public positions in Montluçon and elsewhere, first those whose names figure very highly and of which have been the subject of very delicate attention and also the following names of the families who live outside of Montluçon and whose names have been supplied to me by M. Cornet of Ermagne, such as: Saquet, the General Berruyer, commander of the Legion of Honour, Jean Justin, the Assistant Chief of Police, Breton, Langelier-Bellevue, Boudier, of Villers, of Sainte-Georges, Fradier, Delome, Dumont, Fabouet of Boutetand Foyelle.

In any case, the documents which follow serve to provide new proof of that which has already been established for some time, especially since the publication of the *Genealogy Dictionary* of Mgr. Tanguay, that our ancestors were not nomads or beggars, but that, on the contrary, many belonged to the first families of France. This important fact would come out again, more so, if our Canadian sons would go visit the country of their French ancestors and research the Archives records. The Canadian researchers should not expect to find the history of their family all written out for them in each village, town, or city by a writer as authoritative as M. Des Gozis who published the history of Montluçonnais of 1490 to 1497, however, knowledgeable people confirm that there exist very learned genealogists in each Department. The difficulty is to get to know them. They do their work in silence, without any fame or posterity from their work.[26]

In his book *L'Album de la famille Girouard*, Désiré Girouard also makes mention of Doctor Achille Girouard, born in 1829, son of a doctor in Chartres. (Translation by the author)

His father had two brothers, one a lawyer and the other a merchant, both of whom died without children. The name of the family is today carried by the Doctor Achilles and the descendants of his brother Édouard, Doctor at Evreux. Henri, the grandson of Édouard, was born in 1880 and is the father of Pierre and Emile. This Dr. Achille does not descend from Jean Girouard, married to Petronille Geongeon, ancestor of the Canadian branch in France, but may possibly descend from a brother of Jean, the Girouard sculptor, or from an Acadian branch which returned to France and remained.

The genealogy and roots in France of the France-Canadian branch in Québec can be summarized in the chart "fc" (abbreviation for French-Canadian) that follows. This Canadian Girouard branch, which provided the Girouard families with some of its most famous people in France, will be prominent in the Québec chapter. *[In this chart I use the spelling of 'Geongeon' for the maiden name of Pétronille, because Désiré Girouard uses this spelling, from records in France in his book,* La Famille Girouard en France, *(1902). In his other two works,* La Famille Girouard, *(1884, and* L'Album de la Famille Girouard, *Désiré uses other spellings: for example, in* La Famille Girouard *he uses 'Georgeau' on pages 1 and 19; In* L'Album de la Famille Girouard *he uses 'Georgeon', beginning on page 6. I will use this spelling on the Canadian branch chart—B.G.]*

France

6 THE FRENCH CANADIAN GIROUARD BRANCH IN MONTLUÇON, FRANCE

Note: For descendants of Antoine see Canadian master chart and subcharts in Québec Chapter. Information based on 1. Désiré Girouard's booklet entitled *La Famille Girouard en France*, 1902, 2. Article in *Nova Francia*, Vol. 32, 1926-27, pp. 39-45 (the children descending from each of the blocks of this chart are discussed in paragraph form in the the text of the France chapter.) Research of William D. Gerrior, *Awakenings*, 2002.

Lfc	Mfc	Nfc	Ofc	Pfc	Qfc	Rfc	Sfc	Tfc	Ufc	Vfc
1]	Notes: François, born 1705, was: 1. Clerk to The King of France (1726). 2. Administrator of the lands of the Marquis of Bellenaves 3. Tax Collector for the estate of Murat, 1741. 4. King's representative in matters of Land and Water and of Montmaraud, 1744. 5. He was also recorded as an Aministrator on Bellenave's land, France. He donated a house for the sick and poor people.				? 1721 Jean Girouard Lord of Boisrolin King's Counsellor Comptroller of Riom m. Pétronille Georgeon 1690					
2]			1736 - Marie - Madeleine Girouard of Boisrolin m. Pierre of St-Martine Lord of Trimouille, Comptroller of the King's Treasury at Terdat 1726	1705 - 1786 François,Lord of Bouchet and Arvigny, Montrognon, also lived in Paris m. Catherine Marie Lucile Chambaud 1730 at Beaune Paris	Paris 1693 - 1738 Pierre Lord of Boisrolin & Marie Burel Terray m1. Marie Burel m2. Françoise Périer	1696 - 1767 Antoine Girouard departed to Québec to establish the first French Canadian Girouard branch m. Marie Anne Barré Montréal 1723				
3m1]					1720 - 1784 François Alexandre of Boisrolin Judge, Aministrator, 1755 m. Antoinette Barbe Bertin living at Montmauraud 1747	Catherine Marguerite m. Paul Gilbert Alamargot 1741				
3m2]				1737 Marie Pétronille Girouard of Boisrolin m. François Pailleret 1755	↔	François - 1747 died young				
4]					1751 Gilbert of Boisrolin	1749 Angélique Françoise Girouard of Boisrolin No children	Note: Any trace of the descendants of Gilbert and Angélique, if any, seem to have been lost.			
5]					Other descendants, if any, are unknown in France at this time				FRENCH CANADIAN BRANCH IN FRANCE ANTOINE	

© *Awakenings Girouard/Giroir... Routes and Roots*

Achille Girouard, Doctor at Chartres

Photo of the Honour Room and families of Belliveau and Landry, who attended the Master chart plaque unveiling ceremony.

CONCLUSION

We have explored both the Acadian and the French Canadian Girouard/Giroir/(e)... origins in France.

The whole experience in France and consequent contacts has been a very rewarding and worthwhile adventure for me and has greatly enhanced this book concerning the rich history, culture and heritage of the Girouard/Giroir(e) family. These trips to France have rekindled the interest of the Girouard/Giroir(e) families in France, and this in turn has increased interest in North America.

Two different events symbolize this continued interest in France:
First we have the unveiling of the Acadian Girouard, Giroir(e), Gerrior...Master Chart, following the 1990 first international reunion of the family, at la Maison de l'Acadie, attached to the old church at La Chaussée, France. A special thanks to Michèle Touret, Directrice de la Maison de l'Acadie, and Baudouin de La Bouillerie, owner of la Château de la Bonnetière whose wife, Marie was born a "Giroir". This event would not have been possible if it were not for the interest and kindness of Andrée and Yvon Gombert of Châtaneuf les Martigues, France who attended the first international reunion in 1990 in Antigonish, Nova Scotia and brought the master chart plaque back to la Chaussèe at La Maison de L'Acadie.

The unveiling of the bronze master chart plaque which now adorns the wall in the Honour Room of la Maison de l'Acadie, was an emotional ceremony, attended by two Acadian families who were visiting on this day, the Belliveau and the Landry families of Campbellton, New Brunswick, Canada, both of whom have links to the Girouard family in Canada.

Unveiling of the plaque by Madame Touret, in the presence of Baudouin de la Bouillerie and families mentioned above. Andrée Gombert presenting.

One of the most recent signs of this spirit and awakenings, which I believe may have been sparked by one of my visits to France, is the following article:

A Giroire Family Trace Their Ancestors
In 1826, Frumence Giroire married Marie Clément. They had 6 children. M. Guy Secq of Saint-Jean-de-Sauves is among his descendants. Last year his daughter was employed as a hostess at the Maison de l'Acadie when a Canadian came along who was also a Giroire descendant and through conversation it became evident that they had some common links. But was this Canadian a cousin of the local Giroires? He then agreed that if his family could trace their ancestry back to the point where he had arrived, he would gladly arrange with the family in Canada, which is very large, for exchanges amongst cousins. M. Guy Secq did not hesitate and on Sunday he hosted a reunion of the descendants of Frumence Giroire in order to identify as many links as possible back through as many generations as possible. [see subchart 900-BG] **

Une famille Giroire sur les traces de ses ancêtres

Une rencontre difficile mais très agréable

The second event symbolizing this continued interest is the family reunion held in France

En 1826, Frumence Giroire, épouse Marie Clément. Ils ont 6 enfants. Parmi les descendants, M. Guy Secq de Saint-Jean-de-Sauves. L'an passé, la fille était employée comme T.U.C. pour l'accueil à la maison de l'Acadie. Un Canadien s'en vint, qui descendait lui aussi des Giroire. De fil en aiguille dans la conversation, on en vint à constater des liens communs. Mais ce Canadien était-il un cousin des Giroire de ce coin ? Il déclara alors à cette jeune fille que si sa famille pouvait établir une ascendance certaine jusqu'au point où lui en était arrivé, il établirait volontiers avec toute la famille qui est forcément grande au Canada, des échanges entre cousins. M. Guy Secq n'a pas hésité. Et dimanche il réunissait toute sa famille à savoir les descendants de ce fameux Frumence Giroire et de Marie Clément pour essayer d'établir tous les maillons manquants jusqu'au plus grand nombre de générations. Certes, il n'est pas facile de se lancer comme ça dans la généalogie. D'ailleurs Giroire, comment écrit-on cela sur les registres ? On trouve au moins trois façons d'écrire ce mot. Mais en réunissant toutes les bonnes volontés, bientôt verra-t-on beaucoup de cousins canadiens arriver dans notre région.

In addition to these two events, I know, from the keen interest and diligent correspondence of Guy Secq and Gaston Giroir, Baudouin and Marie de la Bouillerie, Andrée Gombert, Jean-Pierre Giroire, Pierre Giroir, René Giroire, Michèle Touret and many others, that research will continue to develop with regards to the Girouard/Giroir(e) families in France. The most complete work can only be accomplished through sharing what we know with others and working together with all interested parties, to build the great mosaic of our family.

Now, we are ready to follow our Girouard ancestors on their voyage from France to North America.

11

Port Royal and old Acadie

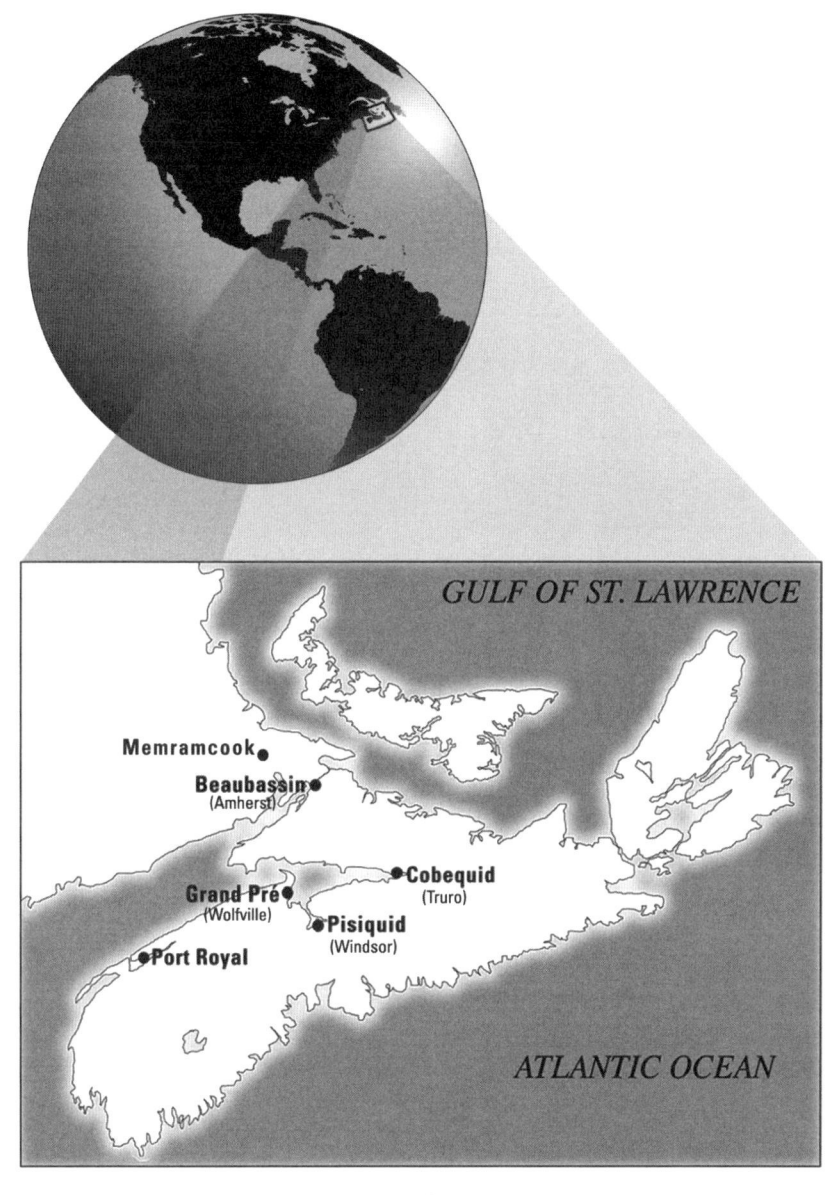

THE SETTLEMENT AT PORT ROYAL

During the 17th century, settlers arrived from different parts of France in a region of the New World which they called *Acadie* (Acadia), which gradually became associated with the regions known today as the Maritime Provinces of Canada,

Acadian Awakenings: An Acadian Family In Exile

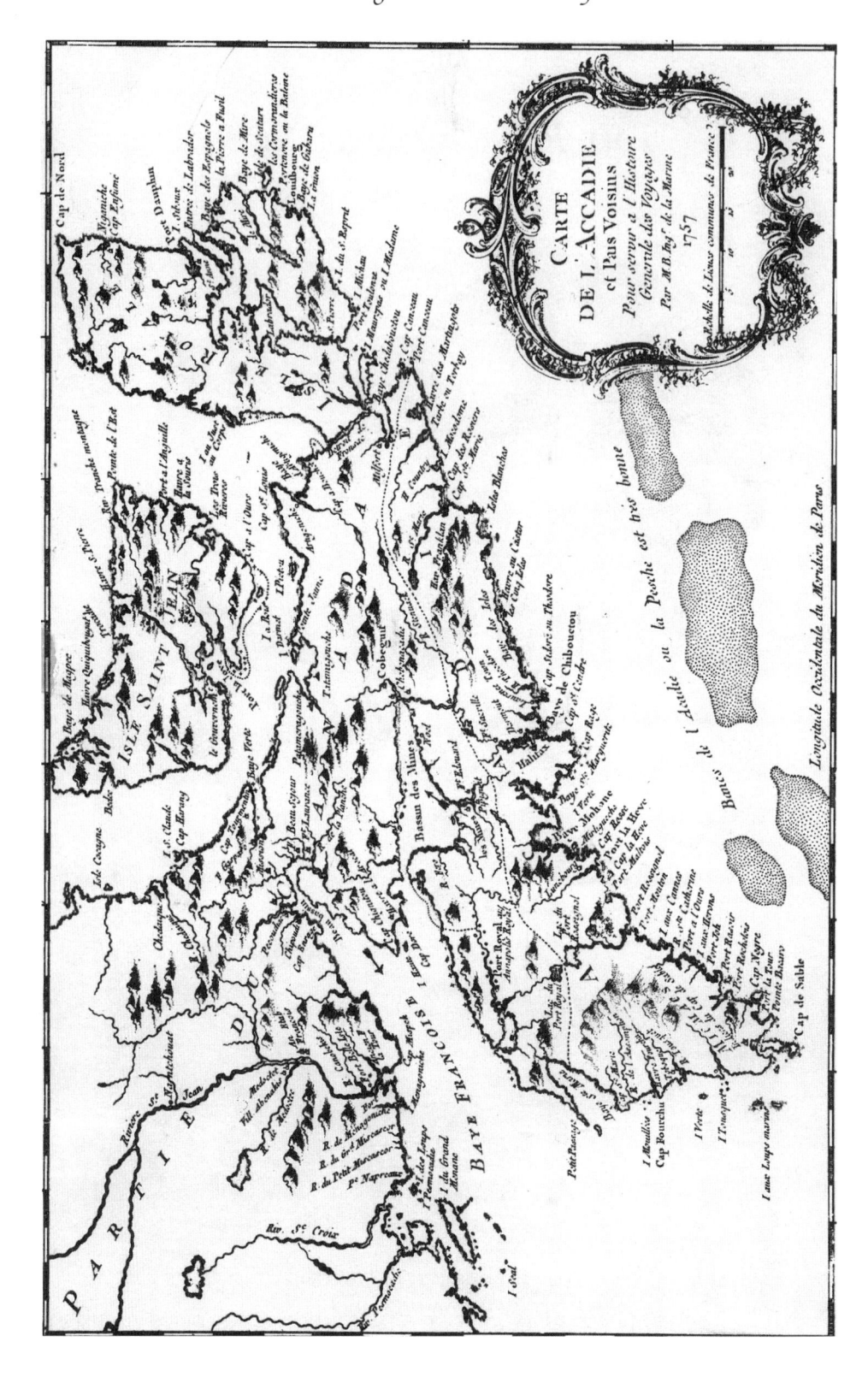

Opposite: Map of L'Accadie[sic], 1744 by Bellin "Carte de l'Accadie Dressé sur des Cartes et Plans de la Marine"

National Archives of Canada NAC –19267.

and the northern part of Maine, including Mount Desert Island. People from France who settled the area after 1632, primarily in what is now mainland Nova Scotia, were known as Acadians. They developed a unique way of life, which found expression in a distinctive lifestyle, language, customs and beliefs which endure to this day.

In the early 17th century France was determined to strengthen her political and economic position in the New World through colonization. Traders and men of influence received commissions to establish settlements, in exchange for the rights to profit from the rich fisheries and fur trade. In April, 1604, several of these men, Samuel de Champlain, Pierre du Gua, Sieur de Monts, the Sieur de Poutrincourt and Jean de Biencourt, with their crews and settlers, sailed from Le Havre, France, for Acadia. They landed at La Hève (another spelling for "Le Havre", meaning harbour), Acadia, in May. After a month or so exploring the coasts and inlets of the new land, the two ships sailed around the southern tip of the province into the Bay of Fundy, which they named Baie Française. On the northern side of the bay, they discovered a wide river, presumably the Saint John River. Later they discovered l'Ile Sainte-Croix, (St Croix Island). Here they settled for the winter, reasoning that the island would provide protection from the native peoples, although, as they later found out, the Mi'kmaq were very friendly and peaceful in this area.

Following a very harsh winter, during which scurvy took the lives of 36 men, they moved everything to the north side of the Annapolis Basin, to a site known today as the Habitation, Port Royal.

Sally Ross and Alphonse Deveau, in their award-winning book, *The Acadians of Nova Scotia Past and Present*, provide us with a description of Champlain's arrival at the Annapolis Basin, translated from his diaries. These offer a great deal of information and many descriptive passages on the landscapes and geography of Nova Scotia, documented during Champlain's various expeditions:

Continuing two leagues on the same course, we entered one of the finest harbours I had seen on all these coasts, where a couple of thousand vessels could lie in safety. The entrance is eight hundred paces wide, which I named Port Royal. Into it fall the rivers, one which is called Equille...[1]

Here they built a fort in 1604, calling it the Habitation. Champlain also wrote the following about the Annapolis area:

At the east is a river between the said mountains and hills, in the which ships may sail for fifteen leagues [30 miles] or more, and in all this distance is nothing on both sides of the river but fair meadows, which river was named L'Équille, because of the first fish taken therein was an *Équille* [sand eel]. [2]

Elizabeth Ruggles Coward in her book, *Bridgetown Nova Scotia, Its History to 1900*, continues from Champlain's diary of the following summer:

> ... At the very beginning we were desirous to see the country up the river, where we found meadows, almost continually above twelve leagues [36 miles] of ground, among which brooks do run without number, which come from the hills and mountains adjoining. The woods were very thick on the water shores and so thick that sometimes one cannot go through them... but mountains be not perpetual in the country: Within three leagues [9 miles] of our dwelling, the country through which L'Équille passeth is all plain and even. I have seen in these parts, many places where the land is the fairest in the world. But the perfection thereof is that it is well-watered.[3]

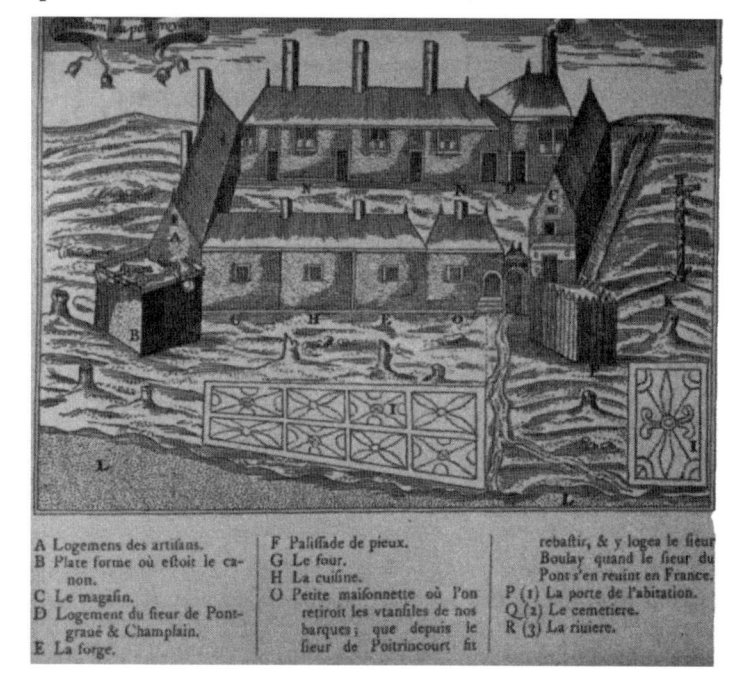

Samuel de Champlain's plan of the Port-Royal habitation, 1613
A. Artisan's lodging
B. Platform for cannon
C. Storehouse
D. Lodging of Gravé & Champlain
E. Forge
F. Palisade of stakes
G. Oven
H. Kitchen
I. Gardens
K. Cemetery
L. Water of the basin
M. Drainage ditch
N. Dwelling
O. Small building for rigging of pinnaces

C8760/From a copy at the National Archives of Canada, original held at the National Library of Canada, Bibliothèque nationale du Canada.

Above: Port Royal Habitation drawing

courtesy of NAC-8760

Opposite: Map based on Mitchell 1733 Map of Annapolis River
Source: Information from Nova Scotia Museum History Collection

Following pages: Mitchell 1733 map of Annapolis River with corrections and notes by the Placide Gaudet map of Annapolis River with his notes in Appendix)

courtesy of. (NAC)

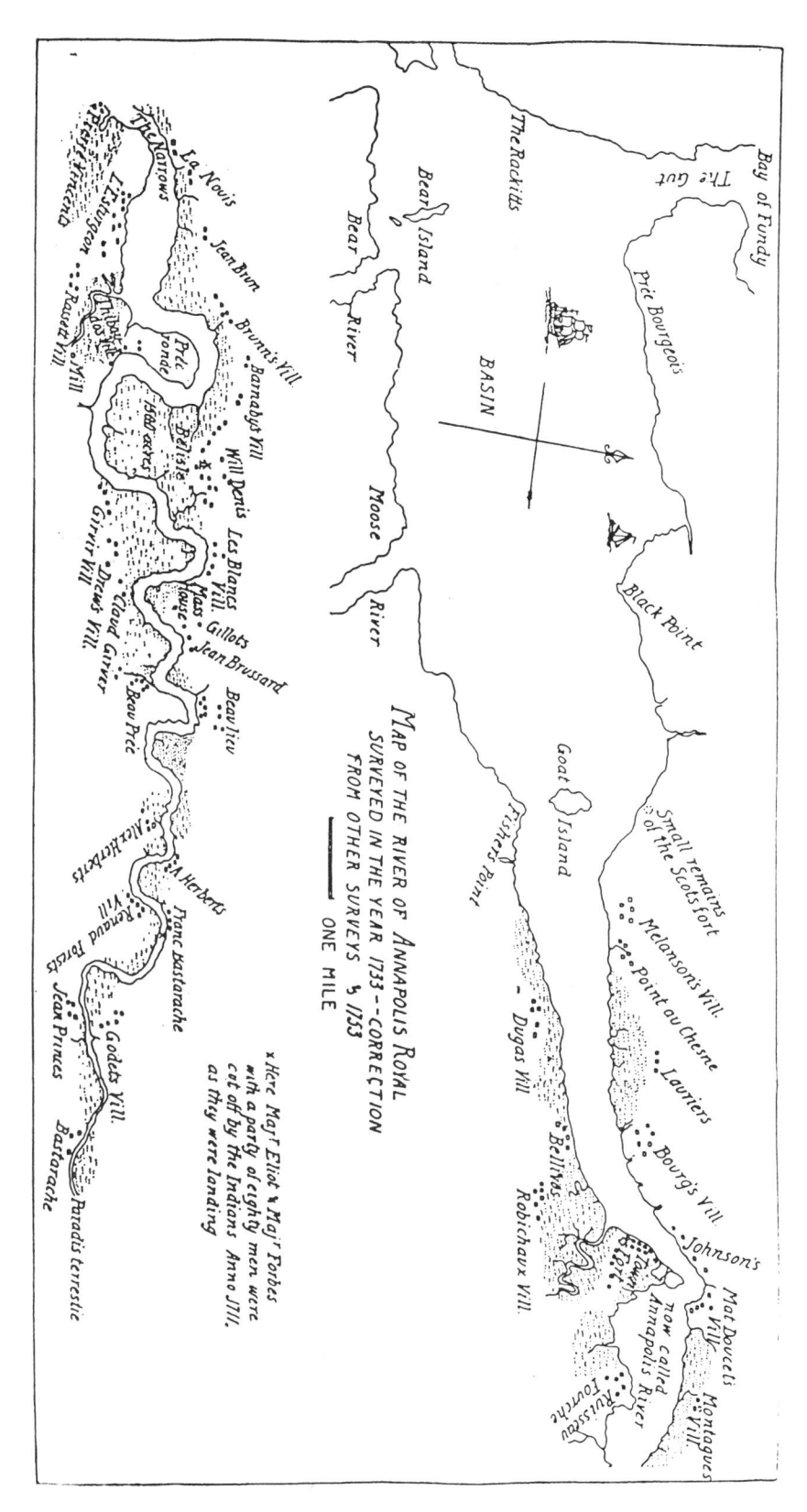

Port Royal and old Acadie

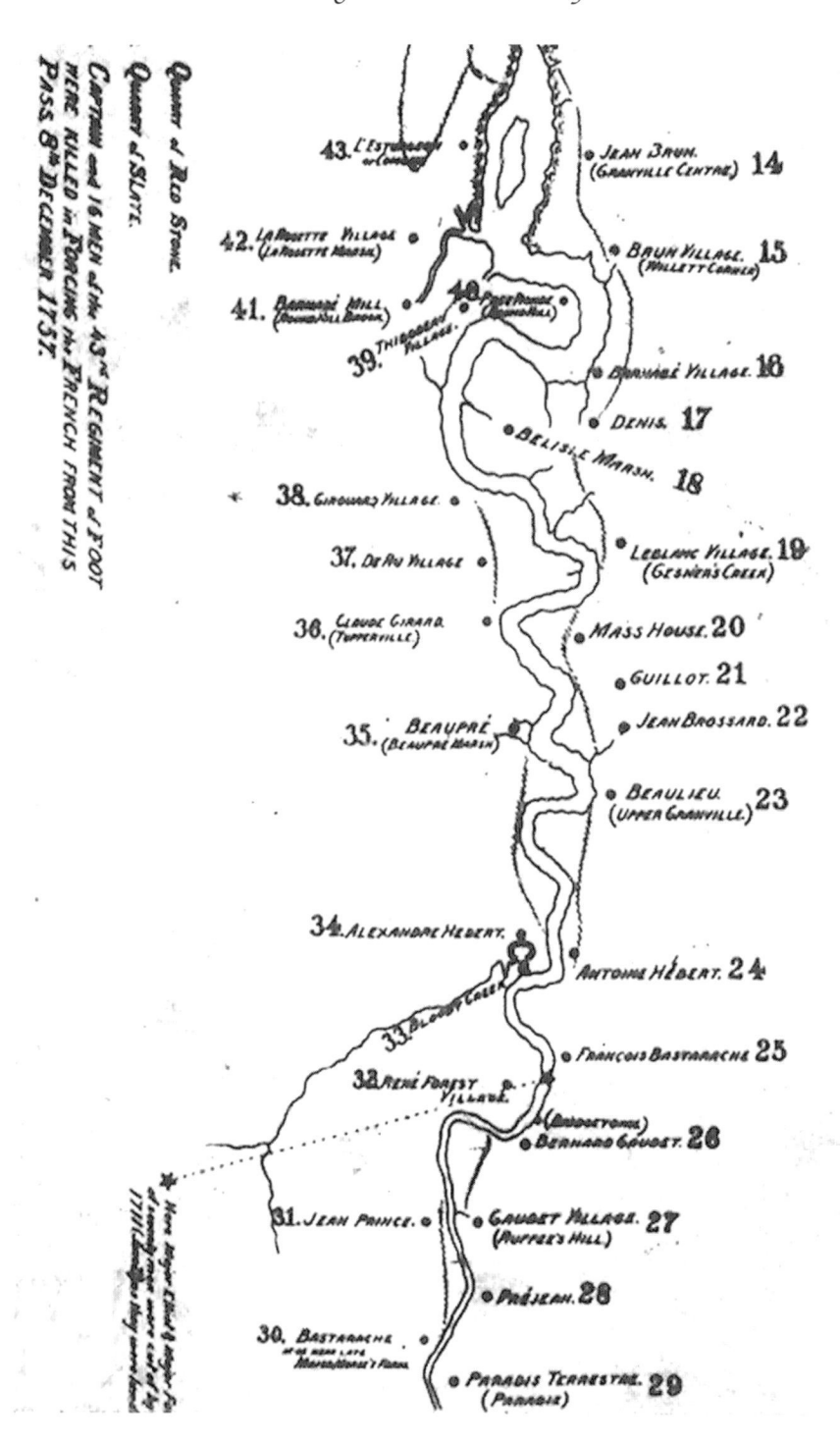

Map of Acadian Villages along the Annapolis River

Left margin annotations (top to bottom):
- Quarry of Red Stone.
- Quarry of Slate.
- Captain and 16 men of the 43rd Regiment of Foot were killed in forcing the French from this Pass 8th December 1757.
- Here Major Elliot & Major [...] of [...] were killed by [...] 1711 [...]

Villages (left side, top to bottom):
- 43. L'Estringeon [or Couveau]
- 42. La Rosette Village (La Rosette Marsh)
- 41. Barnabé Mill (Bornabéhill Brook)
- 40. Pine Ridge (Round Hill)
- 39. Thibodeau Village
- 38. Girouard Village
- 37. De Rou Village
- 36. Claude Girard (Tupperville)
- 35. Beaupré (Beaupré Marsh)
- 34. Alexandre Hébert
- 33. Bloody Creek
- 32. René Forêt Village
- 31. Jean Prince
- 30. Bastarache [at or near late Mansel Morse's Farm]

Villages (right side, top to bottom):
- 14. Jean Brun (Granville Centre)
- 15. Brun Village (Willett Corner)
- 16. Barnabé Village
- 17. Denis
- 18. Belisle Marsh
- 19. LeBlanc Village (Gesner's Creek)
- 20. Mass House
- 21. Guillot
- 22. Jean Brossard
- 23. Beaulieu (Upper Granville)
- 24. Antoine Hébert
- 25. François Bastarache
- 26. Bernard Gaudet (Bridgetown)
- 27. Gaudet Village (Ruffee's Hill)
- 28. Préjean
- 29. Paradis Terrestre (Paradis)

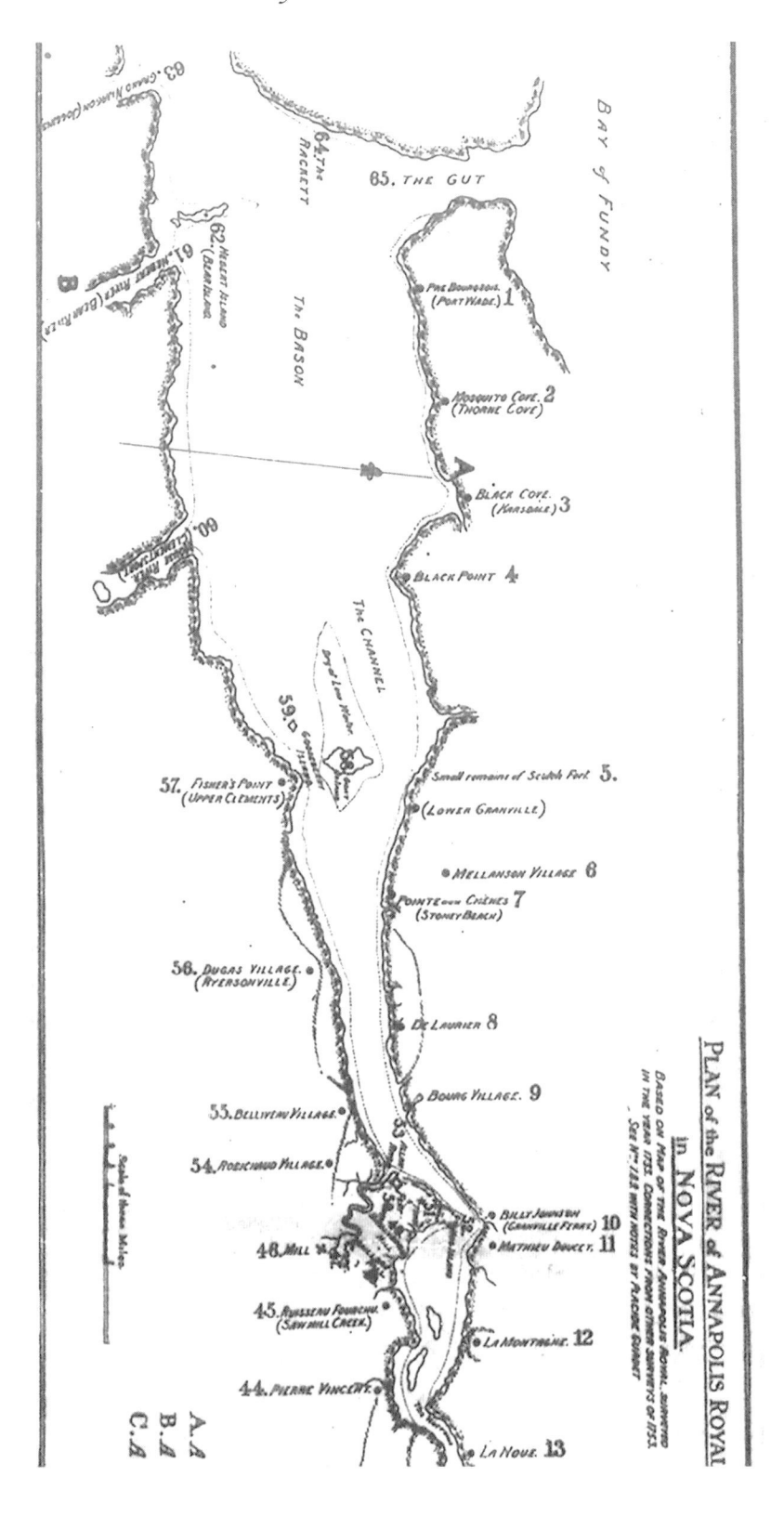

Port Royal and old Acadie

Above: Habitation fortress, Port Royal.
At left: Harbour basin at Port Royal viewed from Habitation.

Thinking of wars back home, and of the economic hardships endured by many of their compatriots, the French felt that they had discovered a paradise. In fact, a place on the upper part of the river is still called Paradise today, as it was named on Mitchell's 1733 map.

Champlain and his men established *l'Ordre du Bon Temps*, (Order of Good Cheer), to pass the time in winter and raise the spirits of everyone. Jean Daigle, in his article "Acadia 1604-1763", in *Acadians of the Maritimes*, provides us with more information concerning the winter months:

The winter of [1606-1607] was more successful for the colony's inhabitants. Marc Lescarbot, a Lawyer, arrived in 1606, whipped up enthusiasm and presented the first theatre performance in North America- le Théâtre de Neptune. Samuel de Champlain founded the "Ordre du bon Temps" (Order of Good Cheer).... [4]

The author with his wife Audrey at Port Royal, during their honeymoon. Little did I realize then, that I was destined to be doing this work today!

156

The oldest social club in Canada: l'Order du Bon Temps. Painting by C.W. Jeffrys.

Each week one person took his turn at creating the best food and music for the group. This competition provided laughter, stories, music and entertainment so that everyone had a good time. Today an "Order of Good Cheer" certificate is given by the province of Nova Scotia to all non-residents visiting our province for the first time, a remembrance of things past in the age of modern tourism.

In 1606, Louis Hébert, a pharmacist, and Marc Lescarbot, a lawyer and writer, arrived, and the following year, Champlain left to become the founder of Québec. Poutrincourt returned to France in 1607 to receive Royal confirmation of the grant of Port Royal, and on February 25, 1610, departed from Dieppe, France with his oldest son, Charles de Biencourt, and a number of settlers, among whom were Claude de La Tour and his son Charles, later Governor of Acadia. *[Charles de la Tour is related to the Girouard/Girroir(e) family through the marriage of his granddaughter to Alexander Girouard. [AMC Block C-3a]— B.G.]*

Bergitta Wallace explores the history of this period in "*An archeologist discovers Early Acadia*". The following is excerpted from her work

While establishing himself at Port Royal d'Aulnay made a financially useful family alliance when he married Jeanne Motin. . . . Through Jeanne, d'Aulnay became allied with other influential habitation owners, in Acadia.

D'Aulnay was not the only contender for control of Acadie. A royal decree issued by the French king granted a portion of the land

Portrait of Charles de Menou, Sieur d'Aulnay et de Charnesay. A late nineteenth-century overpainted photographic image on wove paper. Location of original portrait unknown.
New Brunswick Museum, Webster Canadiana Collection, W987

assigned to d'Aulnay to Charles De La Tour, of Cape Sable seigneury. This development, as well as differences in regional origin, personality, and religious sect, launched the two men on a lifelong conflict. The struggle took place on two fronts: via diplomatic maneuvering at the court in France and warfare in Acadie.[5]

In 1613, the Habitation was destroyed by the British. What was useful was saved, and the rest burned by Captain Samuel Argall of Virginia who, with his fleet, set out to eradicate all the French settlements along the coast. Gone was the Port Royal settlement, where the first registered baptism in North America had taken place, (that of Membertou, chief of the Mi'kmaqs, and 20 of his family, on June 24, 1610). Today a replica of Champlain's original Habitation, built to be as exact as possible by the Canadian government in 1939, stands on the same site.

De Monts had sailed back to France in September 1606 and never did return to Acadia. Poutrincourt again returned to France in July of 1611, with a load of furs, leaving his son in charge of the little colony. After the destruction of the Habitation, Charles de Biencourt, with his close companion Charles de la Tour and a few others, survived in Acadia thanks to their Indian friends.

Under British rule, in 1621, William Alexander obtained a charter from King James I to establish a Scottish settlement in the former Acadie, naming it *Nova Scotia* (New Scotland). The Scots fort of 1628, under the command of Alexander's son, was located only a short distance from the Port Royal Habitation site. A monument marks the site today. In 1632, however, the colony was returned to France by the Treaty of St-Germain-en-Laye, and most of the Scots returned to Scotland.

Isaac de Razilly had received a commission in 1630 to found a settlement in La Hève, (today's LaHave, in Lunenburg County), and brought over tenant farmers from the western part of France, (areas like Poitou, Charentes and Vendée), some of whom knew how to dyke marshland farms in France, a skill they had originally learned from Dutch engineers brought in by Henri IV. Although La Hève provided for good fishing grounds, it was not as ideal a setting for farming.

Port Royal, unlike the rocky Atlantic coast, had many tidal marshes along the Annapolis Basin and river shoreline. These marshes were large, treeless, stone-free plains that were well suited for farming, once dykes had been built to prevent the high Fundy tides from flooding them twice daily.

De Razilly died prematurely at La Hève in July, 1636, and was succeeded by his cousin Charles d'Aulnay de Charnisay, who had arrived with him in 1632. Birgitta Wallace provides the following information regarding D'Aulnay:

[He was] an aristocrat who could trace a noble lineage back to the time of the Crusades; he was a member of one of the most influential families at the French Court. The powerful Cardinal Richelieu, known for his victory over the Huguenots in la Rochelle, was one of his relatives. D'Aulnay grew up in the family estates at La Chaussée, Martaizé and Aulnay near Loudun…[6]

That year, d'Aulnay built the second Port Royal fortress and buildings at the place

D'Aulnay and his wife, Jeanne Motin, with three of their children at Port-Royal.

Courtesy of Parks Canada - Artist: Terry MacDonald - 1988 - #H 03 03 01(02)

now commemorated as Fort Anne National Historic Park, about seven miles east of the original Habitation on the south shore of the Annapolis River. In the same year, Jeanne Motin arrived on the *Saint Jehan*, with other settlers. She became d'Aulnay's wife, and they had nine children, (four sons who died in French wars, four daughters who became nuns, and a child who died in infancy and was buried at Port Royal). Thus d'Aulnay left no descendants in Acadia except a *Métis* (a child of d'Aulnay and a Mi'kmaq woman), named Doney.

D'Aulnay recruited a number of Acadians from the Seigniory of Aulnay in France, which he looked after for his mother. The Girouards, like the Aucoins, worked on d'Aulnay's seigniories in France, and so it is very likely that François Girouard *dit* La Varenne (also called 'la Varenne'), was a passenger on one of these voyages, with Razilly and/or d'Aulnay. Léopold Lanctôt[7] states that Girouard came to Port Royal with Jacob Bourgeois, military surgeon, and that both arrived in 1642 with Charles de Menou, Sieur d'Aulnay-Charnisay, Governor of part of Acadia. D'Aulnay drowned in 1650, and his bitter rival, Charles de La Tour, married his widow, Jeanne Motin, three years later, when he was 60 years old. This marriage assured de la Tour control of almost all of the colony. Jeanne Motin was his third wife, and gave birth to five children, from whom thousands of Acadians descend today. Two of their daughters married sons of Baron Philippe Mius D'Entremont, La Tour's major-general, whom La Tour had brought to Acadia in 1651.

De la Tour is the only member of the Acadian élite of those early days to have left descendants who can be traced as far back as 1610. He built two forts, Fort St. Louis, at what is now Sand Hills, Villagedale, at Cape Sable, NS, and Fort Sainte-Marie (later Fort La Tour) at Portland Point, Saint John, New Brunswick. Remnants of the latter, in particular, can be visited today. He died in 1663 in Acadia. *[One branch of the Girouards [AMC Block D-3a] can claim to descend from him.—B.G.]*

Robert Sedgwick of Massachusetts took Port Royal in 1654, but the Treaty of Breda, in 1667, returned Acadia to France yet again. Many battles were fought at or near Port Royal during the following years. *[Some of those battles were likely well known to the Girouards in Giroir Vill/ Girouard Village at Port Royal, although they, like most Acadians probably rarely took an active part in the fighting—B.G.]* The French colony remained relatively small; by 1671, the Acadians still numbered only about 500, as compared with a population of more than 50,000 in the New England colonies.

On October 13, 1710, however, Port Royal, under Governor Daniel Auger, Sieur de Subercase, was finally surrendered to Colonel Nickerson's English expedition, after a two-week siege with little ammunition and food remaining. The French garrison had only 160 men while the English expedition had 3,400 soldiers and 30 ships. Subercase marched his men out of the fort with arms and baggage and "all the honours of war". Most were sent back to France.

Port Royal was renamed Annapolis Royal in honour of Queen Anne of Great Britain, and Acadia became Nova Scotia. Annapolis Royal was left in the hands of Colonel Samuel Vetch of Massachusetts, and the key to the old fort was carried to Boston. *[In 1922, the Massachusetts Historical Society sent the key back to the Fort Anne museum, where it may be seen today.—B.G.]*

The colony of Acadia, from the beginning, had been hotly contested by England and Scotland as well as France. For Acadians, however, like the Girouards, it became quickly their only land, their own country—as it had been for the original inhabitants, the Mi'kmaq and Maliseet. From the first, the Mi'kmaq were friendly to the French and hostile to the English. After the English took the fort in 1710, the Mi'kmaq constantly harassed members of the garrison who went up the river for wood and provisions. In 1711 some seventy soldiers were fired upon by the Indians, lying in ambush for them on the north side of the river.

The battles continued, even after the Deportation. The battle of Bloody Creek in 1757 was yet another example of this rivalry. The native people in this engagement were from Maine, under the command of Anselme, son of the Baron de Saint-Castin, one of the great military leaders of the old Acadie, who had married an Indian at Penobscot. Of a party of British soldiers, in two flat boats and one

Port Royal and old Acadie

whaleboat, only one man returned to *the fort. Forty men were taken prisoners, eighteen were killed (including two officers), nine men and two officers were wounded and ransomed. Major Alexander Forbes, the fort engineer, was in command of the soldiers, and though wounded seven times, he gained the opposite bank and refused to surrender. Finally, he was killed by an Indian who swam the river with a pistol in his mouth and a tomahawk in his hand. The spot is marked by a cross on Mitchell's map of the river, drawn in 1733.*[8] *[A monument has been erected, and still stands at one of these battle locations of 1757, not far from Tupperville on highway #201.— B.G.]*

The Plaque reads:
Bloody Creek-
Commemorating the combat between British garrisons of Annapolis Royal and allied French and Indians in the half century of conflict for possession of Acadia on the north bank of the Annapolis River, June 10, 1711 and here, Dec.8, 1757.

LIFE IN ACADIA BEFORE THE DEPORTATION

A useful summary of pre-Deportation Acadian life, based on information from archaeological digs [9] in the Belle-Isle area, at the narrows of the Annapolis River just across from Giroir Vill / Girouard Village, appears in a series of three information sheets published by the Nova Scotia Museum.

These sheets gain further clarity, and can be more appreciated by referring to the paintings of artist Azor Vienneau. These works were made for a series of educational films on the life of the Acadians before Deportation, called *Premières Terres Acadiennes*, and approved by the Nova Scotia Museum. Very careful attention was paid to detail: the paintings are based largely on historical research and on the results of the Belle-Isle archaeological dig.

Farming

Farming was a major part of the livelihood of the Acadians. But they were not farmers in the common sense of the word clearing land to make their fields. They made use of a system of dyking to create their fertile fields, using knowledge and skills that were familiar to them from France. The high tides and great marshlands of Port Royal made this location ideal to apply these techniques. It is likely part of the reason the site was chosen in the first place. Upon arrival, the Acadians knew exactly what to do and began the process of dyking immediately.

As we know, the Acadians settled on the shores of rivers, which emptied into the Bay of Fundy, or Baie Française, as it was called during this period. The Bay of Fundy, because of its funnel-like shape, has very high tides, which also affect all

"Early Acadia (1635-1755), The Harvest," artist: Claude Picard Sainte- Basile, NB.
Courtesy of Parks Canada

the rivers connecting to it. The following diagrams help explain the methods used to build the dykes.

At high tide, these rivers would overflow their banks at various points, covering a considerable area of lowlands, or marshes. When the tide went out, these lands were still wet with leftover salt tidewater, a spongy, marshy terrain which was built up from layers of fine rich soil due to the twice-a-day ebb and flow of tidal action over many centuries.

To make use of these rich lands the Acadians built dykes, or long walls around the perimeter of the lands affected in this manner. The dykes were so well compacted and tight that they stopped the river water from flooding these lands as the tide was rising. The Acadians then hand-dug canals or ditches on this land, each draining towards an *aboiteau*, a one-way door or gate, which lead back out to the river. In this way, the rain and snow would wash the salt off the land, into these canals and back out to sea through the *aboiteau*. (See fig 1) The drainage would occur only at low tide, when there was no salt water on the sea side of the gate, and the salt river water could not come back in when the tide was rising because the doors only opened one way. As the tide came in, the salt water would put pressure on the one-way gate, causing it to close and pressing the seal even tighter as the tide came up, putting more pressure on the gate. After two years of this land drainage process, the silty soil on the marshes became de-salted and dry, and these marshes thus made excellent rich soil for farming.

Methods of dyke building

Figure 1: Dyke gate

Figure 2: low tide before any dyking

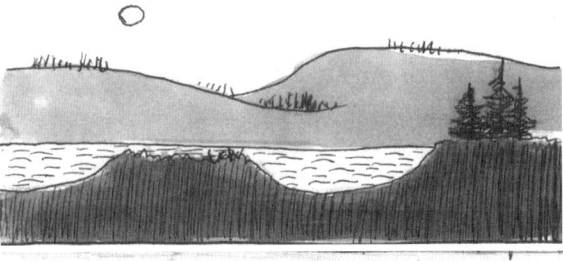

Figure 3: high tide before any dyking

Fig. 4 high tide, after dyking.

Fig 5 - one method of constructing Acadian Dykes.

Fig 6 – second method

sketches by Margaretha van Gurp

The Acadians repairing a dyke, Belle-Isle, NS, across from Giroir Vill/ Girouard Village around 1720. Artist: Azor Vienneau.

Nova Scotia Museum historical collection.

Acadians Salt-marsh haying, Belle-Isle, N.S. across from Giroir Vill / Girouard Village around 1720 Artist: Azor Vienneau.

Nova Scotia Museum historical collection..

Farming on the drained, fertile side of the dykes, aerial view
Nova scotia Museum historical collection..

Sometimes the dykes were built by driving five or six rows of logs in the ground, laying other logs one on top of the other between these rows, filling all spaces between the logs with well-packed clay and then covering everything over with sods cut from the marsh itself. Sometimes dykes were built by simply laying sods over mounds of earth.[10]

The Acadians were called lazy by settlers from other communities. They were referred to as *defricheurs d'eau* (clearers of water) because they built dykes and cultivated the natural meadows and marshes, rarely clearing the upland forests for agriculture purposes...[11]

For example, it is the complaint of Governor de Broullan in 1701 that

...they [the Acadians] are found retreated to small portions of land, although their concessions are large ....[12]

Upon deeper reflection, it is obvious that the Acadians used the higher ground just above the marsh for their houses and buildings, to guarantee a dry location. Rather than being lazy, they were simply good readers of their landscape, being in harmony with it, and knowing well how to harness the natural resources around them. Considering the agricultural methods of the period, the marshlands were more efficient and more productive than clearing uplands for agricultural purposes.

Sally Ross and Alphonse Deveau give the best rationale possible for the Acadians in this regard, quoting an original source, the Sieur de Dièreville, who arrived at Port Royal in 1699 from Normandy, and who is credited as being the most important source of first-hand description of life in the settlements of Rivière Dauphin (Annapolis River). Dièreville writes the following concerning their efficiency and their hard work:

It costs a great deal to prepare the lands which they wish to cultivate. To grow Wheat, the Marshes which are inundated by the Sea at High Tide, must be drained; these are called Lowlands, and they are quite good, but what labour is needed to make them for cultivation! The ebb and flow of the Sea cannot easily be stopped, but the Acadians succeed in doing so by means of great Dykes, called Aboteaux [sic][13]

Coarse salt hay (*spartina*) on the seaside of the dykes, which grew in the marshes in the salt water ebbing of the tides, was another natural resource that the Acadians quickly harvested. During the low tide the *spartina* was exposed. The Acadians cut the salt hay and piled it on "staddles" (platforms), which they built to keep it above the highest seasonal tidemark, so it could stay dry. They later baled the hay and stored it in barns to feed their animals all winter. Thus it was not necessary for them to slaughter their cattle for lack of winter fodder, as it was in most of the New England colonies. Consequently, unlike the New England colonies, they were not dependent on receiving new cattle from Europe each spring to replace those they had to slaughter the previous fall. This provided the Acadian colony at Port Royal with stability and self-sufficiency.

The Acadians soon had finer grasses growing on the dry landside of the dykes replacing the *spartina* hay, which had always flourished in the tidewaters, although they continued to harvest it on the seaward side of the dykes.

Before 1755, the Acadians lived largely self-sufficient lives on their marshland farms. They tilled the soil and it yielded abundant crops of wheat, oats, barley, rye, peas, corn, flax and hemp. They also kept gardens in which they grew beets, carrots, parsnips, onions, chives, shallots, herbs, salad greens, cabbages and turnips. Cabbages and turnips seem to have been particularly important in their diet.

The Acadians kept cattle and sheep, as seen from the census documents. Pigs roamed freely in the forest behind the houses, and also fed on kitchen scraps and, in winter especially, on leaves and peelings from the cabbages and turnips stored in the gardens and covered with straw until needed. The Acadians seem to have eaten a lot of pork but relatively little beef, preferring to keep their cattle for milk, as working animals, (i.e oxen) and for trade.

The Acadian life was a hard life but a good one in many ways. They understood their landscape, and made it work for them. In a land where regulations were kept to a bare minimum, the settlers could supplement their needs by hunting and fishing as well as berry picking and making various liquids. They brewed their own beer from branches of fir trees, and dried fruit and berries as food

Those Acadians who devoted their lives to farming were very busy, depending on the season. Their day consisted, for the most part in dyke-building, making hay, fencing, house- and barn-building, cutting firewood, clearing land in wooded areas, gardening, hunting and looking after domestic animals, making candles, soap, butter, dye, clothing. Also they prepared and preserved food, and made furniture, tools, and toys in their leisure time, depending on weather and crops. This would also certainly be true for the Girouard pioneers who lived at Port Royal and later moved to Beaubassin, which was first established around 1671, and those who moved again to Memeramcouq (Memramcook) in 1700.

Houses

The NS Museum pamphlet *The Acadians: Settlement*, gives an informative description of how the Acadians worked together, in particular, for special events such as weddings and related house-building activities:

Like many people isolated by circumstances, the Acadians had a strong sense of community and performed many tasks together. One of the most important of these was the regular maintenance of dykes. Another, which was much enjoyed, occurred when a young couple married. The whole village would gather to help clear land and to build a house for them. It became an occasion for work, fun, food and celebration. Fiddles and jawharps often provided music on these occasions. [14]

In 1983, the Nova Scotia Museum's archaeological dig at Belle Isle revealed a well preserved house foundation, which measured 11.5 m x 7.5 m. (roughly 35 ft x 22 ft) on the outside perimeter. The foundation was fieldstone, two rows deep and three to four courses high, suggesting a somewhat larger one-room house than expected from written descriptions of this period.

The thick foundation wall also suggested that heavy timbers had been used for the frame of the house. Also, indirect evidence, in the form of the relatively small

Acadians, building a home, Belle-Isle, NS, circa 1720. Artist: Azor Vienneau.
Nova Scotia Museum historical collection

Acadian Awakenings: An Acadian Family In Exile

Exterior of early Acadian house, recreated from archaeological excavations at the Belle-Isle site just across the river from Giroir Vill / Girouard Village.
Artist: Azor Vienneau.

Nova Scotia Museum historical collection.

Interior of early Acadian house, recreated from archaeological excavations at the Belle-Isle site just across the river from Giroir Vill / Girouard Village. Artist: Azor Vienneau.

Nova Scotia Museum historical collection

quantities of stone and brick and the large quantity of nails found on the site, indicates the walls were not made of stone, but that wood was used for building material for construction of frame and walls.

A great deal of clay walling material called *bousillage*, made from local clay mixed with marsh hay for strength, was found at the site, indicating that the inner walls were probably covered with this clay. One intact surface of the walling material had been treated with a white clay slip, giving a plaster-like finish, while the opposite side still retained wood-grain impressions, suggesting that the outside wall was wood, and that the *bousillage* had been applied to the wooden walls on the inside of the house. The interesting implication here is that the house would have been reasonably bright and pleasant on the inside. Fragments of cut and bundled marsh hay were also found, suggesting this readily available material had been used to thatch the roof.

The base of a combined circular oven and fireplace was the most unique architectural discovery at Belle-Isle. This particular design is not found anywhere else in North America. Such clues, although scanty, provided the archaeologists with a pretty clear picture of what this house looked like, so clear in fact that the NS Museum artists had little difficulty in reproducing what the house may have looked like, both inside and out.

Many other household items were found, such as scissors, fishhooks, two jaw harps, knives and spoons, and various dishes, that help give us a clearer picture of Acadian life. Most of these items were made by the Acadians themselves, but many iron, steel, and glass items were manufactured in England, France, Spain, Germany, Holland, and New England. Once we realize this, it modifies our idea that the Acadian communities were completely cut off from the rest of the world in the 17th century.

Another interesting class of objects found was animal bones, 96% of which are from domestic animals. The bones came from cheaper cuts of the carcass, suggesting that the Acadians sold or traded the choicer cuts of meat for things they needed.

A full and detailed account of all findings is contained in the NS Museum Curatorial Report # 48 by David Christianson, Nova Scotia museum Curator of Archaeology, director of this very significant project. [15]

The village of Belle-Isle was the richest and largest village of Port Royal, and not all that was found would be typical of other villages. Belle-Isle was just across the river from Giroir Ville/Girouard Village. It would be interesting to explore Giroir Ville/Girouard Village in the same manner, particularly given that the Girouards/Giroirs were allied to Emanuel Le Borgne, Sieur de Belle-Isle, by the marriage of Alexandre de Ru Girouard to Le Borgne's daughter Marie. Considering also that Alexandre de Ru and other brothers, along with their father Jacques (Jacob) Girouard, were living on lands previously owned by d'Aulnay, the second Governor of Acadia, this area would not only be of interest to the Girouards but to all Acadians. D'Aulnay's homestead would have likely been comparable to that found at Belle-Isle. [This topic is presented in the epilogue from the research of Régis Brun, Archivist, Université de Moncton, Centre d'études acadienne.]

It has been recorded that after the death of d'Aulnay, 1650, Le Borgne, a French merchant who had lent d'Aulnay a considerable amount of money, arrived at Port Royal to protect his interest in Acadie. There he took control of the land granted to d'Aulnay, in particular at Port Royal. [16]

I maintain, based on the information collected to date concerning the Belle Isle and Giroir Vill/Girouard Village connection, that it is likely that both Belle-Isle and GiroirVill/ Girouard Village (Tupperville) belonged to d'Aulnay and were taken over by Emanuel Le Borgne. Later, he would have given the land across the river to his daughter, Marie and her new husband, Alexandre de Ru Girouard, (part of the extended family, including Alexandre's parents, brothers and sisters, most of whom established at Giroir Vill/ Girouard Village). Hopefully, archaeological work will continue on Acadian sites along the Annapolis River, and the connection of Giroir Vill/Girouard Village and Belle-Isle to d'Aulnay, in particular, will inspire and encourage further research at Giroir Vill/Girouard Village, as expressed by the NS Museum:

We have learned a lot that we didn't know before. But the archaeologists are quick to point out that the farm at Bellisle was only the home of one pre-Expulsion Acadian family. Although the excavation has told us at great deal we should not be to quick to generalize from this one example to the whole of Acadie. In other words, the work has just begun.[17]

Family Life
Acadians had large families. When a son married, he would settle some distance from his father's house and start another little village. Any group of two or three houses was called a village. In the census of 1671 there were 361 souls and in 1686 almost double that: 622 souls including 30 soldiers. By 1733, when Mitchell's map was drawn, there were small Acadian villages as far away as Paradise.

Acadian villages, including Giroir Vill / Girouard Village, as seen from the Port Royal map, formed little family hamlets—a sort of clan or extended family concept that was very common in France:

The extended family. . . gathered at the same hearth and under the same roof, a large social group, based on several generations, with the old parents, the married children and their spouses, the youngsters of the different couples. . . . A patriarchal image dominated by the noble figure of the head of the family, who decides at once the destiny of each one, directs the management of the farm, allots the tasks and chooses his successor. These solidly established family communities, that were generally linked to the possession of a domain, were encountered in many of the provinces [Old France]. It is possible that they were that in the 16th and 17th centuries, the form most often seen south of the Loire.[18]

The area south of the Loire was the genereal vicinity of many of the Girouard, Giroir, Giroire and other first Acadians: the departments of Vienne, Deux-Sèvres, and Vendée. There is further evidence of this kind of extended family and support for each other in this last will of Michel Haché Gallant, married to Anne-Marie Cormier, the daughter of Thomas Cormier and Madeleine Girouard [AMC Block C-2].[19]

```
                    LAST WILL and TESTAMENT
                              +
Desc.: HACHE'-GALLANT, MICHEL I (PQ-NS-ISJ)        a/k/a: L'ARCHE, LARCHE'
                                                          ACHEE, BALLONS
b. : ca 1660-63      @: TROIS RIVIERE, QUE, CAN ; c. 24 APR 1668 TROIS RIVIERE
m.1: 1690            @: BEAUBASSIN, ACADIA (AMHERST, NOVA SCOTIA)
m.2:                 @:
m.3:                 @:
d. : 10 APR 1737     @: RIVIERE du NORD, PEI *(DROWNED) Int 17 JUL 1737 Port Lajoye
F/ : PIERRE L'ARCHE     M/: ADRIENNE LANGLOIS

Spouse 1: 1 CORMIER, ANN-MARIE
   "   2:
   "   3: -
1 b.: 1674           @:              d.: pre 1739    @: PEI
2 b.:                @:              d.:             @:
3 b.:                @:              d.:             @:
F/1 : 1 CORMIER, THOMAS              M/: 1 GIROUARD, MADELEINE
Children
  I.D.   Name           Born       Died             Married
  1      MICHEL II      1691                        MADELEINE LeBLANC
  2      JOSEPH         1693       1746             MARIE GAUDET
  3      MARIE          1694       pre 16 SEP 1749  1) 1715 FRANCOIS POIRIER
                                                    2) 1729 RENE RACICOT
  4      JEAN BAPTISTE  1696       pre 1752         1719 MARIE-ANGIE GENTIL
  5      CHARLES        1698                        1727 BENEVIEVE LAVERGNE
  6      PIERRE         1700       pre 1760         1726 CECILE LAVERGNE
  7      ANNE           1702       3 AUG 1763       1719 JOSEPH PRETIEUX
  8      MARGUERITE     1705                        1)1725 PIERRE JACQUEMIN
                                                    2) *     dit LORRAIN
  9      JOSEPH-FRANCOIS 1707                       ca1725 ANNE BOUDROT
         a/k/a Francois-Joseph
  A      MAGDELEINE **  1709                        1733 PIERRE DUVAL
  B      JACQUES        1712                        MARIE-JOSEPHTE BOUDROT
  C      LOUISE         1715       29 OCT 1779      1735 LOUIS BELLIVEAU

* 8      MARGUERITE                                 * 2)1739 ROBERT ANGO dit CHOISY

: ** a/k/a Madeleine.  All b. at Beaubassin, Acadia.

    Michel was a most practical man, attested to by the following last will and
testament. Rec from MEMOIRES DE LA SOCIETE' GENEALOGIQUE CANADIENNE-FRANCAISE,
1956, Vol. VII, p 95. / GALLANT-FERLAND by Yvonne Dolbec Gallant Martel BFA# 108

    "Obligation of a yearly pension of 10 livres by each of the undersigned:
    On this day, 17th November 1736, in the presence of Fr. Angelique Collin,
Recollet of the Province of Britany, missionary and chaplain of the King at Port
Lajoye, Bishopry of Quebec, in the absence of a notary to pass the following act
between Michel Hache' and Anne Cormier, his wife, of the first part, and his
children on the second part, herein named, who agree to the following:
    Be it known that all the named children are obligated to give their father
and mother during their lifetime, the sum of 10 livres tournois each year,
commencing as of this date.  Furthermore, the named children renounce the
inheritance of their father and mother after their parents' death, they, the
parents, being free by the present document to give their estate to the one of
their children whom they will determine appropriate.
    It is further agreed by the said Michel Hache' and Anne Cormier.... with
their children that when one of the parents dies, the said children will pay
only half of the above named sum of 10 livres to the other parent."

                        Submitted By Peter Gallant Berlo 116L
```

Last Will document of Michael Hache Gallant

Women's Role

The early settlements in Acadie (i.e. Champlain's expedition and others) were almost exclusively male, and it was assumed that men in these frontier establishments would intermarry with the native population. From 1632 onward, settlements became more permanent, however, and land was brought under cultivation by entire families who were recruited to come to the new colony.

Brenda Dunn, in her article "Looking into Acadia", in *Aspects of the Lives of Women in Ancienne Acadie* explains how French law ensured that women were respected in their own right.[20] Legally, men and women were both considered minors until the age of 25, or marriage, whichever came first. Even after marriage, though, women continued to be known by their original family surname, although the name of the married couple was the husband's. The custom of Paris provided for a marriage contract to be drawn up before a couple wedded, and that marriage established a community of goods between the couple. Neither husband nor wife could conduct propert transactions without the others's written consent.

Marriage contracts usually stipulated that, on the death of one spouse, one half of the couple's property was to be inherited by the survivor, and the other half divided equally among the children, male and female. This meant that widows and widowers had legal autonomy, at least until remarriage (which was almost inevitable). There appear to have been very few single women in Acadie; perhaps the pressures of survival in the new land demanded partnership.

Sally Ross and Alphonse Deveau point out that:

The family was the cornerstone of Acadian life in the seventeenth and eighteenth century. By 1650, some 50 families were living in or near Port Royal and constituted the foundation of the Acadian People.[21]

Brenda Dunn elaborates on women's roles as follows:

Women obviously played important roles in a society based on family and kinship networks. There were few aspects of Acadian life that they were not involved…there was very little variety in Acadian Christian names. The majority of Acadian women were named Marie, Anne, Madeleine, Cécile, Jeanne or Françoise. One of the reasons for this repetition was the children often took their godparents names. Wives kept their maiden names all their lives…[22] *[This custom accounts for the fact after the death of François Girouard we see his wife's name Jeanne Aucoin, recorded as "Vve Aucoin" (the widow Aucoin) in the census.—B.G.]*

Widows in seigneurial families were exceptions, known as "Madame" rather than widow, as seen in the 1707 census where we find "Mde le Belleisle widow", "Mde Freneuse", …along with "widow Naguin".

Although Acadian society was more egalitarian than that of France in the late seventeenth and eighteenth centuries, there was some stratification. The upper level consisted of families that had been granted seigneuries, such as the Mius d'Entrements, la Tours and the Damours. While a seigneurial grant gave them status, it did not mean that they were wealthy. Families that were prosperous and respected in the community such as the Bourgeois, the Melansons, the Robichauds [and the Girouards–Claude Girouard was an Acadian Deputy as we shall see later-BG] but who lacked seigneurial grants were also part of the elite. To these groups could be added the French officials and Military officers assigned to the colony before 1710, many of whom married Acadian women[23] *[such as Jacques Girouard who married Anne Petitpas 1707, daughter of Claude Sieur La Fleur, Secretary for the King at Port Royal according to the research of Edward Lavin Girroir [24]—B.G]*

Acadian women led extraordinarily busy lives. Families were large; many women were married in their teens, and continued bearing children well into their forties. Certainly, these large families meant that the small settlements were full of close kin who could help care for the youngest children, but women were also largely responsible for producing domestic necessities themselves. They spun, dyed and wove wool and flax for clothing, tended gardens, cooked and baked, and helped as necessary with other, heavy labour.

Speaking of the household inventory of Marguerite de Sainte étienne de la Tour, widow of Plemarais, made at Port Royal, 1707, Brenda Dunn continues as follows:

The household goods included a handworked tablecloth and six handworked napkins. There were also two irons, which came in pairs so that one could be heated while the other one was in use. These household objects give us an idea of the technology available to Acadian women who were noted for their industry, especially as it related to the domestic chores of cooking and making clothing for their large families.[25]

The reader should also refer back to the interior and exterior of Acadian homes by Azor Vienneau presented earlier in this chapter for more detail concerning the role of women as interpreted in these paintings.

Many people are interested in knowing more about the Acadian dress of the period. Brenda Dunn expresses her views, based on the information presently available:

The everyday dress of the eighteenth century Acadian women is believed to have been a linen chemise, worn under either a vest or a jacket with a woven wool or linen skirt often striped. An apron, neck scarf and cap would complete the outfit. No respectable women of the period would have been seen with her head uncovered. It is possible that different regions of France had a distinctive style of cap. Knit stockings and wooden shoes were worn for everyday wear. Leather shoes were probably worn on occasions such as attending Church.[26]

As they did in France, women worked in the fields at harvest-time. In Acadia, however, it appears that they were also responsible for culling the fish entangled in the weirs at high tide, and they are known to have used canoes.

Obviously, for most Acadian women, there were few luxuries and little time for ceremony. A mid-18th-century visitor from New England commented on the few, cracked china cups of one household, and the rough-and-ready dress of the women. Women wore wooden shoes at work, as men did, another custom which drew the visitor's comment.

There were a few exceptions, however, as Brenda Dunn points out: "Some of the administrator's wives did enjoy silks, beads and laces imported from France, as well as the occasional trip back to France itself. Most women, however, although their legal status and many traditions were informed by the customs of the mother country, made their lives entirely within the close community of Acadie".[27]

Nicknames

Many Acadians bore certain common Christian names such as François and Pierre and Jean, so nicknames helped to resolve this confusion. Nicknames were often short and easy, and defined the individual by some known characteristic or character trait, which made it easy to remember that person.

Nearly every Acadian had a nickname, and often these were used as surnames (e.g. Alexandre Girouard *dit* du Ru, was often recorded as simply "Du Ru"— his nickname. Thus we have Du Ru village, also recorded as 'Drews Vill' on the 1733 Mitchell map. I believe this name was derived from the last syllables of his nickname. He is elsewhere known as Sieur du Ru or sometimes just DeRu or Du Ru.).

Community Life

As previously discussed, the building of dykes and houses were two major community events in which Acadians demonstrated their support for each other and their community spirit by coming together as friends, neighbours and extended family to complete the task at hand. This would be true whenever there were big tasks to be accomplished such as the cutting and storing of hay. Jean Daigle describes this vital community spirit:

Despite the continual attacks and looting—Port Royal was attacked once in 1704, twice in 1707 and again in 1710—the Acadians held firm. They had developed an ability to resist and adapt that kept these difficulties from becoming insurmountable. The system of family organization goes a long way toward explaining how the inhabitants of the Bay of Funday could cling to a territory coveted by several great powers for over 150 years.

Community life in Acadie. (Artist: Azor Vienneau.
Nova Scotia Museum historical collection.

Port Royal and old Acadie

Limited immigration to Acadia meant that, after three or four generations, all inhabi... the various settlements were related to one another (uncle, cousin, distant cousin) etc. As is always the case in this type of rural society, the emotional and blood ties created by kinship formed a basis for the establishment of a system of mutual aid, solidarity and independence, in which the wealthier distributed their surplus to those whom war or natural disaster had touched. This homogeneity created what is commonly called the Acadian extended family, a traditional society that was able to resist the great social upheavals of the period, thanks to its natural resources.[28]

Religion was a very important part of Acadian life. Sally Ross and Alphonse Deveau quote Father Petit, a priest who in 1676 became pastor at Port Royal, and who was named the first Vicar-General by Bishop Saint-Villier of Québec:

One sees no drunkenness, nor loose living and hears no swearing or blasphemy. Even though they spread out four of five leagues along the shores of the river, they come to church in large numbers every Sunday and on Holy Days.[29]

The Acadians were very friendly with the Mi'kmaq, who helped them in many ways to survive this new land. They traded with the Indians, New England colonies and other French settlements. As power shifted back and forth between France and Britain, the Acadians welded closer and closer together, almost oblivious to the governing power and the long transition periods, while developing a unique character and way of life.

The objects illustrated in this painting represent artifacts recovered from Acadian archaeological sites [sites near Giroir Ville / Girouard Village] or listed in the inventories of ships that actually traded with the Acadians. Artist: Azor Vienneau
Nova Scotia Museum historical collection

...tion on trade comes from the NS Museum publication, *The*

...ns were remarkably self-sufficient, there were some things they ...emselves, and for these needs they established trading links with ...r French settlements. Molasses, cooking pots, broad axes, clay ... and rum came from New England. Through Louisburg they ...cottons, thread, lace, firearms, and religious items from France.

Acadians were fond of smoking (both men and women smoked). Their clay pipes came mostly from England, although at times they did fashion their own, using local red clay. In return for these items, the Acadians traded grain from their fertile reclaimed marshlands, their cattle which were healthy and well-fed on salt-marsh hay, and furs they had obtained from trapping and trade with the Micmac.

We also know some of the Girouards in the early 1700's made their livelihood from the sea as captains of vessels, such as Pierre Girouard [AMC Block E-3b] and François Girouard [AMC Block F-3b]. Certainly these Girouards would also spend a great deal of time in the winter months, as boat builders, a trade, which they obviously knew well. This tradition would be handed down to a number of their descendants.

Government under British Rule

During the periods when power was in transition from English to French rule and vice versa, the Acadians learned self-government. Soon they had spread out to Beaubassin, Grand Pré, Pisiquid, Cobequid, Memramcook and the Peticodiac Rivers. All these Acadian villages were far from the seat of government at Port Royal, and were for all practical purposes, autonomous. According to Jean Daigle, "The Acadians had little contact with the administration, preferring to call on their own people in case of problems like land boundaries."[30] He goes on to elaborate:

Because it preferred to look at its own interest, the Acadian extended family joined by ties of blood and affection, devoted all its energy to developing a lifestyle that was totally original in North America for the period. From their experiences with salt marshes in France, the Acadians constructed dikes to reclaim alluvial land from the Baie Française (Bay of Fundy). This form of agriculture guaranteed self sufficiency despite the vicissitudes of war...[31]

This independence was clearly demonstrated in their refusal to pay taxes, as Daigle further illustrates:

... In fact, the English authorities admitted that they had received only 30 pounds sterling in 1732 [for taxes levied on the Acadians], and 15 pounds in 1745. Once again, the failure of taxation and landholding policies shows that the Acadians lived beyond English authority... the Acadian community would prefer to turn within itself to solve these questions with the village priest or patriarch who had above average education or experience which, in their eyes, replaced formal authority. It may be said that the Acadians set up a system of government parallel to the one established by the English...[32]

Because the communities were widely spread out, and in order to communicate and maintain relations with the Acadians, the British authorities at Annapolis Royal found it necessary to appoint deputies to represent each of the villages, or sections, along the Annapolis River. The Deputies were responsible and answerable to the English Council, or Board of Governors, to represent the concerns of the Acadians in their community.

According to Daigle there were 24 delegates, six from Annapolis, 12 from Les Mines and two from Beaubassin. As Daigle puts it

They [the Deputies] were usually selected from among those Acadians enjoying the greatest influence in their community and were periodically convened by the government to consider various matters. It was they who, on several occasions, refused on behalf of the Acadian people to swear an unconditional oath of loyalty. [33]

Claude Girouard — Acadian Deputy, 1732

From the minutes of the English Council at Port Royal, now held at the Public Archives of Nova Scotia[34], it appears that Claude Girouard [AMC Block I-3a] was one of these Acadian leaders, nominated by his fellow Acadians in Port Royal and appointed as a Deputy on Nov. 11, 1732, by the English governing Council at Port Royal. Claude was living in Giroir Ville / Girouard Village at this time. (All of his generation is accounted for on my genealogy charts, based on these census records, so by process of elimination, we know that Claude Giroard, as it is spelled in this document is Claude [AMC Block I-3a], son of Jacques Girouard and Marguerite Goutrot).

Even their enemies recognized Acadians as a peaceful, hard-working community. British Governor Lawrence, the chief architect of Deportation, addressed them in May 1750.

My friends, we are all well aware of your industry and your temperance, and that you are not addicted to any vice or debauchery. This Province is your Country: you and your fathers have cultivated it; naturally you ought yourselves to enjoy the fruits of your labour. [35]

Moyse de les Derniers, one of Lawrence's chief assistants, and eyewitness to many sad scenes, wrote:

They were the most harmless and most virtuous I have ever known. They lived in a state of perfect equality of person, without distinction of social rank. Setting little value on luxuries and even ordinary conveniences, were quite satisfied with a very simple way of life. They were especially remarkable for the high quality of their principles. I cannot remember a single case of illegitimate birth among them. Their knowledge of agriculture was extremely limited; still they were able to obtain large crops from their marshlands. They were healthy people, able to withstand great fatigue and many of them lived to a ripe old age, and this without the help of medical doctors. Really, if ever there was a people that would remind one of the "Golden Age", it was the old Acadians. [36]

In *"En Amerique"*, E. Rameau de Saint-Pierre speaks of the early Acadian life:

The Acadians had arrived at a situation where no one was poor, no one was rich. There was much economic uniformity in the people. Family life was simple but cheerful and little troubled by futile desires of worldly advantage. Was this not real civilization and real wealth? They loved their land; they loved their family and their ancient traditions. After the chores of the day, neighbourly gatherings usually occupy their evenings, of which they were fond. [37]

Some descriptions in Henry Longfellow's wellknown poem "Evangeline", written around 1897, although they are thought to be largely idealized, were apparently not far from reality. For example, Longfellow writes:

Thus dwelt together in love these simple Acadian farmers,
Dwelt in love of God and man.
Alike were they free from fear that reigns with the tyrant, and envy, the vice of republics.
Neither locks had they to their doors, nor bars to their windows; but their dwellings were open as day and the hearts of the owners;
The richest was poor, and the poorest lived in abundance. [38]

D.C. Harvey in *The French Regime in Prince Edward Island*, comments further, as follows:

On the other hand Forant, Franquet and Provost all found the Acadians strong, vigorous, obedient, intelligent, handy with an axe, submissive to religion, even a little superstitious. These three officials agree that the Acadians were not so much 'lazy' as inclined to avoid hard labour and to concern themselves only with the necessities of life, leaving the luxuries to those who valued them more highly. . . .
The Acadians, although good-natured, were not always easy to manage. They submitted more readily to gentleness than to violence, those officers were most successful with them who showed affability rather than firmness. [39]

Obviously the Acadians were not always easy to manage. In 1731, when George Mitchell, a deputy of the Surveyor-General of Woods, was ordered to survey the woods and lands on both sides of the river, the inhabitants were ordered to plant poles to show their boundaries to the surveyor. At first, many refused to do this.

Alexandre de Ru Girouard, in the company of the heads of various Annapolis River families, among them his brothers François, Guillaume, and Charles, had taken the oath of allegiance to the King of England in December 1729. In December 1731, however, Alexandre de Ru refused to permit English surveyors to survey his land, fearing, with good reason, that they were planning to take the Acadian lands. His son Louis and his brothers Jacques and François also refused to allow the surveyors on their land.[40] In order to make an exact plan of the river the surveyor hired a boat and four men, besides an interpreter, to accompany him to try to resolve some of these problems.

The English government also had to contend with some of the priests, who they regarded as activists encouraging English hatred among the Mi'kmaqs. They accused the priests of advocating the use of the sword rather than the cross. They were very important leaders for the Acadians who turned to them for advice, counsel and religious guidance.

The Mass House (church) of St-Laurent was located directly across the river from Claude Girouard's home, according to Placide Gaudet's notes on the 1733 Mitchell map. Acadians came here from both sides of the river to attend service.

I can imagine a very peaceful picture when this scene comes to my mind: A calm, warm, Sunday morning, when the river water flows gently and all one can hear is the sound of oars and paddles in the water as the Girouard families, other Acadian families and perhaps some Mi'kmaq, are heading across the river in their Sunday best with family members of all ages. On the other side of the river, smoke is rising from the chimneys and other families are walking to church. No wonder the Acadians felt happy and prosperous in the country they were building, around Port Royal and in the Annapolis Valley!

From Placid Gaudet's notes, in particular #20 on the 1733 Mitchell map, *(see appendix 4)*, we learn that the church was destroyed in 1736, after the priest was arrested and accused of inciting the Indians and French inhabitants to revolt against the English garrison.

This was not the first time such accusations had been made. Some documents indicate that on an earlier occasion one of the Girouard ancestors was also accused, when there were concerns about the priest inciting the native Indians.

From the minutes of H.M. Council at Port Royal, Aug. 27, 1724, we have indications that Alexandre Girouard de Ru [AMC Block C-3a] may have been involved. Alexandre, living along the Annapolis River (see Placid Gaudet's note # 37 of the Annapolis River, 1733 Mitchell map), was accused of assisting the priest, Fr. Charlemagne, to encourage seven Indians to attack the English at Port Royal and Canso. Remembering that Alexandre du Ru lived just across the river from St. Laurent Church at Port Royal, it is likely that he was very close to the priest.

In this document Alexandre Girouard (Du Ru) is described as a "poor innocent fellow" by the Acadian Deputies, in an attempt to win pity for him and a pardon by the English, for his accused acts. But we know from other documents that Alexandre was married to Marie Le Borgne, daughter of Alexandre Le Borgne and Marie de Saint-Etienne de la Tour, Sieur de Belle-Isle, the largest village in Port Royal, and that she was the granddaughter of Charles de La Tour, one of the first Governors of Nova Scotia. Alexandre himself was the grandson of François Girouard, one of the wealthier inhabitants of the settlement, according to land and cattle assets etc. From all this information, we know that Alexandre (who also had the title of Sieur de Ru), was not a "poor ignorant fellow" at all.

In March 1733, we have a record of land rents and seigneurial rents being paid by Girouards to the English government. Obviously some of the Girouards were a stubborn, though principled lot. Another Girouard had challenged Governor Crosby of Port Royal in Council, over a disputed piece of property in Port Royal.

The Gerrior brother, James (Jacques; or Jacob) and his brother François Giroard [AMC Block F-3b], had begun building a house on this property, having made a written agreement for the same with the owner, the widow Renée Gotrot. But it seems that Lady Renée later sold the same land to Governor Crosby of Port Royal. The stubborn Gerrior brothers would not appear in Council, even when summoned by the English government, but were represented by François Bourgeois, although he was found for some reason to be unauthorized to represent them.

Excerpt from Minutes of Council (1730-1742)[2], year 1724[3] Nova Scotia Archives concerning Alexandre Girouar (alias) (Drew) being examined about his voyage with the Priest to The Mines

Port Royal and old Acadie

> At a Council held at the Honourable L.t Governors Own house in His Majestys Garrison of Annapolis Royall on Munday the 4.th Day of March 173¾ at 3 o' the Clock P. M.
>
> Present
> His Honour the L.t Governor of the Province
> Major Paul Mascarene   Will.m Shirreff Secretary
> John Adams Esq.r   Henry Cope Esq.r
> William Skeen Esq.r   Otho Hamilton Esq.r
>
> His Honour Acquainted y.e Board that Prudane Robichaux and John Duon whom he had Commissioned to Receive and Collect the Seigniorial Rents of this River Were Come And as they had Given him in their Acco.ts thereof And Wanted Acquittances for y.e Same, He had Therefore judged Proper to Lay the same before them that Cognizance may be taken of the Annual Amount thereof And of the Real Quantity [380] Quantity that he had Received from the said Rent Gatherers for and On Acco.t of His Majesty that a State from thence may be made in Order to be Transmitted home by the first Opportunity • • •

Rent gathers Acco.t of the Seigniorial Rents laid before the Board.

> The petition of Paul Boudrot Being read & He Call'd before y.e Board*
>
> Order'd that a Summons be Sent for Both Partys for to Appear before y.e Board by y.e first of Dec:r next at furthest
>
> Then was Read Jn.o Depuis petition Complaining ag:st y.e Pobomcoups as aforesaid & he y.e S:d Dupuis & M:r Charles Dentremon of Pobomcoup, being both present & Examined thereon And it [450] And it being Said that M:r Pobomcoup had by Lease Lett to farm y.e Said Land to Alex:r Giroar for Twelve Years, it was Judged proper that the Said Giroar & his Wife Should be sent for to appear before y.e Board tomorrow June y.e 17:th 1736 at 10 A. M: till which Time Adjourned;

Jn.o Depuis & Pobamcoups Difference.

[C-3A]

> Being mett according to Adjournm.t the partys being also present, as also M:r Alex.r Giroar and his Wife, the Niece of Said M:r Pobomcoup, who produced a Lease dated 17:th July 1735, for Said Land in favour of Herself & Husband for 12 Years, they being thereby to pay to y.e S:d Pobomcoup 14 Bushells of Wheat *per* Annum in Consideration of that Rent to have also y.e preference of S:d Land if it should be at any Time offer'd to be Sold; Which being Consider'd as also M.r Dupuis Allegation of M.r Pobomcoups having Verbally Leas'd to Him 32 Years agoe S:d Land for 8 Bushels *per* Annum, & that He would not turn Him out, untill He or Some of His Children Should Settle thereon, & what M.r Charles Dentremont advanced in answer thereunto, as his Deceas'd ffather's Reason for dispossessing the Said Jn:o

Excerpt from Minutes of Council, 1733 concerning Land Rents and seigniorial rents paid by Alex Giroar [Girouard] [AMC Block C-3a].

181

Habitants bringing their yearly rents to the seigneur. Artist: Margaretha van Gurp.

MOVEMENT AND TRAVELS OF GIROUARDS BEFORE DEPORTATION
Census records (1671, 1689, 1693, 1698, 1700, 1701, 1703, 1707, 1714, 1728, in Acadia) and other related documents (i.e. sworn statements at Belle-Ile-en-Mer) help us to trace the roots and routes of our first Girouard ancestors in North America, up to the time of the Expulsion.

The master chart gives the big picture, or the bird's-eye view. The reader should constantly refer to the AMC (row 2) to help visualize the footsteps of each of the brothers and sisters of the second generation, to rows 3a and 3b when following the movement and travels of the 14 children of the third generation, and to row 4 as we follow the deportation and migrations of the children of the fourth generation. Further official documents for reference for these generations (and all generations on the AMC) can be found in the appendix of this book entitled "References for each block of the AMC".

The First Generation: François Girouard and Jeanne Aucoin
Port Royal

The Girouards were among the first families in Acadia. According to Léopold Lanctôt,[41] François Girouard arrived in Port Royal in 1642, with Jacob Bourgeois, his good friend and Military Surgeon at Port Royal, both arriving with Charles d'Aulnay, governor of part of Acadia. We have a sworn statement by Jacob Bourgeois that he arrived in 1642 with D'Aulnay:

Today the thirty-first day and last day of the month of July, 1699, in front of us, Mathieu de Goutin, Con. Du Roy, Lieutenant General, civil and criminal, Sieur Jacques Bourgeois states under oath that he established in this country, saying he came here in 1642 to establish and

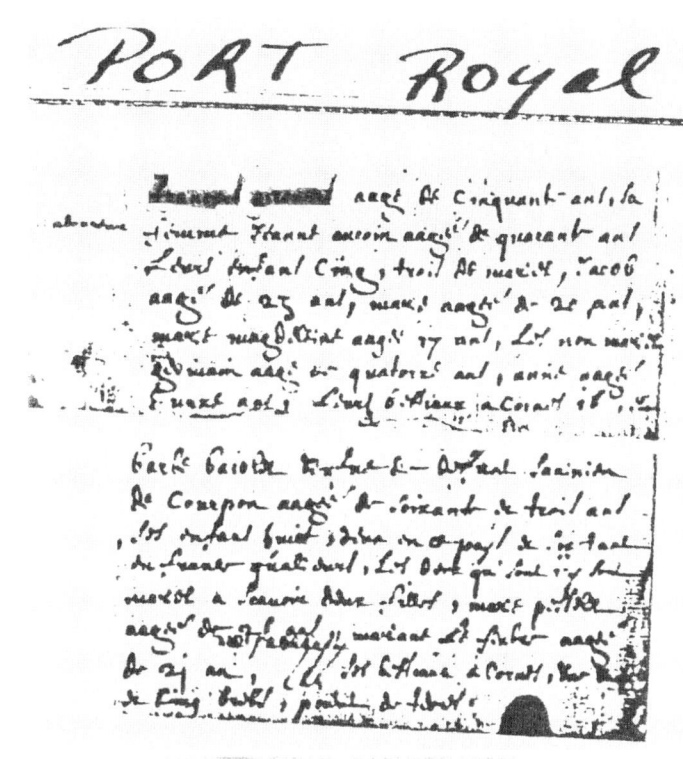

Port Royal and old Acadie

Excerpt from the original census document, 1671, Port Royal for François Girouard and his family. "François Girouard aged 50, labourer, his wife Jeanne Aucoin age 40, their children of which three are married: Jacob age 23, Marie age 21, Marie Madeleine age 17, those not married: Germain 14 years old, Anne 5 years old. Livestock: 16 cattle and 6 sheep, 8 arpents of land". (trans.) [sic]

THE GROWTH OF THE POPULATION

Acadia again became a French colony, with the advantage of passing from the administration of a company to a direct administration by the king.

The king appointed a governor but, unfortunately, did not make any effort at colonization. Acadia was left to its own resources, with about seventy families established here and there at La Heve, Pobomcou, Riviere Saint-Jean, and the great majority at Port Royal, the administrative center.

To make up for the neglect, however, the colony enjoyed a twenty year period of peace, during which time it had an opportunity to flourish.

It has been seen that very few of the settlers who came with Poutrincourt remained to colonize Acadia. The first Acadian families actually date from the expedition of Razilly, in 1632, when several men of nobility came to Acadia. They also descend from the Scotch colonists of 1627; the French who came with d'Aulnay between 1636 and 1649, and from an expedition conducted by de la Tour in 1651.

In 1671 a census of Acadia was made by M. de Grandfontaine, and deposited in the archives of the ministry of the colonies at Paris and is here reproduced:

PORT ROYAL

Jacob Bourgeois, druggist, 50; wife, Jeanne Trahan; children: Jeanne 27, Charles 25, Germain 21, Guillaume 16, Marguerite 13, Francois 12, Anne 10, Marie 7, Jeanne, cattle 33, sheep 24.

Jean Gaudet 96; wife, Nicole Colleson: child: Jean 28; cattle 6, sheep 3.

Denis Gaudet, 46; wife, Martine Gauthier; children: Anne 25, Marie 21, Pierre 20, Pierre 17, Marie 14; cattle 9, sheep 18.

Roger Kuessy 25; wife, Marie Poirier; child: Marie 2; cattle 3, sheep 2.

Michel de Foret 33; wife, Marie Hebert; children: Michel 4, Pierre 2, Rene 1; cattle 12, sheep 2.

Widow Etienne Hebert 38; children: Marie 20, Marguerite 19, Emmanuel 18, Etienne 17, Jean 13, Francoise 10, Catherine 9. Martin 6, Michel 5, Antoine 1; cattle 4, sheep 5.

Antoine Babin 45; wife, Marie Mercie; children: Marie 9, Charles 7, Vincent 5, Jeanne 3, Marguerite 1; cattle 6, sheep 8.

Olivier Daigre 28; wife, Marie Gaudet; children: Jean 4; Jacques 2, Bernard 1; cattle 6, sheep 6.

Antoine Hebert, cooper, 50; wife, Genevieve Lefranc; children: Jean 22, Catherine 15; cattle 18, sheep 7.

1671 full census taken from The True Story of the Acadians by Dudley LeBlanc.

practice his profession as medical surgeon, for Monsieur d'Aulnay, who was the governor general in this country. *[It is likely that François named his first son Jacob in honour of his good friend Jacob Bourgeois. —B.G.]*

The first written record of François Girouard and Jeanne Aucoin appears in the 1671 census records of Port Royal. The original of this earliest Acadian census, recorded by Fr. Molin, is in the Archives of Paris, but a copy is available in the Public Archives of Nova Scotia.

From the declarations given at Belle Ile-en-Mer, France, in 1767, (sworn statements by those Acadians who were brought to France by Louis XV), the first François Girouard in Acadia was referred to as both François and Jacques Girouard *dit* "La Varenne". As we discovered, there are many places in France named Varennes or La Varenne.

The measure of wealth for a farmer at the time was in the land and animals he owned. François Girouard is listed as having 16 cattle and 6 sheep, and 8 arpans [arpents is the common spelling today in French] of land being cultivated, a rather well off family for the time.

François is here reported as having 12 sheep, although both Steven White and Léopold Lanctôt list six sheep in the 1671 census. (This part is not legible on my copy of the census).In the 1678 census, François is listed with 18 cattle and 15 arpans of land. In a later (1686) census, François and his family are listed having 13 cattle, 16 sheep, eight pigs, five arpans of land and one gun. François is listed as 70 years old in this census, although he should have been 65 years old, if age 50 was correct in the 1671 census. This clearly shows that the Acadians would often give only, as was common at the time, approximations of their age based on memory.

Jeanne Aucoin's sister Michelle was married to Michel Boudrot, who was born approximately 1631,

F-2

Jacob Girouard 23; wife, Marguerite Gauterot; child: Alexandre; cattle 7, sheep 3.

Pierre Vincent 40; wife, Anne Gaudet; children: Thomas 6, Michel 3, Pierre 2, and one daughter; cattle 18, sheep 9.

Pierre Martin 40; wife, Anne Oxihnoroudh; children: Pierre 10, Rene 8, Andre 5, Jacques 2; cattle 11, sheep 9.

Vincent Brot 40; wife, Marie Bourg; children: Antoine 5, Pierre 1, and 2 daughters; cattle 9, sheep 7.

Daniel LeBlanc 45; wife, Francoise Gaudet; children: Jacques 20, Etienne 15, Rene 14, Andre 12, Antoine 9, Pierre 7, and 1 daughter; cattle 17, sheep 26.

Michel Poirier 20; cattle 2.

Barbe Baiols, widow of Savinieu de Courpon; 8 children in France, and 2 daughters married in this country; cattle 1, sheep 5.

Antoine Gougeon 45; wife, Jeanne Chebrat; child: one daughter; cattle 20, sheep 17.

Pierre Commeaux, cooper, 75; wife, Rose Bayols; children Etienne 21, Pierre 18, Jean 14, Pierre 13, Antline 10, Jean 6, and 3 daughters; cattle 16, sheep 22.

Jean Pitre, edge tool maker, 35; wife, Marie Bayols; children: Claude 9 months, and 2 daughters; cattle 1.

Etienne Commeaux 21; wife, Marie Lefebre, child: one daughter; cattle 7 sheep 7.

Charles Bourgeois 25; wife, Anne Dugast; child: one daughter; cattle 12, sheep 7.

Barnabe Martin 35; wife, Jeanne Pelletrat; children: Rene 8 months, and one daughter; cattle 3, sheep 2.

Clement Bertrand, carpenter, 50; wife, Huguette Lambelot; cattle 10, sheep 6.

Antoine Bellineau 50; wife, Andree Guion; children: Jean 19, and one daughter; cattle 11, sheep 8.

Rene Landry 53; wife, Perrinne Bourc; children: Pierre 13, Claude 8, and five daughters; cattle 10, sheep 6.

C-2

Thomas Cormier, carpenter, 35; wife, Madeleine Girouard; child: one daughter; cattle 7, sheep 7.

Rene Rimbaut 55; wife, Anne Marie; children: Philippe 16, Francois 15, and three daughters; cattle 12, sheep 9.

Abraham Dugast, gunsmith, 55; wife—Doucet; children: Claude 19, Martin 15, Abraham 10, and five daughters; cattle 19, sheep 3.

Michel Richard 41; wife, Madeleine Blanchard; children: Rene 14, Pierre 10, Martin 6, Alexandre 3, and three daughters; cattle 15, sheep 14.

Charles Melancon 28; wife, Marie Dugast; children: four daughters; cattle 40, sheep 6.

Pierre Melancon, tailor, refused to answer.

Etienne Robichaud told his wife that he did not want to give account of his cattle and his lands.

Pierre Lanaux or Lanoue, cooper, sent word that he was feeling fine and he did not want to give his age.

THE HABITATION OF POBONCOM NEAR THE ISLAND OF TOUQUE'

Phillippe Mius, squire, sieur de Landremont ou de Dantremont, 62; wife, Madeleine Elie; children: Abraham 13, Phillippe 11, another of 17, and two daughters; cattle 26, sheep 25.

AT CAP NEIGRE

Armond Lalloue, sieur de—53; wife, Elizabeth Nicolas; children: Jacques 24, Armond 14, Arnault 12, and two daughters.

AT RIVIERE AUX ROCHELOIS

Guillaume Poulet, his wife and one child.

Copy of original record of death of Jacob (Jacques) Girouard.[AMC Block F-2] "On Oct. 27, 1703, Jacob Girouard died after having the last sacraments of the Church. His body is buried in the cemetery on the 28th of the same month. F. Filix Parin, Recollect. »

Copy of original document of the death of Jeanne Aucoin "On April 18, 1718, I buried Jeanne Girouard, widow of the father of the Girouards, more than 90 years old. F. Justinneu Duand, Recollect Missionary."[4]

and arrived in Acadia in 1642. He was appointed Lieutenant General and Judge at Port Royal, and died there, according to the 1718 census, when he was 90 years old. Jeanne, listed as widow of François in the 1693, 1698, and 1700 census records, died in Port Royal, 1718. Her oldest son, Jacob, had died 15 years before her.

The Second Generation: Extended Family, and the Aucoin link Port Royal, Grand Pré and Beaubassin

After the children of Jeanne and François Girouard had married and built their own homes, the couple lived by themselves at Port Royal.

Their children did not go far away, however. The oldest son, Jacques, and the youngest daughter, Anne-Charlotte, with her husband, Julien Lord (t), remained on the family land, on the north side of the Annapolis (Dauphin) River, almost across from the fort of Port Royal, just east of Isle des Cochons. According to a later census, after François Girouard died, Jeanne was living with her daughter, Charlotte and son-in law, Julien Lord, in the old homestead of François Girouard.

The François Girouard lands were probably getting crowded, not only because of the couple's own children, but also because of extended family resulting from the children of the second marriage of Jeanne Aucoin's mother.

Jeanne Aucoin had, of course, been born in France, the youngest daughter of Martin Aucoin Sr, who married Marie Salle, daughter of Jean-Denys Salle and François Arnaud, in France around 1617. Marie Salle was born in Cougne in the neighbourhood of La Rochelle in Aunis, France. There were three children of the marriage: Michelle b. 1618; François b. 1622 and Jeanne b. 1631. Martin Aucoin died in France before 1633, and his widow, Marie Salle, married Jean-Claude Landry, having a son, René Landry *dit* le Jeune, born in 1634 at La Ventrouze, in Poitou, France.

Between 1640-1641, Marie Salle and her second husband, Jean-Claude Landry, emigrated to Port Royal. They brought with them the three children of her first marriage: Michelle Aucoin (age 22), François Aucoin (age 18) and Jeanne Aucoin (age 8), as well as their son, René Landry. There also came with them three children of Jean-Claude Landry, by his previous marriage: Perrine Landry (age 29) and her husband, Jacques Joffriau; 22-year-old twins, Antoinette Landry and Rene Landry dit L'Ainse. Jean-Claude's sister, Marguerite, had already established at Port Royal with her husband, Robert Martin.

The Aucoins and the Landrys made the voyage on one of two ships bringing a number of colonists and provisions to Port Royal around 1640,1641: the *Saint-Françoys* and the *Saint-Jean*.

In the spring of 1641, Michelle Aucoin married Michel Boudrot and Antoinette married Antoine Bourg. Marriage dispensations, obtained because of consanguinity, prove that Antoinette was sister to both René Landry *dit* L'ainé and to René Landry *dit* Le Jeune, and that René Landry *dit* Le Jeune was a half-brother to Michelle, Jeanne and François Aucoin.

Léopold Lanctôt, in his book, *Familles Acadiennes*, from which the above information is taken, indicates that all of these families above were living as close neighbours. The in-laws and the children of Jeanne Aucoin and François Girouard appear to have all in common farmed the land of François Girouard, as was so often the custom in large extended families. The widowed Marie Salle appears to be living with her granddaughter, Marguerite Boudrot, as of 1671, since the census of that year shows that the following families were all living on the homestead of François Girouard and Jeanne Aucoin:[42]

François Bourg, his wife Marguerite Boudrot, and their two children; Marie Salle, widow of Jehan [Jean]-Claude Landry; François Girouard and his wife Jeanne Aucoin, with their five children, three of whom are married: Marie, with her husband Jacques Belou, and one child; Jacob and his wife, Marguerite Gautrot, with their son, Alexandre. Madeleine, the other married daughter, was at this time living with her husband, Thomas Cormier, on six acres of land further away from this site, in Port Royal.

The 1671 census reports:

Jacques Belou [AMC Block B-2], 30 years old, cooper (barrel-maker) is listed with his wife Marie Girouard, 20 (François' daughter), 1 daughter: Marie. Livestock: 7 cattle, 1 sheep.

Jacques Girouard [AMC Block F-2] also known as Jacob, is listed as 23 years old, son of François, with wife Marguerite Gauterot, 17, and one son Alexandre. Livestock: 7 cattle, 3 sheep and no land. *[The center column of the AMC gives my own direct link to Jacques Girouard and Marguerite Goutrot. Of course everyone descending from any block on the master chart below Jacques Girouard in row two, is also a descendant of Jacques Girouard and Marguerite Gautrot. Their descendants today are dispersed all over the world, and we will trace many of them throughout this work.—B.G.]*

Thomas Cormier [AMC Block C-2], 35 years old, carpenter, is listed with wife, Madeleine Girouard, age 17, 1 daughter, age 2. Livestock: 7 cattle, 7 sheep and 6 arpans of land being cultivated. *[Also listed on this census are Francis (François) Pellerin and wife, Andrée Martin. After the Deportation we find the Gerriors and the Pellerins living in the same area of Guysborough County, in Larry's River. They may have had common ties before Deportation.—B.G.]*

None of the young Girouard families had any land of their own but each family had its own cattle and livestock to help work the land and feed the families. This certainly makes it clear why Jacques (Jacob) Girouard and his wife Marguerite Goutrot, who later had a total of 14 children, had to move from the paternal land of François, to a new location (Giroir Vill /Girouard Village) six km eastward on the river, just across the river from Belle-Isle marsh and the Port Royal Church. This move would have been necessary to provide land for Jacques and his children, because obviously his father's land would not have been large enough to support the heavy use of his own family and the extended family. Jacques Girouard's oldest son, Alexandre, must have already established in this new Girouard location because we see a separate listing on the map for Alexandre de Ru, in addition to Giroir Vill /Girouard Village.

For four generations, Girouards lived peacefully in Port Royal, knowing of their ancestors through oral tradition, at least as far back as their common great-grandparents, François and Jeanne Girouard.

There were exceptions, however, to the tendency of the extended family to remain on the original land of François Girouard and Jeanne Aucoin. We know that, as of 1671, one of François' daughters, Madeleine Girouard married to Thomas Cormier, established at Beaubassin (today known as Amherst, NS), quite far away from Port Royal, and that Marie Salle's daughter, Michelle Aucoin, lived at the opposite end of Port Royal from François Girouard and Jeanne Aucoin.

Marie Salle's only son by her first marriage, François Aucoin, died leaving a son, Martin Aucoin, who is the ancestor of all the Aucoins of Acadia. (The name of François' wife is not known; both of Martin's parents had probably died before the 1671census since their names do not appear). Martin Aucoin m. Marie Gaudet, daughter of Dennis Gaudet and Martine Gautier in 1672 at Port Royal. Martin does not appear on the 1671 census, probably because it does not mention single boys who at the time of the census were not living at home but may have been involved in the fishing industry or the fur trade, and were therefore either in the woods hunting or out in their fishing boats, trying to earn a living.

Around 1680, Martin Aucoin moved his family to Basin des Mines (today's Minas), 100 km east of Port Royal. The reason was simple—Port Royal had become too crowded. Later Martin firmly established in Grand Pré with his family, 17 children in all *(see appendix)*.

In the 1686 census at Grand Pré, Parish of Saint-Charles-des-Mines, we find: Martin Aucoin (age 35) Marie Gaudet, his wife (age 27). Their children: Martin, (age 12), Marie (age10), Michel (age 9), Isabelle (age 7), Louise (age 4), Alexis and Augustin (age 2). Livestock: 15 head of cattle, ten sheep. The family appears again on the 1693 census, indicating their established roots in Grand Pré, while also indicating that one of the twins, Augustin, had died.

Girouard Lands in Port Royal

The reader should refer to the two maps of Annapolis River presented at the beginning of this chapter: (1) the 1733 Mitchell map of Port Royal and the Dauphin River, 1733, and (2) the same map with corrections and annotations by Placide Gaudet. The following descriptions are taken from Gaudet's notes on the 1733 map and plan, from Rev. Donald J. Hébert's book, *Acadians in Exile*. [43] (I have inserted the AMC references in these notes; see appendix for notes on other family names on the map).

36 **Claude Girouard** [AMC Block I-3] son of Jacques (Jacob) Girouard and Marguerite Gautrot, and grandson of François Girouard and Jeanne Aucoin was born at Port Royal in 1683. He died March 14, 1738.

37 **De Ru Village**- Alexandre Girouard [AMC Block C-3], surnamed De Ru was born in Port Royal, 1670. He was brother to Claude Girouard in #36 above. He died Sept, 1744 in Port Royal.

38 **Girouard Village** was settled by Jacques Girouard [AMC Block F-2], who was born in Port Royal in 1648. He was the eldest son of François, a native of France, and Jeanne Aucoin. He was the father of the above-mentioned Girouards. He died in the year of 1703, leaving fourteen children. Six of his sons settled on the south side of the river.[44] *[see row 3 and 4 of the AMC to locate all fourteen children.— B.G.]*

Since my visit in 1984 I have learned much more about Giroir Vill/Girouard

Port Royal and old Acadie

Village, or Tupperville, and have been in contact with Regis Brun[45], an author and archivist in Moncton, New Brunswick. His research on land ownership of the Annapolis River Acadian "plantations" (villages) before 1763 includes the first owners or Grantees of Several Plantations and the owners of the same lands in 1734.

The following table of Girouard locations is excerpted from Brun's exciting research, which reveals important information regarding our Girouard ancestors. I have inserted square brackets with information to link my charts and maps to his

Name and Map References of Several Plantations	First Grantees Land Owners	Land Owners in 1734
La Montain [Montagne] [Placide note # 12 on Mitchell map, 1733-BG]	Jacques, Pierre, & Charles Lord François Girouard (c. 1621-1693) & Jeanne Aucoin [AMC block F-1]	Michael Boudreau
Notre Dame Delavent [in Giroir Vill, Mitchell map, 1733 and Placide Gaudet's note #12 Girouard Village on Mitchell map, 1733 with corrections-BG]	Monsieur d'Aulnay [second Governor of Acadie] [1605-1650]	Jacques Girouard [also known as Jacob in some records and written as Jacob on the Delabat map showing "La ferme "-BG]
La Terre Rouge [located in Giroir Vill, Mitchell map, 1733 ; see also Gaudet note 12 , to Mitchell map. See also Drew on Mitchell map and DeRu Village, Gaudet note 37 to Mitchell map-BG]	Jacques Girouard (1648-1703) & Marguerite Gouthrot (1655-1700) [AMC Block F-2]	Alexandre Girouard [1671-1744], [AMC Block C-3a] and François Girouard [1680-1752] [AMC Block F-3b] and brothers. [See rows 3a and 3b of the Girouard Acadian Master Chart [AMC] for all the brothers and sisters of Alexandre and François-BG]
Pointe-des-Rouseaux [Located at the lower end of Giroir Vill, Mitchell map, 1733 and also refer to Gaudet note 12, Girouard Village on Mitchell map.—BG]	Julien Lord (1654-1724) & Charlotte Girouard (c.1660-1742) [AMC Block E-2]	Charles Girouard [1689-1742] [AMC Block C3b] Guillaume Girouard [1686-1757] [AMC Block J-3a]

189

research; otherwise, this document is Brun's research work, and reproduced with his permission and kindness.

Certainly this information enriches the Girouard history and heritage. Also it is interesting to note the link of the Girouard family to the land of Monsieur d'Aulnay, second Governor of Acadie, providing more support to the theory that this family came to Port Royal with d'Aulnay from the segneurie of Aulnay, La Chaussee and Martaizé, as Massignion has suggested. Brun's research also increases interest in possible archaeological exploration in this area, since d'Aulnay's homestead would be of interest, not only to the Girouards but to many other Acadian families.

Of the five children of the second generation of Girouards in Acadia:

The first child of the second generation of the Acadian Master Chart Anne Charlotte m. Julien Lord [AMC Block E-2] and remained in the old homestead of her parents for about 25 years, while looking after her widowed mother, who died in 1718. They inherited the old homestead and lived there with their family.

The second child of the second generation of the Acadian Master Chart Jacques (Jacob)[AMC Block F-2] remained in Port Royal until his death in 1703. In 1671, the Jacob Girouard family was living on the Girouard land at Port Royal just across from the fort about two km east of Isle aux Cochons (Pig Island) on the north side of the Dauphin River, (now known as the Annapolis River). This location, called Village de la Montagne, was named after Julien Lord *dit* la Montagne[46], who had inherited this domain.

The other three children of François Girouard and Jeanne Aucoin, Germain (m. Marie Bourgeois), Madeleine (m. Thomas Cormier), and Marie (m. Jacques Blou), all later established at Beaubassin.

Rows 3a and 3b of the AMC show the third generation of Girouards to be born in Port Royal, the fourteen children of Jacques (Jacob) Girouard, (the oldest son of François Girouard and Jeanne Aucoin), and his wife, Marguerite Goutrot. Jacques and his family later moved upriver (about 12 km east, on the south side of the river from Village de la Montagne) to establish at a place which is recorded as "La Ferme" on a 1710 map by the French surveyor Delabat.

This area and the surrounding land were the beginning of Giroir Vill/Girouard Village, consisting of the homes of Jacques Girouard and of some of his children. It was almost directly across the river from the small church in Port Royal. In this section we will look a little closer at both of these Girouard settlements with the aid of the following maps.

The land concession of François Girouard and Jeanne Aucoin (shown as *veuve* François Girouard on maps above) was fifteen arpents (a little more than half a mile) along the shore of the river, and extended back to the interior of the forest. Jacob's grant, located in present-day Tupperville, ran 30 arpents (a little more than a mile or 1.6 km) along the river and extended 60 arpents inland towards the forest (a little more than two miles). He constructed dykes to reclaim the land previously covered by the high-tide salt water, built his house on the upper lands and planted some fruit trees. (See *verger*, French word for apple orchard, marked on preceeding Lanctôt map).

Nine-tenths of these lands would have been forest, according to Léopold Lanctôt.[47] However, the Acadians cultivated the lowland marsh area, using their expertise in dyking to reclaim the marshland as fertile farms.

In the 1671 census we learn that the extended Girouard family included the oldest son, Jacob, and his wife Marguerite Goutherot. Jacques Belou, son-in-law of François and Jeanne, is also living as their neighbour, owning cattle but no land. This indicates they were helping François to develop his farm, and living from the produce of his land. François died 1693, and other census records and maps indicate Charlotte and her husband Julien Lord, were living in the homestead with her mother Jeanne, now referred to as the widow François Girouard.

With regards to seigneuries, Jean Daigle states:

> The seigneurial system created by the home government to divide the land, distribute it and organize new settlers had little effect in Acadia. A number of seigneuries were granted at Port Royal, Beaubassin and along the St. John River but minimal attention given by the seigneurs to their affairs, the various squabbles between them and their tenants, and the inhabitants' refusal to comply with their orders meant that even though seigneuries existed on paper, they had practically no influence on the daily lives of the settlers. The inhabitants lived apart from the seigneurial system.[48]

Acadian families, at Port Royal.
Courtesy of Léopold Lanctôt,[5] Familles Acadiennes Vol. I, p.88 and Marc Vielleux, Éditions du Libre Exchange

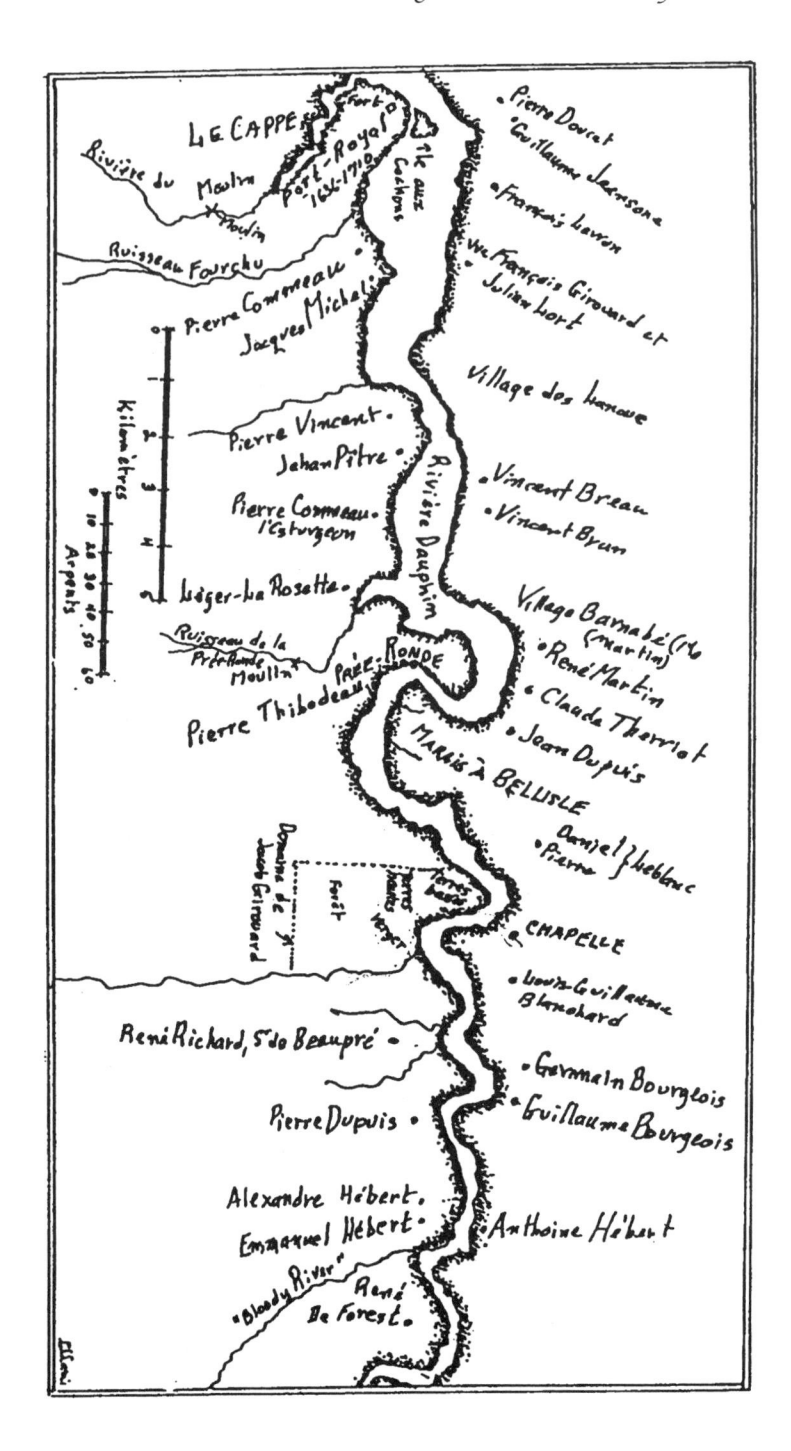

Map of the Domaine of the Girouards, from Familles Acadiennes I, p.277.
       Courtesy of Léopold Lanctôt, and Marc Vielleux, Éditions du Libre Exchange[6]

I learned in telephone conversation with Léopold Lanctôt, August, 2002, that he compiled and drew his own maps based on factual information that he found in the National Archives during his research.

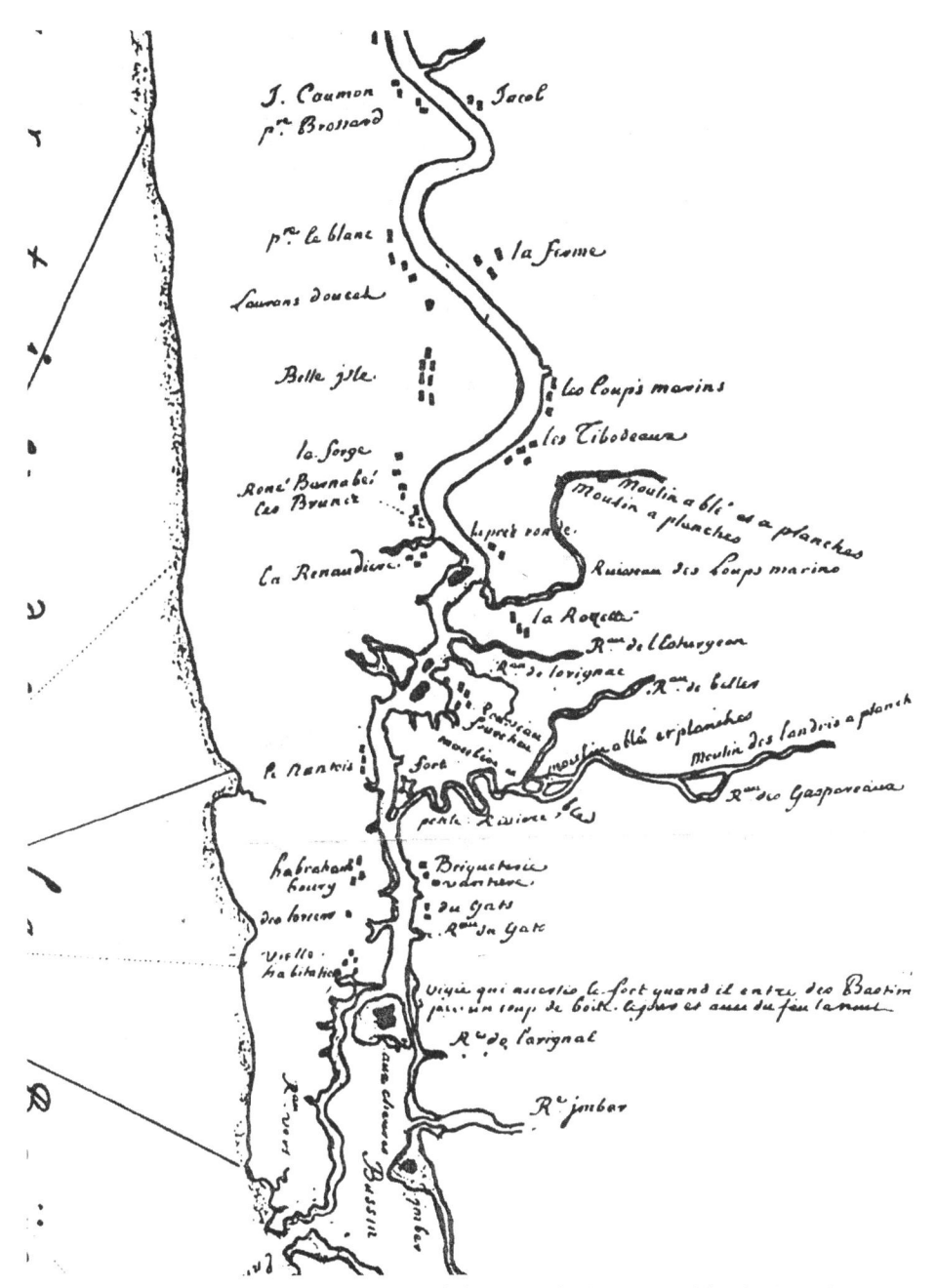

Map of Annapolis River near Port Royal showing "la ferme" and land of Jacob [Girouard], by Delabat.

In a footnote, Daigle tells us there is no comprehensive work on the seigneurial regime in Acadie and he goes on to cite some limited sources which help to clarify. Only Jacques and his sister, Anne Charlotte, and some of their children remained in Port Royal.

The 1686 census in Port Royal shows both of these families and their parents as follows:

François Girouard 70 years old [this age appears to be inaccurate by 5 years]; Jeanne Aucoin 55 years of age. Five married children. 1 gun, five arpans of land being cultivated, 13 cattle, 16 sheep, and 8 pigs.

Julien Lort [Lord], 32, and wife Charlotte Girouard, 26. Four children: Alexandre 10, Jacques 8, Pierre 5, Marie 2. *[Julien Lort's nickname, 'Lamontagne', was a war name. He came to Acadia in 1670 as a soldier with the knight Hector D`Andigné sieur de Grandfontaine. He was one of the rare inhabitants of Port Royal who knew how to write, having signed his name in his own handwriting in the census records of 1668, 1700 and 1701. He lived with Anne Charlotte and her parents at La Montagne in Port Royal.—B.G.]*

Jacques Girouard 38, and wife Marguerite Gautrot, 32. Nine children: Alexandre 16, Pierre 14, Jacques 12, Jean 10, François 6, Claude 3, Guillaume 3 months, Marie 8, Marguerite 4.

1 gun, 10 arpans of land being cultivated, 13 cattle, 15 sheep, 9 pigs.

The 1700 census at Port Royal provides the following information:

> Att a Council held by order of the Honble Lieu.^t Govr Armstrong, at his own House in the Garrison of Annapolis Royall on Munday the 11th Septem.^r 1732
>
> Present
>
> His Honour The Lieu.^t Governor of the Province
> Major Paul Mascarene   Will. Shirreff Secry
> William Skene Esqr   Otho Hamilton Esqr
>
> His Honour acquainted the Board, that he had Caused three orders, Agreed to by the advice of the Council to be published vizt One in Relation to the Magazine intended to be Built at the Grand Pré of Menis, One in Relation to Wood Sold by the Cord, and Incroachments made on the Kings High way, and the third for the Inhabitants of this River to Chuse New Deputys Upon the Complaint of these Now in Office, as also in Relation to the ffrench half Bushell And that for Answer thereunto the Inhabitants had made an Answer, which he laid before the Board, for them to Consider, Whether it was a Complyance to his Said orders, [Order in Relation to the Magazine at Menis, one in Relation to Wood and incroachments on the Kings high way & a third for Chusing New Deputies approved of in Council.]
>
> ¹ See Fisher, True History of the American Revolution, Ch. II.
>
> 264   *Nova Scotia Archives.*
>
> and therefore ordered Both his orders and their said Answer, to be Read. Which being done, the Board Refer'd the Consideration thereof till 3 o Clock P. M; and ordered that the Deputys be then present

Claude Girouard is chosen as Acadian Deputy. He died in 1738, according to the notes accompanying Mitchell's 1733 map.

Here is the official account from the Council Minutes as well as minutes from another council meeting, concerning farm rents to be paid by James Gerrior to Madame Belle-Isle.

And Both the Instructions and Advertisem.t being Read, they were approved of

And as mr Winniett had Sent word by the Constable that he was Busy, and that his own affairs would not allow him to be present at the Board, his Said Excuse was ordered to be minuted *Mr. Winniett's Excuse for not attending the Board.*

Then adjourned till 3 o Clock P. M.

Att 3 o Clock P. M., the Same Members present, The Board took into Consideration the Inhabitants Answer to his Honours aforesaid order for Chusing Deputys; and they having Chosen Prudent Robicheaux, Alexander Hebert, Nicholas Gautier, Peter Lanow, Joseph Bourgeois, Claud Girourd, William Blanchard; and Prudent Robicheaux Jun.r, altho not [318] Not altogether Conformable to His Honours orders It was Judged proper to accept thereof, and that his Honour might Give his Approbation to the Same, and his Honour did Accordingly Approve thereof, and Recommended to them the Duty upon them, and the faithfull Execution of their office *the Inhabitants answer for Chusing New Deputys Considered.*

And According to his Honours aforesaid order, for making an Annual Choice, It was agreed upon by his Honour (by and with the advice of the Board) with the Deputys present, that the annual Day for the Election of New Deputys Shall be always hereafter on the Eleventh of october, in Commemoration of the Reduction of this place, Provided that it be not on the Lords day, Commonly Called Sunday, and that then it Shall be on the Munday following, and that the Deputys in office Shall always Give Notice thereof to the Governor thirty Days before the time then Agreed upon, in order to have his orders for the Same *the Day Appointed for the Chusing of Deputys.*

Then his Honour Represented to the Board the Difficulty of having a Quorum, mr Adams being frequently through the Infirmity of old age, not able to Give his Attendance; and that Seeing mr Winniet, by his frequent Excuses, that his Bussiness could not permitt him to attend the affairs of the Government, his Honour therefore desir'd the Advice of the Board *Motion for Chusing a New Member of Council.*

Att a Council held at the Honourable Lieut Governor Armstrong House on Wednesday the 28th of June 1732

Present

His Honour the Lieut Governor of the Province
Major Paul Mascarene | William Shirreff Secry
John Adams Esq.r | Otho Hamilton Esqr
William Skeen Esq.r

Then was Read a Petition from one James Goussell against John Prince Both of this River Inhabitants, In Relation to the Exchange of Some Ground In Which Said Gousell Complaining, That the land that the Said Prince had Given him in Exchange was what he found Belonged to himself at that time, & not to the Said Prince; and therefore prayed a New Division of their lands *Prince and Goussells affair Referred to the Deputys.*

Orderd that their Difference be Refer'd to Some of the Deputys viz.t Sandrew Manuell Joseph Bourgioug¹ William Blanchar and Claud Girroir

Then was order'd to be Read mr Jennings Petition. Which by the Minute of Council the 9th of August 1731 was order'd to be laid before them, and mr Handfeild Being *Mr Jennings affair laid Before the board.*

¹ Last part of name blotted.

Council minutes (1720-1742)[7] concerning Girouard land disputes [Note the spellings in this 1734 document: first 'Gerroir', which is very similar to my family spelling of 'Gerrior' used in Guysborough County branches and later, James is referred to as 'Girroir', which is the same spelling presently used in Tracadie and Isle Madame. So in

---

314   *Nova Scotia Archives.*

At a Council held by Order of the Hon.ble Gov.r Armstrong at his own house within his Majestys Garrison of Annapolis Royall on Saturday 15.th ffebruary 173¾ at 10 oClock A. M.

                                      Present [405][1]

              Present

         The Hon:ble the L.t Gov.r of the Province
W.m Skene Esq.r   Eras.s Ja.s Philipps Esq.
W.m Shirreff *Secretary*
Henry Cope Esq.r   Otho Hamilton Esq.r

Governor Cosbys Petition for a patent for Widow Le Bats Land.

The Board being Sat, there was laid before them for their consideration a Memoriall of Maj.r Alex.r Cosbys L.t Gov.r of the Garrison of Annapolis Royall praying a patent for Some land now in his possession, having purchased part of the Same of Renneé Gotrot widow to the Deceased John Le Bat.

The Said Reneé Gotrots deed of Sale to Gov.r Cosby for the same Land. An Agreement between Reneé Gotrot of the one part & James Giroard & ffrancis Giroard on the other part for the Said Lands. The S.r de Bell Isle's Grant for the Said lands to the Said John le Bat. Also the Said S.r de Bellisle's Widow's Contract to the Said Le Bat An Examination taken by Cha.s Tallard of the said Reneé Gotrot before two of the Deputies by order of the Honble Gov.r Armstrong

Geroards the Defend.s

[D34] &
[F-3b]

All which being read, Gov.r Cosby with Pierre Lanow & W.m Burgeois for James & francis Giroard's Appeared before the Board, And having heard what they had to Say further on Said papers, it was found that Said Burgeois had no Authority to Act or Say any thing in behalf of the Giroards, And therefore Lanow who was Summon'd by L.t Gov.r Cosby, being Ask'd whether he had any knowledge of the Giroard's having performed that [406] that part of the Contract by building the house therein mentioned, he Answered, that they had not, because they had not finished the Same

Two pages blank, fastened together with wax.

Minutes of H. M. Council, 1720-1742.   315

Whereupon his Hon.r the L.t Gov.r of the Province finding that there were none to represent the S.d Giroards, thought proper to Adjourne the Board till Saturday next the 22.d Ins.t And then Ordered M.r Secretary to Summons the partys to Appear that day with all their papers & Such other witnesses as knew anything of the Affair in dispute with Reneé Gotrot. L.t Gov.r Cosby & the Said Giroards And Also Ordered that Mr Secretary Should minute down that James & Francis Giroards should Each of them pay a pistole to the Constable for their Contempt in not Appearing

                  (signed)
                          L: Armstrong

this one document James Girouard appears as 'Gerroir', and 'Girroir', although we know his grandparents were François Girouard and Jeanne Aucoin. Thus it seems the spellings of the name at this early time in Port Royal, were just as interchangeable as we find in early documents in France. It must be concluded that these new spellings did not develop in Isle Madame and Tracadie after the Deportation, but were used very early in Port Royal. Remember also that the name (geirrior-the o is like a stylised "d "with two dots above it) was a feminine form of geirhildr[8] (itself possibly an early spelling for Girouard), an early Norse personal name. Could this geirrior be a lingering feminine form of the Norse name?—B.G.]

* * *

294   *Nova Scotia Archives.*

the Amount of the Seignr.ll Rents. Prudane Robichaux's Acco.ᵗ Amounting to forty one Bus.ˡˢ And Seven Eights of Wheat fiffty six ffowles four Partridges five shill & ten pence Cash on Acco.ᵗ of Rent; and Two pounds thirteen Shillings for fines of Alienation, being Read: As also that of John Duon's, Amounting to Eighty Bus.ˡˢ. ¼ Bus.ˡˡ of Wheat, Seventy Nine fowles, Thirteen Shill & four pence on Acco.ᵗ of Rent, And Eight pounds seven Shill

the Boards Opinion Directing that the Rents may be Reduced to money And that such are not as yet pd may be paid and that the Rent gatherers Acco.ts may be Examined by a Comity of Council. and Sixpence for Fines of Alienation: The Board Are of Opinion that the Governor should give his Receipt for the sum And Quantity of the sev.ˡ Species he had Rec.ᵈ from yᵉ Rent-gatherers And in the State of Acco.ᵗˢ to be Transmitted to be Only Charged Accordingly And that Such of the Rents as are out standing may be paid in And placed to Acco.ᵗ As soon as possible And That the said Rents may be Reduced to Money Viz.ᵗ by Reckoning the Wheat at 50.ᵈ Hens at 18.ᵈ Pullets at 5.ᵈ Partridges at 5.ᵈ the present Currant prices of these Species Amongest the Inhabitants And not According to the price they went at formerly in time of the ffrench Viz.ᵗ yᵉ Wheat at 40.ᵈ And Hens at 10ᵈ *per* Report thereof Made by Mʳ Duon

Order'd that an Order be sent to the Richards of Beauprée Renny fforest And James Gerroir & Such [381] Such others as had not paid their Rents to Appear before the Council to Show Cause why they do not pay As the Other Inhabitants have Done Conformable to the Governors Orders

Order'd that a Comity of Council be Appointed to Examine the Rent-gatherers Acco.ᵗˢ And Compare them with the Minutes taken of the Contracts in the Secretarys Office And the State M.ʳ Secretary has made of the Same

Order'd that William Shirreff, Major Henry Cope, Erasmus James Philipps and Otho Hamilton Esq.ʳˢ be the Members of yᵗ Comity

                  (signed)
                       L: Armstrong

At a Council held at the same place on Wednesday the 10ᵗʰ Day of April 173⅔ at 10 o' the Clock A. M.

Minutes of H. M. Council, 1720-1742.

His Honour the L.ᵗ Governor of the Province and the Same Members Present

the Comitys Report of the Seignʳˡˡ Rents laid before the Board. The Board being sett Major Paul Mascarene who was Appointed in the Room of Mʳ Shirreff Who could not Attend the Comity, Appointed the 4.ᵗʰ Day of March last, for Examining the Rent Gatherers Acco.ᵗˢ of the Seigniorial Rents, Laid before the Board the Comitys Report thereof, Which being Read And Orderd to be keept upon file, It was Agreed that According to the Examination taken of M.ʳ Belisles Case conformable to the Minute of Council the 9.ᵗʰ of January last, His Hon.ʳ the L.ᵗ Governor of the Province Might give An Order to the [382] The Inhabitants of Beaupré, Renny fforest and James Girroir to pay to her the said M.ʳˢ Belisle the Whole of their Rents they Appearing, without Any Contradiction as Yet to be farm Rents and Not what they Call Seigniorial Rents And to Continue to pay her the same till his Majestys pleasure be thereon Known

the Inhabitts of Beaupree Renny fforest & James Girroir Orderd to pay M.ʳˢ Belisle their whole Rents.

197

Julien Lort, 46, and wife Charlotte Girouard, 38. Children: Alexandre 24, Jacques 21, Pierre 18, Louis 5, Marie 13, Madeleine 8, Marguerite 2. Jeanne Aucoin, 69, widow of François Girouard and mother of Charlotte, is living with them. (A daughter Anne, 13, is omitted but is mentioned in 1701 census). 15 cattle, 34 sheep, 20 arpans in value, 2 guns.

[I met with Francis Lord of San Diego, CA, in 1991, while he was on vacation in Halifax. He is a descendant of Anne Girouard and Julien Lord as follows:
[AMC Block E-2] **Anne Girouard**, daughter of Francois Girouard and Jeanne Aucoin, m. Julien Lord dit Lamontangne. Eleven children: 1. Charles (b. 1704) m. Marie Doucet; 2. Louis (b. 1693); 3. Anne m. M. Doucet (1698 census); 4. Magdeline (b. 1692); 5. Alexander (b. 1676) m. Françoise Bariault; 6. Pierre (b. 1681); 7. Marie (b. 1687) m. Jean Doucet; 8. Jean-Baptiste (b. 1695) (1698 census); 9. François; 10. Margarete; 11. Jacques (b. 1678) m1. Anne Comeau, m2. Charlotte Bonnevie (see also 1693 census Port Royal).

Child # 11 Jacques Lord, son of Anne Girouard and Julien Lord, m1. Anne Comeau and m2. Charlotte Bonnevie. Seven children: 1. François (b. 1739); 2. Claude (b. 1735); 3. Jacques (b. 1709); 4. Charles (b. 1722); 5. Josephe (b. 1725) m. Jos Garneau; 6. Marie Blanchard; 7. Honoré (1742-1818) m1. Appolline Garceau, m2. S. La Faille, m3. M. Babin.

Child #11-7 Honoré Lord (1742-1818). Seven children: 1. Marie m. P. L'Ecuyer; 2. Henri; 3. Henrietta; 4. David m. E. Toupin; 5. Edouard (1807); 6. …Mile m. Juliane Roy; 7. Jean-Baptiste m. Marie Ligny (PQ).

Child # (11-7)-7 Jean-Baptiste Lord m. Marie Ligny, PQ, having a child by the name of Aubin Lord (1809-1889) m. Madeleine Roy, 1831, Bourbonnais, ILL. Four children: 1. Alexander; 2. Joseph; 3. David; 4. Edward (1835-1915) m. Henrietta Piedalue.

Child# (11-7-7)-4 Edward Lord m. Henrietta. Five children: 1. Leo; 2. Frank; 3. Ellen; 4. Lilly; 5. Clovice Edward (1865-1934) m. Hannah Powers.

Child # (11-7-7-4)-5 Clovice Edward Lord m. Hannah Powers. Six children: 1. Robert; 2. Mary Alice; 3. Dr. Maurice Powers; 4. Russell Glenn Clovis; 5. Elizabeth; 6. Francis Evarette Lord, San Diego (who has provided this information)[49] *. [Of course all of the Lord family would, in a similar way, also be Girouard descendants.—B.G.]*

In 1645, Jacob Bourgeois Sr. was named Lieutenant of Port Royal and his uncle, Germain Doucet *dit* Laverdure, was named Major of Port Royal.

His son, Jacob Bourgeois Jr., a very close friend and companion of François Girouard, was military surgeon for the garrison at Port Royal, and also was involved in coastal navigation in the Bay of Fundy. In addition he was an excellent farmer, and the richest resident in Port Royal with 20 acres of land, 33 cattle and 24 sheep. Jacob Bourgeois was responsible for initiating and establishing the new colony at the head of Chignectou Bay, in a place named Beaubassin (Beautiful Basin), now called Amherst, NS. He noticed the potential of the fertile land at Beaubassin during his sea excursions (his coastal navigation would have made

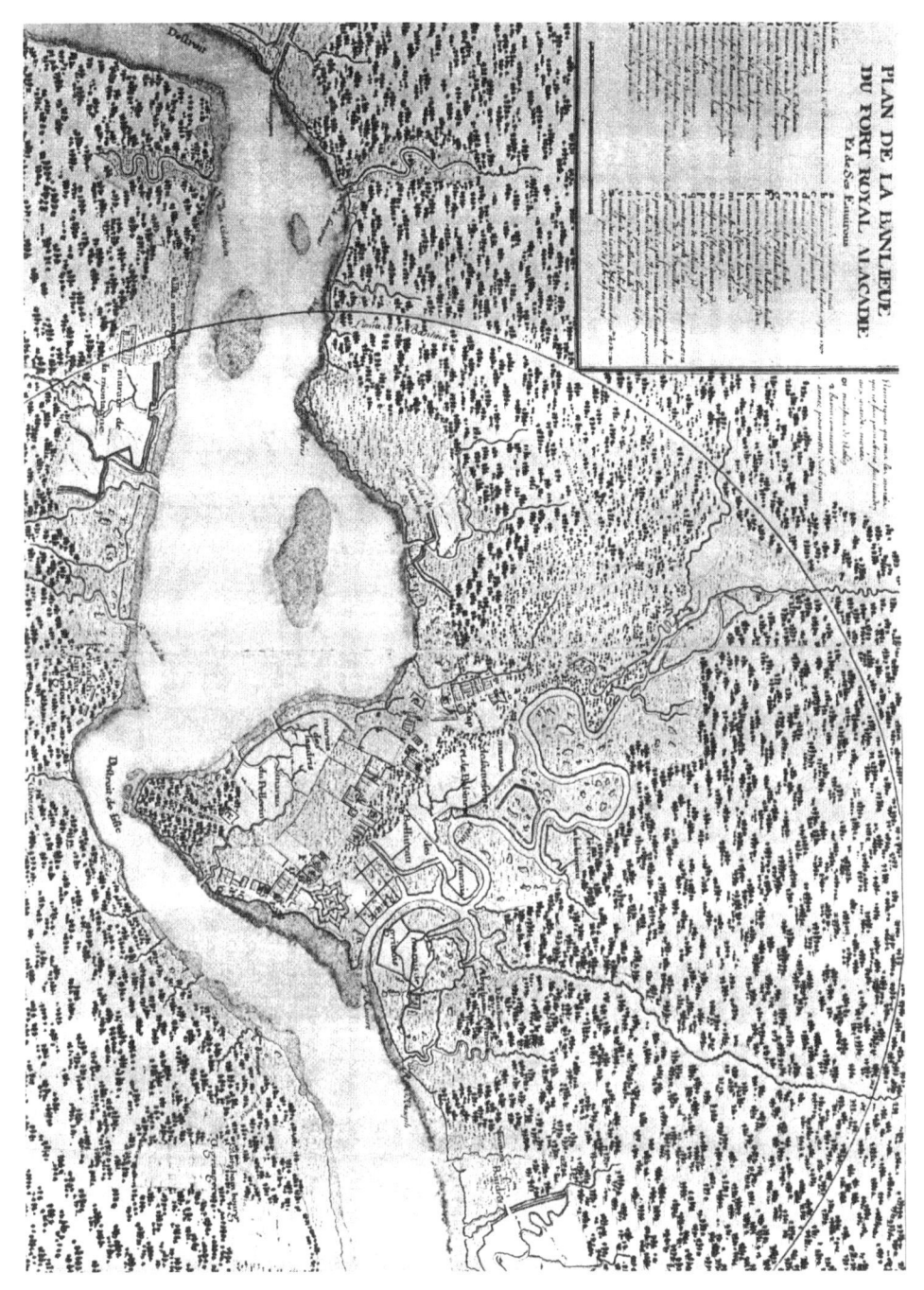

Plan de la Banlieue du Fort Royal A L'Acadie 1708.
courtesy of the National Archives of Canada

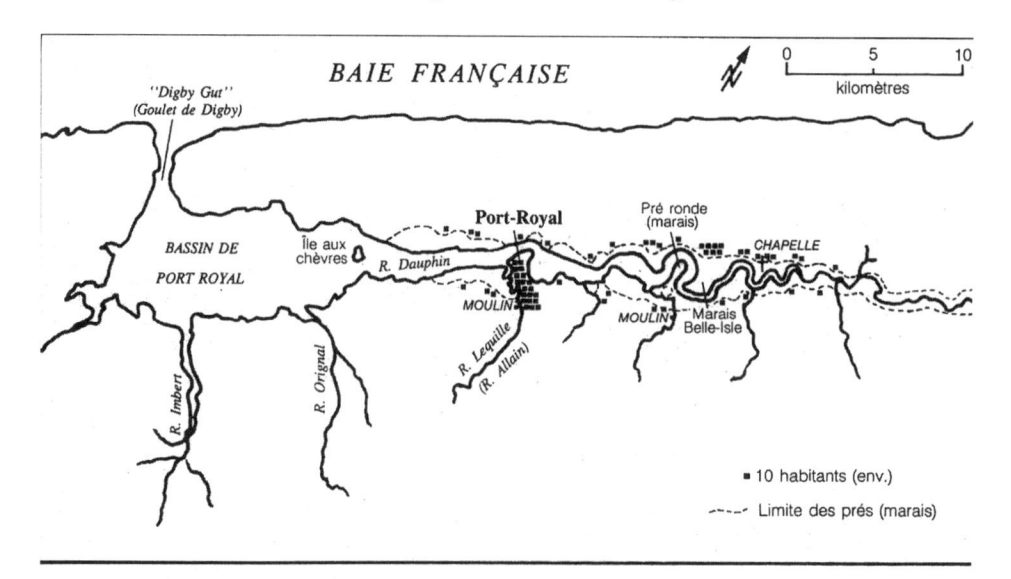

*Le bassin de Port-Royal au tout début du XVIIIe siècle.
Carte refaite à partir de deux cartes du livre de A.H. Clark,*
Acadia: The History of Early Nova Scotia, p, 122 et 136.

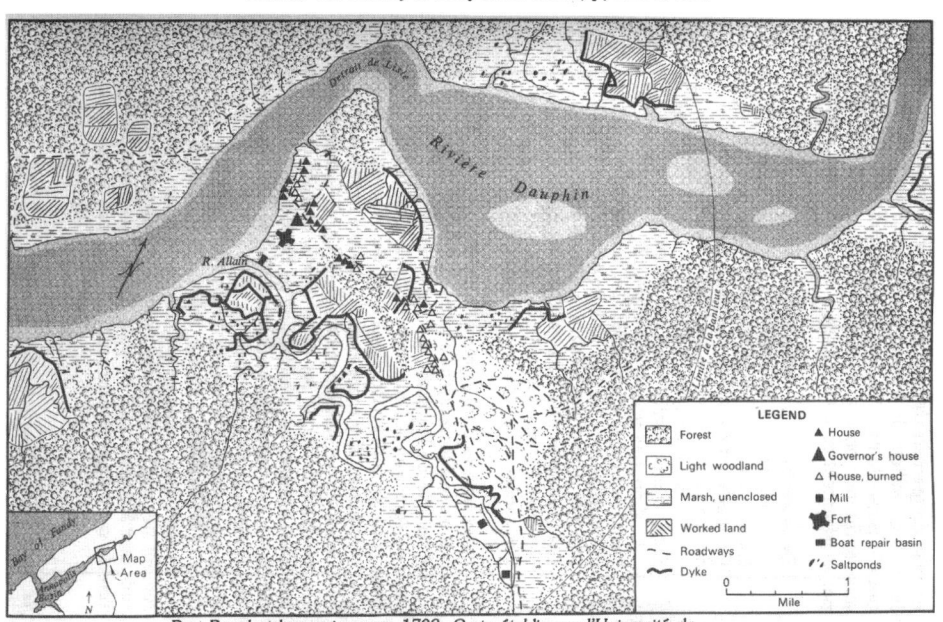

*Port-Royal et les environs en 1709. Carte établie par l'Université de
Wisconsin d'après une carte de la Marine.*
A.H. Clark, Acadia: The Geography of Early Nova Scotia, p. 136.

The map on the previous page shows the Port Royal Fort in 1708 (St. Anne Fort in Port Royal today), and surrounding area, with dykes and marshlands (marais). The old homestead of François Girouard and Jeanne Aucoin is named La Montagne after Julien (Lort) Lord dit la Montagne who married Charlotte. Charlotte and Julien lived in the old homestead, looking after Charlotte's widowed mother until she died in 1718. Seeing the relative close proximity of the Pellerins and the Girouards, it is no surprise that the Girouard and Pellerin descendants both re-established in the same region of Larry's River, years after the Deportation and migrations.

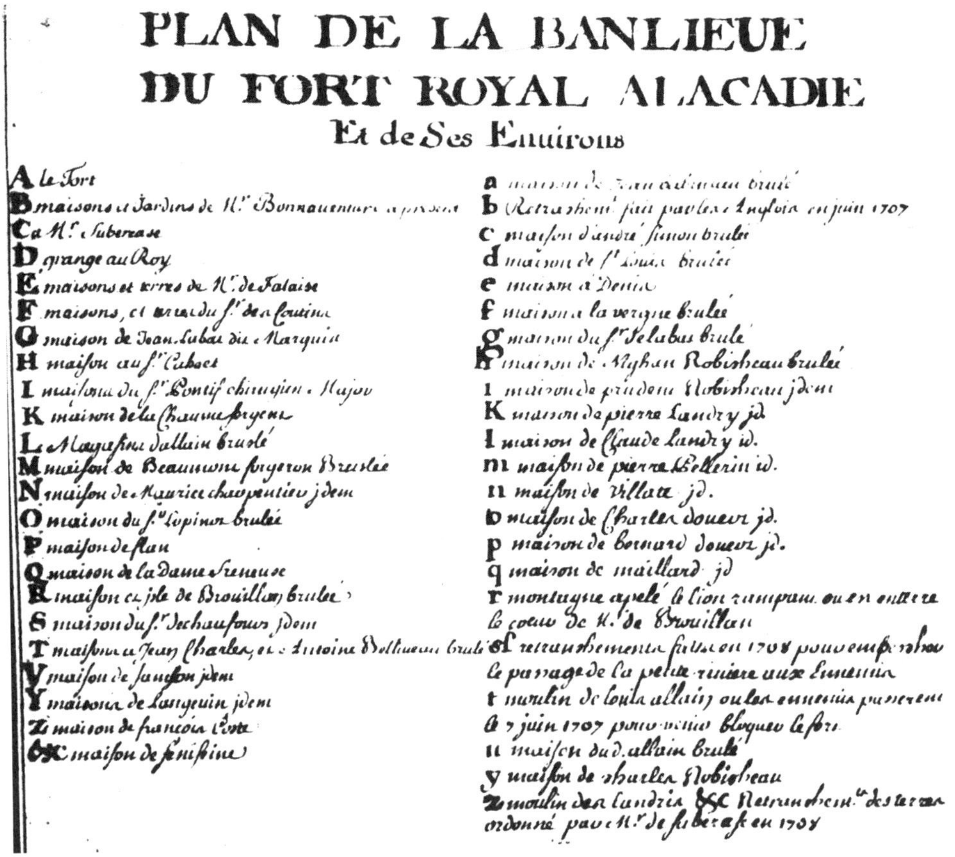

PLAN DE LA BANLIEUE DU FORT ROYAL A L'ACADIE
Et de Ses Environs

[Legend of map locations, largely illegible handwritten French text listing properties labeled A through Z and a through z, identifying houses, gardens, and features such as "Le Fort", "grange au Roy", maisons of various inhabitants, including Bonnaventure, Suberase, de Falaise, Jean Lubas dit Marquis, and others — many marked "brulé" (burned).]

him very familiar with all the inlets and bays in the area), and in order to provide a good future for his children, he decided this was the place to begin a new colony.

According to Paul Surette,[50] Germain Girouard, son of François, married Marie Bourgeois, the widow of Pierre Syre, and the daughter of Jacob Bourgeois Jr. The couple established at Beaubassin, along with two daughters of François: Marie Girouard (married to Jacques Blou and Madeleine (married to Thomas Cormier). Jacob Bourgeois' sons, Charles, Guillaume and Germain, and all the men, helped him dyke this land and prepare the colony to receive the new families.

In order to help defray the cost of building the new colony at Beaubassin, Jacob Bourgeois sold Isle Aux Cochons (Pig Island) in the Dauphin River, originally conceded to him by Charles de la Tour, to Étienne Pellerin.

There were approximately 60 inhabitants at Beaubassin in 1687. Two years later, in 1689 the population was 150. In 1701 there were approximately 320 inhabitants, and in 1707 the population was 271.[51]

In the 1686 census at Beaubassin, we find:

Germain Girouer, 30 years old, and wife Marie Bourgeois 32 [AMC Block D-2] Children: Germain 4, Agnès 7 months.
Children of Marie Bourgeois and of Pierre Syre: Jean Syre 15, Guillaume 6, Pierre. 1 gun, 4 arpans of land, 8 cattle, 3 sheep, 4 pigs.
Thomas Cormier and wife Madeleine Girouer, 37, [AMC Block C-2] Five daugh-

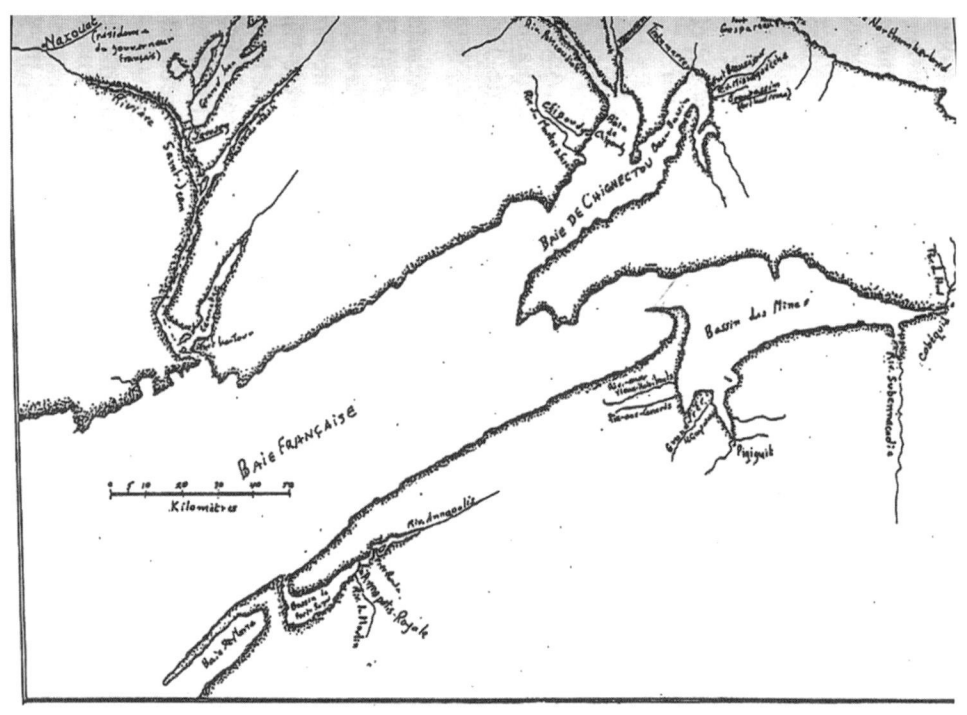

Carte n° 11 – La Région de Beaubassin au XVIIIe siècle

Map of Bay de Chignecou, and Beaubassin region.
Courtesy of Léopold Lanctôt,[8]Familles Acadiennes Vol. I, p.237 and Marc Vielleux, Éditions du Libre Exchange

ters and François 16, Alexis 14, Germain, 10, Pierre. 30 cattle and 10 sheep.
Jacques Blou and wife Marie Girouer [AMC Block B-2] Two daughters and a son. 15 cattle and 18 sheep.

In summary we have the following information on these three children of François Girouard and Jeanne Aucoin:
Third child of the second generation of the Acadian Master Chart: Marie Girouard (spelled Girouer in census of 1686) [AMC Block B-2], daughter of François Girouard and Jeanne Aucoin, married Jacques Blou around 1669, Port Royal, are later living in Beaubassin (1686, and 1689 census) at La Butte, (Amherst NS), near the border between Nova Scotia and New Brunswick. One daughter, Marguerite Gaudet m. Anselme Boudreau. *[Marie Thérèse Sauze and her cousin Andrée Gombert of France, who attended our reunion descend from Marie and Jacques Belou, and also tie into the line of Madeleine Girouard and Thomas Cormier see below. There are also many branches descending from this block in the Chéticamp region. —* B.G.]

Fourth child of the second generation of the Acadian Master Chart: [AMC Block C-2]: Marie-Madeleine Girouard, daughter of François Girouard and Jeanne Aucoin, married Thomas Cormier around 1668 at Port Royal; they were later living in Beaubassin (Ouechcoque), not marked but across the water to the east of

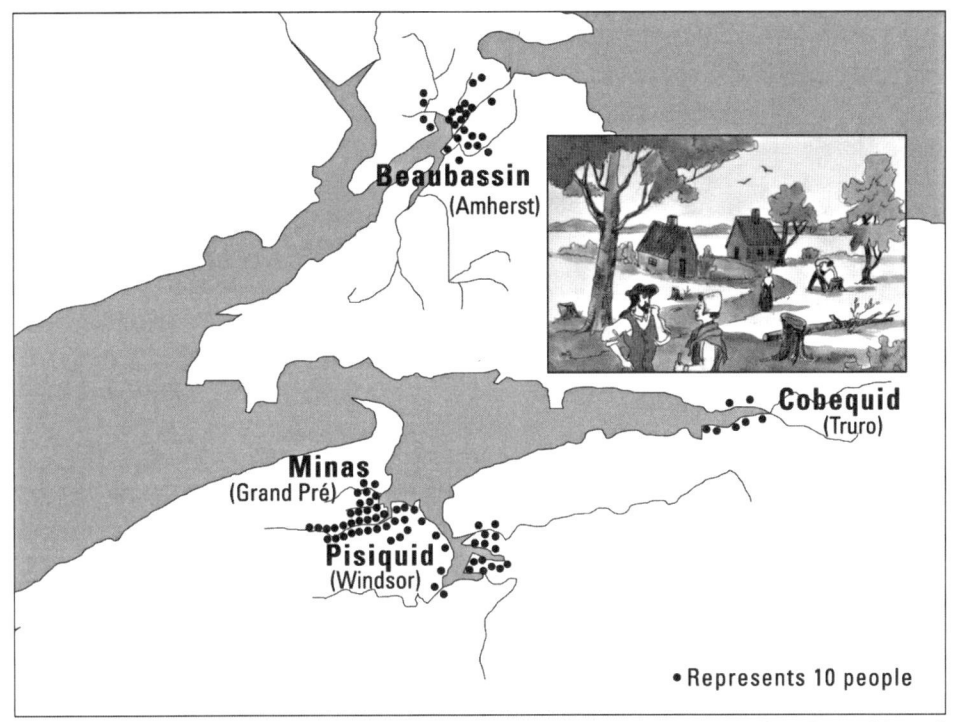

Map of population expansion, 1670-1710 at Beaubassin, Pisiquid and Cobequid based on map by the University of Wisconsin, Cartographic Laboratory, from Donald Hebert's book, Acadians in Exile[9], Sketch insert is by Margaretha van Gurp.)

Menoudie and south of La Butte on Paul Surette's map. (1686, 1689 census). Madeleine Girouard and Thomas Cormier were among the richest and most successful inhabitants of Beaubassin.[52] Marie (Madeleine) Girouard is recorded as widow of Thomas Cormier in the census records of 1683, 1698, and 1700.

[I learned at la Maison d'Acadie in la Chaussée, France, that Andrée Gombert and her cousin Thérèse, who both attended our first international reunion in 1990 in Antigonish, also descend from Madeleine Girouard and Thomas Cormier. Here is the genealogy of their direct line:

[Madeleine, daughter of Madeleine Girouard and Thomas Cormier, married Michel Boudreau circa 1690 having one child, Anselme Boudreau. See also [Block P201-3 of subchart 201]. Anselme married Marguerite Gaudet circa 1725 and in turn had a child Joseph Boudreau who married Jeanne Marie Haché 1761, Restigouche. Their child, Marguerite Boudreau, m. Michel Pitre, at Caraquet, NB, having a child named Michel Pitre m. Luce Haché 1825 (Petit Rocher) NB. Their son, Joseph Pitre, m. Hélène Haché 1862, Bathurst, NB. Their daughter, Theresa Pitre m. Jean Nier, Chatham, NB having a daughter, Marie Thérèse Nier, who married Alesis Andrieu 1937 at Marseilles, France. Their daughter is Andrée Andrieu m. Yves Gombert 1960, having two children: Frédéric Gombert, and Allain Gombert at Chateanneuf Les Montaignes (France). Marie Thérèse Nier has a sister, Hélène, who is the mother of Marie Thérèse Sauze, first cousin of Andrée Gombert. Marie Thérèse Sauze m. Jean Chiocca (La Playne).

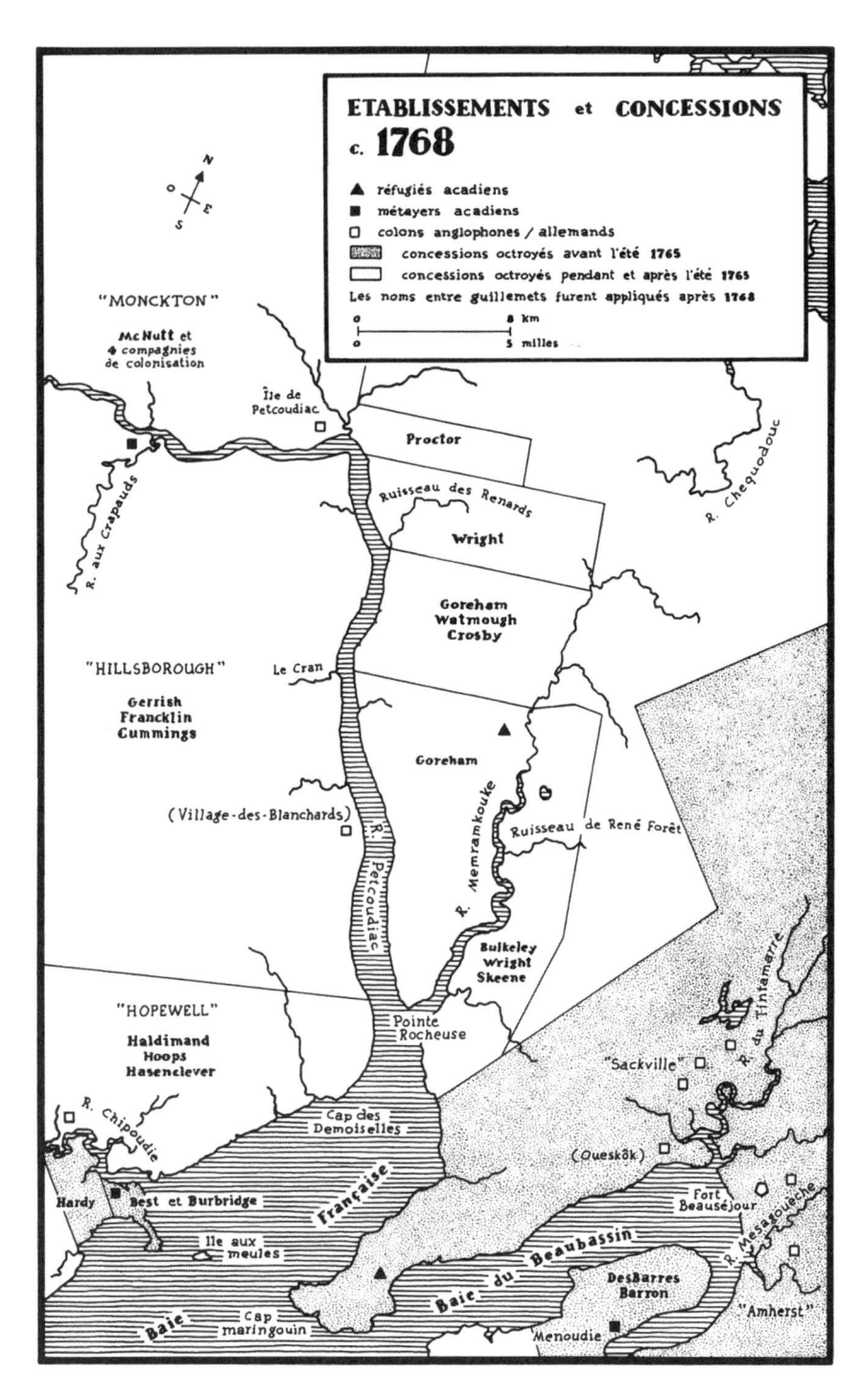

Map showing Beaubassin.
Courtesy of Paul Surette, Le Grand Petcoudiac, Histoire des Trois-Rivières[10] Vol. III, p. 38.

There are also a great number of branches of this block [AMC Block C-2] in Chéticamp, Nova Scotia, consisting mostly of Chaisson descendants (See Nova Scotia and PEI book, Antigonish County chapter, concerning the Romard family of Cape Breton who also link to [AMC Block G-5] in later generations of this branch from [AMC Block C-2]).

I have been in contact recently with another descendant of Madeleine Girouard and Thomas Cormier [AMC Block C-2]. Her name is Elaine Avery, granddaughter of James Avery à (Alexander Avery & Elizabeth Deslauriers) à (Benjamin Avery & Angelique Fougère) à (Joseph Fougère & Marguerite Charpentier) à (Georges Charpentier & Anne Cyr) à (Jean-Jacques Cyr & Marie-Josephe Hébert) à (Pierre Cyr & Claire Cormier) à (Thomas Cormier & Marie Madeleine Girouard [AMC Block C-2]).

Also I have been in contact with William R. Stringfield, another present-day descendant of this branch who provided me his direct line in the following way:

Another branch from Madeleine and her husband Thomas Cormier [AMC Block C-2]: Anne Marie Cormier, daughter of Madeleine Girouard and Thomas Cormier, m. Michael Haché Gallant having one child: Jean-Baptiste Haché m. Anne-Marie Gentil, Beaubassin, 1784. Also see [Block U201-4 of subchart 201]). They were also recorded in Nantes, France. Their son, Joseph Achée (Haché) b. Isle St-Jean, Acadia, m. Marie Dumont (who descends from Jacques Belou and Marie Girouard [AMC Block B-2]. Josephe Achée was on the ship Le Bon Papa from France to Louisiana, 1785. Their daughter, Isabelle Achée, m. Joseph Calandro at St James Parish, LA in 1794, having a daughter, Félicité Calandreau m. Jean-Baptiste Burat. Six children: 1. Mélasie m1. Isidore Barrons m2. Cyprien Burat; 2. Constance or Hortance Burat m. Joseph Gauthier (1817); 3. Marie-Louise m. François Barrons 1860; 4. Marie-Elodie m.1. Aristide Grandpré and m2. Pierre Léon Burat; 5. Jean Sylvain Burat (b. 1834); 6. Clément Laurent (b. 1836); Adeline Burat (b. 1839); Jean Darsino (b. 1840).

Child # 1 Mélasie m.1. Isidore Barrois had one child, Octave Barrois who married Clémence Barrons. From m2. Cyprien Burat, the following children six children were born: 1. Cyprien Napoléon Burat m. Victoria Gauthier; 2. Elénore Burat m1. Pierre Léon Burat; 3. Hubert; 4. Pierre Romene Burat m. Emma Endoyie Burat; 5. Norbert «Villere» Burat m. Odile Léoda Buras; 6. Marie-Julie Burat

Child # 2 Constance "Hortance" Burat m. Joseph Gauthier. Five children: 1. Victoria Madeline Gauthier m. Cyprien Napoléon Burat; 2. Josephine Theotisia Gauthier m. Thomas Maliden; 3. Marie-Louise "Azéma" Gauthier, m. Antoine Joseph Burat; 4. Joseph Rosemond Gauthier m. Louise Meyer; 5. Clementine Rosalie Gauthier m. Andrew Viner Sconvich

Child # 3 Marie-Louise m. François Barrois. Five children: 1. Jean Ulysse Barrois; 2. François D. Barrois (1850-); 3. Marie Clémence Barrois m1. Octave Barrois; 4. Augustin m. Gertrude Treadaway; 5. Adrien Barrois m. Isabelle Elizabeth Burat

Child # 4 Marie-Elodie m1. Aristide Grandpré. Two children: 1. Joséphine Léon Grandpré m. Gaspard Smith; 2. Amelia Elodie Buras m. Jean Lucia Burat

In addition, I have contacted two more of the present-day descendants of Madeleine Girouard and Thomas Cormier [AMC Block C-2], and have received

	L201	M201	N201	O201	P201	Q201	R201	S201	T201	U201	V201
2]	Note: First names in each block of this chart are all Girouard descendants of Madeleine Girouard and Thomas Cormier. These descendants however no longer carry the Girouard name, because of marriage.					1654 - Madeleine m. Thomas Cormier	→ REFER TO [BLOCK C-2] OF MASTER CHART OF WILLIAM D. GERRIOR. Reference: Research of William D. Gerrior, *Acadian Awakenings*, 2002. Purl Brook, Antigonish, NS. Also Wm. Stringfield and Rose Seeley survey returns [Block U201-4 of subchart 201].				Sarah Agnes Gallant MacNeil [Block Q201-9].
3]		1688 - 1690 Jeanne	1682 - Pierre m. Catherine LeBlanc	1676 - Germain m. Marie LeBlanc 1704	1669 - Madeleine Cormier m. Michel Boudreau	1674 - Anne Marie Cormier m. Michel Haché Gallant 1690	1670 - François m. Marguerite LeBlanc	1672 - Alexis m. Marie LeBlanc 1697	Claire	1686 - Marie m. Jean Baptiste Poirier	1686 - Agnès m. Pierre Poirier
4]	Anne Marguerite	1698 - Charles	1693 - Joseph	1691 - Michel	Madeleine	1713 - Jacques Haché Gallant m. Marie Josèphe Boudrot	1715 - Louise	1708 - François	1694 - Marie	1696 - Jean-Baptiste Ref: Survey form returns of Wm. Stringfield and Rose Seeley	Pierre
5]	1754 - Madeleine	1751 - Geneviève	1751 - Anne	1748 - Cyprien	1736 - Jacques Philippe	1749 - Charles Gallant m. Félicité Gouthrot	1738 - Marie Jeanne	1740 - Joseph	1743 - François	1744 - Charles	
6]	Pierre	1795 - Charles	1790 - Marguerite	1780 - Félix	1779 - Marthe	1792 - Simon Haché Gallant m. Isabelle Gaudet	1776 - François Mathurin	1782 - Mathurin	Marguerite	1785 - Jacques	Joseph
7]						Simon Gallant m. Agnès Benoit					
8]	Ide	Johanna	Wilfred	Elizabeth	George	Simon Gallant m. Alice Cook	Henri	Minerva	Murray	Raymond	
9]	George	Simon	Joseph	Hilda	Frédéric	Agnès Gallant m. Andrew MacNeil	Walter	Idella	Lillian	Marcella	Melvina
10]					Gregory Gerard	Andrew Joseph McNeil m. Claire Campbell	Kevin Joseph	Marilyn Doreen	Mary Pauline	Melvin	
11]					Megan Louise	Andria Joan McNeil	Rachael Gean				ACADIAN GIROUARD DESCENDANTS Subchart #201 Linking to [AMC Block C-2]
					New Glasgow	New Glasgow	New Glasgow				

© *Acadian Awakenings Girouard/Giroir... Routes and Roots*

information from both: Sarah Agnes Gallant MacNeil, Purl Brook, Antigonish County, NS, and also Rose Seeley of Fox Point, NB. [See subchart 201. —B.G.]

Fifth child of the second generation of the Acadian Master Chart [AMC Block D-2]: Germain Girouard, son of François Girouard and Jeanne Aucoin, born approx 1657, married Marie Bourgeois, daughter of the well-known surgeon of Port Royal, Jacques Bourgeois Jr. Jacques was the chief developer and person in charge of [53] the Beaubassin colony. This family of Germain Girouard and Marie Bourgeois logically therefore moved to the new community of Beaubassin and appear on the 1686 census in Beaubassin, just south of the Mesagouèche River (see square block on Paul Surette's map of Acadian hamlets, next to the location where Fort Lawrence was later built). Marie Bourgeois is shown on the 1680 census in Beaubassin, and is recorded as a widow in the 1700 census. The daughter, Agnès of Germain Girouard [AMC Block D-2] married to Abraham Gaudet is also recorded in 1707 census as well as her brother, also named Germain m. Jeanne Barrieau (Barrilot) on the census of 1714 at Beaubassin (see subchart 202 of the Acadian Québec book).

Michel Girouard, son of Germain Girouard and Jeanne Barrilot, m. Marie Thibodeau. They were recorded at La Butte in the Beaubassin area.[54] (La Butte is due south along the shore from the Mesagouèche River in the basin leading into Menoudie.

François *dit* Beauséjour, another son of Germain and Jeanne Barrilot, living north of Beaubassin, married 1. Marie Poirier 1735 and m2. Catherine Josette in 1762.[55] François's son Joseph m. Anne Desmoliers was recorded at Notre Dame, PQ.[56] His descendants established in Du Lac, Deux Montagnes, to the west of Montréal, and include the well-known Patriot leader, Joseph Girouard. This is the "Patriot" branch in Québec. [Subcharts for this branch #202 in the Québec volume, traces this Girouard branch to present day.]

I have also corresponded with Jeanne Decarrie, Chateauguay, PQ, descendant of Germain Girouard, [AMC Block D-2] of the second generation of the AMC and whose genealogy I have traced to the present generation.[57] [See Québec volume, Acadian chapter, subchart 202.]

This effectively means we have representation to present day, from each of the five children (male and female) of the second generation of Girouards in Nova Scotia, linking all to the first generation, François, dating back from the early 1600's in France. These connections back to the earliest generations of the master chart are very important.

The Girouards at Port Royal: A Well Connected Family
It is interesting to note that succeeding generations of Girouards continued to prosper, and remain connected to government, nobility and/or military leaders through marriage.

Germain Girouard [AMC Block D-2] married Marie Bourgeois, daughter of Jacques Bourgeois, military surgeon at Port Royal, founder of the new settlement of Beaubassin and one of the most prosperous inhabitants of Port Royal in 1671.

Jacques Bourgeois was a very good friend of François Girouard, as both were brought to Port Royal by Charles de Menou d'Aulnay in 1642, according to Léopold Lanctôt.[58] (This statement, although probable, is not supported by any reference, but in phone conversation with the author, he informs me that his research was completed many years ago and many of the documents that he used at the National Archives have since been misplaced or lost. Security today is much tighter).

Thomas Cormier, who married Germain's sister, Madeleine Girouard [AMC Block C-2], had first established at Port Royal but is later recorded as one of the richest and most prosperous inhabitants of Beaubassin. According to Bona Arsenault, "Jacques Bourgeois, one of the most prosperous inhabitants of Port Royal began developing a new colony. . . Thomas, one of his son-in-laws, soon became one of the most well-to-do members of the colony [Beaubassin]. . ." In actual fact, Thomas was not the son-in-law of Jacques Bourgeois, as Bona Arsenault states here, although his wife's brother, Germain (married to Jacques' daughter Marie) was. Of course they were all living close together, as extended families would naturally do in these times.

Anne (Charlotte) [AMC Block E-2], born approximately 1659, married Julien Lord (Lort or Laure) *dit* Lamontagne.

Jacob Girouard's son, Alexandre Girouard *dit* de Ru [AMC Block C-3a] married into the de La Tour family. His wife, Marie Le Borgne de Belle-Isle, was granddaughter of Charles de La Tour, first Governor of Acadie, being the child of his daughter, Marie de St-Étienne de la Tour and her husband Alexandre, Sieur de Belle-Isle, Governor of Port Royal. Another of Jacob Girouard's sons, Jacques, married Anne Pettipas [AMC Block D-3a], daughter of Claude Sieur Lefleur Pettipas, administrative officer for the King at Port Royal.[59] He had arrived in 1645 at Port Royal and was *Notaire Royal* (barrister and solicitor) and Chief Clerk of the Tribunal.

Third Generation of the Acadian Master Chart
Port Royal, Grand Pré, Beaubassin, Memramcook, Québec, France

The 14 children of Jacques Girouard, the eldest son of François Girouard and Jeannne Aucoin, and his wife, Marguerite Gauterot, were all born in Port Royal. (In order to show all of the children, it has been necessary to arrange them along two rows, 3a and 3b of the Acadian Master Chart, since each row is only 11 blocks across). Use the Master chart to help track all 14 children.

At Port Royal
Six of the 14 children of Jacques Girouard and Marguerite Gautrot are recorded at Port Royal in 1714 as follows, and will be presented according to the places where their routes took them, not by order of age or place on the AMC.

[1/14] Alexandre de Ru Girouard [AMC Block C-3a], *son of Jacques Girouard and Marguerite Gautrot* m. Marie de la Tour, granddaughter of Charles de la Tour. As far as I am aware, he did not move from Port Royal. However, one of his daughters, Marie, is recorded at Beaubassin with her husband, the surgeon of Beaubassin, Jean Mouton. Her son Charles was also listed in the Grand Pré records and later the family is recorded in Louisiana[60], after Deportation. Alexandre's son Pierre m. Jeanne Martin and the family were deported to Philadelphia. At least two of the other sons, Félicité and Joseph are recorded as married in the West Indies (Félicité at St. Môle, St. Dominique), and there is a strong possibility that his two sisters were also there, named Nathalie and Marie Josèphe but not identified any further.

One of the grandsons of Alexandre de Ru, Jean Charles Girouard à Louis à Alexandre established in Montréal, Notre Dame, PQ. (There is apparently a branch of this family today in the county of Montcalm, according to genealogist, Rev. Harvé Richard, in his article: "Coin Généalogique". I have not heard from this branch in all my surveys, despite the fact that it would be the only line of this branch carrying the Girouard name. Nevertheless there will likely be many further connections as a result of the wide distribution of this book).

From Janet Jehn's book, *Exiles in the Colonies*, we see that two of the children of Alexandre de Ru Girouard were deported to Connecticut: Jeanne Girouard m. François Forest; the family is recorded in Connecticut, 1755, then later at Assomption, PQ. Her sister, Madeleine Girouard m. Charles Blanchard; they are recorded in Connecticut, 1755, and later in St. Antoine de Chambly, PQ, 1768. A third daughter, Marie-Josèphe m1. Louis Dugas, and m2. Thomas Jeansone, and is recorded in the New England Colonies in 1755, appearing later at St. Jacques and L'Achigan, PQ in 1767.

We know from Léopold Lanctôt that the family of Marie-Josèphe Girouard and Thomas Jeansone, (son of Guillaume Jeansone and Isabelle Corporon), having unsuccessfully petitioned to be sent back to France from Connecticut, made the long trek through the woods, rivers and mountains, along with several other families to L'Assomption, PQ.[61]

It appears that some of Alexandre's children were held prisoner at Fort Beauséjour, during the Deportation years. The name 'Amand' is one that does not occur often in the Acadian Girouard branches. I know of one descendant named Amand, who was grandson of Alexandre via his father Louis, married to Marie Blanchard. The name Amand occurs in the prisoner list at Fort Beauséjour, with Marguerite and Joseph Girouard. From other records we know that Amand à Louis à Alexandre has a brother Joseph and an Aunt Marguerite, so this is likely the family on the prisoner list. There is also an Amand recorded in France around the Chatellerault area. Could it be this same Amand, born 1736 (See [AMC Block C-3a] in the Québec volume, with more detail regarding the possible connection to the Montcalm Girouards in Québec, and France chapter.

The following is the genealogy of Alexandre (de Ru) Girouard:

Alexandre (de Ru)Girouard [AMC Block C-3a] m. Marie Le Borgne. Eleven children: 1. Alexandre b. 1696; 2. Jeanne b. 1709 m. François Forest 1727; 3. Cécile b. 1721 m. Louis Dugas (five children: Marie-Josèphe, Rosalie, Benjamin, Joseph, Jean-Baptiste); 4. Marie-Josèphe b. 1716 m1. Louis Dugas, 1734, m2. Thomas Jeansone, 1742; 5. Bernard (1697-1703); 6. Pierre b. 1718 m. Jeanne Martin, P.R., 1743, Deported to Philadelphia (four children: Nathalie, m. Jean-Baptiste Bujeau, 1763, Philadelphia, Pa., Charles b. 1747, Marie-Josèphe b.1750, and Félicité); 7. Marie Girouard b. 1693 m. Jean Mouton, Surgeon at Beaubassin; 8. Madeleine b. 1700 m. Charles Blanchard, 1718; 9. Marguerite m. Alexandre Guilbault, 1734; 10. Angélique b. 1708; 11. Louis b. 1705 m. Marie-Josèphe Blanchard at P.R., 1727 (nine children: Pierre b. 1751, François b. 1748, Jean-Charles, b. 1743, m. Anne Ouvray, 1772 at Montréal, Notre Dame, according to Loiselle notes, Joseph b. 1731, Jean-Baptiste b. 1741, Félicité b. 1739, Isabelle b. 1739, Amand b. 1736, Anne b. 1733). *Also see subchart 204 in Louisiana volume.*

Child # 2 **Jeanne Girouard** [Block M204-4], b. 1709, Port Royal m. François Forest, 1727, Port Royal. Nine children: 1. Paul Forest b. 1729, Port Royal; 2. Marie Marguerite Forest b. 1730 m. Jean-Baptiste Poirier, ca.1730, Isle Royale; 3. Charles Forest, b. 1733, Port Royal m1. Marie-Joseph Robichaud, ca. 1755 m2. Isabelle Dugas; 4. Jean-Baptiste Forest b. 1736 m. Marie Hébert, 1767, L'Assomption, PQ; 5. Simon Forest b. 1738, Port Royal, m. Rosalie Richard, 1763, L'Assomption PQ (Jolliette) (one child: Marie b. 1772, m. François Perreault); 6. Elizabeth Forest b. 1741, Port Royal, m. Martine Goudreau, ca., 1765, Massachusetts, in exile; 7. Félicité Forest b. 1743, Port Royal, m. Joseph Mirault, 1766, Connecticut; 8. Madeleine Forest b. Port Royal m. Jean-Pierre Poirier ca. 1753, Beaubassin; 9. François Forest b. 1750, Port Royal, m1. Marie-Jos Robichaud, m2. Félicité Dugas.

Child # (2-2) **Marie-Marguerite Forest**, m. Jean-Baptiste Poirier. Three children: 1. Marie-Madeleine; 2. Jean-Baptiste; 3. Marie-Marguerite.

Child # (2-3) **Charles Forest**. One child: 1. Monique m. Lazare Poirier.

Child # (2-8) **Madeleine Forest** m. Pierre Poirier. Seven children: 1. Marie-Angélique b. 1759 m. Gabriel Benot; 2. Pierre m. Marie-Rose Bergeron; 3. Marie Josèphe m. Frances Pellerin; 4. Jean-Baptiste Poirier m. Madeleine Bergeron; 5. François; 6. Joseph m. Marguerite Bergeron; 7. Marie-Anne Poirier m. Jean-Baptiste

Pellerin.[62]

Child # 6 **Pierre Girouard** [Block Q204-4 of subchart 204] m. Jeanne Martin, Port Royal, 1743. Three children: 1. Charles 1747, deported to Philadelphia. 2. Nathalie b. 1744, deported to Philadelphia. 3. Félicité m. Nicolas Demmars m2. Jean-Baptiste Bariteau, deported to France, St-Dominque, and Môle, St-Nicolas, in the West Indies. *See Louisiana volume for more details.*

Child # 7 **Marie Girouard** [Block S204-4 of subchart 204] m. Jean Mouton, Surgeon at Beaubassin; Ten children: 1. Jean Mouton b. 1712 m. Marguerite Poirier, 1734, Beaubassin (three children: Marie-Madeleine, Jean François, and Marguerite m.1755 Jean Girouard-see marriage record at Beaubassin in Port Royal section of the book); 2. Jacques Mouton b. 1714, Beaubassin m. Marguerite Casey, 1734, Beaubassin (four children: Marguerite m1. Jean L'Oiseau and m2. Armand Robichaud, Jean D. Mouton, b. 1740, Beaubassin m. Isabel (Elizabeth), Bastarche, Madeleine, and Anne); 3. Charles Mouton m. Anne Comeaux (one child: Georges m. Nathalie Gaudet); 4. Joseph Justinien Mouton; 5. Marie-Joséphine; 6. Marguerite m. Jean Hébert, 1743, b. 1724, Port Royal (one child: Etienne Hébert m. Marie Joseph Lavergne); 7. Anne b. 1729 m. Joseph Grégoire Richard, 1749, Port Royal; 8. Salvador b. 1730 m. Anne Bastarache, 1752, Port Royal (four children: Marin m1. Marie Joseph Lambert, m2. Marguerite Bernard, Marie Geniève, Céleste Anne Prexede, an Jean Mouton, b. 1755, d. Louisiana 1834, m. Marie-Marthe Bordat); 9. Louis b.1731 d. Louisiana, m. Marie Modeste Bastarche at Restigouche ca. 1760 (three children: Anne Charlotte m. Xavier Terriot, David, Elizabeth, Isabelle m. Pierre Blanchard). 10. Pierrre b. 1732 m. Marie Thibodeau.[63]

Child # 9 **Marguerite Girouard** [Block V204-4 of subchart 204] m. Alexandre Guilbault, 1734, Eight children: 1. Amand b 1734 m. Françoise, Notre Dame PQ, m2. Marie-Charlotte (Billy) Carpentier; 2. Joseph m. Madeleine Bertrand; 3. Charles Guilbault, b. 1739; 4. Joseph (1741-1757) d. at Québec, PQ; 5. Théotiste b.1746; 6. Jean (1749-1757) Québec, PQ; 7. Grégoire, b. 1750 m. Agathe Hus dit Millet, 1771, Sorel, PQ; 8. Ludivine b.1752)

[2/14] Jacques Girouard, [AMC Block D-3a] *son of Jacques Girouard and Marguerite Gautrot* m1. Anne Pettipas, m2. J. Amirault, living at Port Royal. All his children however are recorded at Beaubassin. His son, Pierre and his wife Marie Granger were deported to New York[64]. One other son of Jacques Girouard and his second wife J. Amirault, was Jean, married to Margaret Mouton in January 1755, at Beauséjour, very close to the time of the Deportation of 1755.   Jacques Girouard married Anne Pettipas and was deported to France. *Also see Gaudet's notes on Girouards as well as Bergeron.* Jacques and his second wife, Jeanne Amirault, and their son, Joseph, are recorded in St. Louis, New Orleans, La., where Joseph married Irsule Trahan. The genealogy of Jacques Girouard is as follows:

Jacques Girouard, [AMC Block D-3a], m1. Anne Pettipas m2. Jeanne Amirault. Nine children from his first marriage. 1. Madeleine b. 1717, Port Royal m. Joseph

Comeau, 1739, Port Royal (seven children: Madeleine, Anne, Jean-Baptiste, Isabelle Modeste, Joseph, Marguerite); 2. Elizabeth b. 1715, Port Royal, m. Michel Lambert, 1743, Beaubassin (two children: Madeleine and Amand); 3. Charles b. 1707, Port Royal; 4. Marie-Josèphe b. 1713 m. François Forest Beaubassin (one child: Rosalie Forest); 5. Marguerite, b. 1706, Port Royal, m. Jaques Forest, 1726, Port Royal, m2. Pierre Doiron, Beaubassin (four children: Marie b. 1742, d. at the General Hospital of Québec, 1760, Jean m. Marie-Jeanne Forcier, St-Michel d'Yamaska, Joseph Forest m. Agathe Badayac, 1765, Yamaska, PQ; 6. Joseph b. 1729 m. Irsule Trahan, St. Louis, La. 7. Jean b. 1728 m. Marguerite Mouton, M'ck, Beauséjour, 1755; 8. Pierre m. Marie Blanche Granger b. 1753 (their son being François b. 1753) They were deported to New York; 9. Anne Girouard m. Joseph Forrest (four children: Pierre, Catherine, b. 1744 m. Louis Marits, 1762 L'Assomption, PQ, Hélène, and another Catherine).

I quote genealogist Bergeron here regarding Jean Girouard and Margaret Mouton to point out how fortunate the Girouards are to have such a precious document as part of their Acadian heritage (translated by the author):

Nevertheless, having quoted Roy for perhaps too long, we will have to omit other historical notes to at least condense two very rare Acadian documents, which have in fact to do with our Girouards. The first concerns the marriage contract between Jean Girouard, son of Jacques and Jeanne Mireault of Beauséjour and Margaret Mouton, daughter of Jean and Marguerite Poirier; the second although less important, also concerns a marriage contract of Anne Nuriat, widow of Charles Girouard, who is to remarry. . . . Jean Girouard, her brother-in-law intervenes as a witness. When we realize that from the old Acadie, only 57 pieces of strictly notarial documents were saved, there is reason to be jealous of the Girouards, who themselves can claim two of these relics.

Port Royal and

I have traced the names given in these m
and confirmed the relationships of all involved
any trace of this branch after the fifth generat
Mouton go, having married only just before the
brother Pierre end up? We know his brother Pierre
deported to New York[65] and perhaps they were co1
British culture in New York. We do know they had a s
another brother, Joseph[66] born in 1729, who, as mentio.
St. Louis, La. The official marriage record is reproduced

```
January 25, 1755 (the year of the 1st Gre⸍        ₋aval)
```

"**WERE PRESENT** Jean Mouton and Margueritte Poirier, his wife, whom he authorizes for the present undertakings of this place of Beauséjour, speaking for their daughter who is present and with her consent, on one part...

And Jean Girouard, son of the late Jacques Girouard and of Jeanne Mirau (sic), living in this said place of Beauséjour, speaking for himself and in his name and of his own consent, on the other part...

The said parties with the advice and consent of their parents and friends and with the permission of M. de Monsieur de Vergor Du Chambon, knight etc... and The King's Commander for all of french Acadia, witnessed on behalf of the said Jean Girouard, by Chanverlange Le Vasseur his brother-in-law and Jacques Vigneau, and on behalf of the said Margueritte Mouton, by Jacques Bourgeois her cousin... have made the following accords and conventions...

Namely:... legitimate marriage to (illegible word) be celebrated and solemnised before our Holy Mother the Church... the sooner (sic) it can be accomplished and will take place between them, their said parents and friends...

To, as will the said future spouses, live and be in full communion of goods and property in the said community, on the day of the celebration of the said marriage, following the custom of Paris, without being held accountable for one and other's debts assumed before the said future marriage...

..and because of the close friendship that the said future spouses promise to each other... have made or will make by these proceedings, to whomever survives the other... irrevocable gift and in the best form that a gift can take, of all the possessions of the community they will form, where (?...) on the day of his death, assuming however that there does not exist any children born (sic) or to be born in legitimate marriage, in which case the present gift shall... be deemed null and void...

..Signed and sealed at Beauséjour on the afternoon of January twenty-five of the year seventeen hundred and fifty-five - completed by Courville, Public Notary of the said place who has signed along with M. de Vergor, and Mr. Barbuty and Mr. Nioche (2 habitual names without any family links), witnesses (here: two other names made illegible through photocopying, except for the following:) Poirié, Jean Girouard and Margueritte Mouton, future spouses, Le Vasseur, Jacques Vigneau, Jacques Bourgeois et Jacques Mouton having declared being unable to (sic) sign, of this enquiry, Reading accomplished according to the ordinance. - A proper dismissal, a word crossed out.

The official marriage record of Joseph Girouard and Irsul Trahan.

Opposite: sketch by Margaretha van Gurp

who married Anne Marie Nuriat is the grandson of Germain ...ock D-2] and his wife Marie Bourgeois, via the father of Charles- who is married to Jeanne Barrieau (Barrilot).

must be remembered however that Jean Girouard, husband of Margaret ...outon, had five stepsisters and one stepbrother via the first marriage of his father, Jacques Girouard to Anne Pettipas, and that descendants of these stepchildren are living today in Québec. *[see Québec volume with reference to one of these stepsisters, Marguerite Girouard m. Jacques Forrest. One of their direct descendants, Denis J. Taylor, recently contacted me.—B.G.]*

[3/14] Claude Girouard [AMC Block I-3a], son of Jacques Girouard and Marguerite Gautrot m. Elizabeth Blanchard and stayed at Port Royal. He died in 1738.

His son Joseph Girouard was deported to MA, 1755, in Boston, 1763, and later he established in St. Ours, PQ, in 1767, where his Uncle Guillaume's family had located an earlier [AMC Block J-3a] branch.[67] (*See Québec volume for subchart 207 for this branch, presented up to the 1950-60's.*)

Three of Jacques and Marguerite's other children, Guillaume, Charles and François, remained in Port Royal at least until 1714, and moved later to Memramcook, where they are recorded in the 1752 census. These three, along with their brother, Pierre [AMC Block E-3b], all of whom we know were in Memramcook at this time, and their children (six boys, all married with their own families), and the four Girouard daughters of Claude and Guillaume, (Anne, Françoise, Marie, Anne), and the extended family of grandparents etc., account for the 15 families, recorded heading for Memramcook in 1752, three years before the actual Deportation.[68] I claim this identification because of the context, the census records and the fact that these closely related families would very likely be trying to stay together as one extended family, supporting and helping each other through the misery. The girls married, respectively, Dupuis, Jean Richard, Pierre Pellerin, and Honoré Blanchard.

Let's look a little more closely at these families.

[4/14] Guillaume Girouard [AMC Block J-3a], *son of Jacques Girouard and Marguerite Goutrot*, m. Marie Bernard and was in Memramcook in the 1752 census. Paul Surette makes reference to Guillaume Girouard and his brother Germain beginning the colonization of the great marsh of Beaubassin, in 1708[69], so they were there long before moving to the Memramcook area. Guillaume later continued to Québec, establishing a branch of Girouards at St- Ours, PQ and the surrounding area, some of whom later went on to establish a branch in Rhode Island. *See subchart # 208, and related information and references, up to present day in the Québec book in the appendix.*

Opposite page: Map of Memramcook River, courtesy of Paul Surette [11] taken from his book Atlas de l'établissement des Acadiens aux trois rivières du Chignectou 1660-1755, *p. 85, Les editions d'Acadie, 1996.*

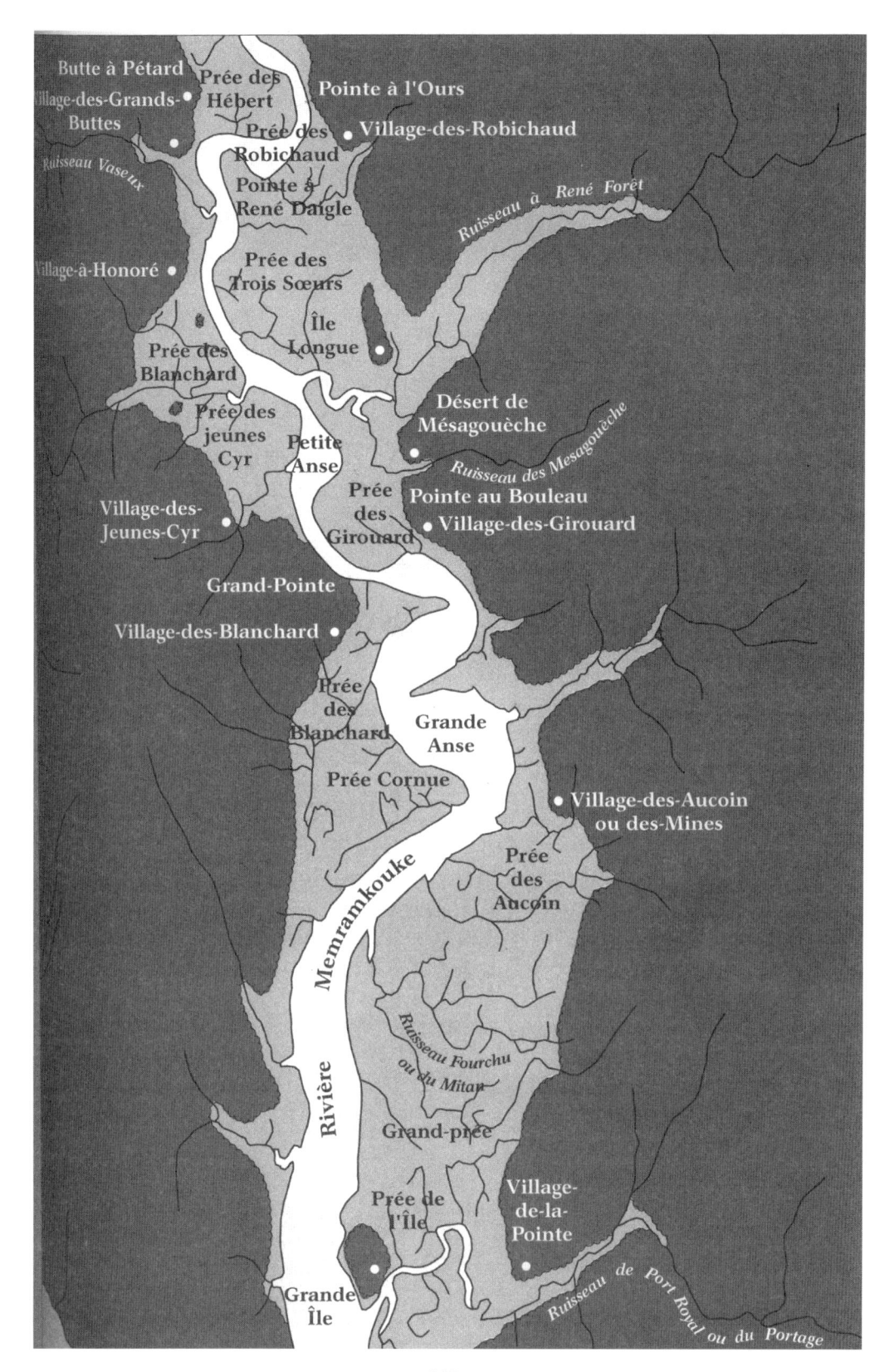

Port Royal and old Acadie

[5/14] Charles Girouard [AMC Block C-3b], *son of Jacques Girouard and Marguerite Goutrot*, m1. Anne Bastarache, m2. Marie J. Pitre at Port Royal in 1744. His son François m2. Catherine Martin, 1754, at Port Royal. Another son of Charles and Anne Bastarache, Charles m. Marie Thibodeau was recorded at Beaubassin and his brother, Joseph Bistet Girouard, was also at Beaubassin and later at the St. John River, 1767. Joseph Bistet Girouard, according to Paul Surette[70], was moving his family to the Memramcook area at La Petite Anse, in 1742. Bistet Girouard later established as one of the first pioneers of Bouctouche, NB.

It appears that the Girouard family was involved in the taking of the transport ship *Pembroke*, (below) no matter which version of the story is used.[71] One of Joseph (Bistet) Girouard's daughters, Anne Girouard, married Pierre Belliveau, cited by Gaudet as hero of the taking of the transport ship, the *Pembroke*, during the Deportation. However, in the same document, Gaudet mentions the Acadian captain John Beaulieu as also being aboard the *Pembroke*. It is this John Beaulieu who is referred to by Mary Weekes as the (Girouard) hero of the *Pembroke*. As a sea captain, he would likely be at the head of any action. This Jean Girouard *dit* Beaulieu [AMC Block F-4m1] would be first cousin to Joe Bistet, since his father François [AMC Block F-3b] was brother to Charles [AMC Block C-3b] the father of Joe (Bistet) Girouard. Jean Girouard *dit* Beaulieu was also referred to as 'Mangeau' according to Stephen White.[72]

In *Acadian Betrayal*, Mary Weekes notes a reference by Gaudet, which supports Jean Girouard (Beaulieu) of Tracadie as hero of the Pembroke story: "The factual material forming the background of this story checked with Placide Gaudet's *Report concerning Canadian Archives*, 1905, Vol 11, p xxix."[73]

Two other daughters of Joseph (Bistet) Girouard, and therefore granddaughters of Charles, Rosalie Girouard m. Charles (Charlitte) LeBlanc and Marie Madeleine Girouard m. Charles Joseph Bastarache, were among the first settlers in Bouctouche. *See [AMC Block C-3b] in the Founders of Bouctouche section of the New Brunswick volume, for further related information on these Girouards).*

A number of Charles Girouard's other children were deported to South Carolina: Natalie, Gregoire, Bonnaventure, Basile, Madeleine, François. The last child, François, had a son Joseph Amable, who we find in the West Indies. Anne Girouard, daughter of Charles Girouard and his first wife Anne Bastarache, m. Pierre Pellerin (Jean-Baptiste and Marie Martin) at Port Royal in 1745, so the family is still at Port Royal at this time. The last record at Port Royal of this family is that of François, son of Charles and Anne Bastarche, when he married his second wife, Catherine Martin, 1754. Obviously he was not with the group of Girouards who migrated to Memramcook in 1752. We can assume he was deported from Port Royal, since he appears on the 1763 census in South Carolina. *See [AMC Block C-3b] in New Brunswick volume for further information.*

[6/14] François Girouard [AMC Block F-3b], *son of Jacques Girouard and Marguerite Goutrot*, m1. Anne Bourgeois, m2. Marie Guilbeau. He was at Port Royal and recorded later, 1752, at Memramcook, coming from Port Royal. His son Jean-Baptiste [AMC Block F-4m1] is recorded at Memramcook, and later (1763) on the prisoner list at Fort Beauséjour, with his family as noted earlier in this chapter. *[This Jean-Baptiste Girouard is in my direct line of the AMC.-B.G.]* From Beauséjour, the families were apparently taken to Halifax as prisoners, where they stayed for several years (probably engaged by the English to help construct and repair roads, forts etc.). There is a record of the marriage of one of Jean-Baptiste's daughters (Marie Girouard m. to Basile Goutrot in 1770) and the birth of another daughter, Annastasie, in the year 1770 in Halifax, recorded by Rev. Charles Bailey *(see Antigonish and Guysborough book for more detail).*

We have a record of this family of Jean-Baptiste Girouard and Madeleine LeBlanc [AMC Block F-4m1] at Chezzetcook, where they stayed with a number of other Acadian families for seven years. Here we have records of baptisms performed by old Jean-Baptiste Girouard (Girroir) in the absence of the priest. *(See details in Antigonish and /Guysborough chapters of NS volume.)* Finally we have a record of this family establishing at Tracadie, in Antigonish County, Nova Scotia. From here stem the branches established in Guysborough County, at Larry's River, Lundy, and Charlos Cove.

All of this is related in another rare and valuable document for the Girouards— the interview with Captain Girroir of Tracadie, Nova Scotia, by Edmé Rameau,[74] a historian hired by the government of France in the 19th century to gather information on the Acadians after Deportation.

In the 20th century, many of the descendants of the Girroirs, Gerriors, Gerroirs in Tracadie and the closely related Guysborough branches migrated out of these root areas to Halifax, Sydney, New Glasgow, Stellarton, and Trenton, Nova Scotia and other parts of Canada and the United States in search of work. The genealogy for all of these branches is given in the AMC, including my direct line in the centre column of the AMC and includes every block of the AMC from the 5th to the 12th generation and their related subcharts and genealogical block information presented in paragraph form in the Nova Scotia/Prince Edward Island book. Their complete story unfolds for each block of the AMC.

François's son Pierre [AMC Block C-4m1] who was at Memramcook with his father and who is also brother of Jean of Tracadie[75], separated from them and continued to Québec, establishing at Deschambault on the St. Lawrence River in the year 1760.[76] His son Jean-Baptiste m. Agatha Boisell, 1785, at L'Assomption Deschambault, PQ. Another son of Pierre via his first marriage to Marie-Josèphe Forest, was Pierre Charles, who also established at Québec. I have received no further record or connection from this branch. *See the genealogy block information for [AMC Block C-4m1] in the Québec book.*

Another son of François is Joseph [AMC Block J-4m1], brother of Jean Girouard of Tracadie. He established at Québec. Joseph Girouard married for the second time to Marie J. Arseneau, in Québec City, and their children and grandchildren are located in Notre Dame, Montréal, St-Jacques de Montcalm St-Etienne, St-Phillipe and La Prairie. *See chart and map of this branch, presented in the Québec volume to present day.*

The two sisters of Jean-Baptiste of Tracadie, granddaughters of Jacques Girouard and Margaret Goutrot, are Marie-Madeleine [AMC Block E-4m1] and Anne-

Hélène [AMC Block H-4m1]. Anne-Hélène Girouard m. Charles Benoît was at Memramcook. *(See Benoît on Paul Surette's map)*. Both were at Québec in 1757, 1758.[77]

Having now accounted for the six children of Jacques Girouard and Marguerite Goutrot [AMC Block F-3] of the third generation of the AMC, who stayed at Port Royal until at least 1714, and having presented the movement of their descendants, I now turn my attention to two of the fourteen children who settled at Grand Pré.

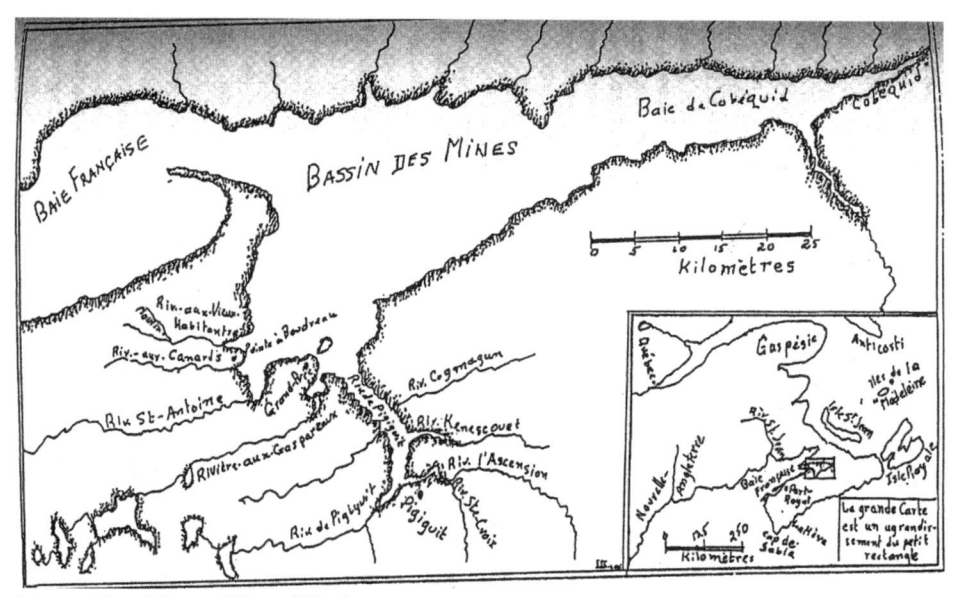

Map of Les Mines (Grand Pré)
Courtesy of Léopold Lanctôt, Familles Acadiennes Vol. I, p.75, and Marc Vielleux, Éditions du Libre Exchange.

Sketch of St. Charles Church, Grand Pré. Artist: Evelyn Oakley

218

At Grand Pré
Many Acadians left the region of Port Royal for the Mines (Grand Pré region). Also see previous map in which each black dot on the map represents 10 persons. Here we find Denis Girouard [AMC Block B-3b] and his brother, Pierre Girouard [AMC Block E-3b].

[7/14] Denis Girouard [AMC Block B-3b] *son of Jacques Girouard and Marguerite Goutrot*, m. Marguerite Barrieau 1709 and died in the same year of 1709 at Grand Pré. Marguerite m2. Louis Philippe Douaron, 1712,[78] and at least five of their children were part of the emigration to Ile St-Jean (PEI) with their parents.

[8/14] Pierre Girouard [AMC Block E-3b] *son of Jacques Girouard and Marguerite Goutrot* m1. Marie Comeau and m2. Marie Douaron (or Doiron). We have record of this Pierre Girouard with his first wife, Marie Comeau, and one boy and one girl, at Kinscour in the 1701 census (Grand Pré). According to the 1709 and 1712 census, Marie Douaron b. 1694 at Pisiquit was married at Grand Pré on November 14, 1709 to Pierre Girouard, widower of Marie Comeau. In the 1714 census, Pierre is recorded at Pisiquit Rivière with his second wife, Marie Douaron[79]. He was later recorded at Isle Madame with his family.

One of Pierre's sons, Claude Girouard, had a son in turn named Pierre Girouard m. Cécile Detcheverry, who established the Isle Madame, N.S. branch of Girroirs. This later Pierre is first recorded at Petit de Grat in 1752 (2125-1 Placide Gaudet). The baptisms of his children were recorded by L'Abbé Charles-François Bailey, at Gabarus, Cape Breton, Nova Scotia. One of the Girroirs of the Isle Madame branch, James (Jacques) Gerrior settled in Georgetown, Prince Edward Island, establishing one of the PEI Gerrior branches. Again, documents refer to this same person interchangeably as James or Jacques. See charts 163, Isle Madame and 162, PEI in the Nova Scotia, PEI book, to follow these branches through to the present day.

Many of the descendants of this PEI branch have in recent years migrated to the mainland Nova Scotia, mostly to the Trenton, New Glasgow and Stellarton area, following employment. Their roots are in Georgetown, PEI, as far back as their great-grandparents James Gerrior and Anne Wolf, but from that point back they are rooted in the Isle Madame branches where their earlier ancestors settled after Deportation. Some descendants of this branch still live in Georgetown and surrounding areas of PEI. The descendants of this branch still carrying the surname, however, are located today only on the mainland of Nova Scotia, for the most part in the Trenton, New Glasgow and Truro areas.

One of the sons of Pierre, [AMC Block E-3b], is Louis Paul Girouard b. Grand Pré m. Marie Thibodeau, daughter of Charles Thibodeau and Françoise Comeau. He is recorded with his family in Île Saint-Jean (Prince Edward Island), 1752 on the north side of the Macpec River, (Malpèque à Île Saint-Jean), "having cleared an acre of land since the previous July when they came to this place", according to the 1752 census by Sieur de la Rocque, 1752). Louis and his wife, Marie Thibodeau, and six children were recorded in this census: Gervais 8, Firmin 3, Charles 8 months, Marguerite 15, Anne Théodose 13, and Marie-Joseph 6. After the fall of Louisbourg, they are refugees at Baie des Chaleurs, NB, and following this, after the Deportation, we find the family in Halifax. They later moved to Petitcodiac River, NB, then to Bouctouche, NB, in 1789/90 where he established the Girouard branches of New Brunswick. His son, Paul Gervais Girouard, and grandsons, Béoni, Benjamin, Pierre and Joe Bob all received title to land that year in Bouctouche—80 acres of land to the head of each family, 40 acres per person. *See Paul Surette's map,[80] , and charts numbered in the 300, 500, 600, 700 series in the New Brunswick volume for more details covering these branches to present day.*

Louis Paul Girouard's other son, Firmin, was deported and later is recorded living at Donaldsonville, Louisiana, acquiring a lot of land on the west bank of the Mississippi River. *See chart number 162.1 and the Louisiana book and appendix 5.*

Pierre had another son, Honoré (uncle to Firmin, brother of Louis Paul above) who was also deported and is found in St-Malo, France where his son Prosper is married. Prosper's sister Hélène Judith and her family are recorded in Cenan, near Châtellerault, France in the same vicinity as la Ligne Acadienne, having also been deported back to France. Honoré's family, 30 years later, voyaged from France to Louisiana establishing the Giroir branch in Louisiana, retaining this spelling of the family name, conforming to the way the name was spelled on the passenger list made up in France. Despite this, we know for certain they are the same "Girouard" family who, after the initial Deportation from Nova Scotia, were sent back to England, then later to France. *See charts 162.1 for both Girouard and Giroir branches in the Louisiana book for more details. The children of Pierre [AMC Block E-3b] can be found in subcharts 300,500,600,700 of the New Brunswick volume, subchart 163 and 164 of the Nova Scotia & Prince Edward Island volume and subchart 162.1 and 162 .6 of the Louisiana volume.*

During my trip to Louisiana for the Congrès Mondial Acadien in 1999, I did some research at the West Baton Rouge Museum, Port Allen, La. I met Jeannie Giroir Luckett, the education curator of the museum, who gave a personal tour of the museum to Alex Giroir of Pierre Part, La., and me. Here I found one of the original Acadian registers of St-Charles-des-Mines, Grand Pré region of Acadia. The register was brought to St. Gabriel Parish, La, via an English schooner carrying Acadians who were initially deported to Maryland, and then migrated to Louisiana, arriving in New Orleans on this vessel July 12, 1767. The register has remained in Louisiana to the present day. In this document we find the family of our Pierre Girouard discussed above. The original records were displayed in a glass showcase, and copies of the record were made first in 1978, for interested researchers, and then reprinted in 1988 with a third printing in 1999 for that year's Congrès. Here are excerpts from records of the Girouard, Giroir families at Grand Pré confirming the information above concerning all of Pierre Girouard's family [AMC Block E-3b], whose descendants are later established in Isle Madame, NS, PEI, New Brunswick and Louisiana as explained above.

I have retained the spellings as they appear in the documents. Girouar sometimes appears as Giroir or Girouard. Note also the use of the trema (two dots above the letter u) in the family name, originally found in France, still used during this period in Acadia. The following abbreviations are used.

spo=sponsors
SGA =St. Gabriel Church Parish, Louisiana

Bn.=born
bt.=baptised
bur.=buried
d.-died
wit=witness
sig =signed

Grand Pré Records Excerpts, p. 80, 81 Diocese of Baton Rouge Catholic Church Records, Acadian Records, 1707-1748, Vol. 1 Revised third printing 1999:[81]

Charles Girouar (Pierre Girouar and Marie Douaron) bn. 30 Sept. 1710, bt. 26 dec. 1710, spo. Charles Douaron and Margueritte Pinet (SGA-1,19) (SGA-1,19).
Denis Giroüar, husband of Margueritte Barillot, bur. 28 Dec. 1709, d. 26 Dec. 1709, wit. none given (SGA-1,25)
Denis Girouar (Jacques Girouar and Margueritte Gotrot) habitants de Port Royal) m. 17 Oct. 1709 Margueritte Barillot (Nicolas Barillot and Marie Hébert, habitants of Pigiguit) wit. {+}Pierre Giroüar; {+}Nicholas Barillot; {+} Jacques Granger; sig. {+} Denis Giroüar; {+} Margueritte Barillot (SGA-1,58).
Étienne Giroüar (Pierre Giroüar and Marie Commeaux) bn. 21 Dec. 1708, bt. 14 April 1709 spo. Étienne Commeaux and Suzanne Breaux (SGA-1,10)
Jacques Girouard, age ca 22 (Pierre Giroaurd and decd. Marie Caumau, of the parish of L'Assumption de Pigidy) m. 31 July, Marie Boisseau, age ca 18 (François Boisseau dit Blondin and Anne Saunié) wit. {+} Thomas Douaron; {+} François Boisseau; Estienne {+}Girouard; Estienne Racois (s); sig. {+} Jaques Girouard; {+} Marie Boisseau (SGA-2, 220)
Jean Giroir (Pierre Giroir and Marie Douaron) bn. 18 May 1729, bt. 6 June 1729, spo. Jean Boudrot and Catherine Meunier (SGA-2, 91).
Magdelaine Girouard (Pierre Giroaurd and Marie Douaron) bn. 24 May 1719, bt. 24 June 1719 wit. Nicholas Barrilot and Marie Granger (SGA-2, 14)
Marie Joseph Girouard (Pierre Girouard and Marie Douaron) bn. 27 Oct. 1717, bt. 1 May 1718 spo. Jacques Terriot (s) and Marie Douaron (SGA-2,6).
Pierre Giroüar, widower of Marie Commeaux (Jacques Giroüar and Margueritte Gotrot, habitants of Port Royal, m. 14, Sept 1709 Marie Douaron (Jean Douaron and Marie Trahan, habitants of Pigiguit) wit. {+} Jacques Granger; {+} Jean Douaron; sig. {+} Pierre Giroüar Marie Trahan (sic) (SGA-2, 58)
Pierre Girouard, age 18 to 19, bur. 27 Jan. 1719, d. 26 Jan. 1719, wit. none given (SGA-2,170)
Veronique Giroüar (Pierre Giroüar and Marie Douaron) bn. 1 march 1712, bt. 3 April 1712, spo. Sieur Mouton, chirurgien, and Angelique Douaron; sig. Jean Mouton (s) (SGA-1, 36)...
On page 165 of the same volume, (1707-1748), in the Mouton family section, we find the following entry:
...Jean Mouton (Sieur Jean Mouton, chirurgien des Mines, and Marie Giroüard) bn. 19 Nov. 1712, bt. 20 Nov. 1712 spo. Monsieur Delatour, Lieutenant of the naval detachment company and Seignior in part of Acadia and Marie Giroüard. (SGA-1, 37). .[sic]

[This Marie Girouard married to Jean Mouton is the daughter of Alexandre de Ru Girouard and Marie La Borgne. [AMC Block C-3a] who was the granddaughter of Charles de La Tour and whose family I have presented in this chapter. So we see again the Girouard family is connected in high places early in Acadia. – B.G.]

At Beaubassin

Two of the 14 children of Jacques and Marguerite Gauterot moved to Beaubassin to join their Uncle Germain [AMC Block D-2] and their aunts: Marie, married to Jacques Belou [AMC Block B-2] and Madeleine, married to Thomas Cormier [AMC Block C-2]. Both families were already established at Beaubassin, as a result of the move of the second generation. They first appear on the census in Beaubassin in 1686.

[9/14] Germain Girouard, [AMC Block D-3b] *son of Jacques Girouard and Marguerite Gauterot*, m. Marie Doucet and moved from Port Royal to Beaubassin. He is recorded there on the 1703 and 1714 census, long before the Deportation years.

In Paul Surette's recent book, *Atlas de l'Établissement des Acadiens aux trois rivières du Chignectou 1660-1755*, he mentions that Germain, and his brother Guillaume, the youngest sons of Jacques Girouard and Marguerite Gauthrot, along with their future brothers-in-law, residing at Nanpanne (near Amherst, NS), began the colonization of the great marsh of Beaubassin, between its northwest border and the Tintamarre River.

Germain [AMC Block D-3b] was now with his Uncle Germain [AMC Block D-2], his wife Marie Bourgeois and their son Germain who married Jeanne Barrilot. The family of the older Germain [AMC Block D-2] as mentioned, had moved to Beaubassin as part of the second-generation movement.[82] One of the sons of Germain [AMC Block D-3b], also named Germain, married first to Marie Arsenault and married a second time to M. Henry, was living in Sackville, Beaubassin area, and later is found established in St-Hyacinthe, Québec. Another son, Claude, was a refugee at Saint-Chambly, Québec; another son Joseph, married to Agnes Gaudet, established at St-Antoine-sur-Richelieu, Québec. A daughter, Anne, married to Pierre Gaudet, was deported to France where we find them recorded at La Rochelle and Nantes. Also another son, Pierre m. Marguerite Gaudet, in PEI, 1752 and they are recorded later in France.[83] *See Québec volume and appendix 5 for details on these numerous Québec descendants, found on subchart #213 and related block genealogy information from various subcharts up to present day, in many cases.*

Another son of Germain Girouard [AMC Block D-3b] is Michel Girouard, m. to Marguerite Haché-Gallant, who is also found in Beaubassin region in 1755 at Veshcaque (on Paul Surette's map). Michel married in 1745 and is found at Gentilly, Québec. *Subcharts 217, 218 in appendix 5 trace this illustrious branch of Acadian Girouards to present day in Québec.*

[10/14] Marguerite Girouard [AMC Block H-3a], daughter of Jacques Girouard and Marguerite Gautrot m. Louis Doucet (à Pierre Doucet à Germain Doucet) ca. 1702, and she and her husband joined her brother Germain at Beaubassin, being found on the census of Beaubassin in 1707. Stephen White gives the following references: Port Royal census, 1678,6a; 1686, 12a; 1698, 24a; census Beaubassin, 1714. There are seven children: 1. Pierre (census Beaubassun 1714) m. Marie-Anne Richard (Martin & Marguerite Bourg); d. Nov. 8, 1746; 2. Louis (census Beaubassin, 1714); 3. Marguerite m. (according to A. Godbout) ca. 1726, François Poirier (Michael & Marie Chaisson); 4. Madeleine (census Beaubassin, 1771, census, Fort Beauséjour, 1762) m. (according to A. Godbout) ca. 1733, Michel Richard (Martin & Marguerite Bourg); 5. Marie b. ca. 1714, (census of Beaubassin, 1714), m1. (according to A. Godbout) ca. 1731, Jean-Baptiste Gaudet (Pierre & Cécile Mignot); m2. (register of Nicolet, June 27, 1763, Charles Orillon dit Champagne (Charles & Marie-Anne Bastarache) widow, Anne Richard; Marie died and was bur. (register of Nicolet, Nov. 30/Dec.1, 1789) and the approximate age of 75; 5. Joseph (according to P. Gallant) m. ca. 1738, Isabelle Elisabeth Carret (Pierre & Angélique Chaisson), d. between 1746 and 1750; 6. Madeleine, born and bap. Aug. 9/10, 1722, godparents François Poiriers, son of Michael and Madeleine Doucet, daughter of Louis Doucet, (Beaubassin census register).[84] I have no further trace of the family descendants to date.

Concerning the remaining children of Jacques and Marguerite, we have the following information:

[11/14] **Jean Girouard [AMC Block E-3a]**, *son of Jacques Girouard and Marguerite Goutrot*, was born 1676, at Port Royal. No further information on this Jean Girouard.

[12/14] **Anne-Marie Girouard [AMC Block G-3b]**, *daughter of Jacques Girouard and Marguerite Goutrot*, was born 1697 at Port Royal. She died at 12 years of age.

[13/14] **Marie Girouard [AMC Block G-3a]**, *daughter of Jacques Girouard and Marguerite Goutrot* was born in 1678, m. Jacques Granger at Port Royal. Nine children: 1. one son b. before the census of 1701; 2, one daughter b. before census 1707; 3. Marie, Annapolis (Maryland) 1763; m. Joseph-André LeBlanc (André & Marie Dugas) July 29, 1726 at Grand Pré; 4. Charles b. ca. 1705, m. Marie-Josèphe Daigre (Bernard & Angélique Richard) at Grand Pré, Feb. 17, 1738 ; d. before census of July, 3, 1763; 5. Pierre born and bap. Grand Pré register Feb. 6, 1708 (godparents: Pierre Thériot & Anne Bourgeois); 6. Jean-Baptiste born and bap., Grand Pré register, Aug. 18, 1710 (godparents: Jean Melanson who signed and Marguerite Richard) [Georgetown, Maryland] 1763; m. Grand Pré register, July 9, 1736, 25a, Marie-Josèphe Gautrot (Pierre & Marie-Josèphe Bugeaud (disp. 3-3 cons); 7. Joseph born and bap. Grand Pré register, Feb. 26, 1713 (godparents: M. Baudoin master surgeon at Québec who signed and Marie Girouard, wife of Mouton); m Marguerite Thériot (Jean & Madeleine Bourg) Grand Pré register, Nov. 20 1734 (disp.3-4 cons.); d. before June 30,1763; 8. Marguerite m. Grand Pré register, Jan.22, 1742, Joseph Daigre (Bernard & Angilique Richard), d. before Mar. 5, 1764; Bénoni born and bap. Grand Pré register, Jan. 4/5,1720 (godparents: Joseph Granger & Marguerite Bourq); m1. Grand Pré register, Oct. 15, 1742, 21 a,

Elisabeth Thériot (Jean & Madeleine Bourg) disp. (4-4 cons.); m2. ca. 1750 Anne Richard; d. before census of Jan. 1, 1752.[85] I have no further record of this family to date.

[14/14] Madeleine Girouard [AMC Block H-3b] *daughter of Jacques and Marguerite Gauterot,* was born in 1695 at Port Royal and m. Pierre Richard. *[This family is particularly significant in the genealogical study of the Girouards, because they were deported to France and it is the declaration (sworn legal statement) of Pierre Richard which states that his wife's grandfather, Jacques François dit La Varenne, came to Port Royal from France with his wife Jeanne Aucoin. This important statement tells us that our first François at Port Royal came from a place called La Varenne in France. It also states, however, that he arrived with his wife, which if true would be a contradiction to other information claiming he married at Port Royal.—B.G.]*

Thus are the travels, movements and general directions of the 14 children of the third generation and of their descendants to present day. Of course the descendants of one of these 14 children François Girouard [AMC Block F-3b] married to Anne Bourgeois, are shown in every block of the AMC below the third row, to present day in the centre column. Also, via the expansion in each of the blocks to the left or right of the centre column using corresponding subcharts and genealogical block information in paragraph form, we are also able to trace each of these lateral blocks on the Girouard Acadian Master Chart, [AMC] to present day for the most part. This tracing is accomplished in each of the books throughout the five book series.

The details of each branch above appear in the next four volumes, depending on where they established after Deportation and migrations. This present book is limited as in the above section in tracing only the early generations (first, second, third, and fourth generations of the AMC). These generations only are the subject of our present focus, concerning the travels of the Girouard families before, during and after the Deportation. There is still more to come in this chapter!

The Fourth Generation of the Acadian Master Chart

Paul Surette's maps give an excellent overview of the many places in the Beaubassin and Memramcook areas where the Girouards established or were refugees before and during the Deportation year of 1755. I have supplemented the maps with some photos, taken during a personal guided tour of these areas with Paul Surette, whom I met at a meeting of family co-ordinators for the Congrés Mondial, 1994, in New Brunswick. Looking at the map we see the Girouards and the Aucoins remained in close proximity to each other, even at this point.

In his most recent book, *Atlas de L'Établissement des Acadiens aux trois Rivières du Chignectou,* (1996), Paul Surrette gives more detailed maps and descriptions of the places where the Acadians, mostly those of the fourth generation, were established in the region of the three rivers of the Chignectou, during the 1755 Deportation. One of these rivers, the Memramcook River, is of particular interest during the time leading up to and including the Deportation of 1755.

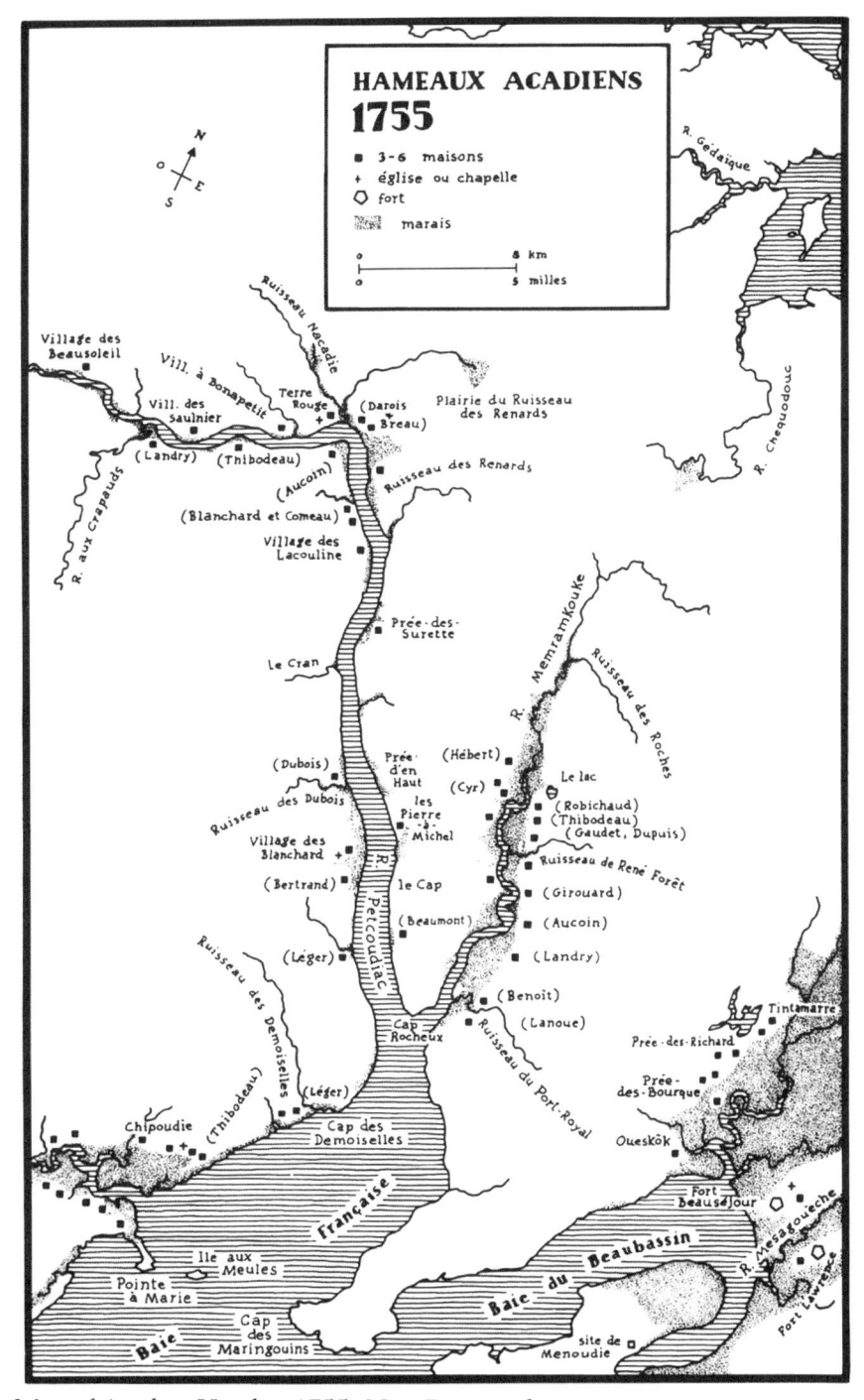

Map of Acadian Hamlets 1755, New Brunswick.
Courtesy of Paul Surette[2] Le Grand Petcoudiac, 1763-1832, Histoire Des Trois Rivieres, Vol. III, p. 15.

Following page: author's photos accompanying Paul Surette's map of Acadian Hamlets, 1755

Above - first photo: Marshland of Girouard Hamlet, just above Aucoin Hamlet shown on map and old Memramcook River Bridge. (where the following Girouard descendants resided: John Baptiste à François à Jacques [AMC Block Q-4m1]; Guillaume à Guillaume à Jacques descending from [AMC Block J-3a]; Pierre à François à Jacques [AMC Block C-4m1]

Port Royal and old Acadie

Opposite - second photo: Site of Girouard houses during this period (see square dot marked Girouards on Paul Surette's map). First Church of Memramcook was on same site according to oral tradition

Opposite - third photo: View of the Memramcook great marsh, from the location of Anne-Hélène Girouard and Claude H. Benoît. [AMC Block H-4m1] à François and Anne Bourgeois. (See Benoît square dot on map). This Anne-Hélène was sister to Jean à François and Pierre à François above.

Opposite - fourth and fifth photos on the bottom of page: Marsh of Joe Bistet Girouard, son of Charles à Jacques [AMC Block C-3b] (see square marked Cyr on Surette map). Photo taken not far from the church in Memramcook as seen in photo.

Above - top photo: Marshland of Germain à François [AMC Block D-2]. (see square dot next to Fort Lawrence on bottom right corner of Paul Surette's map.)

Above - middle photo: View of marshland of Jacques Belou and Marie Girouard à François [AMC Block B-2] at La Butte (Amherst Point), just south of Mesagouèche River. (not shown on map but this is located along the shaded shoreline, just south of letter "F" in Fort Lawrence on Surette map.).

Above - bottom photo: Rich marshland of Thomas Cormier and Madeleine Girouard [AMC Block C-2] at Ouechcoque, just below La Butte on map, across the water and east of Menoudie in Beaubassin.

Above - first photo: Overlooking Beaubassin, from marshlands of Michel Girouard and his wife Marguerite Haché-Gallant at Vechcaque (Oueskôk) on map. Michel is son of Germain Girouard à Jacques [AMC Block D-3b].

Above - second photo: Marshlands of Germain Girouard [AMC Block D-3b] à Jacques at Tintamarre; just south of Tintamarre is the land of Germain à Germain à Jacques. [AMC Block D-3b].

Census Records

The following excerpts are from census records showing Girouards located at Port Royal, Beaubassin and Beauséjour, Le Lac, Tintamarre census. They give a sense of the reality of our ancestor's existence in Acadie, representing their last mark so to speak. These census documents have been reduced in size because of space constraints, but are still readable for the avid researcher who is used to straining his or her eyes. I have made notations, to match them up to my genealogy and to the AMC.

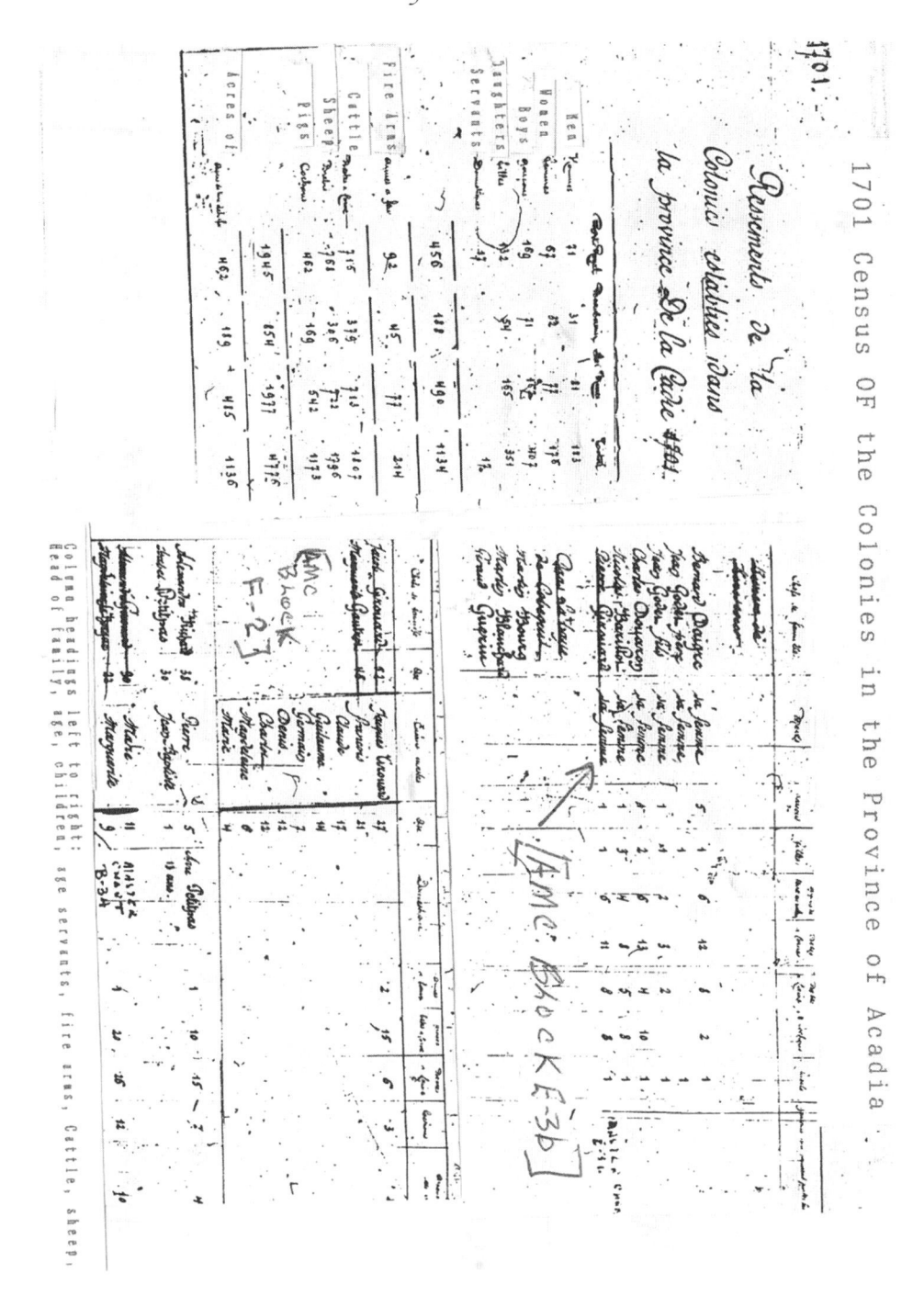

Port Royal census 1701 shows Pierre Girouard and his wife [AMC Block E-3b] family of Jacques Girouard and Marie Gouthrot [AMC Block F-2]

Following page top: Port Royal Census in Acadie 1707 shows Widow Girouard [which would be Jeanne Aucoin [AMC Block F-1]]; Jacques Girouard and his wife [AMC Block F-2], Alexandre Girouard and his wife [AMC Block C-3a]

Census of Port Royal in Acadia 1707

1707 Census of Beaubassin

Column headings left to right are: boys over 14, Boys under, girls over girls under, _____, Land value, Cattle, sheep?, pigs.

This page bottom: Beaubassin census in 1707 shoes Louis Doucet and Marguerite Girouard [AMC Block H-3a] Abraham Gaudet and Agnes Girouard, daughter of Germain Girouard [AMC Block D-2] Germain Girouard and his wife [AMC D-3b]

*Census at Beauséjour (Pointe de Beaubassin) shows: At Beaubassin, Charles Girouard
At Le Lac: François Girouard and Jacques Girouard*

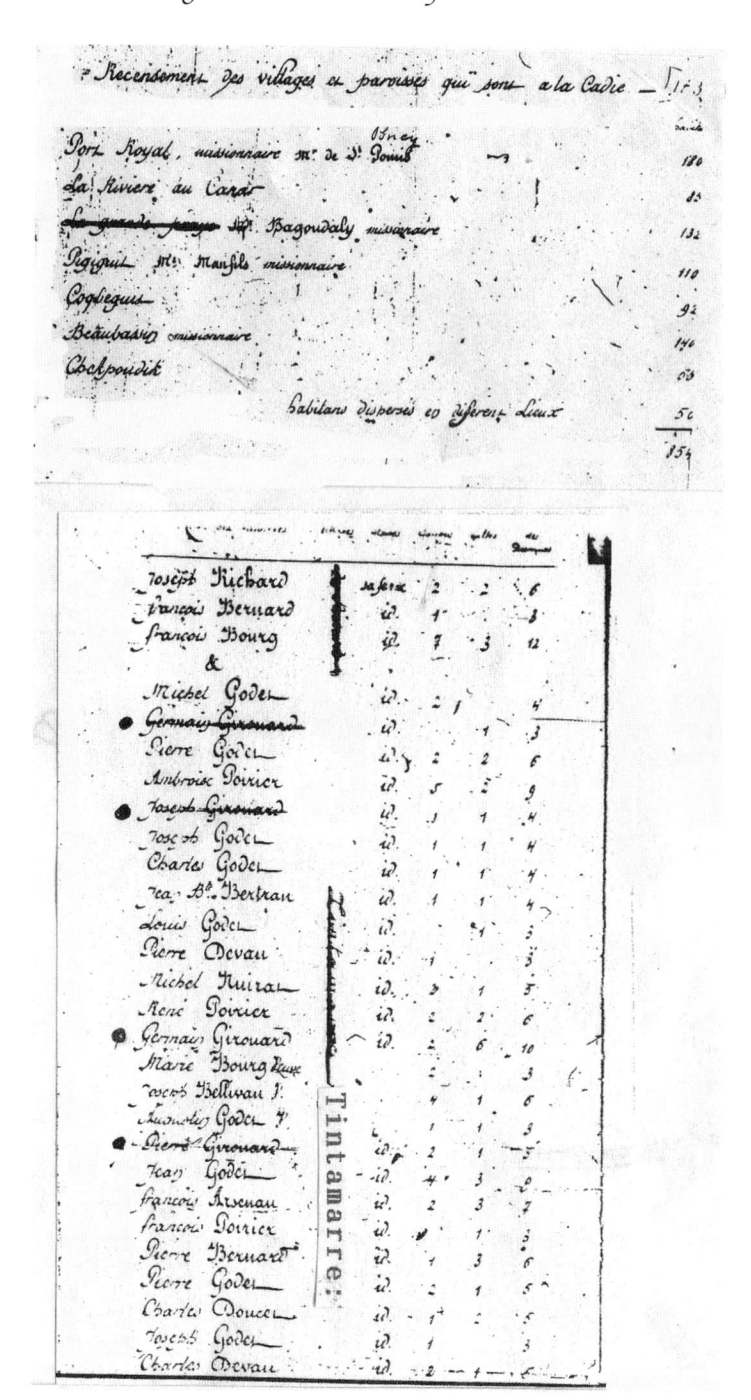

Above: Census at Beauséjour (Pointe de Beaubassin) shows:
At Tintamarre: Germain Girouard and family, Joseph Girouard and Family; and another Germain Girouard; as well as Pierre Girouard

Opposite: Memramkouke at the first long elbow in the River, 1750, Paul Surette map.
Base map courtesy of Paul Surette, *Atlas de l'Establishment des Acadiens aux trois rivières du Chignectou 1660-1755*, p.1.[13]

Port Royal and old Acadie

Paul Surette, in his recent book, *Atlas de l'Establishment des Acadiens aux trois rivières du Chignectou 1660-1755*, gives an excellent, detailed account of all establishments of Acadian families surrounding the three rivers of Chignectou, one of which is the Memramcook (Memramkouke) River establishments, where as we know, a number of Girouard families were established at the time of the Deportation.

The children of 'marriage age' at this time would be the fourth generation of Girouards. We will now have a closer look at these fourth-generation descendants, for the most part in the Memramcook region, in excerpts which I have translated from Paul Surette's book, and combined with my genealogical chart references and notes. Paul Surette uses the old spelling of 'Memramkouke' which I will retain throughout the following section.

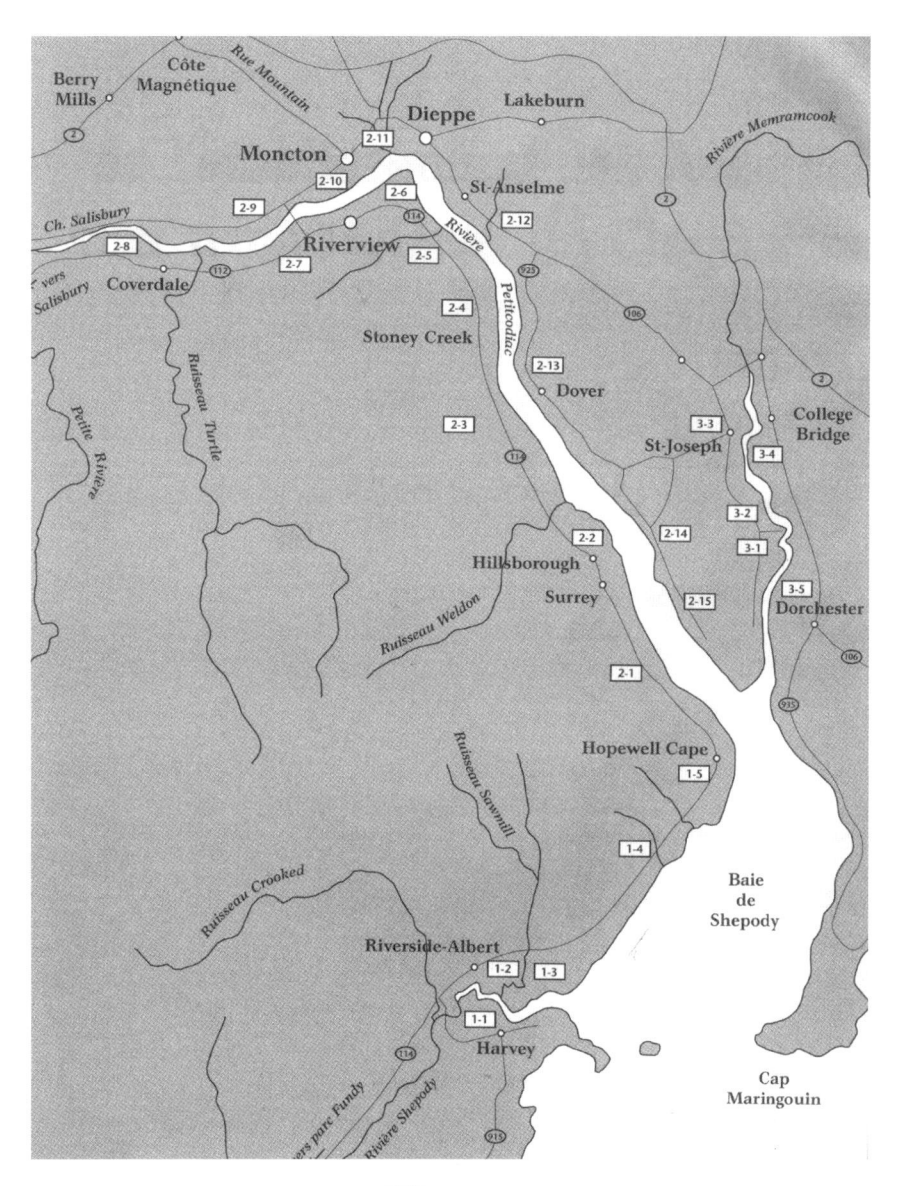

233

Pointe au Bouleau (Bouleau Point) [86]
[translations of excerpts from research of Paul Surette]

In 1729 the children of the three Dugas sisters, who had left this region, planned to return to this location which their fathers had prepared for them in Memramkouke. The three Dugas sisters were Françoise Dugas m. René Forêt à Michel Forêt, Agnès Dugas m. Michel Thibodeau à Pierre Thibodeau, and Madeleine Dugas m. Jean Hébert à Emmanuel Hébert.

One of the children of Françoise Dugas, Joseph Forêt, who himself was father of three children, surely would have reclaimed his land for his children, but he died at 32 years of age. His cousin, Madeleine Hébert, married René Daigle, and his cousin Joseph Thibaudot, established there early.

The Thibaudot clan, to whom these colonists belonged, then offered to their family allies, the Blanchards, who were frustrated with their land at Peticoudiac, the option of choosing land on the opposite side of the Memramkouke River.

Around 1732, several young Blanchard men began work across from the upsteam area of Pré de Trois Soeurs. Participating, were of course, three of the sons of the late Jacques Girouard and Marguerite Gautrot. [AMC Block F-2]. The Girouards and the Blanchards were allied through marriage as seen in the relationships of two of the following three Girouard brothers, sons of the late Jacques Girouard, and Marguerite Gautrot:

1) François Girouard [AMC Block F-3b] father of eight children at this time, married to Anne Bourgeois

2) Charles Girouard [AMC Block C-3b] married Anne Bastarache

3) Guillaume Girouard [AMC Block J-3a] m1. Marie Bernard, m2. Anne Renauchet (whose son Guillaume was married to Anne Blanchard, 1735).

In this same year, Anne Bourgeois, wife of François Girouard, gave birth twice in the space of eleven months. Her health gradually deteriorated and she died a year and a half later, 1735.

This same year one of the three Dugas sisters, Madeleine, with her husband, Jean Hébert and her future son-in-law, Cyr, established themselves at the old site where their daughter, Madeleine already resided, and took for themselves, one of the spots designated for the Blanchards at the foot of the Grands-Buttes. The Blanchards protested and prepared a counter-strategy: As of 1737, Honoré à Antoine Blanchard and some family allies returned to the upstream site, next to the lands that they had lost, while their close relatives planned to occupy the other neighbouring sites. In order to come to Memramkouke, the widower, François Girouard [AMC Block F-3b] adopted a more subtle strategy: He allied himself to one of the other founding families, in this case, one of Forêts descending from the oldest of the Dugas sisters, Françoise Dugas. François Girouard [AMC Block F-3b] courted the widow of Joseph Forêt à René, who was Marie Guilbeau, and married her in 1737. In 1739, the Blanchards and their allies went as far as the High Council in Port Royal with their grievances against the Héberts. Other sons of Antoine Blanchard prepared a site for their families, further downstream, at the north entry of Grande Anse, on the south side of Grand-Pointe.

In January, 1740, the new wife of François Girouard, former widow of Joseph Forêt à René, gave birth to a girl, Marie-Josèphe Girouard. The couple planned to marry their children from their first marriages (the Forêt and Girouard children) and establish them at Memramkouke on the marsh of the first Forêt founder in this region.

All of the children of René Forêt resisted. The sons claimed the original site and the oldest sisters demanded their portions for their oldest sons. However, Pierre Girouard [AMC Block C-4m1] second surviving son of François Girouard, became engaged to his stepsister Marie-Josèphe Forêt, daughter of Marie Guilbeau (Guibaut), and her former husband, Joseph Forêt, and therefore inherited part of the paternal Forêt property rights at Memramkouke.

Soon after, Pierre's cousin, Guillaume à Guillaume Girouard whose sister, Marguerite, was engaged to Jean-Baptiste à Antoine Blanchard, became engaged to Anne Blanchard, à Pierre, cousin to Jean-Baptiste Blanchard, and married in 1745. *[Refer to subchart 208 linking to [AMC Block J-3A] in the Québec Acadian book for these and other relationships of this family in Memramkouke.]*

Later, the two Girouard cousins had difficulty finding a place in the long marsh on the original Forêt land. Firstly, the clan Forêt did not let them on their former original site, on either side of the main brook, one side being where Trois Soeurs (three sisters) were established and the other side being the colony at Mésagouèche, where none of the descendants of these colonists had come back to work the land, and which remained in ruins.

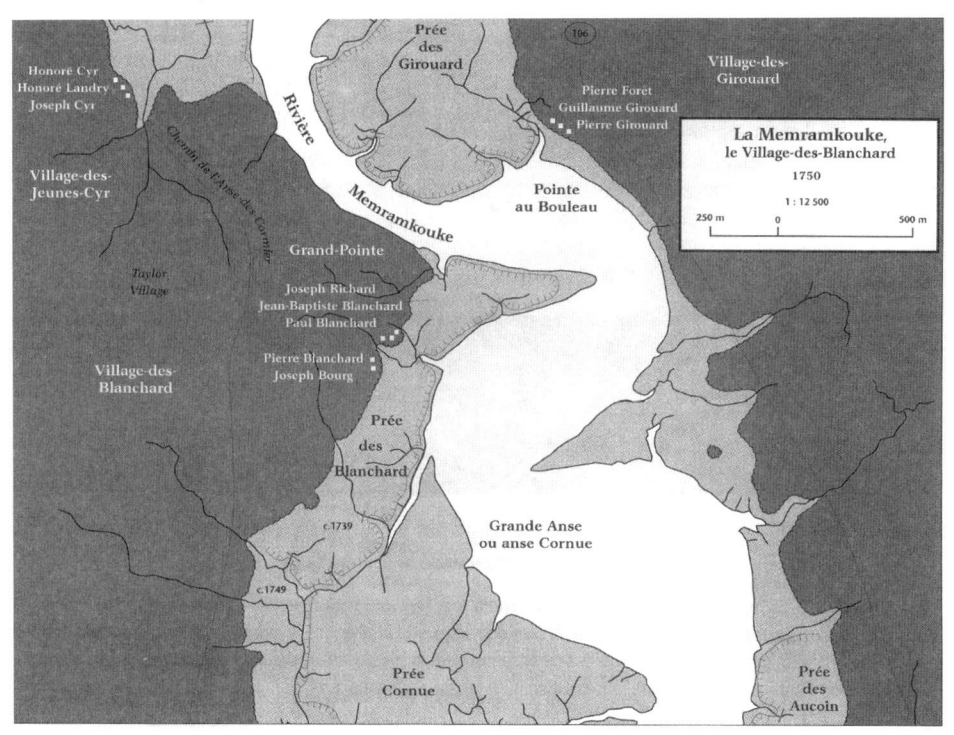

Memramkouke, Blanchard Village,
Courtesy of Paul Surette, *Atlas de l'Establishment des Acadiens aux trois rivières du Chignectou 1660-1755*, p.179.[15]

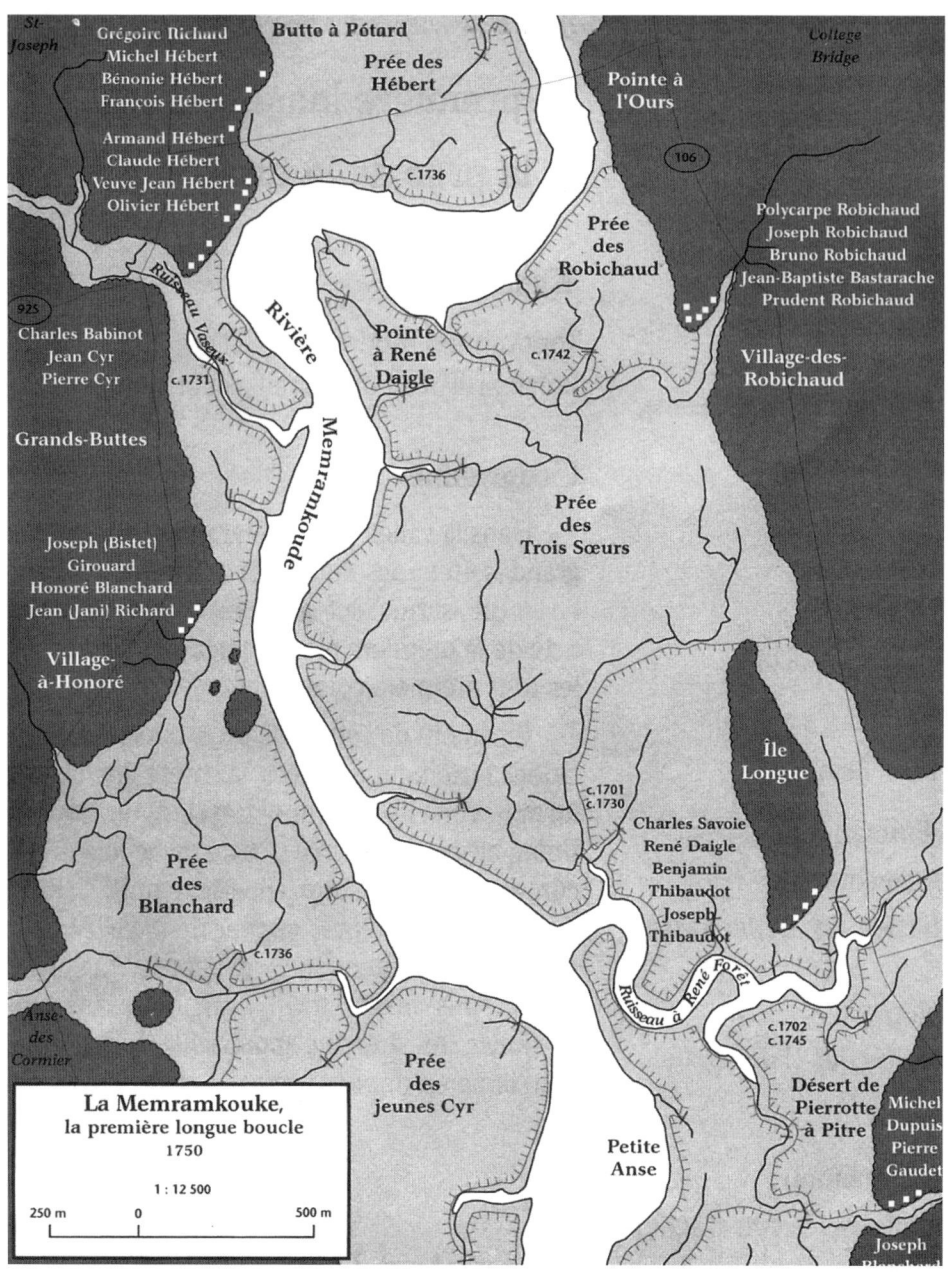

Map of The Memramkouke River area.[16]
Courtesy of Paul Surette, *Atlas de l'Establishment des Acadiens aux trois rivières du Chignectou 1660-1755*, p.190.[17]

Also, the oldest sons of the Forêt daughters, cousins of Marie-Josèphe, took over the upstream area. The only remaining lands were downstream at the far end of the marsh area at Pointe au Bouleau. It is here the Girouard cousins built their homes. They began to enclose the end of the pré (marsh) up to the area, which marks the boundaries of the former portion of desert of Mésagouèhe.

In February of 1743, at Port Royal, Abbé DesEnclaves married Pierre Girouard and Marie-Josèphe Forest [AMC-Block C-4m1]. In the course of the following year, this couple moved to Memramkouke near their cousin. Guillaume, who was living alone at the time in his home. The same Abbé DesEnclaves married Guillaume and Anne Blanc. *Subchart 208 linking to [AMC Block J-3a] in the Québec Acadian book.*

In the meantime, two brothers of the couple, Pierre Girouard and Marie-Jos. Forêt, rejoined them at Point au Bouleau. The oldest brother of Marie-Josèphe Forêt courted Elizabeth LeBlanc, daughter of Jean-Simon à Pierre and allied to the Blanchards. He built a home in Memramkouke near one of his sisters.

This war ended in 1748 and during the following years several new colonists moved their families here. Pierre (Placide) Gaudet, Michel Dupuis and Joseph Blanchard all established nearby, at Désert de Mésagouèche. Honoré Lanoue, and Claude Benoit married to Anne Hélène Girouard [AMC Block H-4m1] a sister of Pierre Girouard, rejoined their respective brothers at Grande Iles of the Grand-Pré near the Ruisseau de Port Royal (Port Royal Brook).

In June, 1748, the Abbé DesEnclaves married Pierre Forêt and Isabelle LeBlanc and the couple established at Point au Bouleau. During this time, a younger brother of Pierre Girouard, Jean-Baptiste Girouard [AMC Block F-4m1], was engaged and planned to settle at Memramkouke. *[The Tracadie chapter, Nova Scotia and Prince Edward Island book refers to Placide Gaudet's speech in Ottawa regarding this Jean-Baptiste Girouard of my direct line. —B.G.]*

The peace did not last long, because in 1749 the English founded a colony near the Chébouctou Harbour, which they named Halifax. In November, 80 French soldiers occupied Chignectou in order to provide a defence in this region. Shortly after, the Abbé Leloutre and his Indian friends joined them. Having a priest to look after things and a place to worship not only assured that the religion would be practised, but also provided a control point. They increased their numbers. In 1752, the young priest, Abbé Breton François LeGuerre, was assigned to the colonists at Trois Rivière and at Tintamarre. Toward 1753, they chose Pointe au Bouleau for their first place of worship at Memramkouke. So the colonists in Memramkouke, among them the Girouards, erected a simple chapel made from freshly cut green forest wood, on the Point of Bouleau near Village-des-Girouards.[87]

The Village of the Blanchards was located in the upstream section of la Pré Cornue, to the left and at the foot of the higher land of Grand-Pointe. One of the sons of Jacques Girouard, François, who was then the widower of one of the daughters of Germain Bourgeois, remarried the widow of Joseph Forêt, oldest son of one of the three sisters and René Forêt. At this time the second of the three sons of Antoine à Guillaume Blanchard, Honoré Blanchard became engaged to a niece of François Girouard, (Marie-Josephe à Charles Girouard) and along with two of his future brothers-in-law, Charles and Joseph Girouard, came to further develop the land at Petit Anse, just upriver from Grand-Pointe *(see maps on pages 233 and 234)*. He married Marie-Josephe Girouard in 1739. *[Refer to the Louisiana book, subchart 211 or appendix 5, linking to [AMC Block C-3b] showing these relationships and other family links.]*

During this same year, the oldest brother of Honoré Blanchard, Jean-Baptiste Blanchard, began courting another niece of François Girouard, Marguerite à Guillaume Girouard, while her sister, Anne Girouard, was engaged to Joseph à

efer to Block T208 4 of subchart 208] of the
nking to [AMC Block J-3A.]. Both Girouard
Girouard [AMC Block J-3A]. Following Honoré,
Blanchard the youngest and Paul, who was still
 Richard, came to work at Grand-Pointe. They
aboiteaux at this upriver end of Pré Cornue.
cousins of the Blanchards and the Girouards estab-
area. Anne Blanchard, sister of Pierre, began seeing
ouard. *Refer to [Block P208-4 of subchart 208] in Québec
ck J-3a]*. This couple, and Anne's cousin Pierre Girouard
à r.   egan to establish on the opposite side of the river, at Point
au Boule.   *[AMC Block C4-m1] and corresponding block genealogy in
the Québec v..   )*.

At La Petite Anse: Village of Honoré Blanchard[88]
(Refer to subchart 211 of the Louisiana volume and the appendix linking to [AMC Block C-3b] and to Paul Surette's overview map presented earlier).

The Blanchards and several family associates and relatives, the Gaudets, the Girouards, the Dupuis and the LeBlancs, established at la Petite Anse (Little Bay), on the Memramcook River.

Before they completed their work, the husband of one of the three Dugas sisters, Jean à Emanuel Hébert, with the help of his son-in-law, Jean Jacques Cyr, took over the site at the foot of the Grands-Buttes and established there around 1734. The Blanchards protested but did nothing for the moment.

At this time, Honoré, second son of Antoine à Guillaume Blanchard, and Marie-Josèphe Girouard à Charles, brother of François Girouard were engaged. *(Refer to subchart 211 of the Louisiana book and the appendix 5 linking to [AMC Block C-3b])*. The Blanchard clan made a plan to get back their land by occupying the other work locations as soon as possible, by continuing to denounce the theft of their land, even bringing their grievances to HM Council at Port Royal, and finally in a more subtle way, by talking to the other two Dugas sisters.

These strategies determined the future for Honoré Blanchard. His fiancée's uncle, the widower François Girouard, married the widow of the oldest son, Joseph Forêt (à René Forêt, the founder), and she reclaimed the property rights at Memramkouke. Shortly after, his fiancée's oldest brother, Charles Girouard à Charles, became engaged to Madeleine, daughter of Agnes Dugas and Michel Thibeaudot. *(Refer to subchart 211 in the Louisiana book or appenix 5, linking to [AMC Block C-3b])*. Charles Girouard à Charles, and Honoré Blanchard then came to Memramkouke to resume work on the land, beginning at the north of Petite Anse, downstream from the Grands-Buttes where the Héberts and the Cyr brothers established. Immediately following, his oldest brother, Jean-Baptiste, began to court a cousin of Honoré's fiancée, and he too came to the north entry of the Grande Anse to continue on the south flank of the Grande-Pointe.

In January 1739, Honoré and Marie-Josephe Girouard à Charles were married by Abbé Poncy. *(Refer to subchart 211 of the Louisiana book, linking to [AMC Block C-3b])*. Her brother Charles was witness. The couple, at this moment, were

Port Royal and old Acadie

staying in Port Royal. Four months later, at the beginning of May, Charles Girouard married Madeleine Thibaudot. In July the whole clan of Blanchards presented a grievance against the Hébert and Cyr families.

Another brother of Marie-Josephe Girouard, Joseph Girouard *dit* Bistet *(See [R211-4m1 of subchart 211 in the Louisiana book or appendix 5 linking to [AMC Block C-3b])* arrived at Memramkouke to help his brother Charles and his brother-in-law, Honoré Blanchard. Around 1740 he began to court a girl from Beaubassin, Anne à François Doucet of Pont-à-Buhot in Upper Mesagouèche. Joseph Bistet

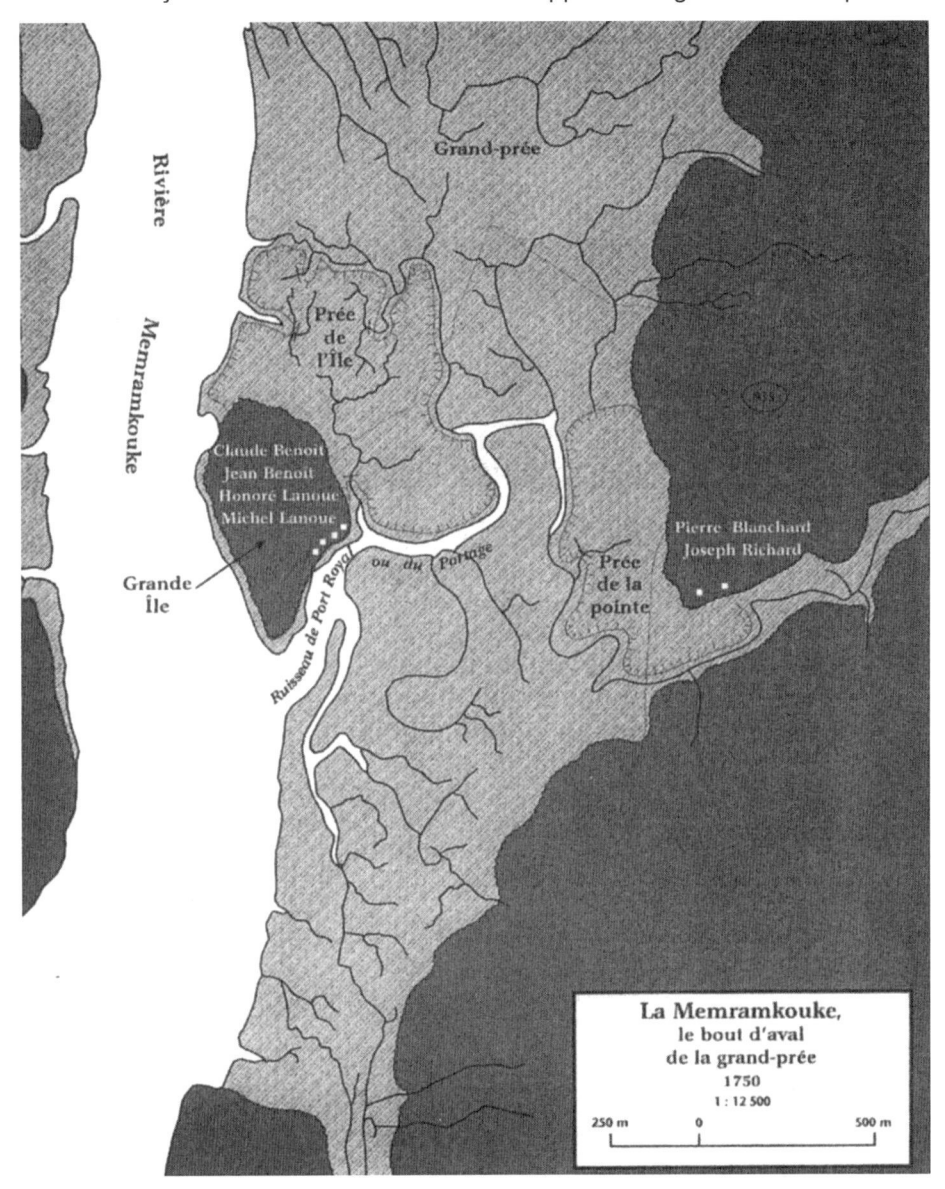

La Memramkouke–le bout d'aval de la Grand-pré (the downstream end of Grand Pré).

Courtesy of Paul Surette, Atlas de l'Establishment des Acadiens aux trois rivières du Chignectou 1660-1755, p.211.[18]

and Honoré Blanchard moved permanently to Petite Anse, around 1742, while the two Girouard cousins of Honoré's wife, Pierre à François Girouard and Guillaume à Guillaume Girouard, were preparing a place on the opposite side of the river, downstream at place called Pointe au Bouleau.

In July 1743, in the Notre-Dame-de-l'Assomption church of Mesagouèche, Father Laboret married Joseph Bistet Girouard à Charles and Anne Doucet. *(Refer to Subchart 211 of the Louisiana volume linking to [AMC Block C-3b])*. While this was all occurring, Françoise à Guillaume Girouard married Jean-Baptiste Richard *dit* Jani (à Michel Richard *dit* Beaupré). *(Refer to subchart 208 of the Québec volume linking to [AMC Block J-3a])*. Jani built a home near Honoré and Bistet Girouard and celebrated his wedding in 1745.

Between these colonists and rivals Hébert and Cyr, henceforth neighbours from upstream to downstream, the relationships stayed tenuous but improved. Toward 1746, one of the daughters of Jani Richard, Madeleine, and one of the sons of Jean Hébert, were engaged. Soon after, the father Hébert died. Time healed the wounds.

The hamlet founded by Honoré grew. His wife, Marie-Josèphe Girouard, who already had one son when she first arrived, gave birth to two more sons, and two daughters. Anne Doucet, wife of Joseph Bistet Girouard, gave birth to a daughter, Anne, in 1748. Françoise (Girouard), wife of Jani Richard, gave birth to a son, Anselme, and then two daughters.

Relatives established in the village and surrounding area. Toward 1744, a sister of one of the cousins of Jani established on the opposite side of the river at Pointe à l'Ours; around 1748, the youngest brother, Joseph, established among the Héberts of Grands-Buttes. Finally, around 1750 one of the younger brothers of Joseph Bistet à Charles, Basile Girouard was a refugee at Memramkouke near his brother. He courted at Vechcaquechiche, the youngest sister of his sister-law, Anne, known as Marie-Josephe, à François Doucet, who he married in 1753. *(Refer to subchart 211 linking back to [AMC-Block C-3b])*.

At La Pré des Trois sœurs

[*The reader should refer to the previous map of "La première longue boucle" (the first long bend in the river), and to the preceding base map of Memramkouke River in full view]. A little further north on the Memramkouke River, just above Village des Girouards, we have the Pré des Trois Soeurs (Meadow of the Three Sisters). (One of the Thibodeau sisters is shown in [Block P202-4 of subchart 202] linking to [AMC Block D-2], the family of Michel Girouard à Germain II à Germain [AMC Block D-2]; also see subchart 202, Louisiana volume or appendix where you will find Michel and his wife Marie Thibodeau of the fourth generation of Girouards).*

Le Bout d'Aval la Grande Ile, et la Pointe d'entrée de la Valée du Portage [89] (Downstream end of Big Island and the entry point of Portage Valley)

In February of 1745 Abbé Des EnClaves married Honoré Lanoue and Agnès Belliveau and exactly one year later he married Claude Benoit and Anne-Hélène Girouard à François and Marie Guilbauld [AMC Block I-4M1] of the fourth generation of Girouards. These couples were living in Port Royal and whenever their husbands found the time and the occasion, they would come to improve their future homesteads at Memramkouke. They signed the peace in October 1748, and the following spring, Honoré Lanoue, Claude Benoit, Pierre Gaudet, Michel Dupuis and Joseph Blanchard moved all of their young families to Memramkouke.

The peace and calm did not last long. In November of 1749, following the plans and the orders of the last governor of Canada, Pierre de la Corne and 80 French soldiers set up camp at Gédaïque to organize a defence for the Chignectou area. The following spring, a series of forts were built along the border that they established (i.e. the Mésagouèche River) at which time they demanded the assistance of the inhabitants. They erected a small fort on la Pointe Rocheuse (Rocky Point), across from Grande Isle.

At the same time, the English set up at the foot of Beaubassin. The French soldiers returned in September and erected a fort on the ruins at Mésagouèche. Then, to force the Acadians who were living on the south side of the river to move to the French side on the north of the Mésagouèche River, the French soldiers and the Indians burned all their villages. . . .

As we can see, Paul Surette's research has greatly enriched the story of the fourth generation of Girouards in the Memramcook area, coming from Port Royal and other parts of Acadie and he does the same for a number of other Acadian families who might be interested in knowing more about their family roots and routes.

WHY DID THE ACADIANS MOVE BEFORE THE DEPORTATION?
Generally speaking, with the English takeover (1654-1670), the Acadians moved further up the Annapolis River for better protection from raids etc. as witnessed by Nicholas Denys at this period. Denys observes that "Since the English have become masters of the country, the inhabitants who had homes close to the fort have, for the most part, abandoned their lodgings and have settled up the river. [90]

This is entirely understandable, considering that another very productive and large marshland, Grand Pré, was not that far away by land. In fact, one could travel upriver by boat to a place now called Paradise at the east end of the Annapolis River and Grand Pré was not far from this point by land.

However, for those Girouards and other Acadians who moved further north of Port Royal to Beaubassin, near the border of today's province of New Brunswick, the situation must have been quite different.

Sea travel would have been the only practical means of travelling and transporting household goods and belongings to Beaubassin, even though some may have taken the long land route. Some of François' grandsons are recorded as sea captains during these early times, so it seems logical that they probably used their vessels to help their relatives to move to Beaubassin.

I firmly believe there is another reason explaining why and how the Girouards moved north. It must be remembered that Germain Girouard married Marie Bourgeois, the daughter of the surgeon, Jacques Bourgeois, who was the chief developer and Seigneur (landowner) of Beaubassin. He would have had access to large ves-

Année 1727

Noms des Batimens	Jauge des batim.	Noms des Capitaines	Lieux de leur Destination
Le Batteau la Suzanne de Québec	20	M⁺ Pierre le Gardeur	Isle Royale
Le navire la Louise de Québec	100	Jean Thibault	Isle Royale
Le Batteau le S¹ Louis de Québec	60	Jean Peillon	Isle Royale
Le Batteau le S¹ Pierre de Québec	90	Louis Hubert de la Croix	Isle Royale
Le Batteau le S¹ Jean de Québec	70	Jacques Badault	Isle Royale
Le B⁺ le Joseph françois de Québec	80	Charles de l'Age	La B...
Le Batteau le S¹ Pierre de l'Isle	30	Charles D'auteuil	Isle Royale
La Goëlette le Dragon Vert de Québec	60	Pierre D'auteuil	Isle Royale
Le Batteau la Concorde de Québec	60	Vigoureux	Isle Royale
La Goëlette la Louise de l'Isle Royale	60	Charles de la Tour	Isle Royale
Le Brigantin le Surprenant de Québec	100	André Galien	I.R. et M. ...
Le Batteau la Concorde de Québec	80	François Pinard	Isle Royale
Le B... le p... ... de l'Isle R¹	50	François Chevalier	Isle Royale
Le Batteau l'Efrouté de l'Isle Royale	60	Pierre Grouard	Isle Royale
Le Brigantin la Veuve du Sage de S¹ Malo	40	Deslauriers le Turp	Isle Royale
Le navire l'Esperance de la Rochelle	130	Claude Habot	S¹ Domingue
Le navire la Patience de Québec	150	Girard Fitzmaurice	I.R. et la Martinique
Le Brigantin la Madeleine de Québec	100	Jacques Grenou	S¹ Domingue

Année 1728

pendant l'année mil sept...

Noms des Batimens	Jauge des batim.	Noms des Capitaines	Lieux de leur Destination
Le Batteau l'Efrouté	50	Pierre Grouard	Isle Royale
Le Batteau le S¹ Antoine	40	Charles la Tour	Isle Royale
Le Batteau le Dauphin	30	Jean la Farque	Isle Royale
La Goëlette La Suzanne	90	Philippe le Gardeur	Isle Royale
Le Batteau l'Efrouté	50	Pierre Grouard	Isle Royale
Le Batteau le S¹ Michel	40	Jacques Pinan Dubré	Isle Royale
Le Batteau le Dauphin	30	Jean la Farque	Isle Royale
Le navire le Jean Caterine	60	Jean Paradis	S¹ Domingue
La Goëlette la Marianne	65	Charles Cheron	...

242

Port Royal and old Acadie

sels to transport supplies, materials, people and animals, from Port Royal to establish the new settlement at Beaubassin. He would have also helped the Girouards/Giroir(e)s obtain land and settle in the new colony. In addition, the Girouard captains would be first to hear of rumours of the British takeover and rising hostility of the English and therefore would have had the advantage of early warning signs, and encouraged his extended family and other compatriots to move further north, away from the English.

Frances Girroir Laboe, [Block R8-9 of subchart 8], of Houston, Texas, the daughter of Senator Edwin Lavin Girroir of Tracadie, quotes oral tradition, passed on to her by her Aunt Rose:

Rose sat down and told all she knew regarding one connection:
"A very prosperous family of Girouards lived near Port Royal—the father was one of the leaders who was treating with the British—after the discussions and the appearance of ships in the area he said, 'There is going to be serious trouble.'

"The family packed what they could carry and set off into the woods. They

Above: Mi'kmaq giving directions to Girouard family. Artist: Margaretha van Gurp.

Opposite: Ships, tonnage, Girouard captains and their destinations-census 1727

found a stream where they could fish, and stayed. They feared the Indians who came by times, but gave them small gifts and were never harmed." Aunt Bessie wrote me: "Girouards [meaning her direct line Girouards / Girroirs—BG] are not from New Brunswick [Beaubassin], but from Port Royal, or near."[91]

To account for the further movement of the Girouard families, I quote from genealogist P. G. Roy:

An official census, made in 1752 and therefore three years before the first phase of the deportation of the Acadians, reveals that 15 Girouard families had taken refuge in the villages of Pointe-de-Beauséjour. [near Beaubassin, named Amherst today].[92]

So the early warning signs referenced in both oral tradition as presented in Frances Laboe's stories and written documents confirming the existence of Girouard captains of ships, seem to give the background and the how and whys for the movement of the 15 Girouard families to Memramcook, three years before the Deportation. Of course, there is also the obvious, basic reason–some of them were unwilling to take the oath of allegiance in order to stay in their country. Fearing reprisals, they began to move north away from the English territory.

According to Placide Gaudet[93], we also find many Girouard families moving north to Memramcook and surrounding area. These families and other Girouard families were also living at one time in La Butte, Tintamarre, (known as Sackville, NB, today), Cobequid (Truro), and Grand Pré area, Pisiguit (Windsor), just prior to the Deportation. *(Refer to preceding census documents and photos presented earlier in the Beaubassin, Tintamarre area.)* Bona Arsenault recorded many families in each of these areas. However, this was not far enough north for their protection from the wrath of the English soldiers, as we shall see.

Thus we see that many of the Girouards had moved out of Nova Scotia before the time of the Deportation—some by ship or small vessel, some by wilderness paths. Not all were successful escaping deportation and imprisonment, as we shall see in more detail in the next section.

The Acadian Neutrality Position and the Oath Of Allegiance

The Acadians had to find a strategy to deal with the alternating power struggles between France and England. Most Acadians claimed neutrality in this struggle, for obvious survival reasons, and the fact that they did not want to fight against their mother country, against soldiers from France, nor did they want to give up their Catholic religion. They led relatively peaceful and very productive lives, little affected by the struggles of the two countries. They valued their family relations, their Roman Catholic religion and their strong independence, all of which guided them and gave them the strength to survive throughout all these changes of command and consequent impositions on their lives.

In regard to the neutrality position, which led to the Acadians being prepared to sign only a conditional oath of allegiance, Jean Daigle quotes Jules Léger "Guides to Understanding the Acadian Dispersion," M.A. thesis Canisius College, 1963:

The refusal of the Acadians to swear this unconditional oath could be interpreted as an act of rebellion, punishable by expulsion, as was threatened by Vetch [Commander]. He later changed his mind, reasoning that if the Acadians were driven out of Nova Scotia, they would move to Cape Breton or New France [Canada] and strengthen French positions there.[94]

Daigle continues to say:

In view of this political situation, it was out of the question for Acadians to swear an unconditional oath of loyalty to a European monarch. Because they were morally certain that they were within their rights, they noted the following points, which they considered most important:

1. The Catholic faith of the Acadians must be respected.
2. The English must acknowledge that Acadians live in an Indian area, and that the Indians, who are totally loyal to France, could retaliate against any Acadian accused of having borne arms against France.
3. The Acadians had their own history that the English should take into account.

Léopold Lanctôt[95] summarizes the situation regarding the oath and related problems:

. . . From 1713-1729 the English Governors attempted to make the Acadians take an unconditional oath of allegiance to the King of England, insisting that the oath of allegiance would guarantee their rights. However, needing the Acadians to provide food for their garrison, and to protect them against the Indians, the English would not allow the Acadians to leave to go to French colonies, a violation of the Treaty clause which gave the Acadians the choice to stay or leave, as decreed by Queen Anne of England. The English began to confiscate the fishing boats, which the Acadians had built, to prevent them from leaving. . .

From the first arrival in 1604, until the Treaty of Utrecht, in 1713, the colony of Port Royal and the surrounding area passed back and forth between French and British control seven times. During this time the Acadians continued to build their peaceful society and families, living in harmony with nature around them and making wise use of all their resources. But the peaceful scene was not to last!

Oath of Allegiance, the English demanding Oath of Allegiance from Acadians, 1730. Artist: Claude Picard, Saint-Bellisle, NB. Series: Deportation of Acadians.
Courtesy of Parks Canada

Across the river is the place called La Montagne named after Julien Montagne, married to Charlotte Girouard, daughter of François Girouard and Jeanne Aucoin. This is the original homestead of François Girouard.

Sketch of the Annapolis River showing the habitation site and later the Port Royal Fort upstream on the opposite side of the river (today called Fort St. Anne in Port Royal, a National historic site; sketch insert): Artist: Margaretha van Gurp

Port Royal and old Acadie

The Deportation
(1755-1763)

Now all was not well in Acadia!

In 1755, the British and French in North America were on the verge of war. Fearing reprisals from both sides and certainly not wanting to fight their own French soldiers, many Acadians again refused to swear an unqualified oath of allegiance, which would force them to take up arms against their own countrymen from France. Consequently, that year, the British authorities in Nova Scotia decided to deport the Acadians, in order to prevent any alliance with the French, and the Deportation began.

Person in charge, reading out the order.

Hear ye hear ye!

"That your Lands & Tenements, Cattle of all kinds and live stock of all sorts are forfeited to the Crown with all your effects saving your money & household goods and your selves to be removed from this Province"

The Deportation Order, 1755, Artist: Claude Picard, Saint-Basile, NB. Series: Deportation of Acadians.

Courtesy of Parks Canada

The homes and settlements were burned in 1755 to discourage any further attempts of the Acadians to return. To Winslow, at Grand Pré, for example, Lawrence wrote:

You must proceed by the most rigorous measures possible, not only in compelling them to embark, but in depriving those who escape of all means of shelter or support by burning their houses and destroying everything that may afford them the means of subsistence in the country.

Many Acadian families were deported, scattered for the most part around various locations on the Atlantic rim. Not all went peacefully. Some families, perhaps hearing early rumours, anticipated the Deportation order, and hid in the woods and/or made their way to French territory in either New Brunswick or Québec, thereby escaping the deportation, as did many of the families of the present Girouard, Girroir, Gerrior descendants in the Maritime provinces and Québec. While some escaped deportation, others were caught on the run as seen in the Memramcook region, previously discussed. Some carried out active resistance to the British like the well known Acadian Joseph Broussard nicknamed Beausoleil, who lived in New Brunswick, on the Peticodiac River.

Ships take Acadians into Exile: Artist: Claude Picard, Saint-Basile, NB Series: Deportation of Acadians.

Courtesy of Parks Canada

Settlements are burned 1755, Artist: Claude Picard Saint-Basile, NB. Series: Deportation of Acadians.

Courtesy of Parks Canada

Acadian Awakenings: An Acadian Family In Exile

Acadian Deportation and Escape, 1755-1785

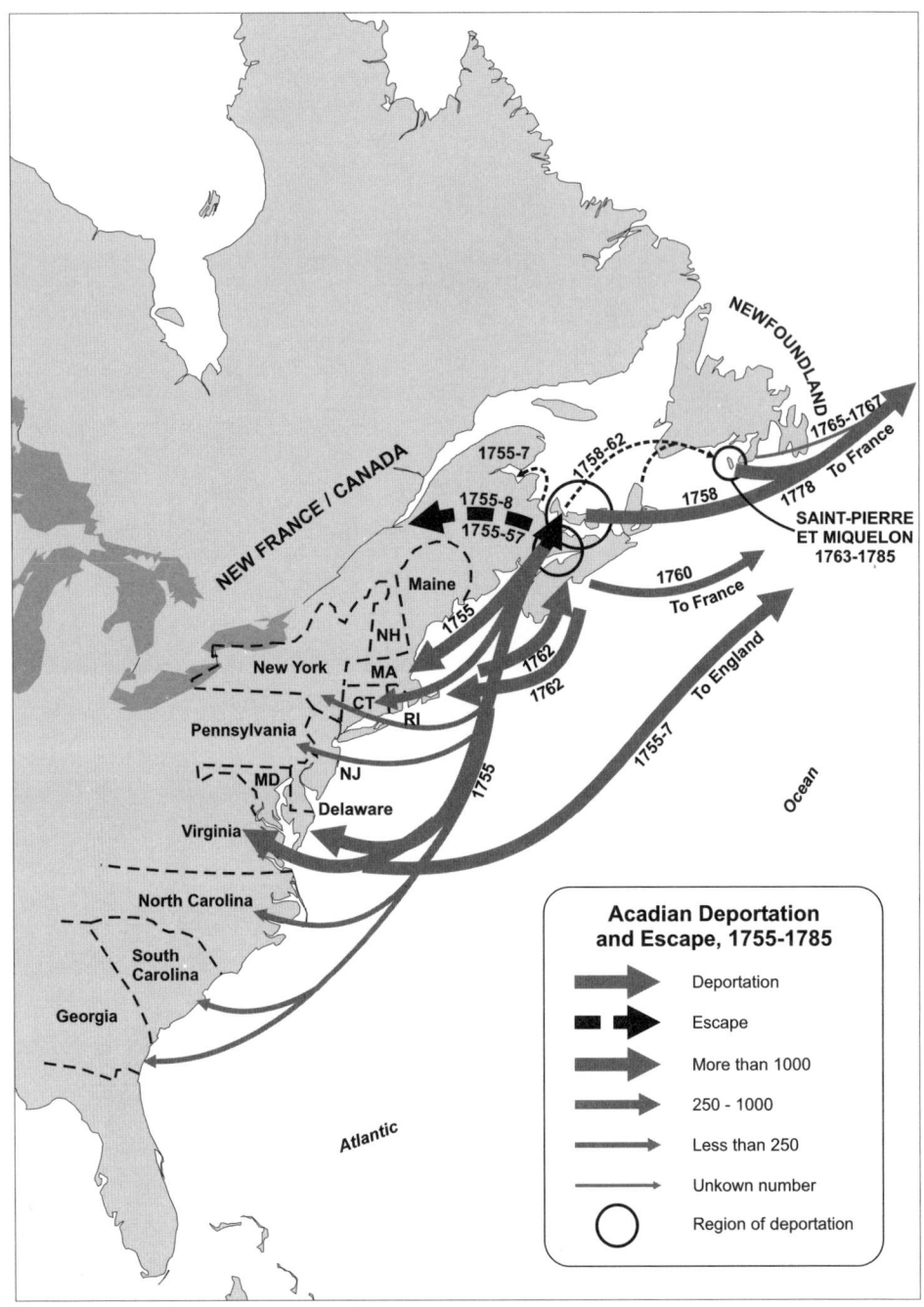

- Deportation
- Escape
- More than 1000
- 250 - 1000
- Less than 250
- Unkown number
- Region of deportation

Deportation from Port Royal

From the exhibition "Acadie, The Odyssey of a People", we learn that the Deportation was carried out by the 250 troops regularly stationed in Nova Scotia, assisted by 2,000 British troops from New England... [96]

Approximately 1,600 Acadians were taken forever from their former region of Port Royal in December, 1755, putting an end to 120 years of Acadian presence. As mentioned earlier the Acadians in the Annapolis Royal area were confined to their homes until the arrival of the transport ships.

Port Royal and old Acadie

Opposite: Map based on the Deportation map appearing in Naomi E. S. Griffiths book, L'Acadie de 1686 à 1784, Contexte d'une histoire, *translation by Kathryn Hamer, Les Editions d'Acadie, 1997-70. Bottom map is MAP Detail from Carte de l'Acadie... 1744*

National Archives NMC –19267

Deportation from Pisiquit
From the Pisiquit area (Windsor, NS) in the fall of 1755, approximately 1000 Acadians were deported.

Deportation from Grand Pré
At Grand Pré (near les Mines) Lieutenant Colonel John Winslow was in charge. He set up his camp near the church at Saint-Charles. On September 5, 1755 Winslow assembled the men and the boys of the area in the church, and read the Deportation order. Approximately 2,200 Acadians were deported from the Grand Pré area between mid-October and the end of December.

Except for the one below, I am not aware of any map which locates the Acadian families living in Grand Pre, in the same detail as those we have for Port Royal. However the following map, which can be found in Brenda Dunn's book, *The Acadians of Minas*,[97] is helpful in seeing the location of various Acadian areas during this period.

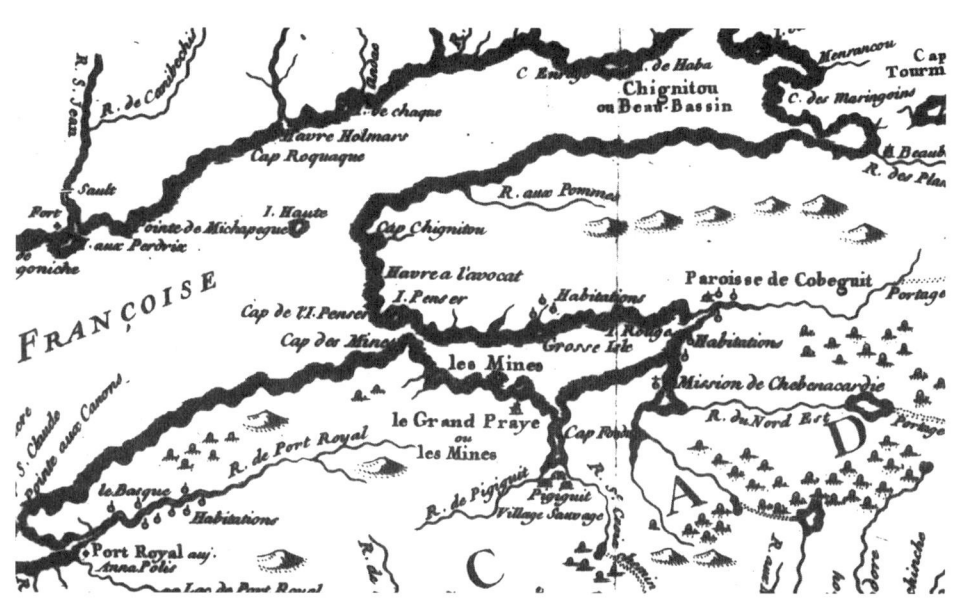

Brenda Dunn explains that in 1707, the date of the last known census during the French period, the Minas Basin population had reached 660 in approximately 105 families. She points out that Minas was usually referred to the Minas Basin area, although sometimes it was used interchangeably with Grand Pré.

Deportation from Cape Sable
Acadians at Cap-Sable were taken prisoner during raids in 1756, 1758, and 1759. They were deported to Boston and France.

Deportation from Fort Beauséjour

In Paul Surette's *Atlas de l'Établissment des Acadiens aux trois rivières du Chignectou 1660-1755*, one finds an excellent, detailed account of a number of the Girouard families during this period, with both text and map visuals. Many other families in the Memramcook and Peticodiac regions are presented with equal detail. I have translated a number of excerpts on the Girouard families, with the assistance of Paul Girouard, Vice-President of our Nova Scotia Girouard/Girroir/Gerrior family organization. Where appropriate I have inserted genealogical links using square brackets. All of these communities or villages on the Memramcook River were under the protection of the French at Fort Beauséjour, which also explains why many Acadians established here, either permanently, or temporarily on their way further northward.

Deportation from the Memramkouke River region

In 1755, British forces came in great numbers, capturing Fort Beauséjour, and renaming it Fort Cumberland. In August, a trap was set, in which they captured, by trickery, two-thirds of the Acadian men of the area, *[including Bistet Girouard of Petite Anse, and without a doubt his brother, Basile]*, after which they summoned the women and children to join their husbands at the fort. Most of the women and children in Trois Rivières refused to obey. The British Commander Monckton sent Frye and 200 soldiers in this region to destroy everything in the colony.

Shortly after noon on September 2, 1755, the largest of the three vessels of the expedition, appeared at the mouth of Memramkouke River, and the military began also to

Lay Waste, Artist: Nelson Surette, Yarmouth, N.S.

Port Royal and old Acadie

burn the villages. Arriving at Pointe au Bouleau, they set fire to four houses *[obviously the Girouards and the Forêt homes]*, and they also set fire to the little wooden chapel which did not burn very well, because of the wet green wood from which it had been so recently constructed.

Paul Surette gives more information regarding the burning of homes:

. . . It was during the completion of this nasty work that British troops were ambushed by the French, and the noise of gunfire during this ambush created a diversion, distracting the other English troops; thus Memramkouke was saved from destruction.

Another detachment destroyed the hamlet of the Blanchards at the foot of the high grounds of Grand-Pointe. Of the Girouard inhabitants of the area, we see that Jean-Baptiste Blanchard (à Antoine) and Marguerite Girouard are later found at Deschambault and Repentigny, PQ. Sons of Paul Blanchard (à Antoine) are found at Saint-Jacques de Cabahannocer, La. Anne Girouard and Joseph Richard are later recorded in St-Servan, France. Pierre à François was a refugee in Québec, Deschambault and L'Assomption. *[Refer to subchart [AMC Block C-4m1], of the Québec Acadian book and related block genealogy information for descendants of this branch].* Guillaume à Guillaume was later recorded in Sainte-Croix de Lotbinière. *See [AMC Block J-3a] and subchart [Block P208-4 of subchart 208] and related genealogy block information in the Québec Acadian book.*

Soldiers burned the four homes in Pré des Trois Soeurs, three of which were inhabited. They then walked back to Barnabé Cove and set fire to everything. Later the disaster-stricken Acadian victims, one of whom appears to be Michel à Germain Girouard, took refuge in the woods in upper Petitcoudiac area where they erected a crude chapel and began a very strong resistance against the enemy. *[It was in this chapel that Father LaBrosse married Marie Girouard à Michel à Germain to Michel Comeau in March 1756].*

During these weeks, some of the Acadian prisoners, for the most part from the Trois Rivières region, dug a tunnel at the south end of the fort. During a hurricane on the night of September 30, 86 Acadians escaped. Bistet Girouard was among them.

A week and a half later, the English military deported 1,100 Acadians from Chignectou, to South Carolina and Georgia. About 300 Acadians had participated in the defence of Fort Beauséjour, and although they contended that they had been forced to fight, British authorities considered them traitors and ordered that they be deported to American colonies furthest away from Nova Scotia. It was from Fort Cumberland that the Deportation was ordered. . . .

Note following prisoner list[98]:

This list of 374 names was sent to the Duc de Niverois with a pathetic appeal to help them get away. Most of these people had moved from Acadia before the exile and were captured on the Memramkouke and Petitcodiac Rivers. Others were from Cocagne and Miramichi. The English authorities considered them prisoners of war and refused to allow them to leave. The next year they were offered land but most of them left clandestinely and reached the Islands of St. Pierre and Miquelon. From there a few went to France, but for the most part went to St. Domingue and then to Louisiana.

Fort Beauséjour collage: photo #1 outside of building: photo#2 grounds inside the fort.

Life at Fort Beauséjour Fort Beauséjour: Artist: Lewis Parker.

Courtesy of Parks Canada.

Fort Beauséjour was the last stronghold of the French which fell to the British in 1755. The painting shows a variety of everyday activities at the fort, one year before its capture.

Between 1758 and 1761, Acadians living along the Saint John, Petitcodiac, Memramkouke, Restigouche and Miramichi rivers, and those coming from Au Lac, La Butte, Tintamarre and Beaubassin were brought to Fort Cumberland as prisoners, as part of the Deportation plan. Here they were held, awaiting more ships to remove them, and were joined as prisoners by other Acadians who had hidden in the woods and/or run northward after the siege in 1755, but were later captured.

[Many of the Girouard families were in these areas. Jean Girouard, my direct ancestor and his family who were living in Memramkouke, appear on the prisoner list of 1763. Some were captured in raids while others surrendered. Some escaped and took refuge in surrounding areas in what is now the province of New Brunswick.

Many Girouards and other Acadians had continued up to Québec (see Québec book), staying temporarily in the Fort Beauséjour area but others were not so fortunate and were captured and held prisoner there.

The list of prisoners at Fort Beauséjour includes my great-great-great-great-great-grandfather Jean-Baptiste Girouard [AMC Block F-4m1] and his family. This would also be the direct ancestor of all the Antigonish County Gerrior/Gerroir/Girroir families, as well as the Guysborough County Gerriors.

I am sure that Jean-Baptiste and family listed here are my direct ancestors and the direct ancestor of all Gerriors in Antigonish and Guysborough because the names on the list are identified in an 1860 interview, conducted by the French historian, Edmé Rameau de St-Père with Captain Joseph Giroire of Tracadie, grandson of Jean-Baptiste Girouard and son of Joseph [AMC Block E-5]. In this interview Joseph states full well that he recognizes his Uncle François and other family members in the prisoner lists. He also confirms that his family came from Port Royal, evading the English, as refugees, according to the stories told to him by his Uncle François.

This Rameau document, which I have translated (see Tracadie Guysborough chapter of the Nova Scotia/Prince Edward Island volume, is a rare and precious document for the Gerrior families of Antigonish and Guysborough counties. It was published in the 32nd notebook of the Société Historique Acadienne, under the title of Notes de Voyage en L'Acadie en 1860, Tracadie, by Rameau de Saint-Père, France.[99] In addition to the above support of this claim, my genealogical research on Jean-Baptiste Girouard's family matches up, with reference to the same names which appear on the prisoner list. Anastasia [AMC Block G-5] of this family does not appear on the list, as she was born later, at Halifax in 1770.— B.G.]

One Girouard descendant, Pierre Cormier. (the great-grandson of Madeleine Girouard [AMC Block C-2] and Thomas Cormier) appears on the prisoner list. He was not in prison for long. According to a story related to me, in correspondence with Pierre's direct descendant, Rose Seeley, Fox Creek, NB, Pierre had other plans.

Pierre Cormier III, grandson of Madeleine Girouard and Thomas Cormier [AMC Block C-2], was born at Rivière Hébert in 1734 married Anne Gaudet at Tintamarre (Sackville) in 1755, who was a daughter of the pioneer from the valley of Memramkouke, taken prisoner in 1755.

LIST OF THE ACADIAN PRISONERS AT FORT BEAUSEJOUR ON AUGUST 24, 1763.
Ref: LEBLANC, Dudley J., "THE ACADIAN MIRACLE"

Jean Babinot	Joseph Gaudet	Louis Gaudet	Pierre Sire	Pierre Melanson	Jean Baptiste Gaudet
Paul Babinot	Magdelaine Gaudet	Marie Gaudet	Anne Sire	Marie Melanson	Anne Gaudet
Silvain Babinot	Joseph Gaudet	Marie		Marie	Marie Joseph
Marguerite	Magdelaine	Magdelaine	Joseph Richard	Jean	Joseph
Domingue	Jean	Jean	Anne Richard	Joseph	Anne
Jean	Blanche	Pontif	Melenne Richard		Magdelaine
Marie	Pierre		Rozalie	Pierre Richard	Nastazie
Jean Baptiste	Pierre Gaudet	Jean Nuirat	Marie	Magdelaine Richard	
Marguerite	Anne Gaudet	Francoise Nuirat	Joseph	Anne	Etienne le Blanc
Charles	Pierre Gaudet	David	Germain	Baptiste	Ysabelle le Blanc
	Marguerite			Jean	Simon
Joseph Suret	Modeste	Joseph Prejant	Michel Sire	Francois	Etienne
Ysabelle Suret	Marie	Marie Prejant	Magdelaine Sire	Michel	Mathurin
	Marie	Agathe Prejant	Genevieve Sire	Marguerite	Joseph
Pierre Paul Douaron			Michel	Bazile	Anne
Marguerite Douaron	Paul Gaudet	Charles Gaudet	Vincent		Marguerite
Marie Douaron	Marie Gaudet	Marguerite Gaudet		Joseph Richard	Magdelaine
Magdelaine	Joseph Gaudet	Felix Gaudet	Jean Girouard - F4M1	Marie	
Pierre Douaron	Pierre	Rosalie	Magdelaine Girouard- F4M1	Marguerite	Amant Lanour
Marguerite Douaron		Pierre	Marie Girouard - D-5	Roze	Marie Lanour
Jacques Douaron	Marguerite Gaudet	Marie	Francoise - F-5	Joseph	
Charles	Dominque Gaudet	Anne	Joseph - E-5		Pierre Chiasson
	Modeste		Modeste	Jean Gaudet	Ozit Chiasson
Joseph Le Blanc	Theotiste	Pierre Gaudet		Jeanne	Michel
Marie le Blanc	Michel	Magdelaine Gaudet	Michel Bourg	Marie	Joseph
Firmin le Blanc		Marie	Marguerite Bourg	Poncy	
Joseph	Rene Poirier	Pierre	Blanche Bourg		
Marguerite	Anne Poirier	Felicite	Michel		
Blangline	Jean Poirier	Mathurin	Magdelaine		
Jean	Marie	Jean	Marie		
	Noemie		Bleme		
	Alexis		Pierre Bourgeois		
	Pierre				
	Joseph		Paul Gautrot		
	Modeste		Anne Gautrot		
	Victor		Joseph		

Port Royal and old Acadie

Jean Dubois	Joseph Boudrot	Pierre Arsenau	Jean Bro
Marie Dubois	Rozalie Boudrot	Magdelaine Arsenau	Marie Bro
Rozalie Dubois	Joseph	Jean	Lucie
Marguerite	Charles	Bazile	
	Marguerite	Louise	Amand Bujeau
Cyprien Dupuy	Anne		Marie Bujeau
Francoise Dupuy	Amant	Claude Boudrot	Adelaide
Magdelaine Dupuy	Thomas	Judith Boudrot	Jean
Jean		Michel	
	Charles Gautrot	Pierre	Jean Cormier
Paul Landry	Francoise Gautrot	Nastazie	Marie Cormier
Magdelaine Landry			Marie
Modeste	Claude Poirier	Pierre Chiasson	Magdelaine
Jean David	Marguerite	Marie Joseph Chiasson	Francois
	Allain	Joseph	Pierre
Pierre Boudrot	Marguerite	Lucie	Nastazie
Magdelaine Boudrot	Louis		Pierre
Hylaire	Charles	Joseph Hebert	
Jean	Marie	Louise Hebert	Pierre Ouel (Noel)
Joseph	Ester	Marguerite	Anne Ouel
	Magdelaine		Pierre
Pierre Rostegui	Jean	Joseph Bourg	Magdelaine
Marie Rostegui		Anne Bourg	Angelique
Francois	Charles Dugas	Michel	
Anne	Pierre Dugas	Abraham	Pierre Bastarache
Jean	Mazarin	Pierre	Anne Bastarache
Marguerite	Ozitte	Anne	Anne
Marie	Jean	Magdelaine	Joseph
		Marie	Ester
Joseph la Pierre	Pierre Melanson	Jean	Ysidore
Rozalie la Pierre	Felicite Melanson		
Magdelaine	Marguerite	Claude Boudrot	Joseph Gueguen
Marguerite	Pierre	Magdelaine Boudrot	Anne Gueguen
Claire	POSSIBLE DESC. OF ALEXANDER C-3A	Marie	Joseph
Anne	Amant Girouard	Marguerite	Jean
Jean	Marguerite Girouard	Louis Allain	Marie
Joseph	Joseph	Anne Allain	
Charles		Magdelaine	Michel Bastarache
Ysabell	Charles Forest	Marguerite	Marguerite Bastarache
	Marie Forest	Benjamin	Felicite
Pierre Rostegui	Jean	Michel	Marguerite
Isabelle Rostegui	Paul	Marie	Marie Roze
Marguerite	Marguerite	Baptiste	Anne
Joseph	Anne	Joseph	
	Modeste		Charles Melanson
Joseph Quessy	Ursule	Jacques Leger	Anne Melanson
Marie Joseph Quessy		Marie Leger	Jean
Marie	Jean Guedry	Charles	Charles
Magdelaine	Marie	Anne Marie Miron	Pierre
Pierre	Jean	Joseph	Anne
Jean Baptiste	Alexandre		
Joseph		Jean Richard	Cyprien Poirier
Etienne	Michel Hache'	Francoise Richard	Cecile
Nastazie	Magdelaine Hache'	Joseph	Pierre
	Felicite	Anne	

I have included a copy of the prisoner list at Fort Beauséjour. Fort Beauséjour National Historic Park is located in Aulac, New Brunswick, 40 km. south of Moncton.

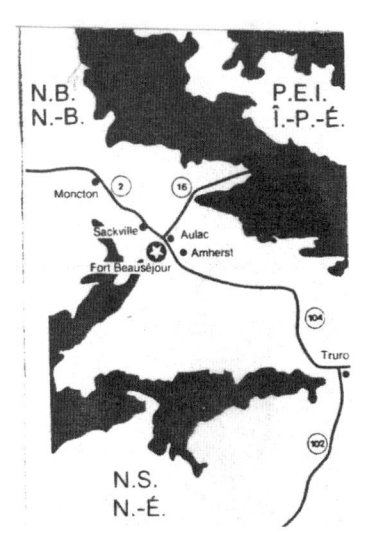

Fort Beauséjour, showing supply rooms which may have been the only protected quarters available at the fort where the Girouard family and other Acadian prisoners would have been held as prisoners.

A few months after his wedding, Pierre Cormier III was imprisoned in Fort Beauséjour, which had become an English prison under the name of Fort Cumberland. Tradition claims that he escaped from the prison; dressed as a woman on the eve of the day he was to board the vessel for his deportation to Georgia. The same tradition claims that he joined two of his brothers who fought with the defenders of Québec in 1759. He had apparently reached Québec with his wife by following a route through the Lowlands (Frédéricton and Madawaska). His first child Pierre IV was born somewhere around Frédéricton, in 1756. Three other children were born around L'Islet (PQ) during ensuing years. Pierre and Ann Gaudet returned to the lowlands around 1760.[100]

According to the missionary priest François Le Guerne, life was pure misery for the Acadians from this point on. Detachments of soldiers went through the countryside to take those who had escaped. But many of the Acadians in the

Beaubassin area, Chipoudy (Shepody), Petitcodiac and Memramkouke rivers hid in the woods, following the advice of the Rev. Le Guerne, who describes the situation as follows.

The Acadians from this point on knew nothing but grief and misery at the hands of the English who have destroyed their houses... and have killed hundreds of people. These attacks continued on all Acadian villages until their final deportation in 1755. In the region of Petitcodiac, Memramkouke, they have burned more than 250 houses and the Catholic Church...

In a letter of 1757, Le Guerne describes the situation as follows:

Hidden and fugitive with them in the woods in fear and misery, I have shared with the Acadians who have stayed, the sad destiny to which they have been brought, helping them with advice and anything else within my ministry. 1756-1757 was extremely hard in the region of Miramichi, Shediac, Bouctouche and Cocagne.... At the embarkation we saw the saddest spectacle. There were children who lost track of their parents.

The Acadians who arrived at the Miramichi River to the north along the eastern shore had an even more dreadful time. Le Guerne further recorded in 1757 that a large number of them had perished from hunger and the harsh previous winter, while still more died of a "horrible contagion". They were forced "to eating the leather of their shoes, carrion and some, even the excrement of animals," he wrote.[101] Approximately 600 Acadians of that group died in the winter of 1755-1756, the survivors leaving in small groups for other regions of New Brunswick, eastern Québec and Ile Saint-Jean. Regarding the rest of the Beaubassin Acadians, Le Guerne wrote:

To save about 100 women and their children, whose husbands were put on the ships, I went to them and after consoling and reassuring them the best I could, I advised them to withdraw to the nearest French territory, which was Isle St-Jean (Prince Edward Island). Many young people, some elderly and five or six men who escaped from Beauséjour began to trek through the swampy woods, a distance of 10 leagues (approximately 30 miles or 48km) to the sea. They remained out of sight of the English for a month before arriving at Baie Verte, where they embarked for Ile St-Jean.[102]

It can readily be seen from the location of the birth place, marriage and death of Jeanne Girouard, daughter of Alexander Girouard de Ru, m. François Forest (*see [AMC Block C-3a] block genealogy presented earlier in this chapter*), that this family must have suffered a great deal of stress and misery from the Deportation and migrations, being scattered far and wide in their travels. Léopold Lanctôt, in his book, *Acadian Families*, gives an account of this family in exile which I have translated here. The story is quite long and detailed, giving us a clear idea of how much suffering and hardships our ancestors experienced.

Family of Jeanne Girouard, daughter of Alexandre de Ru, and their deportation from Beaubassin[103]

In June 1755 a fleet of 33 troop transport ships unloaded 2000 men at Fort Lawrence. Fort Beauséjour, on the other side of the river Mésagouèche, was commanded by Louis Dupont de Vergor. He was assisted by Thomas Pichon, a French trader, who informed the English on the movements of the French troops and on the goings and comings of the Acadians as well as their sentiments and intentions. The Acadians, who hated Vergor and Pichon, refused to take up arms against the English, fearing the reprisals of the English against their families. However 300 Acadians were forced by the French soldiers, on pain of death, to defend Fort Beauséjour. Were François de Forest, husband of Jeanne Girouard, and his sons among these 300? Vergor vainly put the lives of the Acadians in danger because, counselled by the traitor Pichon, he gave up at the first sign of resistance from the shooting of the first cannon ball on the fort. The English renamed Fort Beauséjour as Fort Cumberland.

On July 31, 1755, Lawrence signed the order of deportation of all Acadians to the New England colonies, Maryland, Virginia, the Carolinas and Georgia. The order was transmitted in great secrecy to the Commanders at each post.

In 1755, under the pretext of a meeting necessary to inform the Acadians on the Governors' arrangements to conserve their land, the inhabitants of each region of Beaubassin met at Fort Cumberland. Having no idea of the trap being set for them, 400 heads of families from all over Beaubassin obeyed and went to Fort Cumberland for this meeting. François de Forest, husband of Jeanne Girouard must have been among them with his two married sons. They closed the doors of the Fort, declared them as rebels and made them prisoners. They then announced that all their land and their goods were being confiscated and they would be transported to Isle Royal (Cape Breton, NS today), which belonged to France.

They spent the night at the fort under guard and the next day the British announced that they would be transported, not to Isle Royale but to New England colonies, Virginia, Georgia or the Carolinas.

The Cumberland commander, Winslow, ordered his soldiers to seize all cattle, and to gather all the boys over 16, among them, two sons of François, Jean-Baptiste (age 19) and Simon (age 17). All lived as prisoners until September, either at Fort Cumberland or Fort Lawrence, where they transferred some of the Acadians. The women brought food and other necessary things to their husbands and sons.

Toward the middle of September, the British started to load the prisoners from both forts on the ships; the women and the children were next. Before joining her husband, Jeanne Girouard entrusted at least one of her daughters, Rosalie (age 11) to a relative or friend, who succeeded in escaping the English and headed for Québec. Rosalie married in 1761 at Saint-Pierre-du-Sud, PQ before her parents were able to return from exile. Jeanne took with her, all the other younger children: Marie Elizabeth (age 14) Joseph-Armand (age 13), Félicité (age 12), Madeline (age 8), Basile (age 7) and François (age 5). Jeanne (Girouard) de Forest must have been accompanied by her oldest daughter Marguerite (age 25) who went to join her husband, Dominique Robichaud and her daughters-in-law, Nathalie Hébert, wife of Paul and Marie-Josephte, wife of Charles.

On October 13, 1755, the fleet of ten ships carrying 960 Acadians, set sail for Annapolis Royal, taking on more Acadians from this place on ships that were already overcrowded. The crowding and hording together of families in such confined spaces was horrible and frightening. The ships headed for Georgia and South Carolina. In the month of December, 400 Acadians from Beaubassin, disembarked at Savanah, Georgia. Another 1020 coming from Beaubassin and Annapolis Royal disembarked at Charlestown, in South Carolina.

In Georgia they were dispersed in small groups throughout the Province. In the spring of 1756, the Governor permitted them to build their own boats and in the month of March 1756, nearly all of them embarked for South Carolina. Arriving at Charleston, South Carolina they found their relatives and friends who were deported there. Approximately 300 Acadians from South Carolina joined them to continue their voyage northward to Canada. On April 15 the band of Acadians went to sea in hopes to reach River Saint Jean located in what is now New Brunswick, Canada, which was considered French territory, but only a few were successful in doing so. For the most part the boats were stopped either in New York, or Boston or along the Connecticut coastline.

In New York, in 1756 in the counties of Winchester, Richmond, Suffolk, Kings and Queens, 18 heads of families with their wives and children numbering 93 persons arrived from Grand Pré and were distributed. Louis "Giroid" was among them with his family of six. On another official list of Acadians distributed in the counties of Winchester and Orange, there was a total of 332 Acadians distributed as follows: Winchester 141; Orange 81; Richmond 13; Suffolk 44; Queens 44; and Kings 9. Over 55 minors were bound out. From time to time the Acadians arrived at New York from Georgia.

François de Forest with his wife Jeanne Girouard and family, who had been deported to Georgia or South Carolina, made this voyage with his family. They were among those whose boat was stopped on the coast of Connecticut where François was reunited with his brothers Jean-Pierre, Jacques, and Mathieu and his daughter Marguerite, wife of Dominique Robichaud. At least they had all made the voyage together. In 1763 all of these persons asked to be transported to France.

"General List of Acadian Families, dispersed in the Government of Kenehtoket (Connecticut) who desire to go to France:
The family of Jean-Pierre Fouret, seven persons. . . of Jacques Fouret, consisting of ten persons, Mathieu Forest of six persons, of Dominique Robichaud, eight persons, of François Fournos (Forrest), his wife, two children, four persons."

The Government refused permission to transport them to France. Governor Murray authorized the Acadians to come to establish in the territories of his government. François De Forest and his sons, many of whom were already married, decided to join the Amiraults who were preparing to take advantage of this offer. The caravan met and began the long walk in the spring of 1767. In addition to the Amiraults, this caravan was composed of François De Forest and his wife, Jeanne Girouard and her oldest daughter, Marguerite and her husband Dominique Robichaud. Also there were at least three sons of Jeanne Girouard and François de Forest: Jean-Baptist his wife Marie-Josephte Hébert and their son Joseph (age 2); Simon and his wife Rosalie Richard; François, single (age 17). They accomplished the trek from Connecticut to Montréal by foot.

Upon arrival at Montréal they were directed to Saint Pierre-du-Portage (L'Assomption). The family of de Forest appear to be one of the first to arrive at L'Assomption, Aug., 1767. We don't know for sure if Jeanne Girouard arrived with the family because there was no record of her arrival or later death, indicating that she may have died, like many of her

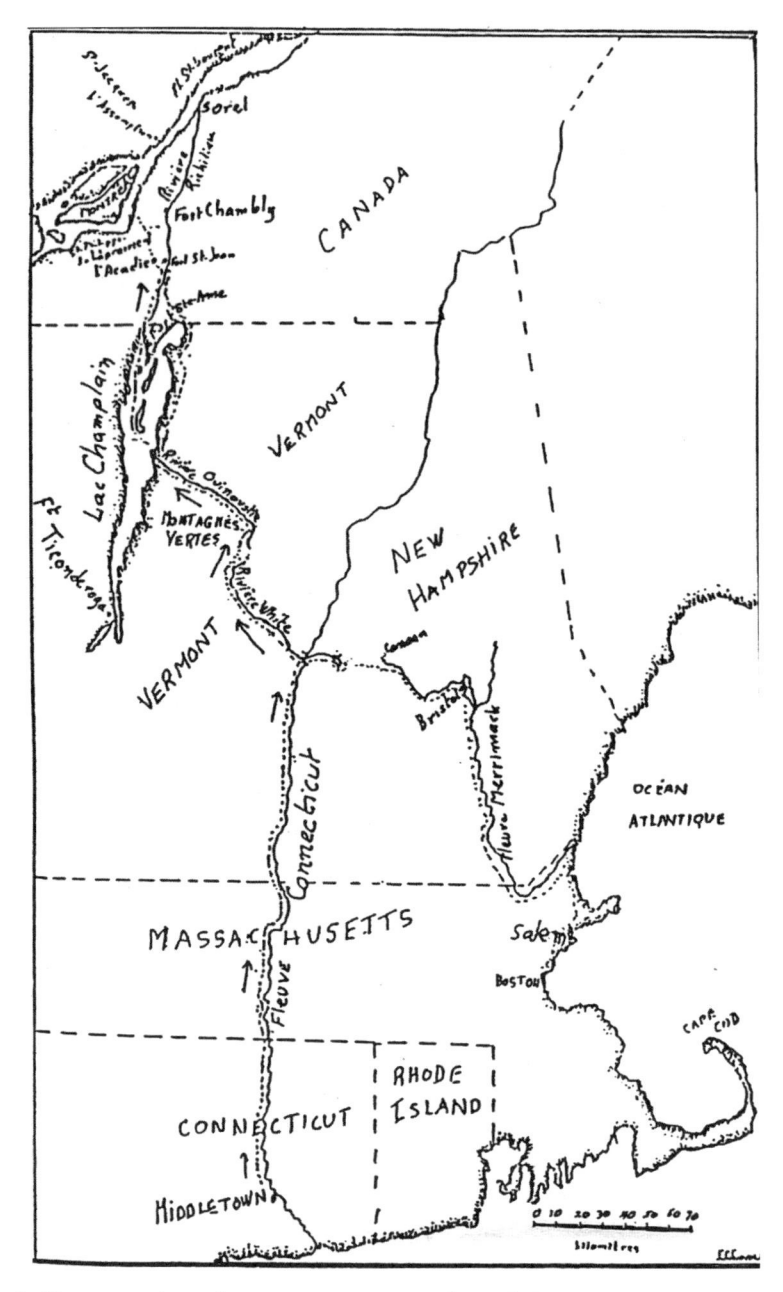

The probable route of Acadians participating in the trek from Connecticut to Montréal, through the woods on foot. Map by Léopold Lantôt. [19]
Courtesy of Léopold Lanctôt, Familles Acadiennes Vol. I, p.27, and Marc Vielleux, Éditions du Libre Exchange.

friends, during the long 800-kilometre trip through the woods. She would have been 58 during this long hike.

François did not arrive with all his children either: His daughter, Felicité, married to Joseph Amirault, arrived in the fall of 1768; his youngest son, Charles did not arrive at Assomption until the end of 1770 or the beginning of 1771; one daughter, Mary Elizabeth married to Marin Gautherot, followed her husband to Deschambault near Québec. Rosalie had been in Saint-Pierre-du-Sud since 1760 or earlier; Joseph-Amand and Basile went to Bécancour, PQ; as for Paul and Madeleine, their whereabouts are unknown.

In 1769, Monsieur L'Abbé Jacques Degeay, Sulpicien, had obtained concessions for the Acadians in the Seigniory of St-Sulpice at Ruisseau Vacher and Ruisseau St-Georges. In addition to the land, the families were also provided with animals, tools, and basic food items to help them work the new land and build homes for their families. The family established in Assomption and, like all other Acadians arriving, were welcomed with open arms and given land.

In 1772, Msgr. Jean Olivier Briand, Bishop of Québec, approved Ruisseau Vacher and Saint-Georges as a new parish which was named Saint-Jacques in honour of Fr. Jacques Degeay who did so much for the Acadians. They gave the Acadians a young parish priest, an Acadian himself, by the name of Fr. Jean Bro (Breault). The first Mass took place below Ruisseau Vacher in the home of Charles de Forest, son of François de Forest and Jeanne Girouard à Alexandre (de Ru) Girouard. They constructed a Church in 1774. François de Forest died in 1777 at St-Jacques, at the age of 75.

In regard to this story, we learn elsewhere in Léopold Lanctot's work[105] that there were other Girouard families involved. Thomas Jeansone, son of Guillaume Jeansone and Isabelle Corporon, who married Marie Josephe Girouard, daughter of Alexandre Girouard and Marie Le Borgne, were hiding in the woods at Port Royal, and were captured by Major John Henfield and his soldiers, in November 1755 and deported on one of the two ships, *Two Sisters* or *L'Edward* to Connecticut, where they were well received and supported as a result of legislation from the government of Conecticut.[106] Later they were part of a group of 666 Acadians who were refused transportation to France, after the peace treaty between France and England, 1763. Marguerite Lort (Lord), daughter of Julien Lort and Charlotte Girouard along with her husband Joseph Amirault were also among those who signed the petition asking to be transported to France. This family group, along with other Acadian families, therefore decided to go to Québec as their alternate choice. However, there were not enough boats available for these 666 Acadians in this group represented in the petition by 119 heads of the families at Connecticut. Determined to reach their objective, they formed part of the caravan on foot to Québec with other Acadians in the same circumstance. They were joined apparently by François de Forest and his wife Jeanne Girouard, another daughter of Alexandre Girouard and Marie Le Borgne.[107]

Deportation from Ile St-Jean (second phase of Deportation) 1758

Anticipating the British actions, large numbers of Acadians moved to Ile St-Jean (Prince Edward Island) to escape the first Deportation in 1755, but many of them did not expect, nor were they successful in escaping the next Deportation, from PEI in 1758. Before we look at the Deportation itself, the following account of some of the hardships of our Acadian ancestors at this time is worth noting.

Many on this trek to PEI, would have been part of a caravan of Acadians, according to Léopold Lanctôt, who researched this topic at the National Archives of Canada. According to my telephone conversation with Léopold Lanctôt in December, 2000, who at the time still resided in Ottawa, some of the original documents are no longer available to the public, except on microfilm, and some have been lost to theft. According to Lanctot:

As of 1710, Acadia had passed into the hands of the English, who constantly harassed the Acadians to take an unconditional oath of allegiance to the British Crown. In 1730 the residents of Mines des Beaubassin [Amherst, near the border of NS and NB] joined with the residents of Pisiquid [Windsor] under order of the government and signed a conditional oath of allegiance, supposedly guaranteeing their rights as citizens, as part of the Treaty, following the capitulation of Port Royal, given under the decree of Queen Anne of England. Charles Douaron, of Pisiquit, *[son of Jehan Douaran and his first wife, Marie-Anne Carol and also his half brother]*, Thomas Cormier m. Anne Girouard *(daughter of Pierre Girouard and Marie Comeau [Block T163-4m1, subchart 163])*, were among those who signed. *[Pierre Girouard and Marie Comeau subcharts 162.1, 162.6, in the appendix and the Louisiana book, and subcharts 300, 500, 600, and 700 of the New Brunswick book.]*

In 1744 the war between France and England flared up again. The Acadians observed their neutrality, but were constantly exposed to the harassment and demands of both the English and the French who often passed through their village. Finally, in 1749 an English flotilla of ships arrived with more than 2,500 persons, anchoring in Chébouctou Bay, south of the Acadian peninsula, just 75 km, by road, from Pisiquit (Windsor). Here they founded, almost overnight, the city of Halifax. The Acadians in Pisiquid now became very anxious, seeing these great numbers of English colonists in such close proximity. Halifax became the capital of Nova Scotia, so named by the English. Conscious of the imminent danger, the Acadians requested permission from the English governor to immigrate to French territory, in particular, to Ile Saint-Jean, which was still held by France. The response of the Governor was to stall, and in 1749 the situation got more threatening when a company of Rangers (Métis and Anglo Indians), commanded by Captain Gorham, arrived at Pisiquid for the sole purpose of ordering the residents to help construct a road from Pisiquid to Halifax.

Without authorization from the governor, who would obviously have refused anyway, Charles Douaron decided to go to Île Saint-Jean (PEI). He would not make this journey by water from Pisiquid because the English had confiscated all the Acadian boats, and the English frigates were constantly crossing the entrance of the Basin of the Mines and could easily apprehend any Acadians fleeing from this place. The only practical means was to go to Cobequid (Truro) by land and then head towards the Northumberland Strait in the hopes of

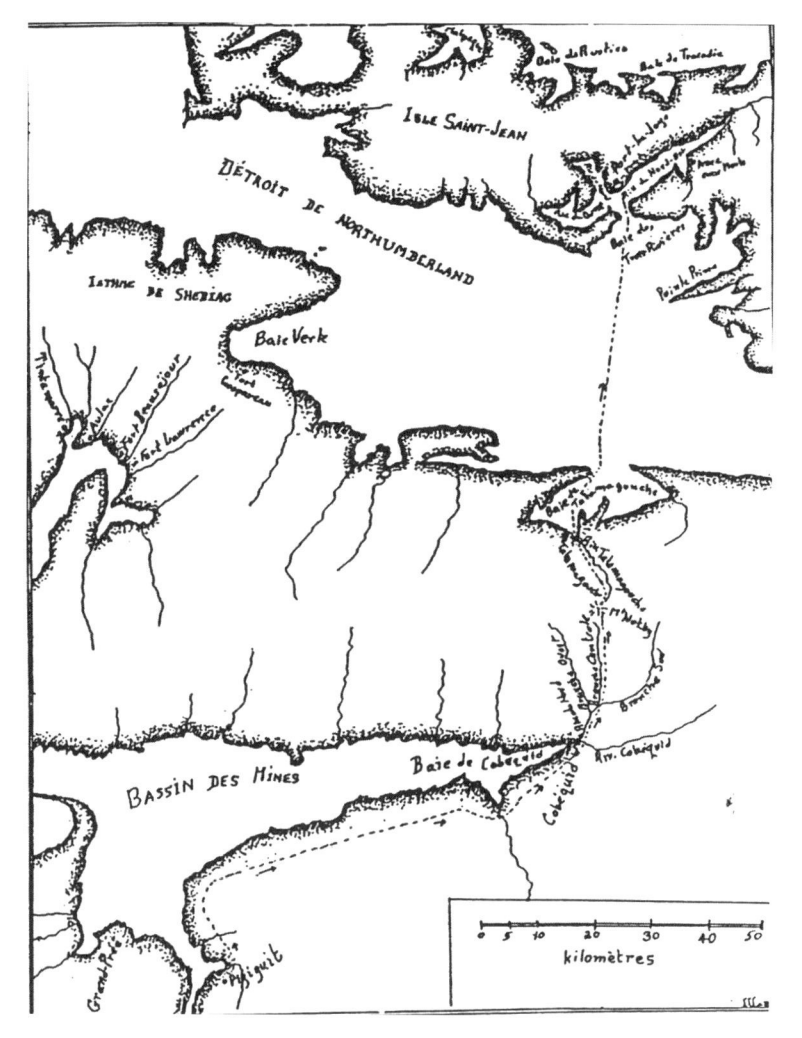

Map of the Emigration of Acadians from Pisiquit (Windsor, NS) and Cobéquid (Truro, NS) to Isle St-Jean (Prince Edward Island), map by Léopold Lanctôt, courtesy of Léopold Lanctôt, Familles Acadiennes Vol. I, p.154 and Marc Veilleux Editions du Libre-Echange[20]

making a night crossing with the help of the boats of French Acadian fisherman based in French territory.

Charles Douaron had a daughter Angéligue and a brother, Noel, already established at Cobequid. They knew among them that the Acadians of this place were preparing to migrate in mass to Île Saint-Jean. Charles decided to join them. With his sons and sons-in-law, *[Thomas Douaron married to Anne Giroir, daughter of Pierre Girouard and Marie Comeau, among them]*, his brothers and almost all the Daigle family, he set off for Cobequid at the beginning of the winter of 1749-50.

The trip was made on snowshoes, dragging all the best furniture and belongings on an Indian dragging train, along with their cattle and sheep. This was a painful and tiresome voyage for the elderly: Charles Douaron, 75 years old, and his wife, Françoise Gaudet, 76 years old. The elderly, the pregnant women and the children took their places on the dragging train, with their baggage. Those in good health were dressed in furs, hoods and mittens, travelled with snowshoes, axe in shoulder strap, gun on shoulders and all with a good sharp hunting knife tucked in their belt.

From time to time the caravan stopped to hunt game to provide food that they could count on during the long trip. In the evening they set up camp. They had to first gather some firewood to keep them warm during the night, and then to cook some meals in their large pots. Then they had to dig a hole in the snow to spend the night, sheltered from the wind and the snow. The trip to Cobequid must have taken fifteen days. (In 1747 the soldiers, not having any household, baggage, elderly, women and children and without the troop of animals which move very slowly, made this trip in nine days, a distance of 80 km).

At Cobequid the Douaron and the Daigle families joined one of the caravans heading for Ile St-Jean. The exodus first started at the beginning of 1749. Charles Douaron must have joined the Thériots who immigrated en masse: his oldest daughter Marie-Angélique, married one of them, Charles Thériot. The families of Charles' brothers, Nöel, Louis, Philippe and his half-brother Charles, the youngest, must have been part of the group. In 1752, we find them all in the same region together in Ile St-Jean.

The Acadians at Cobequid had cleared a road from Cobequid to Tatamagouche Bay on the Northumberland Strait across from Ile Saint-Jean. The road had been constructed, in part, for contraband business with the French colonists of Ile Saint-Jean and of Ile Royale (Cape Breton Island). It was also constructed in the event that they needed a quick escape route, should the English yoke to which they were bound, become intolerable.

The caravan probably divided up into small bands, not too close to one another, so as to avoid attracting the attention of the British. They must have started en route towards the end of March or early April of 1750 because at the end of June 1752, Nöel declares to the census-taker that he had been in Ile Saint-Jean for 26 months. The snow was melting when the caravan left.

The Acadians took everything they could of their personal belongings and furniture, as much as could be piled up on the wagon being hauled by an ox. They had to push in front of them all the animals, including the cattle and sheep and pigs. The elderly, the pregnant women, and the children travelled on horseback or on the wagon. The caravan advanced very slowly on the rough road tracking through the dense forest, strewn with rocks and roots of trees. They followed along the Cobequid River, (today Salmon River) for a short distance, and then they followed one of its tributaries, the North River, up to its source, at the base of the mountain, which today is called Nutby Mount. The further they went, the more difficult it became because they had to cross the chain of mountains at Cobequid. Starting from sea level, the road climbs up to an altitude of nearly 400 meters (1,300 feet) over a horizontal distance of only 25 kilometres. The final leg of the journey is approximately 5 kilometres through the highest part of the mountain, to reach the Tatamagouche Rivière (today Wagh River), which they followed up to its mouth where it meets the Tatamagouche Bay, part of the Northumberland Strait.

During this entire trip from Pisiquid to Cobequid, and then from Cobequid to Tatamagouche (a distance of about 50 km), they did not encounter any English. The English and the Bostonians rarely ventured into the woods in pursuit of the Acadians because they had learned to fear the skilled French marksmen, who from the time of their adolescence, hunted game with the Indians, their friends, who also taught them the secrets of how to ambush, only

Port Royal and old Acadie

possible in these dense forests.

When the Acadians reached Tatamagouche Bay, they hid in the woods awaiting the arrival of a number of small boats piloted by Acadians, who for a number of years had participated in contraband trade with the French colonists, evading the English who were patrolling the Strait. They would transport them in the night to avoid being seen by the English. The group came ashore at Port-la-Joye (today, Charlottetown, PEI), towards the end of 1750. Nöel Douaron and the members of his family went to Pointe-Prime at the entrance of the Bay of Port-la-Joye, while the family of Charles Douaron and of his brothers Louis and Philippe, and their half-brother, Charles (the younger), established along the northeast shore of the river and its tributaries. [109]

From the census records in Ile St-Jean, 1752, taken by Sieur la Rocque, Surveyor for the King of France, we learn the following. Information in square brackets comes from elsewhere in the census as follows:

Thomas Douaron, son of Jehan Douaron and m2. Jehanne Trahan, b. 1699 at Pisiquid m. ca. 1724, married Anne Giroir, native of Acadia, daughter of Pierre Girouard and Marie Comeau, emigrated to PEI in 1750, establishing on the south coast of the North-East River, having six daughters and five boys of which one was married. *(Refer to [AMC Block 164-4m2] of the Isle Madame chapter in the Nova Scotia, Prince Edward Island book).*
Thomas Douaron, half-brother of Charles [who married Françoise Gaudet. Thomas is also a brother to Marie Douaron who married Pierre Girouard, widow of Marie Comeau], is a labourer, native of Acadia, age 53, having been two years in this Country, married Anne Giroir, native of Acadia, aged 48. They have ten children: four sons and 6 daughters: 1. Paul Douran 21; 2. Charles age 14; 3. Alexandre age 12; 4. Jacques age 10; 5. Rose age 22; 6. Magdelaine age 18; 7. Anne age 8. Marie Marthe age 6; 9. Elizabeth age 5; 10. Marguerite age 3.

They have animals with them, an ox, a heifer, a pig and 33 hens. The land where they have established is on the south shore of the North-East River. They had cleared two arpans of land on which they have planted two bushels of wheat.

Véronique Girouard, 45 years old, half-sister to Anne, and daughter of Pierre Girouard and Marie Doiron, is recorded in the 1752 census of Île Saint-Jean (Prince Edward Island), with her husband, Pierre Barieau (Barriaud), age 45, married 1730, G.P. and their children: 2 boys and 7 girls. *(Refer to subchart 164 in the Isle Madame chapter of the Nova Scotia, Prince Edward Island book)*

Louis-Phillippe, b. 1683 m. Nov. 21, 1712, at Grand Pré to Marguerite Barilot, widow of Denis Girouard [AMC Block B-3b] (at least two sons and three daughters migrating to PEI in 1750 with their mother).

Having been successful through all their ingenuity, hard work, hardships and sufferings in escaping the first deportation of 1755 and establishing in PEI, many of these poor souls were not so fortunate during the next phase of the deportation, from Isle St-Jean in 1758.[110]

After the capture of Louisburg in 1758, over 3,500 Acadians in Île Saint-Jean were deported to France. *(See France chapter where I have traced some of our Girouard families from Île Saint-Jean.)*

Deportation from Isle St-Jean, 1758. Artist: Lewis Parker.

Courtesy of Parks Canada

    The North Atlantic crossing must have been a miserable voyage. It is difficult for us to imagine the ravages of the elements and the conditions in the lower hold of a crowded ship on such a long voyage, across the icy cold water of the Atlantic Ocean in the month of December. Seven hundred perished when two of the vessels sank close to the coast of Europe.

    On December 10, 1758, the *Violet* sank with 400 Acadians aboard. Three days later, on December 13, a transport close to southern tip of England sank with 300 Acadians aboard. There was a heroic effort to save the survivors of the *Violet* by the crew of the *Duke Williams*. One lifeboat made it to the English port of Penzance with only 27 survivors of more than 700 Acadians from the two vessels. Another badly battered ship from PEI reached Boulogne-en-Mer, France with 179 survivors.

    We saw in the France section of this volume, documents of Girouard ancestors who were returned to France as part of this deportation. Likely there were some Girouard descendants aboard the two vessels that sank. We do find record of the family of Anne Girouard and Thomas Douaron (of Prince Edward Island) in St-Malo, France, at St-Servan, St-Suliac Parish, and we have record of the family of Véronique Girouard m. Pierre Barrieau, first in France, and later in Louisiana, two families that survived the voyage.

DEPORTATION DESTINATIONS

From the "Odyssey of a People" exhibition,[111] we learn the following facts, which I have summarized below.

Fearing reprisals from both sides, the Acadians had refused to swear an unqualified oath of allegiance, resulting in the Deportation. They were only allowed what personal effects they could carry. All other property was forfeited to the British Crown. Six thousand Acadians (men, women and children) were transported to nine American colonies (as seen on the cover of this book), which were generally not prepared to receive them, and in the process, families were often separated. Some of the 20 transport ships did not reach their destinations.

Massachusetts	900
Connecticut	675
New York	200
Pennsylvania	700
Maryland	860
Virginia	1150
North Carolina	290
South Carolina	955
Georgia	320
Total	6050

Virginia refused to accept the Acadians and they were kept on their ships in port until they were eventually sent to England and kept as prisoners of war until the Treaty of Paris in 1763, when they were sent back to France.

In North Carolina and Georgia, the Acadians were allowed to seek refuge elsewhere. In other colonies they were scattered in small groups. In Léopold Lanctôt's book, *Les familles Acadiennes*, we also learn that in North Carolina the Acadians were permitted to build small boats in which they sailed to Massachusetts, only to have their boats seized by order of Governor Lawrence and to be imprisoned once again.

In Maryland, Pennsylvania, Delaware and Connecticut, the Acadians, or French Neutrals, were not welcomed, being of the Roman Catholic religion. Most of the deported Acadians made their way back to the Bay of Fundy and the St. John River, arriving with only half their numbers after many hardships, sickness and death.

One last story, written by Diana Ross McCain in *Connecticut* magazine, regarding the two American colonies of Maryland and Connecticut, directly involves one of our Girouard ancestors, Jacques Girouard, and his wife Marie Boisseau. In exile the family was separated. From the Girouard names mentioned in this story, I have been able to positively identify this family linking to our same common ancestry at the connecting point of Block U163- 4m1 of subchart 163 in the Isle Madame chapter of the Nova Scotia, Prince Edward Island book, which eventually ties into the AMC at [Block E-3b] (see also the appendix 5 of this book for subchart 163). This story appeared in *Connecticut* magazine, January 1991. I received a copy from Irene Schofield, a Gerrior descendant from Charlos Cove. The author has since kindly provided this article to me with permission to reproduce it here. I have added a map, sketch and AMC references in square brackets where appropriate.

From the Past: The Acadians
Banished from Canada in 1755, they looked to Connecticut for succor. They didn't find much!

by Diana Ross McCain, Connecticut Magazine

Six pathetically wretched strangers—exhausted, destitute, sick, vermin-ridden, nearly naked—turned up in Woodbury on Jan.2, 1757. Paul and Theotiste Landry and their baby, along with Theotiste's parents, Jacques and Marie Girouard and their infant, had journeyed hundreds of miles by land and sea all the way from Maryland in anguished search of two of the Landrys' children and five of the Girouards'. The children had been separated from their parents and sent to an unknown destination more than a year earlier, in one of the cruelest episodes in North American history: the expulsion from Nova Scotia of thousands of inhabitants of French descent by the British administration.

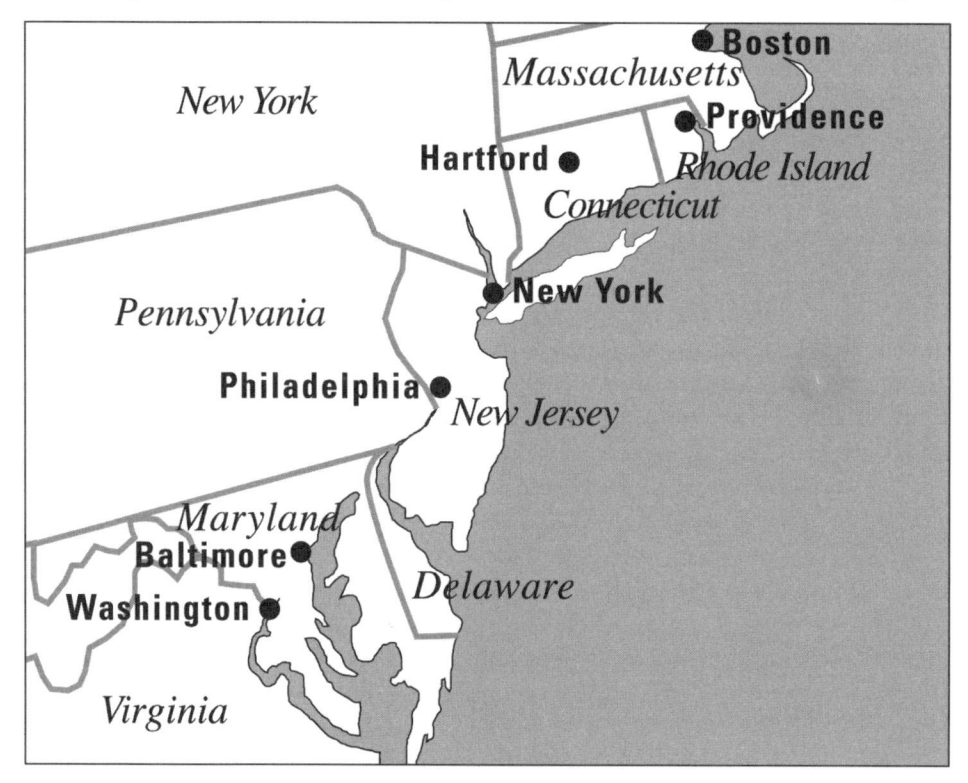

Two years earlier, the Landrys and Girouards had been among an estimated 9,000 to 18,000 residents of French ancestry in the region of Nova Scotia called Acadia, which had been under British control since 1713 as a result of the Treaty of Utrecht with France. Under the terms of the treaty, French inhabitants were guaranteed by Protestant Britain the right to retain their lands as British subjects and to practice their Roman Catholic faith.

The following decades were uneasy ones for Acadia's French-speaking inhabitants, as relations between France and Great Britain remained hostile. The British feared that the Acadians might aid the French and their Indian allies, so they required them to take an oath of allegiance to the British monarch. The Acadians were willing to take it so long as it contained a condition that they not be required to bear arms. To swear an oath without such a condition might, they feared, lead to their being forced to wage war on fellow Frenchmen. From their insistence on this condition, Acadians came to be called French Neutrals.

Time ran out for the French Neutrals in the summer of 1755, as France and Great Britain were once again poised to go to war. In the course of asserting their domination of Acadia, British troops captured a French fort and found 300 French Neutrals inside. Although the Neutrals claimed they had been forced on pain of death to assist in the fort's defence, their presence made them terribly suspect. Making their position even more precarious was a longstanding British lust for their lands.

Nova Scotia Gov. Charles Lawrence, a man with a reputation for harshness, quickly brought the issue to a head. In July, 1755, he demanded that the French Neutrals swear an unconditional oath of allegiance. When they refused, he activated a plan, two years in the making, for a "final resolution".

It was a brutally simple scheme: All French Neutrals would be banished from the land they and their forefathers had occupied for more than a century. They would be dispersed among His Majesty's North American colonies so that they would never be able to return to Acadia nor join fellow French in Canada. All their land and livestock were to be confiscated. Their houses, their barns, their crops—all were to be torched, to ensure that any who managed to escape the round-up would have no means of survival and nothing to return to. (English-speaking Protestants would be recruited to occupy their lands.)

"It will be necessary to keep this measure as secret as possible," wrote Lawrence in a letter outlining his plan on July 31, 1755. Toward that end, in August and September, he had French Neutral men and boys summoned to a number of locations. One was the church in the village of Grand Pré where on Sept.5, British Lt. Col. John Winslow told 418 French Neutrals that they had been convened to hear "His Majesty's Final resolution to the French Inhabitants: of Nova Scotia," which was "that your Lands and Tennements, Cattle of all Kinds and Live Stock of all Sortes are forfitted to the Crown with all your other Effects, Saving your money and Household Goods, and you your Selves to be removed from his Province."

"I am...Directed to allow you Liberty to Carry off your money and Household Goods as many as you Can without Discommoding the Vessels you Go in," Winslow continued. "I shall do everything in my power . . . that whole familys shall go in the Same Vessel." Meanwhile, armed soldiers had been positioned outside, and the doors and windows barred.

Yet as it turns out, Winslow was lying. Contrary to what he told his captive audience, his orders had not come from the king. In fact, a communiqué from the British secretary of state directing Lawrence to handle the French Neutrals' situation with the "greatest caution and prudence" was at that moment on its way from London, but arrived too late to have any impact on their fate.

And so it was that a total of 6,000 French Neutrals were herded onto ships during the last four months of 1755 and shipped to British colonies to the south. In a number of instances, sometimes intentionally, other times by happenstance, husbands, wives, and children were placed on different vessels, their destinations unknown to one another. (Many French neutrals never set foot on land again; inadequately clothed for an ocean voyage late in the year, some perished from exposure, while others died from smallpox.)

[Thus, Paul and Theotiste Landry and one child, along with Jacques and Marie Girouard [Block U163 – 4m1 of subchart 163] were sent to Maryland, while Marie Girouard's 76-year-old father, Francois Boisseau, with five of the Girouards' children and two of the Landrys', just 5 and 7 years old, were among 672 individuals who sailed in December on three ships bound for Connecticut.]

The Connecticut General Assembly, aware by October of what was occurring in Nova Scotia, authorized the governor to issue orders necessary to handle any French Neutrals allotted to Connecticut. The first ship to reach these shores, carrying 300 exiles, arrived in New London on Jan. 21, 1756, notes G. Philip Hebert in an article in the *Connecticut Maple Leaf* magazine, published by the French-Canadian Genealogical Society of Connecticut. The second ship sailed into New London on May 22, 1756, after a nightmarish voyage. Blown off course, it had ended up in Antigua, where many of the deportees contracted smallpox and died. The survivors were sent to the original destination of Connecticut. If, when and where the third ship made land here has not been recorded.

With one shipload of French Neutrals on their doorstep and more expected any day, the General Assembly in January, 1756 appointed a committee to oversee distribution of the exiles, anticipated to number about 400 total, in groups of three to 19, among 50 different towns. It also issued directives to the towns to support the French Neutrals "as tho' they were inhabitants of such town."

The Assembly compassionately directed the committee to take care "that no one family of them be separated and sent into two or more towns" but it also decreed that "to prevent said French people making their escape out of this colony. . . .none of them be allowed to depart out of the Respective Towns where they shall belong" unless they received written permission.

Each town made its own arrangements for the newcomers' food, clothing, shelter, medical care, and sometimes employment and education. Guilford, for example, voted on April 13, 1756, that the selectmen shall "put out to service so many of the French Family which is amongst us as they can dispose of without cost to the best advantage to free the Town from charge." This means French Neutrals would be bound out to households that would, in return for their labor, shelter and support them, a common expedient for supporting the poor. Hartford built a separate house for its 13 French Neutrals, and the selectmen were directed to try to find them work.

Woodbury's allotment of nine exiles included, Francois Boisseau, his five Girouard grandchildren and his two Landry great-grandchildren, who were "poor, naked, and full of vermin" according to a report to the General Assembly by the Woodbury selectmen, "unable to Support them Selves or even to Subsist by them Selves in one family if everything needful was found for their Support." [sic] Woodbury considered the children "as town poor."

The youngsters were sent to school, where they learned easily, and picked up English customs and language so quickly that by early 1757, according to the selectmen's report, many had "lost their mother tongue."

The father searching for his children who were separated at the time of Deportation. Artist: Margaretha van Gurp.

Meanwhile in Maryland, the Landrys and Girouards were frantically trying to locate their sons and daughters.

Appeals to the governor of Maryland that they be allowed to search for their children were denied–until the governor heard that the children had been sent to Connecticut. He then granted the parents a travel pass. They set out with the Landrys' new baby, born in Maryland (the child sent with them probably having died) and with the Girouards' infant, also born in Maryland.

It proved to be an arduous voyage. At last, devoid of everything but hope, they reached New London, then went on to Woodbury, where "to their great joy" they were reunited with their children.

Woodbury provided a house and necessities for the new arrivals until Colonial officials could decide what was to be done with them. But to the distress of their parents, the children remained with the masters to whom they had been bound out. Finally, in desperation, the parents seized the children and brought them back to the house Woodbury had provided.

Then, when the parents "refused to let them (the children) return to their master," continues the report, officials took them away by force. That this was accomplished "much to the joy of the children" must have been an agonizing blow to the parents.

Finally, determined not to bear any more than its fair share of the French Neutral burden, Woodbury asked the General Assembly either to reimburse it for the cost of supporting the extra French Neutrals; send one of the newly arrived families to Litchfield or New Milford, neither of which had been assigned any French Neutrals; or send the newcomers back to Maryland. The Assembly responded by sending Paul and Theotiste Landry and their child to New Milford, and Jacques and Marie Girouard to Litchfield. With their children left behind in Woodbury, the Landrys and Girouards pressed their case with the General Assembly. In May, 1757, Paul Landry petitioned the Assembly to have his children live with him in New Milford, quoting the Assembly's directive that French Neutral families not be broken up among towns. In October, Jacques Girouard petitioned the Assembly that his family too be allowed to live together. From archives, it is assumed that both requests were granted, and that the families were ultimately reunited.

Overall, there was little chance that the French Neutrals, even if distributed in small numbers, would be successfully integrated into Connecticut society, due to centuries of warfare and hatred between France and England. A particular thorn was the exiles' Roman Catholic faith, which Connecticut Congregationalists so loathed that French Neutrals were denied the services of a priest for marriages and baptisms. (The Roman Catholic Church authorized laymen to perform conditional marriages and baptisms for the faithful in exile, with the hope they might someday be validated by a priest.)

Added to these hostilities was the fact that "all the Acadian families were property owners and rather prosperous farmers back in Nova Scotia and that the life of abject poverty–their treatment as town paupers–certainly was no inducement for assimilation," notes Father Hector Hebert, a Jesuit priest whose collection on French Neutrals in Connecticut is housed at the French-Canadian Genealogical Society in Tolland.

The French Neutrals' uneasy visitation ended seven years after it began. In February, 1763, "the Treaty of Paris brought peace between France and England and put an end to French power in America," and thus, "The Acadians could no longer be considered a menace, and there was no good political reason for keeping them out of Canada or Nova Scotia," notes Arthur Doughty in *The Acadian Exiles.* "Almost immediately those in exile began to seek new homes among people of their own race and religion." A list compiled in 1763 of French Neutrals in Connecticut hoping to go to France—a voyage that was never made—included 666 names, among them the Landrys and Girouards.

Connecticut natives were probably pleased at the prospect of the French Neutrals departing, from a mixture of emotions that included antipathy for the exiles' alien culture and religion, gratitude for being relieved of the cost of their support, and perhaps sympathy for their plight. Several towns assisted French Neutrals seeking to leave, such as Waterbury, which in 1763 voted, "to give the French family in this Town, in order to transport said French Family into the Northward country, not exceeding ten pounds, including Charitable Contributions." Yet this largesse was not universal. Requests to pay their passage to Canada submitted by groups of French Neutrals to the General Assembly in 1766 and 1767 were denied. In June, 1767 a group of 240 somehow managed to pay for their exodus to Québec.

The "Northward country" was not the only destination for the families. As early as 1764, a number left for the West Indies. Paul and Theotiste Landry and their family, now grown to five children, as well as Jacques Girouard, his wife and three of their children, were among those who went to Santo Domingo,(Saint-Domingue) according to Stephen White, genealogist at the Centre d'Etudes Acadiennes at the Université de Moncton in New Brunswick.

But two of the Girouard children were among the handful of French Neutrals who remained in Connecticut. Sybil Girouard married Thomas Harrison in 1764, had several children in Litchfield, and died in 1845. Philemon Girouard, who would have been 6 or 7 at the time of the expulsion, stayed in Woodbury, where he died in 1801 at age 52. Perhaps Philemon and Sybil were among the children who so quickly assimilated that they found their own parents strangers when they arrived to claim them.

Still, most French Neutrals considered Connecticut a land of unhappy exile, best abandoned as soon as an opportunity arose. Yet the long-

APPENDIX

Acadians Aboard the Sloop *Dolphin*, William Hancock, Master

Captain's Spelling	Correct French Spelling	Wife	Children
Peter Gold	Pierre Gourde	1	3
Joseph Purye (1)	Joseph Poirier	1	2
John Purye (1)	Jean Poirier	1	2
Joseph Purye' (2)	Joseph Poirier	1	1
Joseph Purye (3)	Joseph Poirier	1	3
Francrway Purye	François Poirier	1	1
Peter Purye (1)	Pierre Poirier	1	7
Paul Purye (1)	Paul Poirier	1	4
John Purye (2)	Jean Poirier	1	0
Balone Duset	Benoni Doucet	1	3
Mich¹ Durna	Michel Bernard	1	3
John Burns	Jean Bernard	1	1
Paul Duran (1)	Paul Durand	1	3
Paul Duran (2)	Paul Durand	1	3
Joseph Duran (1)	Joseph Durand	1	1
Peter Busher	Pierre Boucher	1	1
Paul Purye (2)	Paul Poirier	1	4
Joseph Duran (2)	Joseph Durand	1	6
Jolour Lundrie	Jolour Landry	1	3
Joseph Abar	Joseph Hébert	1	3
Glod Abar	Claude Hébert	1	1
John Purye (3)	Jean Poirier	1	0
John Duron	Jean Durand	1	6
Peter Tebuthu	Pierre Thibodeau	1	0
Peter Purye (2)	Pierre Poirier	0	0
Charles Brown	Charles Brun	1	2
Joseph Purye (4)	Joseph Poirier	1	1
Andrew Leblang	André Leblanc	1	2

(From the *Council Journal*, Anno., 1755, pp. 478-479.)

[65]

EXILE WITHOUT AN END

Acadians Aboard the Ship *Cornwallis*, Andrew Sinclair, Master

Captain's Spelling	Correct French Spelling	Wife	Children
John Multon	Jean Mouton	1	10
John Lewis	Jean Louis	1	1
Joseph Kasey	Joseph Quesny	1	5
Peter Dermer	Pierre Demers	1	8
Joseph Grangie	Joseph Granger	1	8
Jorotan Lavoa	Jorotan Lavoie	1	6
Francis Purye	François Poirier	1	10
Mich¹ Wair	Michel Mayer, Douaire	1	7
John Day	Jean Daigle	1	4
Paul Lavoy	Paul Lavoie	1	3
Jarman Carry	Germain Carrier	1	2
Marran Liblang	Marran Leblanc	1	5
Alex¹ See Curmie	Alexandre Cyr? Cormier	1	7
Joseph Curmie	Joseph Cormier	1	7
Alexander See Casie	Alexandre Cyr? Quesny	1	6
Charles Burvoe	Charles Belliveau	1	8
Jarman Furrie	Germain Fournier	1	5
Abrance Skison	Abrance Chiasson	1	5
John Dupio	Jean Dupuis	1	2
John Furrie	Jean Fournier	1	10
John Carrie	Jean Carrier	1	8
Tako Bonvie	Tako Bonnevie	1	4
Alex¹ See	Alexandre Cyr?	1	10
Peter Lambeer	Pierre Lambert	1	7
Charles Duzie	Charles Dasy	1	9

(From the *Council Journal*, Anno., 1755, p. 480.)

APPENDIX

Acadians Aboard the Sloop *Endeavour*, James Nichols, Master

Captain's Spelling	Correct French Spelling	Wife	Children
Line Ougan	Line Hugon	1	3
Peter Ougan (1)	Pierre Hugon	1	5
James Ougan	Jacques Hugon	1	2
Peter Ougan (2)	Pierre Hugon	1	1
John Corme	Jean Cormier	1	7
Mich¹ Corme	Michel Cormier	1	1
John Multon	Jean Mouton	1	3
John Jenvo?	Jean Jeanveau ou Juneau?	1	0
Glod Toudeau	Claude Trudeau	1	3
Paul Morton	Paul Martin	1	5
John Morton	Jean Martin	1	0
Innes Woirt	Innes Ouellette?	1	4
Jeremiah Duset	Jérémie Doucet	1	5
Joseph Care	Joseph Carrier	1	4
Charles Benn	Charles Aubin	1	2
John Dupe	Jean Doutre ou Dupuis	1	8
Francis Lopeors	François Laperre	1	3
Francis Lablong	François Leblanc	1	0
Joseph Lablong	Jean Leblanc	1	2
Simon Leblong	Simon Leblanc	1	2
Charles Furne	Charles Fournier	0	1
Peter Morton	Pierre Martin	0	0
John Blonchin	Jean Blanchet	0	0
Mich¹ Depe	Michel Dupuis	0	0
Joseph Leger	Joseph Léger	0	0
Alexander Commo	Alexandre Comeau	0	0
John Balleo	Jean Belliveau	0	0
Joseph Peters	Joseph Pitre	0	0
Michael Hache	Michel Haché	0	0
Peter Hache	Pierre Haché	0	0
Peter Curme	Pierre Cormier	0	0
Francis Duset	François Doucet	0	0
John Curme	Jean Cormier	0	0
Peter Robert	Pierre Robert	0	0
Peter Oben	Pierre Aubin	0	0

EXILE WITHOUT AN END

Captain's Spelling	Correct French Spelling	Wife	Children
Michael Lapeire	Michel Lapierre	0	0
Michael Pore	Michel Poirier	0	0
John Creman	Jean Grenon	0	0
John Shesong	Jean Chiasson	0	0
Peter Burswoy	Pierre Bourgeois	0	0

(From the *Council Journal*, Anno., 1755, p. 520.)

Acadians Incapable of Labor, Sick or Infirm, January 28, 1756

As Spelled in Record	Correct French Spelling	Wife	Children
John Giroire	Jean Girouard	1	2
Gabriel Goslin	Gabriel Gosselin	1	0
Widow of John Sevoirs	Vve Jean Savoye		3
Herman Doucit	Herman Doucet	1	6
Frances Vincent, widow	Françoise Vincent		2
Chas Ignace Carree, lunatic	Charles Ignace Carrier		0
John Cormy	Jean Cormier	1	7
Peter Hugon	Pierre Hugon	1	2
Joseph Cormy	Joseph Cormier	1	4
Peter Corniew	Pierre Cornue	1	5
Marguerite Aucon [husband left behind]	Marguerite Aucoin		2
Widow Aucoin¹	Vve Aucoin		3
Margaret Tebodeau	Marguerite Thibodeau		1
Joseph Cornieu	Joseph Cornue	1	2
Paul Poirey	Paul Poirier	1	3
Bellony Doucet	Benoni Doucet	1	3
Joseph Poivereau	Joseph Poivereau		1
Charles Douert [and aged mother]	Charles Douaire		6
Francis Poivereau	François Poivereau	1	1
Gould²	Gourde		2

¹ In addition to her own children an unidentified orphan is listed.
² "An old man," not named, is mentioned in the care of this family.

Names of some Acadian families who were passengers on a number of ships heading to various locations during the Deportation, from Chapman J. Milling, in his Exile Without an End.[112]

Ships Names and Destinations.	Number of Days Victualled	Tons.	Men.	Women.	Sons.	Daughters.	Total.	
The Helena, for Boston	28	166	52	52	108	111	323	
The Edward, for Connecticut	28	139	41	42	86	109	278	
The two Sisters, for Ditto	28	140	42	40	95	103	280	
The Experiment, for New York	28	136	40	45	56	59	200	St. Christopher.
The Pembroke (a) for North Carolina	42	139	33	37	70	42	232	
The Hopson, for South Carolina	42	177	42	46	120	134	342	
A Schooner, for Ditto	42	30	1	1	4	3	9	
Vessels, seven	238	927	251	263	539	611	1664	

"I am informed, that several of these unhappy people died on their passage; that many of them are suspected to have found means to escape [only those on board the Pembroke, and now live with the remaining fugitives [48 families] in the mountains.'

I am not aware that the King's instructions to Governor Cornwallis, in 1749, and Governor Hopson in 1752, relating to the Acadians were ever quoted by previous historians.

APPENDIX

As Spelled in Record	Correct French Spelling	Wife	Children
Louis Hougin	Louis Hugon		4
Jerman Forryns*	Germain Foret		3
John Louizeau	Jean Lizot		3
Joseph Ducont	Joseph Ducont	1	6
Ignace Nuriat	Ignace Nuirat	1	2
Joseph Hubert	Joseph Hubert	1	3
Francis Leblanc	François Leblanc		
Abraham Soysant	Abraham Soysant	1	6
Peter Lambert	Pierre Lambert	1	2
Alexander Cumon	Alexandre Commant, Comeau		0
Charles Bruyn	Charles Brun		0
Francis Moses	François Moyse		0
Michael Richard	Michel Richard		0
Basil Grevoir	Basile Grégoire		0
John Blanchard	Jean Blanchard		0
Peter Bourgeois	Pierre Bourgeois		0
Michael Lambiert	Michel Lambert		0

*Both persons apparently deceased or separated, since children are listed as "Three small Children of Jerman Forrys's".
(From the Council Journal, Anno., 1754, pp. 62-63.)

74   EXILE WITHOUT AN END

Numerical Census Figures on Acadians in South Carolina

Nov. 17, 1755, to Jan. 1756. Acadians aboard the *Two Brothers, Dolphin, Cornwallis, Endeavor, Syren and Hopson* 944
April 14, 1756, report of Governor James Glen to the Lords of Trade:
First arrivals 1000
Parties arrived from Georgia 200
June 16, 1756, report of Governor William Lyttelton to Lords of Trade. Exclusive of transient parties from Georgia, total landing at different times in South Carolina 1027
Acadians remaining at time of report 645
Shipped off or escaped 273
August, 1756, Dispersed to various Parishes by Act of Assembly 645
To country Parishes 516
Remaining at Charles Town 129
March, 1759, report of Committee appointed to inquire into present state of Acadians in Charles Town 340
July 12, 1760, report of Committee appointed to inquire into present state of Acadians in Charles Town 210

With the permission and courtesy of Parks Canada and the Lefebvre Monument Society, inspired by the plaque of 300 names exhibited at Grand Pré National Historic site, we have record of the following 300 Acadian families in Acadie.

Noms de familles acadiennes au XVIIIᵉ siècle
Acadian Family Names of the 18th Century

Il reste peu de souvenirs tangibles de la période qui a précédé la Déportation. Toutefois, grâce à des documents historiques, nous connaissons la plupart des noms de famille de colons acadiens. Un grand nombre de ces noms sont encore répandus dans les communautés acadiennes des Maritimes et témoignent de la survivance du peuple acadien. Certains de ces patronymes ont également survécu en Louisiane, en France et au Québec où ils perpétuent le souvenir de la Déportation des Acadiens et des migrations qui l'ont suivie.

Cette liste d'environ 300 patronymes a été établie à partir de registres paroissiaux, de relevés de recensement et d'autres documents acadiens/néo-écossais de la première moitié du XVIIIᵉ siècle. Tous les noms des familles acadiennes de civils, dont on sait qu'elles ont vécu dans la colonie entre 1700 et 1755, y figurent. La liste ne comprend pas les noms des membres de la garnison française qui ont servi en Acadie et ceux de leurs familles.

Little physical evidence remains of pre-expulsion Acadia. However, most of the family names of the acadian settlers are known from historical documents. Many of these names continue in today's Maritime Acadian communities, dramatically illustrating a people's survival. Acadian names also survive in areas such as Louisiana, France, and Quebec, a legacy of the Acadian Deportation and subsequent migrations.

This list of approximately 300 family names was drawn from parish records, census records and other documents from Acadia/Nova Scotia in the first half of the 18th century. All Acadian civilian families known to have lived in the colony at any time between 1700 and 1755 are included. The list does not include the families of the French garrison which served in Acadia.

Abbadie, de Saint Castin d'Allain
Amirault dit Tourangeau
Angou dit Choisy
Apart
Arcement
Arosteguy
Arseneau

Arnaud
Aubois
Aucoin
Ayot
Babin
Babineau dit Deslauriers
Barillot

Noms de familles acadiennes au XVIIIe siècle
Acadian Family Names of the 18th Century

Barolet
Bastarache dit (Le) Basque
Bastien
Belliveau dit Bideau
Belliveau dit Blondin
Belou
Benoit dit Labrière
Bergereau
Bergeron d'Ambroise
Bergeron dit Nantes
Berrier dit Machefer
Bernard
Bertaud dit Montaury
Bertrand
Bézier dit Touin dit Larivière
Blanchard
Blanchard dit Gentilhomme
Bodard
Boisseau dit Blondin
Bonnevie dit Beaumont
Bonnière
Borel
Boucher dit Desroches
Boudrot
Bourg
Bourgeois
Boutin
Brassaud
Brasseur dit Mathieu
Breau
Broussard
Brun
Bugaret
Buisson
Bugeaud
Buote
Buteau
Cahouet
Caissy dit Roger
Calvé dit Laforge
Carré
Caylan
Célestin dit Bellemère
Cellier dit Normand
Chauvet
Chênet dit Dubreuil
Chesnay dit Lagarenne
Chiasson dit La Vallée
Chouteau dit Manseau
Clémenceau
Cloistre
Coignac
Comeau
Cormier dit Rossignol
Cormier dit Thierry
Corne
Corporon
Cosset
Coste
Cottard
Cousin
Crépaux
Creysac dit Toulouse
Cyr
Daigre
D'Amours de Chauffours

Noms de familles acadiennes au XVIIIe siècle
Acadian Family Names of the 18th Century

D'Amours de Clignancour	Fontain dit Beaulieu
D'Amours de Freneuse	Forest
D'Amours de Louvière	Forton
D'Amours de Plaine	Fougère
Daniel	Fournier
Darois	Froiquingont
David dit Pontif	Gadrau
Delisle	Galerne
Denis	Gallé
Denys de Fronsac	Garceau dit Boutin
Derayer	Garceau dit Richard
Deschamps dit Cloche	Garceau dit Tranchemontagne
Desgoutins	Gareau
Desmoillons	Gaudet
Deprés	Gauterot
Deveau dit Dauphiné	Gauthier
Dingle	Gentil
Doiron	Giboire Duvergé dit Lamotte
Dominé dit Saint-Sauveur	Girouard
Doucet dit Laverdure	Gisé dit Desrosiers
Doucet dit Lirlandois	Godin dit Beauséjour
Doicer dit Mayard	Godin dit Bellefeuille
Druce	Godin dit Bellefontaine
Dubois	Godin dit Boisjoli
Dubois dit Dumont	Godin dit Catalogne
Dufaut	Godin dit Châtillon
Dugas	Godin dit Lincour
Duguay	Godin dit Préville
Duon dit Lyonnais	Godin dit Valcour
Duplessis	Gosselin
Dupuis	Gourdeau
Egan	Gousman
Flan	Gouzille

Errata

Noms de familles acadiennes au XVIIIe siècle
Acadian Family Names of the 18th Century

Grandmaison (Terriot dit Guillot dit)
Granger
Gravois
Grosvalet
Guédry dit Grivois
Guédry dit Labine
Guédry dit Labrador
Guédry dit Laverdure
Guéguen
Guénard
Guérin
Guérin dit Laforge
Guilbeau
Guillot dit Langevin
Guy dit Tintamarre
Guyon
Haché dit Gallant
Hamel
Hamet
Hamon
Hébert dit Manuel
Hélys dit Nouvelle
Henry dit Robert
Hensaule
Héon
Heusé
Hugon
Jeanson
Joseph
Kimine
La Barre
Labat, dit Le Marquis, de La Bauve
La Chaume

La Croix
La Lande dit Bonappetit
Lambert
Lambourt
Landron
Landry
Langlois
Lanoue
La Pierre dit La Roche
La Vache
Lavergne
La Vigne
Lebert dit Jolycoeur
Le Blanc
Le Blanc dit Jasmin
Le Borgne de Belisle
Le Clerc dit Laverdure
Lecul
Léger dit La Rozette
Le Jeune dit Briard
Le Juge
Le Marquis dit Clermont
Le Mire
Le Neuf de Beaubassin
Le Neuf de Boisneuf
Le Neuf de La Vallière
L'Enfant
Le Poupet de Saint-Aubin
Le Prieur dit Dubois
Le Prince
Leroy
L'Eschevin dit Billy
Le Vanier dit Langevin

Noms de familles acadiennes au XVIIIe siècle
Acadian Family Names of the 18th Century

Lavasseur dit Chamberlange
Levron dit Nantois
Loiseau
Long
Longuepée
Loppinot
Lord dit La Montagne
Lucas
Maffier
Maillet
Maisonnat dit Baptiste
Malboeuf
Mangeant dit Saint-Germain
Marcadet
Marchand dit Poitiers
Marres dit La Sonde
Martel
Martin
Martin dit Barnabé
Massé
Massié
Mathieu
Maucaire
Mazerolle dit Saint-Louis
Melanson dit Laverdure
Melanson dit La Ramée
Mercier dit Caudebec
Messaguay
Meunier
Michel dit La Ruine
Migneau dit Aubin
Mignier dit Lagassé
Mirande

Mius d'Azit
Mius d'entremont de Plemarais
Mius d'entremont de Pobomcoup
Monmellian dit Saint-Germain
Mordant
Morin dit Boucher
Morpain
Moulaison dit Rencontre
Mouton
Moyse dit Latreille
Naquin dit L'Étoile
Nogues
Nuirat
Olivier
Onel (O'Neale)
Orillon dit Champagne
Oudy
Ozelet
Part dit Laforest
Pellerin
Petitot dit Saint-Sceine
Petitpas
Pichot
Picot
Pincer
Pinet
Pitre dit Marc
Poirier
Poitevin dit Cadieux
Poitevin dit Parisien
Poitier
Porlier
Poujet dit Lapierre

Noms de familles acadiennes au XVIIIe siècle
Acadian Family Names of the 18th Century

Lavasseur dit Chamberlange
Levron dit Nantois
Loiseau
Long
Longuepée
Loppinot
Lord dit La Montagne
Lucas
Maffier
Maillet
Maisonnat dit Baptiste
Malboeuf
Mangeant dit Saint-Germain
Marcadet
Marchand dit Poitiers
Marres dit La Sonde
Martel
Martin
Martin dit Barnabé
Massé
Massié
Mathieu
Maucaire
Mazerolle dit Saint-Louis
Melanson dit Laverdure
Melanson dit La Ramée
Mercier dit Caudebec
Messaguay
Meunier
Michel dit La Ruine
Migneau dit Aubin
Mignier dit Lagassé
Mirande

Mius d'Azit
Mius d'entremont de Plemarais
Mius d'entremont de Pobomcoup
Monmellian dit Saint-Germain
Mordant
Morin dit Boucher
Morpain
Moulaison dit Rencontre
Mouton
Moyse dit Latreille
Naquin dit L'Étoile
Nogues
Nuirat
Olivier
Onel (O'Neale)
Orillon dit Champagne
Oudy
Ozelet
Part dit Laforest
Pellerin
Petitot dit Saint-Sceine
Petitpas
Pichot
Picot
Pincer
Pinet
Pitre dit Marc
Poirier
Poitevin dit Cadieux
Poitevin dit Parisien
Poitier
Porlier
Poujet dit Lapierre

Port Royal and old Acadie

Noms de familles acadiennes au XVIIIe siècle
Acadian Family Names of the 18th Century

Poupart	Savary
Préjean dit Le Breton	Savoie
Prétieux	Semer
Pugnant dit Destouches	Serreau de Saint-Aubin
Racois dit Desrosiers	Sicot
Raymond	Simon dit Boucher
Renaud dit Provençal	Soulard
Richard	Soulevant
Richard dit Sansoucy	Surette
Richard dit Beaupré	Tandau
Richard dit Boutin	Terriot
Richard dit Lafont	Testard dit Paris
Rimbeau	Thébeau
Rivet	Thibault
Robichaud dit Cadet	Thibodeau
Robichaud dit Niganne	Tillard
Robichaud dit Prudent	Tourneur
Rodohan	Toussaint dit Lajeunesse
Rodrique dit de Fonds	Trahan
Rousse dit Languedoc	Triel dit La Perrière
Roy dit La Liberté	Turcot
Rullier	Turpin dit La Giroflée
Saindon	Vallois
Saint-Étienne de la Tour, de	Vescot
Saint-Julien de La Chaussée, de Samson	Viger
	Vigneau dit Maurice
Saulnier dit Lacouline	Villatte
Sauvage dit Forgeron	Vincent dit Clément
Sauvage dit Chrystophe	Voyer

COURTESY OF AND REPRODUCED FROM PLAQUE BY
LES PRODUCTIONS LA SOCIÉTÉ DU MONUMENT LEFEBVRE INC.

INSPIRÉE DE L'EXPOSITION DU LIEU HISTORIQUE NATIONAL DE GRAND-PRÉ
INSPIRED BY THE EXHIBIT AT GRAND-PRÉ NATIONAL HISTORIC SITE

COURTESY OF
PATRIMOINE CANADIEN PARCS CANADA
CANADIAN HERITAGE PARKS CANADA

Milling gives a detailed summary of the Deportation, which I have translated as follows in chart form. [115]

Deportations (1755-1758)

Embarkation	Number	Departure	Destination	Arrival
Beaubassin, Beauséjour	500	Oct. 1755	Charleston, S.C.	Dec. 1755
"	200	Oct. 1755	North Carolina	Dec. 1755
"	400	Oct. 1755	Savannah, Ga	Dec. 1755
Pisiquit, Cobequid	493	Oct 1755	Annapolis, Md.	Nov. 1755
"	860	Oct. 1755	Boston	Nov. 1755
"	156	Oct. 1755	Philadelphia	Dec. 1755
"	200	Oct. 1755	Williamsburg, Va.	Jan. 1756
Grand Pré	206	Oct.-Dec. 1755	Boston	Nov. 1755
"	420	"	Baltimore, Md	Nov. 1755
"	298	"	Philadelphia	
"	1140	"	Williamsburg, Va	Dec, 1756
Port Royal (Annapolis Royal)	323	Dec. 9, 1755	Boston	Feb. 1756
"	558	Dec. 9, 1755	Connecticut	Feb. 1756
"	200	"	New York	"
"	351	"	Charleston, S.C	Feb. 1756
"	232	"	North Carolina	"
Total	6 537*			
Isle St-Jean(PEI)	3 500	Aug. 1758	France	Dec. 1758
Total	**10,037**			

* This figure of 6 537 varies from the figure on the "Odyssey of a People" poster, given as 6,050 a difference of about 500 and differs again from the figure 6,950 given in the book *The Acadians of the Maritimes Thematic Study*, edited by Jean Daigle[116]. It should also be noted that the place of embarkation is not always the place where the Acadians lived.

It is important to realize that the Acadians were deported to regions much more populated. They must have been overwhelmed in a dominantly Protestant, English-speaking world, but also they must have been shocked by the sheer population of these colonies. Jean Daigle gives some comparative population figures for the Acadian and American colonies and those of New France (Canada) in "Acadia, 1604-1763".[117]

Year	Canada (New France)	Acadia	American Colonies
1608	28	10	100
1640	220	200	28 000
1680	9700	800	155 000
1710	16 000	1700	337000
1750	55 000	8000	1 200 000

Naomi Griffiths[118], from a report of Jean Daigle and Robert LeBlanc, gives a good summary of the Acadian situation in terms of the distribution of the Acadians by the end of the Deportations in 1763 as follows.

Distribution of Population in 1763
1. Massachusetts   1000
2. Connecticut   650
3. New York   250
4. Maryland   810
5. Pennsylvania   400
6 South Carolina   300
7. Georgia   200
8. Nova Scotia   1,250
9. St John River   100
10. Louisiana   300
11. France   3,500
12. Québec   2,000
13. Prince Edward Island 300
14. Bay des Chaleurs   700

"*Migrations and return, 1755-1800*". Artist: Claude Picard, Sainte Basile, New Brunswick, *Deportation of Acadians*.

Courtesy of Parks Canada

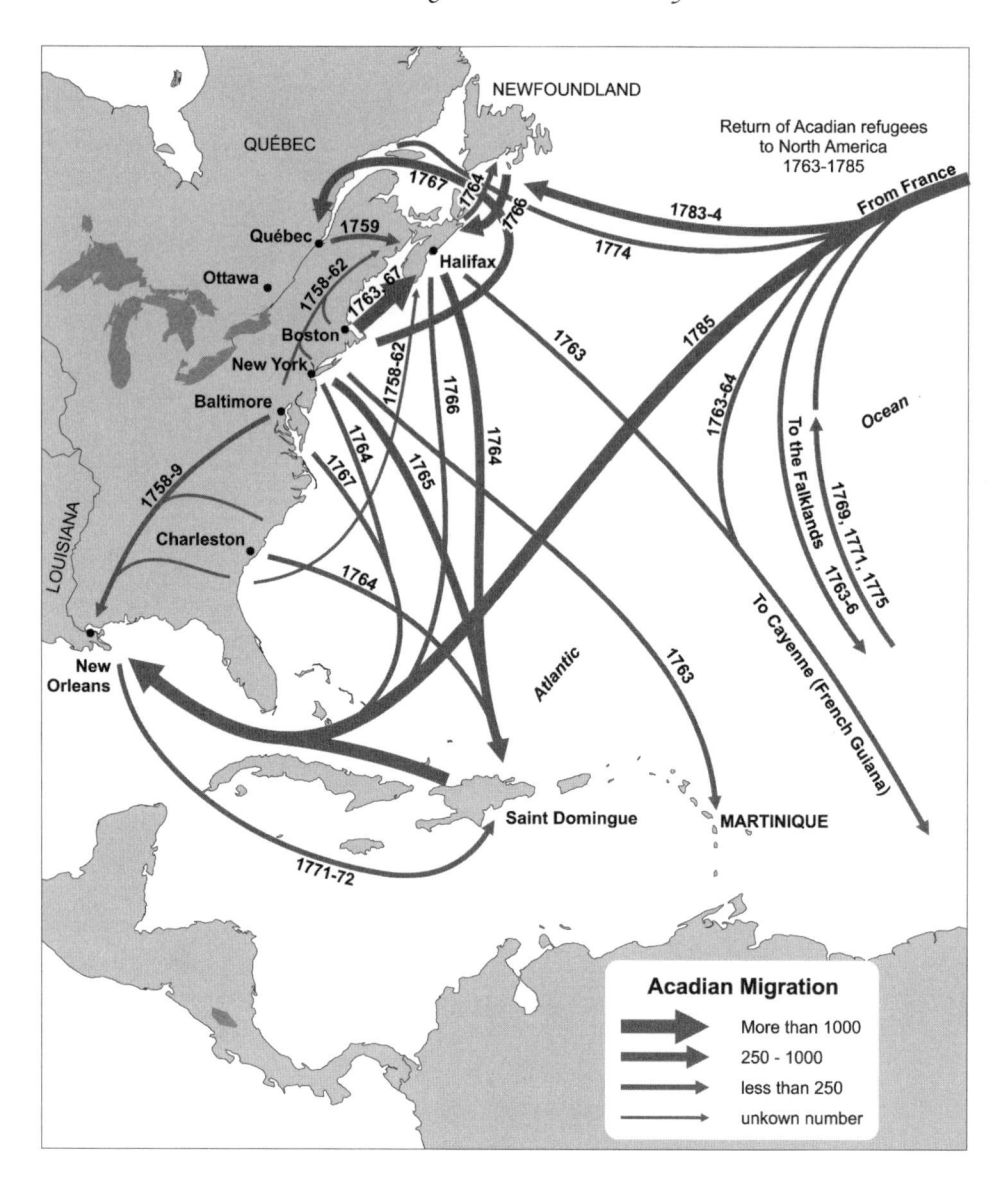

Acadian Migration, 1758-1785

Map of MIGRATIONS AND RETURN: 1763-1800, based on map by Naomi Griffiths in her book entitled L'Acadie de 1686 à 1784, Contexte d'une histoire.

"The Return" Artist: Nelson Surette, Yarmouth, Nova Scotia

awaited exodus did not always end happily; Paul Landry and Marie and Jacques Girouard survived eight years in exile in Connecticut ,only to die in Santo Domingo within months of their arrival.

We learn the following facts from the "Odyssey" exhibition.

The Deportation order remained in effect from 1755 to 1764. Altogether a total of 10,000 Acadians were deported, most of them to the American Colonies south of Nova Scotia…From 1756 to 1763, as Acadians either surrendered or were taken prisoner, they were held in Fort Edward near Windsor (Pisiquid), Fort Cumberland in Amherst, formerly called Fort Beauséjour at Annapolis Royal and at Halifax. A final deportation to Massachusetts in 1762 failed when the colony refused the Acadians and sent them back to Nova Scotia. [114]

Part of the culture shock would also have been due to the loss of their priest and the interruption to their religious weekly masses, which brought their families together on a regular basis in prayer. In addition they were surrounded by a dominant culture that held a different religion and who were mostly very negative towards the Roman Catholic, French-speaking Acadians.

As indicated on the "Odyssey" poster, "The migrations that followed the Deportation were extremely complex. They spanned two generations, spread through the North American Colonies and reached as far as Europe, the West Indies, Louisiana and even the Falkland Islands."

At St. Pierre et Miquelon
Between 1763 and 1765, some of the Acadian exiles moved from Nova Scotia, Massachusetts and France to Saint Pierre et Miquelon, two small French islands off Newfoundland. Others followed later. Their troubles had just begun. Because of wars and shifting political alliances, some of these exiles had experienced five and six migrations by the end of 1816. [119]

From the 1767 census of Isle Miquelon, Bona Arsenault records a Girouard widow, not giving her first name, born 1724 coming from Fort Beauséjour after 1755. She had four children with her: Dominique, 1752; Modeste, 1754; Théotiste, 1759; Michel, 1762.

I have been able to determine that this is the family of Pierre and Marguerite Gaudet, also recorded in the PEI census of 1752, and in France[120]. Pierre was the son of Germain Girouard and Marie Doucet [AMC Block D-3b] and see subchart #216 in Québec book and in the appendix. Gaston Giroir sent me records of some Acadian Girouards in France in which Pierre Girouard and Marguerite Giroaurd appear. These families were not linked at the time to our François Girouard and Jeanne Aucoin. But with Gaston's notes and my own research records here, I was able to positively identify the above family in France as descending from François. *See[Block R213-4 of Subchart 213] in the Québec book linking back to [Subchart AMC Block D-3b].*

The above family was transported to France and recorded living at Cherbourg. The mother was still a widow at this time. This family was now recorded as "Giroire". The children are as follows: 1. Dominique, 20 years of age, recorded as a navigator; 2. Théotiste 19, a dressmaker. [121]

We learn the following from the "Odyssey of a People" display.

In France
Approximately, 1,100 Acadians who had been refused entry to Virginia during the Deportation of 1755 were sent to England where their numbers were eroded by illness. At the end of the war in 1763 some 750 survivors were repatriated to France.

In the decade that followed 1755, France received over 3,000 Acadian exiles from Nova Scotia, Île Saint-Jean and England. After a number of settlements failed, many Acadians left for other French colonies and Louisiana *[refer to France chapter for more details of the Acadian Girouard, Giroir, Giroire ancestors who belong to this migration.]* [122]

In Louisiana
After a number of settlement plans failed in France, many Acadians left for other French colonies, in particular for Louisiana.

. . . Louisiana became the focal point of the Acadian exiles and their migrations. Approximately 1,500 Acadians arrived from the American colonies, West Indies and Nova Scotia between 1763 and 1767, but the largest group, nearly 1,600, were Acadians who came from France in 1785. Smaller groups followed them over the next few years. They were welcomed in the Spanish colony of Louisiana, which had been French until 1762 and encouraged Roman Catholic settlers.[123]

I have learned that Prosper Giroir and his family came to Louisiana from France more than 25 years after being exiled to France, (either via Virginia and England, or directly from Isle St Jean). He obviously wanted to rejoin relatives in Louisiana—his cousin Firmin Girouard and his family, who had been separated from him during the Expulsion of 1755 and deported to Louisiana.

The "Odyssey of a People" exhibition also discusses the Acadians who went to French West Indies, French Guiana and the Falkland Islands

In French West Indies: St. Domingue, Guadeloupe, Martinique, Ste. Luce
. . . Acadians arriving in the French West Indies from the American Colonies and Nova Scotia suffered in the tropical climate, and hundreds died. Most of the survivors subsequently relocated in Louisiana and in the American Colonies. *[See Louisiana book for more details]*
In French Guiana
. . . One of the many unsuccessful settlement efforts brought 138 Acadians from France to the tropics of French Guiana in 1763-64, where many died. The survivors were repatriated to France.
In the Falkland Islands (Iles Malouines)
Between 1763 and 1766 several Acadian families migrated to the Falkland Islands from France, only to return after 1767, when France recognized Spain's claims to the Islands. . . [124]

Canada—Migrations in the Maritimes and Québec
Some Acadians returned to Canada (by land or sea or a combination of both) to their former land of Acadie. Some migrated to Québec and some migrated back to old Acadie from Québec. Pierre-Maurice Hébert, in *Les Acadiens du Québec* [125] provides maps showing the Acadian routes, arriving at Québec overland following rivers, or by sea along the eastern coast of the American colonies and then up around the mainland of Nova Scotia to the St. Lawrence River , or a combination of both of these routes in some cases. In the "Odyssey" exhibition we learn the following:

Those Acadians who fled to Québec in 1755 were later joined by numbers of refugees from Nova Scotia, Île Saint-Jean and American colonies. Some returned from France in 1774 and established at Gaspésie, PQ. By the end of the eighteenth century, some 8000 Acadians were permanently established in Québec, representing approximately 1/3 of the population.[126]

Other Acadians simply came out of hiding in the woods to make their way to one of to these two regions— Québec or the Maritimes.

Many Acadians, longing for their homeland of Acadie, managed to return from the American colonies in the years following the peace of 1763. Others arrived from Québec, Saint Pierre et Miquelon, and France to join compatriots in remote areas of Nova Scotia: Tracadie, Pomquet, Isle Madame, Chéticamp, Chezzetcook, Torbay and also further north, in what is now known as New Brunswick. As the "Odyssey" exhibition explains, "By the early 19th century, the migrations were over. Although the Acadians were scattered around the Atlantic rim, their sense of their own identity remained intact".

The Acadians began the work of building new communities in their new surroundings wherever they re-established. They were not given back their original lands, except for those in the very prosperous Acadian region of West Pubnico and surrounding area, who returned to their old lands after the Deportation. The Acadians in this region are an exception to the general pattern of return which other Acadians experienced.

According to Jean Daigle:

Following the Treaty of Paris (1763), British authorities allowed the Acadians to return to the Maritime provinces on condition that they swear an oath of allegiance and settle in small groups. The Acadians complied since France had been defeated. [127]

Petit Joseph Comeau and his son Henry in Comeauville, Baie Ste. Marie, Digby County, NS, 1948.
This photograph is typical of the Acadian farming communities after the deportations and migrations ended, and up until the late 1950's. Petit Joseph Comeau is the father of Joseph Comeau, who married my aunt, Martina Gerrior, of Larry's River in 1948. Petit Joseph Comeau is also uncle to Daniel Comeau, who is presently the Co-ordinator for the Central region of Nova Scotia for the Congrès Mondial Acadien, 2004. Daniel participated in our International Reunion, 1990 in Antigonish.

Consequently, under these orders, most of the Acadians chose to re-establish away from the English communities, where they could live together, according to their own value system, without outside interference. They naturally remained somewhat aloof from any surrounding English communities and English government for quite some time because of their traumatic experiences. Many Acadian communities continued in their traditional occupation of fishing, which has always been a part of their history.

Madeleine Girouard and Charles LeBlanc
During and After Deportation

One particular branch of the Girouard family, who migrated back to the St Mary's Bay region of Clare—the family of Madeleine Girouard [AMC Block E-4m1] of the fourth generation and Charles LeBlanc (à Pierre à Daniel LeBlanc and Françoise) had a very interesting and revealing history during the Deportation and consequent migrations, and one of their descendants was to play a major role in the history of Acadians, becoming the first Acadian Bishop. The story of Bishop Edouard LeBlanc's Girouard ancestors during and immediately after the Deportation is based on my own research, and an article by Placide Gaudet.

The LeBlanc genealogy of this branch has already been researched, for the most part, and is available from the Acadian Archives of the Université Saint-Anne genealogical collection, in Church Point, Nova Scotia. Since the Bishop carries the LeBlanc surname, all the LeBlanc descendants have every right to be very proud of their ancestor. At the same time, Bishop Edouard LeBlanc was no less a Girouard descendant, so the Girouards can also rightly feel very proud of him. In addition, we have discovered a huge branch of LeBlanc cousins with whom we now can share our heritage as Girouard descendants. Let us first explore the story of Charles LeBlanc and Madeleine Giroaurd, the ancestors of the first Acadian bishop, Edouard Alfred LeBlanc, descending from [AMC Block E-4m1] the fourth row of my Acadian Girouard master chart.

Madeleine Girouard [AMC Block E-4m1], spouse of Charles LeBlanc, is the great-granddaughter of the first François Girouard and Jeanne Aucoin, through her father, François m. Anne Bourgeois, son of Jacques Girouard and Marguerite Goutrot. *[This couple can be found on the fourth row of my Girouard Acadian Master Chart.]*

Madeleine was sister to Jean-Baptiste Girouard [AMC Block F-4m1], who arrived at Tracadie, NS in the late 1700's. *[The Guysborough County and Antigonish County branches both link to this same Jean-Baptiste, who is of the author's direct line.[* Madeleine had two other brothers, Joseph Girouard m. Françoise Blanchard, and Pierre Girouard m1. Marie-Josephe Forest and m2. M. Doucet who both established at Québec. *[Their genealogies are followed in the Québec volume].* Madeleine also had a sister, Anne-Hélène m. Claude H. Benoit and another sister, Marie-Madeleine m. Claude Gaudet both of whom established in Québec, and who have already been mentioned in relation to the Deportation from the Memramcook region.

In the following passage from Placide Gaudet we find a great deal of informa-

	L80	M80	N80	O80	P80	O80	R80	S80	T80	U80	V80
4]		Research of William D. Gerrior *Acadian Awakenings* 2002. Information collected from the Centre Acadian collection, Université de Ste-Anne, Chruch Point, Clare, Nova Scotia and from Dr. Neil Boucher's Doctoral Thesis, 1993 Acadian Nationalism and the Episcopacy of MSGR. Edouard Alfred LeBlanc, Bishop of Saint John, New Brunswick (1912-1936): A Maritime chapter of Canadian Ethno-Religious History.		1716 - 1805 Madeleine Girouard Charles (Chat) LeBlanc 1717 P.R. St. Bernard		→Refer to Chart . Girouard/LeBlanc branches in St. Bernard, NS, and L'Anse- des- LeBlanc, N.S		**[Block E-4M1] of the Acadian Master**			
5]				1742 - Felicité LeBlanc m. François Comeau (*dit*) Maza	1740 - Pierre LeBlanc m. Marie Praxède Belliveau	1736 Charles (Charitan) LeBlanc m. Anne Melanson St. Bernard	1748 - Joseph (*dit* Joppe) Leblanc m. Anne Doucet	1744 - Marie Modeste Madeleine LeBlanc m. Frédéric (*dit* Soudic) Belliveau			
6]			1796 - Madeleine Leblanc m. Germain (*dit* Benjamin) Belliveau 1780	1783 - Anselme (Captain) LeBlanc m1. Anne Gaudet 1808 m2. Anastasie Belliveau 1815	Nathalie LeBlanc m. Charles Marin Belliveau (*dit* Sucre)	1786 - Joseph (*dit* Morrison) LeBlanc m. Rosalie Theriault, 1813 L'Anse-des-Leblanc	1788 - Charles (Chat) LeBlanc m. Marie Melansons 1825	1781 - Marie LeBlanc m. Jean (*dit* Jeaneau) Comeau	1796 - Jean Baptist (*dit* Bonni) LeBlanc (n.m.)	1826 - Pierre Corneille Leblanc m. Seraphie Melanson	
7]		1834 - Jovite Eustache (Captain) LeBlanc m1. Marie Elizabeth Comeau m2. Léonise Gaudet 1813	1820 - Marie (nm)	1818 - 1898 Elizabeth (nm)	1816 - Edouard (*dit* Dike) m. Dorothée Gaudet	1824 -1891 Luc LeBlanc m.Julie Vitaline Belliveau 1854 at St. Bernard	1814 - Thérèse Charlotte LeBlanc m. Jovite Belliveau	1821- Mathurin Toussant (*dit* Torine) LeBlanc m. Catherine LeBlanc	1827 - Madeleine LeBlanc m. Hilaire Comeau	1829 - Anne- Léonise LeBlanc (nm)	
8]					1864 - Jean Baptist LeBlanc m. Clara Lovitt	1870 - Edouard Alfred LeBlanc First Acadian Bishop 1912	1859 - 1862 Madeleine LeBlanc	1862 - Rosalie LeBlanc m. Louis à Charles Thériault			
9]				Marguerite LeBlanc m. François Comeau							St Bernard/L'Anse - des-LeBlanc Girouarrd/LeBlanc Descendants Linking to [AMC Block E-4M1]

© *Acadian Awakenings Girouard/Giroir… Routes and Roots*

Port Royal and old Acadie

tion on the travels of Charles LeBlanc and Madeleine Girouard, during the Deportation period.[128] I have added a few visuals to augment this already very detailed and well-written account of this family.

It appears that an ancestor of Bishop Charles Edouard LeBlanc came to St. John as a refugee from Annapolis in 1756 and spent some years near Richibouctou... His Lordship, Bishop LeBlanc is a thorough French Acadian on both his mother and his father's side. He is of the seventh generation from Daniel LeBlanc, who was born in France, 1626, and married there in the spring of 1650 to Françoise Gaudet, immigrating a few months later, with his wife to Port Royal, NS, establishing some miles up the river from the fort, on the north side. Daniel LeBlanc was one of the notable men of his day, so much so that in May, 1690, when Sir William Phipps attacked and took the fort at Port Royal, he was among the six persons chosen by Phipps to form a council to govern the country until an English Governor could be appointed. Daniel had a family of seven children: six sons and one daughter. Pierre, the youngest of the family was born in 1664, and married twice. His last wife was Marie Thériault, by whom he had six children: three sons and three daughters. The oldest of the sons was Charles LeBlanc, born September 26, 1706 and married in 1735 to Madeleine Girouard. They had a family of several children, one of whom was called Charles like his father; Charles Jr was born 1736 near Belle Isle, on the other side of the Annapolis River. The second Charles was married to Anne Melanson, 1780. One of the sons of this union was Joseph *dit* Morrison born 1786 m. Rosalie Thériault, by whom he had ten children, Luc (Luke) born 1824, being one of these ten children. Luke married Julie Belliveau and settled in Ohio after his marriage, on the township line between Digby and Clare, where he died 1891. His wife died in 1897 and was buried by her youngest child, who had just been appointed parish Priest of St. Bernard, and who became the Bishop of St. John.

In 1755, Charles, husband of Madeleine Girouard, escaped deportation by fleeing with his wife and children over the North Mountain in Annapolis County.

Some two months later, with a party of 120 Acadian refugees on board fishing boats, he went from Port Morden, which was their hiding place, down the shore of the Bay of Fundy

Major Point, Clare, Digby Co., N.S.

Acadian Cemetery at Major Point.

as far as Little Passage, by which they entered into St. Mary's Bay. Ascending the bay a number of miles and being overtaken by a snowstorm, they landed on a point called Major Doucet's Point, midway between Yarmouth and Annapolis Royal.

There they spent the winter of 1755 and 1756. Early in the spring of 1756, LeBlanc and his companions went back aboard their fishing boats, descended St. Mary's Bay and entered the Bay of Fundy by the Grand Manan, and from there came to St. John where they remained for a few weeks. Before leaving St. John, the party divided. Some of them went up river as far as Nerepis, where they met some of their compatriots, who had embarked from Annapolis on the scow *Pembroke* on December 8, 1755, bound for North Carolina, but who while on the voyage seized the ship and brought her to St. John where she arrived with 286 Acadian families on February 8, 1756.

These families, joined by some of those with Charles LeBlanc, afterward went to the province of Québec, where their descendants are very numerous.

Charles LeBlanc and the remainder of his party left St. John in the fishing boats, and followed the course of the bay, entering Cumberland Basin, then ascended to the Pedcoudiac River as far as the bend where Moncton is now situated, and stayed there a short time. Afterward they crossed through the woods to Cocagne, Kent County, a few miles north of Shediac, where they found several families of Acadian refugees and went with them to Miramichi. After a short stop there, the party again divided, some stopping there while Charles LeBlanc and his family and Jean Belliveau and others came to Richebouctou and ascending the Aldoune River, remained there with other refugees from 1756 to 1760.

At this date they participated in the arrangement made between the Acadians at Miramichi, Richibouctou, Bouctouche, Cocagne, with Col. Frye, who was commanding Fort Beauséjour. They went to Cumberland and from there back to Annapolis Royal again where they remained until permitted to occupy lands on the south side of St. Mary's Bay, now forming the municipality of Clare, which were issued by the English authorities. LeBlanc

Anse-des-LeBlanc

settled near the border of the townships of St. Clair and Digby at a place now called l'Anse-des-LeBlanc or LeBlanc's Cove, which is near the Church at St. Bernard and some two miles from Weymouth Bridge.

From Rev. C.J. d'Entremont's records, held at the Acadian Museum in West Pubnico, we also have the following notes regarding Madeleine Girouard and Charles LeBlanc:

Charles *dit* Chat, son of Pierre and Madeleine Bourque, was born Sept 26, 1716 Port Royal, of the second wife, Françoise Thériault. *[some discrepancy here, as Placide states he was born 1706]*. He married Madeleine Girouard, January 2, 1735. He was one of the first colonists of Baie Ste-Marie and his name is among the 200 acres of land in the concession of the Township of Clare, accorded June 1775. His lot was number seven, located in L'Anse-des-LeBlanc, after which this area derived its present name.

Charles LeBlanc died at St. Bernard, NS, on September 30, 1805 at the age of 89. His burial records are found at Ste-Marie, giving his age to be 91, which is an error of two years. His wife preceded him by three months, according to her burial record, here translated by the author.

June 8, 1805. The body of Madeleine Girouard was buried in this parish of Ste-Marie, spouse of Charles LeBlanc, who died at the age of nearly 90 years of age. Mother, grandmother, great grandmother and great-great-grandmother, she has a total of 180 children, grandchildren, great-grandchildren and great-great-grandchildren, of which 150 are living in this Parish, forming 35 families.
Signed François Comeau
Signed Sigogne, Priest

This branch of the fourth generation of the Acadian Master Chart, who settled near Comeauville by Belliveau's Cove, in St. Bernard, NS, are, as we have seen, the descendants of Charles LeBlanc and Madeleine Girouard (the daughter of François Girouard and Anne Bourgeois). They escaped Deportation, according to Rev. C.J. D'Entremont, and fled towards Miramichi. In the Annapolis census of 1763, this family, including six children are recorded. Charles was still in Annapolis in 1769 when two of his children married there. In 1770 he only had two children left with him. It is then that he went to nearby St. Mary's Bay to settle at St. Bernard, at a place which has ever since been called L'Anse-des-LeBlanc, (LeBlanc Cove). He died there, Oct. 30, 1805 at the age of 89, less than four months after his wife, Madeleine Girouard, who was buried on June 8. Charles was known as 'Cha', pronounced 'shaw', from the first three letters of his name. He and Madeleine are the ancestors of the first Acadian Bishop, Msgr. Edouard LeBlanc, who was the Bishop of St. John, N.B. from 1912–1935.

All the LeBlanc descendants of this branch in St. Bernard and later in L'Anse-des-LeBlanc, stemming from Charles LeBlanc and Madeleine Girouard, are, as mentioned earlier, also Girouard descendants. Consequently, there are many parallel lines of descendants who are also Girouard descendants, from the brothers and sisters in each generation of this direct line (i.e. the brothers and sisters of the Bishop Edouard LeBlanc, the brothers and sisters of his father Luc, of his grandfather Joseph and the brothers and sisters of his great grandfather Charles Jr.). All of the origins of these branches are shown on a subchart 80, which I have created for these branches. The corresponding genealogical information related to each block of subchart 80 is traced in many cases by the LeBlanc genealogical records held at Université Sainte Anne. All descendants of the LeBlanc branches of each block of this subchart 80 are also Girouard descendants.

Normally I would present this information concerning post-Deportation descendants such as Bishop Edouard LeBlanc in the Nova Scotia and Prince Edward Island book. However that book is organized by seven root areas where family still carrying the surname Girouard/Giroir(e) Gerrior name, re-established. Because the Girouard /LeBlanc descendants of Charles LeBlanc and Madeleine Girouard branch no longer carry the Girouard name and because this branch remained relatively close to the Port Royal area, compared to other Girouard descendants in Nova Scotia who settled in the North of the province, I believe it is more appropriate for me to present this branch at this time, in this section of this book.

The historian Dr. Neil J. Boucher, vice-president of Université Sainte-Anne and also a board member for the 2004 Congrès mondial acadien (World Congress of Acadians), researched and defended his doctoral thesis on the topic of "Acadian Nationalism and the Episcopacy of Msgr. Edouard Alfred LeBlanc". Much detail and documentation are provided in this thesis regarding the first Acadian Bishop. Except where otherwise indicated, Dr. Boucher's thesis is the source of the following information. I have added a photo of Bishop LeBlanc, which was obtained during one of my research visits to Université Sainte-Anne.

Edouard Alfred LeBlanc
à (Luc LeBlanc & Julie Vitaline Belliveau) à (Joseph LeBlanc *dit* Morrison &

Rosalie Thériault) à (Charles LeBlanc Jr. & Anne Melanson) à (Charles LeBlanc & Madeleine Girouard) [AMC Block E-4m1]

We learn from Neil Boucher that Joseph LeBlanc *dit* Morrison moved his family inland from St. Bernard to Weaver Settlement around 1820. They had seven children, the seventh child being, Luc LeBlanc b. 1825 who became the father of Bishop Edouard Alfred LeBlanc. Luc married Julie Vitaline Belliveau, daughter of Joseph-Charles Belliveau and Marguerite Comeau. Here they purchased 160 acres of land. The family settled in Port Royal or Annapolis area after the Peace of Paris ended the Seven Years War. Father Bailly, missionary priest, married two of Luc's children in the fall of 1769:

Photo of Bishop Edouard Alfred LeBlanc: Courtesy of Archives, Université Sainte Anne. Church Point, Clare, Digby County, Nova Scotia.

Register de L'Abbé Bailley (1773-1783): 1. Madeline LeBlanc, daughter of Charles LeBlanc and Madeleine Girouard, m. Frédéric Belliveau; 2. Pierre LeBlanc m. Marguerite Belliveau.

The Belliveau descendents from these two branches would thus also be Girouard descendants.

Rev. Edouard Alfred LeBlanc was educated in his early years at Weaver Settlement schoolhouse commencing in the mid 1870's. The Tupper Laws of 1864 created a system of publicly funded schools where English was the only language of instruction. For Acadian students who only spoke French, this was a complex learning environment where teachers had to use English texts and translate information, while at the same time attempt to teach their students to communicate in English in written and oral form, forgetting the fact that no education with regard to their own Acadian cultural background was included. Despite the limitations for Acadians, students with standardized English texts celebrating English culture and history, some students were successful. Edouard Alfred LeBlanc was one of a few who progressed to high school at Weymouth Bridge High School and then to the school at Meteghan River. After that he was a clerk for some years. At the age of 19 he abandoned his business pursuits and attended St. Joseph's College in Memramcook. He advanced to grade ten in 1889. In 1890 he was able to continue his studies at the newly constructed Collège Sainte-Anne, in his home region of

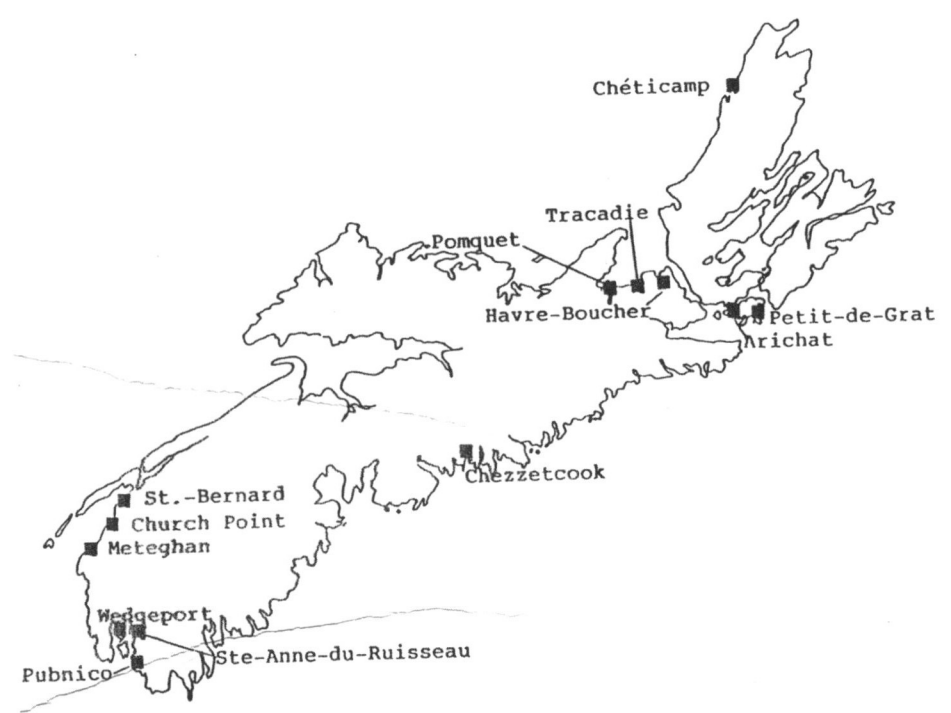

Map of Nova Scotia showing region of St-Bernard. Source: Dr. Neil Boucher's Doctoral thesis: "Acadian Nationalism and the Episcopacy of Msgr. Edward Alfred LeBlanc"

Clare in Digby County. He was one of the first group of 61 students when Université Sainte Anne first opened its doors. He excelled, winning many top honours and prizes for excellence in his academic studies as well as his religious studies, over the four years with the Eudist priests as his mentors, and naturally attracted the attention of the Directors, looking for possible candidates for the priesthood. In 1895, after graduating from the Collège Sainte Anne, he continued his theological studies at the newly constructed Holy Heart Seminary in Halifax, taught again by the Eudists priests, being one of five students accepted that year. After three years in the seminary, Edouard Alfred was ordained at St. Mary's Cathedral, Halifax, by Monsignor O'Brien, June 29, 1898.

On Sunday July 10, 1898 he celebrated his first Mass at the nearly sixty-year-old St. Bernard Church, which was filled to capacity and overflowing

A few weeks after his ordination, the future Bishop of St. John was sent to Meteghan as curate to Father James Daly, where he remained until 1901. Then he was appointed parish priest at Caledonia, a purely English-speaking congregation in the electoral district of Shelburne and Queens. From there, in 1906 he was transferred to the parish at Salmon River in the Municipality of Clare, Digby County. The following year, 1907, he was appointed by His Grace Archbishop McCarthy of Halifax, as pastor of St-Bernard's church, in his native parish.

One of his greatest projects in the parish of St-Bernard, commencing upon his arrival, was his vision and mobilization of the local community, to raise funds and

Above left: The first stage of completion
Courtesy of Université Sainte-Anne, Pointe de l'Eglise

Above right: Second stage of completion, with its towers complete.
Courtesy, Université Sainte-Anne, Pointe de l'Eglise

construct a new church to replace the old church which could no longer meet the needs of the increasing population. However, his vision was that of a European Cathedral rather than the parochial church usually found along the coast of Saint Mary's Bay. Consequently, thirty-two years later, the last of 8,000 blocks of granite, was placed. He was not in the parish for all this time, since his nomination to be Bishop came two years after the construction began.

To have an Acadian Bishop had been a dream of the Acadian society for a long time and it was not achieved overnight or without extreme persistence and hard work over a long period of time, on the part of those Acadian nationalists who were lobbying the local Church hierarchy and ultimately the Pope for this position. The struggle was a long process, involving a number of trips to Rome to

Increase and decrease of ethnic population in Nova Scotia between 1871 and 1911[66]

	Population 1871	Population 1911	% Increase or decrease
English	113,520	177,701	+56.5%
Scottish	130,741	145,535	+11.3%
Irish	62,851	54,244	-13.6%
Acadian	32,833	51,746	+57.6%

Population charts of ethnic groups (1871-1911) statistics researched by by Neil Boucher.

see the Pope and the building up of a large file concerning this request. These efforts occurred in a sea of Irish domination in the hierarchy of the Church.

But the Acadian dream was gathering strength and also attracting national interest, even from Prime Minister Sir Wilfred Laurier, who was very supportive to this cause. He attended the Fourth National Acadian Convention in Isle Madame, Cape Breton, Aug. 15,16, 1900, during the height of the Acadian Nationalist movement. For the first time, the topic regarding the Bishop and other hierarchy appointments within the Church was on the Convention agenda.

During this period of lobbying for an Acadian Bishop, the Maritimes witnessed a rebirth of the Acadians on the national stage which strengthened their cause and now, the issue which had been a regional concern, had become a national issue and this fact put more pressure on the hierarchy of the Church to make a favourable decision, providing a Bishop from the ranks of Acadian Priest of the province.

It is important to note, as Neil Boucher points out in his thesis, that this issue was not a language issue, but a cultural equality issue: A French Canadian Bishop would not suffice… On the other hand, to accept a French Canadian Bishop would be an acknowledgement of Acadian inferiority within French speaking groups; it would be adding insult to injury.[129]

The Acadian leaders were finally successful in 1912 when the Bishop of Toronto died, setting off a chain of other appointments and therefore giving the Pope an opportunity to fulfil his promise to provide an Acadian Bishop from the ranks of the Acadian priesthood. As Neil Boucher writes:

The year 1912 constituted a watershed in Acadian socio-religious history. The enthronement of Monsignor LeBlanc was regarded by many contemporaries as the zenith of nationalist fervor prevalent in Acadian society during the three previous decades.

I would like to introduce another important Gerrior link here, by expanding on Dr. Boucher's comment above, and mention that this dream for an Acadian Bishop was planted even earlier in the mind of another Acadian Priest, Father Hubert Girroir, originally of Tracadie, NS, one of those staunch nationalists mentioned earlier. Fr. Giroir first made reference to this dream in his capacity as Rector of the Cathedral at Arichat during the years 1853-1863. An article written by Diocesan Historian, Antigonish, NS, A.A Johnston, describes his enthusiasm in this regard and clearly implies that this dream began almost fifty years before the actual appointment of the first Acadian Bishop in 1912.

Father Girroir was a zealous apostle for the spread of education among the Acadians of eastern Nova Scotia and he gladly seconded the educational endeavours of his bishop. Throughout his life he worked resolutely for the betterment of his fellow Acadians, trying to overcome great obstacles. He saw and he told the people that without education they could never compete economically, socially or politically with their neighbours of other national descents, and that without education they could not hope to produce from their own ranks a sufficient supply of French-speaking priests or give to the Church, within a reasonable length of time, an Acadian Bishop. [130]

Sally Ross refers to these two Acadian men, Fr. Hubert Giroir and Bishop Edouard LeBlanc, as the two "human milestones" in the rebuilding of Acadian society in Nova Scotia, in her illustrated study, *Rebuilding a Society: The Challenges faced by the Acadian Minority in Nova Scotia during the First Century after Deportation, 1764-1867*.[131]

Concerning Father LeBlanc, Neil J. Boucher continues to describe his challenges:

As the first Acadian Bishop, there were high expectations of him from the Church to promote Catholicism and from the Acadian Nationalist to promote the Acadian people and culture. His diocese was an ethnic mix, dominated by most of the town's Irish Catholics, thus his position required sensitivity, understanding and a broad outlook.

The Bishop's rather tall stature and his firmness may have given him an authoritarian appearance to some, but his firmness was not marked by aggressiveness. He was calm, gentle and composed in his personality, diplomatic and cautious in his approach to problems—all necessary characteristics when dealing with national issues, and all reasons why he was chosen as Bishop. He was tolerant, for he would have accomplished little for the Acadians as Bishop if he were otherwise.

As Dr. Boucher points out, "A fiery approach to opponents and critics would not be what was needed to advance Acadian aspirations in the early 1900's".

Bishop LeBlanc was tested at the very beginning of his post by the problem in Moncton, New Brunswick, where the Acadians of St. Bernard parish wanted to establish their own Acadian parish with their own Acadian priest. He received letters on the matter even before he was Bishop.

Bishop LeBlanc was a nationalist in his own manner. To further the Acadian identity, for him, meant to build French Catholic institutions. He believed that this was the best way to assure linguistic and cultural survival for the Acadian parishioners of his jurisdiction. His initiatives in the founding of L'Assomption Parish in Moncton, his work to have an Acadian enthroned on the Chatham See, his initiative in the founding of the order of the French-teaching Sisters, and his collaboration with Msgr. Patrice Alexandre Chaisson [another Girouard descendant—see Antigonish chapter of NS volume] to have an Acadian Archdiocese erected in New Brunswick, all bear witness to his own style of nationalism.

He witnessed the downsizing of the nationalist movement, which occurred in the post-1912 era, when national conventions had reached their apex, and lost momentum. For this reason, some may view Bishop LeBlanc as a transitional figure whose career reflected a necessary, transitional stage in the evolution of Acadian self-assertion. During Bishop LeBlanc's era, the Church was the chief vehicle to assure the survival of Acadians, supporting Acadian health, education and welfare. The State would not become involved in those fields for another thirty years. Neil Boucher summarizes LeBlanc's work as follows:

It is in this interim period between the victories of the early 1900's and the new orientation at mid-century, when the functions of the state were set in motion, that LeBlanc's style of nationalism made its mark. Like many of his contemporaries in social leadership positions of the

Maritimes in this period, LeBlanc fitted well into the mainstream of an ideology that could still be labelled as conservative.

His strength, based on his educational training and the thinking of his time, was in building up Church structures and services, in French, to support the Acadian communities under his jurisdiction.

This completes the research to date concerning the illustrious family of Charles LeBlanc and Madeleine Girouard [AMC Block E-4m1], and their descendants on the French shore of Clare, Digby County, Nova Scotia. Subchart 80, presented at the beginning of this section, allows us to trace the genealogy of each person in each block, for the most part, to the present day.

CONCLUSION

The migrations and movements of the Girouards were in many ways typical of many other Acadian family migrations. There are other Acadian villages and towns in Nova Scotia where other Acadian families settled, and re-established after the Deportation. To show the overall picture in Nova Scotia I will present a map of the seven root areas where Acadians in Nova Scotia, for the most part, permanently re-established. This map is based on the research of Sally Ross and Alphonse Deveau in their book *The Acadians of Nova Scotia, Past and Present*,[132] which won both the Evelyn Richardson Award and the City of Dartmouth Book and Writing Award, and my own research in the enlargement maps for the two Acadian communities of Larry's River, in the Torbay region of Guysborough County, and the Chezzetcook region of Halifax County.

The French language has gone through different degrees of change in each of these root areas, due to the dominant English culture and to the varying levels of communication within the province and the varying infrastructure and local resources which affect each community's ability to develop organizations to combat this process. In all seven communities, however, there is an obvious pride in their Acadian roots, and a strong appreciation for the sacrifices of their ancestors.

It is important not to forget the maternal lines, even though they may not carry the family surname of our first Acadian ancestor, in any of its various spellings. Some of the maternal lines of the Girouard/ Giroir(e) families, carrying other family names like LeBlanc via marriage, settled in the St. Bernard, Clare region in the south of the province, and account for numerous Girouard descendants in that area. Similarly, we have many Girouard descendants on the other maternal side, now carrying the names of Chiasson and Romard, who established in Chéticamp, Cape Breton, at the other end of the province. (*See Nova Scotia book for these links*). Of course the list goes on and on. . . . and it is very important not to forget these descendants who are just as much Girouard /Giroir(e) in bloodlines as those who carry the actual surname.

For the most part, however, the descendants still carrying the family name of Girouard/Giroir/Gerrior/Girroir(e) re-established permanently in the following seven major root areas in Canada and the United States after Deportation and migrations. Of course, we also believe there may still be many Acadian descendants who re-established in France.

Girouard/Giroir Distribution-Telephone Directories, 1990.

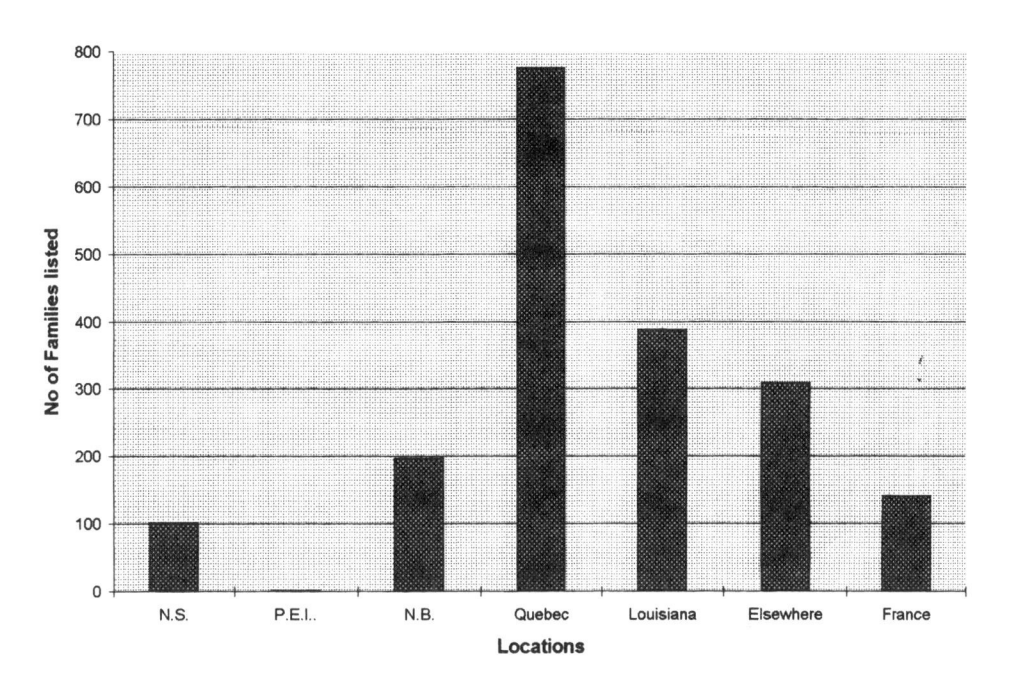

Girouard/Giroir Distribution-Telephone Directories, 1990.

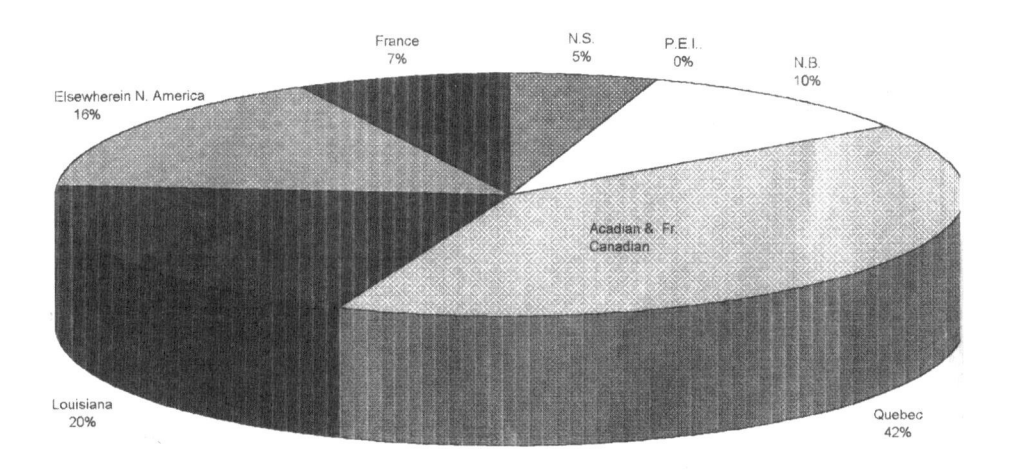

Acadian Awakenings: An Acadian Family In Exile

```
Girouard, Giroir(e)...
families established
in seven root areas
after deportation


1. Tracadie, Antigonish Co., NS
2. Larry's River, Guysborough Co., NS
3. Isle Madame, Richmond Co., NS
4. Prince Edward Island
5. New Brunswick
6. Quebec
7. Louisiana
```

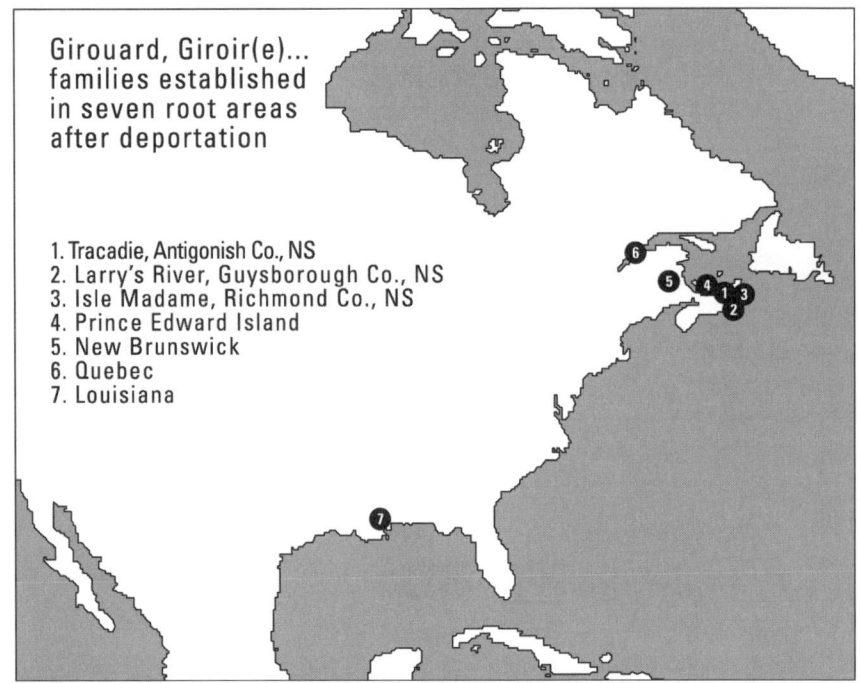

Map of seven root areas where the Girouard, Giroir(e)... descendants re-established after deportation and migrations, in North America:

The seven root areas where the Girouard, Giroir(e),Girroir, Girrior, Gerroir, Gerrior, Gerrier families re-established:

1. Antigonish County, NS—Tracadie, Heatherton and Merlin. One branch, from Joseph Nicholas Giroire [AMC Block E-5]. *Girroir, Girrior, Gerroir, Gerrior are the most common spellings used. However some branches in the USA spell their name as Gerrier.*

2. Guysborough County, NS—Larry's River, Charlos Cove and Lundy. One branch, from François Giroire [AMC Block F-5], brother of above Joseph Nicholas Giroire. *Descendants of this branch spell their surnames as "Gerrior", although early records show a number of different spellings, including Girouard.*

3. Richmond County, NS—Isle Madame: West Arichat, Arichat and Port Royal. (One branch, from Pierre [AMC Block E-3b], great-uncle of the two brothers, Joseph Nicholas and François, in Antigonish and Guysborough, above.) *Girroir, Girrior, Gerrior spellings are the most common in this branch.*

4. Prince Edward Island—Georgetown and Summerside. One branch, James Gerrior [subchart 164], descending from the same Pierre [AMC Block E-3b]. Many descendants today are in Trenton and New Glasgow, NS, and the USA. "Gerrior" *spelling is the most common, although Gerrier is a spelling used for some of these branches in the USA.*

5. New Brunswick—Along the Atlantic coastline of the province, there are four branches, from the four sons of Paul Gervais Girouard: Benjamin, Pierre, Joe Bob and Béoni, all descending from Pierre, above [AMC Block E-3b]. This is the second largest concentration of Acadian Girouards in North America. Descendants of the daughters of Joe Bistet Girouard are Girouard descendants also, carrying the name of LeBlanc and Bastarache, founding families of Bouctouche. *Girouard spelling is used only in New Brunswick.*

6. Québec—along the St. Lawrence River and its tributary rivers, there are six Acadian Girouard branches. The following descendants of each of the blocks listed in the master chart established in Québec.
1 Germain Girouard [AMC Block D-2]
2 Alexandre Girouard [AMC Block C-3a] *[There should be descendants in the Montcalm region of at least one of Alexandre's sons, recorded in Québec; I have not been successful in contacting them to date—B.G.]*
3 Jacques Girouard [AMC Block D-3a]
4 Claude Girouard [AMC Block I-3a]
5 Guillaume Girouard [AMC Block J-3a]
6 Germain Girouard [AMC Block D-3b].
   Joining them later in Québec were
7 Pierre Girouard [AMC Block C-4m1] and
8 Joseph Girouard [AMC Block I-4m1].
Québec thus has the largest concentration of Acadian Girouard descendants in North America. *Girouard spelling only is used in Québec although very early records show Giroir*

7. Louisiana—along the Mississippi and Bayous is the third largest concentration of Acadian Girouards/Giroirs in North America. These represent two branches, Honoré Giroir and Firmin Girouard, both of whom descend from Pierre [AMC Block E-3b]. *Girouard and Giroir spellings are both common.*

In the forty years that followed the Deportation, Acadians grew rapidly in number, with large families. In 1803, New Brunswick had approximately 3,038 Acadians; Nova Scotia 3,937 and PEI 353, amounting to nearly 8,000, or 8% of the overall regional population, and nearly as many as were exiled during the Deportation years.

Throughout the nineteenth century the Acadian population continued to grow.

Map of re-establishment Acadian communities in Nova Scotia, in seven root areas, based on research of Sally Ross, Alphonse Deveau and, Bill Gerrior, the author of this book.

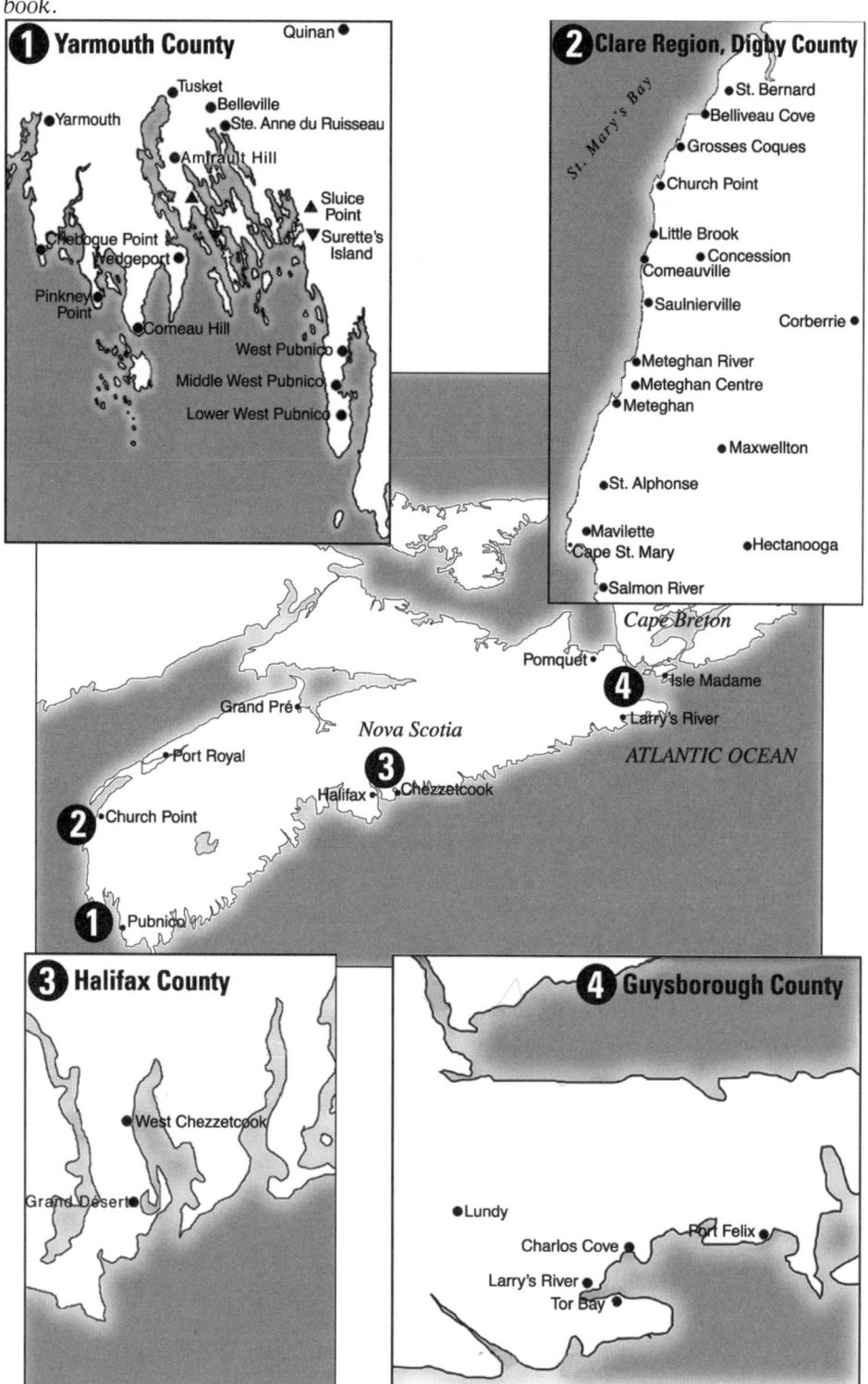

Port Royal and old Acadie

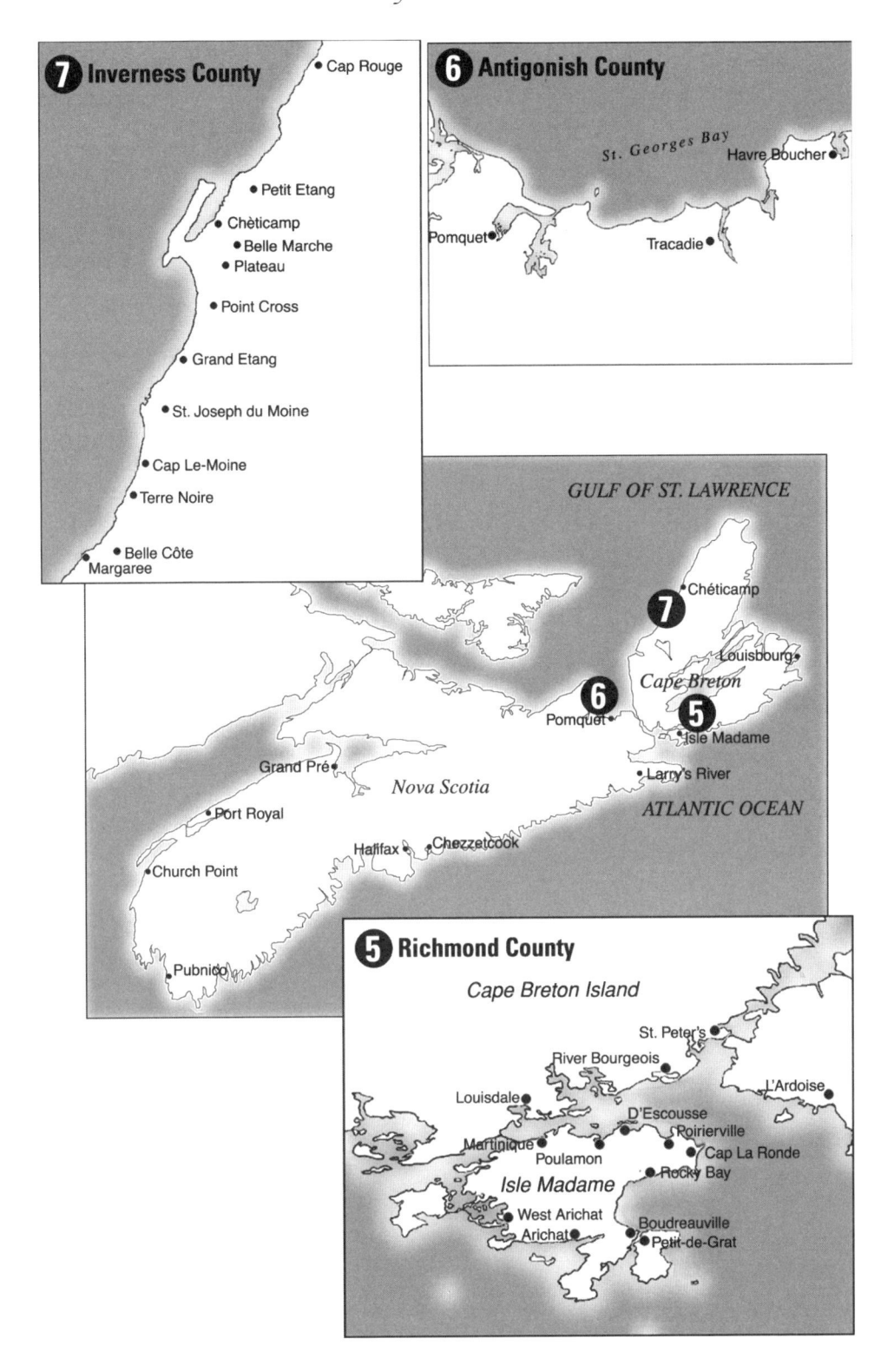

DISTRIBUTION OF GIROUARDS/GIRROR/GIRROIR/GERRIOR(E) TODAY

Combining smaller regions into a larger unit—which we are accustomed to doing in Canada—New Brunswick, PEI and Nova Scotia can be considered under one heading: the Maritime Provinces.

The picture then looks like this. The Maritimes Provinces, taken together have eight branches carrying the family name after Deportation and migrations. Québec has eight branches, but since some of these branches were established there before Deportation, in the second and third generation, they are now more populous than the eight branches in the Maritimes which established around the fourth and fifth generations; Louisiana with its two branches would be third in size of these distribution areas in North America.

And so, as you see, we Nova Scotia Gerriors still know how to manoeuvre the statistics to survive, by grouping together when we have to compete for numbers with any of our larger neighbours! Statistics can always be manipulated to tell you what you want to hear. *C'est la vie!*

In all these areas, however, migration in the last century has been into major cities and towns, accounting for a great deal of assimilation, and leaving those Acadians remaining in the root areas constantly struggling to protect and promote the uniqueness of their Acadian culture.

EPILOGUE

Giroir Vill/Girouard Village (Tupperville) Today

The foundation of the homestead of François Girouard and Jeanne Aucoin at La Montagne, (marked François Girouard and Julien Lort on Lanctôt's map), is about 1.6 km. north of the causeway at Granville Ferry. The land is just to the right of the main road in a cleared field, having two quonsett huts adjacent to the site, which were used as restaurants at one time. The land today belongs to Linda Walker, who inherited it from her father, Joe H. Casey, former M.L.A. for Annapolis West. This is the land of our first ancestor, the place which is named la Montagne on some old maps of the 17th and 18th centuries.

In doing some initial research in the area, with the help of Richard Laurin, who is a tour guide for today's Acadians visiting their roots in Acadie, we discovered in an open field to the left of the half-round restaurants, what we believe to be the original foundation of the home of our first Francois Girouard and Jeanne Aucoin, (occupied later by their daughter Charlotte Girouard and her husband, Julien Lord *dit* La Montagne). *Refer to the fort map at Port Royal, which shows La Montagne presented earlier in this chapter.*

The family, as discussed, moved up stream to establish Giroir Vill/Girouard Village, now called Tupperville, in Annapolis County. Tupperville is 16 km. east of Annapolis Royal, and 9.6 km. west of Bridgetown on Highway 201, approximately 360 metres from the Tupperville School Museum.

By using the 1733 map and today's map of Nova Scotia, one can easily find this exact location, by following highway #201 and comparing the turns on the river to the actual turns on the road following the river. You will find yourself in the community of Tupperville.

In 1984, as part of the preparation for the 1985 reunion, my son Steve and I planned a trip to the Annapolis Valley to find the location of Giroir Vill/Girouard Village, further upriver on the south side, where François' son, Jacques, later established his family. Because of the shape of the river and the excellent 1733 map based on Mitchell's survey, with corrections from other maps and surveys of 1753, which I obtained from the National Archives in Ottawa, we were easily able to locate the area known as Giroir Vill/Girouard Village in 1733. This location is also marked as Giroir Vill on another early map of the period. [133]

Since my first visit in 1984, I have learned much more about Giroir Vill/Girouard Village, through the help of Marion Inglis who presently owns and farms the land where Giroir Vill/Girouard Village once lay. This land has been in her husband's family for over two hundred years.

Top photo: Two restaurants to the right of Foundation site. Half-round buildings (quonsett huts) mark the site and fields showing the foundations in the area.
Next: Foundation depression at the site of François Girouard's former homestead
Above left: Series of trees planted to act as a fence to contain cattle.
Above right: Series of trees planted to act as a fence to contain cattle.

I first visited Mrs. Inglis and some of her family at the Inglis farm in Tupperville on November 13, 2000, and it was clear from her warm welcome that she was very much interested in all of the history and heritage of her community and of the Acadian Girouard pioneers of this region. She is the chairperson of the Tupperville School Museum and has been very active in preserving local history. Her committee consists of a very active and knowledgeable group of residents interested in preserving the history and culture of this area.

I was introduced to Marion Inglis by Richard Laurin, a former Parks Canada tour guide at Grand Pré. He operates a company called Novacadie, which offers private tours at Port Royal and other locations in Nova Scotia and New Brunswick, especially designed for Acadian families who wish to know more about their routes and roots, and the original locations of their first ancestors in Acadie. Richard is particularly interested in developing tours designed for the Girouard/Giroir(e) descendants, and he was aware, as a result of his tours in the area of Port Royal, that Mrs. Inglis' ancestors were among the very early owners of the former Giroir Vill/Girouard Village land, from shortly after the Deportation to the present day.

Mrs. Inglis' home is located further west than the riverside location which my son Steve and I had originally visited in 1984, but still on Giroir Vill/Girouard Village land, off Route # 201 through present-day Tupperville.

I visited and interviewed Mrs. Inglis again on November 30, 2000. I was able to trace the ownership of the Giroir Vill/Girouard Village lands after the Deportation with the help of Mrs. Inglis and her family, and official documents which I obtained from the Western Region Land Information Centre.[134]

The chain of ownership of the Inglis house can be traced from shortly after the Deportation of the Acadians in 1755, to the present day, as follows, with the direct line of Carmen Inglis, (Marion's husband) marked in bold.

OWNER	PERIOD OF OCCUPATION
Joseph Rice	1777—1839
Phillip Inglis (great-grandfather of Carmen Inglis)	1839—1841
Elizabeth Inglis	1841—1887
Charles Inglis (grandfather)	1887—1887
James Alfred Inglis	1887—1923
Lalia A. Woodbury	1923—1933
Joseph William Inglis, Jr., also known as William Joseph, farmer (father)	1933—1938
Carmen Inglis, farmer	1938—1963
Carmen and Marion Inglis	1963—

Acadian Awakenings: An Acadian Family In Exile

Opposite page: View from Giroir Vill /Girouard Village (now Tupperville) in Annapolis Valley. The river is the Annapolis River.
#1 Downriver (westward) toward the basin and Port Royal Fort.
#2 River, eastward toward the town of Paradise.
#3 Northward from Giroir Vill /Girouard Village with North Mountains in background.
#4 From Giroir Vill /Girouard Village looking south away from the river toward higher ground and forest area, with present dwelling.

In the historical description of the land in the documents, we have the following comments:

When Joseph Rice came to this area he purchased a goodly amount of La Ferme Marsh and built a house. In his will of 1830, he leaves rooms in his house or any built on the property to Elizabeth Dowling, a widow. It is possible that she was the widow of his brother, Eleazer. He leaves the farm to Phillip Inglis, husband of Elizabeth Dowling Rice, the second. According to present owner, there was an older house on the property. It is possible that Phillip built this house after he got possession of the farm. After Phillip's and his wife Elizabeth's deaths, the property was officially divided among their children *(B.97, p. 229.)* although some already had possession. Charles signed off his rights to his brother, James Alfred. This included the house. In Alfred's will in 1923 he leaves the property to his niece, Lalia Woodbury, daughter of his brother, John, who looked after him and his brother, William.

Ginette Arsenault, Program Director for the (Congrès mondial acadien) CMA2004 The World Congress of Acadians 2004, meeting with Marion Ingles and some of the committee members and supporters at the school museum in Tupperville. Myself and L. to R.: Michael Tupper, Jeff Achenbach, Perry Everett, Anthony (Toni) Napoli, Ginette Arsenault, Janie (Inglis) Barkhouse, Natalie Robinson, Marion Inglis and Loretta Tugles.

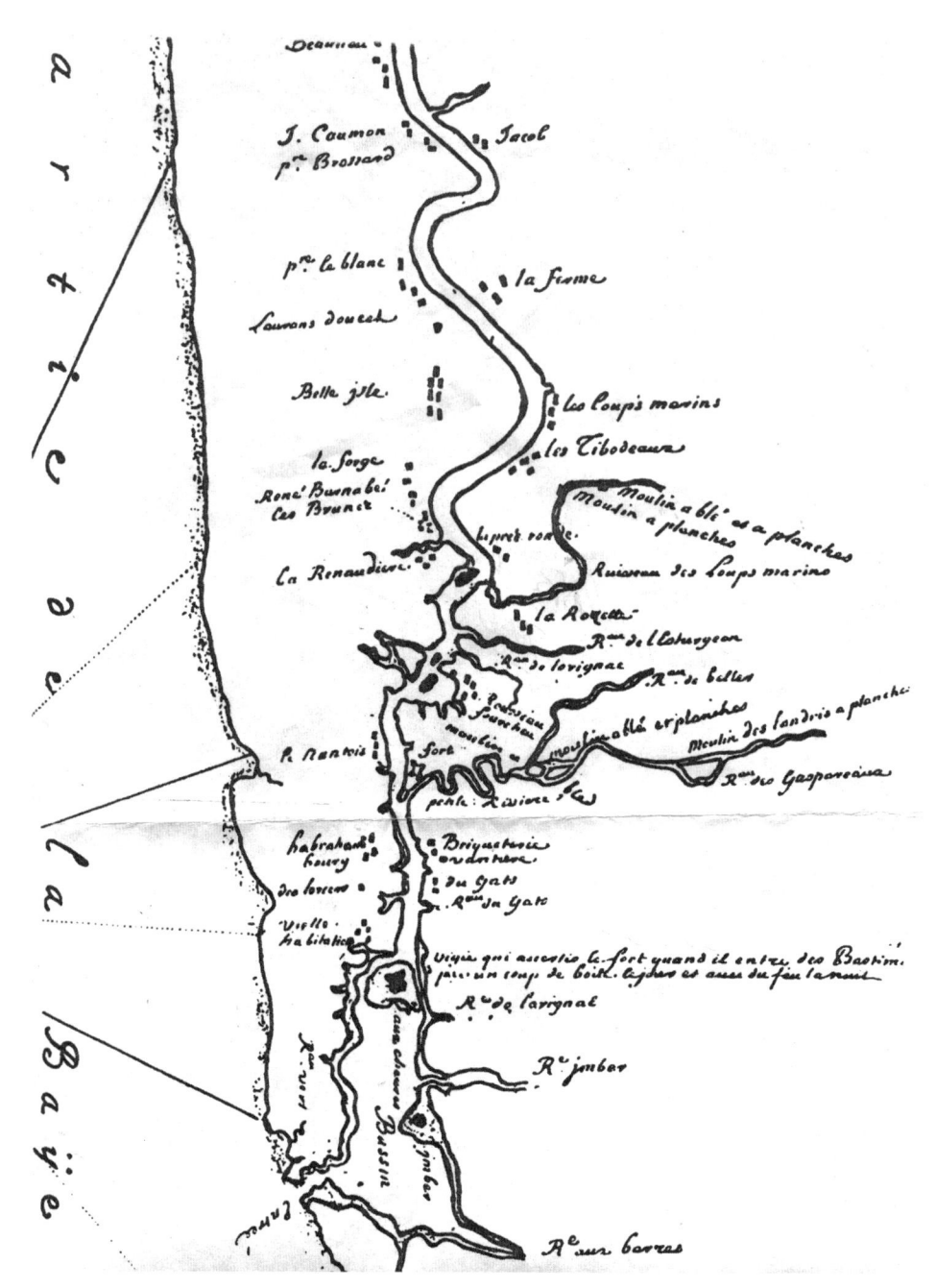

Port Royal, 1710, showing La Ferme and Jacob Girouard's house location (map by French engineer Delabat)

Another document from the Land Information Centre records the sale of La Ferme Marsh in 1784, by William and Lydia Laurence to Joseph Rice, along with some other bordering lands. According to this deed, La Ferme Marsh, which Joseph Rice purchased, was forty-eight rods in width.

In combination, these documents, maps and aerial photos provide us with proof beyond a doubt that the land presently owned by the Inglis family was the land owned by our Acadian ancestors, Jacques (*dit* Jacob) Girouard, son of François Girouard and Jeanne Aucoin, the first Girouard family in Acadia. Two of these maps also show Alexandre *dit* du Ru Girouard [AMC Block C-3a], son of Jacques Girouard and Marguerite Gouthrot, and his brother Claude Giroir [AMC Block I-3a], also son of Jacques (Jacob) Girouard.

Mrs. Inglis had one tour-bus visit with many Acadians/Cajuns from Texas and

Aerial photo Giroir Vill/Girouard Village "la ferme" area. The present-day Inglis Farm and homestead, 1992, is enclosed in the white border. The "X" marks the apple orchard, site of one of the Girouard foundations.

Acadian Awakenings: An Acadian Family In Exile

The following photo collages will give the reader some idea of the great beauty, productivity and fertility which still exist on this ancient farm, and the importance of the old Acadian Girouard sites on this property.

Inlgis Farm sign at Marion Inglis' fruit and vegetable roadside barn stand

Two-hundred-year-old homestead on the Inglis Farm and Mrs. Marion Inglis in her home during our visit

Photos by Steve Gerrior, son of the author

Port Royal and old Acadie

Below: part of fruit stand collage
The Inglis fruit stand in front of the Inglis house demonstrates that this farm is still producing beautiful vegetables and fruit.

Photo by Steve Gerrior

Louisiana, including possibly at least one Girouard descendant. At the end of their tour of the Giroir Vill/Girouard Village farmland, (the Inglis Farm), the group stood in a circle, holding hands, around the Girouard cellar foundation, near the barn foundation in the old apple orchard—a very emotional experience, said Mrs. Inglis.

This apple Orchard has very old trees and is likely part of the same orchard which is shown on the Léopold Lantôt's map of Jacob Girouard's land earlier in this chapter. The scene might look like this in the 1600's and early 1700's

There are other foundations, just above the Girouard marsh on the upper

Depiction of the seventeenth century Acadian families in an orchard at Port Royal.
Courtesy of Parks Canada - Artist: Terry MacDonald - 1988 - #H 03 03 01(03)

Photo collage opposite:
#1 Mrs Inglis also pointed out, to Richard Laurin and I, the old French well which was filled in for safety reasons, but which we were able to easily see, by just lifting the sods It was located close to the old Post Road.
#2: Mrs. Inglis also pointed out the nearby barn foundation. It is overgrown now, but she remembers in her youth, in the 1930's and 40's, seeing the foundation and hearing the farmers speak about the old French barn next to the house foundation.
#3 Foundation location where the group of Cajun visitors stood holding hands. This is in the present large apple orchard across the main road from the Inglis home.
#4 Mrs. Inglis said this plant blooms annually in the spring in a beautiful pink flower, and appears nowhere else on the farm but over this ancient Acadian Girouard foundation.
#5 View of a field, with North Mountain in background and sheep in foreground, much like those François Girouard owned, 250 years earlier. Photo taken from the French well site.

All photos by Steve Gerrior

Port Royal and old Acadie

#1 #2

#3

#4 #5

Acadian Awakenings: An Acadian Family In Exile

land, below the tree-line at the foot of the South Mountain. Mrs. Inglis and her grandson, Gregory helped us find these two original Giroir Vill/Girouard Village foundations by taking us across the main road from her house to another road leading back toward the South Mountain (the Old Post Road). From there, her grandson, Gregory, took us on a road to the left of a "No Trespassing" sign, staying close to a wire fence, leading down towards the marsh stopping at a fork in the road where we found the first Girouard foundation, an indentation in the ground now covered, with four or five trees around the perimeter.

#1

#2

#3

Port Royal and old Acadie

Opposite page: #1 The road starting from the main highway which begins just across the main #201 highway from the end of Marion's driveway. As you are walking up the road, make a left and follow the road next to the fence which takes you to a fork in the road, where you will find the next Acadian Girouard cellar foundation.
 # 2 Arriving at the fork, or Y in the road, you will find the first Girouard foundation.
 # 3 Richard Laurin in the foundation depression

Below #4 Bill standing in the foundation depression. It was a bit of an eerie feeling standing in the middle of this foundation, as I reflected back to our ancestors.
 # 5 The second Girouard foundation. We took the left fork at the Y in the road for about 30-45 metres to a large marker tree (see photo) Then we went into the woods to the right of this tree about 3-4.5 metres.
 # 6 There we found the second old Girouard foundation—again an indentation in the ground, over which trees had grown around the perimeter.

#4

#5

#6

Acadian Awakenings: An Acadian Family In Exile

The Girouard house foundations were located on the upper land above the marsh, matching Lanctôt's description accompanying the Girouard map.

Below #1 I have marked the foundation locations with an x looking up from the marsh
 # 2 Looking over the marsh at the North Mountain from the marsh below the Girouard foundations.
#3 Giroir Ville/Girouard Village marsh, looking at North Mountain from another location on the marsh.
 # 4 Walking up the road from the Girouard marsh. The "x" marks the location of the Girouard foundation that we found.

#1

#2

#3

#4

Recent research on the Land at Giroir Vill /Girouard Village (Tupperville)
Before I begin to explain the research itself, I must begin by setting the stage and tone of this research.

Cluny Maher, a resident of Tupperville, a well-known artist, and strong supporter of my research in this area, is very much in touch with the land and the landscape in the Annapolis River region, depicting many beautiful scenes in his paintings. He is a keen observer of the different forms that land takes throughout time and the seasons. His son, Daniel (Danny), has the same keen observations it seems, according to the following excerpts taken from his master's thesis written for Technical University of Nova Scotia, 1993, which his father shared with me during one of my research visits to Tupperville.

I find in this writing, a deep and profound rationale, expressed most elegantly, for the research that I am presently doing concerning the land of our first ancestors in the Annapolis River region. Let me share some excerpts from Daniel Maher's writing. His thesis, primarily referring to the Annapolis Valley region is entitled "The Place a Name Makes". On the first page he states, "The landscape is a vessel. It is a treasury of hundreds of years of human investment. In all senses of the word, it is an archive."

He goes on to quote Chief Seattle. "The earth is rich in the lives of our kin". He then expresses an idea, which is part of what I am trying to achieve—a link or connection to the past, through a study of the land where our ancestors first established in North America. "The landscape reaffirms an auspicious continuity of time and a connectedness of all things. . . ."Daniel continues by quoting Guy Debar. "When confronted with an unfamiliar or especially rich environment, we do begin to perceive in a fuller way: to see, hear, smell, taste, and touch our environment... [135]

Further, he quotes J. Douglas, *Landscapes of the Mind*, (1990) to illustrate his point of land connectedness and rootedness:

The modern mid-twentieth-century novel reflects not only the growing placelessness of our civilization, but also the inevitable sense of loss that placelessness generates: moreover, we are confronted by the inevitable place-loss, itself a kind of self-loss, which comes from our loss of childhood ... [*i.e. that the land has a greater appreciation, as we move from childhood to adulthood and get further away from our roots in place and time—interpretation by BG]*

Daniel Maher goes on to say:

As adults we search for a much deeper understanding of our environment, beyond mere perception towards an essence of reality. . . .It must become an intellectual understanding …we need to be compassionate; we need to make connections; we need to be self-critical; we must perceive the world as a whole…. To cosmocize our landscape we must go beyond a catalogue of what is. We need to know why and why not something else…It [the study of our environment] must be an interdisciplinary examination spanning all fields of study, from geology to literature.

This introduction, so beautifully expressed in these excerpts, set the stage for my research of the land in Giroir Vill/Girouard Village and LaMontagne in the Annapolis River region, and may give the reader an appreciation for the challenge and the responsibilities that many archaeologists face in their professional work as they explore these very old Acadian sites, the beginnings of Acadian culture and heritage in North America. Like the surgeon, the work of the archaeologist is so delicate that one slip of the knife could mean death of a valuable artifact, which might interpret part of the mystery of our ancestors' existence. This is a painstakingly slow process, and we all must be very patient.

So let me begin now with an explanation of my present research: With regard to both of these locations—Giroir Vill/Girourad Village and La Montagne—there is an exciting possibility of some archaeological exploration in the near future, with the lead coming from Jonathan Fowler, an archaeologist in Nova Scotia who has devoted a great deal of time researching Acadian sites in this province. Over the past two years Jonathan Fowler has been responsible for archaeological research at Grand Pré National Historic Park. In collaboration with the National Historical Site Director, Donna Doucet, this research has attracted the attention of many people interested in the history of Acadia, and has received wide media coverage.

Jonathan Fowler is very interested in the Giroir Vill/Girouard Village site, and has indicated to me that he would like to proceed with some initial exploration of the various sites sometime in the near future. The Nova Scotia Museum has also indi-

Jonathan Fowler reflects on some of the exciting findings at Grand Pré

cated an interest in my research. Remember that Belle Isle, just across the river from Giroir Vill/Girouard Village, was the site of an important archaeological dig under the direction of David Christianson, Curator of Archaeology, Nova Scotia Museum.

In connection with this research, Ron Robichaud, teacher at the Nova Scotia Community College, Centre of Geographic Sciences (COGS), Lawrencetown, NS, attended a presentation that I was giving at Grand Pré National Park, and thought that this research of the Girouard foundations would be an excellent mapping project for one of his senior students. Mr. Robichaud also has a keen interest in the Port Royal Acadian sites, as his own ancestors are also named on the 1733 Mitchell map.

Senior student Marcel Gelinas produced the following map, using research data which I provided and his own fieldwork, using a commercial GPS instrument. His work confirmed the accuracy of my rough-copy mapping of the research, since his independent field data matched my data, using a handheld GPS instrument. This map, which Marcel produced under the direction of Ron Robichaud, proved to be an excellent project and was proudly displayed at the end-of-year functions. It will be useful for future research as the project develops. Copies were provided to David Christianson, Curator of Archaeology for the Nova Scotia Museum historical collection, and to Jonathan Fowler for his records. I am grateful to Ron Robichaud for initiating this project and monitoring its progress to the end result!

Visiting Giroir Vill/Girouard Village (Tupperville)
With the assistance and support of the Tupperville Museum committee, we hope to place a monument on the former Giroir Vill /Girouard Village farmlands at the Tupperville School Museum, which is itself already recognized as a municipal heritage property. This legacy is very important to our family internationally. We are very fortunate indeed that this book, *Acadian Awakenings: Roots and Routes*, and the bronze plaque of the Acadian Master Chart will both be displayed inside the museum to provide more detailed background for the permanent monument outside the museum.

The museum is an important place for our Acadian families to visit, and also a place to learn more about the Planter and Loyalist families who settled here after the Acadians. These links are enriching to both cultures and families of present-day descendants; more sharing of this nature, in my opinion, would be beneficial to a number of Acadian and Planter families in the Port Royal area. This site will be a permanent historic site for the Acadian Girouard family as a result of this partnership and interest from both cultural groups. Please keep this in mind while planning your vacation around the World Congress!

During the Girouard family reunion in 2004, we hope to have Jef Achenbach, a member of this vibrant and active museum committee, construct an actual full-sized model Acadian home near one of our original Acadian Girouard/Giroir foundation sites. Jef is an expert in the building of Acadian homes with *bousillage* and thatched roofs, as well as Acadian clay ovens—a wonderful, sensory, hands-on

Acadian Awakenings: An Acadian Family In Exile

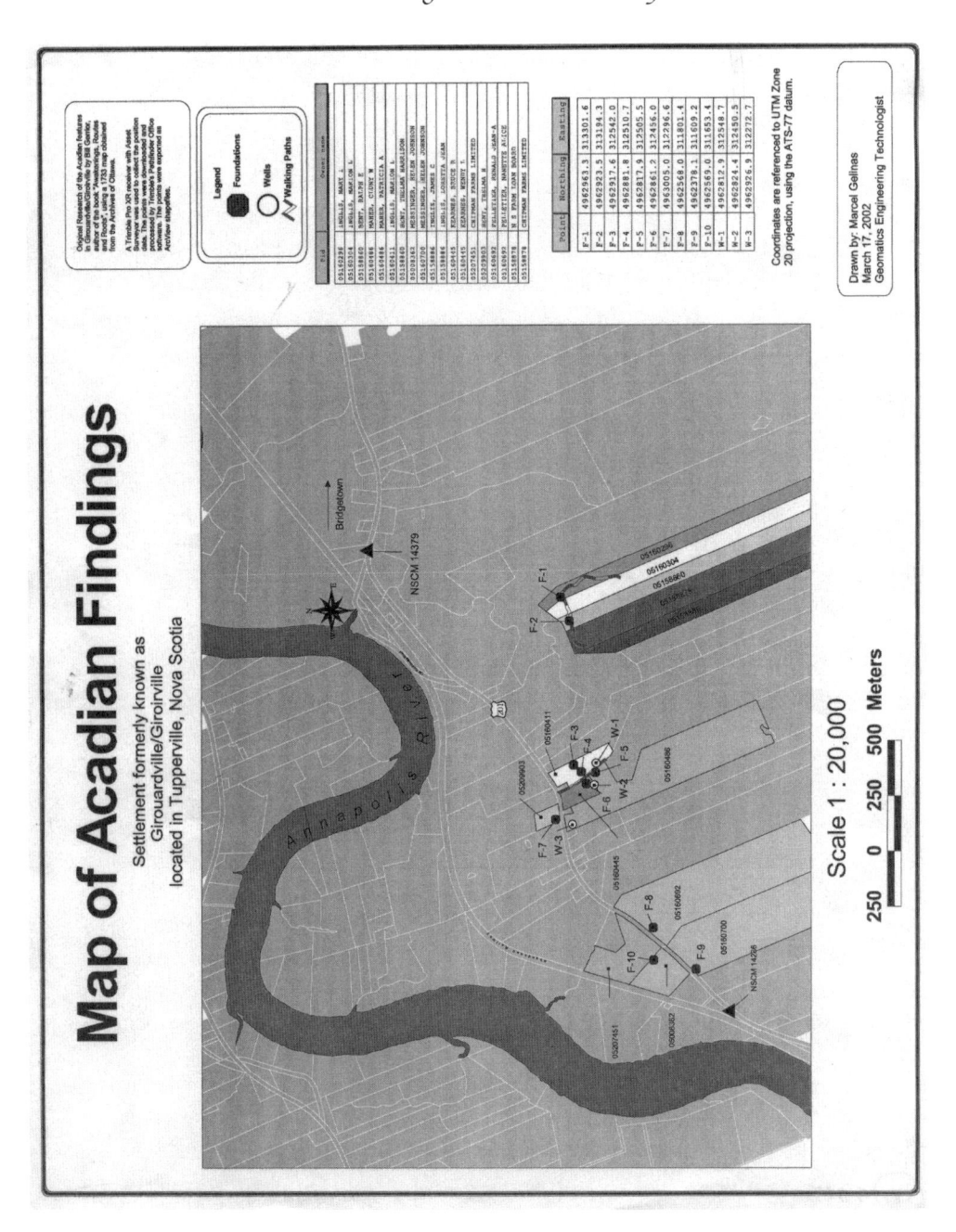

Giroir Vill / Girouard Village foundations, as mapped by Marcel Gilinas

experience which both my sister, Evelyn Oakley, and I were fortunate to experience. The Tupperville museum offers an annual workshop in building these clay ovens. The clay ovens are the ones visible at the back of the Acadian home, in the painting by Azor Vienneau, presented earlier in this chapter. The clay is taken from the Terre Rouge River, which is the river located on the Giroir Vill/Girouard Village farmlands, identified on some maps because of its importance as a source of the red clay necessary for constructing Acadian bake ovens, and in the construction of homes.

Here are a few images of this wonderful day-long workshop, given by Jef Achenbach & Perry Everett, which my sister, Evelyn and I attended, with others, including a baker from France who now resides in Nova Scotia.

Tupperville School Museum circa 1858

Tupperville School Museum, ca. 1858 a registered Municipal Heritage Property.
Courtesy of ink sketch artist: Janie (Inglis) Barkhouse

Below: The workshop brochure cover page.

Courtesy of Tupperville Museum.

Opposite top: The author, while collecting red clay from the river bank, could not resist a dip in the Terre Rouge River, where the first families of Giroir Vill/Girouard Village in the late 1600 and early 1700's must have done the same.- Photo by Jef Achenbach
Opposite middle: mixing the clay must have been a social event for family members, I am sure. L to R: Jean-Marc Riant, Evelyn Oakley, Perry Everett, Bill Gerrior and Darrel Boudreau.
Opposite bottom: Bill, Jef and Perry putting on the dome over the sand mound, which was used to create the cavity in the oven.

Photo credits for all photos of clay workshop activities - except Terre Rouge River : by John Paull

Tupperville School Museum presents June 10, 2001

Acadian Oven-Building Workshop

WORKSHOP LEADERS

JEF ACHENBACH
PERRY EVERETT

CONTACT INFORMATION

Jef Achenbach
c/o Annapolis Thatching Co-op Inc.
Phone: 902-532-2749
E-mail: j.achenbach@ns.sympatico.ca

Tupperville School Museum Coordinator
E-mail: tuppervillemuseum@auracom.com

NOVA SCOTIA
Tourism and Culture

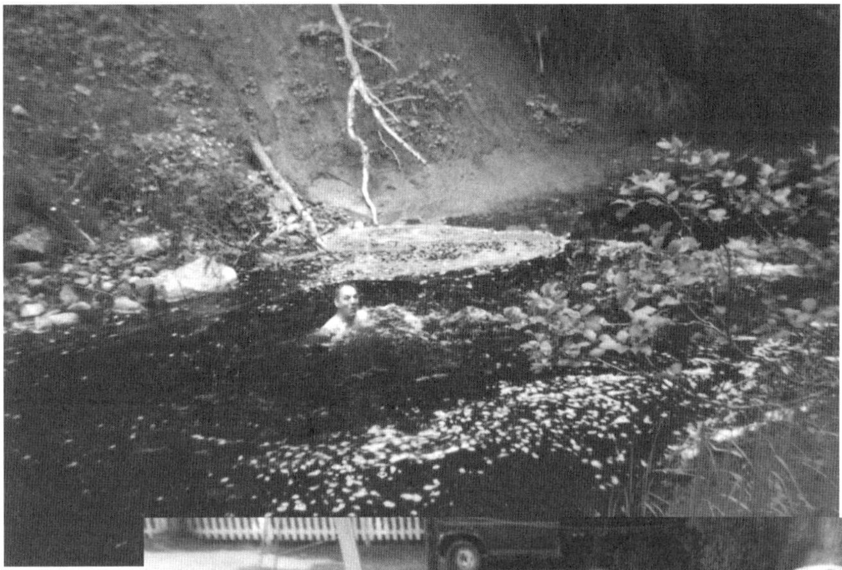

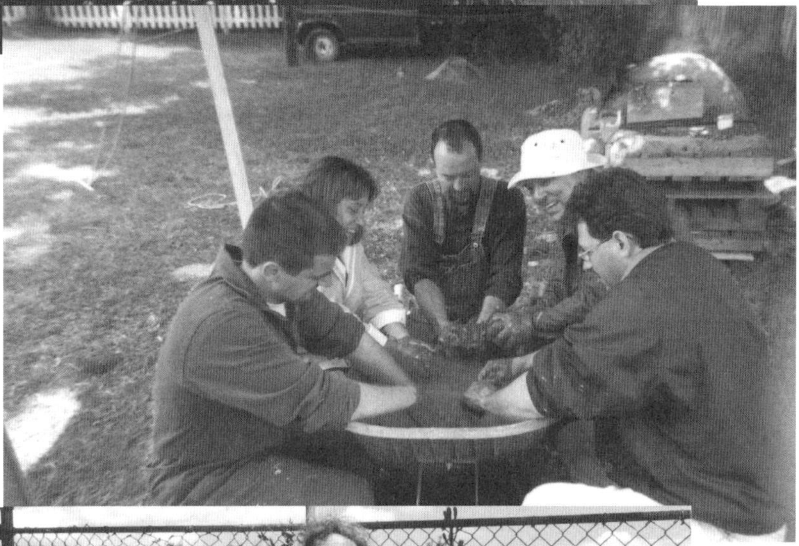

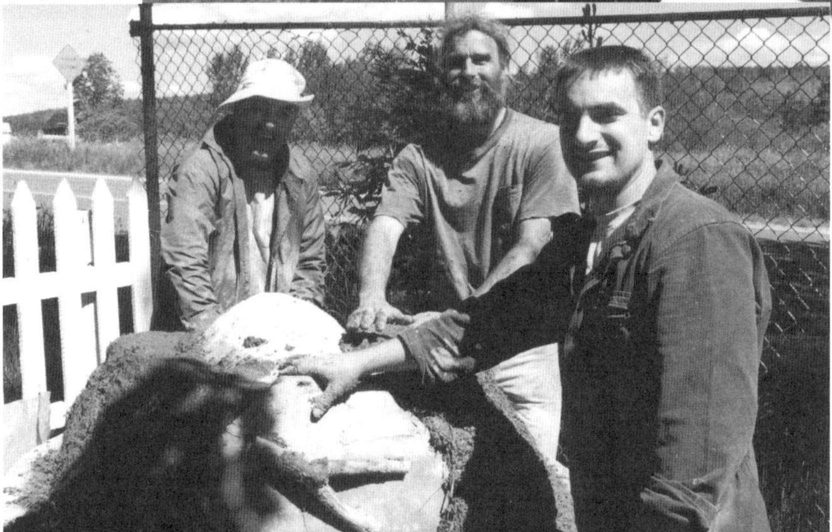

Jean-Marc Riant, of France, residing in Lunenburg (a professional baker).

Opposite top: the sand mound was shovelled out after the clay dried and fired up until the oven was at maximum heat then the fire material is removed and the door cover put on.
Opposite middle: the oven will retain its heat for a long time, allowing the baker to mix his dough and bake as many loaves of bread as needed.
Opposite bottom: The bread is baked and as you can see turned out great!

Below: Letter from John Paull, a visitor to the museum on the day of the workshop.

Mr. Jef Achenbach,
R.R. #1, Annapolis Royal,
NS B0S 1A0

Friday, June 15, 2001

Dear Jef,

I enjoyed meeting you and your friends last Sunday. I do hope that I was not too disruptive regarding your clay oven building project.

Joan and I enjoyed the loaf of bread, the difference in texture and taste resulting from the clay oven baking was palpable and very enjoyable.

As promised, I enclose the photos I took at Tupperville. Sorry they're not more professional. If by chance you'd like more prints just send me an e-mail quoting the number on the back of the print(s) in question, and I'll be happy to oblige.

Sincerely,

John H. Paull

Acadian Awakenings: An Acadian Family In Exile

Research trip to Bouctouche Acadian Museum, New Brunswick, to share ideas and plan more exciting Acadian workshops at Tupperville. Left to Right: Committee members of the Family Association of Girouard, Giroir, Gerrior: Gisèle (Girouard) Nowlan, Fernand Girouard (Vice President), Maurice Girouard (President). Tupperville Museum Committee: Jef Achenbach, Jo Stern, David Scarratt (with nice French hat). Second Row: Anthony (Tony) Napoli, Michael Tupper, Susan Olin and Bill Boucher (Bouctouche Museum Society).

Courtesy of Marian Inglis, President of Tupperville Museum Committe

Mrs. Inglis, who lives on the old Giroir Vill/Girouard Village land at Tupperville, is very open to having any Girouard descendants visit her farm to learn more about their history and heritage. However, as visitors can appreciate, she operates a busy farm and requires at least two weeks notice for visits off-season. Otherwise, during the regular tourist season of May (Apple Blossom time) until mid-October, the best option is to arrange a tour through Novacadie Tours, Richard Laurin's company, which has pre-arrangements with Mrs. Inglis for visits and tours. The tour information is customized for each Acadian family in Port Royal (and other Acadian sites). The Girouards/Giroirs are among the first Acadian families to be researched for these specialized tours, because I have been collaborating with Richard Laurin, providing information from my research. This information is for the benefit of all our Girouard Giroir(e) visitors, ensuring that Richard has extensive knowledge of the family links, in addition to his own research of the area, regarding our roots and routes, heritage, genealogy and established international Acadian links.

General tour: Greetings and introductions plus a brief history of the farm. Also shown are sprayer, storage barn and containers ranging in size from old fashioned apple barrels to bushel boxes to 18 bushel bins. You can look at a quince tree, which many people have never seen, then walk along the orchard road to see a variety of apples, peaches, plums, pears strawberries, raspberries, cherries and blueberries from which you can pick whatever is in season. [No wonder our Acadian ancestors had need for little—on this beautiful fertile soil, they grew mostly everything they needed to survive -BG]. There is a tour of the old Acadian cellar, which we now know is likely the foundation of Alexandre du Ru Girouard's homestead of the 1700's, located in the present apple orchard. The Old Post Road, which used to run between Halifax and Yarmouth, is adjacent to this site. You will get a brief glimpse inside the Inglis Farm Market and a look at a 200-year-old Bough Sweet apple tree. The tour then goes to the other end of the orchard for a view of the Annapolis River. In the distance one can see the rock where, according to oral tradition, the ancestors of the present owners, over a hundred years ago, found French coins, believed to have been buried by the Acadians on their way to boats on the river at the time of the Expulsion.

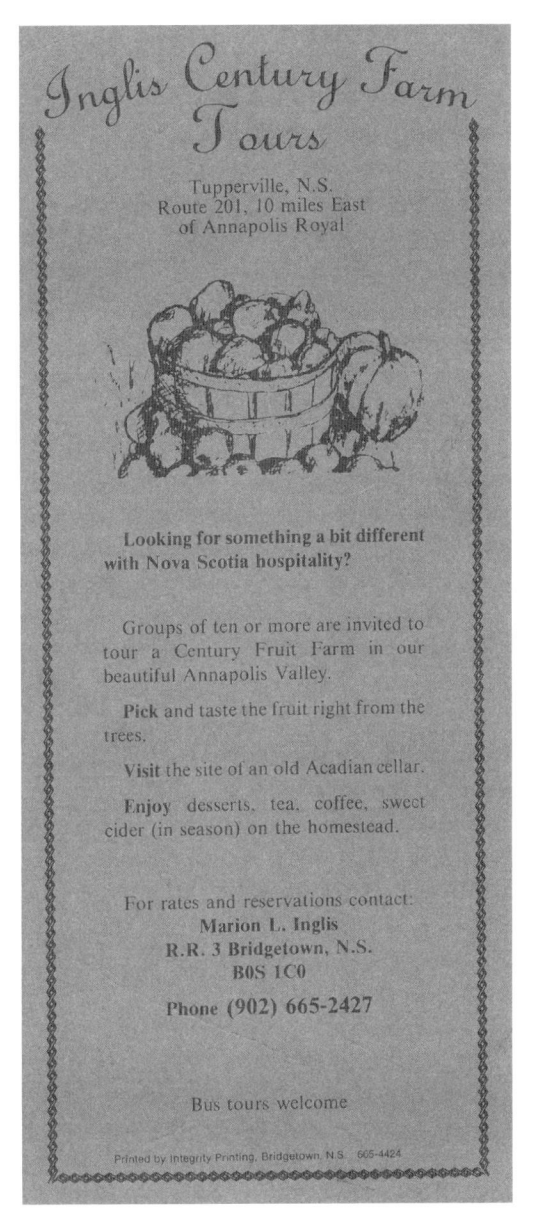

Brochures of Mrs Inglis

Refreshments: The tour includes a morning or afternoon tea, following the tour on the Century Farm lawn. Served buffet style, tea features seasonal desserts, teas, coffee and sweet cider made on the farm. Before you leave you are given recipes from the farm to take home as a souvenir of your visit.

Acadian Awakenings: An Acadian Family In Exile

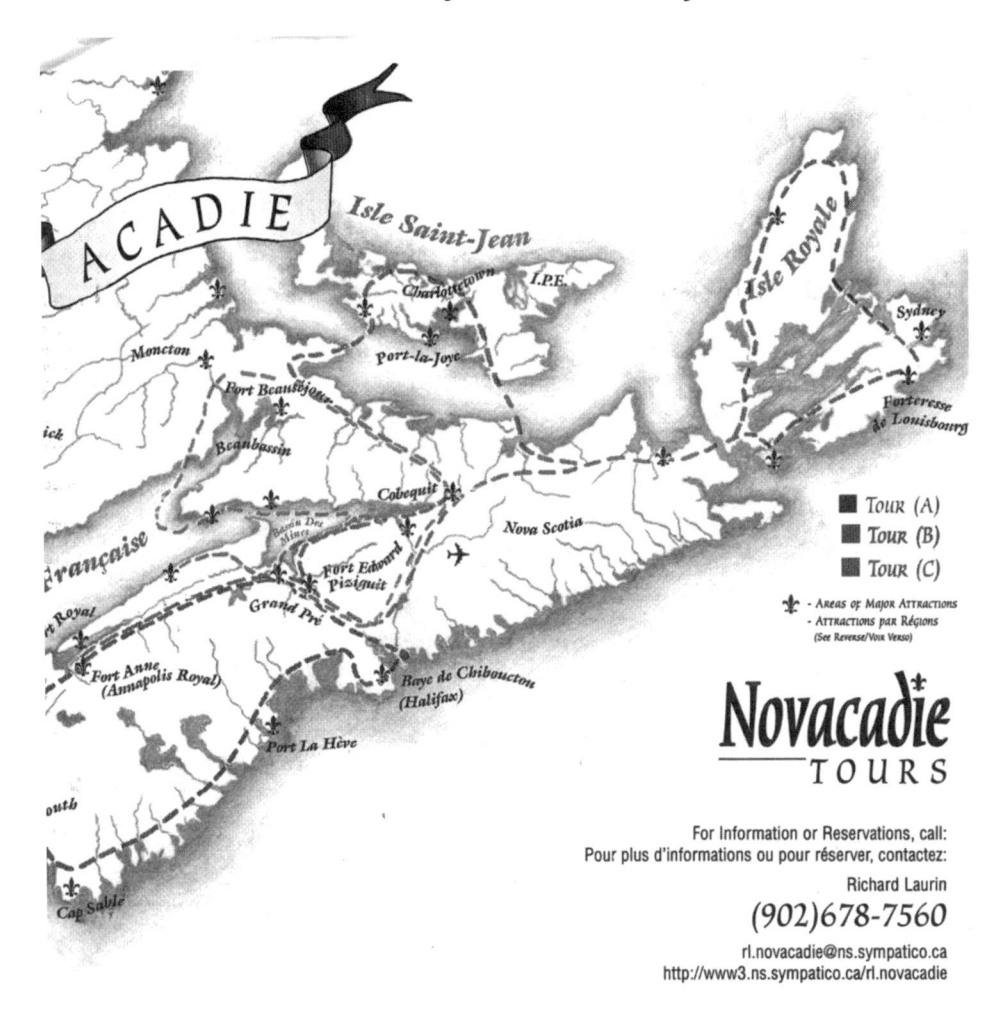

Novacadie TOURS

For Information or Reservations, call:
Pour plus d'informations ou pour réserver, contactez:
Richard Laurin
(902)678-7560
rl.novacadie@ns.sympatico.ca
http://www3.ns.sympatico.ca/rl.novacadie

Brochure provided by Richard Laurin.

Lafayette Region, Louisiana bus tour at Tupperville, NS during summer 2002.

Richard Laurin showing what is believed to be an old Acadian well on Bruce and Wendy Kearnes property adjacent to Marion Inglis' farm.

Marion cooking up the stew

Tour group lunch at the home of Marion Inglis

Concerning the Tours at Tupperville (Giroir vill/Girouard Village, I would like to present a very moving experience in the form of a poem, written by Hanson Paul LeBlanc, Jr., as a result of his visit to the land of his ancestors, the first progenitor being Daniel LeBlanc.

Being at Tupperville at the same time as of one of the most recent Novacadie Bus tours, Marion Inglis invited Hanson Paul LeBlanc to join the group and Jef Achenbach provided him with many points of reference in old Acadie to explore. The following poem concerns his reflections on some of these varied and deep emotional moments.

Insert Photo: Hanson Paul LeBlanc Jr. of Louisiana, Marion Inglis and Jef Achenbach, Tupperville, NS, at the Inglis farm.

ACADIE
(A Visit Home)
by Hanson Paul LeBLanc
Dedicated to Jef Achenbach and Marion Ingles

Acadie...Acadie
I've stood the ground
My Fathers stood
Acadie...Acadie

Sailed the Gut of Digby
Walked the street St. George
Viewed the Marsh Bellisle
The dykes of toil still guard

Strolled the creek of Gesner
And the Rivière Dauphine
Yes, I've stood the ground O' Daniel
Acadie...Acadie

Marveled the inventions
...oven attached to hearth
Adaptations...ox yoke
Ingenuity...aboiteau

Oh! the surprise you saved
On yonder hill...Grand Pré
The Cross of Deportation
Landlocked...denied to me

Fence post my companion
...grief inside released
Know my distant Fathers
Know...my Acadie

Forthcoming is your story
Associates...if not kin
Fan a flame...unknowing
That comes from deep within

Already they are giving
A light to show our way
Oh, your story, my dear Fathers
No longer a distant day

> Hanson Paul LeBlanc, Jr.
> Faubourg de la Boucanede la Louisianne

Acadie (A Visit Home) explained by Hanson Paul Jr.
From childhood I've longed to know 'To whom did I belong?' Even though the value of family was strong in my heritage, visits to grandparents was an every weekend experience from my earliest memories, family was somehow just not big enough.

In the LeBlanc family, an annual 'Family reunion' was begun in the early '50's. Never-the-less, there existed within me a strong sense of something more that was never satisfied by family gatherings. Answering that longing was effectively denied by the Family's motivation to move on, to progress in the American way. This motivation was expressed directly in statements by the accepted family leader, my Uncle Percy, i.e. "I'm not looking back, I'm moving forward", in response to inquiries as to where did I come from. The acceptance by the family that my generation would not be taught the mother tongue, in compliance with the 1920's Louisiana law that forbid the speaking of French on the school ground, further eroded my opportunities to discover and answer my inner longings.

It is this backdrop, along with my family genealogy work and history gathering that nudged me towards this visit home and the tremendous emotional experience that accompanied my Nova Scotian odyssey.

The poem
...Acadie...Acadie...this name was all that would emerge as I first viewed, from a distance, the Cross of Deportation. Gut wrenchingly these words gushed from my throat as I supported myself on the fence post that separated me from the memorial, hardly visible, without the aid of binoculars. This was my first inkling that there was something inside that needed to be released in written form. I seldom refuse such an urge. Within days I had given the first rudimentary drafts to the recent acquaintances I dedicated the poem to, Jef Achenbach, who guided, shared, and informed tremendously my visit and Marion Inglis who graciously invited me to join a tour group, for whom she had opened her property for a visit of an Acadian homesite (unexcavated foundation).

Sailed the Gut of Digby... Digby Gut, entranceway to the Annapolis Basin and Port Royal first experienced by the progenitor of the Acadian LeBlancs, Daniel LeBlanc possibly in 1644.

Walked the street St. George...oldest street in Canada, in Port Royal (Annapolis Royal) along which there are buildings, which Daniel would have visited.

Viewed the Marsh Bellisle

the dykes of toil still guard... As an incentive to come to Acadie recruits such as Daniel were promised a piece of land in return for dyke building and fur trapping. Daniel's homesite was just upriver of Bellisle Marsh where he toiled on the dykes to reclaim the marsh for farming. [This was just across the river from Giroir Vill/ Girouard Village (Tupperville) - BG]

Strolled the Creek of Gesner... Daniel's homesite is on a branch of Gesner's Creek which empties into **...the Rivière Dauphin** (Annapolis River)

Marveled the inventions

...oven attached to hearth of Acadian home...this is a uniquely Acadian. Jef suggests that this lean-to, as shown in the picture, would eventually be enclosed to accommodate a grandmother or whomever who might come to assist a mother with a sick child as in winter this would be the warmest room for convalescing.

Adaptations...ox yoke... On the forested North and South mountains the trees grew tightly packed. To harvest them ox teams were used. The large, common ox yoke used in farming and towing wagons, etc. were unusable in the forest. An adaptation, attaching the yoke to the horns and reducing its horizontal length, accommodated the tight quarters the team worked in.

Ingenuity...aboiteau... Dyke building techniques were brought over from Europe however, in Holland the water was pumped out with windmills, in Acadie the flapper valve of the aboiteau allowed the process of leaching the salt from the marsh by allowing fresh water to flow out of the marsh while denying the tide back in.

Oh! the surprise you saved
On yonder hill...Grand Pré
The Cross of Deportation
Landlocked...denied to me...Jef reminded me to ask to see the memorial cross near Grand Pré National Site that marks the departure point of the Acadians. I got choked-up just asking. The attendant walked me over to a corner of the deck, to a set of field glasses. After aiming and adjusting she directed me to peer through. In the distance was the cross. Hardly able to talk I blurted out 'I'm sorry, I've written about it and I'm overwhelmed.
Walking across the parking lot with my own binoculars, I approached the barbed wire fence and again observed the cross. By now I was grief struck and sobbing...Acadie...
with the **fence post my** (lone) **companion.**

Know my distant Fathers...I talked to my ancestors then

Associates...if not kin... By the time the words were down there were words to the people I met that gifted me with a memorable experience.

Conclusion:

This then is the recent research at Port Royal, in the Annapolis River region, with a focus on Giroir Vill/Girouard Village (Tupperville) and La Montagne near Grandville. I must say it has been an enriching experience working with the museum committee at Tupperville and their wonderful hospitality, interest and support. I look forward to future research in a continuing, collaborative approach, sharing each other's culture, friendship and wonderful, varied personalities skills and talents in the process. I would like to conclude with a song evoking the memory of the hardships of our ancestors, but at the same time celebrating these new findings and links to our heritage.

This song means more to me now than it ever did before; it is easy to see quite clearly why Acadians identified with the song " Un Acadien Errant",. (A Wandering Acadian), which was adapted from the song "Un Canadien Errant". In fact this song was one of the songs considered for the Acadian national anthem, at the Second National Acadian Convention, at Miscouche, Prince Edward Island, although the committee, in final analysis, chose "Ave Maria Stella". This gives the reader an idea of the strong sentiment this song carried for the Acadians.   The song was very appropriately sung at the first Maritime Provinces Reunion by Sharon Aucoin, accompanied by her husband, Marcel Aucoin, (both of whom have always been very close friends of ours in Halifax).

Marcel is originally from Chéticamp, Cape Breton. His European roots are in France, at La Rochelle, and of course he is connected to the first François Girouard via his connection to Jeanne Aucoin, the wife of François. Our families must have been destined to be together since both Sharon and Marcel were involved in the first two reunions in Nova Scotia. It was very appropriate that the Gerriors and the Aucoins were celebrating and remembering this moment together.

I have had the words for this song translated to give non-French-speaking readers a general idea of the meaning. For singing purposes, it is not possible to retain the rhyme scheme in the English translation. So sing it in French and refer to the English translation for the meaning, since the written music is also provided. It will always remind you of the great sacrifice our ancestors made and how we came to be where we are today.

Port Royal and old Acadie

UN ACADIEN ERRANT

Refrain	Chorus
Un Acadien errant	A wondering Acadian
Banni de ses foyers	Banished from his home
Un Acadien errant	A wondering Acadian
Banni de ses foyers	Banished from his home
Parcourait en pleurant	Crying as he's traveling
Des pays étrangers	Through strange countries
Parcourait en pleurant	Crying as he's traveling
Des pays étrangers	Through strange countries
Un jour, triste et pensif	One day sad and thoughtful
assis aux bords des flots	Sitting along side of the river
Un courant fugitif	To the fugitive current
Il adressait ces mots	He addresses these words
Si tu vois mon pays	If you see my country
Mon pays malheureux	My unhappy country
Va dire à mes amis	Go tell my friends
Que je me souviens d'eux	That I remember them
Pour jamais séparé	For never separate
Des amis de mon coeur	Your friends from your heart
Hélas où je mourrai	Alas, wherever I die
Je mourrai de douleur	I'll die in sorrow

"Un Acadien Errant"

Having evoked the past and many sacrifices of our ancestors, I have been motivated to preserve our Acadian culture and heritage for the future by contributing to its richness through this volume and the four volumes to follow in the series. Throughout this work, I have always felt that it is very important in our culture, as in all cultures, to provide models for our youth to look to with pride. It is by coming together at family reunions and celebrating all of these things that we instill in our youth the love of their ancestors and the confidence in their own abilities to take an active part in building our society and a better future for themselves and their descendants. In the words of a grade four poem which will I always remember, I address these words to our youth

When I hear the old men	When I hear the people
Telling of heroes	Praising great ones
Telling of great deeds	Then I know that I too
When I hear that telling	Shall be esteemed
Then I think within me	I too when my time comes
I too, am one of these.	Shall do mightily.

International Family Reunion 1990

At family reunions we constantly learn more of our past, and some of those heroes that the last poem speaks about, while celebrating the present, meeting relatives near and far, and sharing more of our culture. In this way we help rebuild it for the future.

This is the moment when all the dry genealogy comes to life and where people have an opportunity to laugh, dance, sing, tell stories and learn more about themselves as part of the larger family of which we are all part: the Acadians or the French Canadians, whatever the case may be. So my focus has been on the past, only so we can more meaningfully celebrate who we are today, and plan for who we may want to be in the future.

Here are some excerpts from family reunions, 1985, 1990 news clips, including the program of the First International Family reunion. These collages help convey the concept of rebuilding our culture and celebrating the present and the future. In each of the four upcoming books, I will present more details of reunions concerning Nova Scotia/Prince Edward Island, New Brunswick, Québec and Louisiana.

INTERNATIONAL REUNION - INVITED GUEST LIST

Hon. John M. Buchanan
Premier of Nova Scotia

Mayor Colin H. Chisholm
Town of Antigonish

Hon. Guy LeBlanc
Minister of Community Services and
Minister Responsible of Acadian Affairs

Mr. Francis LeBlanc
Minister of Parliament,
Ottawa

Mr. Jean-Denis Comeau
Assistant to Minister of Acadian Affairs

Mr. Paul Comeau
Executive Director, Fédération acadienne
de la N.-É.

Fr. Frank Morley
St-Peter's Parish
Tracadie, N. S.

Mr. Daniel Comeau
Regional Coordinator for
Halifax/Dartmouth, FANE

Fr. Donnelly
St-Peter's Parish
Tracadie, N. S.

Rev. Vernon Fougère
Vicar General
Diocese Antigonish

Mr. Hyland Fraser
Warden of Antigonish

Mr. Bill Gillis
M.L.A. Antigonish

Hon. Roland Thornhill
Minister of Tourism

Ms. Barbara LeBlanc
Superintendent of Grand Pre
Historic Park

Mr. Robert Bullen
FANE Representative, Antigonish

WELCOME/BIENVENUE TO THE FIRST INTERNATIONAL ACADIAN REUNION OF GERRIOR, GIROIRE, GIROIR, GIROUARD, GIRROIR, GERROIR ETC...

HIGHLIGHTS OF THIS SPECIAL WEEK-END

Friday, July 27, 1990

06:00 - 08:30 pm
- Registration, Wine & Cheese, Bar, Social, Souvenirs etc...at Bloomfield Centre.
- Open air sounds of "Strait Area Scottish Strings" and Acadian fiddle music in Bloomfield Centre.

08:30 - 08:40 pm
- Opening welcome by Mayor Chisholm of Antigonish, or his Deputy Mayor. Introduction of Guests.

08:40 - 09:30 pm
- Introductory remarks and welcome by Bill Gerrior and announcements.

09:30 - 10:30 pm
- Order of Good Cheer. Certificates presented by committee and special guests to pre-registered descendants in the province of Nova Scotia for the first time.
- Explanation of charts, relationship of various branches, genealogy overview and heritage, slide presentation etc...

10:30 - 10:45 pm
- Presentation of Plaques:
- Minister of Acadian Affairs, Guy LeBlanc, is presenting a plaque in honor of Senator Edward Lavin Giroir, 2nd Acadian Minister in the Nova Scotia Legislature. This plaque will be presented to Dr. MacDonnell, the Senator's nephew.
- Vicar General for the Diocese of Antigonish, Rev. Vernon Fougère is presenting two plaques in honor of Rev. Hubert Girroir, the first Acadian priest of Antigonish Diocese. These plaques will be presented to Fr. Conrad P. Giroir of West Arichat and Fr. Donnelly of Tracadie.

10:45 - 11:00 pm
- Guy LeBlanc, Minister of Acadian Affairs, Francis LeBlanc, Member of Parliament, Paul Comeau, Executive Director of Fédération Acadienne and Bill Gerrior will be presenting a plaque to the delegates from France.

11:00 - 11:10 pm
- Bluenose Ceremony (Fun Welcoming Ceremony)

11:00 pm -01:00 am
- Dance Troupe "Dance Interplay"- directed by Marie (Gerrior) Nugent. Also Acadian step dancing by John W. Gerrior and Joe Gerrior.

Saturday, July 28, 1990

09:00 - 10:00 am
- Social - Music by: Gerrior Family Band - Verna (Gerrior) - Gionet, Vincent Gionet, Marcel & Sharon Aucoin, Reg & Barbara Gerrior, Evelyn (Gerrior) Oakley, Herman Gerrior, Mike Gillis, Bill Gerrior, Tom Rusinak and John S. Gerrior.

10:00 - 11:00 am
- Late registration - Bloomfield Centre

10:00 - 11:00 am
- Branch photography -- see schedules "Please be on time"

01:00 - 06:00 pm
- Family Picnic - Tracadie, N.S.

08:30 pm- 01:00 am
- Dance at Bloomfield Centre featuring the River Band from Larry's River, The Gerrior Family Ensemble, Acadian Fiddle Music by John S. Gerrior and son Reg Gerrior.

Sunday, July 29, 1990

10:00 am - 12:00 pm
- A time to share notes, review genealogy, displays and collecting addresses etc... Those interested meet at Bloomfield Centre.

01:15 pm
- Mass at Cathedral co-celebrated by Fr. Conrad Giroir, West Arichat, Fr. Douglas Murphy, Larry's River, Fr. Frank Giroir, Louisiana and other clergy T.B.A. After mass, all branches will proceed to the St-F.X. Stadium for final large group photo. There will also be a draw for the Air Canada tickets between Canada and France.

HUGS, KISSES, GOODBYES

Weekend Program for the First International Reunion, 1990, St Francis University, Antigonish, Nova Scotia and St Peter's Church Parish Grounds, Tracadie, Nova Scotia.

Acadian Awakenings: An Acadian Family In Exile

1640's — International Reunion — 1990
Antigonish — Nova Scotia — Tracadie

DESCENDANTS 1990 Girouard · Gerroir · Girroir · Girouard 1640's DESCENDANTS

A GATHERING OF THE CLAN

by MARILYN SMULDERS
Special to The Daily News

The descendants of Francois Girouard — 800 strong — are having a reunion

MORE THAN 225 years ago, Bill Gerrior's ancestral family was torn apart by the expulsion of the Acadians from Nova Scotia. Some fled to New Brunswick, Prince Edward Island and Quebec, some settled in Louisiana and other parts of the eastern seaboard and some did, somehow managing to keep their roots intact in Nova Scotia.

But 1990 marks a coming together for the Gerrior family. More than 800 descendants of Francis Girouard, a farmer who stepped off a boat in Port Royal in 1647, will be gathering in Antigonish for a family reunion from July 27 to 29.

"The impetus for the reunion comes from the deportations but the focus is on family, on heritage," says Bill Gerrior, prime mover behind the reunion.

Oddly enough, not all Girouards will have the same surname as their great, great, great, great, great, great, great granddaddy.

Name misspelled

Over the years the Girouard name has been misspelled and some versions have managed to stick. Some of the spellings that survived the past four centuries include Gerrior, Gerroir, Geroir, Giroire, Girroir and last but not least, Girouard.

Bill Gerrior notes that in one family several generations back, three children had recorded their name three different ways. It's no wonder then that so many different versions exist today. The name itself means a descendant of Gerald, a name given to a man who's a capable warrior.

Bill is a Girouard junkie. Nestled into the corner of a comfortable sectional, he finds himself surrounded by thick red volumes of family history. A junior high school principal at Timberlea Junior High, 45-year-old Bill compiled these books himself. They contain branches of the family tree that date back 12 generations from Francois in the 800's to Bill's own children Steve, 18, and Suzanne, 17.

Bill caught the genealogy pox several years ago and he's been happily afflicted ever since. While teaching grade six in Hubbards, he took his students on a

Bill Gerrior has amassed plenty of documentation in tracing the branches of his family tree.

of Nova Scotia in Halifax to research their community and family. Bill took the exercise to heart, looking up his own name.

Since that time, Bill has scoured census roles, buried himself in church records and scanned hundreds of microfiche screens. He's talked to senior Girouard members for any clues they could provide in bringing hazy family branches into focus. His research has taken him to France, Louisiana and Quebec.

For several years after starting his research, Bill was stumped. Tracing forward from the 17th century and backward from the present day, he couldn't seem to find the missing link somewhere in the middle. The confusion came in the mid-1700's, which was the same time the English were expelling the Acadians from Nova Scotia.

Bill got his breakthrough from 104-year-old Laguit Girroir Pellerin of Larry's River. Still "as sharp as a whip," she was able to point Bill to Tracadie. Once he got a hold of Tracadie's church records, Bill not only

Jean Baptiste Girouard, he uncovered a legend as well.

In 1755 or thereabouts, Jean Baptiste and his family fled into the woods to avoid deportation. Discovered later on, the Girouards were imprisoned at Fort Beausejour near Amherst while British soldiers figured out what to do with them. Eventually, they moved through the province, to Chezzetcook and then to Tracadie.

But the more romantic version of Jean Baptiste's whereabouts was discovered in a book at the Public Archives.

Led mutiny

"According to legend," begins the passage, Jean Baptiste led the mutiny of the English ship called the Pembroke en route to Louisiana with its cargo of Acadians. He turned the boat around to New Brunswick and landed it in Saint John, where the Acadians dispersed into the forest. In this version, there's no mention of prison and somehow Jean Baptiste makes it back to Nova Scotia.

Baptiste live in Larrys River, Lundy and Charlos Cove. Many retain their Acadian heritage and are French-speaking.

Bill delights in digging up lost family stories — the gems in every serious genealogist's crown. But the brightest gem of all will be the reunion itself.

It's not the first reunion for the Girouard clan, but it's certainly the largest. In 1985, a family reunion attracting 600 descendants from the Maritime provinces was held at St. Francis Xavier University in Antigonish. This time around, Bill's research allowed him to invite even more people. Descendants will be arriving from France, Quebec, the U.S. as well as the three Maritime provinces.

Singsongs, dances, picnics, group photographs, special presentations by local politicians and a family mass are just a sampling of what's in store during the three-day event. Air Canada "the official airline carrier for all participants," is even kicking in complimentary tick-

"I have so many fond memories from the first reunion that I just can't wait for this one," says Rita (Girouard) Kay, who descends from the New Brunswick branch of the family. "We sure owe Bill a debt of gratitude; without him, I wouldn't have experienced this great joy."

At a time when families are breaking up more frequently and the concept of the extended family has been largely relegated to history, a family reunion takes on greater significance.

"Life is so busy today; we're all in our own little worlds. Sometimes you don't even take time out to see a brother who may live only two blocks away," says Anne Marie Schroeder of Dartmouth, Bill's first cousin. "I'd love for my children to have a special feeling for their cousins — the same warm feeling I had growing up."

Christine Morin of Bedford, part of the Prince Edward Island branch of the family, was taken aback by her children's interest. All four of her children, in their 20's, are coming home to Nova Scotia for the reunion.

Basic curiosity

"It means so much to all of us to be together, to be a family. We're all looking forward to meeting relatives we didn't even know existed."

Paul Comeau, executive director of the Acadian Federation of Nova Scotia, believes the Girouard family's wholehearted response to the reunion reflects people's basic curiosity to find their place, their identity. This drive appears to be even stronger among Acadians, he says.

"Really very little has been published. Even in the school system, I remember studying from a history book, *My British Heritage*, says Comeau, who hopes other Acadian families will follow the Girouard example and organize their own reunions.

As for Bill, researching and organizing his family reunion has been a labor of love. And he's not worried he'll be suffering from Girouard withdrawal when it's all over. His immediate family has drawn closer in the months and weeks preceding the reunion and Bill says those bonds will only get stronger.

Besides, he plans on writing a book and that should keep him whittling at the Girouard family tree for some time yet.

Far left: Robert Gerrior, Deputy Mayor of Antigonish
Near left: Bill Gillis, M.L.A., Antigonish
Right: Bill Gerrior, Chairman of Reunion

344

*Registration booths for each of the seven root areas in North America: Antigonish County, NS; Guysborough County, N.S; Isle Madame, N.S; Richmond County, N.S; Prince Edward Island; New Brunswick; Québec; Louisiana and special guests from France.
At right: Daniel Comeau F.A.N.E. representative*

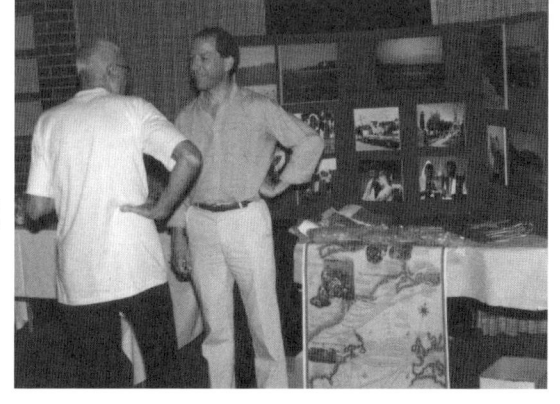

Master chart Plaque being presented to France. l to r: Paul Comeau, President of F.A.N.E. (Federation of Acadians of Nouvelle Ecosse-Nova Scotia); Francis LeBlanc, Member of Parliament; Hon. Guy LeBlanc, Minister of Acadian Affairs, Andrée Gombert (Girouard descendant) from France and her husband Yves Gombert.

The author's family presenting him with gold plated Master Chart.

l to r: Michael Oakley, (brother-in-law); brother, Herman; nephew, Vincent; sisters: Delores, Evelyn, Verna, Theresa; brother, Tom; son, Steve; brother, Reg; Dad (John S. Gerrior) (d); Mom (née Mary Beatrice Fougère) and Bill.

Port Royal and old Acadie

Above: Dr. MacDonell receiving plaque, from Hon. Guy LeBlanc and Bill Gerrior. Commemorating Senator Edward Lavin Girroir.

At left: Fr. Conrad P. Girroir receiving plaque, from Vicar General, Rev. Vernon Fougère, commemorating Fr. Hubert Girroir

At right: the author's father, John S. Gerrior

Above L to R: Brother Herman Gerrior, guitar; brother Reg Gerrior, fiddle; Dad (John Sylvester Gerrior) fiddle.

Above: The author's sister, Marie (Gerrior) Nugent (3rd from top left), Director of the Dance Troupe called Dance Interplay Association in Sydney, N., S. who performed very entertaining Multicultural dances.

Above left: Sharon Aucoin, Master of Ceremonies for Bluenose induction of descendant's skit. Above right: Marcel Aucoin, Corker of Port Royal, for Bluenose induction Ceremony skit

Top to bottom: New Brunswick, Louisiana, Guysborough County, Isle Madame (left) and Prince Edward Island (right). Top of next page: Québec and France together, then Antigonish County..

Top stage photo: Musician friends and family musicians: at Picnic under the tent: l to r: Bill's brothers, Herman Gerrior, lead guitar; Reg Gerrior, lead guitar; Mike Gillis, percussion; Tom Rusinak, saxophone; Marcel Aucoin, base.
Bottom stage photo: Reg Gerrior, Donna and John (Wilmer) Gerrior, first cousin, and Bill Gerrior (author).

Port Royal and old Acadie

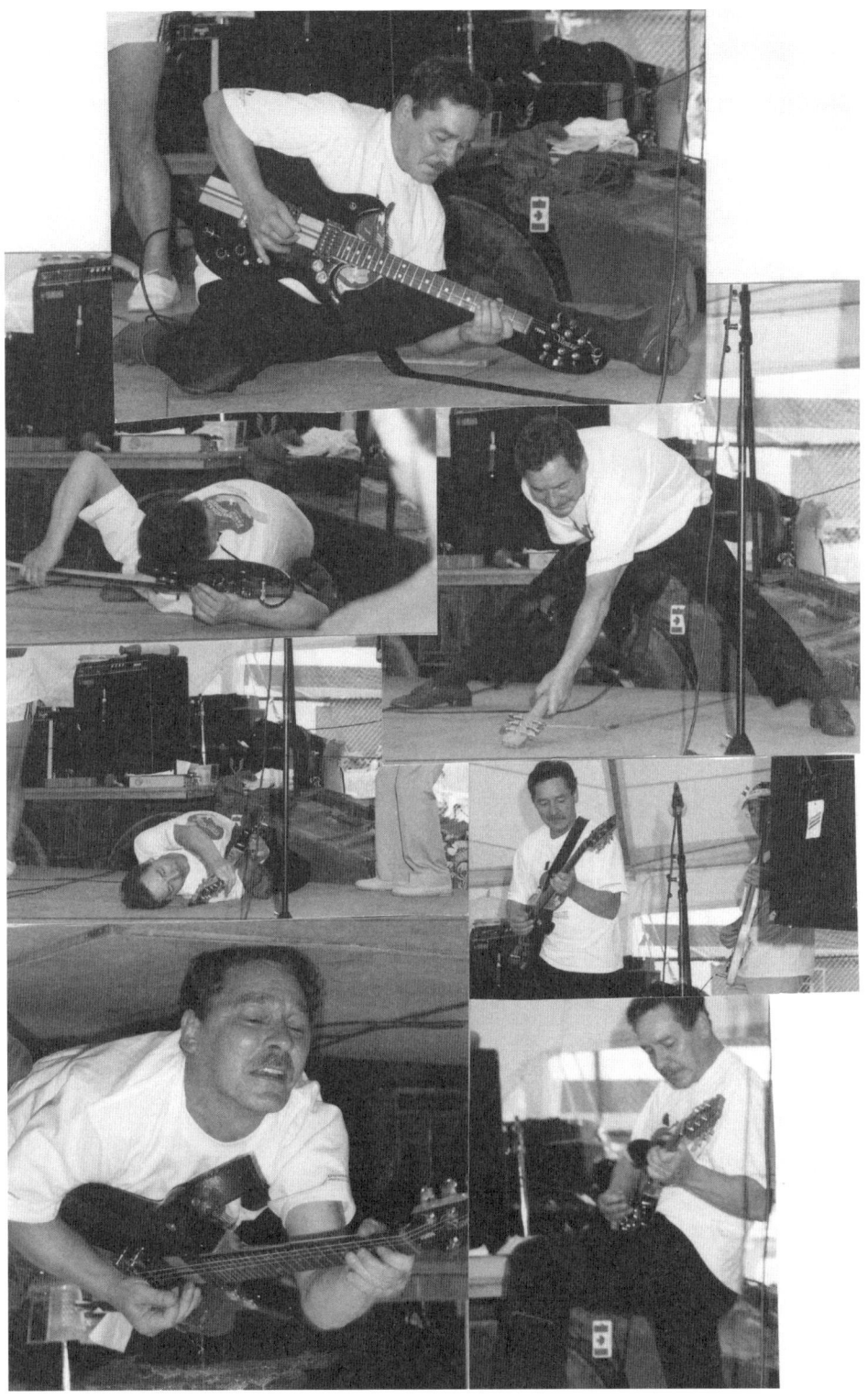

Author's brother, Reg Gerrior, renown for his Guitar Act, during his singing of classic rock song, Johnny B Good.

Acadian Awakenings: An Acadian Family In Exile

Port Royal and old Acadie

Words by Lisa Pellerin, music to the tune of "World turned upside down"

Above: Troy Pellerin, B.J. Pellerin, Sherry Pellerin, Lynn (Avery) Moulstone and Lisa Pellerin.

Opposite page top l to r: Music by the author's sister, Verna (Gerrior) Gionet; nephew, Vincent Gionet; sister, Evelyn (Gerrior) Oakley, & author's father, John S. Gerrior missing from this photo). Words composed by cousin, Florence Cummerson
Opposite page bottom: Québec Descendants of Gabriel Girouard and his sisters along with Don Girouard and his wife Marie-Claire and Don's brother Paul Girouard singing tribute song to the tune of the French traditional song entitled "Chevaliers de la Table Ronde".

Acadian Awakenings: An Acadian Family In Exile

(top left: Bill Gerrior receiving Cajun T-Shirt from Louisiana Giroir descendant, Marianne Arata; Top right Bill Gerrior receiving cowboy hat from Calgary Girouard descendants; left middle and top middle: Shirley and Cyrus Giroir sporting their Louisiana colours of Yellow and White along with Ida and Buddy Hyver of Louisiana; bottom left: Leah Oakley Acadian face painting; bottom right Derick Pellerin and friend.

At right: River Band

Port Royal and old Acadie

Top photo" Closing Mass: Co-celebrated by descendants: Fr. Murphy, Larry's River, N.S; Fr. Conrad Girroir, West Arichat, Isle Madame, N.S; Fr. Frank Giroir, Louisiana; Photos on right: descendants as readers; bottom photo: members of St. Peter's Church Choir, Larry's River, N.S.

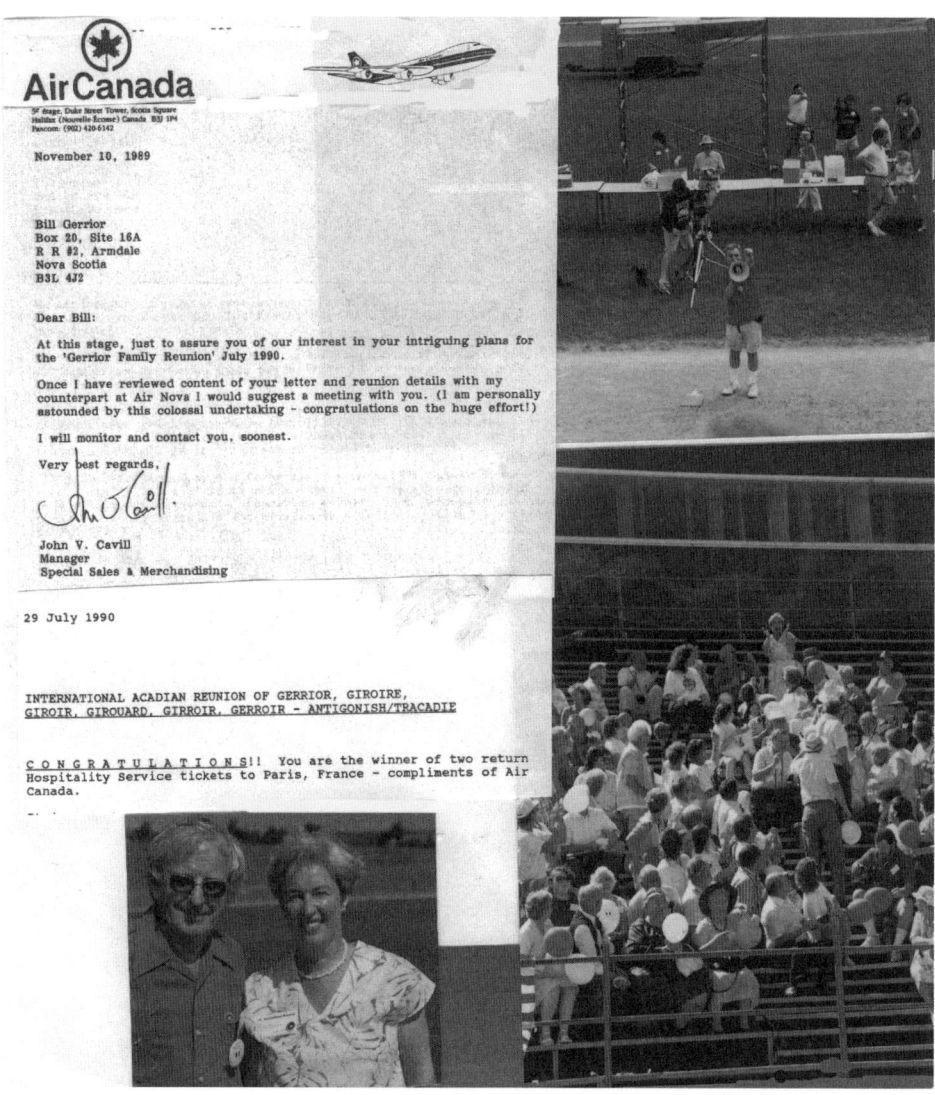

Above left: Judge Jean Girouard and his wife Andrée. Above right: Andrée's reaction to their names being announced as the winning couple. Below: closing photo.

All reunion photos courtesy of Peter Tenwald.

In the appendix the reader will find samples of subcharts I have designed in conjunction with the Acadian Master Charts to trace all the Acadian Girouard, Giroire families in North America back to François Girouard and Jeanne Aucoin. They function in the same way as the master chart. I have found that when all the facts are known regarding any Acadian Girouard Giroir, Girroir(e) family in North America today, regardless of where they have been scattered and took root, they unbelievably have connected to one of these blocks on this one-page Acadian Master Chart. Similarly, the same is true for the French Canadian master chart leading back to Antoine Girouard and the Belgium master chart leading back to Pierre Realh.

Lastly, the subcharts are very easy for the professional genealogist or family to read, because they are organized and read in the same way as the master chart. The reader should note the following pattern which makes the charts easily understood: On all of the subcharts, any particular row represents the brothers and sisters of the generation numbered on the left side of that row and the parents of all these brothers and sisters in this row are always located in the block directly above the male person in the centre column of this row. There is direct descent only in the centre, shaded column of all subcharts, allowing us to therefore trace any block in any row, back to the first person at the top of the centre column of the chart. There is no direct descent in any of the other columns of the subcharts. Like the master chart, the surname is not used in any of the blocks of the chart since it is assumed all have the same family name (regardless of spelling).

Most importantly, I have also provided an alphabetical index for all names appearing on all subcharts and master charts, according to the first name appearing in each of the blocks. This index gives the chart (s) where this person is located as well as the root location. (e.g. Louisiana, Antigonish ,etc.)

This brings to a close our discussions on the Acadian Girouard/Giroir(e)/Gerrior families before, during and immediately after the Deportation, with their numerous migrations and wanderings, searching for lost family members and for a place to take root, now that they were no longer being chased, hunted, imprisoned, or banished from their original lands in Acadia. The next four volumes will focus on the same family after the Deportation and follow their roots and routes to the present day, celebrating the international linking together after almost 250 years of separation begun in 1755.

Volume 2: Nova Scotia and Prince Edward Island
Volume 3: New Brunswick
Volume 4: Québec: Acadian branches and French Canadian branches
Volume 5: Louisiana

PREVIEW
OF THE NEXT FOUR BOOKS

In the next four volumes, with reference to the Acadian Girouards, I will trace as many of the blocks of the subcharts and master charts as possible, in the seven root areas of North America where they established or took root and wherever else in this world that their routes have taken them. This will be accomplished using charts and block genealogy in paragraph form, linking our ancestors on the many charts to present day descendants, while integrating family photos where provided, as well as all the stories, history and heritage that I have collected over the past twenty years, related to the particular region and the families, thus providing an enriched, cultural and historic family mosaic on which to solidly base the proud heritage of the Girouard, Giroir(e)... families, while at the same time, creating an international identity for our family. Also the French-Canadian branches from France and Belgium branches from Liége, Belgium will be followed to present day in the same manner. This is all accomplished as follows.

Volume II- Nova Scotia and Prince Edward Island

CHAPTER 1 ANTIGONISH COUNTY, NOVA SCOTIA

The settlement, after deportation and migrations, of Acadian Girroir/Gerrior(e) descendants of François and Jeanne Aucoin, in root Area # 1, Tracadie, Antigonish County, Nova Scotia.
Regions: Tracadie •Big Tracadie •Merland •Heatherton, NS, migrating to other centres in North America

Highlights: Jean Baptiste Girouard, the first Girouard of Tracadie •maps • genealogy from 1640 to 2002 • history • illustrated stories • prominent individuals • links to Guysborough Co. branches • France Historian, Rameau's visit to Tracadie, NS • MLA, Placide Gaudet's speech in Ottawa, re: Girouards-in part • Fr. Melanson's record at Chezeetcook of the first Jean Baptiste Girouard of Tracadie • Mary Weekes article, The settlement of the Girroirs • Justice of the Peace and Acadians in Politics • Senator Edward Lavin Girroir • Fr. Hubert Girroir and the struggle for French Language Education for Acadians• Ship Captains of old and new • migration of families to U.S.A. and their part in the USA Military • war heroes • reunion photos.

CHAPTER 2: GUYSBOROUGH COUNTY, NOVA SCOTIA

The Settlement, after deportation and migrations of Acadian Gerrior descendants of François and Jeanne Aucoin in root area # 2, Guysborough County.
Regions: Larry's River • Lundy • Charlos Cove •Port Felix •Guysborough Co. N.S migrating to Halifax, New Glasgow, Stellarton, Sydney, Nova Scotia and in

other parts of Canada and the U.S.A. wherever their routes lead them.

Highlights: Luc Gerrior, the first ancestor in Guysborough Co., • History of the region • old maps • genealogy of all branches from 1640 to 2002 • photos of ancestors and descendants today • Acadian history and illustrated feature stories of prominent descendants • links to origins in Tracadie, Antigonish Co. • the author's family and all other branches in Guysborough Co. • connections to the Avery, Manette, Richard, David, Pellerin, Fougère, Pettipas, Delorey, Murphy and other families in regions • Larry s River Celebrations • the role of the Church in these Acadian regions of Guysborough Co. • Councillors • family links to Provincial, national and international personalities in the entertainment world •reunion photos

CHAPTER 3: ISLE MADAME, Cape Breton

The Settlement, after deportation and migrations, of Acadian Girroir, Gerroir, Gerrior descendants of François and Jeanne Aucoin in root Area # 3 Arichat, West Arichat, Isle Madame, Nova Scotia,

Regions: Arichat, West Arichat, Petit de Gras, Port Royal, Cape Breton and migrations elsewhere.

Highlights: Pierre Girouard (Girroir), the first to establish at Isle Madame • history of the region • old maps • individual family genealogies of all branches from 1640 to 2002 • original master chart genealogy system establishing international links and international family identity for all Isle Madame descendants • old photos of ancestors and recent photos of family descendants • Acadian history • Acadian illustrated feature stories of prominent descendants • Captains of seafaring vessels • Boat building • War heroes • international mathematics award winner • Acadian monument and the White Masses • The struggles of Fr. Hubert Girroir, first Acadian parish priest of Arichat promoting French education and Acadian identity • Fred Gerrior the Whistler • Fr. Conrad P. Gerrior keeper of the Acadian Girroir culture and genealogy of Isle Madame- a legend in his own time • reunion photos.

CHAPTER 4 PRINCE EDWARD ISLAND

The settlement, after deportation and migrations, of Acadian Gerroir descendants of François and Jeanne Aucoin returning in root Area # 4 Prince Edward Island, and all their descendant in the Canada and the U.S.A.

Regions: Georgetown • Summerside

Highlights: Georgetown and Summerside: The first Girouard, Paul Girouard (Gerrior) to establish permanently in Prince Edward Island came from Isle Madame • history of the PEI region • old maps • individual family genealogy of all branches from 1640 to 2002 • original master chart genealogy system establishing international links and international family identity for all Prince Edward Island descendants • old photos of ancestors and recent photos of family descendants • Acadian history • Acadian illustrated feature stories of prominent descendants • Ship Captains • Reunion Photos ,1985, 1990.

PHOTO AND NEWS CLIP.

VOLUME III NEW BRUNSWICK

The settlement, after deportation and migrations, of Acadian Girouard descendants of François and Jeanne Aucoin, in root Area # 5 New Brunswick, and all their descendants in the Canada and the U.S.A.

Regions: Bouctouche • Ste-Marie-de-Kent • St-Antoine (Girouard descendant) • St-Paul • Lagacéville • Sheila • Neguac• Chatham •Tracadie, NB

Highlights: Louis-Paul Girouard the first to establish permanent roots in New Brunswick. • History • old maps • individual family genealogies of many branches from 1640 to 2002 • original master chart genealogy system establishing international links and international family identity for all New Brunswick descendants • old photos of ancestors and recent photos of family descendants • Acadian history • Acadian illustrated feature stories of prominent descendants • early French Education opportunities for some Acadians • Acadians in Politics • many firsts for the Girouards • Agriculture • maple syrup cabins (Joe Allain) • renown Sculptor Marie-Helene Allain (Girouard descendant) • reunion photos • Tribute to Founders of Bouctouche including two Girouard mothers • Bouctouche honors the first Acadian M.LA, Gilbert Girouard • The ballot box brawl • the first two National Conventions of Acadians • war hero, Pius Girouard • Dr. Edgar Girouard, key person in genealogy links in New Brunswick • millionaire descendant • reunion photos • USA Space program and Acadian links to New Brunswick Girouard Family • family reunions reunions • The first World Congress of Acadians 1994

VOLUME IV: QUÉBEC

The settlement, after deportations and migrations of Acadian descendants of François Girouard Aucoin and Jeanne Aucoin in root area # 6: PQ; the settlement of descendants of French Canadian branch of Girouards originating from Antoine Girouard directly from France and the descendants of Belgium, French-Canadian Girouards, descending from Pierre Realh directly from of Liége Belgium- and all their descendant in the Canada and the U.S.A.

Acadian Branch Regions: Deschambault. • Lotbinière • Deschaillons • Les

Becquets• Bécancour • St-Ours-sur-Richelieu •St-Antoine-sur-Richelieu • St-Jude • St-Barnabé • La Présentation • St-Hyacinthe • Marieville • St Phillipe • L'Acadie • St-Eustache • Deux-Montanges • Eustache • St-Benoît • Drummondville • Victoriaville •Arthabaska • Tetford Mines • Warwick • Asbestos • Sherbrooke • Montréal • Québec city and migrating to various other centres in PQ, Ontario and in general in many parts of Canada and USA wherever their routes lead them

Chapter 1, volume IV: Acadian Girouards of Québec.

Highlights: There are nine branches of the Acadian Master Chart that established permanent roots in Québec. The first Acadian Girouard of this number appears to be Germain III à Germain II à Germain [AMC Block D-3b] who married 1733 at Notre Dame Church, establishing at St-Hyacinthe, PQ

Early history • the Patriots (Jean Joseph Girouard) battles, imprisonment, executions and expulsion • maps • individual family genealogies of many branches from 1640 to 2002 • original master chart genealogy system establishing international links and international family identity for all Acadian Québec descendants • photos of ancestors and descendants today • Acadian illustrated feature stories of prominent descendants • early French Education opportunities for some Acadians • Acadians in Politics • Joseph Éna Girouard colleague and close family friend of Prime Minister Wilfrid Laurier of Canada • The Louis Réal question • Girouard pioneers in Québec • War Heroes: René de la Bruère Girouard • Luc Girouard, Pioneer of Vernon, B.C • Gold rush years • the history and development of the town of Drummondville from its first electrical lights, Joseph Éna Girouard its first Mayor.

Chapter 2, Volume IV: French-Canadian Branches Girouards in Québec originating from France and From Belgium

French-Canadian Branch Regions: Salaberry de Valleyfield, •Beauharnois • St-Timothé • Dorval • St-Benoit •Deux Montagne and migrating to various other centres in PQ, Ontario and in general in many parts of Canada and USA

Highlights: maps • family research and genealogy of Supreme Court Judge Désiré Girouard • individual family genealogies of many branches from 1640 to 2002 • original master chart genealogy system establishing international links and international family identity for all French-Canadian descendants of Antoine Girouard • illustrated feature stories of prominent descendants • life of Messire Antoine Girouard founder of St Hyacinthe College and monument statue in his honor • French-Canadian descendants in Politics • war heroes: Sir Percy Girouard, Governor of Kenya, Africa, his involvement with Prime Minister of England Sir Winston Churchill; the role of the railway during the Boer war • Judge Jean Girouard, descending from Jean Baptiste and Brigitte Monpetit, whose genealogy is expanded in subchart 2000, is the key genealogist and link today between Acadian and French Canadian Branches internationally • Family Reunion 1979 of descendants of Jean Baptiste Girouard and Victoria Legault (chief organizers Laurent and Bruno Girouard) • family reunion of the descendants of the five sons of Laurent Girouard and Parmélie Rollin. This Laurent descends from another Laurent, son of Joseph Girouard and Josephe Bleau [FCMC Block O-4] (chief organizers: Amand Girouard, Cécile Girouard and Armand Girouard Lafrenière)• The first Family reunion recorded with representation from both the French Canadian Branch and Acadian branches of Girouards at Quatre Vents, Dorval, and PQ. Sept 14, 1907.

Chapter 2 volume IV Québec French-Canadian branches descending from Pierre Realh, Liége Belgium

Important birth record and related genealogy establishing this branch which to date has never been published to my knowledge • Belgium Master chart • genealogy from 1726 to 2002 of known descendants of this branch.

VOLUME V: LOUISIANA

The settlement, after deportation and migrations, of Acadian Girouard and Giroir descendants of François and Jeanne Aucoin, in root area # 7, Louisiana and all their descendants in Canada and the U.S.A. and wherever their routes have taken them in the world.

Acadian /Cajun Regions: Donaldsonville •Plequemine • Paincourtville Plattenville •Pierre Part •la Fourche •St-James •Houma •Gibson • Bayou Black •Bayou Tortue •Bayou Teche• Franklin •St-Martinville • Broussard •Breau Bridge • Lafayette •Kaplan •Baton Rouge •New Orleans • Gretna •New Iberia •Thibodeaux and migrating to neighboring states in USA such as Texas and other states, wherever their routes led them.

Highlights: The evolvement of French language of the Acadians or Cajuns in Louisiana • Firmin Girouard is the first to establish in Louisiana, 1766 • Prosper Giroir is the first of the Giroir branches to arrive in Louisiana, 1785 • Description of the relationship between the Giroir branches and the Girouard branches • Acadian Girouards in the West Indies connected to the master chart • Description of how both branches arrived in Louisiana: Firmin Girouard by overland route and Prosper Giroir by boat from France, 1685 • maps • individual family genealogies of many branches of both Girouards and Giroirs from 1640 to 2002 • original master chart genealogy system establishing international links and international family identity for all the Louisiana Girouard and Giroir Acadian /Cajun descendants • old photos of ancestors and recent photos of family descendants • Acadian/Cajun history • Acadian illustrated feature stories of prominent descendants • visits with families and interviews • two complete sections, one on Giroir and the other on Girouard families.

The Giroir Branches: • Tour of some Acadian Giroir regions with Mary Jane Siracusa chief organizer of the family reunions in Louisiana • a meeting with some very interested Cajuns • Giroir and Girouard family genealogists in New Orleans • Profile of Alex Giroir who preserves an important part of the Cajun culture in Louisiana• visits with some Cajun Giroir families and including many interviews • a Cajun dance• Visiting the French Quarter in New Orleans with some hot Cajun Music • a Cajun Giroir cook out down on the bayous • A boat tour of the Bayous • hunting alligators • Some Acadians find rich oil fields on their land • former alderman of Morgan City, Cyrus Giroir and the meeting of his family and many other Giroir branches. Estilitte Giroir branches • Etienne Giroir Branches • Joseph Damase Giroir Branches • François and Madeleine LeBlanc Giroir branches • François Appolinaire Giroir branches • Family reunions of the Giroirs and Girouards and the Second World Congress of Acadians in 1999, Louisiana.

The Girouard Branches: The early history of this Firmin Girouard branch in Canada at Grand Pré, PEI, Restigouche, New Brunswick • Visit to many Girouard homes in Louisiana with accompanying interviews • the attempted lynching of the Parish Priest • The Old plantation home in Broussard restored and a visit with its present owner Terry Girouard • Girouard Cattle ranching, and champion horsemanship • a Fais do-do experience at Whisky River • sugar cane farming • Adolphe Girouard branches • Leonce Girouard branches • Joseph Oscar Girouard branches • Dupré Girouard branches .

Girouard, Girroir, Gerrior, Organization Committee for the World Congress of Acadians, 2004 Nova Scotia. Left to Right: Front Row, l to r: Steve Gerrior, Father Conrad P. Girroir, Robert Girroir, Daniel Stewart.
Back Row, l to r: Paul Girouard, Bill Gerrior, Jeanne LeJeune, Carol (Gerrior) Finch, Anne-Marie (Comeau) Schroeder, Anne Marie (Fougere) Long; Nina Long, Michael Pellerin. Absent from Photo: Christine Oderkirk, Fernand Girouard, Brad Comeau and Brad Pellerin.

See you all in Nova Scotia CMA 2004 !

Preface Endnotes

1 Mary Weekes, "The Settlements of the Gerriors in Tracadie", Dalhousie Review, July 1950, Archives of Nova Scotia., call # F 90015. Vol. 30 #2 pp. 163-167,

Introduction Endnotes

1 (Into) Sally Ross and Alphonse Deveau, *The Acadians of Nova Scotia, Past and Present*, Nimbus Publishing, 1992, p.121

Family Endnotes

1. Honourable Désiré Girouard, *La Famille Girouard*, Étude Généalogique, la Branche Canadian, privately published, 1884, pp 10,11
2. Extrait du *Dictionnaire Géographique et typographique*, concerning the village of «Le Girouard», which I found at the Mairie in «Le Girouard, during my trip in 1988.
3. Rev. Henry Barber M.D., F.S. *A British Family Names, Their Origin and Meaning*, with lists of Scandinavian, Frisian, Anglo-Saxon and Norman names, second edition, enlarged, London Elliot stock, 62 Paternoster Row, E.C., 1903.
4. Lovette Jailler, Extrait de la revue "La Bouillaie des Ancêstres" no. 51, deuxième trimestre, 1993, for interpretation of words, "girouette, giver and Geroir".
5. Honourable Désiré Girouard *La Famille Girouard en France*, Lévis, *Bulletin des Recherches Historiques*, 1902, 7.
6. Information provided by Sovereign, 583 Boundary Road, Cornwallis, and Ontario. I have been unable to contact this company, however they state that it is an interpretation by heraldic researchers using the authentic sources indicated. This copy Coat of Arms information was provided to me by Jean Marie Girouard, Longueuil, PQ.
7. This information was provided by Sovereign. However as mentioned in footnote 6 above, I have not been able to contact this company. This copy was provided to given to me by Bernard Girroir of Tracadie, Nova Scotia

France Endnotes

1 *Acadian Réveil* The Acadian Cultural Society, Société Culturelle Acadienne. Post office Box 53, Marlboro, Massachussetts, 01752, USA.
2 *Bulletin de la Société des Antiquaires de L'Ouest et Musée de Poitiers*, 3 trimestre de 1966, Tome VII quatrième Serie, p.564
3 Catherine Petit, *Les Acadiens, Piétons De l'Atlantique, Guide Des Acadiens en France*, Ace, 1984, Paris, compositions-impression, Mame-Tours, printed in France,

as well as information provided by Michèle Touret, Diretrice of the Syndicat d'Initiative (Tourist Bureau) of Loudun.

4 These excerpts are taken from information provided to me by Michele Touret, produced by the organization, *Les Maison de l'Acadie*.

5 Geneviève Massignon, *Les Parlers Français d'Acadie*, Enquête Linguistique, 2 volumes,Paris, Librairie C. Klincksieck, pp. 36, 37, Volume 1

6-70 Ibit B. p. 68

7 Extrait du *Dictionnaire Géographique et typographique*, concerning the village of "Le Girouard", which I found at the Mairie in "Le Girouard.". I have since found the name Girouard, Giroir(e) also used in many documents dating back to 1100 in information provided to me by Lucienne (Giroire) Doussin of Parthenay, Deux Sèvres, from well documented sources in France which have already been referenced toward the end of this chapter. All spellings of Girouard, Giroir(e)… in these documents seem to be equally authentic and verify their early use in France and their interchangeability.

8 "Genealogical notes" of Lucienne (Giroire) Doussin of Parthenay, passed on to her by R. Giroire, (relation to her as yet unkown) the reference given to this document held in the Public Archives collection of France and the information was published by the *Archaeological Society of Poitiers*, which is quoted here. Parthenay is in the Department of Deux Sèvres

9 All of these, which I couldn't explore because of my time restraints, are subjects for future research.

10 *Généalogie des familles acadiennes établies à Belle-Isle-En-Mer, France, 1767*, Archives département de Morbihan,1978, Public Archives of Canada, (Mg 6, A6, series E)

11 Catherine Petit, *Les Acadiens Pietons de L'Atlantique*, 1984, Ace Editeurs, composition-impression Mame-Tours, printed in France.

12 *Généalogie des familles acadienes, établies à Belle-en-Mer, France, 1767*, Archives département de Morbihan (Vannes), 1978, Public Archives of Canada, série E

13 Catherine Petit, *Les Acadiens Pietons de L'Atlantique*,1984 Ace, Editeurs, composition-impression Mame-Tours, printed in France.

14 "Genealogy research notes charts and information" provided to me by Gaston Giroir, La Boulonière, 37270, Larcay, France.

15 Albert J. Robicheaux Jr., *The Acadian Exiles in Saint-Malo (1758-1785)* Vol. III, Acadian Marriages p. 935

16 Albert Robichaux, *The Acadian Exiles of Châtellerault, (1772- 1785)*.

17 Ship List: Courtesy of the Président of L'Association Régionale de l'Ouest des Amitiés Acadiennes (AROAA), based in Nantes. Monsieur Gérard Braud sent a copy to Marie-Jeanne Gambini, a teacher in Marseilles, who sent it to May Jane Siracusa, from whom I received this copy.

18 Albert J. Robichaux Jr. These records are found in three books by whose titles are as follows: *The Acadian Exiles in St-Malo, 1758-1785; The Acadian Exiles in Nantes, 1775-1785; The Acadian Exiles in Châtellerault*, and the "genealogy research information" provided to me by Gaston Giroir of La Boulonnière, Larcay, France.

19 Gerard–Marc Braud, *From Nantes to Louisiana*, translated by Julie Landry, La Rainette, Inc. 1999, p.5.

20 Catherine Petit, *Les Acadiens Pietons de L'Atlantique*, 1984, Ace Editeurs, composition-impression Mame-Tours, printed in France.
21 Reference to Law Court change of name from Giloir to Girouard, Châtellerrault, in Mairie of Scorbe-Cl.- was provided to me by "research notes" of Gaston Giroir.
22 Brigitte Wallace, with introduction by Barbara LeBlanc, Edited by Margaret Conrad, Curatorial Report Number 87, one of Three Illustrated Studies: "An Archaeologist Discovers Early Acadia P. 12
23 Mrs Provost et Roman d'Amat, Extract of the *French Biographical Dictionary*, Paris 1985, Volume 16, page 302. provided to me by Gaston Giroir. This same reference also confirms all of the information regarding the Girouard master sculptors which were also included in the documents of R Giroire provided to me by Lucienne (Giroire) Doussin. Guy Secq, cousin of Gaston Giroir, visited Prières (Morbihan) in July, 1992 but was unable to find any record of the death of Jean Girouard.
24 The title "Honourable" is given in Canada to citizens in high public office. Some - like the Prime Minister of Canada - are officially referred to as "Right Honourable"; others - ministers of the Crown, Supreme Court of Canada judges - are referred to as "Honourable". The Supreme Court of Canada is the highest court of Federal jurisdiction in the Federal system.
25 Honourable Désiré Girouard, *La Famille Girouard en France*, privately published 1902, Lévis, PQ, *Bulletin des Rechereches Historiques*, 1902. This article referenced here, is a translation for the most part of this 15 page booklet.
26 136.*Bulletin des Recherches Historiques*, 1902. pp. 6, 7 concerning *La famille Girouard en France*, Lévis, PQ, Honorable Désiré Girouard

Port Royal and old Acadie Endnotes

1 Sally Ross, Alphonse Deveau, *The Acadians of Nova Scotia, Past and Present*, Nimbus, 1992, p. 9.
2 Elizabeth Ruggles Coward, *Bridgetown, Nova Scotia, Its History to 1900*, Kentville Publishing Company Limited, 1955, p. 5
3 Elizabeth Ruggles Coward, *Bridgetown, Nova Scotia, Its History to 1900*, Kentville Publishing Company Limited, 1955, p. 5
4 Jean Daigle, "Acadia, 1604-1763, An Historical Synthesis", The Acadians of the Maritimes A Thematic Study, edited by Jean Daigle, Centre d'études acadiennes, Université de Moncton, Moncton, NB, published by authority of the Minister of Environment, 1982, p. 19
5 Brigette Wallace, "An Archaeologist Discovers Early Acadia", with introduction by Barbara LeBlanc, Edited by Margaret Conrad, Curatorial Report Number 87 Three Illustrated Studies, p. 16.
6 Brigette Wallace, "An Archaeologist Discovers Early Acadia", with introduction by Barbara LeBlanc, Edited by Margaret Conrad, Curatorial Report Number 87 Three Illustrated Studies, p. 15
7 Léopold Lanctôt, Familles Acadiennes tome I, Éditions du Libre-Échange, Veilleux, impression à demande Inc. ,Boucherville, Québec 1994. p 271.

8 Elizabeth Ruggles Coward, Bridgetown Nova Scotia, Its History to 1900, p. 7

9 David J. Christianson, Curatorial Report Number 48, Belleisle, 1983: Excavations at a Pre-Expulsion Acadian site July 1984, Nova Scotia Museum, 1747 Summer Street, Halifax, NS, Canada, B3H3A6.

10 Info, "The Acadians, Two, Farming", Nova Scotia Museum publication.

11 Info," The Acadians, Two, Farming", Nova Scotia Museum publication.

12 J. D'Entremont, "Census of Port Royal", 1678, French Canadian and Acadian Genealogical Review, Vol. VIII, no. 1(Spring 1979, pp. 57 and 59.).

13 Sally Ross, Alphonse Deveau, The Acadians of Nova Scotia, Past and Present, Nimbus, 1992, p. 33.

14 Info, "The Acadians One: Settlement", Nova Scotia, Museum publication.

15 David J. Christianson, Curatorial Report # 48, Belleisle, 1983: Excavations at a Pre-Expulsion Site, July 1984

16 Jean Daigle, "Acadia, 1604-1763, An Historical Synthesis", The Acadians of the Maritimes, A Thematic Study, edited by Jean Daigle, Centre d'études acadiennes, Université de Moncton, Moncton, NB, published by authority of the Minister of Environment, 1982, p. 23

17 Info, "The Acadians Three, The home", Nova Scotia Museum publication

18 Georges Duby, Histoire de la France rurale, Paris, Seuil, 1975, Tome 2, pp. 277-278.

19 Peter Gallant Berlo, article in Le Réveil Acadien, Page 11. Nov., 1988

20 Brenda Dunn, " Looking into Acadie, Nova Scotia Museum, Aspects of the Lives of Women in Ancienne Acadie", with introduction by Barbara LeBlanc, Edited by Margaret Conrad, Curatorial Report Number 87 Three Illustrated Studies, pp 29-51

21 Brenda Dunn, "Looking into Acadie, Nova Scotia Museum, Aspects of the Lives of Women in Ancienne Acadie", with introduction by Barbara LeBlanc, Edited by Margaret Conrad, Curatorial Report Number 87 Three Illustrated Studies, pp 29.

22 Brenda Dunn, Looking into Acadie, Nova Scotia Museum, Aspects of the Lives of Women in Ancienne Acadie with introduction by Barbara LeBlanc, Edited by Margaret Conrad, Curatorial Report Number 87 Three Illustrated Studies. p. 30

23 Brenda Dunn, Looking into Acadie, Nova Scotia Museum, Aspects of the Lives of Women in Ancienne, Acadie, with introduction by Barbara LeBlanc, Edited by Margaret Conrad, Curatorial Report Number 87 Three Illustrated Studies. pp. 29,30

24 Edward Lavin Girroir, "Genealogical research of the Girouards", Centre d'études acadienne, Univeristé de Moncton, N-B.

25 Brenda Dunn, "Looking into Acadie, Nova Scotia Museum, Aspects of the Lives of Women in Ancienne Acadie", with introduction by Barbara LeBlanc, Edited by Margaret Conrad, Curatorial Report Number 87, Three Illustrated Studies p 35

26 Brenda Dunn, "Looking into Acadie, Nova Scotia Museum, Aspects of the

Lives of Women in Ancienne Acadie", with introduction by Barbara LeBlanc, Edited by Margaret Conrad, Curatorial Report Number 87, Three Illustrated Studies p. 37

27 Brenda Dunn, "Looking into Acadie, Nova Scotia Museum, Aspects of the Lives of Women in Ancienne Acadie", with introduction by Barbara LeBlanc, Edited by Margaret Conrad, Curatorial Report Number 87, Three Illustrated Studies p. 37

28 Jean Daigle, "Acadia, 1604-1763, An Historical Synthesis", The Acadians of the Maritimes, A Thematic Study, edited by Jean Daigle, Centre d'études acadiennes, Université de Moncton, Moncton, NB, published by authority of the Minister of Environment, 1982, p. 32

28 Léopold Lanctôt, Familles, Acadiennes, Éditions du Libre-Échange, Veilleux, impression à demande Inc., Boucherville, Québec 1994, p. 31

29 Sally Ross, Alphonse Deveau, The Acadians of Nova Scotia, Past and Present, Nimbus, 1992, p.48

30 Jean Daigle, "Acadia, 1604-1763, An Historical Synthesis", The Acadians of the Maritimes, A Thematic Study, edited by Jean Daigle, Centre d'études acadiennes, Université de Moncton, Moncton, NB, published by authority of the Minister of Environment, 1982, p. 40

31 Jean Daigle, "Acadia, 1604-1763, An Historical Synthesis", The Acadians of the Maritimes A Thematic Study, edited by Jean Daigle, Centre d'études acadiennes, Université de Moncton, Moncton, NB, published by authority of the Minister of Environment, 1982, p. 18

32 Jean Daigle, "Acadia, 1604-1763, An Historical Synthesis", The Acadians of the Maritimes, A Thematic Study, edited by Jean Daigle, Centre d'études acadiennes, Université de Moncton, Moncton, NB, published by authority of the Minister of Environment, 1982, p. 40

33 Jean Daigle, "Acadia, 1604-1763, An Historical Synthesis", The Acadians of the Maritimes A Thematic Study, edited by Jean Daigle, Centre d'études acadiennes, Université de Moncton, Moncton, NB, published by authority of the Minister of Environment, 1982, p 36

34 Minutes of H. M. Minutes of Council 1720-1742, found at Public Archives of NS (PANS), p. Call number F100N 85V 253. Initially, a copy was provided to me by Raymond Girouard, Alymer, P.Q a New Brunswick descendant.

35 Hannay, History of Acadians, p.367.

36 Edmé Rameau de Saint Père, « Une Colonie Féodale en Amerique », 93-94. The original manuscript may be seen at the Public Library of Halifax.

37 Edmé Rameau de Saint-Père, « Une Colonie Féodale en Amerique », p. 89

38 Henry Wadsworth Longfellow, Evangeline, a tale of Acadie, illustrated addition, introduction by Dr. C. Bruce Ferguson, Nimbus Publishing Limited, 1951.

39 D.C. Harvey, The French Regime in Prince Edward Island, p. 210

40 Léoapold Lanctôt, Familles acadiennes, tome Éditions du Libre-É...change, Veilleux, impression à demande Inc. ,Boucherville, Québec 1994. p. 281.

41 Léoapold Lanctôt, Familles, Acadiennes, tome I, Éditions du Libre-Échange, Veilleux, impression à demande Inc.,Boucherville, Québec 1994, p. 93.

42 Léopold Lanctôt, Familles acadiennes, tome I , Éditions du Libre-É...change, Veilleux, impression à demande Inc.,Boucherville, Québec, 1994. p.33.

43 Donald J. Hebert, Acadians in Exile, Rev. Hebert Publications, P.O. Box Cecilia, Louisiana, 70521.,

44 Placide Gaudet "notes to accompany plan of Annapolis River" and my research information based on master chart references.

45 Régis Brun, Les Acadiens avant 1763, a research, which is soon to be published. Mr. Brun, an archivist and researcher, Centres d'études acadiennes, Université de Moncton, kindly shared his working draft of his research with me for inclusion in this book.

46 Léopold Lanctôt, Familles acadiennes, tome II, Éditions du Libre-Échange, Veilleux, impression à demande Inc. , Boucherville, Québec, 1994. p.156

47 Léopold Lanctôt, Familles acadiennes tome I, Éditions du Libre-Échange, Veilleux, impression à demande Inc. ,Boucherville, Québec, 1994, p.271.

48 Jean Daigle, "Acadia, 1604-1763, An Historical Synthesis", The Acadians of the Maritimes A Thematic Study, edited by Jean Daigle, Centre d'études acadiennes, Université de Moncton, Moncton, NB, published by authority of the Minister of Environment, 1982, p. 32

49 Francis E. Lord, Genealogy: "The descendants off Julien Laure, the pioneer Lord in North America." Mr. Francis E. Lord resides in Casa de les Campanas, San Diego I have also corresponded with François E. Lord, who is a descendant of one of the children of the second generation in Port Royal. I met, Francis E. Lord, with some of his relatives, in Halifax in 1991. I also have correspondence from the husband of his daughter, Margaret Lord, who is Lowell E. Salyards, Rochester, NY. Both Lords are descendants of Julien Lord and Anne Charlotte Girouard, [E-2] of the master chart. Anne Charlotte Girouard is the sister of the above Marie, Madeleine Germain, and Jacques of the second generation of Girouards on the master chart. Lowell also sent me Part I of René Gervais Lord and his Descendants or The genealogy of Eugène Francis Gervais and His Brothers and Sisters by Brother Bernard Gervais, C.S.C., published January 1956, Conrad Publishing Co. Bismark N.D. (300 years of the Gervais Roy Clan).

50 Paul Surette, Atlas de l'établissement des Acadiens aux trois rivières du Chignectou 1660-1755, Les Éditions d'Acadie, 1996, Moncton New Brunswick.

51 Andrew Hill Clark, Acadia: The Geography of Early Nova Scotia, pp 127,129-130, referenced in Donald Heberts book Acadians in Exile.

52 Bona Arsenault, History of the Acadians, p.47.

53 William R. Stringfield, Le Pays des Fleurs Oranges (the land of Orange Blossoms), A Genealogical Study of Eight Creoles Families of Plaquemines Parish, Louisiana, the Buras (Burat), Barrois, Fontenelle, Collette, Crosse, Cavalier, Frederick, Martin, Vinet, LaFrance and Dobard, Gateway Press, Inc, 1989, Baltimore MD. Willam R. Stringfield corresponded with me providing information on the Buras (Burat) family. William R. Stringfield resides in , Buras, La. He has provided much information regarding his direct line to Madeleine Girouard.

54 Placide Gaudet, "Girouard Genealogy Research", p. 2119-1 and Edward Lavin Girroir's genealogy research.

Endnotes

55 Genealogy cards on Québec Girouards received from Dr. Edgar Girouard, Moncton, which I referenced to my genealogy information and master chart system. I have copies of the original cards. The researcher of these well-organized genealogical cards is unknown to date.

56 Loiselle "Genealogy notes on the Girouards" p. 00180, Laval University, Archives, St. Foy, PQ.

57 Jeanne Décarie, Montréal, Québec, H1M 2Z5. I interviewed Jeanne Décarie, at her home in Montréal, and she provided a great deal of information on her branch in Québec, which is presented in the Québec book.

58 Léopold Lanctôt, Familles Acadiennes tome I, Éditions du Libre-Échange, Veilleux, impression à demande Inc., Boucherville, Québec, 1994, tome I, p. 271

59 Edward Lavin Girroir's genealogy research of his branch of Girroir's in Tracadie, NS. The originals are held at the Centre d'études acadiennes at the Université de Moncton, on large sheets, which were subsequently reduced and reformatted. Edward Lavin Giroir was the son of Senator Edward Lavin Girroir of Tracadie, NS. I received his charts from Bernard Girroir in Tracadie.

60 Janet Jehn , Exiles in the Colonies p. 27.

61 Léopold Lanctôt, Familles Acadiennes tome I, Éditions du Libre-Échange, Veilleux, impression à demande Inc.,Boucherville, Québec, 1994. pp. 329-333.

62 (References for descendants of children #2,3,8 are taken from Family Tree Maker, Broderbund, 1995, World family Tree, pre-1600 to present day, Vol I. Descendants of Alexandre Girouard, tree # 4512.

63 Family Tree Maker Broderbund, 1995, World family Tree, pre-1600 to present day, Vol. II Descendants of Alexandre, tree #'s 2487,1040, 3250. Also web page of Pierre Girouard à Onil à Alfred [Block P217-6m2 of subchart 217]. http://membes.xoom.com/pierre G/html/frcs/surnames.htm.

64 Placide Gaudet's research on "Girouard genealogy", p.2192. Ottawa National Archives, Call no. C-2239 Micro.

65 Placide Gaudet, "genealogy of the Girouards" pp. 2130, 2138, 2144, 2156; Bona Arsenault genealogy, chapter on Port Royal Girouards; Bergeron, Le Grand Arrangement des Acadiens Vol 1V, The Girouards..

66 Placide Gaudet's research on the "Girouard genealogy", p. 2192. Ottawa National Archives, Call no. C-2239, Micro.

67 Placide Gaudet and Adrien Bergeron, see chart 207 for detailed reference.

68 Adrien Bergeron, Le Grand Arrangement des Acadiens au Québec. La famille Girouard, Vol. IV.

69 Paul Surette, Atlas de l'établissement des Acadiens aux trois rivières du Chignectou 1660-1755, Les Éditions d'Acadie, 1996, Moncton New Brunswick, p. 18.

70 Paul Surette, Atlas de l'établissement des Acadiens aux trois rivières du Chignectou 1660-1755, Les Éditions d'Acadie, Moncton New Brunswick, p.22, 1996.

71 Cahier de La Société Historique Acadienne, Vol. IV No.1 (avril, mai, juin),1971. Notes de Voyage de Rameau in Acadie, 1860, Université de Moncton, pp 21-30.

72 Stephen A. White, Dictionnaire Généalogique des Familles acadiennes, Centre D'études acadiennes, 1999, Vol. I, p 731.

73 Mary Weekes, Acadian Betrayal, and Toronto: Burns & MacEachern, 1955- Author's note section, also held at the CEA.

74 Cahiers de la Société hitorique acadien,Vol. IV, no.1 (avril, mai, juin, 1971), Notes de Voyage de Rameau in Acadie, 1860 pp 35-40

75 " Placide Gaudet's Speech given in Ottawa" (see Antigonish chapter of Nova Scotia Prince Edward Island Book, concerning the Tracadie, Nova Scotia Girouards for contents and reference to Jean-Baptiste Girouard in Memramcook).

76 Loisele "Notes on Girouard Genealogy", Québec National Archives, Laval University St. Foy, PQ, P. 00179 also Placide Gaudet, p. 2132, 2177, 2188.

77 Placide Gaudet's research on the "Girouard Genealogy" 2187-1, 2187-2, 2187-3.

78 Léopold Lanctôt, Familles acadiennes Tome I, Veilleux, impression à demande Inc.,Boucherville, Québec, 1994, p.150.

79 Léopold Lanctôt, Familles Acadiennes, Tome I, Veilleux, impression à demande Inc.,Boucherville, Québec, 1994, pp. 149, 151.

80 Paul Surette, Le Grand Petcoudiac, 1763-1832, Histoire des Trois-Rivieres Vol. III, Les Éditions d'Acadie, Moncton, New Brunswick 1996.

81 Grand Pré Records, Diocese of Baton Rouge, Catholic Church Records, Acadian Records, 1707-1748, Vol. 1, Revised, third printing 1999, Excerpts, p. 80, 81.

82 Census records of 1707, 1714, Beaubassin.

83 Gaston Giroir, correspondence and research notes of Girouard, Giroir(e) family in France. Gaston is a resident of France.

84 Stephen A. White, Dictionnaire Généalogique des Familles Acadiennes, Centre D'études acadiennes, 1999, Vol. I, p. 543.

85 Stephen A. White, Dictionnaire Généalogique des Familles Acadiennes, Centre D'études Acadiennes, 1999, Vol. I, p. 766.

86 Paul Surette, Atlas de l'établissement des Acadiens aux trois rivières du Chignectou 1660-1755, Les Éditions d'Acadie, Moncton, NB, 1996, Les Éditions d'Acadie, Moncton, NB, 1996, pp. 181 and pp 202-204.

87 Paul Surette, Atlas de l'établissement des Acadiens aux trois rivières du Chignectou 1660-1755, Les Éditions d'Acadie, Moncton, NB, 1996, ibid., p. 21, 24.

88 Paul Surette, Atlas de l'établissement des Acadiens aux trois rivières du Chignectou 1660-1755, Les Éditions d'Acadie, Moncton, NB, 1996, p.183.

89 Paul Surette, Atlas de l'établissement des Acadiens aux trois rivières du Chignectou 1660-1755, Les Éditions d'Acadie, Moncton, NB, 1996, p. 213.

90 C. J. D'Entremont, Nicolas Denys, Sa Vie et Son Oeuvre, Yarmouth, N.E., L'Impr. Lescarbot, which appeared as part of a bibliography from La Société Historique Acadienne les Cahiers-janvier, 1987 vol. 18, no. 1, pp. (33-35) Moncton, New Brunswick, Translation: M. J.P. Dinwoodie #7L.

91 Frances G. Laboe (Girroir), sister of Senator Edward Lavin Girroir, Westbrae Parkway, Houston Texas, USA.

Endnotes

92 Genealogist P.G. Roy, p. 9, quoted in Adrien Bergeron, "La famille Girouard" in Le Grand Arrangement des Acadiens au Québec vol.IV.

93 Placide Gaudet's research on Girouard genealogy, Ottawa National Archives, Call no. C-2239 Micro.

94 Jules Léger, "Guides to Understanding the Acadian Dispersion", M.A. thesis Canisius College, 1963:

95 Léopold Lanctôt, Familles Acadiennes tome I, Éditions du Libre-Échange, Veilleux, impression à demande Inc., Boucherville, Québec, 1994, p.230.

96 Acadie, The Odyssey of a People, Environment Canada, Canadian Parks service, Research by Brenda Dunn, James E. Candow, Graphic Design: Cardinald Design, Illustrations: Claude Picard, Lewis Parker, Bernard Lee Blanc, Percy Walsh; Formative Evaluation: Acadian Consultative Committee, Centre of Acadian studies, (Stephen White & R. Gilles LeBlanc); Project manager: William H. Nethery, A.R.O. Interpretation. Project inspired by Robert G. LeBlanc's research: revised edition, 1993.

97 Brenda Dunn, The Acadians of Minas, revised edition, 1990, published under Minister of Environment, Ottawa, Sudiers in Archaeology, Architecture and History, originally published National Parks and Sites Branch, p. 6.

98 Le Réeveil Acadien, Acadian Cultural Society, (Société Acadiene), Fitchburg, Ma. USA . November 1986, article submitted by Patricia Bolton #132 for the membership newsletter publication.

99 Archives Nationales de France, Fonds des Colonies, quoted in the 7th edition of the Société Historique Acadienne, March 1965-Moncton, NB, Canada, C12-Vol.1, fol. 22-26

100 Notes of Rose Seeley, RR#1, Fox Creek, N.B

101 Bona Arsenault, History of the Acadians, 1978, pp. 160, 161

102 Bona Arsenault, History of the Acadians, 1978, p. 135

103 Léopold Lanctôt, Familles Acadiennes tome I, Éditions du Libre-Échange, Veilleux, impression à demande Inc., Boucherville, Québec 1994, pp.238-242.

104 Léopold Lanctôt, Familles Acadiennes tome I, Éditions du Libre-Échange, Veilleux, impression à demande Inc., Boucherville, Québec, 1994,. p27

105 Léopold Lanctôt, Familles Acadiennes, tome I, Éditions du Libre-Échangec, Veilleux, impression à demande Inc., Boucherville, Québec 1994, p 329

106 Léopold Lanctôt, Familles Acadiennes tome I, Éditions du Libre-Échangec Veilleux, impression à demande Inc., Boucherville, Québec, 1994, p. 152-157

107 Léopold Lanctôt, Familles Acadiennes tome I, Éditions du Libre-Échangec, Veilleux, impression à demande Inc., Boucherville, Québec, 1994, pp. 329 –333.

108 Léopold Lanctôt, Familles Acadiennes tome I, Éditions du Libre-Échangec Veilleux, impression à demande Inc., Boucherville, Québec, 1994 p. 154

109 Léopold Lanctôt, Familles Acadiennes tome I, Éditions du Libre-Échangec, Veilleux, impression à demande Inc., Boucherville, Québec, 1994, pp. 152-157.

110 Léopold Lanctôt, Familles Acadiennes tome I, Éditions du Libre-Échange, Veilleux, impression à demande Inc., Boucherville, Québec, 1994, pp152-156

111 Acadie, The Odyssey of a People, Environment Canada, Canadian Parks service, Research by Brenda Dunn, James E. Candow, Graphic Design: Cardinald

Design, Illustrations: Claude Picard, Lewis Parker, Bernard LeBlanc, Percy Walsh; Formative Evaluation: Acadian Consultative Committee, Centre of Acadian studies, (Stephen White & R. Gilles LeBlanc); Project manager: William H. Nethery, A.R.O. Interpretation. Project inspired by Robert G. LeBlanc's research: revised edition, 1993.

112 Chapman J. Milling, Exile Without An End, Bostick & Thornley, Inc., Columbia, South Carolina, 1943, pp. 64-74.

113 Les Productions, La Société, du Monument Lefebvre, inc. C. P. 360 Saint-Joseph, N-B, E0A2Y0.

114 Acadie, The Odyssey of a People, Environment Canada, Canadian Parks service, Research by Brenda Dunn, James E. Candow, Graphic Design: Cardinald Design, Illustrations: Claude Picard, Lewis Parker, Bernard LeBlanc, Percy Walsh; Formative Evaluation: Acadian Consultative Committee, Centre of Acadian studies, (Stephen White & R. Gilles LeBlanc); Project manager: William H. Nethery, A.R.O. Interpretation. Project inspired by Robert G. LeBlanc's research: revised edition, 1993.

115 Acadie, The Odyssey of a People, Environment Canada, Canadian Parks service, Research by Brenda Dunn, James E. Candow, Graphic Design: Cardinald Design, Illustrations: Claude Picard, Lewis Parker, Bernard LeBlanc, Percy Walsh; Formative Evaluation: Acadian Consultative Committee, Centre of Acadian studies, (Stephen White & R. Gilles LeBlanc); Project manager: William H. Nethery, A.R.O. Interpretation. Project inspired by Robert G. LeBlanc's research: revised edition, 1993, p.35.

116 Muriel K. Roy, "The settlement and Population Growth", The Acadians of the Maritimes A Thematic Study, edited by Jean Daigle, Centre d'études acadiennes, Université de Moncton, Moncton, NB, published by authority of the Minister of Environment, 1982 p.153.

117 Jean Daigle, "Acadia, 1604-1763, An Historical Synthesis", The Acadians of the Maritimes A Thematic Study, edited by Jean Daigle, Centre d'études acadiennes, Université de Moncton, Moncton, NB, published by authority of the Minister of Environment, 1982, p. 31

118 Naomi E. S. Griffiths, L'Acadie de 1686 à 1784, Contexte d'une histoire, translation by Kathryn Hamer, Les Éditions d'Acadie, 1997 p. 86.

119 Acadie, The Odyssey of a People, Environment Canada, Canadian Parks service, Research by Brenda Dunn, James E. Candow, Graphic Design: Cardinald Design, Illustrations: Claude Picard, Lewis Parker, Bernard Lee Blanc, Percy Walsh; Formative Evaluation: Acadian Consultative Committee, Centre of Acadian studies, (Stephen White & R. Gilles LeBlanc); Project manager: William H. Nethery, A.R.O. Interpretation. Project inspired by Robert G. LeBlanc's research: revised edition, 1993.

120 Albert J. Robichaux Jr., The Acadian Exiles in Châtellerault 1773-1785 records in which Dominique Giroire married to Agnes Broussard of Archigny, Vienne). Dominque (absent) and Agnes Brossard, and his wife were were all in the third Convoy leaving Châtellerault, France, Dec. 1775. Also research notes of Gaston Giroir records this family in France.

Endnotes

121 Milton Rose Jr. and Norma, Gaudet Reider, The Acadians in France, 1762, - 1776, Vol. I

122 Acadie, The Odyssey of a People, Environment Canada, Canadian Parks service, Research by Brenda Dunn, James E. Candow, Graphic Design: Cardinald Design, Illustrations: Claude Picard, Lewis Parker, Bernard LeBlanc, Percy Walsh; Formative Evaluation: Acadian Consultative Committee, Centre of Acadian studies, (Stephen White & R. Gilles LeBlanc); Project manager: William H. Nethery, A.R.O. Interpretation. Project inspired by Robert G. LeBlanc's research: revised edition, 1993.

123 Acadie, The Odyssey of a People, Environment Canada, Canadian Parks service, Research by Brenda Dunn, James E. Candow, Graphic Design: Cardinald Design, Illustrations: Claude Picard, Lewis Parker, Bernard LeBlanc, Percy Walsh; Formative Evaluation: Acadian Consultative Committee, Centre of Acadian studies, (Stephen White & R. Gilles LeBlanc); Project manager: William H. Nethery, A.R.O. Interpretation. Project inspired by Robert G. LeBlanc's research: revised edition, 1993

124 Acadie, The Odyssey of a People, Environment Canada, Canadian Parks service, Research by Brenda Dunn, James E. Candow, Graphic Design: Cardinald Design, Illustrations: Claude Picard, Lewis Parker, Bernard LeBlanc, Percy Walsh; Formative Evaluation: Acadian Consultative Committee, Centre of Acadian studies, (Stephen White & R. Gilles LeBlanc); Project manager: William H. Nethery, A.R.O. Interpretation. Project inspired by Robert G. LeBlanc's research: revised edition, 1993

125 Pierre-Maurice Hébert, Les Acadiens du Québec, Éditions de L'Écho, Montréal, Québec, 1994, pp. 37,38, 39.

126 Acadie, The Odyssey of a People, Environment Canada, Canadian Parks service, Research by Brenda Dunn, James E. Candow, Graphic Design: Cardinald Design, Illustrations: Claude Picard, Lewis Parker, Bernard LeBlanc, Percy Walsh; Formative Evaluation: Acadian Consultative Committee, Centre of Acadian studies, (Stephen White & R. Gilles LeBlanc); Project manager: William H. Nethery, A.R.O. Interpretation. Project inspired by Robert G. LeBlanc's research: revised edition 1993.

127 Jean Daigle, "Acadia, 1604-1763, An Historical Synthesis", The Acadians of the Maritimes, A Thematic Study, edited by Jean Daigle, Centre d'études acadiennes, Université de Moncton, Moncton, NB, published by authority of the Minister of Environment, 1982, p. 19

127 Léopold Lanctôt, Familles Acadiennes tome I, Éditions du Libre-Échange, 1994. p 271.

128 Rev. C.J. d'Entremont, article on the Ancestors of Bishop Edouard LeBlanc called "Heritage", The Vanguard newspaper, Yarmouth, NS March 14,1989, p. 14 b.

129 Neil J. Boucher, Doctoral Thesis, 1993 Acadian Nationalism and the Episcopacy of MSGR. Edouard Alfred LeBlanc, Bishop of Saint John, New Brunswick (1912-1936): A Maritime chapter of Canadian Ethno-Religious History, p. 121,122.
 ibid. p. 39.

130 Agnus Anthony Johnston, "unpublished notes on The Immaculate Conception Parish, West Arichat, N.S." Diocesan Historian, Antigonish, N.S, given to Fr. Conrad Girroir for a speech that he was preparing, for the parish's centennial and subsequently forwarded to me.
131 Sally Ross, "Rebuiding a Society: The Challenges Faced by the Acadian Minority in Nova Scotia during the first Century after the Deportation, 1764-1767" with introduction by Barbara LeBlanc, Edited by Margaret Conrad, Curatorial Report Number 87, Three Illustrated Studies, p. 53.
132 Sally Ross, Alphonse Deveau, The Acadians of Nova Scotia, Past and Present, Nimbus, 1992 pp. 77,89,105,115,127
133 Mitchell 's original 1733 map
134 Inventory site for present owner, Marion l. Inglis, Bridgetown RR#3, original owner Joseph Rice-Micro fiche reference number: 43-02-01567, Village of Tupperville, Annapolis Co; Land deed recorded, Jan. 28, 1784, From William and Lydia Lawrence to Joseph RICE- La Farme Marche, 48 rods in width.
135 Guy DeBord, Comments on the Society of the Spectacle, translated by Malcolm Imerie, London,Verso, 1990

Endnotes for Port Royal Captions

1. National Archives of Canada, original held at the National Library of Canada, Originally from a drawing by the author in Les Voyages du sieur de Champlain Xaintongeois, captain for the King, divided into two books, by Samuel de Champlain (Paris, 1613)
2. Minutes of H. M. Minutes of Council 1720-1742, Public Archives of NS (PANS), p Call number F100N 85V 253.
3. Minutes of H. M. Minutes of Council 1720-1742, Public Archives of NS (PANS), Call number F100N 85V 253.
4. Ray Girouard, Aylmer Québec, one of our committee-at-large members, sent this copy to me.
5. Léopold Lanctôt, Familles acadiennes, tome II, Éditions du Libre-Échange, Veilleux, impression à demande Inc. ,Boucherville, Québec, 1994, p. 88.
6. Ibid p. 277
7. H. M. Minutes of Council 1720-1742, Public Archives of NS (PANS), p. call number F100N 85V253 pp.314, 315.
8. Léopold Lanctôt, Familles acadiennes tome I, Éditions du Libre-Échange, Veilleux, impression à demande Inc., Boucherville, Québec, 1994 Vol. I, p. 237.
9. Map is based on a map by the University of Wisconsin, Cartographic Laboratory, from Donald Hebert's book, Acadians in Exile.
10. Paul Surette, Le Grand Petcoudiac, 1763-1832, Histoire des Trois-Rivieres

Vol. III, Les Éditions d'Acadie, Moncton, NB, 1996, Moncton, New Brunswick Vol. III, p. 38 .

11. Paul Surette, Atlas de l'établissement des Acadiens aux trois rivières du Chignectou 1660-1755, Les Éditions d'Acadie, 1996, Moncton, New Brunswick, p. 85.

12. Paul Surette, Le Petcoudiac (1763-1832), Histoires des Trois Rivières, Dieppe, NB: la Ville de Dieppe, 1985. Vol. 3, p. 15.

13. Paul Surette, Atlas de l'établissement des Acadiens aux trois rivières du Chignectou 1660-1755, Les Éditions d'Acadie, Moncton, NB, 1996, p.1.

14. Ibid, p. 181 and pp. 202-204.

15. Ibid, p. 179.

16. Ibid p. 190.

17. Ibid p. 190.

18. Ibid p. 211.

19. Léopold Lanctôt, Familles Acadiennes tome I, Éditions du Libre-Échange, Veilleux, impression à demande Inc., Boucherville, Québec, 1994, p. 27.

20 Ibid p. 329.

21. Chapman J. Milling, Exile Without An End, Bostick & Thornley, Inc., Columbia, South Carolina, 1943, pp. 64-74.

22 . Les Productions, La Société, du Monument Lefebvre, inc. C. P. 360 Saint-Joseph , N-B, E0A2Y0.

List of Appendices

0. Patrons
1. Acadian Master Chart cross-reference to all subcharts in all volumes of this book.
2. All subcharts cross-referenced to Acadian Master Chart block which they expand.
3. References for each block of the Acadian Master Chart.[AMC]
4. Placide Gaudet's notes to accompany the Plan of Annapolis Royal.
5. Subcharts referenced in Port Royal an old Acadie chapter
6. Girouard, Grrrior Giroir… place-names
7. Letters and surveys in preparation for Family reunions
8. Alphabetical index by first name of all ancestors/descendants in each block of all charts.

Appendices

*Patrons ********With special thanks*

Antigonish County Branches:

In memory of
Hubert William
Girroir, Tracadie
-Dallas & Hebert Asselstine
Edmonton, Alberta

Donna (Girroir) Bankoff
& Marvin
Green Brook, New Jersey

Josephine Elsie (Tramble) Munson
 & James
Arizona

Sarah Agnes (Hache-Gallant) MacNeil
Antigonish, N.S.

In memory of
Francis (Girroir) Laboe
Houston, Texas

Ingrid Hoover
Casco, Wisconsin

Rebecca & Paul Lafrance
Oshawa, Ontario

Karen & Kaye Girroir
Watertown, Mass.
In memory of Francis J. Girroir

William Rice
Winthrop, Mass.
In memory of great-grandmother.
Marie Angelique Gerrior

Mary V. Tanner
Welland, Ontario

Susan April Thiboult
Auburn, New Hampshire

Guysborough County Branches:

Arthur D. & Mary Gerrior
North Weymouth, Mass.

Theresa & Don Adams
Halifax, N.S.

Blanche & Arnold Hughes
Chezzetcook, N.S.

Marcel & Sharon Aucoin
Halifax, N.S.

Jude & Vaughnie Avery
Larry's River, N.S.

Reg & Camilla Avery
Halifax, N.S.
In Memory of Blanche

Bob and Anna Bunton
Beverton, Ontario

Carlene Duval
Campbell River, B.C.

Jean (Robertson) Boyle
Belleville, Ontario

Karen & Raymond Delorey
Larry's River, N.S.

Bill & Marilyn Gerrior
Ottawa, Ontario

Mary L. Gerrior
Stellarton, N.S.

Thomas & Barbara Johnston
Wakefield, Mass.

Acadian Awakenings: An Acadian Family In Exile

Patrons *********With special thanks*
Guysborough County Branches:

Joseph & Marie Butler
Quincy, Mass.

In memory of Irene (Gerrior)
and Les Johnson

Thomas & Barbara Johnston
and family

Claire (Pellerin)Hagen
LeDuc, Alberta

Ernestine Jackson
Peabody, Mass.

Julene F. Raichle
Reading, Mass.

Jean & Alphonse Pitts
New Glasgow, NS.

In memory of
Laura E. Ottaway
-Vernon Ottaway
Saint John, N. B.

In memory of Roland Morley
-Joanne Morley
and family
Lunenburg, Mass.

Estelle & Bill MacMaster
Dartmouth, NS.

Marie Gerrior Nugent
Sydney, NS.

Bazil & Grace Pellerin
Larry's River, NS.

Gordon & Mary Pellerin
Larry's River, NS.

In memory of Percy Pellerin
Larry's River, N.S.
- family
Donald Pellerin
Larry's River, N.S.

In memory of
Joanne Pellerin
-Blair Pellerin and family
Larry's River, N.S.

Dianne Pellerin
Larry's River, N.S.

In memory of Brad Pellerin
-Margaret Anne Pellerin
and family
Larry's River, N.S.

In memory of Cyril Pellerin
-Esther Pellerin and family
Halifax, N.S.

Earl Pellerin
Larry's River, N.S.

Evelyn & Michael Oakley
Halifax, N.S.

Carlene & Bernard Martin
Peabody, Mass.

In memory of
Ethel & Margaret Murphy
-Nina Murphy
Larry's River, N.S.

Mike R. Gerrior
Collingwood, Ontario

Mary L. Gerrior
Stellarton, NS.

Appendices

Patrons ********With special thanks
Guysborough County Branches:

Richard J. & Doris Butler
Quincy, Mass.

Brad & Winni Comeau
Dartmouth, N. S.

Delores & Mike DeRepentigny
Kamloops, B.C.

John W. & Donna Gerrior
Shediac, N.B.

Joseph A. & Dorothy Gerrior
Collingwood, Ontario

Herman & Avis Gerrior
Truro, N.S.

Reg & Barbara Gerrior
Halifax, N.S.

Thomas G. Gerrior
Halifax, N.S.

Verna A. Gionet
Halifax, N.S.

Vincent Gionet
Halifax, N.S.

In memory of
John S. Gerrior
-Mary Beatrice Gerrior
 and family, Halifax, N.S.

Shirley & Salvadore Branco
Andover, Mass.

In memory of Martina (Gerrior)
Comeau
-Anne Marie & Dieter Schroeder
and family
Dartmouth, N.S.

Larry & Claire Sheppard
Rockport, Mass.

Sharon Slate
Beverly, Mass.

Ruth Taylor
Wakefield, Mass.

Blanche & Pat Tully
Dartmouth, N.S.

P. E. I Branches:

Milton Gerrior
Oakville, Ontario

Christine (Morin) Oderkirk
Bedford, N.S.

Isle Madame Branch:

Fr. Conrad P. Girroir
West Arichat, N.S.

Cornelius & Emma Boucher
Isle Madame, N.S.

Richard & Grace Brindle
Kingston, N.H.

Ronald P. & Regina Brindle
Babylon, New York
In memory of
Florence Zenobie Gerrior.
Paul J. Brindle and Charles Brindle

Elaine Marney
Epping, N.H.

Acadian Awakenings: An Acadian Family In Exile

Patrons ********With special thanks*

Clifford & Pattie Gerrior
& Clifford J. Gerrior (Sr)
Brockton, Mass.

Jean LeJeune
Isle Madame, N.S.

Mary Cecile (Gerrior) Latimer
Sydney, N.S.

Mary Anne Gilbert
Acton, Mass.

Barbara (Gerrior) Butterfield
Bow, New Hampshire

Jeannette (Gerroir) & Joe Mury
West Arichat, N.S.

Edward F. White
Canton, Mass.

Phylis A. Tatten
Leominister, Mass.

New Brunswick Branches:

Raymond J. Girouard
Aylmer, P.Q.

Aurea & Aurele Maillet
Moncton, N. B.

Violette Girouard
Sheila, N. B.

Dr. Edgar Girouard
Moncton, N. B.

George & Amerylis Girouard
Moncton, N.B.

Laurie and Pamela Girouard
Maple Ridge, B.C.

Annette Girouard Richard
Richibucto, N.B.

Leonard Girouard
Saint John, N.B.

Gary & Suzanne Girouard
Charlesbourg, P.Q.

Maurice Girouard
Dieppe, New Brunswick

Rita and Leslie Kay
Halifax, N.S.

Fernand & Emerise
Girouard & family
Moncton, N.B.

Bernard Girouard
Fairfax, U.S.A.

Québec Branches:

Annette Girouard
Richibucto, N.B.

Gabriel & Paulette Girouard
Laval, P.Q.

Suzanne (Girouard) Robert
St. Hyacinthe, P.Q.

Therese Girouard & Adrien Boucher
Saint Hyacinthe, P.Q.

Appendices

*Patrons ********With special thanks*

Québec Branches:
Albert & Claire Girouard
Pointe-Aux-Trembles, P.Q.

Norman & Dagmar Girouard
Fort Lauderdale, FL.

Laurie Girouard
Maple Ridge, B.C.

Desirée & Esmé Girouard
Ottawa, Ontario

André Girouard
Sudbury, Ontario

In memory of Pierrette Girouard
Ste-Marie
-Richard Ste-Marie and family

Paul & Paulette Girouard
Halifax, N.S.

Lise Girouard Jourdain
Rivière du Loup, P. Q.

Denise Girouard Wall
Providence, R. I.

Louisiana Branches:

In memory of
Cyrus Giroir
- Shirley Giroir
and family
Morgan City, La.

Lorina & Harry J. Giroir
Houma, La.

Frank J.(Sr.) & Evelyn Giroir
Metairie, La.

Leona & William Knight Bledsoe
Long Beach, California

Delores Emily, Guillory Dekko
Haily, Idaho

In memory of
Stella (Girouard) Hébert
-Barbara Gail and family
Houma, La.

Leonie J. & Theresa Giroir
Morgan City, La.

Howard J. Giroir
Houma, La.

Louis E. Giroir Jr. & Jamie
Round Rock, Texas

Wanda (Girouard) Dore
Broussard, La.

Ida & Buddy Hyver
Metairie, La.

Charles Joseph Rodriguez

Mary Jane Siracusa
Houston, Texas

Taylor Rock
Lafayette, La.

Shirley Daspit (Giroir) Vicknair
Baton Rouge, La.

APPENDIX 1

CROSS REFERENCE OF [AMC] BLOCKS TO SUBCHART NUMBERS FOUND IN EACH CHAPTER OF THE BOOK

	A	B	C	D	E	F	G	H	I	J	K
1]		Research of William D. Gerrior, *Acadian Awakenings*, 2002				François see Master Chart & P.R. Ch. 2,3	Note1: Referring to the Acadian Master Chart-This chart gives a cross-reference between each block of the Acadian master chart and its corresponding subchart(s) numbers, and/or its corresponding genealogy contained in block information. The block information is the genealogy in paragraph format in the text, relating to various blocks of the master chart and various blocks of the subcharts. Also the chapter in which you can find the indicated subchart or block genealogy information is indicated in each block below. Note 2: In each of the blocks on this chart, the abbreviation Ch. means "chapter". Not 3: Note: Block info is genealogy in block paragraph form given in the text of each chapter				
2]		Marie Block info traced to the 11th generation present day, France Ch. 2	Madeleine Subchart #201 traced to the 11th generation present day, France Ch. 2	Germain Subchart #202 traced to the 13th generation present day Québec Ch. 10	Anne Block info traced to the 9th generation present day France Ch. 2	Jacques See Master Chart & P.R. Ch. 3 To present day Direct line in this centre column to the author of this book	Marie m. Jacques Granger No further information	Marguerite m. Louis Doucet No further information	Claude Subchart #207 to the 12th generation, present day Québec Ch. 10	Guillaume Subchart #208 to the 12th generation, present day. Québec Ch. 10	
3a]		Note: Descendants of Alexandre (C-3a) also in West Indies LA Ch. 12	Alexandre Subchart #204 to the 5th generation France Ch. & Québec Ch.	Jacques Block info to the 5th generation Québec Ch. 10	Jean no further information	↔					
3b]		Denis (d) at 21 years of age in same year of his marriage. at Grand Pré No children Port Royal Ch. 3	Charles see block info for this block (C-3b) in the N.B. Ch. & chart #211 traced to the 6th generation LA. Ch. 12	Germain Subcharts #217, #218 traced to the 10th & 11th generation, present day. Québec Ch. 10	Pierre Subcharts #163,164, 162; 162.1; Mad./PEI. Ch. & LA. Ch. Also #300's, 500's, 600's, 700's N.B. Ch. 8 traced to 11th and 12th generations, present day.	François See Master Chart Port Royal Ch. 3	Anne-Marie Traced to the ninth generation.	Madeleine sworn statements Belle-Ile-En-Mer FR. Ch. 2			
4m2]			West Indies		Marie Josèphe No further information	↔	Nathalie m. Amable Blanchard Dep. S.C.				
4m1]	1711 - Marie-Madeleine (d) early	1709 - 1721 François	Pierre Block info. traced to 5th generation Québec Ch. 2	1714 - 1716 Charles	Marie Madeleine m. Charles LeBlanc Port Royal Chapter Traced to present day Subchart # 80	Jean Baptiste See Master Chart Ch. 3	Marguerite No further information	Anne-Hélène Traced to Memramcook River NB Ch.8 & PQ Ch. 10	Joseph Subchart #216 to the 6th generation Québec Ch. 10		

Appendices

5]					Marie Block info. to the 11th generation, present day Ant. Ch. 5	Joseph Subcharts #0,1#,#4,#5,# 8 to the 11th generation, present day Ant. Ch. 5	François See Master Chart Ant. Ch. 5	Anastasie Block info. to the 12th generation, present day Ant. Ch. 5	Marie-Madeleine Block info. to 4th generation France Ch. 2			
6]						Marie Sophie No further information	Luc See Master Chart Ant. Ch. 5	Juliette m. Michel Petipas No further information	Marie Marguerite Block info. to the 12th generation, present day Guys. Ch. 6			
7]	Frédéric Subcharts #35, 36 From the 12th generation to present day Guys. Ch. 6	Vénérande Block info. Traced to present day Guys. Ch. 6	Francis Subchart #34 to the 12th generation, present day Guys. Ch. 6		Marcelline Pierre died young	Isidore Subcharts #31, 32 and Block info. to the 12th generation, present day Guys. Ch. 6	Abraham See Master Chart Guys. Ch. 6	Joseph Subchart #48 to 12th generation, present day Guys. Ch. 6	Maximin Subchart #33 to the 11th generation, present day Guys. Ch. 6	Jean Baptiste Block information & Appendix for 9th generation	Marguerite No further information	Henrietta No further information
8]					Dennis A. Subchart #67	Luke A. Block info. to the 12th generation, present day Guys. Ch. 6	William A. See Master Chart Guys. Ch. 6	Michael A. Subchart #72 to 13th generation, present day Guys. Ch. 6	Benjamin A. Block info. to the 12th generation, present day Guys. Ch. 6	Julie Block info. to the 12th generation, present day Guys. Ch. 6	Delia Block info. to the 12th generation, present day Guys. Ch. 6	Adele Block info. to the 10th generation, present day Guys. Ch. 6
9]		Helen		William (d) at young age	Adelina, Lena Block info. to the 12th generation, present day Guys. Ch. 6	Simon Block info. to the 13th generation, present day Guys. Ch. 6	Jeffrey See Master Chart Guys. Ch. 6	Allan Subchart #95 To the 12th generation, present day Guys. Ch. 6	Agnes Block info. to the 11th generation, present day Guys. Ch. 6	Tom (d) young	Geneva Not married USA	
10]		Helen Block info. to the 12th generation, present day Guys. Ch. 6		Hubert (d) at young age.	Martina	William Not married d) at 25 yrs. of age.	John S. See Master Chart	Tom Block info. to the 13th generation, present day Guys. Ch. 6	Cecelia Block info. to the 13th generation, present day Guys. Ch. 6	Clara Block info. to the 13th generation, present day Guys. Ch. 6	Anna	
11]		Theresa Block info. to the 13th generation, present day Guys. Ch. 6		Thomas Gerard (d) infancy	Herman Block info. to the 13th generation, present day Guys. Ch. 6	Reg Block info. to the 13th generation, present day Guys. Ch. 6	William D. (Bill) See Master chart Guys. Ch. 6	Delores Block info. to the 13th generation, present day Guys. Ch. 6	Verna Block info. to the 13th generation, present day Guys. Ch. 6	Tom Block info. to the 13th generation, present day Guys. Ch. 6	Evelyn Block info. to the 13th generation, present day Guys. Ch. 6	Marie Block info. to the 13th generation, present day Guys. Ch. 6
12]							Steve Block info. Guys. Ch. 6	Suzanne Block info. Guys. Ch. 6				**APPENDIX 1 ACADIAN MASTER CHART TO SUBCHART CROSS-REFERENCE**

©*Acadian Awakenings Girouard/Giroir... Routes and Roots*

385

Appendix 2
Subchart # Cross Reference to Master Chart Block

Cross Reference of all Subcharts with the master chart block which they expand

Subchart # Master Chart Block

Antigonish County Subcharts
0   BlocK[E-5] Ant. N.S.
1   [E-5] Ant.
4   [E-5] Ant.
8   [E-5] Ant.
10 [E-5] Ant.

Guysborough County Subcharts
20 [H-6] Guys. N.S.
31 [E-7] Guys.
32 [E-7] Guys.
33 [H-7] Guys.
34 [C-7] Guys.
35 [A-7] Guys.
36 [A-7] Guys.
48 [G-7] Guys.
67 [D-8] Guys.
72 [G-8] Guys.
76 [G-8] Guys.
95 [G-9] Guys.

Clare & P.Royal,N.S. Subchart
80 E-4m1] Port Royal
201 [C-2] Port Royal

Prince Edward Island
162 [E-3b] P.E.I.

Isle Madame,N.S. Subcharts
163 [E-3b] Isle Mad
164 [E-3b] Isle Mad

New Brunswick Subcharts
300 [E-3b] N.B.
309 [E-3b] N.B.
315 [E-3b] N.B.
500 [E-3b] N.B.
514 [E-3b] N.B.
523 [E-3B] N.B.
527 [E-3B] N.B.
542 [E-3b] N.B.
600 [E-3b] N.B.
700 [E-3b] N.B.
705 [E-3b] N.B.
706 [E-3b] N.B.
711 [E-3b] N.B.
717 [E-3b] N.B.
724 [E-3b] N.B.
729 [E-3b] N.B.
737 [E-3b] N.B.

Louisiana
162.1 [E-3b] LA.
162.6 [E-3b] LA.

West Indies Subcharts
204 [C-3a] W.Ind.
211 [C-3b] W.Ind.

France Subcharts
400 Deux Sèvres FR.
420 Parthney Fr.
800 (Sculptors) FR.
900 (Vienne) FR.
Fc (France-Canadian)

Québec Acadian Subcharts
202 [D-2] P.Q.
Block info [D-3a] P.Q.
207 [I-3A] P.Q.
208 [J-3A] P.Q.
213,217,218 [D-3b] P.Q.
Block info [C-4m1]P.Q.
Block info [J-4m1]P.Q.
3001 [Girouard /Rodier]

Québec French-Canadian
2000 [N-5a] P.Q.
3006-Pierre Realh of Liége, Belgium.

*All these subcharts are connected to the Acadian Master Chart **[AMC]** except for the last subchart 2000 which expands [Block N-5a] of the French Canadian Master chart**[FCMC]** descending from Antoine Girouard, France. Also the France charts 400 and 900 refer to France only. Block info is text genealogy expanding blocks in paragraph form for all other blocks.

Appendices

Appendix 3

References for each Block of the Acadian Master Chart [AMC]

Abbreviations

b.   = born
bap. = baptised
bur. = buried
ca. = circa (around)
cem = cemetery
Co. = County
d.   = died
d/o = daughter of
m.   = is or was married to; is or was mate of
n.m. = not married
p.   = page
pp. = pages
Vol. = Volume
( ) = names appearing in brackets are the parents
tome = volume

Place Names

Ant. = Antigonish, NS
C.B. = Cape Breton, NS
GP   = Grand Pré
Guys. = Guysborough, NS
FR.   = France
La.   = Louisiana
Mass. = Massachusetts
NB   = New Brunswick
NS   = Nova Scotia
PEI   = Prince Edward Island
PR   = Port Royal
PQ   = Province of Québec
Qué   = Québec
Tr.   = Tracadie NS
W.A. = West Arichat, Isle Madame, Cape Breton NS
dit   = nicknamed (called) or from a place called

Sources:

Cen. = Census records
Décl. = Declarations (sworn statements about family relations) of Acadians who were deported back to France (statements taken at Belle-Isle-En-Mer).

PAC = Public Archives of Canada
PANS = Public Archives of Nova Scotia
S.H.A = Cahiers de la Société historique acadienne.
reg. = Parish or Church Register
RG. = (Record Group)-Marriage and baptism records on microfilm at the Provincial Archives of Nova Scotia, in Halifax (PANS)

Locations of original sources concerning the early generations of Acadians:
(Taken from Acadian parish registers which give births, baptisms and deaths)

1) *Registers of the oldest parish, Saint Jean-Baptiste de Port Royal*, are at the Provincial Archives of Nova Scotia, in Halifax.

2) *The registers of Saint-Charles des Mines in Grand Pré* went to Iberville, in Louisiana and can now be found at the New Orleans Archives.

3) *Registers of three other Acadian Parishes: Cobequid (Truro), Pisiquid (Windsor) and Saint Joseph de la Rivière aux Canards*, were lost. Cobequid registers were never found while the Rivière aux Canards registers were carried by deported Acadians to Virginia, following them to England and finally to France. Accidentally, Mgr. Tanguay discovered them in 1867 in Paris, but they were lost again.
Most of the residents of Cobequid and of Pisiquid fled to PEI around 1750, in which case, the 1752 census in PEI lists most of the families from Cobequid and Pisiquid and therefore helps to replace these lost registers.
    The second parish in Grand Pré was called Saint-Joseph-de-la-Rivière-aux-Canards as mentioned above and here the Acadians are traced with the help of the Belle-Île-en-Mer. sworn statements, stating their family names and relationships. These relationships concerned a great number of families in the Grand Pré region who were deported to Virginia in 1755, then to England and finally to France, after the Treaty of Paris of 1763.
    The Archbishop's Archives in Québec has some of the original Beaubassin parish registers, dating from the end of the 17th century.

Early generations (generations 1 to 4 of the master chart)
I have conducted my research at the Provincial Archives of Nova Scotia (PANS), Centre d'études acadiennes, Moncton, NB and the National Archives of Canada (NAC) and related church documents, census records, maps etc. using both primary and secondary sources. I cross-referenced this research, concerning the first four generations of the AMC with research records of professional genealogist, Stephen A. White, Centre d'études acadiennes, Université de Moncton via his his research work for his publication, *"Dictionnaire généologique des familles acadiennes"*. In addition I have consulted the research of other professional genealogists, such as Placide Gaudet and Bona Arsenault concerning the Girouards, and the research work of Paul Surette, Léopold Lanctôt, Loiselle and Bergeron, all professionals in their field of study, and many others as referenced in the text. Consequently, I have been unable to trace most of the blocks concerning genera-

tions 1 to 4 on the Acadian Girouard Master Chart [AMC] to present day.

Later Generations (generations 5 to 12 of the master chart)
For generations 5-12 of the master chart, I have researched primary references, mostly church registers in Tracadie, Nova Scotia, Larry's River, and Port Felix, Guysborough County, Nova Scotia, the latter records being held at the Cathedral in Canso, Nova Scotia, as well as numerous interviews and correspondence with many descendants. (surveys and letters, genealogical charts etc.) As well, I researched civil census records and land grants. As a result, I have been able to trace many branches of the majority of each of the AMC Blocks (Rows 5 to 11 on the master chart), to present day, with documented references.

Summary of master chart in general- In each of the five books, I refer to the master chart [AMC], using various subcharts and related genealogical block information in the text, linking to each block in these charts. I have also collected numerous survey forms etc. from descendants of each block of the Acadian Master Chart [AMC].

The Acadian Master Chart blocks therefore represent a base or foundation for all the corresponding branches in North America, descending from each of the AMC Blocks of the 12 generations of this Acadian Master Chart. All other master charts presented in this book for non-Acadian branches of Girouards are organized in the same way.

All Acadian Girouards, Giroirs, Gerriors, Girroirs, Gerroirs etc. in North America descend from one of these AMC Blocks of the 12 generations shown on the Acadian Master Chart and ultimately trace back to the one François Girouard and Jeanne Aucoin coming to Port Royal from France. I hope the following references for the master chart will serve as solid and accurate starting points for anyone wishing to do further research of the family related to any Block of the Acadian Master Chart..

1st Generation of the Acadian Master Chart
[AMC Block F-1] François Girouard dit La Varenne m. Jeanne Aucoin:
References:
Placide Gaudet genealogical collection of the Girouards, microfilm: C-2238 to C-2241, pp. 2108, 2166 PAC, p. 2136 Placide claims François is from Paris. [I believe this could be ultimately true, before the Loudun location, based on references and other information of other Girouards located near Paris, France, which I have found in my research. Placide does not provide a reference for this statement.]
François b. ca. 1621. PR cen. 1671, 50 yrs. old, cen. 1686, 70 years old; labourer; (Décl. BIM) PR d. before cen. of 1693. Cen. taken in 1671 and 1686 by Fr. Moulin. (PANS).
Jeanne Aucoin b. ca. 1631, d./bur, PR reg., April, 1718 at 90 years of age.
François Girouard arrived from France, most likely from La Chaussée area, Department of Vienne in the region of Loudun (ref: *Les parlers Frances d'Acadie* Vol.

I by Geneviève Massignon (Paris), p. 67,- The actual origins of French Acadians.
Stephen A. White, *Dictionnaire généologique des familles acadienne*, (1636-1714), Volume I: A-G and Volume II: H-Z, Centre d'études acadiennes, Université de Moncton,1999, Vol. I p.718.
Bona Arsenault, *History of Acadians*, Éditions Leméac, 1978, p. 38.
Bona Arsenault, *Histoire et Généalogique des Acadiens*, Éditions Leméac, 1978, *Tome 2, Port Royal, Annapolis Royal, Nouvelle Ecosse, p. 567*.
Léopold Lanctôt, *Familles Acadiennes*, Éditions du Libre-Échange, 1994, Tome I. p. 271.

2nd Generation of the Acadian Master Chart
(Children of François Girouard and Jeanne Aucoin) [AMC Block F-1]

[AMC Block B-2] Marie Girouard, daughter of François Girouard and Jeanne Aucoin, m. Jacques Blou.
References:
Placide Gaudet, genealogical collection of the Girouards, p. 2108 PAC.
Stephen A. White, *Dictionnaire généologique des familles acadienne*, 1636-1714, Volume I: A-G and Volume II: H-Z, Centre d'études acadiennes, Université de Moncton, 1999, Vol. I p.719.
Bona Arsenault, *Histoire et Généalogique des Acadiens*, Éditions Leméac, 1978, *Tome 2, Port Royal, Annapolis Royal, Nouvelle Ecosse, p. 568*.
Léopold Lanctôt, *Familles Acadiennes*, Éditions du Libre-Échange, 1994, Tome I, p. 274.

[AMC Block C-2] Marie-Madeleine Girouard, daughter of François Girouard and Jeanne Aucoin, m. 1668 Thomas Cormier
References:
Placide Gaudet, genealogical collection of the Girouards, p. 2108 PAC.
Stephen A. White, *Dictionnaire généologique des familles acadienne*, 1636-1714, Volume I: A-G and Volume II: H-Z, Centre d'études acadiennes, Université de Moncton, 1999., Vol. I, p. 719.
Léopold Lanctôt, *Familles Acadiennes*, Éditions du Libre-Échange, 1994, Tome I, p. 275.
Bona Arsenault, *Histoire et Généalogique des Acadiens*, Éditions Leméac, 1978, *Tome 2, Port Royal, Annapolis Royal, Nouvelle Ecosse, p. 568*.

[AMC Block D-2] Germain Girouard, son of François Girouard and Jeanne Aucoin, m. Marie Bourgeois.
References:
Stephen A. White, *Dictionnaire généologique des familles acadienne*, (1636-1714), Volume I: A-G and Volume II: H-Z, Centre d'études acadiennes, Université de Moncton , 1999, Vol I, p. 727.
Léopold Lanctôt, *Familles Acadiennes*, Éditions du Libre-Échange, 1994, Tome I, p. 275.

Bona Arsenault, *Histoire et Généalogique des Acadiens*, Éditions Leméac, 1978, *Tome 2, Port Royal, Annapolis Royal, Nouvelle Ecosse*, p. 568.

[AMC Block E-2] Anne (Anne-Charlotte) Girouard, daughter of François Girouard and Jeanne Aucoin, m. Julien Lord dit Lamontagne.
References:
Stephen White, *Dictionnaire généologique des familles acadienne*, Volume I: A-G and Volume II: H-Z (1636-1714), Centre d'études acadiennes, Université de Moncton, 1999, Vol I, p.719.
Léopold Lanctôt, *Familles Acadiennes*, Éditions du Libre-Échange, 1994, Tome I, p. 275, 276 and Tome II, pp.156-159.
Bona Arsenault, *Histoire et Généalogique des Acadiens*, Éditions Leméac, 1978, *Tome 2, Port Royal, Annapolis Royal, Nouvelle Ecosse*, p. 568.

[AMC Block F-2] Jacques Girouard, son of François Girouard and Jeanne Aucoin, m. Marguerite Gautrot.
References:
Placide Gaudet, re: Girouard genealogy pp. 2109, 2111, 2113, 2121, 2130, 2187-1.
Also this family is recorded in Church reg.1-vol 26 Church records, Annapolis Royal, 1702-1705 PANS.
Stephen White, *Dictionnaire généologique des familles acadienne*, Volume I: A-G, Volume II: H-Z.(1636-1714), Centre d'études acadiennes, Université de Moncton, 1999, Vol. I, p.719.
Léopold Lanctôt, *Familles Acadiennes*, Éditions du Libre-Échange, 1994., Tome I, p.276, 277, 278.

3rd Generation of the Acadian Master Chart
Children of Jacques Girouard and Marguerite Gautrot [AMC Block F-3b]

Note: As mentioned on the master chart explanation, there were 14 children so it was necessary to use two rows on the master chart (row 3a and row 3b to show all children)-all the names appearing in these two rows are of the third generation and are children of Jacques and Marguerite Gautrot.

[AMC Block C-3a] Alexandre Girouard (dit de Ru or Rue), son of Jacques Girouard and Marguerite, m. Marie Le Borgne.
References :
Placide Gaudet, genealogical collection of the Girouards, pp. 2198, 2113, 2137, 2149, 2141-1, 2141-2, 2116, 2150. PAC.
Marie Le Borgne is the granddaughter of Charles de La Tour, the first governor of Acadia, her mother, Marie, being the daughter of Charles de La Tour. Alexandre appears on the PR census of 1686, 1703, 1707, 1714.
Stephen White, *Dictionnaire généologique des familles acadienne*, Volume I: A-G, Volume II: H-Z (1636-1714), Centre d'études acadiennes, Université de Moncton, 1999, Vol. I , pp. 720,721.

Léopold Lanctôt, *Familles Acadiennes*, Éditions du Libre-Échange, 1994. Tome I p. 281, 282.

Bona Arsenault: Port Royal vol., p.1721. Alexander's son was deported to Philadelphia (Bona Arsenault and PR cen. 1701).

Present descendants living in county of Montcalm and L'Assumption, PQ according to Hevé Richard in "Genealogy Corner" and as confirmed by former priest Mgr. J. A. Richard of Verdun, Montreal in this article. I have not been able to establish this connection in my charts to date.

[AMC Block D-3a] Jacques Girouard, son of Jacques Girouard and Marguerite Gautrot, m1. Anne Petitpas m2. Jeanne Amireau.

References:

Placide Gaudet, genealogy collection on the Girouards, pp. 2130, M'ck pp. 2138, 2144, 2156, 2192. Jacques' son, Pierre m. Marie Granger, was deported to New York, pp 2192, PAC.

Stephen White, *Dictionnaire généologique des familles acadienne*, Volume I: A-G, Volume II: H-Z (1636-1714), Centre d'études acadiennes, Université de Moncton, 1999, Vol. I, p. 720.

Bona Arsenault, *Histoire et Généalogique des Acadiens*, Éditions Leméac, 1978, *Tome 2, Port Royal, Annapolis Royal, Nouvelle Ecosse*, p. 568.

Edward Lavin Gerrior's genealogy research, recorded at Centre d'études acadiennes, Moncton, NB, states that Anne Petitpas, wife of Jacques Girouard, is daughter of Claude Sieur le Fleur, Secretary to the King at Port Royal.

[AMC Block E-3a] Jean Girouard, son of Jacques Girouard and Marguerite Gautrot.

References:

Stephen White, *Dictionnaire généologique des familles acadienne*, Volume I: A-G, Volume II: H-Z (1636-1714), Centre d'études acadiennes, Université de Moncton, 1999, Vol. I, p. 720.

[AMC Block G-3a] Marie Girouard, daughter of Jacques Girouard and Marguerite Gautrot, m. Jacques Granger.

References :

Stephen White, *Dictionnaire généologique des familles acadienne*, Volume I: A-G, Volume II: H-Z (1636-1714), Centre d'études acadiennes, Université de Moncton, 1999, Vol. I, pp. 720.

Bona Arsenault, *Histoire et Généalogique des Acadiens*, Éditions Leméac, 1978, *Tome 2, Port Royal, Annapolis Royal, Nouvelle Ecosse*, p. 569.

Léopold Lanctôt, *Familles Acadiennes*, Éditions du Libre-Échange, 1994. Tome I p. 281, 282.

[AMC Block H-3a] Marguerite Girouard, daughter of Jacques Girouard and Marguerite Gautrot, m. Louis Doucet.

References:

Placide Gaudet, genealogical collection of the Girouards, pp. 2116-1.

Stephen White, *Dictionnaire généologique des familles acadienne*, Volume I: A-G, Volume II: H-Z (1636-1714), Centre d'études acadiennes, Université de Moncton, 1999, Vol. I, p. 720.
Bona Arsenault, *Histoire et Généalogique des Acadiens*, Éditions Leméac, 1978, *Tome 2, Port Royal, Annapolis Royal, Nouvelle Ecosse*, p. 569.

[AMC Block I-3a] Claude Girouard, son of Jacques Girouard and Marguerite Gautrot, m. Elisabeth Blanchard

References:
Placide Gaudet, genealogical collection of the Girouards, pp. 2141-1, 2141, 2116-1, 2150 PAC, states that Claude's son, Joseph Girouard was deported to Mass. USA, 1755 then later is found at St. Ours, PQ, 1767.
Bona Arsenault, *Histoire et Généalogique des Acadiens*, Éditions Leméac, 1978, *Tome 2, Port Royal, Annapolis Royal, Nouvelle Ecosse*, p. 569.

[AMC Block J-3a] Guillaume, son of Jacques Girouard and Marguerite Gautrot, m. Marie Bernard.

References:
Placide Gaudet, genealogical collection of the Girouards, pp. 2255, 2180, 2123, 2142-1, 2142-2, 2152 (Lotbinière). In M'ck, 1752, pp. 2139-2, 2136-2, 2116, PAC. Annapolis Church records (1702-1755) PANS pp 125, 151, 188, 250). m. ca. 1713, Marie Bernard dit Renochet (René & Madeleine Doucet); d/bur Qué. reg. Nov 23/24, 1757 at age 70.
Stephen White, *Dictionnaire généologique des familles acadienne*, Volume I: A-G, Volume II: H-Z (1636-1714), Centre d'études acadiennes, Université de Moncton, 1999, Vol. I, p. 720.
Bona Arsenault, *Histoire et Généalogique des Acadiens*, Éditions Leméac, 1978, *Tome 2, Port Royal, Annapolis Royal, Nouvelle Ecosse*, p. 569.
Bona Arsenault: *Port Royal Volume*, two children of Guillaume, Pierre and William are at Lotbinière PQ, 1762 and at St. Ours, 1767, PQ. Françoise, the sister of William and Pierre, is at Richibucto, NB with her husband Jean-Baptiste Richard after deportation, p.238.
Désiré Girouard in his book, *La Famille Girouard*, presents Louis Girouard and his son, Arthur, on a last page addition to his book and gives the genealogical line of these two Girouards back to a Pierre Girouard m. Théotiste Dupuis, whom I know from my research is the son of William and Marie Bernard of this Acadian Master Chart block.

[AMC Block B-3b] Denis Girouard, son of Jacques Girouard and Marguerite Gautrot, m. Marguerite Barrieau.

References:
Placide Gaudet, genealogical collection of the Girouards, pp. 2136-2, 2159, PAC.
Stephen White, *Dictionnaire généologique des familles acadienne*, Volume I: A-G, Volume II: H-Z (1636-1714), Centre d'études acadiennes, Université de Moncton, 1999, Vol. I, pp. 720.

Léopold Lanctôt, *Familles Acadiennes*, Éditions du Libre-Échange, 1994. Tome I pp. 281, 282.

Bona Arsenault, *Histoire et Généalogique des Acadiens*, Éditions Leméac, 1978, *Tome 2, Port Royal, Annapolis Royal, Nouvelle Ecosse*, p. 569.

[AMC Block C-3b] Charles Girouard, son of Jacques Girouard and Marguerite Gautrot, m1. Anne Bastarache, m2. Marie J. Pitre.

References:
Annapolis PR pp 162,182,240, PANS.
Placide Gaudet, genealogical collection of the Girouards, pp. 2136-2, 2153. Also at M'ck p 2129, PAC.
Stephen White, *Dictionnaire généologique des familles acadienne*, Volume I: A-G, Volume II: H-Z (1636-1714), Centre d'études acadiennes, Université de Moncton, 1999, Vol. I , pp. 721:
Léopold Lanctôt, *Familles Acadiennes*, Éditions du Libre-Échange, 1994. Tome I p. 280.
Bona Arsenault, *Histoire et Généalogique des Acadiens*, Éditions Leméac, 1978, *Tome 2, Port Royal, Annapolis Royal, Nouvelle Ecosse*, p. 570.

[AMC Block D-3b] Germain Girouard, son of Jacques Girouard and Marguerite Gautrot, m. Marie Doucet.

References:
Placide Gaudet, genealogical collection of the Girouards, pp. 2116-1, 2181 (Québec), 2119, PAC.
Lavin Gerrior's genealogy, Centre d'études acadiennes, Université de Moncton p. 3.
Also, in particular, Michel Girouard m. Marguerite Haché Gallant is now believed to be the son of this Germain Girouard and Marie Doucet, rather than François who was his brother, married to Anne Bourgeois, which is the other theory held by Bona Arsenault and others.
Note: This branch has been another trouble spot with professional genealogists for quite some time. There is no marriage record and, in this case, there is also no other clue such as an interview with the French historian, Rameau. So one has to either accept the opinion of genealogist, Bona Arsenault in these situations or the record of an earlier genealogist, Placide Gaudet, who states that Michel Girouard son of Germain Girouard and Marie Doucet were at Veskak 1752, with one son and two daughters. (Placide 2129-1, PAC). However, Placide does not reveal his source for this statement.

Because of the geography of where Germain settled in Beaubassin close to Germain (D-3b) à Jacques at Tintamarre, I will choose Placide's record of Germain as the father who married Marie Doucet. This is in agreement with genealogist Stephen White of Centre d'études Acadienne, Université de Moncton, NB, who presently holds this position on this connection in favour of Germain. This position is also in agreement with Paul Surette who specializes in the Acadian settlements of Memramcook, Beaubassin, and Chipoudy River.

[AMC Block E-3b] Pierre Girouard, son of Jacques Girouard and Marguerite Gautrot, m1. Marie Comeau m2. Marie Doiron.
References:
Placide Gaudet, genealogical collection of the Girouards, pp. 2118-1, 2118-2, 2121 and 2127 give children of m1. and m2., PAC.
 Pierre's family appears in Rivière Pisiquid cen. 1714. Grand Pré Church Records (1702-1755), shows baptisms of his children from 1708-1729 (pp 7, 13, 14, 22, 29, 173, 140 St. Charles Church records). Louisiana census, 1766, St. James, Donaldsonville, shows Pierre's grandson, Firmin, on the right bank of the Mississippi. Pierre Girouard is captain of the ship L'Effroute of Isle Royal-PAC record 1727, p. 80, 81 "Ships, their tonnage, their Captains, and their destinations."
Stephen White, *Dictionnaire généologique des familles acadienne*, Volume I: A-G, Volume II: H-Z (1636-1714), Centre d'études acadiennes, Université de Moncton, 1999, Vol. I , pp. 720, 724.
Bona Arsenault, *Histoire et Généalogique des Acadiens*, Éditions Leméac, 1978, Tome 3, Beaubassin (Amherst, Nouvelle-Ecosse), Grand Pré, pp. 1389, 1390, first marriage at Port Royal, second marriage at Grand Pré.

[AMC Block F-3b] François Girouard, son of Jacques Girouard and Marguerite Gautrot, m1. Anne Bourgeois m2. Marie Guilbeau.
References:
Placide Gaudet records their son, Pierre in Memramcook p. 2121-2. PAC.
Annapolis reg. records their son, Jean-Baptiste b. 1725 p. 217. Canadian Archives series pp. 21, 44. Also Annapolis Church reg. p. 26. (PANS).
Stephen White, *Dictionnaire généologique des familles acadienne*, Volume I: A-G, Volume II: H-Z (1636-1714), Centre d'études acadiennes, Université de Moncton, 1999, Vol. I, p. 721.
Léopold Lanctôt, *Familles Acadiennes*, Éditions du Libre-Échange, 1994. Tome I p. 280.
Bona Arsenault, *Histoire et Généalogique des Acadiens*, Éditions Leméac, 1978, *Tome 2, Port Royal, Annapolis Royal, Nouvelle Ecosse*, p. 569.

[AMC Block G-3b] Anne Marie Girouard, son of Jacques Girouard and Marguerite Gautrot.
References:
Stephen White, *Dictionnaire généologique des familles acadienne*, Volume I: A-G, Volume II: H-Z (1636-1714), Centre d'études acadiennes, Université de Moncton, 1999, Vol. I , p. 721.
Léopold Lanctôt, *Familles Acadiennes*, Éditions du Libre-Échange, 1994. Tome I p. 280.
Bona Arsenault, Port Royal Vol.

[AMC Block H-3b] Madeleine Girouard, son of Jacques Girouard and Marguerite Gautrot, m. Pierre Richard
References:
Placide Gaudet, genealogical collection of the Girouards, re: Girouard genealogy p. 2136-2. PAC.

Pierre Richard supplied the important sworn statements in Belle-Isle-en-Mer, France. In this statement, we find François, his wife's grandfather, referred to as "Jacques dit La Varenne", it thus gives some idea of where François (Jacques) lived in France although, there were many places with similar or the same name in France. This last reference also raises the point that François must have had a second name of Jacques since this same person, "Jacques dit LaVarenne" is referred to as "François" in the PR census of 1671. I conclude that his full name may have been François, Jacques Girouard.

Stephen White, *Dictionnaire généologique des familles acadienne*, Volume I: A-G, Volume II: H-Z (1636-1714), Centre d'études acadiennes, Université de Moncton, 1999, Vol. I , p. 721.

Léopold Lanctôt, *Familles Acadiennes*, Éditions du Libre-Échange, 1994. Tome I, p. 280.

Bona Arsenault, *Histoire et Généalogique des Acadiens*, Éditions Leméac, 1978, *Tome 2, Port Royal, Annapolis Royal, Nouvelle Ecosse*, p. 570.

4th Generation of the Acadian Master Chart
Children of François Girouard m1 Anne Bourgeois m2. Marie Guilbeau [AMC Block F-3b]

[AMC Block E-4m2] Marie-Josèphe Girouard, daughter of François Girouard and Marie Guilbeau.

References:

Stephen White, *Dictionnaire généologique des familles acadiènnes*, Volume I: A-G, Volume II: H-Z (1636-1714), Centre d'études acadiennes, Université de Moncton, 1999, Vol. I , p. 732.

Bona Arsenault, *Histoire et Généalogique des Acadiens*, Éditions Leméac, 1978, *Tome 2, Port Royal, Annapolis Royal, Nouvelle Ecosse*, p. 569.

[AMC Block G-4m2] Nathalie Girouard, daughter of François Girouard and. Marie Guilbeau.

References:

Stephen White, *Dictionnaire généologique des familles acadienne*, Volume I: A-G, Volume II: H-Z (1636-1714), Centre d'études acadiennes, Université de Moncton, 1999, Vol. I , p. 732.

Bona Arsenault, *Histoire et Généalogique des Acadiens*, Éditions Leméac, 1978, *Tome 2, Port Royal, Annapolis Royal, Nouvelle Ecosse*, p. 569.

[AMC Block A-4m1] Marie-Madeleine, daughter of François Girouard and Anne Bourgeois.

References:

Stephen White, *Dictionnaire généologique des familles acadienne*, Volume I: A-G, Volume II: H-Z (1636-1714), Centre d'études acadiennes, Université de Moncton, 1999, Vol. I , p. 731.

Bona Arsenault, *Histoire et Généalogique des Acadiens*, Éditions Leméac, 1978, *Tome 2, Port Royal, Annapolis Royal, Nouvelle Ecosse*, p. 569.

[AMC Block B-4m1] François Girouard, son of François Girouard and Anne Bourgeois.
References:
RG-1, Vol. 26, near end of document PANS.
Stephen White, *Dictionnaire généologique des familles acadienne*, Volume I: A-G, Volume II: H-Z (1636-1714), Centre d'études acadiennes, Université de Moncton, 1999, Vol. I, p. 731
Bona Arsenault, *Histoire et Généalogique des Acadiens*, Éditions Leméac, 1978, *Tome 2, Port Royal, Annapolis Royal, Nouvelle Ecosse*, p. 569.

[AMC Block C-4m1] Pierre Girouard, son of François Girouard and Anne Bourgeois, m1. Marie-Joseph Forest m2. M. Doucet.
References:
Placide Gaudet, genealogical collection of the Girouards, pp. 2129-2, 2148 (M'ck 1752), 2188-1, (Québec), 2177, 2189-1 (L'Assomption PQ), PAC
Stephen White, *Dictionnaire généologique des familles acadienne*, Volume I: A-G, Volume II: H-Z (1636-1714), Centre d'études acadiennes, Université de Moncton, 1999, Vol. I , p. 731
According to the record, Loiselle notes, Québec National Archives, m2. 1760, Deschambault.
Adrien Bergeron, S.S.S. *Le Grand Arrangement des Acadiens au Québec*, p. 14.
Bona Arsenault, *Histoire et Généalogique des Acadiens*, Éditions Leméac, 1978, *Tome 2, Port Royal, Annapolis Royal, Nouvelle Ecosse*, pp. 569, 572.

[AMC Block D-4m1] Charles Girouard (1714-1716), son of François Girouard and Anne Bourgeois.
References:
Annapolis Church records pp. 44, 162.
Stephen White, *Dictionnaire généologique des familles acadienne*, Volume I: A-G, Volume II: H-Z (1636-1714), Centre d'études acadiennes, Université de Moncton, 1999, Vol. I, p. 731.

[AMC Block E-4m1] Marie Madeleine Girouard, daughter of François Girouard and Anne Bourgeois, m. Charles Leblanc.
References:
Placide Gaudet, genealogical collection of the Girouards, p. 2187 also confirms that Charles LeBlanc's parents are Pierre and Madeleine Bourg. Also place of death is given as St. Mary's Bay (St. Bernard) pp. 2187-2, 2187-1, PAC.
Marie Madeleine, spouse of Charles LeBlanc, d/bur., Annapolis Church records p. 159. (according to Placide Gaudet, Reg. Pointe de l'Eglise, June 6/8, 1805 close to age 90.
Also refer to Yarmouth Vanguard, March 14, 1989, Yarmouth. This Charles LeBlanc is the uncle of Madeleine LeBlanc (F-4m1), according to Stephen White.
Stephen White, *Dictionnaire généologique des familles acadienne*, Volume I: A-G, Volume II: H-Z (1636-1714), Centre d'études acadiennes, Université de Moncton, 1999, Vol. I, p. 731.

Bona Arsenault, *Histoire et Généalogique des Acadiens*, Éditions Leméac, 1978, *Tome 2, Port Royal, Annapolis Royal, Nouvelle Ecosse*, p. 572.

[AMC Block F-4m1] Jean-Baptiste Girouard, son of François Girouard and Anne Bourgeois, m. Madeleine LeBlanc.
References:

Jean-Baptiste m. (according to E. L. Girroir, son of Senator Edward Lavin Girroir) ca. 1751 Madeleine LeBlanc (Pierre & Françoise Thériot); Placide Gaudet claims he died at Tracadie, Nova Scotia ca 1808 p. 21; Church records Annapolis p. 217. Stephen White, *Dictionnaire généologique des familles acadienne*, Volume I: A-G, Volume II: H-Z (1636-1714), Centre d'études acadiennes, Université de Moncton, 1999, Vol. I , p. 731. Also Census at M'ck 1728.

Marriage records of this period have been destroyed or lost during the Deportation. In these cases, some genealogists base their point of view on the movements of family groups during this period. Thus it is believed by Bona Arsenault that Jean-Baptiste was the son of Pierre Girouard (brother of François) m2. Marie Comeau who had a son, Jean-Baptiste, b. 1729. His rationale is based on the families of Claude Leblanc who had a daughter Madeleine, and on Pierre Girouard who had a son, Jean-Baptiste, both being in PEI census. His conclusion is that this Jean-Baptiste and this Madeleine Leblanc are from the above two parents.

However, Stephen White had been able to show via consanguinity relations in the marriage documents of Madeleine Leblanc's grandchildren, Julia and Sophie in Chéticamp marriage records, that the father of Madeleine LeBlanc is in fact Pierre, and not Claude LeBlanc from PEI as Bona Arsenault claims.

We also referred to an interview by historian Rameau with Joseph Girroir, Tracadie, grandson of this Jean-Baptiste Girouard and Madeleine LeBlanc. In this interview, Joseph Girroir states that the family was coming from Port Royal and were refugees at Memramcook. ("Notes de Voyage de Rameau en Acadie 1860", SHA. Vol. 1V, 1971 p. 35). This indicates that our Jean-Baptiste Girouard was coming from Port Royal. Among the Girouards, there seems to be only François Girouard and Anne Bourgeois having a son Jean-Baptiste of Port Royal who would have been able to marry with a Madeleine LeBlanc at this time period, according to Stephen LeBlanc, Centre d'études acadiennes, Moncton, NB

[AMC Block G-4M1] Marguerite Girouard b.1733 daughter of François Girouard and Anne Bourgeois.
References:

Placide Gaudet, genealogical collection of the Girouards, p. 2118-3, family at Québec, 1758, PAC.

Stephen White, *Dictionnaire généologique des familles acadienne*, Volume I: A-G, Volume II: H-Z (1636-1714), Centre d'études acadiennes, Université de Moncton, 1999, Vol. I, p. 731.

No further trace.

[AMC Block H-4m1] Anne-Hélène Girouard, daughter of François Girouard and Anne Bourgeois, m. Claude Benoît.
References:
Stephen White, *Dictionnaire généologique des familles acadienne*, Volume I: A-G, Volume II: H-Z (1636-1714), Centre d'études acadiennes, Université de Moncton, 1999, Vol. I, p. 731.
Paul Surette, *Le Grand Peticoudiac, Histoire des Trois Rivières*, Vol. III.-map showing the family living on the shore of Memramcook River.
Bona Arsenault, *Histoire et Généalogique des Acadiens*, Éditions Leméac, 1978, Tome 2, Port Royal, Annapolis Royal, Nouvelle Ecosse, p. 573.

[AMC Block I-4M1] Joseph Girouard, son of François Girouard and Anne Bourgeois, m1. Françoise Blanchard m2. Marie Arsenault
References:
Stephen White, *Dictionnaire généologique des familles acadienne*, Volume I: A-G, Volume II: H-Z (1636-1714), Centre d'études acadiennes, Université de Moncton, 1999, Vol. I, p. 732.
Bona Arsenault, *Histoire et Généalogique des Acadiens*, Éditions Leméac, 1978, *Tome 2, Port Royal, Annapolis Royal, Nouvelle Ecosse, p. 573.*

5th Generation of the Acadian Master Chart
Children of Jean Baptiste Girouard and Madeleine LeBlanc [AMC Block F-4m1]

[AMC Block D-5] Marie Girouard, daughter of Jean Baptiste Girouard and Madeleine LeBlanc, m. Basile Gouthro
References:
Marie b. 1751 (Tracadie, St. Peter's Church records 60 years old at time of death in 1811, pp. 8, 120 Reg. (1817-1857); Marriage in 1770 of Marie Girouard to Basile Goutrot is recorded in Halifax, by L'Abbé Charles François Bailly, missionary register (1768-1773), originally held at Caraquet, NB-translated by Stephen White, Centre d'études acadiennes, Moncton, N. B.; also the Guysborough Deeds office.
Placide Gaudet: It is stated in the marriage record of 1770 above, that Jean-Baptiste and Madeleine LeBlanc, the parents of Marie Girouard, are from " des Mines". Placide Gaudet claims that "Des Mines" here refers to River Hébert area not Grand Pré area or Pisiquid- p. 2164; Rameau's notes: We also know the family was in Halifax area from the interview, mentioned earlier, with Captain Joseph Girroir, (the grandson of Jean Girouard) with French historian, Rameau.

[AMC Block E-5] Joseph Nicholas Girroir, son of Jean Baptiste Girouard and Madeleine LeBlanc, m. Angélique Pettipas;
References:
Joseph Nicolas, b. 1755 (Joseph's age was calculated approximately, from the known age of his wife Angélique Petitpas. Her death is recorded in the Tracadie Church records held at U.N.B., in the second of three books marked "c" (1854-1858) as

having died at 99 years old in 1854. Assuming her husband, Joseph Girroir, was about the same age, he would be born around 1755; Crown Grant of land at Tracadie (PANS)- Joseph Nicholas Girroir's name appears on the land grant in Tracadie (see Antigonish Chapter in Nova Scotia/Prince Edward Island book for more details); Rameau's notes-In an interview with Captain Joseph Girroir, son of Joseph Nicholas and Angélique Petitpas, the name "Joseph Nicholas" Girroir is used when referring to his father thus clearing up the misconception that Joseph and Nicholas were two different persons. It is the same person having the two names "Joseph Nicholas".

[AMC Block F-5] François Girroir, son of Jean Baptiste Girouard and Madeleine LeBlanc, m. Marguerite Petitpas

References:
Tracadie church records: In the death record of Laurent Jacquet, 1819, son of Paul Jacquet and François' daughter, Madeleine, it states " the grandfather" François Girouard was present. Also in the Tracadie church, marriage record of François' daughter, Marie Sophie, to Moise Jacquet, Jan 15, 1816, we find the name of the wife of François where it states the parents are François Gerrior and Margaret Petitpas; also François appears on the Crown land grant in Tracadie with his brother Joseph Nicholas and his father Jean Giroire; in Rameau's notes during an interview with Captain Joseph Girouard, Captain Joseph talks about his uncle "François" Girouard.

[AMC Block G-5] Anastasie Girouard, daughter of Jean Baptiste Girouard and Madeleine LeBlanc, m. Jean Marc Romard.

References:
Charles Bailly register (1768-1773) gives the birth record of Anastasie as 1770, in Halifax.
Journal paper, *"Du Cape Breton Mercredile"*, July, 1982, p.3. Genealogy of Jean Marc Romard by Rev. Charles Aucoin of Chéticamp; Genealogy and family tree of Jean Marc Romard, researched by Alvin Ernest Romard of Cheticamp; *Notre Famille Romard* by Charles D. Roach; Stephen White's research on the probable origin of the Romards in Acadie.

[AMC Block H-5] Marie-Madeleine Gerrior, daughter of Jean Baptiste Girouard and Madeleine LeBlanc, m. Cyprien (Syphrien) Duon.

References:
Placide Gaudet, genealogical collection of the Girouards, p. 2105 records her birth in Oct., 1763, bap. July 20 at Halifax, 1768.

6th Generation of the Acadian Master Chart
Children of François Gerrior (Girroir,Giroir) and Marguerite Petitpas [AMC Block F-5]

[AMC Block E-6] Marie-Sophie Gerrior, daughter of François Gerrior and Marguerite Petitpas, m. Moyse Jacquet.

References:
Marie Sophie m. Moyse Jacquet, Jan. 15, 1816 Tr. marriage reg. Marie's birth is calculated from death record, 1865, in which she is age 66. (Tracadie Church Burials (1860-1916).

[AMC Block F-6] Luc Gerrior, son of François Gerrior and Marguerite Petitpas, m. Ann Jacquet.
References:
Luc b. 1786 (calculated from death record in 1868 at which time it was stated that he was age 82. Tracadie Church Burials.); Cen., 1838, at Big Tracadie PANS RG. , Vol 99; we find the name of Luc Girroir's wife from another record: Abraham Giroir is recorded as son of Luc Girroir and Anne Jacquet (Delorey) in 1817-Tr. Reg. (1817-1824); Rameau's interview with Captain Joseph Girroir (S.H.A. #31-40 p. 38). where Joseph Girroir talks about Luc Gerrior, son of his uncle François Girouard (Girroir) and Marguerite Petitpas.

[AMC Block G-6] Juliette Gerrior, daughter of François Gerrior and Marguerite Petitpas, m. Alex Petitpas.
References:
Juliette b. ca. 1785 calculated from the death record of her husband Alex, recorded in 1868 in Tracadie Church Burials (1860-1915) where it is stated he was age 91 and his wife is given as Juliette Gerrior. Assuming Juliettte to be approximately the same age, the earliest date she may have been born is around 1785, the year of her parents marriage; in 1820 the Tracadie Church records the birth of Marguerite Petitpas from the parents Alex Petitpas and Juliette Girouard. In Rameau's interview it is stated that Luc had three sisters, so from this reference, I assume that Juliette is a daughter of François and not a daughter of his brother, Joseph, who only had one son as far as I know,-Captain Joseph was the person being interviewed by Rameau.

[AMC Block H-6] Marie-Marguerite Girroir, daughter of François Gerrior and Marguerite Petitpas, m. Paul Jacquet (Delorey).
References:
Marie Marguerite Girroir is daughter of François Girouard. This relationship is established from the Tracadie Church records (1817-1824) where François Gerrior is stated to be the grandfather who was present at the death of Laurent Jacquet, son of Paul Jacquet and Madeleine Gerrior. Later, another son by the same name was born in 1827. Marie d. 1848 at age 57 (Tr. reg. held at U.NB, Centre d'études acadiennes).

7th Generation of the Acadian Master Chart
Children of Luc Gerrior (Girroir,Giroir) and Anne Jacquet. [AMC Block F-6]

[AMC Block A-7] Frédéric Gerrior, son of Luc Gerrior and Anne Jacquet, m. Anne (Nancy) Gillis.
References:

Church reg. of La Havre Boucher (1831-1847) belonging to the parish of Tracadie are found at Centre d'études acadiennes, Université de Moncton, NB. At one time, all three parishes including Pomquet and Tracadie, were under one Priest; also at Université de Moncton, the following Tracadie Church records: Book A (1829-1835); Book B (1841-1852); Book C (1854-1858) are found. Eleven more pages belonging to this group of documents are found with the Havre Boucher records above, covering the years (1835-1836); Frédéric Gerrior m. Anne Gillis Feb. 2, 1848, "B" (1841-1852) above, where it states that Frédéric Gerrior's parents are Luc Gerrior and Anne Jacquet and Nancy is the daughter of Duan Gillis and Jane MacDonald. In the 1871 census, Molasses Harbour, pp. 48, 49, Nancy Gerrior, age 42, widow, of Scotch origin, is shown along with her children: William (20), John (16), Abraham (11), Mary (13). Other church records in Port Felix found at Canso also confirm that these same children descend from parents Frédéric Gerrior and Nancy Gillis.

[AMC Block B-7] Vénérande Gerrior, daughter of Luc Gerrior and Anne Jacquet, m. Dennis Linden.
References:
Vénérande, daughter of Luc and Anne Jacquet m. Dennis Linden 1836, son of Henry Linden and Salé____. Book "A" Tracadie reg. held at Centre d'études acadiennes, Moncton NB. Her birth date is calculated from her marriage record approximately, 1816.

[AMC Block C-7] Francis Gerrior, son of Luc Gerrior and Anne Jacquet, m. Julienne Bourke:
References:
Francis Gerroir m. Julienne Bourke May 1, 1829 Tr. Reg. (1829-1845), p. 8. Here it is stated that Francis is the son of Luc Gerroir and Anne Jacquet and Julienne is daughter of the late Ambroise Bourq and Anne Pettipas.-witnesses, Jean Baptiste Culey, Jean Girroir and Luc Girroir.[sic].

[AMC Block D-7] Marcelline Girroir [sic] (1821-1823), daughter of Luc Gerrior and Anne Jacquet, and Pierre Girroir (1828-1830), son of Luc Gerrior and Anne Jacquet,
References:
Tracadie Church register.

[AMC Block E-7] Isidore Gerrior, son of Luc Gerrior and Anne Jacquet, m1. Marguerite Pellerin m2. Caroline George
References:
Isidore b. Sept 20, 1819, Tr. Reg. (1817-1874) p. 15, is son of Luc Girouard and Anne Jacquet; in 1871 census, Molasses Harbour (now called Port Felix), Isidore (Zoar) is recorded as 50 years old and married to Caroline George. The document states Caroline is 37 years old- Reel 138, Marriages (1864-1903) Guysborough Co., RG 32 series WB, Vol 62-65 PANS; PANS, RG. 32, series w, col 33-37, # 128, Guysborough Co.-His first wife's name is given in this document, in the death

record of their daughter Nancy, age 18, where it is stated that Marguerite Pellerin and Isidore Gerrior are the parents; Interview with Abraham Gerrior in Charlos Cove m. Julie Jane Pellerin, and his daughters, who also confirm marriage to m2. Caroline George ("Nanny on the hill"- as she was referred to).

[AMC Block F-7] Abraham Gerrior, son of Luc Gerrior and Anne Jacquet, m. Lavina (Divine) Fougère.

References:
Abraham b. 1817 son of Leck (Luc) Giroir [sic] and Anne Jacquet Tr. Reg. (1817-1824) p. 5; 1871 census of Molasses Harbour (Port Felix) record Abraham Gerrior and his family. stating that Abraham is a boot and shoe maker. His family are: Luke (23), boot and shoe maker, Benjamin (21), Dennis (16), Delia (18), Adele, illegible name (12), illegible name, (8 years old); Notes in the family Bible of Dennis Gerrior, son of Abraham, record Abraham's death as 1895. This Bible is in the possession of one of the descendants of Dennis à Abraham-Daniel Stewart, New Glasgow, one of our committee members for both reunions.

[AMC Block G-7] Joseph Simon Gerrior, son of Luc Gerrior and Anne Jacquet, m1 Adele Belfontaine (Belfonton), m2. Nancy Avery, m3. C. McGillivray.

References:
Joseph b. 1823, son of Luc Giroir [sic] and Anne Jacquet (Delorey), Tr. Reg. p.74; 1871 census, Molasses Harbour, record him as Labourer, age 51 with his wife, Nancy and the following children: Simon (25), Mary (21), Peter (22), Joseph (4), Lawrence (2), Hubert (16), May (9), Catherine (6); Joseph is referred to as both Simon and/or Joseph in various documents. (For example: Marriage record of his son, Simon in 1871 at Port Felix-reel 138, Marriages (1864-1903), Guysborough Co. RG. 32 PANS, show his father (Joseph Simon Gerrior (G-7) of the master chart), as "Joseph" with his first wife Adele Belfonton [sic] (PANS). On p. 153 of (1864-1877) census Reel #19, PANS referring to his other son, Peter and Natalie Avery, it is stated that Peter's father is "Simon".. However in the Port Felix church records, Torbay, Jan 8, 1872, the marriage record of Peter Gerrior to Natalie Avery states that Peter's father is "Joseph". Conclusion: There are not two different persons Joseph and Simon but rather one person known as Joseph Simon Gerrior for [AMC Block G-7] of the master chart, who is sometimes referred to as Simon and sometimes referred to as Joseph. It is from Si<u>mon</u> that I believe these branches were named " à <u>Mon</u>"; Tr. reg., Joseph Gerrior, son of Luc Gerrior and of Anne Jacquet, m1. Jan 12, 1847 to Adele Belfonton (Belfontaine) daughter of Anselme Belfonton and Ozithe (Azithe) Jacquet; Port Felix Church records found at Canso Church (1853-1889) p. 72 of a recopied document, show bap. of Venerante, 1862, daughter of Joseph Gerrior and Nancy Avery [AMC Block G-7]. We know from present day descendants, that Nancy was the second wife of Joseph Gerrior [AMC Block G-7] (ie. In an interview with Barbara Gerrior, of Lundy, descendant of this branch, Barbara confirms Nancy as wife of Joseph Gerrior [AMC Block G-7], mentioning Joseph Lawrence as son of Joseph Gerrior and Nancy Avery. I have recorded the birth certificate she showed me; Interview with Cecilia (Gerrior) Pitts of Rockingham, in Halifax, NS, descendant of this branch, indicates Joseph was

married to C. MacGillivray to whom I have not found any further reference. Cecilia confirms and clarifies many branches as does the correspondence from Josie Doiron, (née Murphy in Larry's River) residing in Isle Madame, Mamie Campbell, of Port Hood, CB., and Cora Mae of Lundy, Guysborough Co.- all descendants of this branch. These branches, originally seeming very complex, are now clarified and referenced.

[AMC Block H-7] Maximin Gerrior, son of Luc Gerrior and Anne Jacquet, m. Helen (Nelly) MacDonald.
References:
Maximin is stated to be son of Luc Gerrior in the civil death records (1860, 1875), PANS. Maximin b. ca 1808 calculated from his death record in 1873 where it is stated that he was 65 years old. Tracadie Reg. burials (1860-1915). His wife is named as Nelly MacDonald. I was able to make contact with a long-lost descendants of this branch in Weymouth, Mass. -Arthur Girroir, one of these descendants whom I contacted and who also attended our International Reunion, confirmed my research notes and clarified names etc.

[AMC Block I-7] Jean-Baptiste Gerrior, son of Luc Gerrior and Anne Jacquet, m. Sophie Pôte (Pottie).
References:
Jean-Baptiste b. 1811, son of Luc and Anne Jacquet-Tracadie reg. at St. Peters Church Rectory, p 11; Jean-Baptiste son of Luc and Anne Jacquet m. Sophie Pôte Sept. 23, 1833, daughter of Bernard Pôte and Margaret Forêt who both appear on the Pottie genealogy charts, as given to me by Janet Pottie Murray, of Halifax. No further reference or trace of this family, except for a daughter Marie A. born 1834.

[AMC Block J-7] Marguerite Gerrior, daughter of Luc Gerrior and Anne Jacquet, m. Joseph Doiron.
References:
Marguerite Gerrior b. June, 1812 daughter of Luc Gerrior and Anne Jacquet Tr. reg., p. 16; Marguerite Gerrior, daughter of Luc Gerrior and Anne Jacquet, m. Joseph Doiron, June, 1834, son of Joseph Doiron and Anne Iva Landry. (Tr reg.)

[AMC Block K-7] Henrietta Gerrior, son of Luc Gerrior and Anne Jacquet.
Reference:
Henrietta b. July 22, 1815 daughter of Luc and Anne Jacquet Tr. reg.

8th Generation of the Acadian Master Chart
Children of Abraham Gerrior and Lavina (Divine) Fougère [AMC Block F-7]

[AMC Block D-8] Dennis A. Gerrior, son of Abraham Gerrior and Lavina (Divine) Fougère, m1. Ellen Delorey m2. Rebecca Bowman.
Reference:
Port Felix Church reg. found at Church in Canso, show bap, 1855, in Larry's River at age of two months. Parents were given as Abraham and Devine Fougère, p 8;

Marriage licences PANS, Reel p. 87; Record of deaths in Tracadie, record the death of Dennis as June 19, 1945. Here it is stated that his wife is Rebecca, née Fougère, having married Bowman, previous to her marriage with Gerrior; In the family Bible, held by descendant Daniel Stewart, is written the date of the second marriage, in 1930.

[AMC Block E-8] Luke A. Gerrior, son of Abraham Gerrior and Lavina (Divine) Fougère, m. Til Hushard.

References:
Luke A. Gerrior b. 1848 (calculated from 1871 Census at Molasses Harbour (Port Felix) where it is stated that he was 23 years old and was a "boot and shoe maker" like his father, Abraham, which is also recorded in this same record of the census; Luke m. Til Hushard, according to my Dad and uncle Tom, as well as Jean Robertson, direct descendant of Luke. Jean also provided some important information and photos of Luke and Til Hushard and family, during an interview I had with her in Halifax; also correspondence with descendant, Debbie Lambert, Frankville, Ant. Co., NS provided many contacts for other descendants of this family branch; Family Bible of Dennis Gerrior gives the date of death of Luke as 1925.

[AMC Block F-8] William A. Gerrior, son of Abraham Gerrior and Lavina (Divine) Fougère, m. Sophie Pellerin:

References:
William b. 1842 birth date calculated from story in Antigonish *Casket-* where it is stated that he died April 21, 1938 at age 96. This record was located on microfilm at St. Francis Xavier University Library. Included was an informative write-up on his life. William was a store owner in Larry's River, originally a fisherman in his younger days, according to the next reference; William A. Gerrior m. Sophie Pellerin, 1868, witnesses, Simon Pellerin, and Delaide Gerrior. (RG 32 series, wb. Vol. 62-65, reel 138, PANS. In marriage records covering period (1864-1903) P. 212 #22, William was recorded as fisherman at Torbay. Sophie Pellerin was sister to Helen Pellerin who married William A. Gerrior's brother, Benjamin Gerrior.

[AMC Block G-8] Michel A. Gerrior, son of Abraham Gerrior and Lavina (Divine) Fougère, m1. Julie Manette m2. Brigitte Haley

References:
Michel b. ca 1843 (calculated from 1871 census, Molasses Harbour, PANS) where it is recorded that Michael is fisherman at age 28, p. 59 #4 of this record; Michel A. Gerrior son of Abraham and Divine Fougère, m1. Julia Manet 1871, daughter of Simon Manet and Julienne Manet-Port Felix Church records p. 227 of marriage records (1853-1879) found at Canso Church Rectory. Julia Manet d. Oct. 28, 1884, Port Felix record at Canso; Michel m2. Brigitte Haley, according to survey returns of Marshall Gerrior, Halifax, direct descendant of this second branch from the second marriage of Michel.

[AMC Block H-8] Benjamin A. Gerrior, son of Abraham Gerrior and Lavina (Divine) Fougère, m. Helen (dit Lacatune) Pellerin.
References:
Benjamin b. 1852, calculated from marriage record at Guysborough in which it states, that Ben is 23 in 1875 and also it states that Ben is a son of Abraham and Divine Fougère-Guysborough Marriages (1864-1903) PANS; also Port Felix records show the above marriage taking place between Ben Gerrior (Tor Bay) and Helen Pellerin, daughter of Simon Pellerin and Gertrude, of Larry's River on Jan. 18, 1875; Marriages in Guysborough PANS-32, Series WB, Vol. 62-65, P. 63 # 17; Benjamin d. 1908, according to family Bible of Dennis Gerrior, his brother, held by a descendant of Dennis, Daniel Stewart, New Glasgow, NS; Laguit (Mary Julien) (Gerrior) Pellerin, daughter of Benjamin, provided much information on the Gerrior connections, being of a very sharp mind at 100 years of age at the time of my interview with her.

[AMC Block I-8] Julie Gerrior, daughter of Abraham Gerrior and Lavina (Divine) Fougère, m. Dan Driscol.
References:
Julia b. May 4, 1862, daughter of Abraham and Divine Fougère (Port Felix Church records); correspondence with Carlene Martin, Mass., U.S.A., 01960, descendant of Julia's sister, Delia, helped confirm this branch in the U.S.A. Julia's child, Eleanor Cullen later married Leo Gerrior, son of Allen Gerrior [AMC G-9].

[AMC Block J-8] Delia Gerrior, daughter of Abraham Gerrior and Lavina (Divine) Fougère, m. Philip Bourgeois
References:
Delia b. 1853 1871 census at Molasses Harbour, Guysborough County states Delia is age 18, daughter of Abraham and Lavina. This is also confirmed by Carlene Martin's family Bible which in addition gives Delia's death date as Oct. 29, 1929. Much information regarding Delia's children and grandchildren is given by Carlene Martin.

[AMC Block K-8] Adèle Gerrior, daughter of Abraham Gerrior and Lavina (Divine) Fougère, m. Gus Bennette.
References:
Adele b. 1858 Port Felix record of baptisms (1853-1873) p. 49 where it is recorded that she is daughter of Abraham Gerrior and Divine Fougère. She was baptised at 2 months on Aug. 29, 1858. I was able to make contact with Adele's grandchildren: William Bennette of Chester, N.H. and his sisters Vangie of Florida and Eveylyn of Derry, N.H. -all confirming the marriage of Adele Gerrior to Gus Bennette having a son, William, born in Larry's River and soon after moving to Derry, N.H., having the above mentioned children.

9th Generation of the Acadian Master Chart

Children of William A. Gerrior and Sophie Pellerin [AMC Block F-8].

[AMC Block B-9] William Gerrior (1878-1878), son of William A. Gerrior and Sophie Pellerin.
References:
William b. Oct.10, 1868, son of William Gerrior and Sophie Pellerin (Port Felix reg, 1853-1872). William died in his early twenties according to my uncle Tom who heard his father talk about him. Also there was another William b. 1873 and a Jeffrey b. 1871, d.1871.

[AMC Block C-9] Helen Gerrior, daughter of William A. Gerrior and Sophie Pellerin, m. Oscar Butler, 1900.
References:
Marriage date taken from their 50th anniversary photo in 1950. Joe Butler, son of Helen, sent me photos and a great deal of family information on descendants of this branch.

[AMC Block D-9] Adélina (Lena) Gerrior, daughter of William A. Gerrior and Sophie Pellerin, m. Archie Butler
References:
Adélina Flora, daughter of William and Sophie Pellerin, bap April 27, 1888 (Port Felix records p 282). Adélina m. Archie Butler and the family lived in Dorchester, Mass. according to Joe Butler, cousin to children of this branch, and according to my discussions with my Uncle Tom, Larry's River. Also information on marriage date was provided by Irene (Gerrior) Johnston, U.S.A.

[AMC Block E-9] Simon Gerrior, son of William A. Gerrior and Sophie Pellerin, m1. Angel Pellerin m2. Madeleine Surette in U.S.A.
References:
Information provided by Irene Johnston, daughter of Simon and information also provided by Sam Gerrior, son of Simon. Also information was provided by the late Lawrence Meuse of St. Anne du Ruisseau, Yarmouth NS, the general vicinity where Simon lived for a time. Lawrence provided information regarding his knowledge of the family. I also interviewed Charles Doucette a neighbour of Simon Gerrior in Eel Brook, near St Anne du Ruisseau, who was very informative regarding his knowledge of Simon Gerrior.

[AMC Block F-9] Jeffrey Gerrior, son of William A. Gerrior and Sophie Pellerin, m1. Anne Fougère, m2. Louise Conway.
References:
Jeffrey, son of William Gerrior and Sophie Pellerin, bap. April 2, 1872 (Port Felix records (1853-1872) also Guysborough census (1864-1877). Jeffrey Gerrior, son of William Gerrior and Sophie Pellerin, m1., 1900, to Anne Fougère, daughter of Joseph Fougère and Marie Delorey. [Marie à "Mocheque"] according to my dad's memory of his grandmother and confirmed by Percy Pellerin of Larry's River.]

Jeffrey m2. Louise Conway, widow of Pat Conway. (L.R. Church reg. P. 3 of marriage record.) Jeffrey d. in Halifax, 1964 (Antigonish newspaper, *The Casket*, Sept. 17, 1964).

[AMC Block G-9] Allan Gerrior, son of William A. Gerrior and Sophie Pellerin, m1. Catherine Pellerin m2. Elizabeth (Lizzie) Pellerin.
References: Allan b. 1873 (Guysborough Co. Census (1841-1877) Reel #119. PANS; Allan m1. Catherine Pellerine (L.R. Church reg. p.46, records the birth of Agnes Gerrior, daughter of Allan Gerrior and Catherine Pellerin, Nov., 1906 who later married Ernest Martin in Sydney area of Cape Breton, NS; Allan married Lizzie Pellerin, 1901, where it is stated that Allan is a widower -L.R. Marriage reg. p. 4; Geneva (Gerrior) Nardocchio, daughter of Allan, and Ruth MacNeil, daughter of Geneva, provided much information regarding this branch. Also, information was provided by Lavin & Emiline Gerrior and their son, Jerome Gerrior and Lavin's brother, Vincent Gerrior.

[AMC Block H-9] Agnes Gerrior, daughter of William A. Gerrior and Sophie Pellerin, m1. Wilber Harding m2. Frank Williams.
References:
Agnes b. Nov 27, 1869 (Port Felix Church records, daughter of William Gerrior and Sophie Pellerin)- witnesses, Simon Pellerin and Michael Gerrior. Also see 1871 census of Guysborough Co. (1864-1877) PANS; Information and photos sent by Joe Butler provided much information on this branch who live in U.S.A. Information on m1. and m2. for Agnes was supplied my cousin, Irene (Gerrior) Johnston, U.S.A.

[AMC Block I-9] Tom Gerrior (d. young), son of William A. Gerrior and Sophie Pellerin,
References:
No documentation, information received from interview with my uncle, Tom Gerrior.

[AMC Block J-9] Geneva Gerrior b. 1885, daughter of William A. Gerrior and Sophie Pellerin.
References:
Geneva, daughter of William Gerrior and Sophie Pellerin, b. 1885 (Port Felix Church reg).

10th Generation of the Acadian Master Chart
Children of Jeffrey Gerrior and Ann Fougère [AMC Block F-9]

All references for my uncles and aunts of the 10th generation are recorded in the L.R. church records of births and marriages as shown in each AMC Block.

11th Generation of the Acadian Master Chart
Children of John S. Gerrior and Mary Beatrice Fougère [AMC Block F-10]

Appendices

All references to this generation are recorded in the following churches of Halifax: St. Mary's Basilica, St Patrick's Church, St Theresa's Church. The dates shown in each AMC Block were given verbally to me from each of my brothers and sisters, with permission to print on charts.

12th Generation of the Acadian Master Chart
Children of Bill Gerrior and Audrey Gray [AMC Block F-11].

Stephen was baptized at St John Vianney Church, Sackville, Nova Scotia, and Suzanne was baptized at St. Michael's Catholic Church, Halifax, NS

Primary Genealogical sources used:
Genealogical primary sources and other related sources used, sections (I-V) are located at Public Archives of Nova Scotia (PANS.)

I.
1) Port Royal census, 1671 by Father of Molin (Original now in Archives at Paris). Also Port Royal census, 1686, 1714, PANS
2) Beaubassin Chignectou census (Amherst, NS) 1672, 1714
3) Cape Sable census 1686 (Charles Le Tour)
4) River Pisiquit (Windsor) census, 1714.
5) Louisiana census, 1766, 1769 St. James Donaldsonville and Convent, on both banks of the Mississippi River, Louisiana.

II.
1) Grand Pré Church Records on microfilm, baptisms, marriages, deaths, 1709, PANS.

III.
Land Papers before 1800 and also early 1800's, Cape Breton.
Land Grants: Giroir, Pettipas, Nicholas and others RG. 20 series A, Vol 32, PANS, Assembly Petitions, 1862, RG. Series P, Misc. A, Vol 18.
A list of people living in Tracadie, 1827, their occupation, Religion, etc. Report of PANS, 1938 pp 56-67 F, 90 N85, Ar2R, 1938.
Petition opposing Confederation, 1865 RGS. Series P., Vol. 19 #11.
Crop failure request for assistance Rg 5, series P, Vol. 85, #2
Ferry service petition Rg 5, Series P, Vol. 67, Z#20
List of persons who suffered by fire in Tracadie 1829, PANS, Vol 2,36, Doc. 12

IV) Minutes of H.H. Council Meetings Annapolis Royal- PANS

Maps
V) Mitchell Map of Port Royal 1733 Provincial Archives of Nova Scotia(PANS); Mitchell Map of Port Royals with notes and changes from Placide Gaudet. National Archives of Canada (NAC).

Appendix 4

Notes to Accompany the Plan of Annapolis Royal
Prepared by Mr. Placide Gaudet,
Genealogist to the Public Archives of Canada

N.B. Notes to be inserted on the north side of the plan of Annapolis River.

1. PREE BOURGEOIS- The marsh at or near Port Wade, here called Prée Bourgeois, was named after Jacques Bourgeois, a native of France, who came to Port Royal in 1642 as a surgeon.
2. MOSQUITO COVE-now called Thorne Cove.
3. BLACK COVE now as Karsdale.
4. BLACK POINT- Probably bears the same name today.
5. SMALL REMAINS OF SCOTCH FORT- This is the site where, in August 1605, de Monts built a fort and a habitation, which were destroyed Nov. 1, 1613 by Samuel Argall. In 1628, Scotch colonists under the command of William Alexander, landed here to form a settlement. In the following summer, more than three or four months after the treaty of peace between France and England, which was signed at Suze, April 24, 1629, a fort called Charles Fort was built by the Scots on the ruins of the one destroyed sixteen years before by Argall. By the Treaty of St-Germain-en-Laye, March 29,1632, Acadie was restored to France. In view of this restitution, the King of England had by an order to Sir William Alexander, dated at the court of Greenwich, July 4 (O.S.)1631, commanded him "to order to George Hume, Knt., or other commanding for you in the said place, to demolish the fort built there by your son, and to remove thence the people, goods, cannon, ammunition, and cattle and other things belonging to this plantation, leaving the limits thereof altogether desert and depeopled, as they were when your sd. Son arrived there to settle in virtue of our commission" (report of the Work of the Canadian Archives for the year 1912, p. 49.) This was done in 1632.
6. MELANSON VILLAGE- Two brothers, Peter and Charles Melanson, natives of Scotland, came to Acadie with their parents in 1657, and settled on the north side of the Annapolis River, a short distance to the east of the Scotch Fort. Peter, surnamed Sieur de la Verdure, born in 1632, married Marguerite Marie d'Entremont in 1665, and settled at Grand Pré about the year, 1680. He became the father of a large family. His brother Charles was born in 1642, and married in 1667 to Marie Dugas. He lived on his father's land on the Annapolis River and had a numerous family. Two brothers, originally Protestants, became Catholics on their marriage, and their descendants are now numerous both in Canada and in the United States.
7. POINT-AUX-CHENES-This place is now known as Stoney Beach.
8. DELAURIER-Nicholas Babineau, surnamed Delaurier, was born in 1653, and married Jeanne Granger. He was the brother of Jean Babineau of Babineau's Hill. His descendants are numerous in New Brunswick.
9. BOURG VILLAGE- Antoine Bourg, born in France in 1609, married

Antoinette Landry and came to Acadie in 1632 with Commander de Razilly. He was the ancestor of the Acadian families of Bour or Bourque, Sieur de Bellehumeur, royal notary of Mines District.

10. BILLY JOHNSON-William Johnson, born about 1686 in Scotland, came to Annapolis as one of the garrison in the year 1711. Soon after his arrival he became acquainted with an Acadian girl, Isabelle Corporon, by whom he had several children, the first of whom was named Marie, born Sept. 9, 1713 and who became the wife of John Davis of the Annapolis garrison. Another was called William, and like his father was known as Billy Johnson. He married Marie Aucoin of Canard River. He is the Johnson referred to in the Journal. The descendants of Billy Johnson, the younger, are numerous in the Province of New Brunswick and Bonaventure Country, PQ, while the Johnsons in the counties of L'Assomption and Montcalm, PQ are descendants of the two brothers.

11. MATTHIEU DOUCET VILLAGE-Mathieu Doucet, son of Pierre and Henrietta Pelletray, was born at Port Royal in 1685. He married at Annapolis Royal, June 15,1712, Anne L'Or, surnamed La Montagne. He was the stepbrother of Germain Doucet, father of Jacques surnamed Maillard. Pierre Doucet, father Germain and Matthieu was born in France in 1621. He was the son of Germain Doucet Sieur de la Verdure, master-at-arms at Pentagoet (Penobscot) in 1640, commanding officer at Port Royal in 1654 and guardian of the minor children of the Governor d'Aulnay de Charnisay who perished in Annapolis River in May, 1650.

12. LA MONTAGNE VILLAGE- Julien L'or, surnamed La Montagne was born in France in 1654, and married Charlotte Girouard at Port Royal in 1655. He died at Annapolis Royal in 1744. His descendants are numerous in the counties of Nicolet and Montcalm, P.Q. The family is now known by the name of Lord.

13. LA NOUE- Pierre Lanoue, a native of France, was born in 1647. he came to Port Royal, and married in 1681, Jeanne Gautrot. His son Pierre, born in 1682, was married on Nov. 21,1722, to Marie Granger, and has many descendants in the Province of Québec, and some in Charlestown, South Carolina.

14. JEAN BRUN- Jean Brun, son of Sébastien Brun and Huguette Bourg, was born at Port Royal in 1682. He married on Oct. 2, 1708, Anne Gautrot, at Port Royal. He died there June 1, 1751, leaving several children whose descendants bear the name Brun and Le Brun.

15. BRUN VILLAGE- This is apparently the homestead of Vincent Brun, who was born in France in the year 1611 and came to Acadie with his wife Renée Breau in 1632. His son, Sébastien, who was born in 1636, married in 1676 Marguerite Bourg. He died August 15, 1728, leaving four sons, each of whom had a large family. Their descendants are scattered throughout the counties of Cumberland, N.S. and Westmorland, N.B. and in the Province of Québec.

16. BARNABE VILLAGE- This village was named after Barnabé Martin, son of the Barnabé Martin who with his brother, Pierre Martin, came to Acadie with Razilly in 1632. Barnabé Martin, the younger, married Jeanne Pelletray 1666. René, his oldest son, born in 1670, married in 1690 Marie Meunier, and settled at this place.

17. W. DENIS- The only mention of this name in the Roman Catholic Church register of Annapolis Royal is in a baptism of a child Jean Pellerin, wife of D'Ouil Denis. Ouil is the phonic sound in French of Will. Who is this William Denis? In all probability he was one of the soldiers of the British garrison at the fort who had married an Acadian and settled among the Acadians. If he had any children their entries of baptism are not recorded in the church register.

18. BELLISLE- This place took its name from Alexander Le Borgne, sieur de Belleisle, born at La Rochelle (France) in 1643, who came to Port Royal in 1668 with the title of Governor of a part of Acadie, granted to him April 4, 1668 by the king of France, at the request of general directors of the West Indies company. This young gentleman was the son of Emmanuel Le Borgne, sieur de Coudray and Jeanne François. Emmanuel Le Borgne, as a creditor of Governor d'Aulnay de Charnisay, came out from La Rochelle to Acadie in 1652, and took possession of all the estates of the deceased d'Aulnay, one of which was a large marsh, containing more than 1500 acres, now known as Belleisle Marsh, and which d'Aulnay had diked and made into a farm. In 1674, Belleisle married Marie de St. Etienne de la Tour and died at Port Royal about 1691, leaving two sons and several daughters.

19. DANIEL LEBLANC, born in France in 1626, came to Acadie with Francoise Gaudet his wife in 1650, and settled on the north–east of Bellisle Marsh about nine miles above the fort. LeBlanc died between the years 1693 and 1698, leaving six sons, four of whom settled in the Minas Basin about 1687. One of the sons became a mariner, and the youngest son, Pierre born in 1644, succeeded to the estate of his father. Pierre LeBlanc died Nov. 4, 1777, leaving eight children, the youngest of whom, named Charles, was born Sept 26, 1805. He was the great–great grandfather of the Right Rev. Dr. Edouard LeBlanc consecrated Bishop of St. John, N.B. December 10, 1913.

20. MASS HOUSE- This chapel stood at the foot of the Marsh on Guillot's land. Its titular saint was Laurent. The date of its erection is not known, but it seems to have been built about 1690, perhaps a few years later. There was a cemetery near it. The parish priest of Port Royal took up his residence here from the surrender of Port Royal, Oct. 1710 to the summer of 1724. Then the British authorities at Annapolis ordered the building to be demolished but this was only done twelve years later, in 1736. It is at this chapel that, three months after the surrender of the fort of Port Royal to Nicholson, Father Justinien Durand, was arrested on a Sunday morning by Captain James Abercromby and brought to the fort and there confined for a month, whence he was taken to Boston by Governor Vetch himself, where he remained a prisoner for ten months. In Dec., 1712, Father Durand was allowed to return to the Chapel of St. Laurent.

21. GUILLOT- Guillot, a diminutive of Guilaume. Guilaume Blanchard son of Jean Blanchard and Radegonde Lambert, was born at Port Royal in 1650, and married in 1673, Hugette Goujeon. Blanchard died about 1716, leaving six sons, the youngest of whom Guillaume, called Guillot was born in 1690. He married Jan. 16, 1714 Jeanne Dupuis and succeeded to his father's estate. He died Feb. 19, 1752.

22. JEAN BROSSARD- This locality was known as Beausoleil. The name was a

surname to the family of Brossard who settled there. Francois Brossard, who was born in France in 1654, took up his residence in this place, 1679. He married in Port Royal, 1680 Catherine Richard and died Dec. 30, 1716. He left six sons, the youngest of whom, called Jean, born March 23, 1705 was the only one of the family who remained in the homestead until expulsion. Pierre Brossard, the eldest, was the father of the famous Beausoleil of Petticoudiac who caused so much trouble to the British during the Seven Years' War.

23. BEAULIEU- Louis Fontaine, surnamed Beaulieu, was born at Port Royal, Aug. 19, 1707. He was the son of René Fontaine. Secretary to Sr. de Subercase, the last French Governor of Acadie, when Port Royal surrendered to Nicholson in Oct., 1710. Louis Fontaine was taken to France by his father and remained there until 1724 when he returned to Annapolis Royal as a domestic of Abbé de Bresslay. He married there, Feb. 10, 1730 Madeline Roy.

24. ANTOINE HEBERT- This village was called after Antoine Hébert, son of Etienne Hébert and Marie Gaudet, natives of France. Antoine Hébert, was born 1670, at Port Royal and married in 1691 Jeanne Corporon by whom he had twelve children.

25. FRANCOIS BASTARACHE-Francois Bastarache, eldest son of Jean Bastarache and Huguette Vincent, was born at Port Royal in 1688. He married in 1714 Agnes LaBauve and died at Annapolis River, Oct 27, 1751.

26. BERNARD GAUDET- Bernard Gaudet, son of Pierre Gaudet, Sr. and Anne Blanchard, born at Port Royal 1673, and married in 1699 Jeanne Terriot. He died March 18, 1757, leaving seven children, whose descendants are numerous in Westmorland County, NB and Montcalm County PQ

27. GAUDET VILLAGE- This was the homestead of Denis Gaudet, who was born in France in 1621, and married at Port Royal in 1645 Martine Gauthier. He died Nov. 21,1709. He was the grandfather of Bernard Gaudet (see note 26).

28. PREJEAN- Jean Préjean, surnamed LeBreton, was born in France in 1641, and married at Port Royal in 1693 Andrée Savoie. He died June 4, 1733, leaving a large family of children and grandchildren.

29. PARADISE TERRESTRE- So far as it could be ascertained by diligent searches, there are no records to show how, why and when this place was called " a paradise upon the earth" by Acadians. It bears now the name Paradise.

30. BASTARACHE- This village was named after Jean Bastarache, surnamed La Basque and Au Basque. Jean Bastarache was born in France in 1661 and married at Port Royal in 1684, Huguette Vincent. He died in 1733 leaving three sons- namely: François, who settled on the north side of the River Annapolis; Jean, born 1696, who escaped the Deportation and went to Québec, where he died in 1757; and Pierre, born in July 1702. The descendants of these three brothers are numerous in the Province of New Brunswick.

N.B. Notes to be inserted on the south side of the plan of Annapolis River.

31. JEAN PRINCE- Jean LePrince, the founder of this village, was born in 1679 at Port Royal. Jacques Le Prince his father was born in France in 1646 and married, 1678, Marguerite Hébert at Port Royal, where he settled. Jean LePrince mar-

ried at Port Royal 1715 Jeanne Blanchard widow of Oliver Daigle. He had five children whose descendants are numerous in the province of Québec, especially in the District of Three Rivers. Mgr. Prince, first Bishop of St. Hyacinthe, was a descendant of Antoine, one of the brothers of Jean LaPrince.

32. RENEE FOREST VILLAGE- René Forest, son of Michel Forest and Marie Hébert, of France, was born at Port Royal in 1670. He married Françoise Dugas and died April 20, 1755, leaving fourteen children.

33. BLOODY CREEK- Two massacres occurred in this vicinity, the first on June 20, 1711, and the other on Dec. 8, 1757.

34. ALEXANDRE HUBERT- Alexandre Hébert, son of Emmanuel Hébert and Andrée Brun, was born at Port Royal in 1686. His father, who removed to Grand Prée, was a bother of Antoine Hébert, who lived on the opposite side of the Annapolis River. Alexandre Hébert was deported in Dec. 1755 being then nearly seventy years of age.

35. BEAUPRE- This village was founded by René Richard, who was born at Port Royal in 1658. He was the eldest son of Michel Richard, a native of France and Madeleine Blanchard of Acadie. René Richard married in 1689 at Port Royal, Madeleine Landry, and his sons took the surname of Beaupré. René Richard, one of them, escaped the Deportation and finally reached Bécancour, where he died in 1776. Joseph Richard, son of René Richard junior, was the great-grandfather of the late Edouard Richard, the historian.

36. CLAUDE GIROUARD- Claude Girouard, son of Jacques Girouard and Marguerite Goutrot, was born at Port Royal in 1684. He married Elizabeth Blanchard in 1709, and died March 14, 1738.

37. DE RUE VILLAGE- Alexandre Girouard, surnamed deRue, was born at Port Royal in 1670. He was a brother to Claude Girouard. (see note 36). He married in 1694 Marie LeBorgne de Bellisle, daughter of Alexandre LeBorgne de Bellisle and Marie de St. Etienne de la Tour. He died Sept. 23, 1744.

38. GIROUARD VILLAGE- This village was settled by Jacques Girouard, who was born at Port Royal in 1648. Jacques Girouard was the eldest son of François Girouard, a native of France, and Jeanne Aucoin, of Acadie. He married in the year 1669 Marguerite Gaudet [Goutrot-BG] and died Oct. 27, 1703 leaving fourteen children. Six of his sons settled on the south side of the river.

39. THIBODEAU VILLAGE- The founder of this village was Pierre Thibodeau, born in France in 1631, and married at Port Royal in 1660 to Jeanne Terriot. He died Dec. 1704, leaving a very large family, whose descendants are today numerous in the Maritimes Provinces, in the province of Québec and in Louisiana. In the church register recording his burial, Pierre Thibodeau is described as "an habitant and miller residing on the upper part of the River Port Royal at the place called Prée Ronde".

40. PREE RONDE (ROUND HILL) - Probably this was one of the farms of the Governor d'Aulnay Charnisay.

41. MILL- (Round Hill Brook) (See note 2, p 118)

42. LA ROSETTE VILLAGE- The name Rosette is a surname given to Jacques Léger, a drummer in the French army in Acadie (see note 1, p. 118)

43. L'ESTURGEON (see note 1 p. 126)

44. PIERRE VINCENT- This village was named after Pierre Vincent, born in France in 1631, and married at Port Royal in 1605 to Anne Gaudet, a native of Acadie. He died about 1677, leaving one daughter and four sons, of whom one died about the age of fifteen years. The remaining three married and had large families. They have descendants in the province of Québec and elsewhere.

45. RUISSEAU FOURCHU –SEE NOTE 1 P. 117.

46. MILL- This mill belonged to Joseph Nicolas Gautier, a native of Rochefort, France, who came to Acadie as a navigator about 1710. He was an educated man and soon became prominent as a merchant, mill-owner and ship-owner. He took up residence at a place called Belair, a short distance from Maillard's Hill. In 1745, he was worth 65,000 *livres* in real estate, but having sided with and assisted Duvirier, Marin and Ramezay in their expeditions against the fort of Annapolis in 1744, 1745, 1747, his properties were confiscated and he was declared an outlaw, and fled from Annapolis a ruined man. He died at the North East River, Île Saint-Jean, April 1, 1752.

47. CAPE- According to a letter from his Honour, Judge A.W. Savary, of Annapolis Royal, "it is called the Cape from where the first road to Halifax starts from the main street of Annapolis into the junction with the other road that leads to Lequille and Halifax. The territory called the Cape embraces both those roads and the settlement on them." In 1714 there were at the Cape forty-one Acadian families forming a population of 207 souls.

48. MAILLARD HILL- see note 1, page 91.

49. BABINEAU HILL- This hill was called after Jean Babineau, born about 1657 in Acadie. In 1691, Babineau married Marguerite Boudrot, widow of Francois Bourg, and died Sept. 5 1741. He was a brother of Nicolas Babineau, surnamed Delaurier, of the north side of Annapolis River.

50. THE FORT- see page 96. In Haliburton's *Nova Scotia* vol. ii, page 160, he states: The fortifications are erected on the southwestern extremity of the peninsula. The works, which have been erected at very great expense, are in a dilapidated condition, the cannon, dismounted, and the whole incapable in the present state of sustaining a defense. The ground on which they are built contains twenty-eight acres of land. One of the last occupants of this old fortress was the Rifle Brigade in 1850 but the post was abandoned soon after on account of the numerous and successful desertions which thinned the ranks of the garrison. The cannon which Haliburton described in 1828 as having been dismounted have disappeared, and nobody seems to know today what has become of them. In recent years the fortifications have been restored by the Dominion Government and are now in an excellent state of preservation.

51. THE TOWN- For a description of the town in 1757, see page 87. The town is built on the extremity of a peninsula, which projecting into the river, forms two beautiful Basins, one above and the other below the town." (Haliburton's *Nova Scotia*, Vol. ii, p 159) In spite of the dignity of old, Annapolis is a small town, but she looms large in the traveler's eyes by reason of the mantle of history in which she wraps herself.

Annapolis do they flood yet feel
Faint memories of Champlain's repeat
of Poutrincourt and d'Ibeville
(Charles G.D. Roberts The Land of Evangeline
p. 21 and 22)

52. HOG ISLAND- see note 3 page 88
53. ALLEN RIVER- This river was called after Louis Allain, born in France in 1654, and married at Port Royal in 1690 to Marguerite Bourg. Allain was one of the leading Acadians of Annapolis Royal, where he died June 15, 1737, leaving one son and a daughter. The descendants of the son are numerous in New Brunswick, in the province of Québec, in Louisiana and other parts of the United States. The daughter, whose name was Marie, married at Annapolis Royal, March 4.

Appendix 5

Sample Subcharts- Early generations refer to Ancestors in Port Royal and Old Acadie as indicated in the text.

	L162	M162	N162	O162	P162	Q162	R162	S162	T162	U162	V162
6]	References: 1. Research of William D. Gerrior. *Acadian Awakenings*, 2002. 2. Interviews, surveys, and correspondence with descendants and census information. Genealogy research notes of Arthur Brian Gerrior of the twelfth generation and Christine (Morin) Oderkirk, descendant of [Block P162-11a].					1752 - 1821 Paul m. Angélique Boucher, 1772 Gabarus, NS Georgetown, PEI	6 REFER TO [BLOCK V163-6] OF SUBCHART #163. Prince Edward Island descendants originate from Isle Madame Branch. References: Stephen White, Centre d'études acadiennes, Université de Moncton, NB for generations 6, 7, and 8 (see notes following chart). For other generations, see archive records, Placide Gaudet p. 2125-1, and 2193; Church records in Isle Madame; interviews with PEI descendants Brian Gerrior, Christine (Morin) Oderkirk, Gloria Hazard, as well as information and photos received via correspondence including survey forms and letters from many descendants.					
7]					Marie -	1772 - 1842 Paul m. Marguerite Bégin	Jean -				
8]					1812 - Angélique m. Charles Broussard 1852 Arichat	1825 - Tranquille François m. Charlotte Cheverry	1807 - Brigitte m. Charles Petitpas 1848 Arichat	1823 - Vital m. Marguerite Coste 1845 Arichat			
9]				Infant died at birth	1849 - 1860 Angélique	1846 - James m. Anne Wolf b. PEI lived at Petit de Grat	1850 - Flora m. Campbell	1851 - Marguerite m. Irénée Aucoin			
10]	1873 - James Henry m. Fanny Perry	1875 - Simon	1877 - Anne Charlotte m. Frank	1878 - Marie Jean	1879 - Tranquille Auguste Mitchell River, PEI	1881 - 1955 Charles Jeffrey m. Mary Burke at Mitchell River PEI b. in Arichat, Georgetown, Trenton, NS	1871 - 1976 John (Capt. Jack) m1. Beronica Marie Perry m2. Cathy Pierre C. Veronica Shoup Georgetown, PEI	1880 - Marie Caroline	1885 - Joseph Honoré Alcide m. _____ Tignish, PEI	Marie Alescia	Allan (d) at 32 n.m.
11a]	1908 - 1961 Sophia m. Fred LaMont	1929 - 1963 Theresa m. M.A. Shirk Trenton, NS	1918 - 1988 Frederic m. Lillian French	1915-1990 Margaret m. Charles Charleton	1904 - 1988 Mary Elizabeth m. Ignatius Farrell	1912 - 1990 Charles Arthur m. Verna Burns Trenton, NS	1911 - 1985 William m. Mary Fougère Georgetown, PEI Trenton, NS	1925 - 1988 Daisy m. Freeman Wells Trenton, NS	1923 - 1988 Marion m. Corey Hartling	1910 - 1978 Joseph Allen m. Anne Gill Mitchell River, PEI Trenton, NS	1906 - 1973 James Jefferey m. Helen Nicholas Mitchell River, Trenton, NS
11b]	1913 - 1977 Sarah (Dolly) m. Ambrose Hines					0					
12]			Charles (d)	Heather Lee m. Joey Earl Agnew Milford, NS	Verna Jeanette m. George Franklin Bates N.G., Trenton	**Arthur Brian m. Jane Elizabeth Pike New Glasgow Ontario**	Russel Matthew m. Cindy Brooks New Glasgow	Robert Burns m1. Cathy O'Laney m2. Tracey Sewell New Glasgow			**PEI BRANCHES Subchart #162 Linking to [AMC Block E-3B]**

©*Acadian Awakenings Girouard/Giroir... Routes and Roots*

	L162.1	M162.1	N162.1	O162.1	P162.1	Q162.1	R162.1	S162.1	T162.1	U162.1	V162.1
3]	References: 1. Research of William D. Gerrior, *Acadian Awakenings*, 2002. 2. Interviews, surveys, and correspondence with descendants of the sixth, seventh and eighth generations.					1673 - Pierre m1. Marie Comeau ca. 1697 m2. Marie Doiron 1709 G.P. Isle Madame, NS M'ck NB	→REFER TO [BLOCK E-3B] OF MASTER CHART OF WILLIAM D. GERRIOR. Note 1: The family of Louis Paul Girouard was in Malpec, PEI, (census 1752 noted in Placide Gaudet's genealogy p. 2128). Firmin, [Block Q162.1-5] appears in the 1766 census in Louisiana, having a lot on the right bank of the Mississippi at St. James (St. Jacques) Donaldsonville. Information sent by Sheila Dusco Girouard, Broussard, Louisiana. Information from Bona Arsenault Vol. 4, p. 2493. Joseph O. Girouard of [Block R162.1-8], was prominent plantation owner. Information from his daughter Stella Girouard and Hebert descendants. Note 2: Pierre Ray [Block Q162.1-7] died of Yellow Fever. Pierre Ray was buried on Girouard farm.				
4m1]				1708 - Etienne	1699 - 1768 Claude m. Marie Madeleine Vincent 1726 at P.R. Aux Mines Isle Madame in 1752, d. at St-Charles de Bellechasse, P.Q	↔	1698 - 1758 Marie m. Jean Trahan ca. 1714 St-Charles de Bellechasse Qué.	1701 - 1719 Pierre	1702 - 1761 Anne m. Thomas Doiron 1724 St-Malo, Fr. (d) at St-Servan, Fr.	1707 -1764 Jacques m. Marie Boisseau 1730 Grand Pré Conn. 1763 Mirebalais	
4m2]			1729 - Jean Baptiste m. Madeleine Boudreau	1723 - Marguerite* m. Bazile Badrot ca. 1743 G.P. Deported St-Malo, 1759 France also at Nantes *(Ref: Gaston Giroir of France)*	1717 - 1764 Marie Josèphe m. Germain Pitre, 1736 at Pisiquid Mirebalais St-Domingue W. Indies	1716 - Louis Paul* m. Marie Thibodeau 1736 He was at Halifax in 1763 PEI, NB and LA. branches	1710 - Charles Grand Pré	1712 - 1768 Véronique* m. Pierre Barilot 1730 G.P. Died 1768, May - France	1714 - 1785 Honoré* m. Marie Joseph Theriot ca. 1740 b. G.P. *Subchart 162.6* St-Malo, Fr. 1759, Plesin, Fr. 1762 Fam. at Louisiana	1719 -1803 Madeleine m. Joseph Leblanc 1740 G.P. *Ref: Bergeron* Died at Carleton, Québec	1732 - Marie m1. Charles Benoit 1755 m2. Charles Landry St-Malo, 1763 F.R.
5]			1746 - 1838 Marie Josephe m1. Michael Duguay m2. Charles Forest	1744 - 1838 Paul Gervais* m. Madeleine Theriault *Originator of NB branches*	1739 - Anne Théodose m1. Pierre Arsenault m2. Laurent 1760 Restigouche, NB	1749 - 1820 Firmin Girouard m. Marguerite Cormier 1771 Migrated Lot 109 St-Jacques LA. Côte Gelée	1737 - Marguerite	1751 - Charles	1761 - Louis Restigouche, NB		
6]	1780 - Marie Mad. m. Jean Bpt. Breaux 1800	1773 - 1801 Jacques* m. Angélique Broussard 1798 St-Martinville Louisiana	1789 - Marguerite m. Joseph Bernard	1783 - Scholastique* m. Jean Bernard 1803 *Lafayette Church V.3 p.160*	1785 - 1815 Félicité m. Benjamin Thibodeau 1805 St-Martinville Louisiana	1776 - Pierre m. Madeleine Thibodeaux 1803 St-Martinville Louisiana	1778 - Joseph m. Marie Anne Landry 1801 Marie, coming from France - Acadian refugee	1787 - Anastasie m. Charles Granger St-Martinville, Louisiana	1771 - 1819 Firmin-Simon m. Adélaide Broussard *Ref: Bona Arsenault* St-Martinville, Louisiana	1792 - Jean Baptiste b. at St. Jacques, Louisiana *Ref: Bona Arsenault*	

Appendices

7]	1816 - Adélaide Aglae m. Camille Broussard 1832 St. Martin, Louisiana	1815 - Clarisse	1813 - 1830 Hilaire (Laf)	1810 Joseph St. Martinville, Louisiana	1811 - Maximilien* m. Carmesile Broussard 1833	1808 - ca 1864 Pierre Ray m. Adéline Melanson 1830 Both died of Yellow Fever.	1804 Simon St. Martinville, Louisiana	1806 - Jean Valmond m. Caroline Taylor (Teller) 1833 b...St. Martinville, Louisiana *Ref: Bona Arsenault*	1821 - 1821 Elina	1821 Madeleine	Drozin *Ref: Henriette & Maxim Girouard*
8]	1830 - Léontine m. Bee Primeaux	1843 - Norbert b. at St. Martinville, Louisiana.	1836 - Elaine (Lina) m. Méance Boulet of Cossinade, Louisiana 1855	1831 - Marie Opiiie m. Antoine Meaux 1851 of Kaplan Louisiana	1841 - Adolphe* m. Clementine Broussard 1870 *Ref: Charts sent by Taylor Rock & Laurence Girouard* Lafayette	1850 - 1937 Léonce (Toutoute) m. Clara Broussard *Ref: Elmer Girouard & Laura Leblanc*	1839 - 1916 Joseph Oscar* m1. Anaise Fedora Girouard à Jean Valmond m2. Cécile Brugere *Ref: Stella Girouard* Broussard, Louisiana	1832 - Adélaide-Ezilda m. Paul Leger 1850 Lafayette Louisiana	1834 - Dupré m. Anastasie Prejean 1839 Broussard Kaplan, LA Vermillion Parish	1852 - Leonard Died of Yellow Fever.	
9]	California		Lora (Sousou) m. Eloige Landry	Annie m. Wiley Rabalais Gueydan	1896 - 1943 Honoré m. Camillia Ozenne	1899 - 1973 Sydney m. Alma Guilbeau	1889 - 1976 Elie m. Lucille Gautreaux Broussard, LA	Nellie m. Winnie Landry (n.c.) Lafayette, LA	Elda m. Camille Broussard		
10]	Harold James m. Sylvia King Lafayette, LA		Nelda Ida Rose m. Jerome Judice Laf., LA	Raymond Joseph m. Rosemae Domingue	Irene m. Pierre Landry Lafayette, LA	Walton Lee m. Julie Domingue Lafayette, LA	Ernest Paul m. Rita Allemand Lafayette, LA	Louis Pierre m. Exarey Ann Dugas Lafayette, LA	Sydney Patrick m. Janell Duhon Lafayette, LA		
11]			Charlene	Catherine	Christine m. James Simon	Hershel Lee Paul m. Brenda Boudreaux	Cynthia Ann m. Malcom Jude Reaux				
12]					Dana m. Darrel Peters	Hershel II m. Lori Smith	Christopher (Twin)	James (Twin)			Girouard Louisiana Subchart #162.1 Linking to [AMC Block E-3b]

© *Acadian Awakenings Girouard/Giroir... Routes and Roots*

419

	L162.6	M162.6	N162.6	O162.6	P162.6	Q162.6	R162.6	S162.6	T162.6	U162.6	V162.6
3]	References: 1. Genealogies to present day provided by Mary Jane Siracusa Gretna La., Howard J. Giroir and Louis Giroir, Round Rock, Texas; and reference to *Exiles at St-Malo*. 2. Also reference to settlement of Prosper's family in *Colonial Settlers Along Bayou Fourche 1770-1798*, by Albert Robichaux; ship's passenger list from France, a copy of which was sent to me by Mary Jane Siracusa, Gretna, Louisiana. 3. Numerous letters, completed survey forms, documents and interviews with Louisiana Girouard, Giroir descendants. 4. Interviews, surveys, and correspondence with descendants of the sixth, seventh, eighth and ninth generations. 5. Research of William D. Gerrior, *Acadian Awakenings*, 2002. 6. *ACADIANS IN CHATELLENAULT, 5TH AND 6TH GENERATION*. 7. Information cross-referenced with various web sites on Girouards and/or spouses maiden name. 8. Genealogy records of Laticia Giroir, Houston, Texas.					1673 - Pierre m1. Marie Comeau, 1698 m2. Marie Doiron 1709 G.P. Isle Madame, NS M'ck NB	→**REFER TO [BLOCK E-3B] OF MASTER CHART OF WILLIAM D. GERRIOR** Notes: 1. Honoré and his wife [Block Q162.6-4M2] and three children: Posper, Hélène-Judith and Eudoxile embarked at St. Malo, France on January 23, 1759 from one of the "five ships". 2. Honoré and his family resided in the following parishes: 1759-1764 - Pleslin; 1764-1772 - St. Suliac (Fr.). Prosper and his family resided in the following parishes in France: 1759-1764 Pleslin; 1765-1770 St. Coulom; 1770-1772 - St. Jouan-des-Guerets. 3. They were on the second convoy in France, from Châtellerault to Nantes November 15, 1785 to prepare for their departure from France to LA. 4. All of generation 6 (row six of this chart) were passengers with their parents Prosper and Marie Dugas, on the ship "La Bergère" departing from France on May 12, 1785 and arriving in Louisiana on August 15, 1785. 5. See also New Brunswick chapter for many other Girouard descendants of Louis Paul [Block P162.6-4M2] and Subchart 162.1 of this chapter for "Giroir" descendents.				
4m1]				1708 - Etienne	1699 - 1768 Claude m. Marie Madeleine Vincent, 1726 at Port Royal. Aux Mines Isle Madame in 1752. d. PQ.	↔	1698 - 1758 Marie m. Jean Trahan ca. 1714 St-Charles de Bellechasse PQ	1701 - 1719 Pierre	1702 - 1761 Anne m. Thomas Doiron 1724 St. Malo (d) at St-Servan, Fr. St. Suliac parish.	1707 - 1764 Jacques m. Marie Boisseau 1730 Grand Pré Conn. 1763 Mirabalais St-Domingue W. Indies	
4m2]		1729 - Jean Baptiste	1723 - Marguerite* m. Basile Boudrot Deported to France at Nantes Ref: *Gaston Giroir of France*	1717 - 1764 Marie Josèphe m. Germain Pitre, 1736 Mirabalais St-Domingue W. Indies	1716 - Louis Paul* m. Marie Thibodeau 1736 at Halifax 1763 PEI - 1752 NB and LA. branches	1714 - 1785 Honoré Girouard m. Marie Josepha Thériot 1740 France (St-Malo) 1759, Ch. deported and died Louisiana 1785		1712 - 1768 Véronique* m. Pierre Barillot 1730 G.P. Died May 1768 France *Genealogy of Carl A. Miller* Grand Pré Marrero LA.	1719 - 1803 Madeleine m. Joseph Leblanc 1740 G.P. Ref: *Bergeron notes* d. Carleton, Qué	1732 - Marie m1. Charles Benoît 1755 m2. Charles Landry 1763 at Pleudihen, Fr. St-Malo, Fr. 1758, 1787	
5]					1758 - Joseph (Died in sea crossing to France) 1758/59		1742 - Hélène Judith* Giroir m. François Blanchard 1763 Pleslin, France Louisiana	1747 - Eudoxile* m. Jean Pierre Hébert 1787 Louisiana Ref: *Folio 872-France, Gaston Giroir*	1752 - 1758 Marie-Anne (Died in sea crossing to France) 1758/59	1754 - 1758 David b. Isle St-Jean Acadie (Died in sea crossing to France) 1758/59	

Additional entry at O/P column row 5: 1761 - 1835 Marie Rose m. François Sébastien Landry 1793 — Pleslin, France Louisiana

1744 -ca1791 Prosper Honoré Giroir m. Marie Dugas 1764 at St-Colombe — France Louisiana

Appendices

6)	1774 -1774 Marie	1771 - 1880 Jeanne (Eleanore) m. Carlos Blanchard 1792	1778 - Pierre (19 years old in 1798 living with brother François in France)	1766 - 1831 Anne-Josephe* m. Fabien Guillot 1797 Ref: letter of Walter I Sathon III	1765 - Marie-Paule* m. Joseph Landry 1788 at Donaldsonville Louisiana b. St. Coloumb France Ref: Stanley Labat	1769 - 1818 Jean Baptiste Giroir m. Elizabeth Landry, 1790	1772 - 1836 François* m. Madeleine Le Blanc 1794 Ref: Survey form of Albert Giroir and Louis Giroir Plattenville Louisiana	1768 - 1772 Joseph Magloire St. Coloumb Fr. Ref: Folio 756 of Gaston Giroir	1766 - 1810 Marianne m. Gregory Landry b. St. Malo France	1766 - 1800 Anne m. Charles Pierre Marc Blanchard 1792	1777 - 1783 Magloire
		St-Jouan Des Guerrets, France	b. Nantes France	France Louisiana	France Louisiana	France Plattenville Louisiana	Plattenville Louisiana			Donaldsonville Louisiana	St. Similien Nantes France
7)	1795 - Louisa m. Joseph Daigle	1797 - 1862 Rosalie Isabel m. Simeon Landry, 1821 Plattenville Louisiana 1792 - Maria Rosa Landry Giroir b. Lafourche, LA	1794 - Marie-Francoise m. Hippolite Landry, 1820 b. Lafourche, LA ------- 1794 - Francisca Elena	1810 - 1854 Ovide Carmilita m. Constant Simoneaux at Plattenville Louisiana b. Plattenville Ref: genealogy of Carla Miller	1804 - Joseph Dumase* m. Carmelite Barillot 1834 at Plattenville Ref: genealogy of Nola Le blanc Labat Jr.	1800 - François Apollinaire m. Théotiste Aucoin 1820	1807 - Etienne* m. Adèle Hebert, 1830, Plattenville, LA Ref: Fr. Frank Giroir's research	1802 - Fabian Lucas 1806 - Constance Francoise 1809 - Malania	1812 - Margarita Abdelarda m. Eugene Dupuis at Plattenville Louisiana 1836	1803 - Delphine Dionisia m. Gregoire-Mathurin Landry 1821 at Plattenville Louisiana	1799 - Jean Baptiste m1. Rosalie-Victoire-Bourg 1821 at Plattenville Loui'sianna m2. Azelie-Eulalie Boudreaux
	Plattenville Louisiana					Donaldsonville Plattenville					
8)	1832 - Jean Baptiste	1829 - 1846 Irma Clotilde m. Auguste Joret b. Ascension Parish, LA	1827 - 1829 Melvine	1821 - Felicite-Adele	1839 - Jean Bapt. m. Marie Clementine Grow Ref: Survey of Lydia Giroir Broussard, Whitney, Texas	1825 - Apollinaire Zephrin m. Armelise Landry (Assum. Census) Paincourtville, LA.	1836 - Louisa Melanie	1839 - Severine Marie	1842 - Julien	1845 - Aurlie Marie	
	Plattenville Louisiana	Plattenville Louisiana		Plattenville Louisiana			Plattenville Louisiana		Plattenville Louisiana		
9)	1851 - Gustelish		1852 - Cordelia	1854 - Marie*	1851 - Justinian-Elfege m. Celima Simoneaux	1858 - Estilette (Stilette) Giroir m1. Céleste Penisson 1880 m2. Corin Ross Ref: Mary Jane Siracusa genealogy records	1864 - Etienne m. Victorine Thériot	1869 - Elfige	1854 - Sophie-Camilla	1859 - 1897 Thelisa-Elisa m. Etienne-Uhyssa Dennison	**Louisiana "Giroir" Branches Subchart #162.6 Linking to [AMC Block E-3b]**
			Assumption Parish Louisiana			Gibson, LA. (Terrebonne)	Bayou Boeuf		Assumption Parish Louisiana	Bayoul'ourse Louisiana	

© *Acadian Awakenings Girouard/Giroir... Routes and Roots*

421

	L163	M163	N163	O163	P163	Q163	R163	S163	T163	U163	V163
3]	Notes: 1. Claude Giroüard m. Madeleine Vincent was at Pisiquit (Windsor) then Isle Madame in 1749, before deportation, then at Beaumont, Québec in 1765. (Reference: Bona Arsenault, Vol 4, Pisiquit.) 2. Claude's children are in row 5. All children in rows 4m1 and 4m2 are children of Pierre [Block E-3b] from his two marriages. 3. Marie Josèphe, [Block S163-5], had a second marriage at Restigouche, Québec, 1759. (Bona Arsenault, Pisiquit, Vol 4.) 4. Research of William D. Gerrior, *Acadian Awakenings*, 2002. 5. Interviews, surveys, and correspondence with descendants of the sixth, seventh, eighth, ninth and tenth generations.					1672 - Pierre m. Marie Comeau 1697 m2. Marie Doiron 1709 *ref : Placide Gaudet p.2115* G.P. Isle Madame, NS M'ck, NB	→**REFER TO [BLOCK E-3B] OF MASTER CHART OF WILLIAM D. GERRIOR.** Subchart showing the maternal Girroir ancestry of Rev. Conrad P. Girroir as well as the ancestry of other descendants in West Arichat, Isle Madame. References: Interviews with Fr. Conrad P. Girroir and his brother, Raymond Girroir, Church Records in West Arichat and Arichat as well as census records. Information and letters from genealogist, Stephen White, Centre d'études acadiennes, Université de Moncton. Placide Gaudet's genealogy of the Girrouards concerning fifth generation at Petit de Grat, p. 2125-1 of Placide, also Placide p. 2162 and Bergeron 1730, referring to Jacques Girouard m. Marie Boisseau [Block U163-4m1] of this subchart. See story concerning this family in Connecticut and Maryland. Also genealogy charts of Stephen Girouard, Allentown, P.A. give reference to Antoine [Block P163-6] of this subchart. [Block M163-4m2] is reference from Gaston Giroir, France.
4m1]					1708 - Etienne G.P. reg.1730 P.R. 1708,1709 census G.P.	1699 - 1768 Claude m. P.R. Marie Madeleine Vincent, 1726 Les Mines, he was at Isle Madame in 1752, d. St. Charles de Bellechasse, Que. *Ref: Stephen White*	1698 - 1758 Marie m. Jean Trahan ca. 1714 St-Charles de Bellechasse Qué.	1701 - 1719 Pierre	1705 - 1761 Anne m. Thomas Doiron 1724 PEI 1752 St. Malo, Fr. at St-Servan, Fr. St-Suliac parish	1707 - 1764 Jacques m. Marie Boisseau 1730 Grand Pré Conn. 1763 Mirebalais St. Domingue W. Indies	
4m2]			ca. 1716 - 1764 Louis Paul m. Marie Thibodeau 1736 at Halifax 1763 PEI - 1752 NB and LA. branches	1710 - Charles Grand Pré	↔	1712 - 1768 Véronique m. Pierre Barilot 1730 PEI 1752 PEI 1752 Disp. Louisianna May 1768 France	1714 - 1785 Honoré* m. Marie Josèphe Thériot ca. 1740 b. G.P. m. Pisiquit d. at St-Malo, France Louisianna	1719 - 1805 Magdeleine m. Joseph Leblanc G.P. 1740 *Ref. Bergeron* d. at Carleton, Gaspesie, PQ	1732 - Marie m1. Charles Benoît 1755 m2. Charles Landry 1763 at Pleudihen, France St-Malo, Fr.	
5]	1729 - Jean Baptiste m. Madeleie Boudreau *ref. Emelie Perkisonn, NB* 1748 - Paraxède	1723 - Margarite m. Basile Boudrot ca. 1743, G.P. Deported to St. Malo, Fr., 1759, Nantes *Ref. Gaston Giroir of France* 1744 - Antoine	1717 - 1764 Marie Josèphe m. Pierre Pitre 1736 Pisiquid d. La Mirebalais 1764 St-Domingue W. Indies 1741 - Bazile	1738 - Sylvain	1729 - Joseph	1727 - Pierre m. Cécile Detcheverry dit Jonis 1751 Petit-de-Grat, C.B. 1752	1731 - Marguerite m1. Jean Pouget (Poujet) 1724 m2. François Aucoin m3. Charles Touzalin She was deported to Fr. and died in Fr. (Census FR. 1781). 1760 - 1843 Victoire m. Michel Pettipas, 1787	1736 - Marie Josèphe m1. M.A. Lorot 1753 m2. J. Bourgeois P.Q. at St-James LA. 1766, 1777 census Marie (d) St-Martinville, 1815, LA. 1763 - Honoré			
6]		Pierre m. Bibienne Poirier Descousse Summerside PEI Branch	1771 - Monique Marie m. Jean-Marie Poirier 1793	1756 - Joseph	1754 - Antoine Ordained in 1785 Nipisiquid, NB	1752 - Jean Baptiste m. Gertrude Landry Isle Madame C.B.	1760 - 1843 Victoire m. Michel Pettipas, 1787 Arichat, NS Tracadie, NS	1763 - Honoré Early Halifax Branch	1765 - 1842 Augustin m. Scholastique Benoit	1767 - Ignace	1752 - 1821 Paul m. Angélique Boucher Gabarus, C.B. Georgetown PEI Branch

Appendices

7]	Margaret m. Louis Thériault	1792 - 1851 Simon m. Angélique LeBlanc	Jean Baptiste m. Angélique Thériault	1799 - 1859 Benjamin m1. Suzanne Boudrot m2. Victoire Thériault	1791 - 1871 Michel m1. Marie Boudrot 1814 m2. Caroline LeBlanc	Rosalie m. Joseph Boudrot	Gertrude m. John Boudrot	Paul - 1848 m. Marine Lavache 1825	Suzanne m. Simon LeBlanc	
8m1]			Gaétome m. Anne Pettipas	Suzanne m. Constance Pettipas	1814 - 1883 Polycarpe m. Sophie Deslauriers 1840 Arichat Ile Madame, C.B.	1820 - 1895 Jean Baptiste m1. Mathilde Fougère 1844 m2. Julie Lajune	1817 - 1906 Henriette m. Firmin Lajune	1822 - 1916 Abraham m1. Emilie LeBlanc m2. Domithilde m3. Olive Marchand	1826 - 1916 Michel m1. Victoire Babin m2. Sabine Poirier m3. Apolline Brian	
9]	Pierre-Louis Arichat	1848 - Adèle m. Frédéric LeBlanc Ref: Ellen Downing	1860 - Sophie Joséphine m. Charles LeBlanc	1843 - Marine Hélène m. Hubert Sampson 1859 Arichat USA Summerville	1841 - 1914 Jean Baptiste m. Martha Lavache 1865 no children Arichat W. Arichat	ca1854 - 1925 William m1. Elizabeth (Louise Anne) Poirier 1881 m2. Elizabeth LeBlanc Isle Madame	1844 - 1910 Jeannette m. Guillaume Laurent Landry	1845 - 1911 Jeffrey (Siffoi) m1. Anne Smith m2. Elizabeth Boucher USA	1856 - Suzanne m. Bell New York, USA	1851 - Paul (Polycarpe) m1. Marie Boutin m2. Marie Frilate USA	1850 - 1869 Marie Ann Barb m1. Felix Coste m2. Charles Genthner 1847 - Honoré
10m1]		1893 - Joseph Thomas West Arichat	1886 - Pierre Alphonse not married	Joseph Alexis 1899 not married	1882 - Wilfred m. Rose Bona USA	1883 - 1980 Mabel m. John Baptiste Girroir Isle Madame	1889 - 1987 Ida (Ada) m1. Boudreau m2. William Leonard m3. Irvin Fratus Cape Cod, USA	Arthance (Hortance) m. Thomas P. Boudreau			
10m2]			Raymond Ref: David Gerrior	1895 - 1976 Leo m. Ann Fortin USA	Alexis -	↔	Mary (Mini) m. Walter Hart Wareham Malden, Mass.	Medord m. Florence Aucoin	Bernadette m. Jack Noonan Plainville, Mass. Attleboro, NC		
11]		Thomas Ref: David Gerrior	1905 - 1931 Marie Elizabeth Petronille m. Alphonse Babin, 1727	1914 - 1989 Marie Eva Mae F.D.J 1912 - William Desiré	1909 - 1992 Pierre Raymond n.m.	1917 - Rev. Conrad Polycarpe Girroir Ile Madame C.B.	Rev. Emedée Thomas Girroir	1906 - 1930 Irène Euclide not married	1902 - 1945 Jean Baptiste Edmond René 1919 - Brigette Annunciata	1922 - 1973 Mary Jane Geneviève m. Harry Helin	
	1911 - 1911 Willie Edward twins d. then 1923-1927 Sophie Eva Mae 1908-1909	Nancy Girroir Sister Superior of Provincial House at Moncton, NB F.D.J., NB								Rev. Conrad (maternal branches) Isle Madame, NS Subchart #163 Linking to [AMC Block E-3b]	

© *Acadian Awakenings Girouard/Giroir... Routes and Roots*

	L164	M164	N164	O164	P164	Q164	R164	S164	T164	U164	V164
3]	References: 1. Research of William D. Gerrior, *Acadian Awakenings*, 2002. 2. Interviews, surveys, and correspondence with descendants of the sixth, seventh, eighth, ninth and tenth generations, census records.					1673 - Pierre m1. Marie Comeau 1697 m2. Marie Doiron, G.F. Isle Madame, NS Mck, NB	☐ REFER TO [BLOCK E-3B] OF MASTER CHART OF WILLIAM D. GERRIOR. Subchart showing the paternal Girroir ancestry of Rev. Conrad P. Girroir as well as the ancestry of other descendants in West Arichat, Isle Madame. References: Interviews with Fr. Conrad P. Girroir and his brother Raymond Girroir, church records in West Arichat and Arichat as well as census records. Information and letters written to Fr. Girroir by genealogist, Stephen White, of Centre d'études acadiennes, Université de Moncton, New Brunswick.				
4m1]				1708 - Etienne		1699 - 1768 Claude m. Madeleine Vincent ,PR 1726 later at Aux Mines & Isle Madame in 1752.d. St-Ch. de Bellechasse	1698 - 1758 Marie m. Jean Trahan ca. 1714 St-Charles de Bellechasse PQ	1701 -1719 Pierre	1702 - 1761 Anne m. Thomas Doiron 1724 PEI 1752 cencus St-Malo, Fr.	1707 - Jacques m. Marie Boisseau 1730 Grand Pré Conn. Mirabalais St-Domingue W. Indies	
4m2]		1729 - Jean Baptiste	1723 - Marguerite m. Basile Boudrot ca. 1743, G.P. Deported St-Malo, Fr. 1759 also at Nantes Ref: Gaston Giroir of France	1717- 1764 Marie Josèphe m. Germain Pitre 1736 Pisiquid d. at Mirebalais St-Domingue W. Indies	1716 - Louis Paul m. Marie Thibodeau 1736 Louis Paul was at Halifax 1763 PEI - 1752 NB and LA. branches	↔	1710 - Charles Grand Pré	1712 -1768 Véronique m. Pierre Barillot 1730 PEI 1752 Grand Pré 1730 d. May 1768 France	1714 -1785 Honoré* m. Marie Josèphe Thériot ca. 1740 b. G.P. d. at St-Malo, France Louisianna	1719 - 1803 Madeleine m. Joseph Leblanc G.P. 1740 Ref: Bergeron d. at Carlton Gaspesie, PQ	1732 - Magie M1. Charles Benoît, 1755 m2. Charles Landry St. Malo, France
5]	1748 - Paraxède	1744 - Antoine	1741 - Bazile	1738 - Sylvain	1729 - Joseph	1727 - Pierre m. Cécile Detcheverry dit Jonis 1751	1731 - Marguerite m1. Jean Pouget 1724 m2. François Aucoin m3. Charles Touzalin She was Dep. to Fr. where she died 1781 (1781 Census)	1736 - Marie Joseph m1. M.A. Lorot 1753 m2. J. Bourgeois at PQ she was at St- James LA. 1766, 1777 census Marie (d) St-Martinville, 1815, LA.			

424

6]	Pierre - m. Bibienne Poirier D'Escousse Isle Madame	1771 - Moniquearie m. Jean Marie Poirier 1793	1756 - Joseph	1754 - Antoine *Ordained 1785 Nipisiquid	1752 - Jean Baptiste Gertrude Landry	1768 - 1843 Victoire m. Michel Pettipas 1787 Tracadie, NS	1763 - Honoré	1765 - Augustin m. Scholastique Benoît Lived in Halifax very early	1767 - Ignace	1752 - 1821 Paul m. Angélique Boucher
7]	Margaret m. Louis Thériault	1792 - 1851 Simon m. Angélique LeBlanc Arichat, C.B.		Jean Baptiste m. Angélique Thériault	1791 - 1871 Michel m1. Marie Boudrot 1814 m2. Caroline Leblanc	1799 - 1859 Benjamin m1. Suzanne Boudrot m2. Victoire Thériault		Rosalie m. Joseph Boudrot	Paul m. Marine Lavache	Suzanne m. Simon LeBlanc	
8]	Marie Joseph	1885 - Albert	1840 - 1861 Benjamin		Daniel m. Marcelline Boucher	1845 - 1912 Désiré m. Marie Geneviève Paon	1881 - Victoire m. Françoise Jacques Marmand	1847 - Charles m. Joseph Lavache	1849 - Jacques Laurent m. Marie McCarron PEI	Jean Baptiste. Hubert	
9]	1886 - Berthe	1883 - Marie Eva	1893 - 1956 Josephine m. Alfred Gilbert USA	Peter		1874 - 1950 Jean Baptiste. m. Mabel Girroir à William à Polycarpe Isle Madame	Gilbert m. Lena Lavandier	Alvina (Mina) m. Amédée Thériault	1881 - Victoria (Tory) m. Joe Millard Boudreau	1875 - Hume	1890 - 1890 Laurent
10]	1911 - 1911 Willie Edward Twins then Eva Mae 1908-09 Sophie 1923-1927	Nancy Girroir Sister Superior of the Provincial House at Moncton, NB F.D.J. NB	1905 - 1931 Marie Elizabeth Pétronille m. Alphonse Babin, 1927	1914 - 1989 Marie Eva Mae F.D.J. 1912- William Désiré	1909 - 1992 Pierre Raymond n.m.	1917 - Rev. Conrad Polycarpe Girroir Isle Madame	Rev. Emedée Thomas Girroir	1906 - 1930 Iréné Euclide not married	1902 - 1945 Jean Baptiste Edmond René 1919- Brigitte Annunciata	Sophie m. John Samson	1922 - 1972 Mary Jane Geneviève m. Harry Helin
											Paternal side of Fr. Conrad P. Girroir and other branches Isle Madame, NS Subchart #164 Linking to [AMC Block E-3b]

© *Acadian Awakenings Girouard/Giroir... Routes and Roots*

Acadian Awakenings: An Acadian Family In Exile

	L202	M202	N202	O202	P202	Q202	R202	S202	T202	U202	V202
2]	References: 1. Research of William D. Gerrior, *Acadian Awakenings*, 2002. 2. Interviews, surveys, and correspondence with descendants of the sixth, seventh, eighth and ninth generations.					1656-1693 Germain m. Marie Bourgeois Beaubassin 1680	→ **REFER TO [BLOCK D-2] OF MASTER CHART OF WILLIAM D. GERRIOR** Québec Acadian branches descending from Germain Girouard married at Beaubassin. (Amherst, NS). Generations 2 to 5 were born at Beaubassin.				
3]				1683 - 1687 Agnès	1685 - Agnès m. Abraham Gaudet 1701	1681 - 1760 Germain II m. Jeanne Barriau 1703					
4]		-	1709 - 1750 Charles m. Anne Nuriat 1738 Port Royal Pt. Beauséjour	1693 - 1776 Marguerite m. Joseph Poirier 1748	1700 - Michel* m1. Anne Marie Nuriat 1737 m2. Marie Thibodeau (2119-1) *Placide La Butte (now Amherst area)* Ref: Paul Surette	1712 - 1790 François (Beauséjour) m1. Marie Poirier 1735 m2. Josephe Boudrot 1762 Que.	1727 - Jacques m. Marie (Barrio) Bourgeois B.B. 1748 Ref: (Tanguay) (Moncton Cards)	Marie Joséphte m. Jean Bapt. Thériot 1745 Beaubassin	1719 - 1719 Aldegonde Beaubassin		
5]	1748 - François	Marie-Blanche m. Louis Perot Chateauguay 1762 St-Sulpice	1741 - Marie Modeste m. Paul Benet 1769 Québec (Bona.A. Vol, 3)	1746 - Catherine 1746 - Joseph	1744 - 1757 François Died at early age at Québec	1738 - Joseph m. Anne Des Mouliers 1766 Qué. N.D. Loiselle notes (00180) p.16	Refer to Loiselle notes on the Girouard genealogy at Québec Archives (Université de Laval) and also Placide Gaudets' Genealogy of the Girouards pp. 2178, 2167. Also Marie Blanche [Block N202-5] and her brother Joseph were listed at Beaubassin by Bona Arsenault, Vol. 3. Michel [Block P202-4] is referenced by Paul Surette section 1.4.1 of his book, *Atlas de l'etablissement des Acadians aux trois rivière du Chignectou 1660-1755*				
6]			1767 - Marie-Anne m. _____ Oliver	1769 - Jean Drowned at Bic	1771 - François Drowned off coast of Spain	1767 - 1800 Joseph m. Marie Anne Baillargé	*La Famille Girouard* by Hon. Désiré Girouard. Placide Gaudet p. 2168 and Loiselle notes p. (00179). Joseph was a Navigator, Engineer and an Architect.				
7]			Marie -	1796 - 1835 Angèle	1797 - 1822 Félicité m. Ignace Dumouchel 1820 St-Eustache, PQ	1795 - 1855 Jean-Joseph Louis m1. Marie L. Félix 1818 m2. Marie E. Barthelot	[Block Q202-7], Jean Joseph, Patriot, Ref: *La Famille Girouard* by Hon. Désiré Girouard; Loiselle notes above; information sent by Laurent Girouard of Montréal and direct descendant of Jean Joseph, Jeanne Décarie, Montréal, PQ Jean-Joseph Girouard was a lawyer at St-Benoit. Deputy (Government Representative) for Lac des Deux Montagnes.				
8m2]			Felicité	Perpétue m. Odilon Dacier	1856 - Marie-Jean m. Marrie Lydia Laviolette	1854 - Joseph m. Celanaire Plessis-Belair	Reference to [Block Q202-8m2], Joseph Girouard is found in *La Famille Girouard* by Hon. Désiré Girouard, Loiselle notes, Lawyer at St-Benoit. Also interviews with Jeanne Décarie, great granddaughter of Jean Joseph Girouard, the Patriot, who has supplied much information and documentation during my visit at her home in Montréal.				
9]				Carmélia m. Pierre Louis Dupuis	Jeanne m. Albert Décarie	1886 - Joseph N.L. m. Berthe Marsolais Lawyer St-Benoit	Reference to [Block Q202-9], Jean Joseph is found in *La Famille Girouard*, Hon. Désiré Girouard p. 32. Joseph [Block Q207-8M2] was also Federal Representative for Lac des Deux Montagnes (MP). Jean [Block P202-8m2] was Dr. and Federal Senator in Longueuil, PQ				Québec Acadian Branch Linking to Subchart #202 [AMC Block D-2]

© *Acadian Awakenings Girouard/Giroir... Routes and Roots*

Appendices

	L204	M204	N204	O204	P204	Q204	R204	S204	T204	U204	V204
3]		References: 1. Research of William D. Gerrior, *Acadian Awakenings*, 2002. 2. *Acadians in Exile*. p. 157 by Rev. Donald Hébert. Louis Girouard and Marie Josephe Blanchard also have the following children: Pierre 1751, François 1748; Jean Baptiste 1741, Isabelle 1739, Amand 1736, Anne 1733, and Jean-Charles 1743 m. Anne Ouvrey 1772, Montréal, N.D. (Loiselle notes). Descendants of this branch are found in County of Montcalm and Assumption, Québec, according to Mgr. J.A. Richard, former Curé of Verdun, near Montréal.				1670 - 1744 Alexandre Sieur de Ru m. Marie Le Borgne ca. 1694	→ REFER TO [BLOCK C-3A] OF THE MASTER CHART OF WILLIAM D. GERRIOR. This family lived at Port Royal up to the fourth generation beginning with François Girouard and Jeanne Aucoin on the master chart.				
4]	1708 - Angélique	1709 - 1767 Jeanne* m. François Forest Dep. to Conn. then at PQ P.R.	1721 - Cécile m. Louis Dugas 1740 P.R.	1716 - Marie Josèphte m1. Louis Dugas 1734 m2. Thomas Jeanson ,1742 New Eng. 1742 P.R.	1697 - 1703 Bernard 1707 - 1720 Marie-Anne	1718 - 1783 Pierre m. Jeanne Martin P.R. 1743 Deported to Philadelphia	1705 - Louis m. Marie Josèphe Blanchard N.Y. 1763 Campfiore, Martinique 1766 W. Indies P.R. 1727	1693 - Marie* m. Jean Mouton 1711 Surgeon at Beaubassin P.R.	1700 - Madeleine m. Charles Blanchard 1718 at P.R. P.R. Conn. PQ 1768	1696 - Alexandre	1713 - 1757 Marguerite m. Alexandre Guilbault 1734 Qué
5]		1 Charles	1757 - Charles Deported to Phil, USA	1750 - Josèphe Marie m. Simon Joseph Castille 1783 St-Domingue, Môle, St-Nicolas, French West Indies *Ref: Acadians in Exile* p. 157 by Rev. Hébert	1744 - Nathalie m. Jean-Baptiste Byjeu Deported to Phil, USA (Ref: Bona Arsenault p. 576 P.R. Volume)	1752 - Félicité m1. Nicolas Demars m2. J. Baptiste Baritou 1786 St-Domingue: Môle, St-Nicolas French West Indies *Acadians in Exile* p. 156	Notes: 1. Felicité [Block Q204-5]. This family was deported to Philadelphia, 1755, (Bona Arsenault). The family was from Port Royal (1701 Census P.R. and Placide Gaudet p. 2149. The second marriage was celebrated in Bordeaux (St-Domingue: Môle, St-Nicolas, French West Indies) (Ref: *Acadians in Exile* by Rev. Donald Hébert p. 157). 2. Josèphe Girouard [Block O204-5] is referenced in *Acadians in Exile* as daughter of Pierre Girouard and Jean Martin on p. 157. 3. Louis Girouard m. Marie Josèphe Blanchard [Block R204-4], uncle of Felicité, also has a daughter Josèphe m1. Germain Gaudet and m2. Christophe Alexis Dumont 1770 at Martinique: St-Pierre of the French West Indies Islands.				
										West Indies **Acadian Girouard Branch** **Subchart #204** **Linking to** **[AMC Block C-3A]**	

© *Acadian Awakenings Girouard/Giroir... Routes and Roots*

	L207	M207	N207	O207	P207	Q207	R207	S207	T207	U207	V207
3]			Research of William D. Gerrior, *Acadian Awakenings*, 2002. Note: Joseph [Block Q207-4] has a cousin Pierre m. Théotiste Dupuis (see Chart #208), but Placide does not give a brother Pierre as referenced in [Block T207-4]. For the moment I will present them as brothers, with references given in [Block T207-4]. Future research is needed to confirm.			1684 - 1738 Claude m. Elisabeth Blanchard 1709 St-Ours	→ **REFER TO [BLOCK I-3A] OF MASTER CHART OF WILLIAM D. GERRIOR.** Québec Acadian branches descending from Claude Girouard. Generations 1 to 5 beginning with François of master chart lived at Port Royal.				
4]			Note: Joseph Girouard and Natalie Leblanc appear on list of Acadians sent to New England, namely Boston Massachusetts 1763. *(ref: Pac, Ottawa)*	Guillaume P.R.	1714 - 1735 Madeleine m. Alexandre Hébert 2197 Placide P.R.	1717 - 1776 Joseph m1. Rosalie Hébert P.R. 1742 m2. Anastasie (Natalie) LeBlanc St. Ours P.R. 1748	1720 François P.R.	1710 Marie Josèphe m1. Charles Landry 1730 m2. Zacharie Thibodeau P.R.	Pierre P.R. accord. to book Ref: St-Denis sur Richelieu 1740 - 1767, Chapter 12		
5m1]					1743 - 1743 Joseph P.R.	↔					
5m2]	1750 - Anne *Ref: p. 188 Acadian Exiles in the Colonies (Janet Jehn)*		Elizabeth m. Francis Duhamel 1787 *(Ref: Bergeron Notes)*	1747 Marie Modeste *Ref: 2150 Placide Gaudet*	1752 - Joseph	1772 - Joseph m. Véronique Hamelin 1796 St-Denis, PQ *Ref: 00179 (Louiselle notes)*	1763 - Jean Baptiste m. Agatha Allaire 1784 *Ref: 00179 (Louiselle notes)* St-Ours, PQ	1769 - Pierre m. Charlotte Duhamel *Ref: 00181 (Louiselle notes)* Grandson in Nashua, N.H.	1754 - Madeleine m. Pierre Sansoucy *Ref: 2150 (Placide Gaudet)* St-Ours, PQ	1756 - Marguerite m. François Gazaille St-Germain 1775	
6]				Edouard m. Josette Comeau 1826 *Ref: 00180 p. 12 (Louiselle Notes)*	Flavien m. Henriette Dupré 1847 *Ref: 00181 p. 19 (Louiselle Notes)* St-Ours, PQ	Moise m. Sophie Comeau 1832 *p. 12, p. 27 (Louiselle Notes)* St-Ours, PQ	Joseph m1. Céleste Laflame 1839 m2. Marie St-Laurent 1841 *Ref: 00182 (Louiselle Notes)* St-Ours, PQ	Jean Baptiste m. Josette Pichette 1823 *Ref: 00133, p. 4 (Louiselle Notes)* St-Ours, PQ			
7]				Paul-Philibert m. Obeline Hébert 1862 St-Ours, PQ	Joseph m. Philomene Jacob, 1860 St-Ours, PQ	Marcel m. Mathilda Dufault 1858 *Ref: 00181 p. 18 (Louiselle Notes)* St-Ours, PQ	Francois m. Adeline Girouard à (Joe & Manuerite Daigle) 1856 St. Jude, PQ				

Notes: 1. Joseph [Block Q207-4], was deported to Mass. 1755; in Boston 1763; and in St-Ours, Québec 1767. (Reference: 2141-1; 2141-2; 2116-1; 2150 Placide Gaudet). Later they established as one of the founding families of St-Denis on the Richelieu River, Québec.

2. Anastasie [Block Q207-4] is the same person as Natalie. Ref: 2167 and 2150 Placide. Also Vol. II, p.15 Bergeron, *Le Grand Arrangement Des Acadiens Au Québec*. This reference provides link between Joseph Girouard [Block Q207-4] and Claude Girouard [Block Q207-3].

© *Acadian Awakenings Girouard/Giroir... Routes and Roots*

Québec Acadian Subchart #207 Linking to [AMC Block I-3A]

Appendices

	L211	M211	N211	O211	P211	Q211	R211	S211	T211	U211	V211
3]	Research of William D. Gerrior, *Acadian Awakenings*, 2002. Joseph Girouard (Bistet) [Block R211-4m1] settled in Bouctouche where his daughters are part of the founding families of Bouctouche, New Brunswick (see NB Chapter). Basile's brother-in-law attended Basile's funeral, [Block P211-4m1] in Carolina and transmitted information to his widow, Marie J. Doucet via the priest connections to Petitcodiac NB. She was at Québec in 1757 where her daughter Anastasie died. She remarried in 1760 to Ignace Coustineau. (Ref: *Fichier généalogique du Père Archange Godbout* p. 1340, Québec Archives.)					1689 - 1742 Charles m1. Anne Bastarache m2. Marie J. Pitre P.R. 1744	→ **REFER TO [BLOCK C-3B] OF THE MASTER CHART OF WILLIAM D. GERRIOR.** Charles Girouard [Block S211-4m1] m. Marie M. Thibodeau had a daughter Jeanne m. Joseph Bonnefou (lawyer). (Ref: *Acadians in Exile*, p. 156), and *The Cajuns*, *Essays on their History and Culture* edited by Glenn R. Conrad, pp. 63-64, 70 of Section III, *The Acadians in St. Domingue* by Gabriel Debien. Charles, [Block S211-4m1], had six other children not as yet traced: Anne 1748, Joseph 1753, Charles 1740, Joseph Timothé 1745, Marie-Rose, Marguerite Serephie 1751 (not shown on this chart). Also see *Atlas de l'établissement des Acadiens aux trios rivière du Chignectou (1660-1755)* by Paul Surette.				
4m1]	Note: Children of Charles and m1. Anne Bastarache are in this row.		1723 - Madeleine m. Joseph Comeau 1749 Dep. to South Carolina P.R.	1731 - 1734 Grégoire P.R.	1728 - Basile m. Marie J. Doucet ca 1753 Died at S. Carolina Memramcook Dep. to S. Carolina, P.R.	1726 - François m1. Claire Richard 1745 m2. Catherine Martin 1754 m3. Marguerite Poirier Dep. to South Carolina 1763 P.R. 1754	1720.... - 1804 Joseph Louis* (Bister) m1. Anne Doucet 1743 Beaubassin m2. Jeanne Béliveau, 1763 Bouctouche (Ref: *Placide*) Memramcook Pisiquit (Windsor) NS	1716 - Charles m. Marie Thibodeau 1739 Memramcook P.R	1717 - Marie Josèphe m. Honoré Blanchard 1739 Bhlanccharde Village Memramrcook P.R.	1722 - Anne m. Pierre Pellerin 1745 at P.R. Deported to Mass. 1755 then at Yamachiche, PQ P.R.	
4m2]			1746 - Nathalie on 1763 cens. S.C. P.R.	1745 - Madeleine S.C. 1763 P.R.	1747 - Anselme P.R.	↔	1748 - Grégoire Dep. to S.C. 1763 P.R.	1748 - Bonaventure S.C. 1763 P.R	Note: Children of Charles and m2. Marie J. Pitre are in this row.	Note: Children of Charles and m2. Marie J. Pitre are in this row.	
5]				1748 - François No more trace of François to date	1751 - Anne	1746 - 1785 Joseph Amable (Carpenter) m1. Mad. Poirier m2. Marie Hosmin 1780 m3. Marie Eve Hofman 1785 West Indies St-Domingue, Môle St-Nicolas	Notes: References for Joseph Amable Giroir and his children as well as the link to this branch are found in *Acadians in Exile* by Rev. Donald J. Hébert, p. 57 which shows records confirming Joseph m. Madeleine Poirier is son of François and Claire Richard. From here the connections to Charles Girouard [Block C-3b] of the master chart are given by Placide Gaudet pp. 2130, 2151, 2153, 2183 and Bona Arsenault's genealogy of the Girouards. Joseph had two other 1/2 sisters from his father François and m2. Catherine Martin. These children were: Marie b. 1754 and Modest b. 1754 (not shown on this chart). Reference to Nathalie, Gregoire and Bonaventure is given in list of Acadians in South Carolina 1763, PAC Ottawa. MG.5, Vol. 451, pp. 77-79.				West Indies ACADIAN GIROUARD GIROIR BRANCH Subchart #211 Linking to [AMC Block C-3b]
6]				Joseph - 1778	1785 Angélique Jeanne Joseph West Indies St-Domingue Môle St-Nicolas	1781 Joseph Mathieu West Indies St-Domingue Môle St-Nicolas	1783 - 1783 Jean Baptiste West Indies St-Domingue Môle St-Nicolas (Died at 29 days old)				

© *Acadian Awakenings Girouard/Giroir... Routes and Roots*

	L208	M208	N208	O208	P208	Q208	R208	S208	T208	U208	V208
3]	Notes: 1. Madeleine Girouard and Michel Martin [Block O 208-4] are named on the Acadian sworn statements at Belle Isle en Mer, France. 2. Pierre [Block Q208-4] was at Lotbinière, Québec, 1762, according to Bona Arsenault, then at St-Ours, 1767. 3. Joseph [Block R208-5] was at Richibouctou, NB after deportation. 4. Louise Girard appears twice on charts - they are two different persons. 5. Marie [Block O 208-4], died at St. Pierre. NF. She was at Kinsale in Ireland, 1765. 6. Interviews, surveys, and correspondence with descendants of the 9th generation. 7. For third and fourth generation, also refer to Atlas de l'établissement des Acadiens aux trois rivières du Chignectou 1660-1755 by Paul Surette: For Marguerite, [Block N208-4] see sec 3.1 of his book; Anne [Block T208-4], sec. 3.1; Guillaume [Q208-3] à Francois, sec 3.1.; François [AMC Block F-3] à Jacques, sec 3.1; Guillaume à Guillaume [Block P208-4], sec.3.44; Pierre [AMC C-4m1] à Francois, sec.3.4); Françoise [Block R208-4] sec.3.2; Charles [Block R211-4m1 of subchart 211] see sec.3.1; Joseph (Bistet) Girouard [Block R211-4m1 of subchart 211] see 3.1. 8. Research of William D. Gerrior, Acadian Awakenings, 2002.					1686 - 1757 Guillaume m. Marie Bernard 1713 called Renochet P.R.	→REFER TO [BLOCK J-3A] OF MASTER CHART OF WILLIAM D. GERRIOR. Québec Acadian branches descending from Guillaume (William) Girouard. Some branches establishing in Rhode Island, USA. Notes: 1. Louis Girouard [Block Q208-8] lived on "Girouard St." in Manville, Smithfield, Rhode Island. 2. Joseph Arthur Girouard was instrumental in building churches and was knighted by the Pope. He taught at Louis Pasteur Institute in Paris. More detail in text.			
4]	1752 - Marie		Marguerite m. Jean Bapt. Blanchard 1743 (Ref: Bergeron Moncton cards) Memramcook	1714 - 1765 Marie Madeleine m1. Michel Martin 1739 m2. Michel Aubois 1754 P. R. Statements Belle-Isle-En-Mer	1721 - 1763 Guillaume m. Anne Blanchard 1745 P.R. according to sworn Statement Belle-Isle-en-Mer (Ref: Bergeron Moncton cards) Memramcook St-Croix de Lotbenière, PQ	1726 - Pierre m. Théotiste Dupuis 1751 P.R. according to sworn Statement at Belle-Isle-en-Mer Memramcook St-Ours, PQ	1724 - 1803 Françoise m. Jean-Baptiste (Jan) Richard, 1745 P.R. according to sworn Statement Belle-Isle-en-Mer Memramcook, Richibouctou, NB	1729 - Anne* m. Justinien Dupuis 1751 P.R. according to sworn Statement at Belle-Isle-en-Mer Memramcook	1716 - Anne* m. Joseph Richard 1758 Memramcook St. Servan France 1758		
5]	1771 Isabelle m. Joseph Gariépy 1793 St-Ours, PQ		Pierre* m. Scholastique Leblanc	1771 - Elizabeth	1769 - 1791 Joseph* m1. Josephte Lord 1791 m2. Marie J. Dupuis Degure 1836 Ref: 00181 St-Ours, PQ	1760 - Jean Baptiste m. Marie Angélique Blouin 1780 St-Ours, PQ		1767 - Marie Modeste m. Louis Duhamel 1788 St-Ours, PQ	1774 - Marie Josephine m. Grégoire Valentin 1795 St-Ours, PQ		
6]			Marie m. Archange C. Payon (Ref: Bergeron) St-Onge, PQ	Eugène m. Emilie Brault 1860 St-Ours, PQ	Charlotte m. André Payan 1891 (Ref: Bergeron) St-Onge, PQ	1784 - Pierre Augustin m. Archange Dufault 1804-1810 Loiselle Notes	Angélique m. François Maurier Lapierre 1802 (Ref: Bergeron) St-Ours, PQ	Thérèse m. J. Chapdelaine 1806 (Ref: Loiselle and Bergeron)			
7]	Geneviève m. Isidore Gravel 1843 (Ref: Bergeron) St-Ours, PQ		Pierre m. Louise Girard 1835 (Ref: 00181) St-Ours, PQ	Joseph* m. Marie Duhamel 1839 (Ref: 00181) St-Ours, PQ	Augustin* m. Delima Bonier 1884 St-Jude, PQ	1818 - François Xavier m1. Marie Louise Girard 1843 m2. Archange Deblois 1858	Jean Baptiste* m. Julienne Sansoucy 1849 St-Ours, PQ	Marie Josephite m. Alex Gerrard 1835 (Ref: Bergeron) St-Ours, PQ	Rosalie m. Charles Larrivère 1846 (Ref: Bergeron, Loiselle notes) St-Ours, PQ	Angélique m. Augustin Blanchet 1830 St-Ours, PQ	

Appendices

					1844 - Louis m. Hermine Cormier 1867 St-Ours, PQ Manville Rhode Island, USA	1883 - Pierre Napoléon	1884 - Joseph Léonidas	1879 - 1985 Adelina	
8]									
9a]	1873 - Anne Isabelle	1872 - Joseph Albert	1870 - Hermine (Marie Alix)	1869 - Mary Louise	1868 - François Louis	1875 - 1953 Joseph Arthur M.D. m. Wavine Brazeau Willimantic, RI Conn. also Manville, RI		Manville, R.I.	
		Manville, RI		Warwick (West) RI					
9b]				1809 - Bernadette	1886 - Georges Rodolphe Manville, RI	↔	1876 - Angélina		
10]				André -	1903 - 1990 Theresa m. Charles Martin	Fernand Louis - 1980 M.D. m. Anita Attleboro Providence, RI	1901 - Gertrude		
							Willimantic Connecticut		
11]					Laurice -	1941 - 1982 Robert (Bo) Louis m. Nancy Howe	Denise m. Daniel J. Wall		
					Plainville, Mass. USA		Providence, RI		
12]						Mark -	Robert Northfield		Québec: Acadian Branch, some descendants in R.I. Subchart #208 Linking to [AMC Block J-4A]
						Minnesota, USA	Minnesota, USA		

References:
1. *Le Grand Arrangement des Acadiens au Québec*, Vol. IV., 1625-1925, Adrien Bergeron, s.s.s.
2. Letters from descendant Denise Wall.
3. *La Famille Girouard* by Désiré Girouard.
4. Placide Gaudet Girouard Genealogy: pp. 2123, 2142-1, 2152, 2155, 2180 Lotbinière, Québec.

©*Acadian Awakenings Girouard/Giroir... Routes and Roots*

	L213	M213	N213	O213	P213	Q213	R213	S213	T213	U213	V213
3]	Reference: Research of William D. Gerrior, *Acadian Awakenings*, 2002. Notes: 1. Marie Josèphe [Block L213-4] died at St-Antoine-sur-Richelieu (parish records). 2. Anne [Block M213-4] was at Fort Beauséjour, 1763 and at Miquelon, 1767 (census records). 3. Michel [Block N213-4] is the son of Germain Girouard and Marie Doucet according to Placide Gaudet. He died at Gentilly, PQ (parish records). 4. Claude [Block O 213-4] died at St-Antoine-sur-Richelieu (parish records). 5. Jacques [Block P213-4] died at St-Antoine-sur-Richelieu (parish records).					1691 - Germain II m. Marie Doucet 1711 Beaubassin L'Islet, PQ	→ **REFER TO [BLOCK D-3B] OF MASTER CHART OF WILLIAM D. GERRIOR.** Québec Acadian branches descending from Germain II Girouard of Port Royal, son of Jacques Girouard and Marguerite Gauterot. Germain II married at Beaubassin. All of the fourth generation were also born at Beaubassin. François [Block Q213-5m2] had one son, Pierre via m2. Amable Raicot,1842				
4]	1734 - 1814 Marie Josèphe m1. Michel m2. Joseph Theriault 1754 St-Antoine sur Richelieu	1721 - Anne m. Pierre Gaudet 1740 Beaubassin, N.B. La Rochelle, and Nantes, France. *(Ref: Notes of Gaston Giroir, Fr.)*	1723 - 1797 Michel* m. Marguerite Haché 1744 According to Placide P. 2129-1 at Viskak, in Beaubassin (near Tintamarre)	1727 - 1816 Claude* m. Marie Bernard 1759 in exile Refugees at Saint-Antoine Chambly, PQ	1727 - 1767 Joseph m. Agnès Gaudet 1750 b. Beaubassin St-Antoine sur Richelieu	ca.1711- 1760 Germain III m1. Marie Arseneau 1733 m2. Maguerite Henry-Robert 1763 Notre Dame church records Beaubassin St-Hyacinthe, PQ	1719 - 1763 Pierre* m. Marguerite Gaudet, 1740 b. Beaubassin PEI Miquelon 1767 Deported to France d. 1763	1733 - 1813 Jacques* m1. Marie Bourgeois m2. Françoise Gaudet 1788 b. Beaubassin *(Ref: 00181)* p. 19 St-Antoine Verchères, PQ	1713 - 1757 Marie Madeleine Gaudet at Beaubassin 1734 b. Beaugassin PQ, 1757	ca 1735 - Marguerite m. Claude Poirier ca 1754 b. Port Royal *(Ref. Stephen White)*	
5m1]	1755 - Madeleine Marie m. Germain Jacques Pisiquid Cap Ignace, PQ	1755 - Marie Françoise m. Charles François Cloutier L'Islet, PQ	1755 - Jacques	1742 - 1757 Rosalie	1734 - Marie Josèphe m. Louis Bernier *(Ref: Bona A.)* Cap St-Ignace Pisiquit Windsor	↔	1748 - Victor m1. Etienne Brasseau 1797 m2. Françoise Archambault *(Ref: Moncton Cards)*	1741 - Pierre m1. Louise Fournier m2. Ann Gamaché Pisiquid Cap St-Ignace, PQ 1763	1744 - Marie-Ann m. Benjamin Dupont 1778 *(Ref: Bergeron genealogy notes)* Cap St-Ignace, PQ	Note: Marie-Josephe, [Block P213-5m1] and her brother Pierre, [Block S213-5m1] were both at Pisiquit (Windsor, NS) *(Ref: Bona Arseneau)*	
5m2]		Joseph * m. Angélique-Charlotte St. Michel Circé, 1793 *(Ref. 00138 p. 45)* St-Hyc., PQ	1765 - Théotiste Romaine m1. J.B. Blanchette 1792 m2. Louise Dusseau St-Hyc., PQ	Charles Amable	Victor m. Marg. Lacoste 1795 dit Languedoc *(Ref: Loiselle Notes)* St-Antoine Verchères, PQ	1769* - François* m1. Marguertie Tétreau 1791 at Beloeil, PQ m2. Amable Raicot 1842 St-Antoine de Chambly	1773 - Marguerite m. Jos Dodelin 1791 St-Hyc. PQ St-Denis sur Richelieu	1785 - Alexis m. Charlotte Sanschagrin 1809 *(Ref: 00183 p. 45)* La Présentation St-Hyc. PQ	M.J. Girouard* m. Joseph Rivet 1797 at St. Hyacinthe, PQ (Notre Dame)		
6]						Jacques m1. Charlotte Guillaume 1811 m2. Josèphine Loyer 1842 St-Hyc, PQ m3. Marg Deschamps 1873	Pierre* m. Marguerite Fontaine 1847 *(Ref: Loiselle Notes 00181 p. 22)* St-Pie, PQ	Marie m. Pierre Guillaume 1834 St. Hyacinthe, PQ			
				François* m1. Angélique Terreau 1838 *(Ref. 00184 p. 47)* N.D. St-Hyc., PQ	Marguerite Giroire m. J.B. Jetro 1820						

Appendices

		Clémentine m. Jean Baptiste Loiseau 1849 St-Pie de Bagot, PQ	Joséphe m. Joseph Martin 1858 St-Pie de Bagot, PQ	↔	Pierre* m. Natalie Decelles Duclos 1856 (Ref. 001808 p. 15) N.D. St-Hyc., PQ	1857 Joseph* m. Emérence Goyer		
7m1]								
7m2]				Timothée m. Adéline Brodeur 1868 (Ref. Moncton Cards) St-Pie de Bagot, PQ	Marie m. Louis Petit 1867 (Ref. Moncton Cards) St-Pie de Bagot, PQ			
			Zoé m. Vincent Meralis 1875 (Ref. Moncton Cards) St-Pie de Bagot, PQ	Ovila m1. Aurore Fontaine 1897 m2. Alphonse Pépin	Dina m. Hermas Marjan 1888			
8]	References: 1. Fourth generation references are combined from Edward Lavin Gerrior and Placide Gaudet's genealogy (pp. 2119-1, 2116-1, 2181, 2129; Bergeron p. 15. 2. *Le Grand Arrangement Des Acadiens Au Québec*, Vol. IV p. 15 by Adrien Bergeron gives an important link of Jacques Girouard [Block S213-4] and Françoise Gaudet to Germain and Marie Doucet. Also marriage of Françoise to Jacques given by 1989 survey form of Pierre Girouard, St-Hyacinthe, PQ. 3. [Block Q213-5m2], François, m. Marguerite Tetreau is given by Richard St-Marie, married to Pierrette Girouard whom I met in Montreal at the Maritime Hotel where we spent the evening discussing genealogy of Girouards. 4. (M213-4) Anne and (R213-4) Pierre, are referenced in correspondence from Gaston Giroir in France. 5. (M3) reference for [Block Q213-6] is given in Loiselle Notes 001808 p. 15. 6. [Block Q213-6] is given by Loiselle Notes 00182 p. 43, 00182 p. 33 and 00181 p. 22. 7. Link between [Block Q213-5M2] and Block (Q213-4) is given by genealogy chart of direct line of Pierrette Girouard m. to Richard St-Marie of Dorval, Montréal, PQ. 8. Generation #6 *(Reference Moncton Cards)*. 9. Generation #5 is found in Notre Dame de. St. Hyacinthe, PQ church records (as indicated in the blocks of this subchart).						Québec Acadian Branch Subchart #213 Linking to [AMC Block D-3b] PQ	

©*Acadian Awakenings Girouard/Giroir... Routes and Roots*

433

	L217	M217	N217	O217	P217	Q217	R217	S217	T217	U217	V217
3]	References: 1. Research of William D. Gerrior, *Acadian Awakenings*, 2002. 2. Interviews, surveys, correspondence with descendants. Notes: 1. Anne [Block M217-4] was at Fort Beauséjour, 1763 and Miquelon, 1767. 2. Michel [Block O217-4] died at Gentilly, PQ (parish records). 3. Claude [Block O217-4] died at St-Antoine-sur-Richlieu (parish records). 4. Jacques [Block S217-4] died at St-Antoine-sur-Richelieu (parish records).					1691 - 1760 Germain II m. Marie Doucet 1711 Beaubassin	→ REFER TO [BLOCK D-3B] OF THE MASTER CHART OF WILLIAM D. GERRIOR. Notes: 1. Québec Acadian branches descending from Germain II 2. Some genealogists hold that Michel Girouard is son of François, but we have not seen any primary documentation to this claim. The belief in Germain as the father of Michel is based on Placide Gaudet's notes (p. 2129-1) of Girouard genealogy and the close proximity of families of Germain and Michel near Viskak and Tintamarre in Beaubassin (Amherst, NS/NB border area). This is the present position held by genealogist Stephen White, Centre d'études acadiennes, Université de Moncton, NB. 3. Michel [Block Q217-4] d. at Gentilly April 22, 1797 at age 74. He was one of the first Acadian families to establish at Becancours, around 1759. References: 1. Reference number of five digits beginning with "00" are from Loiselle notes, Québec National Archives. 2. Joseph II appears at Bécancour Stanfold, Gentilly. 3. Joseph III also shown as (Dede) appearing at Stanfold. 4. [Block M217-6m2], from survey form of André Girouard Gentilly 1828. 5. Block N217-6m2] Loiselle notes 00182, Gentilly, 1845 6. Block R217-6m2] first marriage at St-Pierre Les Becquets, PQ m2 - Loiselle Notes 00184 p. 47. 7. Block Q217-7] m2 at Plessisville, Loiselle notes 00182. 8. Block M217-6m1] Moncton genealogical cards. 9. Block O217-6m1] Québec. 10. Block R217-6m1] Loiselle notes P00183. 11. Loiselle notes (Gentilly records 1784-1914) at Québec National Archives, Université de Laval p. 39. 12. Placide Gaudet Genealogy on the Girouards pp. 2133, 2178 at Beaubassin at Bécancourt. 13. *La Famille Girouard* pp. 37, 38, Désiré Girouard. 14. *Le Grand Arrangement Des Acadiens Au Québec*, by Bergeron. 15. Information and correspondence with Désirée and Esmé Girouard, Ottawa, Ontario.			
4]	1734 - 1814 Marie Josephe m. Michel Gaudet St-Antoine sur Richelieu	1721 - Anne m. Pierre Gaudet 1740 (Ref: Gaston Girour) Beaubassin, NB La Rochelle and Nantes, FR.	1711 - Germain III m1. Marie Arseneau 1733 m2. M. Henry 1763 St-Hyacinthe PQ	1727 - 1816 Claude* m. Marie Bernard 1759 in exile Refugees at Saint-Antoine Chambly, PQ	1727 - 1767 Joseph m. Agnès Gaudet 1750 St-Antoine sur Richelieu where he (d).	1723 - 1797 Michel m. Marguerite Haché Gallant 1744 Died at Gentilly, PQ Beaubassin	1719 - 1763 Pierre* m. Marguerite Gaudet 1740 PEI Miquelon 1767 Dep. to France	1733 - 1813 Jacques* m1. Marie Bourgeois m2. Françoise Gaudet 1788 (Ref: 00181) Beaubassin St-Antoine Vercheres, PQ	1713 - 1813 Marie Madeleine m. Claude Gaudet 1757 PQ	Marguerite m. Pierre Poirier (Ref. Stephen White)	
5]				1749 - 1803 Marguerite	1751 - Rosalie* m. Pierre Chesney Chêné, 1767 Champlain	1750 Joseph I m1. Marie J. Grandbois 1777 m2. Josephte Deslauriers Normandeau 1780 Gentilly	1754 - 1757 Pierre				
6m1]		Rosalie - m. Pierre Chenet (Ref: Moncton Cards)	1780 - Marie m. Jean Baptiste Jeannotte 1804 Gentilly, PQ	1782 - Agatha m. Joseph Genest 1809 (Ref: Moncton Cards) Gentilly, PQ	1781 - Marguerite m1. Gabriel Durand 1801 m2. Joseph Crétien 1817 m3. Vital Bélanger	1778 - Joseph II m. Marie Doucet 1799 Bécancour	1786 - Urban m. Josephte Rivard 1809 Gentilly, PQ				

434

Appendices

6m2]	1790 - Marie-Joseph m. Alexis Turcotte 1812	1803 - Edouard* m. Angélique Lavigueur 1828	1797 - Ambroise* m. Pélagie Lavigueur 1820 m2. Charlotte Lavigueur 1845	Julien* m1. Marguerite Laliberté 1835 m2. Therese Lemay 1885	Gregoire - m. Geneviève Baril 1822	↔	1805 - Isidore* m1. Thérèse Trottier 1826 m2. Carnigan Julie Duclos	1796 - Julie m. Hyacinthe Durand 1816	Adélaïde m. Alexis Bernard 1832	1808 - Geneviève m1. Pierre Laroche 1829 m2. David Fournier 1855 Gentilly, PQ	1794 - Pierre 1813 - 1815 Eugenie 1802 - 1802 child not named
	Gentilly, PQ	Gentilly, PQ	Gentilly, PQ	Gentilly, PQ	Gentilly, PQ			Gentilly, PQ	Gentilly, PQ		
7]			Joseph Marie m. Reine Panneton 1834 Gentilly, PQ	Victor* m1. Caroline Desrochers 1847 m2. Elenor	Edouard* m. Marg. Beaudet 1835 Gentilly, PQ	1802 - 1876 Joseph III m1. Emilie Descormier m2. Mathilde Beaubien	Urbain m. Rosalie Beaufort 1836 Gentilly, PQ	Marie-des-Anges m. Alexis-Hyacinthe Rhéault 1823			
8]		Gertrude (soeur) Ste-Gertrude des Ursulines	Joseph m. Elizabeth Desrocher 1865 Princeville,PQ	Léonise m. Honoré Hébert Princeville, PQ.	Hermine* Emile m. Antoine Gagnon	1826 - 1897 Théophile m. Alexina Pacaud, 1861 Arthabaska, PQ	1824 - 1907 Luc went to Vernon, BC				
9]		Twins	Eva (d)	Marie-Louise Girouard (n.m.)	Amélie m. Sydney Forest*	1882 - 1941 René de la Bruère m. Katherine Grant Perth, ON.	1865 - Raoul* m. Maud Patterson (n.c.) Princeville, PQ.	Aline m. T.E. Griffith* Arthabaska, PQ.			
10]					1910 - Désirée (n.m.) Ottawa, ON	1911 - René Pierre Boucher m. Edith Macneill Smith Falls, ON	1916 - Esmé (n.m.) Ottawa, ON			Québec Acadian Branch Subchart #217 Linking to [AMC Block D-3b]	

© *Acadian Awakenings Girouard/Giroir... Routes and Roots*

	L218	M218	N218	O218	P218	Q218	R218	S218	T218	U218	V218
3]	References: 1. *Le Grand Arrangement Des Acadiens Au Québec*, by Bergeron. 2. *La Famille Girouard*, by Désiré Girouard p. 35. 3. Moncton Genealogy cards submitted to me by Dr. Edgar Girouard of Moncton, regarding some Québec branches. 4. Research of William D. Gerrior, *Acadian Awakenings*, 2002. 5. Interviews, surveys, and correspondence with descendants of the sixth, seventh, eighth and ninth and tenth generations. 6. Marie Josèphe [Block L213-4] died at St-Antoine-sur-Richelieu (parish register) 7. Anne [Block M213-4] was at Fort Beauéjour, 1763 and at Miquelon, 1767 (census records). 8. Michel [Block N213-4], is son of Germain and Marie Doucet, according to Placide Gaudet. He died at Gentilly, PQ(parish records). 9. Jacques [Block S213-4] died at St-Antoine-sur-Richelieu (parish records).					1691 - 1760 Germain II Marie Doucet 1711 Beaubassin	→REFER TO [BLOCK D-3B] OF MASTER CHART OF WILLIAM D. GERRIOR Notes: 1. Québec Acadian branches descending from Germain II 2. Some genealogists hold that Michel Girouard is son of François, but we have not seen any primary documentation to this claim. The belief in Germain as the father of Michel is based on Placide Gaudet's notes (p. 2129-1) of Girouard genealogy and the close proximity of families of Germain and Michel near Viskak and Tintamarre in Beaubassin (Amherst, NS/NB border area). This is the present position held by genealogist Stephen White, Centre d'études acadiennes, Université de Moncton, NB. Joseph Era [Block Q218-8] was a Lawyer, Mayor of Drummondville, PQ and Member of Legislative Assembly of Québec, also a close colleague and personal friend of Prime Minister Wilfrid Laurier (see text). 3. For information on row 6m2 see subchart #217, row 6m2 and related genealogical block information.				
4]	1734 - 1814 Marie Josèphe m. Michel Gaudet 1750 St-Antoine sur Richelieu	1721 - Anne m. Pierre Gaudet 1740 (Ref: Notes of Gaston Giroir, Fr.) Beaubassin La Rochelle, and Nantes, France.	1711 - 1760 Germain III m1. Marie Arseneau 1733 m2. Marguerite Henry, 1763 Beaubassin St-Hyacinthe, PQ	1727 - 1816 Claude* m. Marie Bernard 1759 In exile, Refugees at Saint-Antoine, Chambly, PQ	1727 - 1767 Joseph m. Agnès Gaudet 1767 St-Antoine- sur-Richelieu	1723 - 1797 Michel m. Marguerite Haché Gallant 1745 Gentilly, PQ	1719 - 1763 Pierre* m. Marguerite Gaudet 1740 PEI Miquelon 1767	1733 - 1813 Jacques* m1. Marie Bourgeois m2. Françoise Gaudet 1788 (Ref: 00181) p. 19 Beaubassin St-Antoine Verchères, PQ	1713 - 1757 Marie Madeleine m. Claude Gaudet PQ, 1757	Marguerite m. Pierre Poirier ca. 1754 (Ref: Stephen White)	
5]				1749 - 1759 Marguerite	1751 - Rosalie m. Pierre Chainé	1750 - Joseph I m1. Marie Grandbois 1777 Bécancourt m2. J. Normandeau	1754 - 1757 Pierre				
6m1]				1780 - Marie m. J. Bapt. Jeannot 1804 (Ref: Bergeron) Gentilly, PQ	Marguerite m1. Gabriel Durand Gabriel m2. J. Crétien m3. Vital Bélanger (Ref: Bergeron)	1778 - Joseph II m. Marie Doucet 1799 Bécancour Stanfold	1786 - 1879 Urbain m. Josephine L Rivard 1809 (Ref: 00183) Gentilly, PQ	1782 - Agatha m. Joseph Genest 1809 (Ref: Bergeron Notes) Gentilly, PQ			

Appendices

6m2]	1790 - Marie Josephe m. Alexis Turcotte 1812	1803 - Edouard m. Angeline Lavigueur (Ref: 00182 Loiselle) Survey form of André Girouard pf Broussard, PQ Gentilly, PQ	1797 - Ambroise m1. Pélagie Lavigueur m2. Charlotte Langevin 1845 Gentilly, PQ	Julien m1. Marguerite La Liberté 1835 m2. Thérèse Lemay 1885 Gentilly, PQ	Grégoire m. Geneviève Baril 1822 Gentilly, PQ	↔	1805 - Isidore m1. Thérésa Trottier 1826 m2. Cart. Jul. Duclos St- Pierre Les Becquets m3. M. Poisson 1850 Gentilly, PQ	1796 - Julie m. Hyacinthe Durand 1816 (Ref: Bergeron notes) Gentilly, PQ	Adélaide m. Alexis Bernard (Ref: Bergeron notes)	1808 - Geneviève m. Pierre La Roche 1824 m2. David Fournier 1885 Gentilly, PQ	1794- Pierre
7]		1822 - Charles	1803 - François m. Reine Panneton at Gentilly, PQ,PQ1834	1820 - Victor m1. Caroline Houle 1847 m2. Eleanor Pellitier (Ref: 00182)	1807 - Edouard m. Marguerite Beaudet 1835 (Ref: Louiselle notes)	Urbain m. Rosalie Beaufort (Brunelle) 1836 (Ref: Moncton Cards) Gentilly, PQ Princeville	1802 - Joseph (Dédé) III m1. Emilie Descormier Guillaume 1824 (Ref: 00182 Louiselle notes) Gentilly, PQ, Stanfold, PQ	1805 - 1880 Marie-Des- Anges m. Alexis- Hyacinthe Rheault 1823 Gentilly, PQ	1807 - 1826 Alexis		
8]	1837 - 1837 Luc	1849 - 1883 Elizabeth (Elisa) m. J. Theodore- Agnée Mailhot 1846	M. Félonise m1. Edward Barthell 1879 m2. Philas Sylvain 1906 m3. Narcisse Blais 1927 Princeville,PQ	1839 - Emeline m. Modeste Poisson 1858 (Ref: Bergeron) Princeville, PQ	Adolphe m. Jane Bettez 1876 (Ref. Bergeron) Princeville,PQ	1855 - 1937 Joseph Éna m. Marie Watkins Thetford Mines, Lawyer at Legislative Assemembly,PQ (1896-1889)	1846 - Victor m1. Mélina Auger 1873 m2. Nathalie Daigle 1890 Plessisville,PQ Mégantic,PQ	1841 - Julien m. Adolfe Lecompte 1864 Princeville,PQ Arthabaska,PQ	1848 - Caroline	1838 - 1838 Marie- Adeline	
9]	Gentilly, PQ		1884 - Annette m. Rosario Genest	Louise	1891 - 1980 Wilfred m. Thérésa Marcel 1923 Arthabaska,PQ 1923 Député	1883 - Joseph Arthur R. m. Lucienne Roberge 1912 Thetford Mines,PQ	1885 - Henri Harvey m. Caroline Talbot 1908 Princeville,PQ	1889 - Honoré (Élise) Rasmissen 1921 Drummondville, PQ	Gentilly, PQ	Gentilly, PQ	
10]						André Girouard Professor at Laurentian University, Sudbury, ON (see survey form of 1989)				Québec Acadian PQ Subchart #218 Linking to [AMC Block D-3b]	

© *Acadian Awakenings Girouard/Giroir... Routes and Roots*

437

	L300	M300	N300	O300	P300	Q300	R300	S300	T300	U300	V300
3b]	References: 1. Genealogy charts and research of William D. Gerrior. NB. 2. Research of Dr. Edgar Girouard, Moncton, *Acadian Awakenings*, 2002. 3. Interviews, surveys, and correspondence with descendants of the eighth and ninth and tenth generations. 4. Stephen White's genealogy of the sixth and seventh generations of Girouards of NB, descending from Paul Gervais à Louis Paul à Pierre Girouard, *Cahiers de la Société Historique Acadienne*, Vol. 25, Nos. 2&3 (généalogie des 37 familles hôtesses des "Retrouvailles 94")						→REFER TO E-3B OF MASTER CHART OF WILLIAM D. GERRIOR. Note: From the master chart we see Pierre had three brothers: Germain [AMC Block I-3b], Guillaume [AMC Block I-3a], and Claude [AMC Block I-3a] whose families established in Québec; and in addition, one uncle, Germain [AMC Block D-2] already established in Québec as well as three nephews: Michel, son of Germain [AMC Block D-3b], Joseph [AMC Block J-4m1] and Pierre [AMC Block C-4m1], all of whom established in Québec. One of his brothers, François, [AMC Block F-3b] has all his descendants established in Tracadie NS (Antigonish and Guysborough County branches). One of Pierre's children from ml. Claude Girouard, [Block P300-4m1], establish shed in Isle Madame having a child Pierre m. to Cécile Detcheverry establishing the Isle Madame and PEI branches. Pierre had another son, Honoré Giroir who was deported to France and later voyaged to Louisiana to join Pierre's grandson Firmin Girouard who was already established in Louisiana as a result of deportation and migrations.	1673 - Pierre m1. Marie Comeau 1697 m2. Marie Doiron 1709, G.P.			
						Isle Madame, M'Ck, NB					
4m1]	Note: Block (R300-4m1) - Jean was witness at marriage of Claude. Marie is 60 years in census of 1752, Grand Pré.			1708 - Etienne G.P. Reg. 1730 Census G.P. 1708, 1709 Grand Pré	1699 - 1768 Claude m. Marie Madeleine Vincent from "Les Mines" at PR., 1726 1752 d. St-Ch de Bellechasse	↕	1698- 1758 Marie m. Jean Trahan. She St-Charles de Bellechasse	1701 - 1719 Pierre	ca 1704 - Anne m. Thomas Doiron 1724 St-Malo, France	1707 - Jacques m. Marie Boisseau 1730 Grand Pré, N.C. Placide Bergeron 2162	
4m2]			1729 - Jean Bapt. m. Madeleine Boudreau (Ref: Emelie Perkison genealogy for marriage info.) Reg. Grand Pré 1729	1723 - Marguerite m. Basile Boudrot, 1743 at G.P. Deported to France (Ref: census Pleudihen 1762) France St-Malo 1772 Nantes 1785 FR	1717 - 1764 Marie Josephe m. Germain Pitre 1736 Pisiquid G.P., West Indies 1764	1716 - Louis Paul m. Marie Madeleine Thibodeau 1736 In Halifax 1763 after deportation. Went to Petitcodiac, N.B. then to Bouctouche, 1789	1710 - Charles Grand Pré Census G.P. 1710	1712 - 1768 Véronique m. Pierre Barillot 1730 at Grand Pré Census G.P. 17.2 d. May 1768 France	1714 - 1785 Honoré m. Marie Thériault 1740 Pisiquid Deported to Eng./France (St-Malo) then sailed to Louisiana 30 years later. (Giroir branches)	1719 - 1803 Magdeleine m. Joseph LeBlanc 1740 G.P. (Ref: Bergeron Census 1752) at 33 years old Carleton Reg. 1803	1732 - Marie m1. Charles Benoit m2. Charles Landry
											Census Pleudihen Fr.
5]		Anne -1739 Théodose	1737 - Marguerite	1739- Anne Théodise m1. Pierre Arsenault m2. Laurent Soly (marriage ref: Emelie Perkison) Campbellton NB	1751 - Charles	1744 - 1838 Paul Gervais m. Madeleine Thériault b. Halifax, 1766 Petitcodiac, NB	1749 -1828 Firmin m. Deported to New England States then migrated to Louisiana "Girouard" branches Louisiana	1745 - 1834 Marie Josephe m1. Michel Duguay 1711 m2. Charles Forest	1761- Louis Restigouche NB		
6]	1787 - 1870 Pélagie m. Hubert Cormier, 1804 Founding family Ste-Marie Bouctouche	1770 -1858 Geneviève m. Sylvain Babineau ca. 1792 La Fourche-à-Crapaud Petitcodiac River Grande-Digue, NB	1792- 1819 Bénoni m. Marie Doucet 1813 Grande-Digue, NB	Scholastique m. Charles Léger 1809 (Ref: Emelie Perkison notes for marriage.) Richibouctou, NB	1775 - 1764 Pierre Paul m. Rose Cormier 1796	1784 - 1872 Benjamin m1. Madeleine Cormier 1804 Bouctouche m2. 1821 Adélaïde LeBlanc Richibouctou, NB, 1821	1767 - 1861 Joe (Bob) m. Margaret Cormier ca. 1793 b. Halifax, NS Petitcodiac River Bouctouche, NB	1765 - 1819 Jean Baptiste b. at Hfx. 1789 - 1805 Vénérande m. 1805 François Boucher	1780- 1836 Angélique m. Charles Cormier 1802 Founding family Ste-Marie Bouctouche, NB	1790 - 1855 Charlotte m. René LeBlanc 1807 Bouctouche Founding family Ste-Marie Grande-Digue	1788 - Clothilde m. Paul Mazerolle 1811 (Ref: Stephen White) Bai-Ste-Anne

7m1]	Charlotte m. Joseph Martin 1830 Pointe Sapin, NB	1808 - 1829 Marie-Victoire m. Joseph LeBlanc Memramcook Ste-Marie-de-Kent, NB	1810 - Francine m. Bélonie LeBlanc	1805 - Emmanuel m1. Marguerite Duplesis 1827 m2. Marguerite Leblanc (see Subchart #309)	1812 - 1899 Anselme B. m1. Marguerite Jaillet 1837 m2. Rosalie Bourgeois 1886	1813 - 1895 Athanase m1. Julie Juillet 1837 m2. Françoise Melanson (see Subchart #315)	1815 - Gertrude m. Laurent Goutreau 1848 Memramcook NB	1817 - Siffoi 1807 - Mebain	1819 - Eufrosine	ca1821.- Marie-Blanche m1. John Swiss 1819 m2. Pierre Jaillet 1844
7m2]				Henriette m. Michel LeBlanc	↕	1824 - Olive m. Cyprien Cormier				
8]	1845 - Marie	1840 - 1936 Madeleine Girouard m. Anselme Girouard à Rose (no children) (see Subchart #500) Ste-Marie-de-Kent, NB	1837 - Henriette m. Magloire Girouard à (Hilaire) (see Subchart #523 and 527)	1835 - Magloire m1. Collette Cormier m2. Suzanne Allain m3. Henriette à Joe Rose 1858 (see Subchart #500) Ste-Marie-de-Kent, NB	1838 - 1907 Alexis m. Marie Girouard (Hilaire) 1868 Ste-Marie-de-Kent, NB	1843 - David m1. M. Cormier m2. H. LeBlanc m3. Thodie Robichaud Ste-Marie-de-Kent, NB	1846 - 1885 Gilbert m1. Sophie Baker 1872 First Acadian M.P. for NB Ste-Marie-de-Kent, NB	1849 - 1935 Virginie m. Thomas Allain 1867 Ste-Marie-de-Kent, NB	1841 - Blanche m. Dominique Cormier *Ref: Lorraine Robitaille)*	
9]	1871 - Geneviève m. Onésime Cormier *(Ref: Moncton Cards)*	1899 -1968 Annie m. Marcel Robichaud 1887 -1887 Béatrice	1890 - Elie m. Agnès Daigle 1913 Emma m. Eugène Rainville	1873 - 1938 Joseph (Cyrnac) m1. Collette Cormier 1904 m2. Régina Dallaire Ste-Marie-de-Kent, NB	1869 - 1912 Jacques (James) m. Marie Cormier 1899 Ste-Marie-de-Kent, NB	1875 -1948 Camille m1. Maggie S. Richard Rouville 1902	1874 - 1910 Anselme m. Philomène Bastarache	1880 - 1963 Donat m. Lézainne Anne Pichard 1911	1883 - 1939 Justé m. Evangéline Maillet	1885 - 1976 Albina m. Mélasse Bourque
10]			1927 - Alfreda m. Dr. Paul Bluteau (F.R.C.P.)	Raymond (n.m.)	1899 Arthur m. Léa LeBlanc 1922	1928 -1966 Leo St. Croix Brothers				
11]			Hélène m1. Robert Goutreau m2. Robert Arsenault Barachois	Allain (M.D.) Université de Laval	Edgar (M.D.) m1. Madeleine Dumais 1953 m2. Monique Dumont 1978 Pierre (Dentist) m. Cathy Gaudet Moncton	François At university in PEI	Marc (M.D.) m. Jocelyn LeClair Dieppe, NB	Louise Québec		Benjamin Branch NB Subchart #300 Linking to [AMC Block E-3b]

© *Acadian Awakenings Girouard/Giroir... Routes and Roots*

439

Appendices

Appendix 6

Girouard/Girroir/Gerrior etc. Names and Locations

1) Girouard Street, Poithiers, Department of Vienne, France.
2) Le Girouard Town, Department of Vendée, France.
3) Girouard, area near St-Jean-de-Sauvres, Department of Vienne, France. (See maps in France Chapter).
4) Girouard Street, Montreal, in honor of Supreme Court Judge Hon. Desire Girouard (French-Canadian Branch) and two other locations marked Girouard in surrounding area-see maps in Québec book.
5) Girouard Plaque at the hospital, St. Benoit Deux Montagne, PQ in honor of the generosity and charity of the Patriot, Jean Joseph Girouard. (Acadian Branch).
6) Girouard Street, St-Hyacinthe PQ, in honor of Antoine Girouard (French-Canadian Branch). See also large highway exit sign "Rue Girouard" as one approaches St-Hyacinthe on the Trans-Canada highway.
7) Girouard Street & Girouard Park in honor of Joseph Ena Girouard, the first Mayor of Drumondville PQ (Acadian branch).
8) Girouard Street at the intersection with Laurier Blvd., in honor of Joseph Ena Girouard (Acadian branch), close friend, politician and colleague of Canada's Prime Minister of the period, Sir Wilfred Laurier.
9) Girouard Statue (Antoine Girouard) at St-Hyacinthe College, Girouard Street, St-Hyacinthe PQ (French-Canadian Branch).
10) Girouardville, Bouctouche, NB (Acadian branch).
11) Girouard subdivision, Bouctouche, N.B. (George Girouard).
12) Plaque in Bouctouche, in honor of the first families of Bouctouche. The Girouard wives in this family group, were part of the founding families- the first Acadian mothers of this parish (Acadian branch).
13) Monument plaque in honor of Gilbert Girouard, first Acadian Minister in New Brunswick at Ste-Marie-de-Kent Museum in Bouctouche. (Acadian Branch).
14) Cross on top of Mount Carmel, behind church in Ste-Marie-de-Kent, NB, originally erected in honor of first Mass celebrated in Ste-Marie-de-Kent in home of one of Ste-Marie's prominent citizens, Anselme Girouard (Acadian Branch).
15) Gerrior Rd., Larry's River, Guysborough Co. NS, on original Crown grant of land to the first Gerrior pioneers in Larry's River. (Acadian branch).
16) Half Way House of Joseph Gerrior, which was located at the junction in Lundy, Guysborough Co., in 1870, was the only house in this area. (surveyor A.E.Church map).
17) Girroir Plaque at St. Peters Church, Heritage site, in Tracadie, Nova Scotia, in honor of Rev. Hubert Girroir, renowned leader of his time in Acadian affairs, French education as well as politics of his time.
18) Girroir Plaque in Tracadie, is in honor of Senator Edward Lavin Girroir second Acadian Minister for Nova Scotia. Also in Tracadie, the first frame house was built by Girroirs. It has been well maintained through the years and is still inhabited to present day. The Girroir settlement in Tracadie was very prosperous.

19) Girroir Square, in Malden Mass, U.S.A., in honor of two Girroir brothers who died in France and who were honored for their bravery. (See Isle Madame chapter of the Nova Scotia/Prince Edward Island book).
20) Girouard St-Oka, PQ,- Summer home of Joseph Girouard was located here.
21) Gerrior Subdivision (Harold J. Gerrior West Arichat branch).
22) Girouard Ranch and Girouard Rd., Broussard, Louisiana, named after one of Broussard's early pioneers and leaders of this town as well as a plantation owner- Joseph Oscar Girouard.
 23) Girouard Street, Manville, Smithfield, Rhode Island.
25) Girouard Cup, for soccer in Kenya, Africa, in honor of Sir Percy Girouard.
26) Girouard Street, Nigeria named after Sir Percy Girouard.
27) Mount Girouard, Banff, British Columbia, named after Sir Percy Girouard.

Also for more information on Girouard place names in Québec see http://www.geocities/com/Heartland/Bluffs/2005/rues.html

Appendix 7

Letters, Surveys and Newsclips in Preparation For

7A- The First Maritime Provinces Family Reunion, 1985
and
7B- The First International Family Reunion, 1990

An organizational committee planning the Gerrior Family Reunion met in the Bloomfield Centre on the campus of St. Francis Xavier University. The family's Nova Scotia history traces back to around 1640 when Francois Girouard arrived in Port Royal from the Loudon region of France. Attending the committee meeting are, from left, standing, Brad Pellerin, Dan Stewart, Rev. Conrad P. Girroir, and Brian Gerrior. Seated, Anne Marie Schroeder, chairman William Gerrior and Mary Fougere.

Pioneer family plans reunion in Antigonish

ANTIGONISH — The Gerriors are coming. So are the Gerriores, Girouards, Giroirs, Girroirs and the Gerroirs. A thousand members of the pioneer Acadian family have been invited to a reunion here on the weekend of July 26.

All can trace their family trees back to Francois Girouard who left the Loudon region of France to settle in Port Royal around 1640. One branch of the Gerrior family is directly related to the first governor of Acadia, Charles La Tour.

The reunion idea took root in the efforts of William Gerrior to trace his family geneology. His genealogical research unveiled a number of noteworthy individuals with family branches in Nova Scotia, New Brunswick, Prince Edward Island, other parts of Canada and the United States.

A committee was established to prepare for the reunion which will be held on the campus of St. Francis Xavier University.

The reunion will feature varied events, including a family picnic, an old-fashioned barn dance, a family music concert and celebration of a family mass in conjunction with the celebration of Rev. Conrad Girrior's 40th anniversary in the priesthood.

The organizational committee has prepared information sheets for distribution to family members. These can be obtained by writing to William Gerrior, Box 20, Site 16A, RR2 Armdale, N.S., B3L 4J2.

Committee members are: Anne Marie Schroeder, Porters Lake, Mary Fougere, Tracadie, N.S., Pat Cunningham, Tracadie, the Nardocchio family, Sydney, Dr. Edgar Girouard, Moncton, Danny Stewart, New Glasgow, Rev. Conrad P. Girroir, West Arichat, Brad Pellerin, Larry's River, Coun. Robert Girroir, Antigonish, Brian and Bill Gerrior, Halifax.

Appendices

Questionnaire

Name---------------------------------

RETURN ADDRESS:
    BILL GERRIOR
    BOX 20, SITE 16A
    RR. 2, ARMDALE
    N.S. CANADA
    B3L4J2

Address------------------------------

City/Town----------------------------

Postal Code--------------------------

State------------Phone Area-Code-------- Phone #---------------

1) I am of Acadian Descent (Family settled in present location from Nova Scotia during or after the Acadian Separation in 1755.

    Yes   NO   I don't Know

2) My Family came directly from France to settle here or in the close surrounding area.

    Yes   NO   I don't Know

3) I would be interested in purchasing an Acadian Giroir, Gerrior , Girouard Acadian book when completed. (approximately $30.00-35.00). No commitment by your response here. I simply want an idea of approximate numbers)

    Yes   NO

4) I would be interested in attending a second Acadian Giroir, Girouard Reunion in July of 1990 or 1991 in Nova scotia for all Acadian Girouards in North America- if organized and I receive 8-10 months notice. (Again, no commitment here by your Answer- I simply want an idea of numbers).

    Yes   NO

5) I presently have relatives in the Maritimes. (This Question intended for Girroirs Girouards etc. I missed for first Reunion)

    Yes   NO   If Yes please write name and address of relative on back. Thankyou   Bill Gerrior

1ST MAILING — P2

ADDRESSES - GERRIOR DESCENDANTS   1984

FAMILY TREE
GRID NO.: _____

THE FATHER OF CHILDREN LISTED BELOW IS _____ SPOUSE IS _____
LIVED AT _____   (include maiden name)

THE GRANDFATHER IS _____   SPOUSE IS _____
LIVED AT _____   (include maiden name)

THE GREAT GRANDFATHER (if known) _____   SPOUSE IS _____
LIVED AT _____   (include maiden name)

- If **more information** about the **family tree** is known, please attach pages if necessary.
- If your children have married and have children of their own, please include his/her name on this sheet and attach a separate sheet for their family.

(NAMES & ADDRESSES OF CHILDREN)

1. NAME: _____   SPOUSE: _____
                                            (include maiden name)
   ADDRESS (MAILING) _____   (CITY, TOWN, etc.) _____
   PROVINCE OR STATE _____
   COUNTRY _____   POSTAL CODE _____   PHONE _____
                                                   (include area code)

2. NAME: _____   SPOUSE: _____
                                            (include maiden name)
   ADDRESS (MAILING) _____   (CITY, TOWN, etc.) _____
   PROVINCE OR STATE _____
   COUNTRY _____   POSTAL CODE _____   PHONE _____
                                                   (include area code)

3. NAME: _____   SPOUSE: _____
                                            (include maiden name)
   ADDRESS (MAILING) _____   (CITY, TOWN, etc.) _____
   PROVINCE OR STATE _____
   COUNTRY _____   POSTAL CODE _____   PHONE _____
                                                   (include area code)

If you have more names, please continue on back of this sheet and attach another sheet if necessary.

PLEASE RETURN COMPLETED SHEETS AS SOON AS POSSIBLE (within a week, if possible) TO:

PHONE: 1-902-852-3926

BILL GERRIOR,
BOX 20, SITE 16A,
R.R.#2, ARMDALE, NOVA SCOTIA, CANADA
B3L 4J2.

Appendices

MARITIME PROVINCES ACADIAN GIROUARDS (GERRIORE, GIROIR, GERROIR, GIRROIR, GERRIOR) FAMILY DESCENDANTS

REUNION - JULY 26, 27, 28, 1985 (ST. FRANCIS XAVIER UNIVERSITY, ANTIGONISH, NS)

DEAR RELATIVE,

May I take a moment of your time to talk about the Gerrior family. Because of the great initial response to our first mailing to all Gerriors in the Atlantic Provinces, I have now collected enough addresses to send this flyer to many more descendants of the Gerriors, Girouards, etc., throughout the Atlantic Provinces, and descendants in other parts of Canada and the United States. Thank you for your interest and enthusiasm. For those who did not receive the first flyer, may I introduce myself and explain my purpose and, therefore, everyone will be up to date on all information.

My name is Bill Gerrior, originally from Halifax, N. S.; my father, John Sylvester Gerrior and grandfather, Jeffery, were both from Larry's River, Guysborough County, N. S. I address you as "Relative", since, from my genealogical research of all the Gerriors and related branches, it is obvious that we all stem from the original Francois Girouard who was born in France and arrived in Port Royal, N. S., in the early 1600's. Thus, we are all related either near or far and share a common heritage at some point in the past in Nova Scotia. This thought has motivated me to contact most of the Gerriors, Girouards, etc., families in Nova Scotia and New Brunswick either by phone, in writing, or by personal contact. Please check with all your own relatives to make sure they have received a notice because, with so many people to contact, unintentionally, someone may easily have been missed. These contacts have generated a further interest and enthusiasm for a clan family reunion of all the Gerrior branches and descendants originating from the families now living in the Atlantic Provinces.

Consequently, we have formed a committee with representatives from all areas of the Provinces to help co-ordinate communications to the various branches, to collect information, etc., and to co-ordinate related activities regarding the planned reunion.

The purpose of this flyer is:

(1) To introduce the committee to you.
(2) To announce the plans of the reunion early so everyone can make vacation plans, etc.
(3) To request that you and your family pre-register (see enclosed pre-registration form). In order to make better plans, we need to know, in advance, how many will be attending.

(1) ORGANIZATIONAL COMMITTEE:

1. Anne Marie Schroeder, Porter's Lake (daughter of Martina (Gerrior) Comeau, Larry's River)
2. Mary Fougere, Tracadie, N. S. (daughter of Bertha Girroir, Monastery)
3. Patsy Cunningham, Tracadie, N. S. (daughter of Marjorie Girroir, Tracadie)
4. Nardocchio family, Sydeny, N. S. (Geneva, daughter of Allen Gerrior, Larry's River; Mary and Ruth, granddaughters of Allen Gerrior; Councillor John Nardocchio, husband of Geneva)
5. Dr. Edgar Girouard, Moncton, N. S. (son of Arthur Girouard, Moncton, New Brunswick)
6. Danny Stewart, New Glasgow, N. S. (son of Mary Eldora (Mini) Gerrior, New Glasgow)
7. Fr. Conrad P. Girroir, West Arichat, N. S. (son of Jean Baptiste Girroir, West Arichat)
8. Brad Pellerin, Larry's River, N.S. (son of Clara (Gerrior) Pellerin, Larry's River)
9. Councillor Robert Girroir, Antigonish, N. S. (son of Charles Girroir, Tracadie, Nova Scotia)
10. Brian Gerrior, Halifax, N. S. (son of Charles A. Gerrior, Trenton, grandson of Jeffery Gerrior, PEI)
11. Bill Gerrior, Halifax, N. S. (son of John Sylvester Gerrior, Larry's River)

(2) PLANS FOR REUNION:

We have confirmed the following plans for the Gerrior reunion:

FRIDAY, JULY 26, 1985 - Bloomfield Centre, St. Francis Xavier University, Antigonish, N. S.

- 6:00 - 9:00 P.M. - Meeting of Friends and Relatives <u>Registration</u>, <u>Refreshments</u> and <u>Displays</u>
- 9:00 - 9:30 P.M. - <u>Welcome and Opening Remarks</u>
- 9:30 - 12:00 P.M. - <u>Social and Music</u> (Coffee House Style)
  - <u>Pool</u> available for older children

SATURDAY, JULY 27, 1985 - <u>Free Morning</u> - May we suggest that you have a good sleep or have an opportunity to do some shopping and tour the Town of Antigonish.

- 9:30 - 11:30 A.M. - <u>Late Registration</u>
- 12:30 - 5:00 P.M. - <u>Family Clan Picnic</u> - on the beautiful rustic location of Crystal Cliffs, just 8 miles (18 kms.) outside Antigonish (swimming, games, music, dancing, sing-a-long, etc.; large barn, cookhouse on site. Each family bring along their picnic basket and/or hibatchi barbecue and picnic blankets. This location is a photographer's paradise so don't forget your camera. Musicians, bring your music!
- 5:00 - 7:00 P.M. - <u>Barbecue</u>
- 7:00 - 9:00 P.M. - <u>Acadian film presentation and Gerrior family history sessions</u>
- 9:00 - 12:00 P.M. - <u>Barn Dance</u> featuring Acadian fiddle music and both popular and country music. Fun! Fun! Fun! in the "Barn" at Crystal Cliffs location.

SUNDAY, JULY 28, 1985 - CLOSING - <u>Mass</u> celebrated by Fr. P. Girrior (West Arichat), son of Jean Baptiste Gerrior, on his 40th Anniversary in the Priesthood, and by Fr. Murphy (grandson of Jenny Gerrior, Larry's River), and any other related clergy (T.B.A.)

Mass - 12:00 - 1:00

After Mass - <u>50/50 Draw</u>

<u>Clan Girouard Family Picture</u> in front of Church (a treasure to obtain and possess and to pass on to your children, I'm sure)

<u>Closing Remarks</u> - <u>Good-byes</u> - May we suggest that families plan to visit other parts of the Province of Acadian or family historic interest such as Port Royal, Grand Pre, etc., home towns, (see tourist guide for Nova Scotia).

ACCOMMODATIONS - Families and individuals will be responsible for arranging and booking their own accommodations and meals. Several restaurants and fast-food restaurants are available in the Town of Antigonish. (Only Saturday breakfast and Sunday breakfast need be arranged since the Family Clan Picnic takes care of both lunch and supper for Saturday).

Accommodations are available both at the University Residence and the numerous Motels in the Antigonish area. We strongly encourage families to book the Residence since: (a) it has the best rates (last year, $13.00 per single and $22.00 per double), and (b) it would contribute to the spirit and feeling of togetherness if relatives are all located on the same floor of the Residence (more fun, more time to talk and share good times (memories, etc.). There are no cooking facilities in the Residence and the Caterer has all food rights on campus. There is a lounge on each floor of the Residence. The University will hold a block of rooms open for a limited time only for the Gerrior Clan so BOOK NOW to save disappointment by calling or writing to Dorothy Lander, Residence Manager, St. Francis Xavier University, Antigonish, N. S. (Telephone 902-867-3970). Also, when you book, give some idea of where your grandfather lived in Nova Scotia so that related family branches can be booked in approximately the same area of the Residence.

Other accommodations can be made in town by contacting the following:

Chateau Motel, 112 Post Rd., Antigonish (863-4842)
Claymore Motel, The Mall, Antigonish (863-1050)
Gael Motel, 41 James, Antigonish (363-4212)
Dingle Motel, Lr. South River (863-3730)
Oasis Hotel, South River (863-3557); Wandlyn Inn, 158 Main (863-4001)
Valley View Motel, 295 Hawthorne (863-2939)
Whidden Trailer Court, 11 Hawthorne (863-3736)

MARITIME PROVINCES ACADIAN GIROUARDS (GERRIORE, GIROIR, GERROIR, GIRROIR, GERRIOR) FAMILY DESCENDANTS
REUNION - JULY 26, 27, 28, 1985 (ST. FRANCIS XAVIER UNIVERSITY, ANTIGONISH, NS)
PRE-REGISTRATION FORM

PLEASE RETURN TO: Bill Gerrior,
Box 20, Site 16A,
R. R. #2, Armdale, Nova Scotia,
Canada B3L 4J2.

DEADLINE DATE - Three weeks after receipt of this form.

NAME: _____   ADDRESS: _____
Mailing
My Spouse (if applicable) _____   City, Town _____
County _____
Postal Code _____
Telephone _____

My Father is _____ Spouse _____ Lived at _____

My Grandfather _____ Spouse _____ Lived at _____

I have or will be booking a room at Saint Francis Xavier Residence
Yes /_/   No /_/

I ave or will be booking accommodations in town   Yes /_/   No /_/

Name of Motel _____

I plan to arrive on Friday   Yes /_/   No /_/

I plan to arrive on Saturday   Yes /_/   No /_/

We have tried to keep plans simple and costs as low as possible. The minimum cost is $12.00 per adult and $5.00 per child under sixteen. Any donations are certainly welcomed.

I am enclosing $12.00 for myself and each of the adults listed below and $5.00 for each of the children under 16 (no fee for infants).

The names of persons in my group who will be registering with me are:
(Please write in ages in box after name only if under 16 yrs.)

1. _____ /_/ $ .00   4. _____ /_/ $ .00
      First   Last   Age Amount   First   Last   Age Amount

2. _____ /_/ $ .00   5. _____ /_/ $ .00
      First   Last   Age Amount   First   Last   Age Amount

3. _____ /_/ $ .00   6. _____ /_/ $ .00
      First   Last   Age Amount   First   Last   Age Amount

Please enclose a self-addressed envelope for your receipt and confirmation of registration. This will save a fourth mailing.

Total Amount /_/

Acadian Awakenings: An Acadian Family In Exile

MARITIME PROVINCES ACADIAN GIROUARDS (GERRIORE, GIROIR, GERROIR, GIRROIR, GERRIOR) FAMILY DESCENDANTS

REUNION - JULY 26, 27, 28, 1985 (ST. FRANCIS XAVIER UNIVERSITY, ANTIGONISH, NS)

DEAR RELATIVE,

May I take a moment of your time to talk about the Gerrior family. Because of the great initial response to our first mailing to all Gerriors in the Atlantic Provinces, I have now collected enough addresses to send this flyer to many more descendants of the Gerriors, Girouards, etc., throughout the Atlantic Provinces, and descendants in other parts of Canada and the United States. Thank you for your interest and enthusiasm. For those who did not receive the first flyer, may I introduce myself and explain my purpose and, therefore, everyone will be up to date on all information.

My name is Bill Gerrior, originally from Halifax, N. S.; my father, John Sylvester Gerrior and grandfather, Jeffery, were both from Larry's River, Guysborough County, N. S. I address you as "Relative", since, from my genealogical research of all the Gerriors and related branches, it is obvious that we all stem from the original Francois Girouard who was born in France and arrived in Port Royal, N. S., in the early 1600's. Thus, we are all related either near or far and share a common heritage at some point in the past in Nova Scotia. This thought has motivated me to contact most of the Gerriors, Girouards, etc., families in Nova Scotia and New Brunswick either by phone, in writing, or by personal contact. Please check with all your own relatives to make sure they have received a notice because, with so many people to contact, unintentionally, someone may easily have been missed. These contacts have generated a further interest and enthusiasm for a clan family reunion of all the Gerrior branches and descendants originating from the families now living in the Atlantic Provinces.

Consequently, we have formed a committee with representatives from all areas of the Provinces to help co-ordinate communications to the various branches, to collect information, etc., and to co-ordinate related activities regarding the planned reunion.

The purpose of this flyer is:

(1) To introduce the committee to you.
(2) To announce the plans of the reunion early so everyone can make vacation plans, etc.
(3) To request that you and your family pre-register (see enclosed pre-registration form). In order to make better plans, we need to know, in advance, how many will be attending.

(1) <u>ORGANIZATIONAL COMMITTEE</u>:

1. Anne Marie Schroeder, Porter's Lake (daughter of Martina (Gerrior) Comeau, Larry's River)
2. Mary Fougere, Tracadie, N. S. (daughter of Bertha Girroir, Monastery)
3. Patsy Cunningham, Tracadie, N. S. (daughter of Marjorie Girroir, Tracadie)
4. Nardocchio family, Sydney, N. S. (Geneva, daughter of Allen Gerrior, Larry's River; Mary and Ruth, granddaughters of Allen Gerrior; Councillor John Nardocchio, husband of Geneva)
5. Dr. Edgar Girouard, Moncton, N. S. (son of Arthur Girouard, Moncton, New Brunswick)
6. Danny Stewart, New Glasgow, N. S. (son of Mary Eldora (Mini) Gerrior, New Glasgow)
7. Fr. Conrad P. Girroir, West Arichat, N. S. (son of Jean Baptiste Girroir, West Arichat)
8. Brad Pellerin, Larry's River, N.S. (son of Clara (Gerrior) Pellerin, Larry's River)
9. Councillor Robert Girroir, Antigonish, N. S. (son of Charles Girroir, Tracadie, Nova Scotia)
10. Brian Gerrior, Halifax, N. S. (son of Charles A. Gerrior, Trenton, grandson of Jeffery Gerrior, PEI)
11. Bill Gerrior, Halifax, N. S. (son of John Sylvester Gerrior, Larry's River)

Appendices

(2) **PLANS FOR REUNION:**

We have confirmed the following plans for the Gerrior reunion:

FRIDAY, JULY 26, 1985 - Bloomfield Centre, St. Francis Xavier University, Antigonish, N. S.

- 6:00 - 9:00 P.M. - **Meeting of Friends and Relatives** **Registration, Refreshments** and **Displays**
- 9:00 - 9:30 P.M. - **Welcome and Opening Remarks**
- 9:30 - 12:00 P.M. - **Social and Music** (Coffee House Style) **Pool** available for older children

SATURDAY, JULY 27, 1985 - **Free Morning** - May we suggest that you have a good sleep or have an opportunity to do some shopping and tour the Town of Antigonish.

- 9:30 - 11:30 A.M. - **Late Registration**
- 12:30 - 5:00 P.M. - **Family Clan Picnic** - on the beautiful rustic location of Crystal Cliffs, just 8 miles (18 kms.) outside Antigonish (swimming, games, music, dancing, sing-along, etc.; large barn, cookhouse on site. Each family bring along their picnic basket and/or hibatchi barbecue and picnic blankets. This location is a photographer's paradise so don't forget your camera. Musicians, bring your music!
- 5:00 - 7:00 P.M. - **Barbecue**
- 7:00 - 9:00 P.M. - **Acadian film presentation and Gerrior family history sessions**
- 9:00 - 12:00 P.M. - **Barn Dance** featuring Acadian fiddle music and both popular and country music. Fun! Fun! Fun! in the "Barn" at Crystal Cliffs location.

SUNDAY, JULY 28, 1985 - CLOSING - **Mass** celebrated by Fr. P. Girrior (West Arichat), son of Jean Baptiste Gerrior, on his 40th Anniversary in the Priesthood, and by Fr. Murphy (grandson of Jenny Gerrior, Larry's River), and any other related clergy (T.B.A.)

Mass - 12:00 - 1:00

After Mass - **50/50 Draw**

Clan Girouard Family Picture in front of Church (a treasure to obtain and possess and to pass on to your children, I'm sure)

Closing Remarks - Good-byes - May we suggest that families plan to visit other parts of the Province of Acadian or family historic interest such as Port Royal, Grand Pre, etc., home towns, (see tourist guide for Nova Scotia).

ACCOMMODATIONS - Families and individuals will be responsible for arranging and booking their own accommodations and meals. Several restaurants and fast-food restaurants are available in the Town of Antigonish. (Only Saturday breakfast and Sunday breakfast need be arranged since the Family Clan Picnic takes care of both lunch and supper for Saturday).

Accommodations are available both at the University Residence and the numerous Hotels in the Antigonish area. We strongly encourage families to book the Residence since: (a) it has the best rates (last year, $13.00 per single and $22.00 per double), and (b) it would contribute to the spirit and feeling of togetherness if relatives are all located on the same floor of the Residence (more fun, more time to talk and share good times (memories, etc.). There are no cooking facilities in the Residence and the Caterer has all food rights on campus. There is a lounge on each floor of the Residence. The University will hold a block of rooms open for a limited time only for the Gerrior Clan so BOOK NOW to save disappointment by calling or writing to Dorothy Lander, Residence Manager, St. Francis Xavier University, Antigonish, N. S. (Telephone 902-867-3970). Also, when you book, give some idea of where your grandfather lived in Nova Scotia so that related family branches can be booked in approximately the same area of the Residence.

Other accommodations can be made in town by contacting the following:
Chateau Motel, 112 Post Rd., Antigonish (863-4842)
Claymore Motel, The Mall, Antigonish (863-1050)
Gael Motel, 41 James, Antigonish (863-4212)
Dingle Motel, Lr. South River (863-3730)
Oasis Motel, South River (863-3557); Wandlyn Inn, 158 Main (863-4001)
Valley View Motel, 295 Hawthorne (863-2939)
Whidden Trailer Court, 11 Hawthorne (863-3736)

Acadian Awakenings: An Acadian Family In Exile

THE CASKET, WEDNESDAY, JUNE 13, 1990

1640 INTERNATIONAL REUNION 1990
Welcome GERRIOR • GERROIR • GIROIR • GIROIRE • GIRROIR • GIROUARD

PICTURED at a planning session for this summer's international gathering of the Gerroir families in Antigonish are Paul R. Girouard (seated, left), Claire Hagen, committee chairman Bill Gerrior, committee secretary Anne Marie Schroeder, Rev. Conrad P. Girroir; Rita Kay (standing, left), Daniel Stewart, Mary Fougere, Evelyn Oakley, Brad Comeau, Estelle McMaster, Brad Pellerin, Jean LeJeune, Blanche Hughes, Christine Morin, Ruth MacNeil and Verna Gionet. Other committee members are Dr. Edgar Girouard and Antigonish deputy mayor Robert Girroir.

Acadian Family Plans Int'l Reunion

The pioneer Acadian family of Gerriors (Girroirs, Giroires, Girouards and Giroirs) expects descendants from all over the world to attend the family reunion set for July 27 through 29 at St. Francis Xavier University, with a family picnic in Tracadie, Antigonish County, where one of the family branches settled after the Acadian deportations of the 18th century.

Spearheading the 1990 reunion, which grew out of the 1985 Mairime gathering when over 600 descendants from the Maritimes participated, is Bill Gerrior of Armdale, N.S. Research after the 1985 reunion traced over 1,500 descendants in the North America and France, and the idea of an international reunion was born.

"All Acadian Gerriors, Girouards in North America can now be traced to the same master chart," reunion chairman Gerroir explains. "They are all descendants from the one Francois Girouard who arrived at Port Royal in the 1640s from France, in or near La Chaussee in the proximity of Loudun Dept. of Vienne, France, (about two and one-half hours' drive southwest of Paris)."

Also attending this reunion will be some of the Canadian Girouard branches that arrived directly in Quebec 75 years after Francois arrived in Port Royal. Their first ancestor to arrive in Quebec was Antoine Girouard from Montlucon, Riom, southeast of Loudun, France. At some point in the past in France, researchers believe that there is a common connection. So much has been written in early 1900s by Supreme Court Judge Desire Girouard about the remarkably common physical and character traits, of both these Acadian and Canadian branches. In many cases today, descendants of the Acadian Girouards in Quebec, live in close proximity to the above Canadian descendants.

The reunion activities begin on Friday evening, July 27, with registration followed by a wine and cheese reception. Guests will be greeted by the open air-fiddle music of the "Strait Area Scottish Strings". Dianne Pellerin and daughter Adrienne, Gerrior descendants, are both members of this group. All participants will have, or be supplied with, a master chart as well as their subchart, connecting their branch to the master chart back to Francois of 1640 at Port Royal.

Official welcomes from dignitaries will follow, along with a slide presentation of the Acadian Girouard story, before, during, and after deportation, including songs of the past, Acadian and Scottish fiddle music by the "Gerrior Family"; Acadian dancing by the group, "Dance Interplay", directed by Marie Gerrior (Nugent); displays of history and genealogy, Special Bluenose Ceremony, Order of Good Time Certificates presented from The N.S. Tourist Bureau to all "out-of-province" guests.

Senator Edward Lavin Girrior, second Acadian Minister in the Nova Scotia Legislature (presentation by Minister of Acadian Affairs, Guy Leblanc); and Rev. Hubert Girroir, the first Acadian priest in the Antigonish diocese, and strong supporter of education as well as the Confederation Cause (presentation by Vicar General of Antigonish diocese Rev. Vernon Fougere, Sydney).

Dr. John MacDonell, of Antigonish, will be accepting a plaque in honor of his uncle. Senator Edward Lavin Girroir, the second, Acadian Minister of Nova Scotia.

Also Rev. Frank Morley of St. Peter's Parish, Tracadie, and Rev. Conrad Girroir, of West Arichat, will accept a plaque in memory of Rev. Hubert Girroir.

Saturday, July 28, in the morning, large family branch photos will be taken at the University stadium. A family picnic is being organized in Tracadie with a sing-a-long, Acadian dancing, fiddle music, as well as talent from among many of the descendants who wish to perform. Following the picnic there is a dance at the Bloomfield Center with acadian, cajun, country and pop, music being supplied by two bands, The River Band from Larrys River, Guysborough County, and by the group "The Gerrior Family".

Sunday, genealogy exchange meetings are scheduled from 11-12 a.m-noon with each branch assigned an area to gather more detailed information on its own branch (tape recorders, notepads and an address book are suggested).

The reunion closes with a Mass in the afternoon at St. Ninian's Cathedral, co-celebrated by Gerrior clergy descendants, including Rev. Conrad Girroir, West Arichat; Rev. Doug Murphy, formerly of Larrys River; and Rev. Frank Giroir of Chelsmette, Louisiana, with music co-ordinated by Brad Pellerin.

Finally, after the Mass, the entire group of descendants will pose on the stadium stands for a large group picture. Many of the descendants are expected to continue their historical journey to Grand Pre, Port Royal, and Louisbourg, as well as visit Halifax.

Next year, Bill Gerrior hopes to give some permanance to the moments and feelings experienced at both reunions, by following up with a book, recording all the information, history, reunion activities, genealogy, etc. of the Girouard, Gerrior, Giroir, Girroir, Giroire etc. family.

"Already many descendants have indicated a strong interest in this book," Gerroir says.

For further information on the Reunion, contact Bill Gerrior, Box 20 Site 16A, RR #2, Armdale, N.S., Canada B3L 4J2; (902) 852-3926 as soon as possible.

Appendices

Box 20 Site 16 A
RR # 2 Armdale NS
Canada B3L 4J2
(902) 852-3926
March 28/89

To: All Giroirs, Girroirs, Gerriors, Girourds etc. in the southern states along the eastern coastline of the U.S and in particular, in New Orleans in the state of Louisiana.

Hello:

My name is Bill Gerrior from Halifax County, Nova Scotia. Canada. I have recently researched extensively, the Acadian Giroirs, Gerriors, Girouards etc. with family roots in the Maritime Provinces of Nova Scotia, New Brunswick, and Prince Edward Island. This search concluded with a large Acadian family reunion of many, many branches of this large Family Tree. (see attached.

I have learned from my research that the Acadian name of Giroir, Girroir, Girroire, Gerrior, Girouard etc., all represent the same family regardless of how you may spell it. This fact is confirmed in all the Church records and census records that I have researched. This fact is also Confirmed in a book called "La Famille Girouard", written by the Honorable Desire Girouard, Supreme Court Judge in Quebec around the 1900's. In addition many other references to this fact are made by all reputable authors on Acadian Genealogy. Also it is very clear that all Acadian Giroirs Gerriors, Girouards etc. all descend from Francois Girouard dit (LA Varrene) who married Jeanne Aucoin and who arrived at Port Royal, Nova Scotia in 1640 from La Chausee, near the small village of Varanne, in the region of Loudun, Departement of Vienne, France.(South-West of Paris).

Since the time of the Reunion mentioned above, I have been keenly interested in extending my research to France, the provinces of Quebec in Canada and the many southern states of America and in particular Louisiana where many members of this same family tree were separated during the deportation by the English in 1755. These families still reside in these original areas where they were deported or in close proximity. Although their roots are no longer found in the Maritimes, they are still, nevertheless, part of our family tree and we have shared a common heritage (more than 100 years in Nova Scotia) before the deportation 1755, an of course a common heritage in France.

Two summers ago I began to research the Quebec Archives to link all the Acadian Quebec Girouards to our family tree. I had great success in finding a great deal of information.
I have earlier, sent 900 letters, similar to this one to Quebec Girouards and I have received great interest and response. In 99%

of the time I am able to connect these families to the same master chart which begins with Francois. I am hoping that through this letter to all the Giroirs, Girroirs, Girouards etc. in Louisiana and other parts of the southern and eastern states that I will be able to accomplish the same ie.-connect everyone to the same family tree. In this way I will be able to complete my master chart and also provide you with your own genealogy chart back to 1640.

You may say -Why? The answer is simply that I am very proud of the Acadian family name Giroir, Girroir, Gerrior, Girouard. I have heard and read many admirable deeds and accomplishments related to various branches of this family. I have followed the remarkable survival and progress of these Acadians who were separated during the deportation 1755, and I want to soon have their story recorded in a book which I am also in the process of writing.

As mentioned earlier, as a result of the last genealogical research in the Maritime Provinces, a very successful Reunion was held in 1985, in which more than 600 Acadian Giroir descendants of Francois Girouard 1640, attended. Descendants were from all over Canada and the United States who either lived in the Maritime Provinces, or still had relatives living here. Every family was provided with a master chart and a sub chart which linked their branch to the same master chart of the same family tree. We had a fantastic weekend. For the first time in 350 years of separation we gathered together in the same location(Antigonish just 100 miles north of Halifax N.S.) to share a common heritage and identity, through slides , music, dancing, singing and family picnic.(see enclosed newspaper article).

I know that all the Giroir branches in Louisiana also descend from the same Francois Girouard and were part of the deportation either directly to Louisiana or via one of the southern states then to Louisiana after a short while, or perhaps deported directly to France, then back to Louisiana to rejoin their separated families later.

I suspect that the majority of the branches of Girouards Giroirs descend from Firmin Giroire who I have found on " The census of early Acadian Settlements OF Louisiana- 1766. He is Age 17.

At St. James, Donaldsonville and Convent, Louisiana, right Bank, Firmin is also recorded, at 20 years of age as a soldier of the French Militia , 1770.

Firmin's brother Paul Gervais Girouard has many descendants in New Brunswick, Canada today.

Other Girroir, Gerriors in other States along the eastern and southern coast of United States descend from Acadian Giroir, Girouard. Girroir descendants in the maritime Provinces from which I am sure, I have recorded and can connect if you send me the names of your father, grandfather, etc. and the names of their spouses.

Whatever the case may be, I am very interested in gathering as much information on the above branch and other branches of Giroirs as possible. I would be very interested in corresponding with anyone who has any information to share(either history or genealogy). I would be particularly interested also in hearing from anyone who has done any research themselves or had research done on the Giroirs, GIrouards etc.

Last summer I also visited France at the original location of LA Chausee near Loudun, and spent many enjoyable evenings with a number of Girroire families(they spell their name "Girroire", chatting about our history and about my project over the last few years on the Giroirs, Gerriors. It was a very emotional and exciting time for me as well as for these Gerroire families.
I will be returning this July for three weeks and hope to do further research there.

If you live in the New Orleans area and have a special interest in my project, you can reach me at the Hyatt Regency Hotel in New Orleans(April 29-MAy 5). Phone (504) 561-1234. The room is registered under the name Gerry Carty's group from N.S attending the IRA International Conference. PLease leave your name and phone number and I will gladly return you call as soon as possible. I am very interested in meeting with you and sharing any history and or genealogy.

As you may have guessed, I am also tentatively thinking about a North American wide Reunion of the Giroirs, Gerriors etc. either in the summer of 1990 or the summer of 1991. To help me get ready for this, I am also enclosing a survey form which I hope can be returned to me in two weeks or so. I will use the results of this form for my mailing lists for the above mentioned Reunion. Normally I will notify everyone, ten months in advance. I know that not everyone is able to go to these events, because of illness, trip expenses, etc. However, I could still mail you your genealogy chart and pertinent information if you were interested. What is important is that we share as much of the information that we presently know on the Giroirs(history and genealogy). This is why I am asking you to complete the enclosed form and attach as much as necessary to complete your family tree as far back as possible.

Would you please help me with this big task, by completing the form provided and returning it, and any written information, photos etc., you would like to attach and share regarding your family tree and/or history.

             Yours Sincerely

             Bill Gerrior
PS. Please share this letter with others, I may not have reached.

Adresses-Girouard Descendants   Date--------

Master Chart #-------------

Sub Chart #----------------

My Name is_____My spouse name is_____

(include maiden name if appropriate)

MY Grandfather Or Grandmother(Girouard side)is_____
Spouse Of above is_____ _____
(Include maiden name if applicable)
The above lives/lived at_____

My Great Grandfather (if known)_____
His spouse is_____
Lived at_____

If more information about family tree is known please attach pages if necessary. The more information you give me the better the chances are of connecting to the information I presently have back to 1640.

MY Children are as follows:(FILL COMPLETELY IF Children ARE MARRIED OTHERWISE JUST COMPLETE NAME.)

1) Name _____ Spouse_____
(include maiden name)
ADDRESS_____CITY/TOWN_____-
_____

PROVINCE OR STATE_____
COUNTRY_____ POSTAL CODE_____ PHONE____
_____

PLEASE USE SEPARATE SHEET for other CHILDREN using the above format. Please return information as soon as possible(within two weeks if possible) to: Bill Gerrior,Box 20, site 16 A, RR# 2,Armdale N.S.Canada B3L 4J2.
Phone # 902- 852-3926.

Thankyou for your time in helping to complete the Girouard history and genealogy.

Yours sincerely

Bill Gerrior

Appendices

Questionnaire

Name----------------------------

Address--------------------------

City/Town------------------------

Postal Code----------------------

State------------Phone Area-Code-------- Phone #---------------

RETURN ADDRESS:
BILL GERRIOR
BOX 20, SITE 16A
RR. 2, ARMDALE
N.S. CANADA
B3L4J2

1) I am of Acadian Descent (Family settled in present location from Nova Scotia during or after the Acadian Separation in 1755.

    Yes   NO   I don't Know

2) My Family came directly from France to settle here or in the close surrounding area.

    Yes   NO   I don't Know

3) I would be interested in purchasing an Acadian Giroir, Gerrior , Girouard Acadian book when completed.(approximately $30.00-35.00). No commitment by your response here. I simply want an idea of approximate numbers)

    Yes   NO

4) I would be interested in attending a second Acadian Giroir, Girouard Reunion in July of 1990 or 1991 in Nova scotia for all Acadian Girouards in North America- if organized and I receive 8-10 months notice. (Again, no commitment here by your Answer- I simply want an idea of numbers).

    Yes   NO

5) I presently have relatives in the Maritimes.(This Question intended for Girroirs Girouards etc. I missed for first Reunion)

    Yes   NO   If Yes please write name and address of relative on back. Thankyou   Bill Gerrior

Acadian Awakenings: An Acadian Family In Exile

THE FIRST INTERNATIONAL REUNION OF THE ACADIAN DESCENDANTS OF THE GIROIRE, GIROUARD, GIROIR, GERRIOR, GIRROIR, ETC. FAMILIES

```
Bill Gerrior
Box 20, Site 16A, Brookside
Armdale R.R.# 2
Halifax County, N.S.
B3L 4J2
October 5, 1989
```

Dear Cousins (near and far),

My name is Bill Gerrior from Halifax, Nova Scotia. I was in contact with many families during the preparations for the First Maritime Provinces Reunion held in 1985. Now we are back at it again, preparing for another reunion. Over the past year, I have corresponded with many other Girouard, Giroir, etc. families established outside the Maritimes.

I am happy to announce that we are now in the process of organizing the First International Reunion of all our Acadian Giroire, Girouard, etc. family branches descending from Francois Girouard, dit La Varanne near La Chausee, Loudun area, Dept. of Vienne, France. THE DATES FOR THE FIRST INTERNATIONAL REUNION ARE NOW SET FOR JULY 27, 28, AND 29 OF THIS COMING SUMMER, 1990.

I am pleased to say that we also have some interest and written response from some of the Canadian branches of Girouards who left France 75 years after the N.S. deportation and sailed directly to Quebec. They settled, in some instances, alongside the Acadian Girouards who were stablished there as a result of the 1755 N.S. deportation.

The Canadian Girouards originated from Montluçon Riom area, southeast of Loudun. Their first ancestor in Quebec was Antoine Girouard. At some point in the past, in France, we know there must be some connection between Antoine and the First Acadian Girouard, our Francois. According to the book written in the 1900's by the Supreme Court Judge, Honorable Desire Girouard (a Canadian Girouard) of Quebec, the characteristics of these two branches are compared very favorably with respect to this common link.

The purpose of this letter:
1. To update you on the progress of the research.
2. To tell you our initial plans for the International Reunion.
3. To introduce the committees to you.
4. To request that you and your family pre-register (see enclosed pre-registration form which must be returned within three weeks of this mailing). In order to plan for your maximum enjoyment, it is necessary to know in advance how many will be attending. I am sure you can appreciate the amount of time needed to plan this event.
5. To provide you with some basic information regarding accommodation and transportation. (After our pre-registration is completed, I have arranged for our N.S. Tourist Bureau to send you a complete tourist book on all the aspects of interests, accommodations, restaurants, events, activities, etc. for the summer of 1990 in N.S., including our International Reunion.

I. RESEARCH UPDATE

After our first Maritime Provinces Reunion in 1985 (600 in attendance), I received many letters from descendants who wanted to have another reunion.

Since that time, I have been very fortunate to have been able to extend my research beyond the families who still have roots in the Maritime Provinces, to many other branches in Quebec, other parts of Canada, Louisiana, and many other states of the U.S. These Girouard's, Giroir's, etc. branches no longer have relatives living in the Maritime Provinces because they were part of the deportation of 1755 and established themselves up to present day, in the areas where they were deported. Nevertheless, we now have accurate church records, census records, and family records, etc. which give absolute proof that all these Girouard, Giroir descendants, like the Maritime Province Girouards, Gerriors, etc. descend from these same Francois Girouard form the Dept. of Vienne, who landed here in the Nova Scotia (Acadia) 1640. WE ARE ALL ONE BIG FAMILY, WITH A COMMON HERITAGE, BOTH HERE IN NOVA SCOTIA BEFORE THE DEPORTATION, AND IN FRANCE BEFORE THIS.

Over the past year I have been fortunate enough to visit and make many wonderful contacts with Girouard, Girroire, etc. families in France, Louisiana, and Quebec. I would like to update you on each of these visits. First let me talk a little about France:

FRANCE VISITS AND RESEARCH - During the past year I have visited France twice and found great interest in Loudun and surrounding areas with respect to the Girroire, Girouard, Acadian heritage and their origins in La Chausee. Madame Touret, Director of the Tourist Bureau in Loudun, France, and her husband, Jean, have been eextremely helpful in assisting me with the Girroire, Girouard research in France, by arranging for me to visit many Giroire families during my stay. It was an experience of a lifetime and very moving for myself as well as for the Girroire, Girouard families I visited.

The Tourist Bureau of Loudun also has a special interest in the history of the Acadians since it is from the surrounding area of Loudun (La Chausee, La Varenne, etc. that the very first French settlers voyaged to Nova Scotia. The Girouards, Girroires, etc. are one of the first pioneer families of N.S.

A number of Girroire families from the Loudun area have expressed an interest in attending our International Reunion. These Girroire family descendants have been very hospitable and helpful to me during my stay in Loudun:

Isabelle Sicq (a Girroire descendant); Councillor Boudouin de la Bouillerie and his wife, Marie (Girroire) Proprietors of the Castle "La Bonnetiere" in La Chausee; and Councillor Jean Pierre Girroire and his wife Isabelle; Andree Gombert (Girouard descendant) and husband Yves (southern France) have all been very supportive and helpful in this exciting revival of our family heritage and history in France. Together, the above mentioned committee members will contact all the Gerroire, Girouards in the Dept. of Vienne, France. Madame Touret, Director of the Tourist Bureau Loudun will co-ordinate this committee.

Whether the Girroire, Girouard families from France are able to attend our reunion or not, I wanted all to be aware of our combined interest and pride in our family name and heritage. I also would like to encourage some further research in France with regard to our Family. Further we would like all Girroire and Girouards in France to have an opportunity to be part of the Girroire, Girouard book that's in the making and be able to purchase this book if they so wish, when it is published. Finally, we dearly would love to have as many Girroire, Girouard families as possible, from France, to join us and make this event even more prestigious (this once in a lifetime occasion). I will bring everyone up-to-date in the next letter regarding the progress in France in this regard.

QUEBEC VISITS AND RESEARCH - Since the last reunion, I visited the province of Quebec twice. During my first trip, I visited Quebec and Montreal areas and many of the communities along the St. Lawrence between these two cities where the Girouards settled. I researched our Girouard branches in the Province of Quebec, at the Archives at Laval University. Also, Dr. Edgar Girouard provided me with some cards on the Girouards in Quebec which were passed on to him. Three weeks before my last visit to Montreal, in February of this year, I mailed 1000 letters and survey forms to all telephone book Girouards listed in the Province of Quebec. I received a great amount of information, kindly sent back to me from many interested Girouards responding to my survey. This, along with the information above, allowed me to positively, genealogically trace, four more large Acadian Girouard family branches descending from our master chart, who established in the province of Quebec during and after the deportation and who definitely descend from our same family tree.

Appendices

FIRST INTERNATIONAL REUNION, 1990

Some of these branches descend from the brothers of the first Gerrior, Giroir who established himself in Tracadie, N.S. It was a wonderful feeling to realize again that so many other Girouard branches have been linked. From this initial mailout in January, 1989, over 200 Girouards from Quebec indicated that they would be interested in attending the First International Reunion of the Girouards, Giroirs, Gerriors, etc. This also included a number of Canadian Girouard branches I mentioned earlier. Many Girouards of Quebec have also completed their own genealogy of their branch back to Francois and Antoine if Canadian.

LOUISIANA VISITS AND RESEARCH - Also I had another fortunate opportunity, to make more progress on the Giroir, Girouards in Louisiana, and many other states of the U.S. Last April, I attended an International Conference related to my school work as Principal of a junior high school. The conference was held in New Orleans, Louisiana. I was elated since I had a dual agenda - the conference itself, but also a personal interest of extending my research on the Girouards, Giroirs in Louisiana. Again, three weeks prior to my visit, I sent another 1000 letters and survey forms to all Girouards, Giroirs in Louisiana and other states of the U.S. as well as some western provinces of Canada.

Similarly, I received much valuable feedback from information data, letters, personal genealogies, completed survey forms, inquiries, etc. from many other Girouards, Giroires. Also, I recieved the same from many other southern states of the U.S. and western provinces of Canada (all from the same mail out referred to above); all with the same story when all the pieces are finally fitted together - descendants of Francois Girouard.

As a result of all the contacts mentioned above, I was able to meet with ten or so different Giroir, Girouard family branches in the New Orleans area who themselves had a very strong interest in the family history and genealogy, and were either actively researching themselves or had already completed their own family genealogy.

After a number of meetings with Giroirs, Girouards in New Orleans, a tour of the lands in Louisiana where many of these Acadian Giroir, Girouard families settled, and much information kindly provided by many who responded to my survey letter, we are able to positively trace all these Girouards and Giroir family branches in Louisiana, to our same master chart since they all descend from Francois Girouard, like ourselves in the Maritime Provinces. Again, just as in France and Quebec, it was a feeling of warmth and pride, beyond expression, to meet all of these Girouards, Giroirs, knowing that we all stem from the same root. Over 100 Girouards from Louisiana and many various other States of the U.S. who established roots after 1755 outside the Maritimes, and who were recently contacted in the above survey have indicated that they wish to attend our International Reunion.

Consequently, with everyone's help and contacts made, we are now able to supply all these mentioned Girouards, with a master chart and the appropriate sub-chart which ties into the master chart, tracing each family's genealogy back to 1640 in Port Royal, N.S. - just as we were able to do for our own Maritime Provinces descendants. We are also able to trace many Canadian Branches who descend from Antoine, thanks to the many Canadian Girouards who responded with much information.

So we have made major leaps in our genealogy research and we are getting very close to completion of all our branches stemming from our master chart - our original objective.

I think we can boast, with a certain amount of pride, to be the first Acadian family to have accomplished this genealogical feat in such detail and with such a wide network, thanks to all your help, interest, and willingness to share our collective information with each other to pass down to our own children.

This causes me to think of the line in a Girouard poem (the complete poem I will give to you later). It says:

"Ils ont construit, combattu, defriche' (Translated): They struggled, cleared, constructed
A leurs enfant, ils onto su inculquer   In their children they knew how to instill
Le Grand amour de ce pays immense   A great love for this vast country
Les Girouards, nos ancetres.   The Girouards, our ancestors.

Author unknown. (Complete poem sent to me by Emilie Perkinson, N.B.)

Well that is it for the update on the research. The above represents over 300 Girouards who have indicated an interest in our reunion. Along with the 600 or so we hope to return from the First Maritime Reunion who are either living in the Maritimes or still have descendants in the Maritimes. We are predicting a ball park figure of 800-1000 Girouard, Giroire etc. family descendants for our International Reunion. WE ARE ANXIOUSLY WAITING FOR THE BIG EVENT TO SEE YOU.

II. PLANS FOR THE REUNION

First of all, the Reunion will take place at the same location as our First Maritime Province Reunion:

St. Francis Xavier University, Antigonish (120 miles North of Halifax). The Family Picnic on Saturday will be in the nearby location of Tracadie (the original place of resettlement after the deportation, for the N.S. mainland Gerriors, Giroirs).

ORDER OF EVENTS:

Friday (6 - 9 p.m.) - Meeting friends and relatives. Registration, wine & cheese reception. Various ceremonies, slide presentations, music, displays, etc.
(9 - 9:30 p.m.) - Welcome and Opening Remarks.
(9:30 - 12 mid.) - Social and Music.
Sat. (10 - 12 noon) - Various large group photos by location and family branches taken by our Reunion photographers - "Photo Master" - a treasure for your family memoirs.

(1 - 6 p.m.) - Family picnic, barbecue, music, sing-a-long, bar, etc. - Tracadie, N.S. A very rustic and scenic sight close to St. Peters Church. The Church was built on the original crown grant of land owned and donated to the Church by the Gerriors of Tracadie. The Government has made this Church location an official historic and heritage site.
(7 - 9 p.m.) - Acadian film presentations (Bloomfield Center)
(9 p.m. - 1 a.m.) - Barn Dance - The River Band and other bands T.B.A., popular music, rock-country, Acadian fiddle music, Cajon music, etc.
Sun. (10 - 11:30 a.m.) - Genealogy corner (a place where different branches can get together and discuss their own history genealogy stories regarding their own branch.
(1:30 p.m.) - Family Mass celebrated by Giroir clergy descendants, Fr. Giroir of West Arichat, Fr. Murphy of Pictou, Fr. Giroir of Louisiana and other celebrants to be announced.
(2:30 p.m.) - Photo of entire group after Mass, 50-50 draw, hugs, kisses, goodbyes. Many descendants will want to see more of N.S., P.E.I. and/or N.B. We will send the N.S. Tourist book with all activities and attractions listed (our reunion is listed in this book).

Acadian Awakenings: An Acadian Family In Exile

FIRST INTERNATIONAL REUNION, 1990   Page 3

III. COMMITTEES

Because of the wide spread network needed for the International Reunion, we have established two committees: **The Maritime Provinces Organizing Committee and a Committee at Large**, in various areas of North America and France. They are as follows:

A. **Maritime Province Organization Committee:**

1. Secretary - Anne Marie Schroeder Dartmouth, N.S. 463-7937, (D-10) on master chart, daughter of Martina (Gerrior) Comeau, Larry's River, N.S.
2. Mary Fougere, Tracadie, N.S. 232-2484, (E-5), daughter of Bertha Giroir, Monastery, N.S.
3. Ruth MacNeil, Cape Breton, N.S. 562-6227, (G-9), granddaughter of Allen Gerrior, Larry's River, N.S.
4. Dr. Edgar Girouard, Moncton, N.B. (506) 854-7001, (E-3b), son of Arthur Girouard, Moncton, N.B.
5. Daniel Stewart, New Glasgow, N.S. 755-1367, (D-8), son of Mary Eldora (Mini) Gerrior, New Glasgow, N.S.
6. Fr. Conrad P. Giroir, West Arichat, N.S. 226-2015, (E-3b) son of Jean Baptist Girroir, West Arichat, N.S.
7. Rita Kay (Girouard), Halifax, N.S. 477-2270, (E-3b) daughter of Louis Girouard, N.B.
8. Verna Gionet (Gerrior), Halifax, N.S. 422-9429, (F-10) daughter of John S. Gerrior, Halifax, N.S.
9. Brad Pellerin, Larry's River, N.S. 525-2514, (I-10) son of Clara Pellerin (Gerrior).
10. Councillor Robert Girroir, Deputy Mayor of Antigonish 863-3670, (E-5) son of Charles Girroir, Tracadie, N.S.
11. Evelyn Oakley (Gerrior), Lower Sackville, N.S. 864-0560, (F-10) daughter of John S. Gerrior, Halifax, N.S.
12. Christine Morin, Bedford, N.S. 835-1263, (E-3b) P.E.I. branch, daughter of Mary Gerrior, Trenton.
13. Bill Gerrior, Chairman, Brookside, N.S. 852-3926, son of John S. Gerrior, Halifax, N.S.
14. Jean LeJeune, West Arichat, C.B., N.S. 226-2361, (E-3b) granddaughter of Adele Giroir.
15. Paul R. Girouard, Bedford, N.S. 835-8008, (H-4M1), Quebec Branch, son of Jean Marie Girouard, Longueuil, Quebec.
16. Estelle McMaster, Dartmouth, N.S. 462-3565, (G-10) granddaughter of the late Cecilia Avery (nee Gerrior).

All Area Codes for N.S. are 902.

B. **COMMITTEES - MEMBERS AT LARGE:**

Louisiana

1. Firmin Girouard branches (Louisiana) (E-3b) Dep. 1755
   Paul Richard Girouard and Linda, Gretna, Louisiana (504) 394-3834, son of Paul Roy Girouard, Broussard, Louisiana.
   Sheila Decou (Girouard), Broussard, Louisiana (504) 318-4559, daughter of Paul Roy Girouard, Broussard.
2. Honore Giroir branches (Louisiana) (E-3b) Uncle of Firmin (above)
   Mary Jane Siracusa, Gretna, La. (504) 393-6786, daughter of Beatrice Peebles (Giroir)
   Neva Fraizier, Gretna, La., granddaughter of Justinian Giroir)
   Marianne Areta, Metairie, La., daughter of Andrew Giroir Matairie
   Don J. and Frank Giroir, New Orleans, La. (504) 488-2271 (E-3b), sons of Francois Etienne Giroir, Platinville, La.

France

3. Madame Touret, Loudun Dept. of Vienne Director of the Tourist Bureau, Loudun - Co-ordinator; Isabelle Sicq, St. Jean de Sauves, Dept. of Vienne, France, Girroire descendant; Councillor Boudowin de la Bouillerie and wife Marie (nee Girroire) Moncluton, Dept. of Vienne; Councillor Jean Pierre Girroire and wife Isabelle, Veniers Dept. of Vienne. France - Andree Gombert descendant of Francois Girouard and her husband Yves Gombert, Godu Michel Girroire, Maribeau, Dept. of Vienne.
4. Richard Girouard, Calgary, Canada (403) 244-6228, (D-3b) son of Adrian Girouard, St. Vital, Winnipeg.
5. Raymond J. Girouard, Aylmer, Quebec, Can. (819) 684-6850, (E-3b) son of Alyre Girouard.
6. Denise Wall (Girouard) Providence, R.I., U.S.A. (401) 751-6227, (J-3a) daughter of Dr. Ferdinand, Louis Girouard.
7. Fernand Girouard, Pawtaucket, R.I., U.S.A.; Maxime Girouard, Tucon, Arizona (602) 886-9954, (J-3a), son and daughter of Joseph Honore Girouard.
8. Merilyn Bourbonais, Wauwatosa, Wisconsin, U.S.A. (414) 476-6673, (H-4M1), daughter of Antoinette Louise Girouard.
9. Manon Girouard, St. Hyacinthe, Quebec, Can. (514) 773-4165, (1-3a), son of Jean Louis Girouard.
10. Daniel J. Girouard, Calgary, Alberta, Can. (403) 288-6970, (H-4M1), grandson of Noel Girouard.
11. Desiree and Esmee Girouard, Ottawa, Can. (613) 233-6082, (H-4M1), daughters of Lieut. Colonel Rene Arthur de la Bruere Girouard.
12. Andre Girouard, Sudbury, Ont. Can. (705) 673-3959 (H-4M1), son of Joseph-Arthur Girouard.
13. Jean Girouard (Judge), St. Lambert, Que. Can. (514) 466-1950, Canadian Girouard branch, son of Josaphat Girouard.
14. Robert Girouard (Notaire-Notary), Terrasse Vaudrevevil, Que., Can. (514) 453-1230, (D-3b), son of Alphonse Girouard.
15. A. Brian Girouard, Newmarket, Ont., Can. (416) 853-7247, (E-3b), son of Charles Gerrior, Trenton, N.S.
16. Blanche & Arnold Hughes, Porter's Lake (827-3894); Brad & Winnie Comeau (son and daughter of Martina (nee Gerrior) Comeau.
17. Marie Gerrior, Sydney, daughter of John S. Gerrior; Dianne Clair Pellerine, daughter of   Clara Pellerine (nee Gerrior).

I would like to thank all the members of the organizing committees and the committees at large for their assistance and ask that you keep in touch with your local branches. I would like both the Maritime Organization Committee and the members of the Committee at Large as mentioned above, to send me a wallet-sized photo of themselves, with your pre-registration, so that I can arrange a display for the reunion weekend.

Also, it is very important that all Girouard descendants receiving this letter check with their own close relatives who may wish to attend, but have not received this letter. This letter is not being mailed to all Girroires, Girouards, etc. in the telephone books. That has already been done in past mail outs; i.e., for last reunion and for recent mailouts to Quebec, Louisiana and Southern States - in both cases, I used telephone directories. This letter is being sent only to those Girouards, Girroires, etc. who responded to those past telephone directory mailings. However, it is still impossible to reach everyone even with this method.

Appendices

FIRST INTERNATIONAL REUNION, 1990

V. ACCOMMODATION & TRAVEL

The closest airport to Antigonish is Halifax International (approximately 120 miles). The Acadian Bus Lines goes out of Halifax to Antigonish. The terminal is just across the street from St. F. X. University where our event is being held. Also, there are many car rental businesses from Halifax which I recommend, if you wish to see N.S. and all its beautiful secluded inlets and Acadian villages, towns, etc.

ACCOMMODATIONS: Antigonish is a lovely town with conveniences similar to any small town. There are a number of hotels and motels in and around Antigonish which I will list for you. Families and individuals are responsible for looking after their own accommodation arrangements and meals. Since we expect so many in this small town, it is absolutely necessary that you book accommodations very early and avoid disappointment.

University Residence: Many descendants can book rooms at the University. The accommodations are not that of a hotel but are like any student rooms, with a desk and a single or double bed. There is a common washroom on each floor, one for ladies and one for gentlemen and a common lounge on each floor. The cost is very reasonable at $16.50 per night per person for singles, and $28.50 for doubles (10% tax included and prices subject to change).

For those who find this accommodation suitable, I recommend it highly, since it contributes to the spirit and feeling of togetherness when close relatives are located on the same floor in the residence. We try to book rooms under the same grandfather's name or by area, where possible. This allows you to meet many of your own branch and chat to many relatives.

THE RESIDENCE MANAGER IS HOLDING A BLOCK OF ROOMS OPEN FOR A PERIOD OF FOUR (4) WEEKS AFTER THE DATE OF THIS MAILOUT. After that time the rooms will be available for other groups and then you may not be able to book a room because they may be filled. So don't forget if you are booking the residence, CALL NOW. Please also give your grandfather's or grandmother's name (on the Girroire side) along with the spouse' name and the location where they lived. It would also greatly help us if you would give the Residence Director your master chart number and sub-chart number if I supplied this information to you at the last reunion or in recent correspondence. PLEASE REMEMBER THAT IF YOU REQUIRE A GROUND LEVEL FLOOR FOR PHYSICAL OR OTHER REASONS, LET THE RESIDENCE DIRECTOR KNOW THIS INFORMATION WHEN YOU CALL TO BOOK YOUR ROOM.

The Residence Director looking after reservations for our reunion is ALMA MAC NEIL (902) 867-3970. The Residence Manager is DOROTHY LANDER.

Motels: Motels in and around Antigonish (area code 902 for all calls). Ask the motel clerk to register you also under the name of "The International Girouard/Girroire Acadian Reunion. This will allow us to make a list of where everyone is staying, which makes it easier for relatives to find each other. We will post the list at the Reunion.

    Chateau Motel, 112 Post Road (863-4842)
    Claymore Hotel, The Mall, Antigonish (863-1050)
    Colonial Motor Inn, 41 James, Antigonish (863-4212)
    Dingle Motel, Lower South River (863-3730)
    Oasis Hotel, South River (863-3557)
    Valley View Motel, 295 Hawthorne Street (863-2939)
    Wandlyn Inn, 158 Main (863-4001)
    Whidden Trailer Court - for travel trailers, Center of town, 11 Hawthorne (863-3736)

For more detailed information phone Toll Free Number (check numbers listed on back of this pre-registration form). Perhaps you should copy these numbers before sending this form back to me.

I repeat what I said in our first reunion endeavors (this time with more committment and conviction than ever because of our international status):

"Our own close relatives give this reunion a reason to be, and an event to look forward to, to cherish and pass on to our children. It is even more exciting when this is happening in a cultural atmosphere where other related family branches are sharing this same experience and heritage. We are making history!!!" IT WILL BE A ONCE IN A LIFETIME EVENT!!

So please help us organize for your maximum pleasure, experience and enjoyment BY COMPLETING THE ENCLOSED PRE-REGISTRATION FORM NOW AND MAILING IT WITHIN THE NEXT THREE WEEKS, BEFORE IT GETS MISPLACED OR FORGOTTEN. Thus it is done and we just have to patiently wait until July 27.

Make all cheques or money orders payable to The International Gerrior (or your own spelling) Reunion.

The fee covers all postage involved in the surveys, mailouts, all stationery supplies, rented costs for facilities, refreshments, various decorations, cost for music entertainment, rentals of various equipment needed for the reunion, numerous long distance calls throughout the U.S., Canada and France, printing of various charts and materials, photocopying, genealogy research.

TALK TO YOUR OLDER RELATIVES, PRE-REGISTER NOW, BOOK YOUR ACCOMMODATIONS, DIG OUT THE OLD PHOTOGRAPHS AND GET THEM READY TO BRING AND SHARE WITH OTHERS. MAKE A DISPLAY, IF YOU WISH, ON BRISTOL BOARD, TO HAVE POSTED AT THE REUNION ON OPENING NIGHT.

If you have any history notes or stories or very old pictures you can donate to my collection I would love to receive them. I can't guarantee all material can be used in the book but certainly it would be considered. Make sure all pictures are clearly marked as to who is in the photo, and make sure all notes, etc. are marked as to their owner. These are very valuable papers and photos so please do not send me original printed matter, but a photocopy; and not the original pictures but a print or a negative of the photo. Please send any of the above information with your pre-registration form so that I can have an opportunity to organize all this info for the reunion.

I realize this correspondence is very long but I wanted everyone to be up-to-date on everything.

The next correspondence will be a final update in the spring.

Any donations to our cause can be sent with the pre-registration form. Donations will be used to do further research and to help defray costs of the book on the Girouards, Gerriores. Acknowledgements will be stated in the book by name. So brush up on your French or English, keep to your diet, and take care until then. Thank you all for your interest and enthusiasm, and I hope to see you all in July.

Cousin,

Bill Gerrior

Bill Gerrior

International Reunion

of the

Girroire, Girouard, Gerrior, Girroir, Gerroir, etc. Acadian Family Decendants

July 27, 28, 29, 1990
(St. Francis Xavier University
Antigonish, N.S.

Deadline Date: (3 weeks after receipt of this form, because of long term planning needed).

Name _____
Spouse _____
Mailing Address: Street _____
City/Town _____
Country _____
Postal Code _____
(If applicable) Telephone (___) _____
Area Code

My Father is _____ Spouse _____
lived at _____
My Grand Father _____ Spouse _____
lived at _____
My Great Grand Father _____ Spouse _____
lived at _____

In many places throughout Canada and U.S.A. where Girouards, Giorroires have settled, very often there is a street named after them or a location carrying their name. I have recorded many of these places. If you know of one of these, please drop me a note as to its location and any history that may be attached to the reason for using the Girroire name. Please include any information

Charts
- 99% of all who attended the last Reunion and all who have recently corresponded with me this past year have received a master chart and a hand written subchart/s which tie into the Master chart. PLEASE TRY TO MEMORIZE THESE NUMBERS AND DON'T FORGET TO BRING THE CHARTS WITH YOU TO THE REUNION.

I RECEIVED THE ABOVE CHARTS Yes _____ No _____

If "Yes", MY SUBCHART NUMBER IS _____
(this is the number written under each letter across the very top of the hand printed subchart/s.

My Master Chart # is _____. This is the letter/number such as (D-2) or (E-3B) which is referred to on the hand written chart and this letter/number represents the block on the master chart where your Family branch ties into the master plan of the Family Tree back to Francois 1640.

If "no" to above please include any additional information on your branch. We will keep trying to link up your family genealogically. We have tried to keep plans simple to keep the cost as low as possible. The minimum costs is $25.00 per adult and $13.00 per child 16 or under. A family rate for two adults and two or more children as defined above is maximum of $75.00, regardless of number of children.

Pre-Registration
Please complete and enclose the appropriate amount of money in cheque or money order. THE NAMES OF THE PERSONS IN MY GROUP WHO WILL BE REGISTERING WITH ME ARE:

1) First _____ Last _____ Age _____ $ _____ .00 Amount
2) First _____ Last _____ Age _____ $ _____ .00 Amount
3) First _____ Last _____ Age _____ $ _____ .00 Amount
4) First _____ Last _____ Age _____ $ _____ .00 Amount
5) First _____ Last _____ Age _____ $ _____ .00 Amount
6) First _____ Last _____ Age _____ $ _____ .00 Amount

I registered for the First Maritime Reunion in 1985.
Yes _____ No _____

Reunion Cups
I would like to place an order for my reunion cup, to be paid for at the reunion. These are White and Gold designed cups with Girouard, Girroire, etc spelled in all derivations as well as coats of arms. The date of 1990, the place, etc., "International Reunion" is written around the ridge. A lovely souvenir. (costs $6.00) These must be pre-ordered now so that all cups ordered are sold. They are cups that are designed and produced only for this occasion and cannot be purchased or ordered in any small quantities. Please order now and avoid disappointment, they were a very popular item at our last reunion and we ran out.

Please order me (quantity) _____ Reunion Cup/Cups.
I do not want to order any cups _____

Accommodation
I have or will be booking the Residence at the University. Yes _____ No _____
If NO, I have or will be booking the _____ Motel.

I am living in town and or at (address) _____

Entertainment
If you would like to participate in our Saturday afternoon sing-a-long please indicate below.
I sing _____ I play a _____
I dance _____ other _____

Order of Good Times
Complete this section only if you live outside N.S. I received an "ORDER OF GOOD TIME CERTIFICATE" from N.S. on a previous occasion.
Yes _____ No _____ (the Tourist Bureau only gives these out once to any guest to our province.

Book
If you have already answered this question on your response again, simply so that I have all the information in one location (ie. this form) I would be interested in purchasing a book on the Girroire, Girouard history, genealogy and reunion activities.
Yes _____ No _____. With such a vast amount of info now collected and still coming in, it is very important to record this info in print, to pass on in some organized permanent record form such as a book, showing all our heritage and links as a large family.

462

Appendices

Welcome to Nova Scotia

Nova Scotia, Canada's Ocean Playground, is a 350-mile-long peninsula that beckons the adventurous traveller with beautiful coastal scenery, colourful marine heritage and a lively maritime lifestyle that is as irresistable as the siren-song of the sea.

You'll find quiet coves, picturesque ports, long sandy beaches, and wind-swept headlands. There are exciting modern cities with just the right blend of old and new, and dozens of coastal towns and villages steeped in the traditions of three centuries of seafaring, still telling their tales of schooner races, privateer raids, pirate gold and rum running.

Nova Scotia is surrounded by four bodies of water — the Atlantic Ocean, Bay of Fundy, Northumberland Strait and the Gulf of St. Lawrence — with a coastline that curves, bends and stretches for 4,625 miles.

Nova Scotia has the highest (and lowest) tides in the world, the deepest water this side of the Continental Shelf, the warmest water north of the Carolina's, the most photographed fishing

village in North America, the world's second-largest natural harbour and a hearty highland greeting in Gaelic that means one hundred thousand welcomes.

You can swim, fish, sail, row, paddle and windsurf. There's bird watching, whale watching, raft riding, rock hounding, clam digging and there's something called a tidal bore (a wave of water rushing up river against the current). Honest.

Inland, there are rivers, lakes and streams with salmon and trout; centuries-old forts and churches; magnificent mansions converted to bed and breakfast homes; country fairs and road-side fruit stands.

And, when it's time to celebrate, Nova Scotians know how to throw a party — from the world-famous Nova Scotia International Tattoo to local church strawberry suppers. There are Clan gatherings, dory races, Town Crier competitions, highland games, buskers, barbecues, blueberries and bluegrass.

Our welcome mat is always out and our greeting is always sincere.

Come to the land of 100,000 welcomes — Canada's seaside wonderland — Nova Scotia.

International Reunion

of the
Giroire, Girouard, Gerrior, Giroir, Gerroir, etc.

Acadian Family Decendants
(St Francis Xavier University)
<u>Antigonish, N.S.</u>

Pre-Registration Form

PLEASE RETURN TO: Bill Gerrior
Box 20, Site 16A, RR#2
Arndale,
N.S, Canada B3L 4J2

Deadline Date: (3 weeks after receipt of this form, because of long term planning needed)

CHECK IN is the FREE information and reservations system brought to you by the Nova Scotia Department of Tourism and Culture and the Tourism Industry.

For further travel information, call Check in toll free.

From Nova Scotia, New Brunswick and Prince Edward Island, 1-800-565-7105

From Halifax-Dartmouth area, 425-5781

From Newfoundland and Quebec, 1-800-565-7130

From Central and Southern Ontario, 1-800-535-7140

From Northern Ontario, Manitoba Saskatchewan, Alberta and British Columbia, 1-800-565-7166

From the Continental United States, 1-800-341-6096

From Maine only, 1-300-492-0843

Produced for complimentary distribution by the Department of Tourism and Culture.

463

Acadian Awakenings: An Acadian Family In Exile

<u>INTERNATIONAL ACADIAN REUNION OF GERRIOR, GIROIRE, GIROIR, GIROUARD, GIRROIR, GERROIR, ETC.</u>
<u>JULY 27, 28, 29, 1990 - ST. FRANCIS XAVIER UNIVERSITY, ANTIGONISH, NS & TRACADIE, NS</u>

June 20, 1990

Dear Cousins:

Thank you for your great response. We are anxiously awaiting to see you on the 27, 28, 29 of July. The time is now approaching very quickly!

Our committee has been very busy over the past months preparing, corresponding and contacting many cousins.

We have pre-registered descendants from far and wide - from France, Louisiana and many other states of America, as well as many branches stemming from Quebec and the Maritime provinces (Prince Edward Island, New Brunswick, Nova Scotia) and other central and western provinces in Canada. We are now over 500 pre-registered guests. A party is definitely on! We also expect quite a few registrations on site who will be responding to our news release to 200 newspapers, radio and TV stations here in the Maritimes and Quebec.

*It would also be very helpful to have a brief news release in your own home town area, if outside of the areas listed above. If anyone receiving this letter would like to do this for us we would appreciate your assistance (See enclosed brief news release. Just contact the local newspaper and ask if they would include this notice.

In this way we feel we have done our best to make descendants aware of this "Once in a lifetime event".

If any committee members have not as yet sent me their photos, I would appreciate if you would do this as soon as possible.

ARRIVAL
For descendants arriving at the Halifax Airport, there is an Acadian line bus service to Antigonish which operates daily at a cost of $15.25 one way. Times are 8:40 am daily, 9:35 am daily except Saturday, 1:55 pm daily, 6:25 pm daily except Saturday. The Halifax Airport is about 90 minutes from Antigonish and about 1/2 hour in the other direction from Halifax City.

UPDATE ON ACCOMODATIONS AT UNIVERSITY
There has been a small change in price for rooms at the University, which we mentioned in our first letter as a likely possibility. However, the change is not great and it really seems to be a better deal. The price for a single room was $17.50 + 10% tax = $19.25 but is now $22.40, breakfast included. The price for a double was $15.50 + 10% tax = $17.00 per person, but now is $22.00 per person (includes breakfast). These changes are retroactive for any bookings for the Reunion. For further information or bookings call Alma MacLean at 867-3970. Also, you may inquire about baby sitting arrangements for the weekend

Remember the rooms at the university are student rooms and do not have motel services. You must supply your own soap and towels and there is one male and one female common washroom on each floor. If you have not already booked a room, there are still rooms available at the University but most of the motels are completely booked in Antigonish. However, inquiries could be made to motels in neighboring towns or villages of Tracadie (15 min. away), New Glasgow (1/2 hour from Antigonish) and Truro (3/4 hr. away).

** Enclosed is a map with directions to the University.

One correction to my first letter to keep the records straight: The Canadian Girouards came to Quebec 75 years after Francois Girouard arrived in Port Royal (1640's), not 75 years after deportation (1755).

<u>DON'T FORGET TO BRING YOUR MASTER CHART AND YOUR HAND WRITTEN SUBCHARTS IF YOU HAVE ALREADY RECEIVED THEM FROM ME.</u>

Anyone visiting Port Royal before the Reunion, remember to look for Tupperville on the east side of the Annapolis River across from BellsIsle. Here, on the bend of the river, is where Girouardville or Girroirville was located - known today as Tupperville. (This information from a map dated 1755.)

<u>The following is an update on the agenda for the weekend:</u>

<u>Friday, July 27</u> - When arriving at Antigonish, please use Exit 32 off Trans Canada Highway into Antigonish. If arriving during the day, or before Friday, please go directly to the Morrison Building on the St. Francis Xavier University campus. (see map enclosed) University Campus can be seen from Trans Canada Highway.

If arriving during registration time (6pm - 8:30 pm), please go directly to the <u>Bloomfield Centre</u> for registration and residence accommodation, keys, etc. for room. (See campus map for location Most will be staying in MacIsaac Hall, if you booked in residenc

Appendices

Friday, July 27 — Rooms at the University are very basic with male and female
(continued)   washrooms on each floor and one lounge on each wing. (a double
room is two single beds and a single room is one single bed).
You may wish to bring a portable crib or playpen for small
children and/or sleeping bag for children sleeping with parents.

6:00 - 8:45 pm — Meet the "Straight Area Scottish Strings", Registration, meet
friends and relatives, displays, wine and cheese, listen to the
music of "The Gerrior Family Ensemble", refreshments. Pool is
open 7-8 pm. Children under 12 must be accompanied by an adult.

Please bring photo albums and any history or stories you wish to
share with relatives. (please xerox any notes, newspaper clipp-
ings, etc. you may wish to contribute to our collection. (Put
in envelope and mark Bill Gerrior, c/o Front Desk, Bloomfield
Centre.

8:45 - 9:30 pm — Gather in adjacent Mackay Room for opening remarks and welcomes,
introduction of special guests.

9:30 - 10:00 pm — Genealogy connections, deportation slide and music presentation.

10:00 - 10:15 pm — Special presentations in honour and memory of Senator Edward
Lavin Girroir, second Acadian Minister in the Nova Scotia
Legislature, and Fr. Hubert Girroir, Educational, Religious
leader, Nationalist and leader for the cause of French Language
in N.S. (both descendants of the original Jean Gerrior "Mangeau"
of Tracadie, from which the Guysborough and Antigonish County
Gerrior, Girroir's descend. Special presentation to descendants
from France.

10:15 - 10:30 pm — Order of Good Cheer Certificates to descendants out of province
who have not previously received these on previous occasions.
(pre arranged from info on registration form)

10:30 - 12:00 pm — Special Guests - Corker of Port Royal - Social and Music
(coffee house style), Acadian dancing, John W. Gerrior and
others and various dance displays by "Dance Interplay",
directed by Marie (Gerrior) Nugent.

You will be registering on Friday evening at one of the following registration
tables which represent root areas of early settlement after deportation years:

1) Guysborough County - All descendants roots in Larry's River, Lundy, Charlos
   (colour code-red)   Cove

2) Antigonish County   - All descendants with roots in Tracadie, Merlin,
   (colour code-blue)   Heatherton, Havre Boucher

3) Richmond County   - All descendants with roots in West Arichat, Arichat,
   (colour code-yellow) Port Royal, Petit de Grat, etc.

4) P.E.I.   - All descendants with roots in Georgetown, Mitchell River,
   (colour code-yellow) etc.

5) New Brunswick   - All descendants with roots in St. Antoine, Ste. Marie,
   (colour code-white)   Ste. Anne, Boutouche, Cocagne, Moncton, Shediac, Neguac,
                         Sheila, Lagaceville, etc.

6) Louisiana   - All descendants from Houma, La Fayette, Gibson, Tribodaux,
   (colour code-white   Platinville, St. James, Paincourtville, Morgan City, New
   and yellow)   Orleans and Greater New Orleans area, Kenner, Gretna,
                         Iberville, Broussard, etc.

7) Quebec Acadian -   (Acadian and Canadian Branches)
   (colour code-red   All descendants with roots in Lotbiniere, Deschambault,
   and blue)   Les Becquets, Gentilly, Becancour, Princeville,
                      Plessiville, Victoriville, Athabaska, Tetford Mines,
                      Drummondville, Saint Ours, L'assumptions, Saint Denis,
                      Saint-Antoine sur Richelieu La Presentation, Saint Jude,
                      Saint Barnabe-sud, St. Bernard, Saint Hyacinthe, Warwick,
                      Sherbrook, Saint Pie, Iberville, Longueuil, St. Lambert,
                      Deux-Montagnes, Saint Eustuche, St. Benoit, Valleyfield,
                      Chateauguay, Marieville.

8) France   Dept. de Vienne at Deux Sevres
   (colour code-red,
   blue and white
   hat, with yellow
   shirt or blouse)

We have colour coded each root area, using the colours of the Acadian flag and
it would again be great fun and certainly add to the spirit of the reunion if
you would wear a hat and/or a shirt, blouse or sweater of the colour assigned
to your group above. This helps to quickly identify branches and makes for a
pretty colourful group. If unsure of your root area, please check the alphabetical master list at entrance to Bloomfield Centre, when registering.

Saturday, July 28 - Late Registration

9:00 - 10:00 am - Bloomfield Centre

12:30 - 2:00 pm - at entrance to Picnic at Tracadie - Shuttle service available by bus from Antigonish 12:00 noon to Tracadie, returning at 6:30 pm. Sign up Friday night.

10:00 am - 12:30 pm - Branch Photography - On Football Stadium stands at the University. (beginning with GUYSBOROUGH COUNTY AND ANTIGONISH COUNTY ONLY), Please see schedule on back side for coordination of breakfast and branch photography.
PLEASE ARRIVE FIVE MINUTES BEFORE SCHEDULED TIME
For this reunion, we hired a professional photographer, Peter Tenwolde, who is the owner of a Halifax based company called Photomaster. (See attached information). We encourage you to participate in this service - Freeze your memories with professional quality photos for special events - it's worth it.

1:00 - 6:00 pm - Family Reunion Picnic - Sing-a-long - Come join the fun, come up and sing yourself or dance, etc., if you have a talent. Location - Tracadie, (15 miles from Antigonish on the Trans Canada, heading to Cape Breton, take Monastery exit and make a right turn at the end of this exit, heading to Tracadie - 2 minutes from this exit). The Picnic Site is on recreation land belonging to St. Peter's Parish, overlooking beautiful Tracadie Harbour. This property is part of the original Crown grant of land given to the first Gerrior to arrive in Tracadie (Jean Gerrior) dit Beaulieu, and nick-named "Mangeau", who settled there after the deportation years. The Gerriors later gave this part of their land to the Church.

If families are coming by car, would each family bring what you would normally take to a beach for a picnic, i.e., food for lunch and supper, small barbecue, etc., lawn chair, cooler with drinks, picnic blanket (there are no picnic tables on site, however, some hall tables may be used for such purpose). Bring cameras, tape recorders to catch the sounds of N.S., suntan lotion (for fog burn, ha, ha).

If you are coming from quite far away and/or you don't wish to barbecue, or pack a lawn chair, etc., you may also purchase sandwiches, cold plate, chili, fish chowder, hot dogs, beverages and tea or coffee at the hall canteen on the site at very, very reasonable prices. We hope that people will take advantage of this service or may use a combination of these alternatives so that we can also help support the local Fire Department and women's organization who are providing this food. Bar facilities are also available.

Also, if unable to pack a lawn chair we do have some wooden chairs and some hall tables may be used as picnic tables.

6:00 - 8:30 pm - Return to university or motels, to freshen up and get ready for dance at the University, same location as Friday night at Bloomfield Centre.

6:00 - 8:00 pm - Pool open University

8:00 - 9:00 pm - Pool open for adults only.

8:30 - 1:00 am - Dance at Bloomfield centre, featuring two bands and also enjoy cajun, acadian, popular and country music. Beer and bar available.

Sunday, July 29 -

10:00am - 12:00 noon - Those interested in genealogy and sharing notes, displays, collecting addresses, etc. meet in Bloomfield Centre in Root Area groups. Each group will be assigned a room.

12:00 - 1:00 pm - Lunch on your own at a place of your choice in town.

1:15 pm - Mass at Cathedral co-celebrated by Fr. Conrad Girroir-West Arichat, Fr. Douglas Murphy-Larry's River, Fr. Frank Giroir-Louisiana and other clergy TBA, also with music coordinated by Brad Pellerin with other descendants TBA.

After Mass, all branches will proceed to the field for one large Group Picture. PLEASE STAY FOR THIS GROUP PHOTO BECAUSE I PLAN TO USE IT FOR A FEATURE PART OF OUR BOOK WHICH I WILL BE IN THE PROCESS OF WRITING AFTER THE REUNION. I WOULD LIKE YOU ALL TO BE IN THIS PICTURE FOR THE BOOK.

Appendices

Page 4

After this photo, we will draw for the lucky winner of a pair of tickets, donated by Air Canada. These tickets are for a return trip to Paris from Canada. (See details for criteria, etc. and eligibility at the booth at the Reunion). A special Thanks to Air Canada for their great support of our project.

- 50/50 Draw
- Closing remarks, thank you's, and good bye's. We do suggest that you visit other parts of the Province of Acadian, family or historical interests, such as Port Royal, Louisbourg, Grand Pré and root areas in P.E.I. and New Brunswick.

Reunion cups which were pre-ordered will be given at registration time and may be stored for the evening in the office.

A limited number of extra cups were ordered and will be available on first-come, first-served basis. Florence Cummerson will again make ceramic souvenirs for the Reunion, as well as donate a ceramic lighthouse to be won at the dance.

Security - We cannot be responsible for any loses but would certainly like to return any lost items, so would everyone please mark photo albums, pictures, etc. with name and address. Keys are provided for residence. For your protection, please make sure doors are locked when leaving.

Baby Sitting - A list of babysitters from manpower will be posted Friday in the Residence Office (Morrison House) during the day and the evening at the Bloomfield Centre.

For communications and emergency purposes, PLEASE REMEMBER TO GIVE YOUR HOTEL NAME AND ROOM NUMBER, AND CAR LICENCE AT REGISTRATION.

Looking forward to meeting you all on Friday, July 27.

Cousin Bill
Box 20, Site 16A
R.R.#2, ARMDALE, N.S.
B3L 4J2
(902) 852-3926

BREAKFAST AND PHOTO SCHEDULE
SATURDAY, JULY 28

BRANCH	SATURDAY BREAKFAST	BRANCH PHOTOS
Guysborough County Descendants	8:00 am - Goshen Restaurant on main highway towards Cape Breton, past Antigonish	10:00 a.m. SHARP ST. F.X. FOOTBALL FIELD
Antigonish County Descendants	8:00 am - Goshen Restaurant	10:00 a.m. SHARP ST. F.X. FOOTBALL FIELD
Richmond County (West Arichat) Descendants	9:00 am - Moonlight Restaurant, Main Street, Antigonish	10:30 a.m. SHARP ST. F.X. FOOTBALL FIELD
P.E.I. Descendants	9:00 am - Wandlyn Motel Main Street Antigonish	10:30 a.m. SHARP ST. F.X. FOOTBALL FIELD
Louisiana Descendants	9:00 am - Wandlyn Motel	10:30 a.m. SHARP ST. F.X. FOOTBALL FIELD
New Brunswick Descendants	9:00 am - Claymore Motel (in Mall, Church Street)	10:30 a.m. SHARP ST. F.X. FOOTBALL FIELD
Quebec Descendants	10:00 am - Mother Webbs	11:00 a.m. SHARP ST. F.X. FOOTBALL FIELD
France Descencants	10:00 am - Mother Webbs	11:00 a.m. SHARP ST. F.X. FOOTBALL FIELD

Appendix 8

Alphabetical index of first names found in each block of the master charts and subcharts of all descendants throughout all volumes of this book, carrying the family name regardless of spelling of the surname. The text within the square brackets indicates the place where you will find information presented on this ancestor/descendant. FCMC is presented in the France and Québec volumes. AMC is presented throughout all volumes, and each block of the AMC gives a location, if known.

b.= born
m.= was or is married to or was or is a mate of.
ca. circa (approximately)
Co.=County
Ant.=Antigonish
FR.=France
Guys.= Guysborough
La. = Louisiana
NB.= Province of New Brunswick
NS.= Province of Nova Scotia
PEI.= Province of Prince Edward Island (found in the NS & PEI Volume)
PQ. = Province of Québec
AMC= Acadian Master Chart descending from Francois Girouard and Jeanne Aucoin
FCMC= French–Canadian master chart descending from Antoine Girouard and Anne-Marie Barré
Chart 3006= the Belgium Master chart of Girouards descending from Piere Realh
Sch. = subchart

Note: Approximately 2000 ancestors and descendants appear in this index and all are traced back to 1671 Port Royal, Nova Scotia in the case of all Acadian descendants of François Girouard and Jeanne Aucoin (marked with various subchart numbers or AMC identification) or in the case of the French-Canadian descendants (marked with FCMC; 2000; 3006; or fc). All are traced back to the early 1700's in North America and France. The author has also traced many branches of these 2000 ancestors to present day, in the text of each of the five books. These names on these charts form the basic structure from which the author traces the many branches to present.

If you do not see yourself or any of your ancestors on this list, it does not mean your branch is not included in these books. Your branch will very likely be found in the text of one of these books if it belongs to one of the many branches that the author has traced. If you are not sure of your ancestors' names, contact with the author could help you find these names and therefore find the corresponding chart which applies to your branch. See the author information at the beginning of this book for contacts.

Appendices

If known, the index provides the date born, date of death if known, the spouse's named (s), and the particular subchart (sch.) identification number (or letters in the case of master charts), and the name of places in which you can expect to find some information on this branch. Finally, the last province, state or country abbreviation at the end of the brackets provides the name of the volume where this chart is located and also indicates the geographical location of the descendant. There is a book for each of the provinces (ie. Book Two, Nova Scotia/Prince Edward Island; Book Three, New Brunswick; Book Four, Québec; Book Five, state of Louisiana; and Book One, France (this book). It is in these books that you will find much more detail on various branchs. This alphabetical list is by first name only since every person is a Girouard regardless of spelling.

Abraham b. 1817 d. 1895 m. ca. 1842) Lavina (Devine) Fougère [AMC]
Abraham b. 1822 d. 1916 m1. E. LeBlanc, m2. Domithilde m3. O. Marchand [Sch.163, Isle Madame, NS.]
Abraham b. 1860 d. 1936 m. Hélène Richard, 1885 [Sch. 35, & 36 Guys. Co. NS.]
Abraham (Abie) b. 1871 d. 1947 m. Martha Lavangie [Sch. 31& 32 Guys. Co. NS.]
Abraham b. 1904 d. 1985 m. Julie Jane Pellerin 1929 [Sch. 31, Guys. Co. NS.]
Abraham d. at two years [Sch. 35, Guys. Co., NS.]
Achille b. 1913 d. 1990 m1. Lina Richard, m2 Evelyn Page [Sch. 729, NB.]
Adélaïde Aglae b. 1816 m. Camille Broussard, 1832 [Sch. 162.1, La.]
Adélaïde m. Alexis Bernard 1832 [Sch.217 & 218, PQ., Acadian]
Adélaïde Eusilda b. 1832 m. Paul Leger 1850 [Sch. 162.1, La.]
Adélard b. 1896 d. 1984 m. L. Leduc, 1931 [Sch.2000, and Block N-5 FCMC]
Adélard, not married [Sch.2000, and Block N-5 FCMC]
Adèle b. 1848 m. Frédéric LeBlanc [Sch. 163, Isle Madame, NS.]
Adele b. 1858 d. 1929 m. Gus Benette [AMC]
Adele b. 1873 [Sch. 48, Guys. Co., NS.]
Adelina b. 1879 d. 1985 [Sch. 208, PQ., Acadian]
Adelina b. 1888 (Lena) Flora m. Archie Butler [AMC]
Adolphe m. Jane Bettez, 1876 [Sch. 218, PQ., Acadian]
Adolphe b. 1841 d. 1909 m. 1870 Clementine Broussard [Sch. 162.1, La.]
Agatha b. 1782 m. Joseph Genest 1809 [Sch. 217& 218 PQ., Acadian]
Agathe b. 1815 d. 1900 m. Etienne Caissie, 1834 [Sch. 700, NB.]
Agnès b. 1683 d. 1687 [Sch. 202, PQ. Acadian]
Agnès b. 1685 m. Abraham Gaudet 1701 [Sch. 202, PQ. Acadian]
Agnes b. 1869 m1. Wilbur Harding m2. FrankWilliams. [AMC]
Agnes Sophie b. 1906 m. Ernest Martin [Sch. 95, Guys. Co., NS.]
Agnes Cecelia b. 1902 m. Patrick Pitts [Sch. 48, Guys. Co., NS.]
Aimé b. 1803 d. 1826 [Sch. 542, NB.]
Aimé b. 1813 d. 1824 [Sch. 500, NB.]
Aimé b. 1842 d. m. Sylvia Robichaud, 1870 [Sch. 500 & 514, NB.]
Aimé b. 1870 d. 1922 m. Marie Cormier [Sch. 724, NB.]
Aimé b. 1907 d. 1974 m. Christine Brideau [Sch. 711, NB.]
Alban b. 1893 d. 1974 m. Marion Moore, no children [Sch. 705, NB.]

Albert b. 1879 m. T. Fraizier [Sch. 33, Guys. Co., NS.]
Albert b. 1885 [Sch. 164. Isle Madame. NS.]
Albert b. 1902 d. 1972 m1. S. LaLonde, 1932 m2. H. Gagnier, 1967 [Sch. 2000]
Albert b. 1915 d. 1997 m. Annette Melanson [Sch. 500, NB.]
Alberta m. Roger Beauchamp [Sch. 600, NB.]
Alex b. 1900 d. 1917 [Sch. 600, NB.]
Albina [Sch. 706, NB.]
Albina b. 1885 m. Mélasse Bourque [Sch. 300, NB.]
Albini m. Liliane Lamy, 1968 [Sch. 2000, and Block N-5 FCMC]
Alda b. 1905 d. 1922 [Sch. 527, NB.]
Aldegonde b. 1719 d. 1719 [Sch. 202, PQ. Acadian]
Aldéric [Sch.3001, Rodier Branch, Québec]
Alex b. 1900 d. 1917 [Sch. 600. NB.]
Alex b. 1913 m. Elizabeth Savoie [Sch. 711, NB.]
Alex b. [Sch. 420, France]
Alex Maximin b. 1877 [Sch. 33, Guys. Co., NS.]
Alexander (Leandre) (Soboy) b. 1895 d. 1974 m. Nancy Avery, 1929 [Sch. 32, Guys. Co., NS.]
Alexandre 1670 d. 1744 m. Marie Le Borgne ca. 1694 [AMC & Sch. 204, PQ., Acadian]
Alexandre b. 1696 [Sch. 204, PQ., Acadian]
Alexis b. 1807 d. 1826 [Sch. 217 & 218, PQ. Acadian]
Alexis [Sch. 163, Isle Madame, NS.]
Alexis b. 1838 d. 1907 m. Marie Girouard (Hilaire) 1868 [Sch. 300, NB.]
Alexis b. 1809 d. 1826 [Sch. 218, PQ. Acadian]
Alexis b. 1773 m. Madeleine Landry, 1796 [Sch. 213 & 216 PQ., Acadian]
Alexis b. 1777 [Sch. 213, PQ., Acadian]
Alexis d.1932 m. Exilda Oligny *dit* Livernois [Sch. 2000, and Block N-5 FCMC]
Alexis b. 1785 m. Charlotte Sanschagrin,1809 [Sch. 213, PQ. Acadian]
Alfred (Fred), not married [Sch. 717, NB.]
Alfred b. 1922 d. 1986 m. Annie Richard 1956 [Sch. 523, NB.]
Alfred m. Wanda French [Sch. 500, NB.]
Alfreda b. 1927 m. Dr. Paul Bluteau [Sch. 300, NB.]
Alice b. 1914 m. Clément Leblanc [Sch. 315, NB.]
Alice b.1899, d. 1992 m. Norbert Belliveau [Sch. 706, NB.]
Alice m. Edmond Arsenault [Sch. 737, NB.]
Alice m. Walter Fletcher [Sch. 95, Guys. Co., NS.]
Alice Thoralda b. 1884 m. Bill Shier, no children [Sch. 67, Guys. Co., NS.]
Aline m. T.E. Griffith [Sch. 217, PQ.]
Aline Girouard/Green m. Zénon LeBlanc [Sch. 309, NB.]
Allain (M.D.) [Sch. 300, NB.]
Allan (d) at 32 n.m [Sch. 162, P.E.I.]
Allan b. 1873 m1. Catherine Pellerin, m2. Elizabeth Pellerin [AMC & Sch. 95, Guys. Co., NS.]
Alphie b. 1882 [Sch. 315, NB.]
Alphonsine b. 1886 [Sch. 315, NB.]
Alphie Joseph [Sch. 523, NB.]
Alphonse b. 1843 m. Maria Le Chêne, 1876, [FCMC, PQ.]

Appendices

Alphonse m. Sarah Légère [Sch. 700, NB.]
Alvah J. Kennedy /Stewart b. 1928 d. 1958 m. Betty Hendsbee [Sch. 67, Guys. Co., NS.]
Alvina b. 1917 m. Alin Savoie [Sch. 711, NB.]
Alvina (Mina) m. Amédée Thériault [Sch. 164. Isle Madame. NS.]
Alvina m. Christophe Gadbois, 1891 [Sch. 3001, Rodier Branch, Québec]
Alyre b. 1903 d. 1930 m. Hélène Hébert [Sch. 600, NB.]
Alyre b. 1931 d. 1931 [Sch. 600, NB.]
Alyre Girouard/Green 1922 [Sch. 309, NB.]
Amand b. 1736 [see notes on Sch. 204, PQ., Acadian]
Amand m. Jeanne d'Arc Breault [Sch. 711, NB.]
Ambroise m. Pélagie Lavigueur, m2. Charlotte Langevin 1845 [Sch. 217& 218 PQ., Acadian]
Ambrose Girouard/Green b.1884 m. Julie LeBlanc, 1910 [Sch. 309, NB.]
Ambrose m. Loretta Richards [Sch. 31,Guys. Co. NS.]
Amédée &William (twins) b. 1911 d. 1911 [Sch. 163, Isle Madame, NS.]
Amelia Geraldine [Sch. 76, Guys. Co., NS.]
Amélie m. Sydney Forest [Sch. 217, P.Q Acadian]
Anastasie b. 1760 [Sch. 216, PQ., Acadian]
Anastasie b. 1770 m. 1791 Jean Marc Romard, [AMC]
Anastasie b. 1787 m. Charles Granger, 1810 [Sch. 162.1, La.]
André [Sch. 208, PQ. Acadian]
André [Sch. 400, France]
André b. 1920 d. 1975 , not married [Sch. 523, NB.]
André m. Araceli Jardeleza, 1973 [Sch. 2000, and Block N-5 FCMC]
André Girouard, [Sch. 218, PQ., Acadian]
André Girouard/Green [Sch. 309, NB.]
André m. Léonie Savoie [Sch. 711, NB.]
Andrée m. Richard Stranks, 1991 [Sch. 2000, and Block N-5 FCMC]
Angèle b. 1796 d. 1835 [Sch. 202, PQ. Acadian]
Angélina b. 1876 [Sch. 208, PQ., Acadian]
Angélique [Sch. 33, Guys. Co., NS.]
Angélique b. 1727 d. 1727 [FCMC, PQ.]
Angélique b. 1780 d. 1836 m. Charles Cormier, 1802 [Sch. 300,500,600 &700 NB.]
Angélique b. 1708 [Sch. 204, PQ., Acadian]
Angélique b. 1812 m. Charles Broussard, 1852 [Sch. 162, P.E.I.]
Angélique b. 1812 m. Guillaume Jacquet [Sch. 0,1,4,& 8 Tracadie, Ant. Co., NS.]
Angélique b. 1835 d. 1859 m. Jean Charpentier [Sch. 33, Guys. Co., NS.]
Angélique b. 1849 d. 1860 [Sch. 162, P.E.I.]
Angélique m. David Petitau, dit St-Saens,1793, [Sch. 216, PQ. Acadian]
Angélique Françoise b. 1749 Girouard of Boisrolin, no children [Chart fc, France]
Angelique Jeanne Josephe b. 1785 [Sch. 211, West Indies, La.]
Angélique m. Augustin Blanchet,1830 [Sch. 208, PQ., Acadian]
Angélique m. François Maurier Lapierre, 1802 [Sch. 208, PQ., Acadian]
Angélique m. Joseph Poissant [Sch. 216, PQ., Acadian]
Anita m. Gillis Lussier [Sch. 600, NB.]
Ann Myrtle m. Gregg Robley [Sch. 35, Guys. Co., NS.]

Acadian Awakenings: An Acadian Family In Exile

Anna (Nannie) b. 1879 m. Lawrence Russel [FCMC, PQ.]
Anna b. 1912 d.1996 m. 1937 Basil Doucette [AMC]
Anna m. Eric Roy [Sch. 717, NB.]
Anna m. Telex Boudreau [Sch. 514, NB.]
Anna Marguerite [Sch. 8, Ant. Co]
Anne b. 1722 m. Pierre Pellerin,1745 [Sch. 211, West Indies, La.]
Anne b. 1748 [see notes on Sch. 211, West Indies, La.]
Anne Agnes (Nelli) [Sch. 5, Ant. Co., NS.]
Anne Agnes b. 1910 [Sch. 5, Ant. Co., NS.]
Anne b. 1702 d. 1761 m. Thomas Doiron 1724 [Sch. 162.6 & 162.1 La.; 163 & 164 Isle Madame; 300,500,600 & 700 NB.]
Anne b. 1716 m. Joseph Richard, 1758 [Sch. 208, PQ., Acadian]
Anne b. 1721 m. Pierre Gaudet, 1740 [Sch. 213, 217, &218, PQ., Acadian]
Anne b. 1729 m. Justinien Dupuis, 1751 [Sch. 208, PQ., Acadian]
Anne b. 1733 [Sch. 204, PQ., Acadian]
Anne Josephte b. 1750 [Sch. 207, PQ., Acadian]
Anne b. 1751 [Sch. 211, West Indies, La.]
Anne b. 1766 d. 1831 m. Fabien Guillot [Sch. 162.6, La.]
Anne b. 1766 d. 1800 m. Charles Pierre Marc Blanchard, 1792, [Sch. 162.6 La.]
Anne b. 1794 d. 1875 m. Jean Ravion [Sch. 900, France]
Anne Charlotte b. 1660 d. 1742 m. ca.1675 Julien Lord [AMC]
Anne Charlotte b. 1877 m. Frank [Sch. 162, P.E.I.]
Anne Girouard/Green b. 1882 m. Marcel LeBlanc, 1907 [Sch. 309, NB.]
Anne Hélène b. 1728 m. Claude H. Benoît [AMC]
Anne Isabelle b. 1873 [Sch. 208, PQ., Acadian]
Anne m. Léon DesLauriers, 1874 [Sch. 34, Ant. Co., NS.]
Anne m. Pierre Gaudet [Sch. 202, PQ. Acadian]
Anne MacEachern m. Leonard J. Bowie [Sch. #1 Tracadie, Ant. Co., NS.]
Anne Marie b. 1697 d. [AMC]
Anne Marie m. Timothy Pinstone [Sch. 48, Guys. Co., NS.]
Anne Théodise b. 1739 m1. Pierre Arsenault, m2. Laurent Soly [[Sch. 162.6 & 162.1 La.; 163 & 164 Isle Madame; 300,500,600 & 700 NB.]
Annette b. 1884 m. Rosario Genest [Sch. 218, PQ., Acadian]
Annette m. Henri Richard [Sch. 737, NB.]
Annette m. Joseph Cyrias Blouin, 1939 [Sch. 2000, and Block N-5 FCMC]
Annie Agnes m. Pius White [Sch. 5, Ant. Co., NS.]
Annie b. 1899 d. 1968 m. Marcel Robichaud [Sch. 300, NB.]
Annie b. 1899 d. 1982 m. Jean Baptiste Thibodeau, 1921 [Sch. 705, NB.]
Annie b. 1895 m. Lewis Politesse [Sch. 600, NB.]
Annie m. Wiley Rabalais [Sch. 162.1, La.]
Annie Julia Marguerite b. 1891 d. 1956 m. William H. Burrows [Sch. 35, Guys. Co., NS.]
Ann Marie m. _____ Dockrill, B.C. [Sch. 8, Ant. Co]
Anselme b. ca. 1834 m. Marie Girouard, 1865 [Sch. 500, NB.]
Anselme b. 1747 [Sch. 211, West Indies, La.]
Anselme b. 1824 d. 1887 m. Anne LeBlanc, 1857 [Sch. 717, NB.]

Appendices

Anselme b. 1874 d. 1910 m. Philomène Bastarache *[Sch. 300, NB.]*
Anselme B. b. 1812 d. 1899 m1. Suzanne Jaillet, 1837, m2. Rosalie Bourgeois 1886 *[Sch. 300, NB.]*
Anselme b.1834 m. Marguerite à Anselme Girouard *[Sch. 500, NB.]*
Antoine b. 1696 d. 1767 m. Anne-Marie Barré *[FCMC, PQ.]*
Antoine b. 1723 d. 1723 *[FCMC, PQ.]*
Antoine b. 1729 d. 1762 m. Marguerite Chaperon 1759, 1823 *[FCMC, PQ.]*
Antoine b. 1744 *[Sch. 163 & 164 Isle Madame. NS.]*
Antoine b. 1754 Ordained in 1785 *[Sch. 163, Isle Madame, NS.]*
Antoine b. 1762 d. 1828 m. Marie-Louise Arel, 1793 *[FCMC, PQ.]*
Antoine b. 1817 d. 1817 *[FCMC, PQ.]*
Antoine b. 1836 d. 1904 m. Isabelle Caissy *[Sch. 717, NB.]*
Antoine b. 1864 *[Sch. 700, NB.]*
Antoine b. 1882 d. 1976, did not marry *[Sch. 711, NB.]*
Antoine b. 1892 d. 1975 m. Alice Savoie *[Sch. 700, NB.]*
Antoine b. 1898 m. Exelda Johnson *[Sch. 737, NB.]*
Antoine b. 1902 d. 1953 m. Dorothy Baldwin, 1914 *[Sch. 705, NB.]*
Antoine b. 1905 d. 1984 m. Emilie Savoie *[Sch. 711, NB.]*
Antoine d. 1744 *[Sch. 163, Isle Madame, NS.]*
Antoine Germain b. 1817 d. 1817 *[FCMC, PQ.]*
Antoine Girouard b. 1696 d. 1767 m. Marie Anne Barré, Montréal, 1723 [Chart fc, France]
Antoine Girouard/Green b.1890 *[Sch. 309, NB.]*
Apollinaire Zephrin b 1825 m. Armelise Landry *[Sch. 162.6, La.]*
Appolline b. 1817 m. Tom Roy ca., 1837 *[Sch. 500 & 542 NB.]*
Appoline Hélène b. 1855 *[Sch. 0 Tracadie, Ant. Co., NS.]*
Aquilla b. 1909 m. Edmé Babineau *[Sch. 500, NB.]*
Archange, died young *[Sch. 700, NB.]*
Arthance (Hortance) m. Thomas P. Boudreau *[Sch. 163, Isle Madame, NS.]*
Arthur b. 1876 m. Josephine Godin, U.S.A. *[Sch. 500, NB.]*
Arthur b. 1899 d. 1963 m. Léa LeBlanc, 1922 *[Sch. 300, NB.]*
Arthur b. 1904 m1. Annie Bonenberger, m2. Edmée Goguen *[Sch. 737, NB.]*
Arthur b. 1911 d. 1969 m. Cécile Durand, no children *[Sch. 500, NB.]*
Arthur b. 1944 d. 1979 m. Diane Boudreau *[Sch. 514, NB.]*
Arthur Brian m. Jane Elizabeth Pike *[Sch. 162, P.E.I.]*
Arthur D. m. Mary T. Collins *[Sch. 33, Guys. Co., NS.]*
Arthur William b. 1869 d. 1939 m. Sophie MacDonald *[Sch. 8, Ant. Co]*
Athalie b. 1879 d. 1960 m. Elie Pelletier *[Sch. 900, France]*
Athanase b. 1813 d. 1895 m1. Julie Juillet, 1837, m2. Françoise Melanson *[Sch. 300, 315 NB.]*
Auguste b. 1879 *[Sch. 162, P.E.I.]*
Auguste Girouard/Green m. Marie Richard *[Sch. 309, NB.]*
Augustin b. 1765 d. 1842 m. Scholastique Benoît *[Sch. 163& 164 Isle Madame, NS.]*
Augustin m. Delima Bonier, 1884 *[Sch. 208, PQ., Acadian]*
Augustine Joseph b. 1849 d. 1897, m. Louise Pelletier, 1882 *[Sch. 420, France]*
Auréa m. Aurèle Maillet *[Sch. 737, NB.]*
Aurèle *[Sch. 500, NB.]*
Aurèle b. 1843 *[Sch. 4 & 5, Ant. Co., NS.]*

Aurèle m. Anne- Marie Cormier [Sch. 600, NB.]
Aurlie b. 1845 [Sch.162.6, La]
Aurore b. 1899 m. Ernest Cormier [Sch. 729, NB.]
Baptiste m. Eulalie Barreau [Sch. 400, France]
Basile m1. Angélique Lamoureux [Sch. 213, PQ., Acadian]
Basile b. 1728 m. Marie J. Doucet ca. 1753 [Sch. 211, West Indies, La.]
Basile b. 1741 [Sch. 163, & 164 Isle Madame, NS.]
Béatrice [Sch. 527, NB.]
Béatrice b. 1890 [Sch. 4, Ant. Co., NS.]
Béatrice b. 1897 d. 1913 m. Joe McClure, 1881 [Sch. 600, NB.]
Béatrice b.1887 d.1887 [Sch. 300, NB.]
Béatrice m. Jean- Paul Charron [Sch. 600, NB.]
Bejamin (Benzidore) b. ca 1859 m. Elizabeth Pellerin 1878 [Sch. 32, Guys. Co., NS.]
Bélonie b. 1823 d. 1884 m. Rosalie Desgouffe, 1851 [Sch. 717 &729, NB.]
Bélonie b. 1841 d. 1917 m. Philomène Bastarache, 1878 [Sch. 523, NB.]
Bélonie [Sch. 724]
Ben A. b. 1852 d. 1908 m. 1875 Helen (Lacatune) Pellerin [AMC]
Benjamin (Benzidore) b. 1859 m. Elizabeth Pellerin [Sch. 31,Guys. Co. NS.]
Benjamin b. 1781 d. 1872 m1. Madleine Cormier, m2. Adelaïde LeBlanc [Sch. 300, 309, 315, 500,600 & 700,NB.]
Benjamin b. 1799 d. 1859 m 1. Suzanne Boudrot, m2. Victoire Thériault [Sch. 163, 164. Isle Madame. NS.]
Benjamin b. 1827 m. Victoire Forest, 1859 [Sch. 0, 1, 4 & 8 Tracadie, Ant. Co., NS.]
Benjamin b. 1840 d. 1861 [Sch. 164, Isle Madame. NS.]
Benjamin P. b. 1894 d. 1987 m. Mary Alice Pettipas [Sch. 48, Guys. Co., NS.]
Benoît [Sch. 600, NB.]
Benoît Sauvé [Sch.2000, FMCA]
Bénoni b. 1792 d. 1819 m. Marie Doucet, 1813 [Sch. 600, 300, 500, &700 NB.]
Bernadette b. 1809 [Sch. 208, PQ., Acadian]
Bernadette m. Jack Noonan [Sch. 163, Isle Madame, NS.]
Bernard b. 1697 d.1703 [Sch. 204, PQ., Acadian]
Bernard Girouard/Green [Sch. 309, NB.]
Bernard b. 1941 d. 1991 m. Pearl Rudolf [Sch. 0 Tracadie, Ant. Co., NS.]
Bernice [Sch. 31,Guys. Co. NS.]
Bertha Girouard/Green b. 1911 m. Albert Allain [Sch. 309, NB.]
Bertha m. William Petipas [Sch. 0 Tracadie, Ant. Co., NS.]
Berthe b. 1886 [Sch. 164. Isle Madame, NS.]
Bilianne b. 1843 d. 1875 m. Magloire Jaillet, 1863 [Sch. 523, NB.]
Bill (William D.) author of this book, b. 06/08/44 m. Audrey Gray [AMC]
Bill [Sch. 527, NB.]
Blanche b. 1841 m. Dominique Cormier [Sch. 300, NB.]
Blanche b. 1898 d. 1972 m. Théodore Leduc, 1925 [Sch. 2000, and Block N-5 FCMC]
Blanche m. Arthur Dufence, 1930 [Sch.3001, Rodier Branch, Québec]
Blanche m. Charles Roach [Sch. 711, NB.]
Bonaventure b. 1748 [Sch. 211, West Indies, La.]

Appendices

Brenda *[Sch. 711, NB.]*
Brigitte Annunciata b. 1919 *[Sch. 163, & 164 Isle Madame, NS.]*
Brigitte b. 1807 m. Charles Petitpas, 1848 *[Sch. 162, P.E.I.]*
Brigitte b. 1854 m. Hubert David, 1876 *[Sch. 31, 32 Guys. Co. NS.]*
Bruce *[Sch. 31,Guys. Co. NS.]*
Calixte b. 1876 d. 1880 *[Sch. 523, NB.]*
Camille b. 1875 d. 1948 m. Maggie S. Richard, 1899 *[Sch. 300, NB.]*
Camille m. Laurette Lacroix, 1936 *[Sch.3006, Belgium Branch, Québec]*
Captain Joseph b. 1788 d. 1866 m. Angélique Leblanc, 1809 *[Sch. 0, 1,4,5 &8 Tracadie, Ant. Co., NS.]*
Carmélia m. Pierre Louis Dupuis *[Sch. 202, PQ. Acadian]*
Carmelle m1. Yvon Barriau, 1959 m2. Winston Mathett *[Sch. 711, NB.]*
Carol Jean m. David John Bridges *[Sch. 717, NB.]*
Caroline b. 1838 d. 1882 m. Gédéon Fifre, 1861 *[FCMC, PQ.]*
Caroline b. 1848 *[Sch. 218, PQ. Acadian]*
Casimir m. Louis Gauthier, 1859 *[Sch.3006, Belgium Branch, Québec]*
Catherine b. 1904 m. Joseph Cloutier, *[Sch. 706, NB.]*
Catherine b.1764 m. Charles Dupuis *[Sch. 216, PQ. Acadian]*
Catherine (La Catherine) b. 1865 *[Sch. 48, Guys. Co., NS.]*
Catherine *[Sch. 5, Ant. Co., NS.]*
Catherine *[Sch. 711, NB.]*
Catherine b, 1953 *[Sch. 162.1, La.]*
Catherine b. 1746 *[Sch. 202, PQ. Acadian]*
Catherine b. 1783 d. 1784 *[FCMC, PQ.]*
Catherine b. 1869 m. David Pettipas *[Sch. 0 Tracadie, Ant. Co., NS.]*
Catherine Elizabeth b. 1892 *[Sch. 33, Guys. Co., NS.]*
Catherine Elizabeth b. 1892 d. 1892 *[Sch. 67, Guys. Co., NS.]*
Catherine Jane b. 1906 d.1931 m. _____Caissie *[Sch. 5, Ant. Co., NS.]*
Catherine m Eddie Holland *[Sch. 0 Tracadie, Ant. Co., NS.]*
Catherine m. at Pompaire *[Sch. 400, France]*
Catherine m. 1889 Gus Avery *[Sch. 35, Guys. Co., NS.]*
Catherine m. Malik Bouabdelli *[Sch. 900, France]*
Catherine m. Michel Ceille Biscornet, 1838 *[Sch.3006, Belgium Branch, Québec]*
Catherine m. Pat Petitpas *[Sch. 48, Guys. Co., NS.]*
Catherine Alice b. 1904 *[Sch. 95,Guys. Co., NS.]*
Catherine Patricia m. Vincent McNamara *[Sch. 5, Ant. Co., NS.]*
Cathy *[Sch. 724, NB.]*
Cecelia b. 1901 d. 1989 m. 1921 Bert Avery *[AMC]*
Cécile b. 1721 m. Louis Dugas 1740 *[Sch. 204, PQ., Acadian]*
Cécile b. 1845 d. 1886 m. Henri Mennier *[Sch. 315, NB.]*
Cécile b. 1853 m. Anézyme Cormier *[Sch. 706, NB.]*
Cécile m. Albert Goguen *[Sch. 514, NB.]*
Celina b. 1856 m. Alex Desroches *[Sch. 600, NB.]*
Célina b. 1870 d. 1962 *[Sch. 705, NB.]*
Chantal m. Denis Labbé, 1988 *[Sch. 2000, and Block N-5 FCMC]*

Charlene *[Sch. 162.1, La.]*

Charlene *[Sch. 724, NB.]*

Charles (d) *[Sch. 162, P.E.I.]*

Charles b. 1751 *[Sch. 162.1 Isle Madame .NS.]*

Charles Amable *[Sch. 213, PQ. Acadian]*

Charles Arthur b. 1912 d.1990 m. Verna Burns *[Sch. 162, P.E.I.]*

Charles b 1689 d. 1742 m1. Anne Bastarache. m2. Marie J *[AMC & Sch. 211, West Indies, La.]*

Charles b. 1709 d. 1750 m. Anne Nuriat, 1738 *[Sch.202 PQ.]*

Charles b. 1710 *[Sch. 163 & 164 Isle Madame, CB.; 162.1 &162.6 La; 300-,500,600 &700 NB.]*

Charles b. 1714 d. 1716 *[AMC]*

Charles b. 1716 m. Marie Thibodeau, 1739 *[Sch. 211, West Indies, La.]*

Charles b. 1719 *[AMC]*

Charles b. 1751 *[Sch. 300,500,600 & 700, NB.]*

Charles b. 1822 *[Sch. 217 & 218 Acadian P.Q]*

Charles b. 1847 m. Josèphe Lavache *[Sch. 164. Isle Madame. NS.]*

Charles b. 1902 d. 1923 m. Evelyn Elizianne *[Sch. 527, NB.]*

Charles b. Marguerite b. 1713 d. 1757 m. A Guilbault, 1757 *[Sch. 204, PQ., Acadian]*

Charles Jeffrey b. 1881 d. 1955 m. Mary Burke *[Sch. 162, P.E.I.]*

Charles Edward m. Anastasie Maher *[Sch. 724, NB.]*

Charles Evelyn Elizianne *[Sch. 527, NB.]*

Charles m. Josephte Bodret, 1826 *[Sch.3006, Belgium Branch, Québec]*

Charles m1. Elizabeth Mckeough m2. Helen Landry *[Sch. 0 Tracadie, Ant. Co., NS.]*

Charles, 1740 *[see notes on subchart, Sch. 211, West Indies, La.]*

Charlotte m. Joseph Martin, 1830 *[Sch. 300, NB.]*

Charlotte (Lottie) m. Fred Fenell *[Sch. 36, Guys. Co., NS.]*

Charlotte b. 1790 d. 1855 m. René LeBlanc, 1807 *[Sch. 300,500,600,& 700 NB.]*

Charlotte b. 1843 m. Simon Bonvie, 1869 *[Sch. 34, Ant. Co., NS.]*

Charlotte b. 1880 *[Sch. 48, Guys. Co., NS.]*

Charlotte m. André Payan, 1891 *[Sch. 208, PQ., Acadian]*

Christine b. 1891 *[Sch. 717, NB.]*

Christine m. James Simon *[Sch. 162.1, La.]*

Christine m. Stanley Cox *[Sch. 35, Guys. Co., NS.]*

Christophe b. 1896 d. 1970 m. Elmire Haché *[Sch. 729, NB.]*

Christophe *[Sch. 500, NB.]*

Christopher *[Sch.162.1 La]*

Claire (Nun), Sr. Sylvia-Marie *[Sch. 2000, and Block N-5 FCMC]*

Claire m. Stanley Creamer, 1966 *[Sch. 700, NB.]*

Claire m. Wilfrid Duguay *[Sch. 737, NB.]*

Clara b. 1886 d. 1960, not married *[Sch. 2000, and Block N-5 FCMC]*

Clara b. 1908 d. 1995 m. 1934 Ernest Pellerin *[AMC]*

Clarence (n.m.) *[Sch. 514, NB.]*

Clarence *[Sch. 711, NB.]*

Clarence m. Ethel Avery *[Sch. 76, Guys. Co., NS.]*

Clarence m. Marguerite Lacenaire *[Sch. 600, NB.]*

Clarisse b.1815 *[Sch. 162.1, La.]*

Appendices

Claude b. 1684 d. 1738 m. Elizabeth Blanchard [AMC & Sch. 207, PQ., Acadian]
Claude b. 1699 m. Marie Madeleine Vincent 1726 d.1768 [Sch. 163 &164 Isle Madame, NS; 162.1,162.6 La; 300,500,600 & 700 NB.]
Claude Girouard/Green [Sch. 309, NB.]
Claude b. 1727 d. 1816 m. Marie Bernard , 1759 [Sch. 213, 217, & 218 PQ., Acadian]
Claude [Sch. 600, NB.]
Claudia b. 1899 m. John L. Morris [Sch. 527, NB.]
Claudia m. François Beaulieu, 1964 [Sch. 711, NB.]
Claudine m. Patrick Vignot [Sch. 900, France]
Claudius b. 1917 m. Doris Lirrette [Sch. 500, NB.]
Clémence b. 1815 d. 1893 m. Charles Quevillon,1832 [FCMC, PQ.]
Clément [Sch. 724, NB.]
Clément b. 1878 d. 1949 m. Lucille Belliveau, 1906 [Sch. 717, NB.]
Clément b. 1879 d. 1968 m. Elmire Cormier [Sch. 315, NB.]
Clément m. Thérèse Beausoleil, 1940 [Sch. 2000, and Block N-5 FCMC]
Clémentine m. Jean Baptiste Loiseau, 1849 [Sch. 213, PQ. Acadian]
Cléo m. Jeanne Robichaud [Sch. 527, NB.]
Cléophas b. 1929 d. 1929 [Sch. 523, NB.]
Cloris b. 1895 d. 1925 [Sch. 527, NB.]
Cloris m. Bélonie Melanson [Sch. 729, NB.]
Clothilde b. 1788 m. Paul Mazerolle, 1811 [Sch. 300, 500,600 & 700 NB.]
Clovis b. 1860 d.1947 m. Marie Léger [Sch. 706, NB.]
Coleman m. Anne Ulmon [Sch. 72, Guys. Co., NS.]
Collette m. Simon Leblanc [Sch.500, NB.]
Colette [Sch. 523, NB.]
Collette m. Firmin Savoie, 1894 [Sch. 717, NB.]
Conrad Polycarpe Girroir (Priest) Ile Madame NS. [Sch. 163 maternal Giroir lines, Sch. 164 paternal Girroir Isle Madame, NS.]
Constance b. 1839 d. 1866 [FCMC, PQ.]
Constance Françoise b. 1806 [Sch. 162.6, La.]
Cordelia b. 1852 [Sch. 162.6, La.]
Corinne b. 1923 m. Alfred Niles [Sch. 315, NB.]
Corinne m. Edgar Lebreton [Sch. 711, NB.]
Corinne, not married [Sch. 500, NB.]
Corrine [Sch. 32, Guys. Co., NS.]
Cynthia Ann m. Malcom Jude Reaux [Sch. 162.1, La.]
Cyril James m. Helen Murphy [Sch. 48, Guys. Co., NS.]
Cyrille b. 1856 m. Henriette [Sch. 729, NB.]
Cyrille b. 1875 d. 1943 m. Annie Savoie Le Boutillier [Sch. 711, NB.]
Cyrille Girouard/Green b. 1895 [Sch. 309, NB.]
Daisy b. 1925 d. 1988 m. Freeman Wells [Sch. 162, P.E.I.]
Damien [Sch. 95, Guys. Co., NS.]
Damien b. 1842 [Sch. 700, NB.]
Damien b. 1866 d. 1952 m1. M. Drisdelle, 1891, m2. Domitilde Rousselle [Sch. 700, NB.]
Damien b. 1867 d. 1938 m. Nellie Fury [Sch. 705, NB.]

Damien m. Mini Jones, 1959 [Sch. 700, NB.]
Dana m. Darrel Peters [Sch. 162.1 La.]
Daniel (d) 12 years old [Sch. 5, Ant. Co., NS.]
Daniel [Sch. 729, NB.]
Daniel Alexander b. 1833 [Sch. 33, Guys. Co., NS.]
Daniel b. 1845 d. 1906 m. Marguerite Savoie,1887 [Sch. 500, NB.]
Daniel b. 1885 d. 1979 m. Eliza Delorey [Sch. 33, Guys. Co., NS.]
Daniel b. 1895 d. 1980 m. Eunice McPherson [Sch. 35, Guys. Co., NS.]
Daniel b. 1894 d. 1964 m. Sara Allain [Sch. 514, NB.]
Daniel b. 1910 d. 1989 [Sch. 705, NB.]
Daniel d. 1870 died 12 years old [Sch. 4, Ant. Co., NS.]
Daniel Hugh Stewart m. Shirley Ricketts [Sch. 67, Guys. Co., NS.]
Daniel J (Joseph D.) b. 1881 m. Catherine Delorey [Sch. 5, Ant. Co., NS.]
Daniel m. Marcelline Boucher [Sch. 164. Isle Madame. NS.]
Danielle m. Guy Sauvé, 1984 [Sch. 2000, and Block N-5 FCMC]
Danielle m. Emery Bourque [Sch. 600, NB.]
Danny J. m. Mary Pelly [Sch. 34, Ant. Co., NS.]
Darlene m. Michael Megaffin [Sch. 72, Guys. Co., NS.]
Darren Stewart [Sch. 67, Guys. Co., NS.]
David b. 1905 [Sch. 705, NB.]
David [Sch. 737, NB.]
David b. 1754 d. 1758 [Sch. 162.6, La.]
David b. 1833 d. 1917 m. Marie Richard, 1857 [Sch. 717 & 737 NB.]
David b. 1838 d. 1916 m. Henriette LeBlanc [Sch. 523, NB.]
David b. 1843 m1. M. Cormier, m2. H. LeBlanc m3. T. Robichaud [Sch. 300, NB.]
David b. 1860 [Sch. 31 & 32 Guys. Co. NS.]
David b. 1864 m. Marie Cormier [Sch. 729, NB.]
David b. 1865 d. 1923 m. Marie Genéviève Leblanc, 1890 [Sch. 600, NB.]
David John b. 1852 m. Eliza Jane Reddy [Sch. 4, Ant. Co., NS.]
David John m. b. Eliza Jane [Sch. 5, Ant. Co., NS.]
David b. 1838 d. 1970 m. Carol Debison [Sch. 717, NB.]
David m. Henriette Cormier, 1856 [Sch. 705, NB.]
David N. b. 1850 d. 1932 m. Victoire Pettipas [Sch. 0 Tracadie, Ant. Co., NS.]
Dawn m. Jack Marshall [Sch. 72, Guys. Co., NS.]
Dawn (Bobbie) m. Steve Powell [Sch. 717, N.B]
Debbie m. Arthur Thomas [Sch. 72, Guys. Co., NS.]
Delia b. 1853 d. 1929 m. Philip Bourgeois [AMC]
Delia Humbelina b. 1886 d. 1982 m. Levi Durant [Sch. 67, Guys. Co., NS.]
Delia m. Maxime Arseneau [Sch. 737, NB.]
Délina b. 1880 d. 1966 m. Charles Gaudet [Sch. 523, NB.]
Delores b. 24/04/46 m. Mike de Repentigny [AMC]
Delphine Dionisia b. 1803 m. Gregoire Mathurin Landry, 1821 [Sch.162.6, La.]
Delphine b. 1906 m. Melas Boudreau [Sch. 514, NB.]
Delphine b. 1840 m. Léon Aurillard [Sch. 900, France]
Delphis b. 1883 d. 1966 m. Marie Louise Cuilliérier, 1906 [Sch. 2000, and Block N-5 FCMC].
Denis b. 1688 d. 1709 M. Marguerite Barreau, [AMC]

Denis b. 1850 m. Doucette *[Sch. 500, NB.]*

Denise m. Daniel J. Wall *[Sch. 208, PQ., Acadian]*

Denise m. Gerry Leblanc *[Sch. 600, NB.]*

Dennis A. 1855 d. 1945 m1. 1878 Ellen Delorey m2. 1930 R. Bowman *[AMC & Sch. 67 Guysborough Co., N.S.]*

Dennis David b. 1882 m. Josephine Coakley *[Sch. 67, Guys. Co., NS.]*

Derick m. Liette Blais *[Sch.3001, Rodier Branch, Québec]*

Désanges b. 1804 m. Antoine St-Germain, 1825 *[FCMC, PQ.]*

Désiré b. 1845 d.1912 m. Marie Geneviève Paon *[Sch. 164. Isle Madame. NS.]*

Désiré b. 1874 d. 1937 m. Flavie Cognard, 1896 *[Sch. 900, France]*

Désiré b. 1922 m. Irène Comeau *[Sch. 500, NB.]*

Désiré b. 1836 d. 1879 m1. Mathilda Pratt m2. Essie Cranwill m3. Edith Beatty *[FCMC, PQ.]*

Désiré H. b. 1869 m. Virginia Chambliss, *[FCMC, PQ.]*

Désiré m. Solange Berger *[Sch. 900, France]*

Désirée *[Sch. 95, Guys. Co., NS.]*

Désirée b. 1910 (n.m.) *[Sch. 217, PQ., Acadian]*

Diana *[Sch. 33, Guys. Co., NS.]*

Diane m. Peter Tsitsopoulos *[Sch. 711, NB.]*

Diane Gerrior m. Bernard (Bernie) Jordan *[Sch. 32, Guys. Co., NS.]*

Diane m. Francis Richard, 1963 *[Sch. 76, Guys. Co., NS.]*

Diane m. Tommy Cormier, 1984 *[Sch. 600, NB.]*

Dina m. Hermas Marjan, 1888 *[Sch. 213, PQ. Acadian]*

Dolor b. 1903 d. 1964 m. Simonne Barry *[Sch.3006, Belgium Branch, Québec]*

Dominique m. Yvon Gauthier *[Sch. 900, France]*

Domithilde b. 1810 d. 1812 *[Sch. 700, NB.]*

Domithilde b. 1812 d. 1877 m. Félix LeBlanc ca. 1840 *[Sch. 700, NB.]*

Donald *[Sch. 527, NB.]*

Donald b. 1833 d. 1915 m. Catherine Leeth, 1868 *[Sch. 33, Guys. Co., NS.]*

Donald b. 1924 d. 1986 m. Margaret O'Driscoll *[Sch. 72, Guys. Co., NS.]*

Donald m. Virginia Smith *[Sch. 48, Guys. Co., NS.]*

Donat b. 1880 d. 1963 m. Lézainne Anne Pichard, 1911 *[Sch. 300, NB.]*

Donat b. 1884 m. J. Rosario *[Sch. 514, NB.]*

Dora m. Claude Arsenault *[Sch. 600, NB.]*

Dora Marie b. 1916 *[Sch. 36, Guys. Co., NS.]*

Dorette m. Raymond Briggs *[Sch. 500, NB.]*

Doris m. Robert LeBlanc *[Sch. 527, NB.]*

Dorothy *[Sch. 35, Guys. Co., NS.]*

Dupré b. 1834 m. Anastasie Prejean,1859 *[Sch. 162.1, La.]*

Eddie *[Sch. 33, Guys. Co., NS.]*

Edgar (M.D.) b. 1923 m1. M. Dumais 1953 m2. 1978, M. Dumont *[Sch. 300, NB.]*

Edgar b. 1910 d. 1963 m. Lillianne Arsenault 1932, *[Sch. 717, NB.]*

Edmond b. 1902 *[Sch. 163 & 164 Isle Madame, NS.]*

Edmond b. 1901 d. 1983 m. Rebecca Bourgeois *[Sch. 514, NB.]*

Edmond Girouard/Green b. 1898 d. 1918 *[Sch. 309, NB.]*

Edmond Girouard/Green b. 1919 m. Cora Mae Cormier *[Sch. 309, NB.]*

Edmond m. Claire Ferguson [Sch. 700, NB.]
Edna m. Albert Ranger, 1929, no children [Sch. 724, NB.]
Edna m. Edgar Ferguson, 1942 [Sch. 700, NB.]
Edouard b. 1856 d. 1957 m1. Elizabeth Léger, 1881 m2. Elise Michaud [Sch. 724, NB.]
Edouard b. 1865 d. 1956 m. Mathilda Girouard à David à Marin [Sch. 705, NB.]
Edouard b. 1908 d. 1980 m. Ella Goguen, 1937 [Sch. 514, NB.]
Edouard b. 1803 m. Angélique Lavigueur [Sch. 217 & 218, PQ., Acadian]
Edouard m. Josette Comeau, 1826 [Sch. 207, PQ., Acadian]
Edouard* b. 1807 m. Marguerite Beaudet, 1835 [Sch. 217 & 218, PQ., Acadian]
Edouard b. 1919 d. 1987 m. Loretta LeBlanc, 1940 [Sch. 523, NB.]
Edward (Ned) b. 1833 d. 1927 m. Charlotte Beaumont, 1862 [Sch. 34, Ant. Co., NS.]
Edward Lavin (Sr) (Sentor) b. 1871   d. 1932 m1. L.M. Corbin m2. M. F. [Sch. 8, Ant. Co., NS.]
Edward Lavin (Jr.) b. 1907 m. Mary Dee Buchanan [Sch. 8, Ant. Co., NS.]
Edward m. Yvonne Racine, no children [Sch.3001, Rodier Branch, Québec]
Edward [Sch. 48, Guys. Co., NS.]
Edward & Willie Twins b. 1911 & d.1911 [Sch. 163 & 164, Isle Madame, NS.]
Elaine (Lina) b. 1836 m. Meance Boulet, 1855 [Sch. 162.1, La.]
Elda m. Camille Broussard [Sch. 162.1, La.]
Elenor m. Robert Melanson [Sch. 95, Guys. Co., NS.]
Eléonore b. 1823 m. Gésippe Cousineau, 1844 [FCMC, PQ.]
Eléonore [FCMC, PQ.]
Elévanie b. 1902 (Yvonne) [Sch. 729, NB.]
Elfige b. 1869 [Sch. 162.6, La.]
Elias b. 1937 [Sch. 700, NB.]
Elias [Sch.3006, Belgium Branch, Québec]
Elias m. Paul Pratt [Sch.3006, Belgium Branch, Québec]
Elie b. 1873 d. 1962 m1. Adèle Légère, m2. Agnès Breau [Sch. 527, NB.]
Elie b. 1889 d. 1976 m. Lucille Gautreaux [Sch. 162.1, La.]
Elie b. 1890 m. Agnès Daigle, 1913 [Sch. 300, NB.]
Elie b. 1902   d. 1946 [Sch. 737, NB.]
Elina b. 1821 d. 1821 [Sch. 162.1, La]
Elise b. 1891 d. 1960 m1. Albert Benoît, m2. Leopold Lawrence, 1921 [Sch. 600, NB.]
Elise b. 1890 d. 1936 m. Ernest Cormier, 1906 [Sch. 705, NB.]
Eliza b. 1855 [Sch. 48, Guys. Co., NS.]
Eliza Jane b. 1906 d. 1989 m. Thomas Paul Pellerine,1923 [Sch. 31,Guys. Co. NS.]
Elizabeth 1871 [Sch. 35 & 36, Guys. Co., NS.]
Elizabeth b. 1771 [Sch. 208, PQ., Acadian]
Elizabeth b. 1818 m1 David Cormier, 1838, m2. Daniel Cormier [Sch. 500 & 542, NB.]
Elizabeth b. 1841 d. 1843 [Sch. 34, Ant. Co., NS.]
Elizabeth b. 1843 d. 1845 [Sch. 0 Tracadie, Ant. Co., NS.]
Elizabeth b. 1845 [Sch. 34, Ant. Co., NS.]
Elizabeth (Eliza) b. 1849 d. 1883 m. J. Theddore-Agnée Mailhot , 1846 [Sch. 218, PQ. Acadian]
Elizabeth b. 1853 m. Alexander Richard [Sch. 31,Guys. Co. NS.]
Elizabeth b. 1854 [Sch. 4 & 5 Ant. Co., NS.]
Elizabeth b. 1876 m. Rubien Jaillet [Sch. 315, NB.]

Elizabeth b. 1879 d. 1952 m. Henri Bernard, 1901 *[Sch. 705, NB.]*
Elizabeth Delice b. 1874 *[Sch. 0 Tracadie, Ant. Co., NS.]*
Elizabeth m. Francis Duhame, 1787 *[Sch. 207, PQ., Acadian]*
Elizabeth m. Pite Poisson,1858 *[Sch. 523, NB.]*
Elizabeth Ella. (Betty) m. Dan Lister *[Sch. 35, Guys. Co., NS.]*
Elize m. Tony LeBlanc *[Sch. 706, NB.]*
Ellen Lavina b. 1880 d. 1970 m. Ben Bonvie *[Sch. 67, Guys. Co., NS.]*
Elma Delorey b. ca. 1867 *[Sch. 0 Tracadie, Ant. Co., NS.]*
Elmire b. 1888 d. 1932 *[Sch. 724, NB.]*
Elmire b. 1897-d.1972 n.m. *[Sch. 706, NB.]*
Elmire 1891 m. Joseph Léger *[Sch. 514, NB.]*
Elodie b. 1917 d. 1925 *[Sch. 315, NB.]*
Elvia m. Laurie Arsenault, 1946 *[Sch. 523, NB.]*
Elvina m. Amanda Pratt *[Sch.3006, Belgium Branch, Québec]*
Elzéar b. 1894 d. 1989 m. Emma Lalonde *[Sch. 2000, and Block N-5 FCMC]*
Elzéar m. Amanda Drisdelle, 1943 *[Sch. 700, NB.]*
Emélie b. 1873 m. Cyrille Cormier, 1893 *[Sch. 705, NB.]*
Emeline b. 1839 m. Modeste Poisson, 1858 *[Sch. 218, PQ., Acadian]*
Emery b. 1900 d. 1957 m. Adeline Hart *[Sch. 3001, Rodier Branch, Québec]*
Emery b.1915 d. 1971 m. Blanche Patry *[Sch. 315, NB.]*
Emile b. 1910 d. 1987 m1. Ida Gould m2. Amanda Richard *[Sch. 315, NB.]*
Emile b. 1862 d. 1894 m. Louise Clément, 1887 *[FCMC, PQ.]*
Emilie (Marguerite) b. 1874 d. 1876 *[Sch. 600, NB.]*
Emilien b. 1872 m. R. Marie Bascq *[Sch. 900, France]*
Emilienne b. 1866 m. Jean- Baptiste Poirier *[Sch. 729, NB.]*
Emilienne b. 1886 d. 1963 m. Adrien Redonnet *[Sch. 900, France]*
Emilienne b. 1903 d. 1903 *[Sch. 527, NB.]*
Emma b. 1886 d. 1976, m. Philas Cormier *[Sch. 523, NB.]*
Emma b. 1902 *[Sch. 724, NB.]*
Emma m. Eugène Rainville *[Sch. 300, NB.]*
Emmanuel b. 1805 m1. M. Duplessis, 1827 m2. Marguerite LeBlanc, 1842 *[Sch. 309 & 300 NB.]*
Ena d. infant *[Sch. 700, N.B]*
Eric b. 1901 d. 1989 m. Mildred Blake *[Sch. 729, NB.]*
Ernest *[Sch. 711, NB.]*
Ernest b. 1883 d. 1950 m. Juliette Foucteau *[Sch. 420, France]*
Ernest Chanteloup b. 1882 d. 1951 m. Pauline Parent *[FCMC, PQ.]*
Ernest Paul m. Rita Allemand *[Sch. 162.1, La.]*
Esmée (n.m.) *[Sch. 217, PQ., Acadian]*
Essie Augusta (Gussi) b. 1865 m. Henry-John Skinner *[FCMC, PQ.]*
Estelle *[Sch. 420, France]*
Esther b. 1862 d. 1941 m. Damien Cormier, 1890 *[Sch. 717, NB.]*
Esther b. 1917 m. Louis Gosselin [Sch. 737, NB.]
Esther m. Antoine Larrivé *[Sch.3006, Belgium Branch, Québec]*
Esther m. Damien Cormier *[Sch. 737, NB.]*
Esther m. Louis Yelle *[Sch. 213, PQ., Acadian]*

Estilite Giroir * b. 1858 m1. Céleste Penisson 1880 m2. Corin Ross [Sch. 162.6, La.]
Etienne b. 1708 [Sch. 163& 164 Isle Madame, NS.; 162.1 & 162.6 La; 300,500,600 & 700 NB.]
Etienne b. 1837 d. 1908 m. Josephte Leduc, 1859 [Sch. 2000, and Block N-5 FCMC]
Etienne b. 1864 m. Victorine Thériot [Sch. 162.6, La.]
Etienne* b. 1807 m. Adèle Hebert, 1830 [Sch. 162.6, La.]
Euclide b. 1906 d. 1930, not married [Sch. 163 & 164. Isle Madame. NS.]
Eudoxile b. 1747 m. Jean Pierre Hébert 1787 [Sch. 162.6, La.]
Eufrosine b. 1819 [Sch. 300, NB.]
Eugène b. 1851 m. Léonie Carcaillon [Sch. 900, France]
Eugène Hubert m. Geraldine Reynolds [Sch. 5, Ant. Co., NS.]
Eugene Leo b. 1884 d. 1906 [Sch. 8, Ant. Co]
Eugène m. Emilie Brault, 1860 [Sch. 208, PQ., Acadian]
Eugène m. Hélène Wade [Sch. 700, NB.]
Eugene [Sch. #1 Tracadie, Ant. Co., NS.]
Eugénie b. 1875 m. Pierre Lacenaire [Sch. 514, NB.]
Eugénie Theresa b. 1887 [Sch. 4, Ant. Co., NS.]
Eunice Eva m. Ian McKay [Sch. 35, Guys. Co., NS.]
Euphémie b. 1857 [Sch. 315, NB.]
Euphémie b. 1869 Olivier Cormier [Sch. 500, NB.]
Euphrasie Donat b. 1899 d. 1890 [Sch. 2000, and Block N-5 FCMC]
Eva [Sch.217,PQ. Acadian]
Eva Mae b. 1914 d. 1989, (Nun) F.D.J [Sch. 163 & 164 Isle Madame, NS.]
Evangéline b. 1881 m. Arcade Bastarache [Sch. 500, NB.]
Evariste [Sch. 717, NB.]
Eveline b. 1921 m. Gérald Allain [Sch. 711, NB.]
Evelyn b. 03/11/56 m. Mike Oakley [AMC]
Evelyne b. 1935 d. 1996 m. Eugène Hébert 1959 [Sch. 700, NB.]
Fabien [Sch. 700, NB.]
Fabien b. 1818 d. 1900 m1.Marcelline Allain m2 . Archange Brideau
 m3. Appoline Basque, m4. Odele Maillet [Sch. 700 & 711 NB.]
Fabien Lucas b. 1802 [Sch. 162.6, La]
Felicité Adele b. 1821 d. 1824 [Sch. 162.6, La.]
Felicité [Sch. 202, PQ. Acadian]
Felicité b. 1785 d. 1815 m. Benjamin Thibodeau, 1805 [Sch. 162.1, La.]
Felicité b. 1797 d. 1822 m. Ignace Dumouchel, 1820 [Sch. 202, PQ. Acadian]
Felicité b.1752 m1. Nicolas Demars, m2. J. Baptiste Baritou, 1786 [Sch. 204, PQ., Acadian]
Ferdinand b. 1848 d. 1907 m. Céleste Collette, 1874 [Sch. 500, NB.]
Ferdinand b. 1850 m. Virginie Bastarache [Sch. 315, NB.]
Ferdinand b. 1907 d. 1992 m. Béatrice Goguen, 1937 [Sch. 514, NB.]
Fernand b. 1938 m. Emerise Léger [Sch. 729, NB.]
Fernand Louis M.D. d. 1980 m. Anita Attleboro [Sch. 208, PQ., Acadian]
Fidèle b. 1870 d. 1951 m. Philomène Cormier [Sch. 737, NB.]
Fidèle Girouard/Green (Alyre) b. 1889 d. 1956 m. Emma LeBlanc [Sch. 309, NB.]
Firmin b. 1749 d. 1820 m. Marguerite Cormier, 1771 [Sch.300, 500,600,& 700 NB.; 162.1, La.]
Firmin-Simon* b. 1771 d. 1819 m. Adélaide Broussard [Sch. 162.1, La.]

Flavie b. 1822, died at a young age [FCMC, PQ.]
Flavien b. 1904 d. 1978 m. Denise Colas, 1926 [Sch. 900, France]
Flavien m. Henriette Dupré, 1847 [Sch. 207, PQ., Acadian]
Flora b. 1850 m. Campbell [Sch. 162, P.E.I.]
Florence Aldora Ann Stewart m. William H. Cummerson [Sch. 67, Guys. Co., NS.]
Florestine b. 1900 d. 1983 m. Albert Daoust, 1933 [Sch. 2000, and Block N-5 FCMC]
Floyd b. 1918 d. 1990 m. Elsie Imlay [Sch. 72, Guys. Co., NS.]
Flossie Mae m. Walter Fougère [Sch. 76, Guys. Co., NS.]
France m. Jacqueline Chenault [Sch. 900, France]
Frances Cecelia m. Edouard Laboe M.D. [Sch. 8, Ant. Co., NS.]
Francine b. 1810 m. Bélonie LeBlanc [Sch. 300, NB.]
Francis b. 1805 m. Julienne Bourke 1829 [AMC & Sch. 34 Guys]
Francis (Frank W) b. 1889 m1. M. Richard m2. Eliz. Ryan (Diggans, 1913) [Sch. 36, Guys. Co., NS.]
Francis Xavier b. 1863 m. Ellen Boyle,1890 [Sch. 34, Ant. Co., NS.]
Francis Nicholas b. 1870 d. 1915 m. Theresa Landry [Sch. 0 Tracadie, Ant. Co., NS.]
Francis E. b. 1900 [Sch. 0 Tracadie, Ant. Co., NS.]
Francis m. Alma Riddle [Sch. 95, Guys. Co., NS.]
Francis m. Meta Keller [Sch. 95, Guys. Co., NS.]
Francisco Elena b. 1894 [Sch. 162.6. La]
François b. 1748 [Sch. 204, PQ., Acadian]
François b. 1748 [Sch. 202, PQ.]
François [Sch. 300, NB.]
François Alexandre b. 1720 d. 1784 m. Antoinette Barbe Bertin [Chart fc, France]
François Apollinaire b. 1800 m. Théotiste Aucoin 1820 [Sch. 162.6, La.]
François b. 1771. drowned off coast of Spain [Sch. 202, PQ. Acadian]
François b. 1680 d. 1752 m1. 1708 Anne Bourgeois m2. 1737 Marie Guilbeau [AMC and Sch.300,500,600 & 700, NB.]
François b. 1705 d. 1786, m. Catherine Marie Lucile Chambaud. 1730 [Chart fc, France]
Francois b. 1708 d. 1720 [AMC]
François b. 1712 d. 1790 m1. M. Poirier 1735, m2. J. Boudrot, 1762 [Sch. 202, PQ. Acadian]
François b. 1720 [Sch. 207, PQ., Acadian]
François b. 1726 m1. Claire Richard, 1745 m2. C. Martin, 1754, m3. Marguerite Poirier [Sch. 211, West Indies, La.]
François b. 1744 d. 1757 [Sch. 202, PQ. Acadian]
François d. 1747 [Sch. Fc, France]
François b. 1748 [Sch. 211, West Indies, La.]
François b. 1753 d. 1841 m. 1785 Marguerite Petitpas [AMC]
François b. 1809 d. 1859 m. Rose Pélagie Guilbot [Sch. 400, France]
François b. 1861 [Sch. 724, NB.]
François b. 1889 d. 1957 m. Hélène Collette, 1917 [Sch. 523, NB.]
François b. 1952 d. 1973 [Sch. 2000, and Block N-5 FCMC]
François* b. 1772 d. 1836 m. Madeleine Le Blanc 1794 [Sch. 162.6, La.]
François* b. 1769 m. Marguerite Tétreau dit Jeannot,1791 [Sch. 213, PQ. Acadian]
François b. 1803 m. Reine Panneton, 1834 [Sch. 217 & 218,PQ. Acadian]

François du Buchet b. 1705 d. 1786 m. Catherine Marie Lucile Chambaud, [FCMC, PQ.]
François Girouard of Paris m. ? [Sch. 800, France]
François Louis b. 1868 [Sch. 208, PQ., Acadian]
François m. Adeline Girouard, 1856 [Sch. 207, PQ.]
François Xavier b. 1818 m1. Marie. Louise Girard, 1843, m2. Archange Deblois, 1858 [Sch. 208, PQ., Acadian]
François Xavier b. 1843 d. 1897 m. 1867, Valentine Brunet [Sch. 2000, and Block N-5 FCMC]
François*, dit La Varenne, France b. ca. 1621 d. 1693 m. 1647 Jeanne Aucoin [AMC]
Françoise b. 1724 d. 1803 m. Jean- Baptiste Richard, 1745 [Sch. 208, PQ., Acadian]
Françoise b. 1774 [Sch. 400, France]
Françoise b. 1808 m. Thomas Richard, 1843 [Sch. 700, NB.]
Françoise b. 1848 [Sch. 34, Ant. Co., NS.]
Frank m. Penelope (Penny) Sanborn [Sch. 95, Guys. Co., NS.]
Frank W. b. 1914 d. 1994 (Pop) m. Mary Gurney [Sch. 34, Ant. Co., NS.]
Frédéric b. 1826 d. 1860 m. 1848 Anne (Nancy) Gillis [AMC & Sch. 35 & 36]
Frédéric b. 1832 m. Appollina DesLauriers [Sch. 34, Ant. Co., NS.]
Frédéric b. 1865 m. Eugénie Goguen [Sch. 717, NB.]
Frédéric b. 1881 [Sch. 36, Guys. Co., NS.]
Frederic b. 1918 d. 1988 m. Lillian French [Sch. 162, P.E.I.]
Frumence b. 1844 d. 1922 m. Marie Clément, 1870 [Sch. 900, France]
Gabrielle m. Maurice Martel, 1936 [Sch.3006, Belgium Branch, Québec]
Gabrielle Sauvé [Sch. 2000, FCMC]
Gaétome m. Anne Pettipas [Sch. 163, Isle Madame, NS.]
Gaston m. Ginette Maillard, 1950 [Sch. 900, France]
Gemma [Sch. 706, NB.]
Geneva b. 1885 n.m. [AMC]
Geneva m. John Nardocchio [Sch. 95, Guys. Co., NS.]
Geneviève b. 1808 m1. Pierre Laroche m2. David Fournier, 1855 [Sch.217, PQ. Acadian]
Geneviève b. m. Simon Collette [Sch. 527, NB.]
Geneviève b. 1760 d. 1826 m. André Barron, 1780 [FCMC, PQ.]
Geneviève b. 1770 d. 1858 m. Sylvain Babineau ca. 1792 [Sch. 300, 500, 600, & 700 NB.]
Geneviève b. 1839 m. Maxime LeBlanc [Sch. 315, NB.]
Geneviève b. 1859 m. Pierre Robichaud [Sch. 724, NB.]
Geneviève m. Isidore Gravel, 1843 [Sch. 208, PQ., Acadian]
Geneviève b. 1922 d. 1973 m. Harry Helin [Sch. 163 & 164 Isle Madame, NS.]
Geneviève m. Maxime Arsenault [Sch. 700, NB.]
Geneviève b. 1871 m. Onésime Cormier [Sch. 300, NB.]
Geneviève m. Pierre La Roche, 1824, m2. David Fournier, 1885 [Sch. 217 & 218, PQ., Acadian]
Geneviève Marguerite b. 1730 d. 1799 m. Nicolas Gaudry, 1760 [FCMC, PQ.]
Geneviève Joanne b. 1848 [Sch. 0 Tracadie, Ant. Co., NS.]
George Edward [Sch. 35, Guys. Co., NS.]
George G. m. Florence A. Vachevesse [Sch.34, Guys. Co., NS.]
George Gregory m. May Anita Campbell [Sch. 5, Ant. Co., NS.]
George John Edward b. 1911 d. 1974 m. Marie A. Guimond [Sch. 34, Ant. Co., NS.]
George Joseph (Michael) [Sch. 76, Guys. Co., NS.]

George m. Clara Avery *[Sch. 76, Guys. Co., NS.]*
George m. Shirley LeBlanc *[Sch. 711, NB.]*
Georges m. Alice Hefferman *[Sch. 700, NB.]*
Georges m. Amerylis Berthe, 1950 *[Sch. 523, NB.]*
Georges m. Madeleine LeBlanc, 1867 *[Sch. 523, NB.]*
Georges Rodolphe b. 1886 *[Sch. 208, PQ., Acadian]*
Georgina *[Sch. 542, NB.]*
Georgina m. __ Kelleher *[Sch. 34, Ant. Co., NS.]*
Germain m. Anne Senet, 1802 *[Sch. 216, PQ. Acadian]*
Germain b. 1656 d. 1693 m. Marie Bourgeois *[AMC & Sch. 202, PQ. Acadian]*
Germain b. ca. 1711 d. 1760 m1. Marie Arseneau, 1733, m2. Marguertite Henry-R, 1763 *[Sch. 213, 216, 217 PQ. Acadian]*
Germain II b. 1681 d. 1760 m. Jeanne Barreau *[Sch. 202, PQ. Acadian]*
Germain II b. 1691 m. Marie Doucet 1711 *[AMC & Sch. 213, 217, 218 PQ. Acadian]*
Germaine m. Amer Bréan *[Sch. 309, NB.]*
Gertrude m. John Boudrot *[Sch. 163, Isle Madame, NS.]*
Gertrude (soeur) *[Sch. 217, PQ., Acadian]*
Gertrude b. 1769 d. 1847 m. Toussaint Martin dit Ladouceur November, 1788 *[FCMC, PQ.]*
Gertrude b. 1811 m. Michel Cormier, 1831 *[Sch. 542, 500, NB.]*
Gertrude b. 1815 m. Laurent Goutreau, 1848 *[Sch. 300, NB.]*
Gertrude b. 1840 m. Fabien Bastarache *[Sch. 500, NB.]*
Gertrude b. 1845 m. Clément Goguen, 1871 *[Sch. 309, NB.]*
Gertrude b. 1882 m. Joseph Légère *[Sch. 514, NB.]*
Gertrude b. 1901 *[Sch. 208, PQ., Acadian]*
Gertrude m. John Boudrot *[Sch. 164, Isle Madame, NS.]*
Gilbert d. 2 months old *[Sch. 48, Guys. Co., NS.]*
Gilbert m. Lena Lavandier *[Sch. 164, Isle Madame, NS.]*
Gilbert b. 1846 d. 1885 m. Sophie Baker 1872 *[Sch. 300, NB.]*
Gilbert b. 1885 d. 1957 m. Emma (Rose Anna)Frigault *[Sch. 724, NB.]*
Gilbert b. 1896 m. Sara Arsenault *[Sch. 737, NB.]*
Gilbert of Boisrolin b. 1751 *[Chart fc, France]*
Gilles m. Martine Richard, 1974 *[Sch. 900, France]*
Ginette m. Rémi Boyer *[Sch. 900, France]*
Gisèle m. Henri Nowlan *[Sch. 729, NB.]*
Glen J m. Kathy Hickens *[Sch. 31, Guys. Co. NS.]*
Gloria m. _____ Moore *[Sch. 705, NB.]*
Gonzague b. 1882 d. 1960, not married *[Sch. 523, NB.]*
Grégoire b. 1731 d. 1734 *[Sch. 211, West Indies, La.]*
Grégoire b. 1748 *[Sch. 211, West Indies, La.]*
Grégoire m. Geneviève Baril 1822 *[Sch. 217& 218 PQ., Acadian]*
Gregory *[Sch.3001, Rodier Branch, Québec]*
Guilbert b. 1894 m. Kathleen Baker, no children *[Sch. 48, Guys. Co., NS.]*
Guillaume *[Sch. 207, PQ., Acadian]*
Guillaume b. 1686 d. 1757 m1. Marie Bernard (Renochet) 1713 *[AMC & Sch. 208, PQ., Acadian]*
Guillaume b. 1721 d. 1763 m. Anne Blanchard, 1745 *[Sch. 208, PQ., Acadian]*

Gustelish b. 1851 *[Sch. 162.6, La.]*
Guy m. Nicole Laplaine *[Sch. 420, France]*
Hanah b. 1858 *[Sch. 48, Guys. Co., NS.]*
Harold James (Bim) m. Sylvia Kling *[Sch. 162.1, La.]*
Harry m. Shirley Murphy *[Sch. 32, Guys. Co., NS.]*
Hazel Elizabeth m. Norman Beal *[Sch. 5, Ant. Co., NS.]*
Heather Lee m. Joey Earl Agnew *[Sch. 162, P.E.I.]*
Hector b. 1878 d. 1911 m. Jeanne LeBlanc *[Sch. 527, NB.]*
Hector Henry b. 1884 d. 1939, Dorval *[FCMC, PQ.]*
Hedwidge m. Thedore Jack, 1943 *[Sch. 523, NB.]*
Helen (Ellen) Laura b. 1874 m. _____Dort *[Sch. 33, Guys. Co., NS.]*
Helen b. 1904 d. 1990 m. 1931 Frank Lally *[AMC]*
Helen m. 1900 Oscar Butler Larry's River *[AMC]*
Helen m. Cornelius (Conni) Roach *[Sch. 32, Guys. Co., NS.]*
Helen Rita *[Sch. 76, Guys. Co., NS.]*
Hélène b. 1925 d. 1973 *[Sch. 420, France]*
Hélène b. 1875 d. 1945 m. Joseph Lécuyer *[Sch. 523, NB.]*
Hélène m. George Tanguay *[Sch. 527, NB.]*
Hélène Judith b. 1742 m. François Blanchard *[Sch. 162.6, La.]*
Hélène m1. Robert Goutreau m2. Robert Arsenault *[Sch. 300, NB.]*
Henri (n.m.) *[Sch. 514, NB.]*
Henri Alexandre b. 1850 *[Sch. 420, France]*
Henri Antoine b. 1908 m. Hélène Robichaud *[Sch. 706, NB.]*
Henri b. 1733 d. 1798 m. Marie-Josephte Cousineau 1758 *[FCMC, PQ.]*
Henri b. 1909 d. 1980 m. Aquilina (Lina) Boudreau *[Sch. 717, NB.]*
Henri Harvey b. 1885 m. Caroline Talbot, 1908 *[Sch. 218, PQ., Acadian]*
Henri Jean b. 1767 d.1778 *[FCMC, PQ.]*
Henrietta b. 1815 *[AMC]*
Henriette b. 1805 d. 1826 m. Louis Allain, 1826 *[Sch. 500,and 542 NB.]*
Henriette b. 1817 d. 1906 m. Firmin Lajeune *[Sch. 163, Isle Madame, NS.]*
Henriette b. 1825 m. Moïse Wattier, 1846 *[FCMC, PQ.]*
Henriette b. 1834 d. 1861 m. Marie Savoie, 1860 *[Sch. 309, NB.]*
Henriette b 1837 à Joe-Rose m. Magloire Girouard à Anselme *[Sch. 300, 500 NB.]*
Henriette b. 1840 à Anselme m. Magloire à Hilaire *[Sch.300, N.B]*
Henriette b. 1841 m. Joseph Julien, 1866 *[Sch. 2000, and Block N-5 FCMC]*
Henriette b. 1913 d. 1996 *[Sch. 420, France]*
Henriette b.1863 d. 1866 *[Sch. 600, NB.]*
Henriette m. Michel LeBlanc *[Sch. 300, NB.]*
Henry b. 1895 d. 1991 m. Bertha Lawther, 1919 *[Sch. 724, NB.]*
Henry J. b. 1891 m. Laura Pettipas *[Sch. 48, Guys. Co., NS.]*
Henry Sulpice b. 1830 d. 1830 *[FCMC, PQ.]*
Henry William m. Nancy Walsh *[Sch. 76, Guys. Co., NS.]*
Henry Ambrose *[Sch. 5, Ant. Co., NS.]*
Herman b. 07/04/1949 m. Avis Bona *[AMC]*
Hermine (Marie Alix) b. 1870 *[Sch. 208, PQ., Acadian]*

Hermine Emile* m. Antoine Gagnon [Sch. 217, PQ., Acadian]
Hershel Lee Paul b. 1949 m. Brenda Boudreaux [Sch. 162.1, La.]
Hervé Joseph m. Arlene Kenny, 1956 [Sch. 527, NB.]
Hervé Jr [Sch. 527, NB.]
Hilaire b. 1807 d. 1881 m. Geneviève Allain 1830 [Sch. 500, 523,542, 527, NB.]
Hilaire b. 1813 d. 1830 [Sch. 162.1, La.]
Hilaire b. 1874 d. 1954 m. Emilienne Léger, 1894 [Sch. 527, NB.]
Homère [Sch. 729, NB.]
Honoré b. 1714 d. 1785 m. Marie Thériault, 1740 [Sch. 300,500, 600& 700 NB.]
Honoré b. 1763 d. 1785 [Sch. 163 & 164 Isle Madame, NS.]
Honoré b. 1847 [Sch. 163, Isle Madame, NS.]
Honoré b. 1889 m. Kristine (Élise) Rasmissen, 1921 [Sch. 218, PQ., Acadian]
Honoré b. 1896 d. 1943 m. Camillia Ozenne [Sch. 162.1, La.]
Honoré Eagle [Sch. 500, NB.]
Honoré Girouard b. 1714 m. Marie Josephe Thériot (Theriault)[Sch. 162.6, 162.1 La; 163,164 Isle Madame NS.; 300,500,600 & 700 N.B]
Howard m. Marilyn Rynold 1972 [Sch. 32, Guys. Co., NS.]
Howard Joseph b. 1934 d. 1936 [Sch. 32, Guys]
Hubert b. 1835 m. Brigitte Gouthro, 1886 [Sch. 48, Guys. Co., NS.]
Hubert b. 1918 (d) in infancy [AMC]
Hubert Girroir (Priest) b. 1825 d. 1864 [Sch. 0,1,4,& 8, Tracadie, Ant. Co., NS.]
Hubert Lanigan b. 1877 d. 1946 m. Grace Perreault [Sch. 8, Ant. Co]
Hubert Vincent d. 1947 [Sch. 1 Tracadie, Ant. Co., NS.]
Hume b. 1875 [Sch. 164, Isle Madame, NS.]
Ida Jane m1. Daniel Hurley, m2. Samuel Converse [Sch. 4, Ant. Co., NS.]
Ida b. 1889 d. 1987 m1. __Boudreau, m2 W. Leonard, m3 Irvin Fratus [Sch. 163, Isle Madame NS.]
Ignace b 1767 [Sch. 163, 164 Isle Madame, NS.]
Irma Clotilde b. 1829 d. 1846 m. Auguste Joret [Sch. 162.6, La.]
Iréna m. Léopold Beaudry, 1931 [Sch.3001, Rodier Branch, Québec]
Irene b. 1920 m. Pierre Landry [Sch. 162.1, La.]
Irène b. 1912 d. 1993 m. Bill Anderson [Sch. 315, NB.]
Irene d. 1963 m. ____ Morel [Sch. 35, Guys. Co., NS.]
Irène m. Maurice Pinault [Sch. 900, France]
Irénée b. 1874 m. Euphémie LeBlanc [Sch. 717, NB.]
Irenée b. 1914 d. 1978 m. Emma Boucher [Sch. 717, NB.]
Irênée Euclide b.1906 d. 1930 [Sch. 163 & 164 Isle Madame NS.]
Iroi (Kevin) m. Georgine Richard [Sch. 315, NB.]
Irvin Joseph m. Dorothy Elaine Jones [Sch. 76, Guys. Co., NS.]
Irving b. 1935, d. 1978 m. Helen Richard, 1956 [Sch. 31,Guys. Co. NS.]
Isabell m. Thomas Roach, 1958 [Sch. 711, NB.]
Isabelle b. 1739 [Sch. 204, PQ., Acadian]
Isabelle b. 1771 m. Joseph Gariépy, 1793 [Sch. 208, PQ., Acadian]
Isabelle [Sch. 420, France]
Isidore b. 1819 m1. Marguerite Pellerine 1844, m2. Caroline George 1866 [AMC & Sch. 31 & 32, Guys. Co., NS.]

Isidore b. 1902 m. Emma Léger [Sch. 706, NB.]
Isidore* b. 1805 m1. Thérèse Trottier, 1826, m2. Carignan J. Duclos [Sch. 217 & 218 PQ., Acadian]
Ismérie m. Emile Charles [Sch. 900, France]
J. Edmond b. 1887 d. 1887 [Sch. 705, NB.]
Jacqueline m. Louis Léger [Sch. 729, NB.]
Jacques (James) b. 1869 d. 1912 m. Marie Cormier, 1899 [Sch. 300, NB.]
Jacques b. 1648 d. 1703 dit Jacob m. 1699 Marguerite Gautrot [AMC]
Jacques b. 1674 m1. 1704 A. Petitpas m2. 1725 J. Amireau [AMC]
Jacques b. 1707 d. 1764 m. Marie Boisseau 1730 [Sch. 162.1 & 162.6, La.; 163 & 164 Isle Madame, C. B.; 300,500,600 & 700 NB.].
Jacques b. 1755 [Sch. 213, PQ. Acadian]
Jacques Girouard [Sch.3006, Belgium Branch, Québec]
Jacques Girouard, Sculptor. b. 1669 m. Louise Pain [Sch. 800, France]
Jacques Laurent b. 1849 m. Marie McCarron [Sch. 164, Isle Madame, C.B]
Jacques b. 1727 m. Marie (Barrio) Bourgeois 1748 [Sch. 202, PQ. Acadian]
Jacques* b. 1733 d. 1813 m1. Marie Bourgeois, m2. Françoise Gaudet, 1788 [Sch. 213, 217 & 218 PQ. Acadian]
Jacques* b. 1773 d. 1801 m. Angélique Broussard, 1798 [Sch. 162.1, La.]
Jacques m1. Charlotte Guillaume,1811 m2. Josephine Lover, 1842 [Sch. 213-PQ. Acadian]
James b. 1947 d. 1948 [Sch. 36,Guys]
James Henry b. 1873 m. Fanny Perry [Sch. 162, P.E.I.]
James Jeffrey b. 1906 d. 1973 m. Helen Nicholas [Sch. 162, P.E.I.]
James, twin [Sch.162.1 La.]
James b. 1846 m. Ann Wolf [Sch. 162, P.E.I.]
James b.1947 d. 1948 [Sch. 36 Guys]
James m. Eleanor Smith [Sch. 76, Guys. Co., NS.]
James Stewart m. Audra Ann Scott, 1997 [Sch. 67, Guys. Co., NS.]
Jane [Sch. 542, NB.]
Jane b. 1869 d. 1955 m. Charles Jackson [Sch. 33, Guys. Co., NS.]
Janice m. Stephen Fader [Sch. 31,Guys. Co. NS.]
Jazine b. 1841 d. 1860 [Sch. 705, NB.]
Jean Ann Stewart [Sch. 67, Guys. Co., NS.]
Jean [Sch. 162, P.E.I.]
Jean Baptiste b. 1810 d. 1874 m. Brigitte Montpetit 1833 [Sch. 2000, and Block N-5 FCMC]
Jean Marie b. 1945 m. Blair McNamara [Sch. 5, Ant. Co., NS.]
Jean (Judge) m1. Cécile Drolet, 1949, m2. Andrée Bérard, 1980 [Sch. 2000]
Jean b. 1651 d. 1721 m. Pétronille Georgeon [FCMC, PQ.]
Jean b. 1676 [AMC]
Jean b. 1815 d. 1871 m. Jane Bowie [Sch. 0,1, 4,8, Tracadie, Ant. Co., NS.]
Jean b. 1836 d. 1897 m. Marie Soreau [Sch. 900, France]
Jean b. 1840 d. 1869 [Sch. 33, Guys. Co., NS.]
Jean b. 1863 d. 1871 [Sch. 705, NB.]
Jean b. 1868 d. 1870 [Sch. 527, NB.]
Jean b. 1871 [Sch. 33, Guys. Co., NS.]
Jean b. 1876 [Sch. 706, NB.]

Jean 1778 & 1777 m1 Francoise Pétrault, m2. Madeleine Conte *[Sch. 400 France]*
Jean b. 1905 d. 1987 m. Bertha Collette 1929 *[Sch. 600, NB.]*
Jean b. 1916 d. 1979 *[Sch. 420, France]*
Jean b. 1932 d. 1986 m. Glenys Heaton *[Sch. 600, NB.]*
Jean b.1769 *[Sch. 202, PQ. Acadian]*
Jean Baptiste b. 1760 m. Marie Angélique Belouin, 1780 *[Sch. 208, PQ., Acadian]*
Jean Baptiste b. 1820 d. 1895 m1. M. Fougère, 1844 m2. Julie Lajeune *[Sch. 163, Isle Madame, NS.]*
Jean Baptiste b. 1884 d. 1960 m1. J. Poirier 1909, m2. A. Bourbonnais, 1944 *[Sch. 2000, FCMC]*
Jean Baptiste d. 1912 m. Léa Pelletier, 1898 *[Sch.3001, Rodier Branch, Québec]*
Jean Baptiste m. Marie Hebert, 1845 *[Sch. 216, PQ., Acadian]*
Jean Baptiste m. Mabel Girroir à William à Polycarpe *[Sch. 164, Isle Madame, NS.]*
Jean Baptiste b. 1792 *[Sch. 162.1, La.]*
Jean Baptiste b. 1725 d. 1808 m. 1751 Madeleine LeBlanc *[AMC]*
Jean Baptiste b. 1729 m. Madeleine Boudreau *[Sch. 163& 164 Isle Madame, CB; 162.1 & 162.6 La; 300, 5000, 600 & 700 NB.]*
Jean Baptiste b. 1741 *[Sch. 204, PQ., Acadian]*
Jean Baptiste b. 1763 m. Agatha Allaire, 1784 *[Sch. 207, PQ., Acadian]*
Jean Baptiste b. 1773 d. at 34 years old at La Grace Vachée *[Sch. 400, France]*
Jean Baptiste b. 1783 d. 1783 *[Sch. 211, West Indies, La.]*
Jean Baptiste b. 1806 d. 1818 *[Sch. 700, NB.]*
Jean Baptiste b. 1810 d. 1874 m. Brigitte Montpetit, 1833 *[FCMC, PQ.]*
Jean Baptiste b. 1811 d. 1873 m. 1833 Sophie Pôte *[AMC]*
Jean Baptiste b. 1821 d. 1911 m. Appoline Melanson *[Sch. 717,724, NB.]*
Jean Baptiste b. 1832 *[Sch. 162.6 La.]*
Jean Baptiste b. 1835 d. 1874 m. Marie Leduc, 1855 *[Sch. 2000, and Block N-5 FCMC]*
Jean Baptiste b. 1839 m. Marie Clementine Grow *[Sch. 162.6, La.]*
Jean Baptiste b. 1850 m. Dina Gallant, 1877 *[Sch. 523, NB.]*
Jean Baptiste b. 1862 d. 1912 m. Victoria Legault *[Sch. 2000, and Block N-5 FCMC]*
Jean Baptiste b. ca 1878 d.1958 m. Mary Josephine Crowe *[Sch. 706, NB.]*
Jean Baptiste b.1752 m. Gertrude Landry *[Sch. 163& 164 Isle Madame, NS.]*
Jean Baptiste b.1769 d. 1818 m. Elizabeth Landry, 1790 *[Sch. 162.6, La.]*
Jean Baptiste b. 1799 m1. Rosalie Victoire Bourg, 1821 m2 Azelie E. Boudreaux *[Sch. 162.6 La]*
Jean Baptiste b. 1763 d. 1763 *[Sch. 400, France]*
Jean Baptiste m. Angélique Thériot *[Sch. 163& 164 Isle Madame, NS.]*
Jean Baptiste m. Josette Pichette, 1823 *[Sch. 207, PQ., Acadian]*
Jean Baptiste m. Julienne Sansouçy, 1849 *[Sch. 208, PQ., Acadian]*
Jean Baptiste Hubert *[Sch. 164,]*
Jean Baptiste Hubert b.1841 d. 1914 m. Martha Lavache, 1865 *[Sch. 163, Isle Madame, NS.]*
Jean Girouard m. Pétronille Georgeon, 1690 *[FCMC & Chart fc, France]*
Jean Girouard, Sculptor, b. 1611 d. 1676 m. Joachine Pastureau *[Sch. 800, France]*
Jean Girouard/Green b. 1913 d. 1913 *[Sch. 309, NB.]*
Jean Baptiste b. 1902, d.1945 m. Edmond René *[Sch. 163 & 164 Isle Madame, NS.]*
Jean Louis b. 1776 d. 1837 son of Madeleine m. Jeanne Clisson *[Sch. 400, France]*
Jean Louis b. 1799 d. 1880 m. Edesse Roy, 1831 *[Sch. 700, 705 & 706 NB.]*
Jean m. Charles Gibson *[Sch. 48, Guys. Co., NS.]*

Jean Marie m. Blair Mc Namara [Sch. 5. Ant. Co]
Jean Marie b.1892 [Sch. 36, Guys. Co., NS.]
Jean Marie b. 1856 m. L. Laviolette [Sch. 202, PQ. Acadian]
Jean Marie Girouard b. 1661 d. 1720 m. Marie Roy [Sch. 800, France]
Jean Michel m. Bernadette [Sch. 400, France]
Jean Paul m1. Isabelle LeBlanc, m2. Claudette Godin [Sch. 724, NB.]
Jean René m. Victoire Vineau, 1840 [Sch. 400, France]
Jean Valmond b. 1806 m. Caroline Taylor (Teller), 1833 [Sch. 162.1, La.]
Jean-Charles b. 1743 m. Anne Ouvrey 1772 [Sch. 204, PQ., Acadian]
Jean-Joseph b. 1795 d. 1855 m1. M. Felix 1818 m2. M. Barthelot [Sch. 202, PQ. Acad]
Jeanne m. Albert Décairie [Sch. 202, PQ. Acadian]
Jeanne [Sch. 33, Guys. Co., NS.]
Jeanne b. 1709 d. 1767 m. François Forest [Sch. 204, PQ., Acadian]
Jeanne b. 1897 d. 1982 m. Eric Cormier, 1902 [Sch. 706, NB.]
Jeanne Girouard/Green m. Gérard LeBlanc [Sch. 309, NB.]
Jeanne b. 1771 d. 1880 m. Carlos Blanchard 1792 [Sch. 162.6, La.]
Jeanne m. Joseph Bonnefou [see notes on Sch. 211, West Indies, La.]
Jeanne m. Leonard Gallant [Sch. 514, NB.]
Jeanne m. Marcel Millérioux [Sch. 400, France]
Jeannette b. 1844 d. 1911 m. Guillaume Laurent Landry [Sch. 163, Isle Madame, NS.]
Jeannette m. __Bonnaire [Sch. 700, NB.]
Jeffrey (Siffoi) b. 1845 d. 1911 m1. Anne Smith, m2. Elizabeth Boucher [Sch. 163, Isle Madame, NS.]
Jeffrey 1868 d. 1868 [AMC]
Jeffrey b. 1859 (Siffoi) [Sch. 1 Tracadie, Ant. Co., NS.]
Jeffrey b. 1871 d. 1871 [AMC]
Jeffrey b. 1872 d. 1964 m1. 1900 Anne Fougere m2. 1924 Louise Conway [AMC]
Jérémie b. 1811 d. 1875 m. Hippolyte Picard, 1834 [FCMC, PQ.]
Jérémie m. Esther Handfield [Sch.3006, Belgium Branch, Québec]
Jerome m. Ethel Stewart [Sch. 95, Guys. Co., NS.]
Jimmy b. 1902 d. 1992 m. Stella Decoste 1927 [Sch. 31,Guys. Co. NS.]
Joachim-Amable b. 1737 d. 1830 m. Marie Appoline Cousineau 1768, [FCMC, PQ.]
Joanne (Herb) m. Sherman Richard [Sch. 36, Guys. Co., NS.]
Job b. 1868 [Sch. 717, NB.]
Joe b. 1878 d. 1970 m. Angeline Pero [Sch. 72, Guys. Co., NS.]
Joe (Belou) Johnny b. 1891 m. Mary Jane Pellerin , no children [Sch. 48, Guys. Co., NS.]
Joe (Bob) Marin b. 1767 d. 1861 m. Marguerite Cormier ca. 1793 [Sch. 300, 500, 600,700, 706, 711 737,724 729 NB.]
Joe à Mon b. 1867 m1. Margaret Pettipas, m2. Sophie De Gruchie [Sch. 48, Guys. Co., NS.]
Joe b. 1878 d. 1970 m. Angeline Pero [Sch. 76, Guys. Co., NS.]
John b. 1871 d. 1976 m1. Veronica Marie Perry m2. Cathy Pierre [Sch. 162, P.E.I.]
John [Sch. 36, Guys. Co., NS.]
John [Sch. 5, Ant. Co., NS.]
John [Sch. 700, NB.]
John Alexander b. 1910 d.1988 n.m [Sch. 33, Guys. Co., NS.]

Appendices

John Andrew b. 1918 *[Sch. 36, Guys. Co., NS.]*
John Andrew *[Sch. 76 Guys]*
John b. 1815 d. 1871 m. Jane Bowie *[Sch. 5, Ant. Co., NS.]*
John b. 1855 *[Sch. 35, Guys. Co., NS.]*
John b. 1868 *[Sch. #0 Tracadie, Ant. Co., NS.]*
John b. 1874 *[Sch. 706, NB.]*
John b. 1874 d. 1958 m. Marie Belliveau *[Sch. 737, NB.]*
John b. 1901 (U.S.A.) not married *[Sch. 35, Guys. Co., NS.]*
John Douglas Stewart b. 1923 d. 1977 m. Lelia Bugden, 1945 *[Sch. 67, Guys. Co., NS.]*
John Francis b. 1881 *[Sch. 4, Ant. Co., NS.]*
John Gregory b. 1953 d. 1992 *[Sch. 35, Guys. Co., NS.]*
John Joseph b. 1921 d. 1982 m. Margaret Hale *[Sch. 35, Guys. Co., NS.]*
John m. Roberta Vaughan *[Sch. 48, Guys. Co., NS.]*
John Sylvester b. 1913 d. 1996 m. 1942 Beatrice Fougère *[AMC]*
John Wilfred m. Mabel Bowels *[Sch. 5, Ant. Co., NS.]*
Johnny Girouard/Green b. 1914 d. 1970 m. Joséphine LeBlanc *[Sch. 309, NB.]*
Johnny Green m. Suzanne Allain *[Sch. 309, NB.]*
Jolande *[Sch. 523, NB.]*
Jonas b. 1864 *[Sch. 737, NB.]*
Josaphat b. 1888 d. 1959 m. Sylvia Patenaude, 1912 *[Sch. 2000, and Block N-5 FCMC]*
Joseph *[Sch. 400, France]*
Joseph A b. 1746 m1. M. Poirier, m2. M. Hosmin 1780 m3. M. E. Hofman *[Sch. 211, West IIndies, La.]*
Joseph A. m. Eleanor Malloy *[Sch. 48, Guys. Co., NS.]*
Joseph Albert b. 1872 *[Sch. 208, PQ., Acadian]*
Joseph Albert b. 1893 m. Eva Richard *[Sch. 724, NB.]*
Joseph Alexis b. 1886, not married *[Sch. 163, Isle Madame, NS.]*
Joseph Allen b. 1910 m. Dorothy Fern *[Sch. 95, Guys. Co., NS.]*
Joseph Allen b. 1910 d. 1978 m. Anne Gill *[Sch. 162, P.E.I.]*
Joseph Amable m1. Madeleine Poirier, m2. Marie Hosmin, 1780 m3. Marie Eve Hofman, 1785 *[Sch. 211 West Indies, La]*
Joseph Arthur b. 1872 d. 1973 m. Eliza Jane Macdonald *[Sch. 0 Tracadie, Ant. Co., NS.]*
Joseph Arthur b. 1875 d. 1953 M.D. m. Wavine Brazeau *[Sch. 208, PQ., Acadian]*
Joseph Arthur R. b. 1883 m. Lucienne Roberge, 1912 *[Sch. 218, PQ., Acadian]*
Joseph b. 1668 (Sculptor) m. Marguerite Gautron *[Sch. 800, France]*
Joseph b. 1746 *[Sch. 202, PQ.]*
Joseph b. 1753 *[Sch. 211, West Indies, La.]*
Joseph b. 1756 *[Sch. 163 & 164 Isle Madame, NS.]*
Joseph b. 1758 *[Sch. 162.6, La.]*
Joseph b. 1788 d. 1866 m. Angélique Leblanc, 1809 *[Sch. 0, 1,4,5 &,8 Tracadie, Ant. Co., NS.]*
Joseph b. 1823 m1. 1847 A. Belfontainem, m 2. N. Avery, m3. C. McGillivray Lundy *[AMC]*
Joseph b. 1700 m. Louise Cassiou *[Sch. 400, France]*
Joseph b. 1717 d. 1776 m1. R. Hébert, 1742 m2. Anastasie LeBlanc *[Sch. 207, PQ., Acadian]*
Joseph b. 1720 d. 1804 m1. A. Doucet 1743 m2. J. Béliveau, 1763 *[Sch. 211, West Indies, La.]*
Joseph b. 1727 d. 1767 m. Agnès Gaudet, 1750 *[Sch. 213,217,218 PQ. Acadian]*

Joseph b. 1729 [Sch. 164, Isle Madame, C.B]
Joseph b. 1733 d.. ca.1793 m1. 1752 Françoise Blanchard m2. 1758 Marie Arseneau [AMC & Sch. 216].
Joseph b. 1738 m. Anne Des Mouliers, 1766 [Sch. 202, PQ. Acadian]
Joseph b. 1742 m. Mattherine Rousselien [Sch. 400, France]
Joseph b. 1743 [Sch. 207, PQ., Acadian]
Joseph b. 1752 [Sch. 207, PQ., Acadian]
Joseph b. 1756 [Sch. 164, Isle Madame, NS.]
Joseph b. 1767 d. 1800 m. Marie Anne Baillargé [Sch. 202, PQ. Acadian]
Joseph b. 1768 d. 1772 [Sch. 162.6, La]
Joseph b. 1769 d. 1791 m. Josephte Lord, 1791 [Sch. 208, PQ., Acadian]
Joseph b. 1772 d. 1836 m. Josephte Bleau, 1799 [FCMC, PQ.]
Joseph b. 1772 m. Véronique Hamelin, 1796 [Sch. 207, PQ., Acadian]
Joseph b. 1778 m. Marie Anne Landry 1801 [Sch. 162.1, La.]
Joseph b. 1783 [Sch. 400, France]
Joseph b. 1796 d. 1867 m1. Francois Bouju, m2. Marg. Brossard [Sch. 420, France]
Joseph b. 1803 d. 1885 m1. Rose, m2. Judith Doucet [Sch. 514, NB.]
Joseph b. 1812 m. Elizabeth Dorley [Sch. #1 & 4 & 8, Tracadie, Ant. Co., NS.]
Joseph b. 1830 d. 1920 m. Julia Rodier [Sch.3001, Rodier Branch, Québec]
Joseph b. 1846 d. 1918 m1. Léa Dion, m2. S. Roy, 1875 [Sch. 3006, Belgium Br. Québec]
Joseph b. 1854 m. Celanaire Plessis-Belair [Sch. 202, PQ. Acadian]
Joseph b. 1859 [Sch. 35 & 36, Guys. Co., NS.]
Joseph b. 1877 m. Marie Rose Légère [Sch. 514, NB.]
Joseph b. 1878 [Sch. 315, NB.]
Joseph b. 1881 [Sch. 35, Guys. Co., NS.]
Joseph b. 1884 d. 1955 m. Marie LeBouthillier [Sch. 700, NB.]
Joseph b. 1729 [Sch. 163 & 164 Isle Madame, NS.]
Joseph b. 1872 d. 1962 m. Joséphine Cormier, 1893 [Sch.3001, Rodier Branch, Québec]
Joseph b. 1893 d. 1893 [Sch. 67, Guys. Co., NS.]
Joseph (Cyriac) b. 1873 d. 1938 m1. C. Cormier, 1904, m2. R. Dallaire [Sch. 300, NB.]
Joseph (Dédé) III b. 1802 m1. Emilie Descormier Guillaume, m2. Miltilde Beaubien, [Sch 217,218, PQ., Acadian]
Joseph d. 1778 [Sch. 211 West Indies, La]
Joseph d.1880 m. Marie Roy, 1855 [Sch. 309, NB.]
Joseph Damas* b. 1804 m. Carmelite Barrillot, 1834 [Sch. 162.6, La.]
Joseph Éna b. 1855 d. 1937 m. Marie Walkins [Sch. 218, PQ., Acadian]
Joseph (Gerrior) Herb b. 1921 d. 1957 m. Anna Marie O'Neil [Sch. 36 Guysborough Co., NS.]
Joseph Girouard/Green b. 1888 d. 1953 m. Josephine LeBlanc [Sch. 309, NB.]
Joseph Honoré Alcide b. 1885 m. _____ [Sch. 162, P.E.I.]
Joseph I b. 1750 m1. Marie Grandbois, 1777, m2. J. Normandeau [Sch. 217, 218, PQ., Acadian]
Joseph II b. 1778 m. Marie Doucet, 1799 [Sch. 217 & 218 PQ., Acadian]
Joseph Léonidas b. 1884 [Sch. 208, PQ., Acadian]
Joseph m. Angélique-Charlotte St. Michel ca. 1793 [Sch. 213, PQ. Acadian]
Joseph m. Appoline Benoît Livernois, 1792 [Sch.3006, Belgium Branch, Québec]
Joseph m. Philomene Jacob, 1860 [Sch. 207, PQ.]

Appendices

Joseph m. Elizabeth Desrocher 1865 *[Sch. 217, PQ., Acadian]*
Joseph m. Marie Duhamel, 1839 *[Sch. 208, PQ., Acadian]*
Joseph m. Zoé Dion, 1842 *[Sch. 3006, Belgium Branch, Québec]*
Joseph m1. Céleste Laflamme, 1839, m2. Marie St-Laurent, 1841 *[Sch. 207, PQ., Acadian]*
Joseph m. Philomene Jacob, 1860 *[Sch.207, PQ. Acadian]*
Joseph m1. _____, m2. Françoise Dupuy *[Sch. 420, France]*
Joseph Marie b. 1803 m. Reine Panneton, 1834 *[Sch. 217, PQ., Acadian]*
Joseph Mathieu b. 1781 *[Sch. 211, West Indies, La.]*
Joseph Méderic m. Bertha Racine *[Sch.3001, Rodier Branch, Québec]*
Joseph Magloire b. 1768 d. 1772 *[Sch. 162.6, La]*
Joseph N.L, b. 1886 m. Berthe Marsolais *[Sch. 202, PQ. Acadian]*
Joseph Nicholas b. 1755 d. 1789 m. Angélique Petitpas *[AMC & Sch. 0, 1, & 4, 5, 8 Ant. Co., NS.]*
Joseph Nicolas b. 1812 d. 1871 m. Elizabeth Dorley *[Sch. 0, 1, 4 & 8, Ant. Co]*
Joseph Oscar* b. 1839 d. 1916 m1. Anaise Fedora Girouard m2. Cécile Brugere *[Sch. 162.1, La.]*
Joseph Rose b. 1803 d. 1885 m. Judith Doucet, 1828 *[Sch. 500, 542 NB.]*
Joseph S. b. 1823 m1. A Belfontaine, m2. Nancy Avery m3. C. MacGillivray *[AMC & Sch. 48, Guys. Co., NS.]*
Joseph Thomas b. 1893 *[Sch. 163, Isle Madame, NS.]*
Joseph Timothé, b. 1745 *[Sch. 211, West Indies, La.]*
Joseph b. 1859 *[Sch. 35, Guys. Co., NS.]*
Joseph Villemaire m. Privé, 1818 *[Scht 3006, Belgium Branch, Québec]*
Joseph Wayne m. Charlene Benoît *[Sch. 36, Guys. Co., NS.]*
Joseph William m. Mary Catherine Campbell *[Sch. 5, Ant. Co., NS.]*
Joseph William, died 1.5 yrs. *[Sch. 8, Ant. Co]*
Joseph* b. 1810 *[Sch. 162.1, La.]*
Joseph* b. 1857 m. Emérence Goyer *[Sch. 213, PQ. Acadian]*
Joséphat m1. Alma LeBlanc, m2. Priscilla Léger *[Sch. 706, NB.]*
Josèphate *[Sch. 3001, Rodier Branch, Québec]*
Josèphe b. 1754 *[Sch. 216, PQ., Acadian]*
Josèphe m. Joseph Martin, 1858 *[Sch. 213, PQ. Acadian]*
Josèphe m. Simon Joseph Castille, 1783 *[Sch. 204, PQ., Acadian]*
Josèphe m1. Germain Gaudet, m2. Christophe Alexis Dumont, 1770 *[see notes Sch. 204, PQ., Acadian]*
Joséphine b. 1875 d. 1890 *[Sch. 8, Ant. Co]*
Joséphine b. 1885 m. Isidore Boucher *[Sch. 705, NB.]*
Josephine b. 1893 d. 1956 m. Alfred Gilbert *[Sch. 164. Isle Madame. NS.]*
Josephine b. 1894 d. 1962 m1. George Zerros, m2 Albert Ross *[Sch. 600, NB.]*
Joséphine b. 1897 d. 1917 m. Télex (Télesphore) Cormier, 1916 *[Sch. 705, NB.]*
Joséphine m. Eddie Romans *[Sch. 0 Tracadie, Ant. Co., NS.]*
Josette b. 1934 *[Sch. 420, France]*
Josey b. 1919 d. 1995 m. Sam Delaney 1946 *[Sch. 31,Guys. Co. NS.]*
Josué b. 1883 d. 968 m. Sara Cormier, 1910 *[Sch. 705, NB.]*
Judique b. 1870 d. 1915 m. Olivier Cormier *[Sch. 500, NB.]*
Judith b. 1832 d. 1857 m. Maximin Cormier, 1852 *[Sch. 717, NB.]*

Judith b. 1881 m. _____ Duxbury *[Sch. 717, NB.]*
Jules Edouard b. 1883 m. Anna Poirier *[Sch. 724, NB.]*
Julia Avolona b. 1888 d. 1979 m1. Bill Avery, m2. Henry Casson, m3. Al Fraser *[Sch. 67, Guys. Co., NS.]*
Juliana m. Franky Fougère *[Sch. 514, NB.]*
Julie b. 1796 m. Hyacinthe Durand, 1816 *[Sch. 217, 218 PQ. Acadian]*
Julia (Lyn Julie) m. Troy Snaychuk *[Sch. 717, NB.]*
Julie b. 1844 d. 1846 *[FCMC, PQ.]*
Julie b. 1862 m. _____Driscoll *[AMC]*
Julien (Joseph) b. 1839 d. 1909 m. Aurélie Leboeuf, 1867 *[Sch. 2000, and Block N-5 FCMC]*
Julien 1842, *[Sch. 162.6, La]*
Julien b. 1779 d. 1865 m. Marie-Clémence Lavoie 1801 *[FCMC, PQ.]*
Julien b. 1802 d. 1831 m. Françoise St-Michel 1827 *[FCMC, PQ.]*
Julien m. Adolfe Lecompte, 1864 *[Sch. 218, PQ., Acadian]*
Julien* m1. Marguerite Laliberté m2. Therese Lemay, 1885 *[Sch. 217 & 218 PQ., Acadian]*
Julienne b. 1848 m. Augustin Braud, 1872 *[Sch. 34, Ant. Co., NS.]*
Juliette b. 1785 m. Alex Petitpas *[AMC]*
Juste b. 1883 d. 1939 m. Evangéline Maillet *[Sch. 300, NB.]*
Justinian Elfedge b. 1851 m. Celima Simoneaux *[Sch. 162.6, La.]*
Kathleen m. Fred MacLeod *[Sch. 48, Guys. Co., NS.]*
Kim Marie *[Sch. 35, Guys. Co., NS.]*
Lady Teresa m. Sir Kenneth Canning 1953 *[FCMC, PQ.]*
Larry à Mon (James Lawrence) b. 1860 m. Judith Avery *[Sch. 48, Guys. Co., NS.]*
Larry m. Carol Kirkpatrick *[Sch. 48, Guys. Co., NS.]*
Laura *[Sch. 706, NB.]*
Laura b. 1919 d. 1919 *[Sch. 315, NB.]*
Laura Elizabeth Stewart b. 1924 d. 1995 m. Vernon Ottaway *[Sch. 67, Guys. Co., NS.]*
Laura b. 1876 d. 1938 m. Venture Murphy *[Sch. 32, Guys. Co., NS.]*
Laura May b. 1895 d. 1979, not married *[Sch. 67, Guys. Co., NS.]*
Laure-Anna b. 1894 d. 1971 m. Uldège Saint-Onge *[Sch. 2000, and Block N-5 FCMC]*
Laurent b. 1865 *[Sch. 724, NB.]*
Laurent b. 1890 d. 1890 *[Sch. 164. Isle Madame. NS.]*
Laurent m. Louise Pontbriand, 1942 *[Sch. 2000, and Block N-5 FCMC]*
Laurice *[Sch. 208, PQ., Acadian]*
Laurie m. Donna Leblanc *[Sch. 500, NB.]*
Laurie b. 1925 d. 1978 m. Alfreda LeBlanc *[Sch. 315, NB.]*
Laurie m. Pamela Thorick *[Sch. 737, NB.]*
Laurier m. Cécile Hebert *[Sch. 705, NB.]*
Lavin Edward b. 1867 *[Sch. 0 Tracadie, Ant. Co., NS.]*
Léa m1. Carl William Bauer m2. Ross McBrian *[Sch. 717, NB.]*
Léandre m. Emilie Savoie, 1964 *[Sch. 711, NB.]*
Léandre, no children *[Sch. 3001, Rodier Branch, Québec]*
Lena Geraldine m. Kenneth Avery *[Sch. 76, Guys. Co., NS.]*
Leo b. 1928 d. 1966 *[Sch. 300, NB.]*
Léo b. 1941 d. 1988 m. Huguette Pineault *[Sch. 600, NB.]*

Appendices

Leo b. 1954 d. 1974 *[SCh. 95, Guys. Co.]*
Leo b. 1895 d. 1976 m. Ann Fortin *[Sch. 163, Isle Madame, NS.]*
Leo m. Anne-Marie Robichaud *[Sch. 315, NB.]*
Leo m. Delores Sinitte *[Sch. 0 Tracadie, Ant. Co., NS.]*
Leo Paul m. Angelette Goguen, 1949 *[Sch. 729, NB.]*
Leo Thomas b. 1903 m. Eleanor Cullen *[Sch. 95, Guys. Co., NS.]*
Léon b. 1818 d. 1894 m. Marcelline Cormier *[Sch. 600, NB.]*
Leona m1. Thomas Carr, m2. John Keenan *[Sch. 95, Guys. Co., NS.]*
Leonard b. 1852 *[Sch. 162.1, La.]*
Léonard m. Gisèle Drisdelle *[Sch. 711, NB.]*
Léonce (Toutoute) b. 1850 d. 1937 m. Clara Broussard *[Sch. 162.1, La.]*
Léonie *[Sch. 3001, Rodier Branch, Québec]*
Léonie b. 1892 d. 1969 *[Sch. 705, NB.]*
Léonise m. Honoré Hébert *[Sch. 217, PQ., Acadian]*
Léontine b. 1830 m. Bee Primeaux *[Sch. 162.1, La.]*
Lester m. Audrey O'Leary, no children *[Sch. 48, Guys. Co., NS.]*
Elévanie (Yvonne) b. 1902 not married *[Sch. 729, NB.]*
Lévi m. H. LeBlanc *[Sch. 315, NB.]*
Lewis m. Florence Bourque,1935 *[Sch. 527, NB.]*
Lina (Regina) m1. Bill Noone, m2. Jack Moody *[Sch. 706, NB.]*
Lina b. 1903 m. Ben Robichaud, 1924 *[Sch. 705, NB.]*
Linda Marie m. Ian Pitts *[Sch. 76, Guys. Co., NS.]*
Livain m. Yolande Savoie, 1962 *[Sch. 700, NB.]*
Livia Paul *[Sch. 95, Guys. Co., NS.]*
Lora (Sousou) m. Eloige Landry *[Sch. 162.1, La.]*
Lorraine *[Sch. 737, NB.]*
Lorraine 1919 m. Méderic LeBlanc, 1944 *[Sch. 527, NB.]*
Lorraine m. John Maguire *[Sch. 95, Guys. Co., NS.]*
Louis (Levi) b. 1833 d. 1917 m1. Collette Cormier, m2. Euphémie Jaillet, 1860 1856 *[Sch. 705, NB.]*
Louis ? b. 1610 Beaulieu *[Sch. 400, France]*
Louis b. 1761 *[Sch. 162.1, La.]*
Louis b. 1705 m. Marie Josèphe Blanchard *[Sch. 204, PQ., Acadian]*
Louis b. 1746 d. 1807 m1. M. Bersil, m2. M. Berthault *[Sch. 900, France]*
Louis b. 1761 *[Sch. 300, 500,600 & 700 NB.]*
Louis b. 1833 m. Madeleine Goguen *[Sch. 309, NB.]*
Louis b. 1844 m. Hermine Cormier, 1867 *[Sch. 208, PQ., Acadian]*
Louis b. 1867 d. 1923 m. Emma Alix, 1899 *[Sch.3006, Belgium Branch, Québec]*
Louis b. 1868 d. 1874 *[Sch. 600, NB.]*
Louis b. 1906 d. 1974 m. Louise Robichaud, 1928 *[Sch. 700, NB.]*
Louis b. 1949 d. 1949 *[Sch. 600, NB.]*
Louis Frédéric b. 1839 *[Sch. 420, France]*
Louis Joseph b. 1828 *[Sch. 420, France]*
Louis m. Anaïse Pichereau b. 1876 d. 1953 *[Sch. 900, France]*
Louis Maury b. 1830 d. 1896 *[Sch. 900, France]*

Louis Pascal b. 1735 d. 1796 m. Marie Anne Lamoureux,1761 [FCMC, PQ.]
Louis Pascal b. 1759 d. 1800 m. Madeleine Robert 1784 [FCMC, PQ.]
Louis Paul b. 1716 m. Marie Madeleine Thibodeau, 1736 [Sch. 300,500,600 & 700 NB; 163 & 164 Isle Madame,NS., and 162.1 & 162.6 La.]
Louis Pierre m. Exarey Ann Dugas [Sch. 162.1, La.]
Louis Valentin b. 1830 [Sch. 420 France]
Louisa b. 1795 m. Joseph Daigle [Sch. 162.6, La.]
Louisa Melanie b. 1836, [Sch. 162.6, La]
Louisa b. 1924 m. Aurèle Allain [Sch. 711, NB.]
Louise [Sch. 300, NB.]
Louise [Sch. 523, NB.]
Louise [Sch. 218]
Louise b. 1883 d. 1971 m. René Picard [Sch. 900, France]
Louise [Sch. 48, Guys. Co., NS.]
Louise Girouard/Green [Sch. 309, NB.]
Louise m. Julien Barroux [Sch. 900, France]
Luc b. 1786 d. 1868 m. ca 1800 Ann Jacquet [AMC]
Luc b. 1832 [Sch. 33, Guys. Co., NS.]
Luc b. 1824-1907 [Sch. 217, PQ., Acadian]
Luc b. 1837 d. 1837 [Sch. 218, PQ. Acadian]
Lucien b. 1905 m. Thérèse Fleury, [Sch. 400, France]
Lucien m. Linda Fawcett, 1970 [Sch. 711, NB.]
Lucienne m. Gérard Doussin [Sch. 400, France]
Lucille m. Andrew Proulx 1946 [Sch. 523, NB.]
Luke A. b. 1848 d. 1925 m. Til Hushard [AMC]
Lydia b. 1866 d. 1909 m. Adrien LeBlanc [Sch. 706, NB.]
Lydia m. Jean Guy Richer [Sch. 600, NB.]
Lydia Marie b. 1904 d. 1905 [Sch. 600, NB.]
M. Félonise m1. Edward Barthell 1879, m2. Philas Sylvain 1906 m3 Narcisse Blais,1927 [Sch. 218, PQ. Acadian]
M.J. Girouard* m. Joseph Rivet,1797 [Sch. 213, PQ. Acadian]
Mabel b. 1877 m. Omer Côté [FCMC, PQ.]
Mabel b. 1883 m. John Baptiste Girroir [Sch. 163, Isle Madame, NS.]
Mack [Sch. 542, NB.]
Madeleine [Sch. 717, NB.]
Madeleine b. 1700 m. Charles Blanchard, 1718 [Sch. 204, PQ., Acadian]
Madeleine b. 1714 d. 1735 m. Alexandre Hébert [Sch. 207, PQ., Acadian]
Madeleine b. 1723 m. Joseph Comeau, 1749 [Sch. 211, West Indies, La.]
Madeleine b. 1745 [Sch. 211, West Indies, La.]
Madeleine b. 1754 m. Pierre Sansoucy [Sch. 207, PQ., Acadian]
Madeleine b. 1848 d. 1953 m. Hyppolite Saulnier, 1868 [Sch. 309, NB.]
Madeleine b. 1871 d.1948 [Sch. 31,Guys. Co. NS.]
Madeleine b. 1875 d. 1967 [Sch. 500, NB.]
Madeleine b. 1918 [Sch. 420, France]
Madeleine b. 1840 d. 1936 m. Anselme Girouard à Rose [Sch. 300, NB.]

Appendices

Madeleine b. 1755 m. Germain Jacques *[Sch. 213, PQ. Acadian]*

Madeleine m. Pierre Ste-Martine Terjat,1726 *[FCMC, PQ.]*

Magdeleine b. 1719 d. 1803 m. Joseph LeBlanc1740 *[Sch. 163,164 Isle Madame, NS.; 162.1 & 162.6, La.;Sch. 300,500,600 & 700 NB.]*

Magdeleine b. 1732 d. 1784 m. Jean Cousin *[Sch. 900, France]*

Madeleine b. 1821 *[Sch. 162.1, La]*

Maggie *[Sch. 542, NB.]*

Maggie Gabell b. 1897 d. 1983 m. Gus Van Gothen *[Sch. 67, Guys. Co., NS.]*

Maggie m._____White *[Sch. 72 & 76 Guys. Co., NS.]*

Magloire b. 1887 d. 1908 *[Sch. 711, NB.]*

Magloire b. 1835 m1. Collette Cormier, m2. Suzanne Allain, m3. Henriette Girouard *[Sch. 300, NB.]*

Magloire b. 1837 d. 1918 1. Henriette Girouard 1858, m2. Justine Mélanson *[Sch. 523, 527, NB.]*

Magloire b. 1900 d.1979 m. Eliza Fredette *[Sch. 527, NB.]*

Magloire b. 1909 m. Marie Poirier 1996 *[Sch. 711, NB.]*

Magloire b. 1770 d. 1783 *[162.6 La]*

Magloire b. 1777 d. 1783 *[Sch. 162.6, La]*

Malania b. 1809 *[Sch. 162.6 La]*

Mamie (Nancy Mae) b. 1906 m. Frank Delorey, 1926 *[Sch. 48, Guys. Co., NS.]*

Marc (M.D.) m. Jocelyn LeClair *[Sch. 300, NB.]*

Marc b. 1929 d. 1969 Micheline Monory *[Sch. 900, France]*

Marcel b. 1843 d. 1864 *[Sch.315, NB.]*

Marcel b. 1909 *[Sch. 420, France]*

Marcel m. Germain Robin *[Sch. 900, France]*

Marcel m. Mathilda Dufault, 1858 *[Sch. 207, PQ. Acadian]*

Marcelline b. 1821 d. 1823 *[AMC]*

Marcelline b. 1869 m. Esaïe Vienneau *[Sch. 700, NB.]*

Margaret Avolna Stewart m. Ernest Holland *[Sch. 67, Guy Co.]*

Margaret Anne b. 1883 *[Sch. 4, Ant. Co., NS.]*

Margaret Anne b.1867 m. Peter Fougère 1888 *[Sch. 34, Ant. Co]*

Margaret b. 1850 *[Sch. 48, Guys. Co., NS.]*

Margaret b. 1894 m. David Walter Pettipas *[Sch. 36, Guys]*

Margaret b. 1915 d. 1990 m. Charles Charleton *[Sch. 162, P.E.I.]*

Margaret J. m. Alfred Halbot *[Sch. 48, Guys. Co., NS.]*

Margaret m. Louis Thériault *[Sch. 163 & 164. Isle Madame. NS.]*

Margaret m. Chalmer Hines *[Sch. 0 Tracadie, Ant. Co., NS.]*

Margaret-Marie m. Jaddus Goguen *[Sch. 717, NB.]*

Margaret m. Ronald Doyle *[Sch. 35, Guys. Co., NS.]*

Margaret Mary *[Sch. 724, NB.]*

Margareta Abdelarda b. 1812 m. Eugene Dupuis 1836 *[Sch. 162.6 La]*

Marguerite *[Sch. 213, PQ., Acadian]*

Marguerite *[Sch. 705, NB.]*

Marguerite 1682 m. ca. 1702 Louis Doucet *[AMC]*

Marguerite b. 1693 d.1776 m. Joseph Poirier 1748 *[Sch. 202, PQ. Acadian]*

Marguerite b. 1749 d. 1803 *[Sch., PQ. Acadian]*

Marguerite b. 1723 m. Basile Boudrot, 1743 [Sch. 163 &164 Isle Madame, NS.; 162.11 & 162.6, La; 300,500,600 & 700 NB.]
Marguerite b. m. Jos Dodelin, 1791 [Sch. 213, PQ. Acadian]
Marguerite b. 1731 m1. Pouget 1724 m2. F. Aucoin m3. C Touzalin [Sch. 164. Isle Mad. NS.]
Marguerite b. 1733 [AMC]
Marguerite b. 1737 [Sch. 300, 500,600& 700 NB.; 162.1 La]
Marguerite b. 1749 d. 1759 [Sch. 217 & 218, PQ., Acadian]
Marguerite b. 1756 m. François Gazaille 1775 [Sch. 207, PQ., Acadian]
Marguerite b. 1789 m. Joseph Bernard [Sch. 162.1, La.]
Marguerite b. 1801 d. 1819 [Sch. 500,542 NB.]
Marguerite b. 1812 m. 1834 Joseph Doiron [AMC]
Marguerite b. 1821 d. 1823 [Sch. 1 Tracadie, Ant. Co., NS.]
Marguerite b. 1823 d. 1870 m. Désiré Pettipas, 1823 [Sch. 0, 1,4, & 8, Tracadie, Ant. Co., NS.]
Marguerite b. 1850 [Sch. 1 Tracadie, Ant. Co., NS.]
Marguerite b. 1851 m. Irénée Aucoin [Sch. 162, P.E.I.]
Marguerite b. 1861 m. Maxime Breau [Sch. 737, NB.]
Marguerite b. 1886 census 1891 [AMC]
Marguerite b. 1890 d. 1963 m1. Solomon Gallant, m2. Alphonse Gagnon [Sch. 600, NB.]
Marguerite b. 1781 m1. Gabriel Durand 1801 m2. Joseph Crétien,1817 m3 Vital Bélanger [Sch. 217, 218 P.Q]
Marguerite. b. 1846 m. Calixte Thibodeau [Sch. 523, NB.]
Marguerite d. 1875 m. Eustarache Briand [Sch. 34, Ant. Co., NS.]
Marguerite Giroire m. J.B. Jetro [Sch. 213, PQ.]
Marguerite m. Gilbert Robichaud [Sch. 700, NB.]
Marguerite m. Hazen Smith [Sch. 724, NB.]
Marguerite m. Jean Bapt. Blanchard, 1743 [Sch. 208, PQ., Acadian]
Marguerite m. Normand Desroches, 1964 [Sch. 711, NB.]
Marguerite m. Pierre Poirier, ca. 1754 [Sch. 213, 217 & 218, PQ., Acadian]
Marguerite Serephie, 1751 [see notes on Sch. 211, West Indies, La.]
Maria b. 1845 m. Alexie Girouard [Sch. 523, NB.]
Maria b.1909 m. Léandre Leger [Sch. 315, NB.]
Maria m. Fred Atkinson m. 1969 [Sch. 724, NB.]
Marianne b. 1766 m. Gregory Landry, [Sch. 162.6, La]
Marie [Sch. 162, P.E.I.]
Marie [Sch. 202, PQ. Acadian]
Marie 1906 m. Prudent Bréchoire [Sch. 400, France]
Marie [Sch. 527, NB.]
Marie [Sch. 700, NB.]
Marie Adeline b. 1838 d. 1838 [Sch. 218 PQ. Acadian]
Marie Alescia [Sch. 162, P.E.I.]
Marie Angélique b. 1841 d. 1927 m. Simon Landry [Sch. 0 Tracadie, Ant. Co., NS.]
Marie Angélique b. 1847 m. Rémi Decoste [Sch. 1 Tracadie, Ant. Co., NS.]
Marie Ann Barb b. 1850 d. 1869 m1. Filix Decoste, m2. Charles Genthner [Sch. 163, Isle Madame, NS.]
Marie Anne b. 1876 m. Placide Bastarache [Sch. 527, NB.]

Appendices

Marie b, 1732 m1. Charles Benoît, 1755 m2. Charles Landry, 1763 [Sch. 162.1, 162.6 La.; 163 & 164 Isle Madame; 300,500,600,& 700 NB.]
Marie b. 1698 m. Jean Trahan [Sch. 300 & 600, NB.]
Marie b. 1754 [Sch. 211, West Indies, La.]
Marie b. 12/11/1958 m. Joe Nugent [AMC]
Marie b. 1650 m. ca.1669 Jacques Blou [AMC]
Marie b. 1678 m. ca. 1700 Jacques Granger [AMC]
Marie b. 1695 m. Jean Mouton, 1711 [Sch. 204, PQ., Acadian]
Marie b. 1698 d. 1758 m. Jean Trahan ca. 1714 [Sch. 162.1 162.6, La., 163 & 164 Isle Madame, NS.; 300,500,600 & 700 NB.]
Marie b. 1751 d. 1811 m. Basile Gouthro 1770 [AMC]
Marie b. 1752 [Sch. 208, PQ., Acadian]
Marie b. 1774 d. 1774 [Sch. 162.6, La.]
Marie b. 1799 d. 1820 m1. B. LeBlanc 1820 m2. J. LeBlanc m3. M. Legault [Sch. 500, 542 NB.]
Marie b. 1800 d. 1867 m. Charles Philippe [Sch. 900, France]
Marie b. 1812 m. Nicolas Jacquet [Sch. 0,1,4,& 8 Tracadie, Ant. Co., NS.]
Marie b. 1820 d. 1902 m1. Louis-Laurent Fortier 1842, m2. Benjamin Viau [FCMC, PQ.]
Marie b. 1838 d. 1868 m. Moïse LeBlanc [Sch. 717, NB.]
Marie b. 1845 [Sch. 300, NB.]
Marie b. 1852 d. 1881 m. Thaddie Richard [Sch. 729, NB.]
Marie b. 1856 [Sch. 700, NB.]
Marie b. 1859 m. Antoine Collette [Sch. 527, NB.]
Marie b. 1860 [Sch. 600, NB.]
Marie b. 1872 [Sch. 514]
Marie b. 1874 m. Pacifique Richard [Sch. 315, NB.]
Marie b. 1874 [Sch. 33, Guys]
Marie b. 1900 m. Joe Babineau [Sch. 514, NB.]
Marie b. 1887 m. Daniel Nowlan, 1914 [Sch. 514, NB.]
Marie b. 1928 [Sch. 420, France]
Marie b. 1780 m. J. Bapt. Jeannot [Sch. 217 & 218, PQ., Acadian
Marie Anne b. 1767 m. _____Oliver [Sch. 202, PQ.]
Marie Ann b. 1744 m. Benjamin Dupont, 1778 [Sch. 213, PQ. Acadian]
Marie Anne b. 1707 d. 1720 [Sch. 204, PQ., Acadian]
Marie Anne b. 1752 d. 1758 [Sch. 162.6, La.]
Marie Anne b. 1763 d. 1843 m. Pierre Barsalou, 1784 [FCMC, PQ.]
Marie Anne b. 1904 d. 1980 m. Arthur Brisson 1932 [Sch. 2000, and Block N-5 FCMC]
Marie Anne b.1725 d. 1815 m1. Julien Tavernier 1749 m2. Gabriel Chèvrefils 1767 [FCMC]
Marie Anne m. Victor Dupras [Sch. 737, NB.]
Marie Blanche b. 1861 m. Nazaire Girouard à Bélonie 1885 [Sch. 705, NB.]
Marie Blanche b. 1872 d. 1875 [Sch. 706, NB.]
Marie Blanche b. 1872 m. George Jeté [Sch. 523, NB.]
Marie Blanche m. Olivier Gautreau [Sch. 737, NB.]
Marie Blanche b. 1821 m1. John Swiss, 1819, m2. Pierre Jaillet, 1844 [Sch. 300, NB.]
Marie Blanche m. Louis Perot, 1762 [Sch. 202,PQ.]
Marie-des-Anges b. 1805 d. 1880 m. Alexis Hyacinthe Rheault, 1823 [Sch. 218, PQ. Acadian]

Marie Elizabeth Petronille b. 1905 d. 1931 m. Alphonse Babin, 1927 [Sch. 163 & 164 Isle Madame, NS.]
Marie Caroline b. 1880 [Sch. 162, P.E.I.]
Marie Eva Mae b. 1914 d. 1989 [Sch. 163 & 164 Isle Madame, NS.]
Marie Eva b. 1883 [Sch. 164. Isle Madame. NS.]
Marie Eve b. 1896 d. 1903 [Sch. 514, NB.]
Marie Florence b. 1836 [Sch. 420, France]
Marie Florence b. 1865 d. 1877 [Sch. 5, Ant. Co., NS.]
Marie Françoise b. 1791 Hippolite Landry 1820 [Sch. 162.6, La]
Marie Françoise b. 1755 m. Charles François [Sch. 213, PQ. Acadian]
Marie Geneviève m. Jacques Catudal, 1766 [Sch. 3006, Belgium Branch, PQ.]
Marie Girouard/Green b. 1893 m. Amédée Richard [Sch. 309, NB.]
Marie Jean b. 1878 [Sch. 162, P.E.I.]
Marie Jeanne b. 1784 [Sch. 400, France]
Marie Joseph b. 1790 m. Alexis Turcotte, 1812 [Sch. 217, PQ. Acadian]
Marie Joseph [Sch. 164, Isle Madame. NS.]
Marie Joseph b. 1736 m1. M.A. Lorot 1753 m2. J. Bourgeois [Sch. 163 & 164 Isle Madame, NS.]
Marie Joseph b.1790 m. Alexis Turcotte [Sch. 218, PQ., Acadian]
Marie Josepha m1. John Cresswell Turner, 1961, m2. Peter D. Durlacuer, 1985 [FCMC, PQ.]
Marie Josèphe b. 1717 m. Germain Pitre, 1736 [Sch. 300,500,600 & 700, NB.; 162.1 & 162.6, La.; 163 & 164 Isle Madame NS.]
Marie Josèphe b. 1746 d. 1834 m1. Michael Duguay, m2. Charles Forest [Sch. 162.1, La.]
Marie Josèphe b. 1710 m1. Ch. Landry, m2. Zac Thibodeau, 1730 [Sch. 207, PQ., Acadian]
Marie Josèphe b. 1716 m1. L. Dugas 1734, m2. Thomas Jeanson [Sch. 204, PQ., Acadian]
Marie Josèphe b. 1734 d. 1814 m. Michel Gaudet, m2. J. Theriault, 1754 [Sch. 213, 217 218 PQ. Acadian]
Marie Josèphe b. 1734 m. Louis Bernier [Sch. 213, PQ. Acadian]
Marie Josèphe b. 1746 d. 1834, m1. M. Duguay, 1711, m2. Charles Forest, 1790 [Sch.300,500,60 & 700, N.B 162.1.]
Marie Josèphe b. 1750 [Sch. 204, PQ., Acadian]
Marie Josèphe b. 1761 m. Etienne Turgeon [Sch. 213, PQ., Acadian]
Marie Josèphe b. 1740 [AMC]
Marie Josèphe m. Jean Bapt. Thériot, 1745 [Sch. 202, PQ. Acadian]
Marie Joséphine b. 1872 [Sch. 600, NB.]
Marie Joséphine b. 1774 m. Grégoire Valentin, 1795 [Sch. 208, PQ., Acadian]
Marie Joséphite m. Alex Gerrard, 1835 [Sch. 208, PQ., Acadian]
Marie-Josephte b. 1776 d. 1776 [FCMC, PQ.]
Marie Louise b. 1817 d. 1817 [FCMC, PQ.]
Marie Louise 1892 d 1979 m. Hervé Daoust [Sch. 2000, and Block N-5 FCMC]
Marie Louise b. 1766 d. 1785 [Sch. 400 France]
Marie Louise [Sch. 217 PQ. Acadian]
Marie Luce b. 1802 d. 1832 m. Denis Cormier, 1823 [Sch. 700, NB.]
Marie Lydia b. 1904 [Sch. 600 NB.]
Marie m. Archange C. Payon [Sch. 208, PQ., Acadian]
Marie m. Zoël Girouard à Fidèle à David [Sch. 527, NB.]

Appendices

Marie m. Jean Baptiste Laverdure 1843 *[Sch. 163 & 164 Isle Madame N.S, & svh 13 PQ .]*
Marie m. Pierre Guillaume 1834 *[Sch. 213, PQ. Acadian]*
Marie m1. Joseph Lorenz, m2. Wallace Gracie, m3. Bill Rossbeck *[Sch. 706, NB.]*
Marie m. Edmond à Nazaire *[Sch. 737, NB.]*
Marie m. Louis Petit, 1867 *[Sch. 213, PQ. Acadian]*
Marie m. Terry Lockerbie *[Sch. 34, Ant. Co., NS.]*
Marie Madeleine b. 1714 d. 1765 m1. M. Martin 1739, m2. M. Aubois, 1754 *[Sch. 208, PQ., Acadian]*
Marie Madeleine b. 1762 m. ca. 1778 Cyprien Duon *[AMC]*
Marie Madeleine b. 1695 m. 1712 Pierre Richard *[AMC]*
Marie Madeleine b. 1711 *[AMC]*
Marie Madeleine b. 1713 d. 1757 m. Claude Gaudet *[Sch. 213, 217 & 218, PQ. Acadian]*
Marie Madeleine b. 1716 d. 1805 m. 1735 Charles LeBlanc *[AMC]*
Marie Madeleine b. 1736 m. Pierre of St-Martine *[Chart fc, France]*
Marie Madeleine b. 1780 m. Jean Baptiste Breaux 1800 *[Sch. 162.1, La.]*
Marie Madeleine b. 1654 (m. ca. 1668) Thomas Cormier *[AMC]*
Marie Madeleine b. 1830 *[Sch. 34, Ant. Co., NS.]*
Marie Marguerite b. 1770 d. 1774 *[Sch. 216, PQ., Acadian]*
Marie Marguerite b. 1791 d. 1848 m. ca. 1815 Paul M. Jacquet *[AMC]*
Marie Marguerite b. 1829 *[Sch. 420, France]*
Marie Modeste b. 1741 m. Paul Benet 1769, *[Sch.202 PQ. Acadian]*
Marie Modeste b. 1747 *[Sch. 207, PQ., Acadian]*
Marie Modeste b. 1767 m. Louis Duhamel, 1788 *[Sch. 208, PQ., Acadian]*
Marie Nathalie b. 1819 m. Gilbert Montpetit, 1835 *[FCMC, PQ.]*
Marie Opilie b. 1831 m. Antoine Meaux, 1851 *[Sch. 162.1, La.]*
Marie Paule m. Joseph Landry 1788 *[Sch. 162.6, La.]*
Marie Rose *[see notes on Sch. 211, West Indies, La.]*
Marie Rose b. 1761 d. 1835 m. François Sébastien Landry 1793 *[Sch. 162.6, La.]*
Marie Rose b. 1797 d. 1885 m. Abraham Chase, 1820 *[Sch. 700, NB.]*
Marie Rose b. 1893 m. Joseph Eugène Rousville *[Sch. 717, NB.]*
Marie Sophie b. 1799 d. 1865 m. 1816 Moyse Jacquet *[AMC]*
Marie Ursule b. 1804 d. 1819 *[Sch. 700, NB.]*
MarieVictoire b. 1808 d. 1829 m. Joseph LeBlanc *[Sch. 300, NB.]*
Marie Zita b. 1926 d. 1926 *[Sch. 523, NB.]*
Marie* b. 1855 *[Sch. 162.6, La.]*
Marie Louise Girouard *[Sch. 217, PQ., Acadian]*
Marin b. 1794 d. 1894 m. Suzanne Doucette, 1820 *[Sch. 700,717,724,737,729 NB.]*
Marin b. 1868 m. Eleanor Cormier *[Sch. 724, NB.]*
Marine Hélène b. 1843 m. Hubert Sampson, 1859 *[Sch. 163, Isle Madame, NS.]*
Marion m. Frank Byers *[Sch. 5, Ant. Co]*
Marion b. 1923 d. 1988 m. Corey Hartling *[Sch. 162, P.E.I.]*
Marjorie b. 1934 *[Sch. 5, Ant. Co., NS.]*
Marjorie m. Hughie MacLellan 1955 *[Sch. 32, Guys. Co., NS.]*
Marjorie m. Robert Cunningham *[Sch. #1 Tracadie, Ant. Co., NS.]*
Mark *[Sch. 33, Guys. Co., NS.]*

Mark b. 1970 *[Sch. 208, PQ., Acadian]*
Mark m. Dorothy Dorf 1970, *[FCMC, PQ.]*
Marshal m. Bertha Slaunwhite *[Sch. 72, Guys. Co., NS.]*
Martha b. 1877 d. 1877 *[Sch. 5, Ant. Co., NS.]*
Martha b. 1879 m_____Morrison *[Sch. 5, Ant. Co., NS.]*
Martha Elizabeth m. Louis Eacobacci *[Sch. 33, Guys. Co., NS.]*
Martha m1. Bernard Joseph Gallant, m2. Ray Chiappa *[Sch. 717, NB.]*
Martina b. 1915 m. Joseph Comeau 1949 *[AMC]*
Martine b. 1956 d. 1958 *[Sch. 900, France]*
Mary (Bessie) Elizabeth b. 1885 d. 1963 m. John MacDonell *[Sch. 8, Ant. Co., NS.]*
Mary Aldora (Mini) b. 1890 d. 1969 m. Daniel Hugh Stewart, 1919 *[Sch. 67, Guys. Co., NS.]*
Mary Anne b. 1881 d. 1956 m. John W. Baynard *[Sch. 8, Ant. Co., NS.]*
Mary Alice b. 1910 m. Alice Sampson *[Sch. 31 Guys. Co., NS.]*
Mary b. 1862 m. Michael Avery *[Sch. 48, Guys. Co., NS.]*
Mary b. 1871 m. Martin Pellerin *[Sch. 76, Guys. Co., NS.]*
Mary b. 1879 *[Sch. 36, Guys. Co., NS.]*
Mary b. 1881 m. John Grant *[Sch. 33, Guys. Co., NS.]*
Mary b. 1901 m1. James Smith m2. John Pearce *[Sch. 0 Tracadie, Ant. Co., NS.]*
Mary Catherine (Kay) *[Sch. 35, Guys. Co., NS.]*
Mary Elizabeth b. 1904 d. 1988 m. Ignatius Farrell *[Sch. 162, P.E.I.]*
Mary Elizabeth m. Arthur Babin *[Sch. 95, Guys. Co., NS.]*
Mary Elizabeth b. 1880 m. William Brown *[Sch. 35, Guys. Co., NS.]*
Mary Ellen Stewart m. Chesely Herbert Harris, 1951 *[Sch. 67, Guys. Co., NS.]*
Mary Evangeline b. 1877 d. 1880 *[Sch. 8, Ant. Co., NS.]*
Mary Hélène m. Arthur Petitpas, 1920 *[Sch. 48, Guys. Co., NS.]*
Mary Jane (Jenny) m. William J. Murphy, 1905 *[Sch. 48, Guys. Co., NS.]*
Mary Jane Geneviève b. 1922 d. 1972 m. Harry Helin *[Sch. 163 & 164 Isle Madame, NS.]*
Mary Josephine m. Terry McNamara *[Sch. 5, Ant. Co., NS.]*
Mary L. b. 1884 m. Melville Bell Weekes *[Sch. 4, Ant. Co., NS.]*
Mary Louise b. 1869 m. Lemoine *[Sch. 208, PQ., Acadian]*
Mary m. George Allard *[Sch. 48, Guys. Co., NS.]*
Mary m. Alec Sampson *[Sch. 31, Guys. Co. NS.]*
Mary m. Nicolas Pellerin, 1876 *[Sch. 35 & 36, Guys. Co., NS.]*
Mary m. Pat Lee *[Sch. 717, NB.]*
Mary (Mini) m. Walter Hart *[Sch. 163, Isle Madame, NS.]*
Mary Pélagie (Flossie) b. 1887 *[Sch. 36, Guys. Co., NS.]*
Mary Victoria b. 1879 d. 1971 m. Wm. Tramble, 1898 *[Sch. 34, Ant. Co., NS.]*
Marion m. Frank Byers *[Sch. 5, Ant. Co., NS.]*
Mathieu Jeremy *[Sch. 900, France]*
Mathilda b. 1868 d. 1956 m. Edouard Girouard 1888 *[Sch. 737, NB.]*
Mathilde b. 1862 *[Sch. 706, NB.]*
Mathurin *[Sch. 700, NB.]*
Mathurin b. 1670 *[Sch. 400, France]*
Mathurin b. 1699 m. Louise Pétrault, 1730 *[Sch. 400, France]*
Maureen m. Leo Doiron *[Sch. 1 Tracadie, Ant. Co., NS.]*

Appendices

Maurice b. 1910 m. Gisèle Petrault [Sch. 420, France]
Maurice b. 1910 [Sch. 400, France]
Maurice m. Theresa Rivière [Sch. 400, France]
Maxime [Sch. 900, France]
Maxime b. 1829 d. 1851 [Sch. 309, NB.]
Maxime b. 1860 [Sch. 729, NB.]
Maxime b. 1863 d. 1870 [Sch. 527, NB.]
Maxime b. 1869 d. 1960 m1. Céleste LeBlanc, m2. Adeleine Cormier [Sch. 514, NB.]
Maxime Onésime b. 1885 d. 1975 m. Virginie Robichaud 1906 [Sch. 700, NB.]
Maximilien* b. 1811 m. Carmesile Broussard 1833 [Sch. 162.1, La.]
Maximin b. 1808 d. 1873 m. Helen MacDonald [Sch. 33, Guys. Co., NS. and AMC]
Mebain b. 1807 [Sch. 300, NB.]
Medord m. Florence Aucoin [Sch. 163, Isle Madame, NS.]
Mélanie b. 1878 [Sch. 0 Tracadie, Ant. Co., NS.]
Melas b. 1874 d. 1967 m. Amanda Boudreau [Sch. 729, NB.]
Mélême [Sch. 737, NB.]
Melena b. 1880 m. Antoine Cormier [Sch. 737, NB.]
Mélina m. Nazaire Boyer, 1875 [Sch. 2000, and Block N-5 FCMC]
Mélita m. Léo Pineau, 1969 [Sch. 711, NB.]
Metilda [Sch. 724, NB.]
Melvina b. 1809 [Sch.162.6, La.]
Melvine b. 1827 d. 1829 [Sch. 162.6, La]
Michael [Sch. 31,Guys. Co. NS.]
Michael [Sch. 717, NB.]
Michael Paul Vincent m1. Patricia MacDonald m2. Anna Marie Macbain [Sch. 48, Guys. Co., NS.]
Michel A. b. 1843 d. 1918 m1. Julie Manette, m2. Brigitte Haley [AMC & Sch. 72 & 76, Guys. Co., NS.]
Michel b. 1723 d. 1797 m. Marguerite Haché Gallant, 1744 [Sch. 213, 217 & 218, PQ., Acadian]
Michel b. 1791 d. 1871 m1. Marie. Boudrot 1814 m2. Caroline LeBlanc [Sch. 163 & 164 Isle Madame, NS.]
Michel b. 1858 d. 1931 m. Marie Cormier, 1889 [Sch. 600, NB.]
Michel b. 1859 d. 1940 m. Virginie Cormier, 1880 [Sch. 737, NB.]
Michel b. 1933 d. 1933 [Sch. 600, NB.]
Michel b. 1851 m. Annie Benoît [Sch. 1 Tracadie, Ant. Co., NS.]
Michel m. Annise Bourque [Sch. 600, NB.]
Michel* b. 1700 m1. Anne Marie Nuriat 1737 m2. Marie Thibodeau [Sch. 202, PQ. Acadian]
Michel, b. 1765 d. 1788, [FCMC, PQ.]
Michel b. 1826 d. 1916 m1. V. Babin m2. S. Poirier m3. A. Brian [Sch. 163, Isle Madame , NS.]
Micheline m. Camille Drysdale, 1977 [Sch. 711, NB.]
Mildrid m. William Bowles [Sch. 5 Ant. Co]
Mile [Sch. 729, NB.]
Mini b. 1856 not married [Sch. 0 Tracadie, Ant. Co., NS.]
Mirbain [Sch. 315, NB.]
Modest b. 1754 [see notes on Sch. 211, West Indies, La.]

Moïse b. 1858 d. 1878 *[Sch. 724, NB.]*
Moise b. 1878 m. Juliette Rouvreau *[Sch. 400, France]*
Moïse m. Sophie Comeau, 1832 *[Sch. 207, PQ., Acadian]*
Monique Marie b. 1771 m. Jean-Marie Poirier, 1793 *[Sch. 163& 164 Isle Madame, NS.]*
Monique m. Pierre Poingnant *[Sch. 400, France]*
Nadege m. Serge Aubugeau *[Sch. 900, France]*
Nancy b. 1849 d. 1867 *[Sch. 31, 32 Guys. Co. NS.]*
Nancy b. 1888 *[Sch. 48, Guys. Co., NS.]*
Nancy Girroir, Sister Superior, Moncton *[Sch. 163, Isle Madame, NS.]*
Nancy *[Sch. 164. Isle Madame. NS.]*
Napoléon b. 1897 *[Sch. 737, NB.]*
Nathalie b. 1743 m. Amable Blanchard, 1764 *[AMC]*
Nathalie b. 1744 m. Jean Baptiste Byjeu *[Sch. 204, PQ., Acadian]*
Nathalie b. 1746 *[Sch. 211, West Indies, La.]*
Nathalie b. 1866 m. Michel Bastarache 1887 *[Sch. 600, NB.]*
Nazaire b. 1858 m. Blanche Girouard à Louis, 1885 *[Sch. 705 & 729, NB.]*
Neil b. 1913 m. Irène Allain *[Sch. 500, NB.]*
Neil d. infant *[Sch. 729, NB.]*
Neil Joseph *[Sch. 5, Ant. Co., NS.]*
Nelda Ida Rose m. Jerome Judice *[Sch. 162.1 La]*
Nellie b. 1908 m. Fred LeBlanc, 1946 *[Sch. 705, NB.]*
Nellie m. Winnie Landry (n.c.) *[Sch. 162.1, La.]*
Nicholas dit Réal Girouard m. Anne Galarneau, 1726 *[Sch.3006, Belgium Branch, Québec]*
Noé b. 1872 d. 1953 m. Alvina Goguen *[Sch. 717, NB.]*
Norbert b. 1843 *[Sch. 162.1, La.]*
Norman b. 1952 d. 1968 m. Rosala Poirier *[Sch. 600, NB.]*
Normand *[Sch. 706, NB.]*
Octave b. 1895 d. 1968 m. Nathalie Robichaud *[Sch. 700, NB.]*
Olive b. 1824 m. Cyprien Cormier *[Sch. 300, NB.]*
Olive b. 1825 *[Sch. 542, NB.]*
Olive b. 1832 d. 1916 m. Simon LeBlanc *[Sch. 523, NB.]*
Olivier *[Sch. 542, NB.]*
Olivier b. 1826 m. Geneviève Robichaud, 1861 *[Sch. 717, NB.]*
Olivier b. 1836 d. 1917 m. Henriette Richard 1866 *[Sch. 500, NB.]*
Olivier b. 1840 m. Euphémie Richard *[Sch. 315, NB.]*
Olivier b. 1843 m. Elizabeth Robichaud *[Sch. 309, NB.]*
Olivier b. 1845 d. 1937 m. Ozite Cormier *[Sch. 700, 711 NB.]*
Oscar m. Nora Brown, no children *[Sch. 706, NB.]*
Osite (Osithe) b. 1815 d. 1816 *[Sch. 500, & 542 NB.]*
Ovide Carmilita b. 1810 d. 1854 m. Constant Simoneaux *[Sch. 162.6, La.]*
Ovide m. Simone Beaubien *[Sch. 3001, Rodier Branch, Québec]*
Ovila b. 1891 *[Sch. 2000, and Block N-5 FCMC]*
Ovila m1. Aurore Fontaine, 1897, m2. Alphonse Pépin *[Sch. 213, PQ. Acadian]*
Pacifique b. 1872 d. 1955 m1. Jeanne Légèr, m2. Pulchérie Cormier *[Sch. 737, NB.]*
Paraxède b. 1748 *[Sch. 163 & 164 Isle Madame, NS.]*

Appendices

Patrice b. 1891 d. 1892 *[Sch. 523, NB.]*

Patricia *[Sch. 48 Guys Co.,NS.]*

Patricia Cunningham *[Sch. 1 Tracadie, Ant. Co., NS.]*

Patricia Danial m. Gordon Waring *[Sch. 33, Guys. Co., NS.]*

Patrick b. 1856 *[Sch. 1 Tracadie, Ant. Co., NS.]*

Patrick Henry m. Margaret Mahoney, 1945 *[Sch. 48, Guys. Co., NS.]*

Paul b. 1752 d. 1821 m. Angélique Boucher *[Sch. 163,164 Isle Madame, NS.; 162 P.E.I.]*

Paul b. 1772 d. 1842 m. Marguerite Bégin *[Sch. 162, PEI; 163 & 164 Isle Madame]*

Paul b. 1827 d. 1827 (4 months) *[Sch. 309, NB.]*

Paul d. 1848 m. Marine Lavache 1825 *[Sch. 163, Isle Madame, NS.]*

Paul F. b. 1892 *[Sch. 36, Guys. Co., NS.]*

Paul Gervais b. 1744 d. 1838 m. Madeleine Thériault *[Sch. 300, 500,600, N.B ;162.1 La.]*

Paul Girouard/Green *[Sch. 309, NB.]*

Paul Joseph b. 1917 m. Marg. Ellen Lennon *[Sch. 48, Guys. Co., NS.]*

Paul m. Marine Lavache *[Sch. 163 & 164. Isle Madame. NS.]*

Paul m. May McNeil *[Sch. 1 Tracadie, Ant. Co., NS.]*

Paul-Philibert m. Obeline Hebert, 1862 *[Sch.207, PQ.]*

Paul Polycarpe b. 1851 m1. Marie Boutin m2 Marie Frilate *[Sch. 163 Isle Madame, NS.]*

Pélagie Flossie m. Joseph Richard *[Sch. 36, Guys. Co., NS.]*

Pélagie b. 1787 d. 1870 m. Hubert Cormier, 1804 *[Sch. 300,500,600 & 700 NB.]*

Percy m. Mary Gwendolyn Solomon, 1903 *[FCMC, PQ.]*

Perpétue m. Odilon Dacier *[Sch. 202, PQ. Acadian]*

Peter *[Sch. 164, Isle Madame, NS.]*

Peter b. 1881 *[Sch. 700, NB.]*

Peter Howard *[Sch. 48, Guys. Co., NS.]*

Petre à Mon b. ca. 1851 d. 1925 m1. Avery 1872 m2. G. Pettipas 1901 *[Sch. 48, Guys. Co., NS.]*

Philias b. 1881 d. 1961 m1. Macrine Cormie, m2. Céleste Richard *[Sch. 514, NB.]*

Philias b. 1895 d. 1895 *[Sch. 705, NB.]*

Philippe b. 1919 m. Marguerite Comeau *[Sch. 500, NB.]*

Philippe b. 1836 m. Geneviève Allain, 1855 *[Sch. 705, 706 NB.]*

Philomène b. 1850 m. François Goguen *[Sch. 700, NB.]*

Philomène Minnie b. 1878 d. 1951 m. Calixte Collette *[Sch. 523, NB.]*

Pierre Augustin b. 1784 m. Archange Dufault *[Sch. 208, PQ., Acadian]*

Pierre b. 1701 d. 1719 *[Sch. 162.1,162.6 La.; 163 & 164 Isle Madame, NS.; 300,500,600,& 700 NB.]*

Pierre b. 1794 *[Sch. 217, PQ.Acadian]*

Pierre b. 1751 *[Sch. 204, PQ., Acadian]*

Pierre b. 1754 d. 1757 *[Sch. 217, PQ., Acadian]*

Pierre b. 1768 *[Sch. 216, PQ., Acadian]*

Pierre b. 1817 m1. Elizabeth Webb m2. Marie Pettipas *[Sch. #0, 1, 4, & 8 Tracadie, Ant. Co., NS.]*

Pierre (dentist) m. Cathy Gaudet *[Sch. 300, NB.]*

Pierre *[Sch. 207, PQ., Acadian]*

Pierre Alphonse b. 1899 *[Sch. 163, Isle Madame, NS.]*

Pierre Auguste b. 1841 *[Sch. 420, France]*

Pierre b. 1644 Seigneur de Villiers, Master Sculptor, m. Marie de la Vergne *[Sch. 800, France]*

Pierre b. 1672 m1. Marie Comeau ca. 1699 m2. Marie Doiron 1709 [AMC Sch. 162.1,162.6 La.; 163 & 164 Isle Madame, NS.; 300,500,600,& 700 NB.]

Pierre b. 1693 d. 1738 m1. Marie Burel m2. Françoise Périer [Chart fc, France]

Pierre b. 1708 [Sch. 700, NB.]

Pierre b. 1718 d. 1783 m. Jeanne Martin, 1743 [Sch. 204, PQ., Acadian]

Pierre b. 1721 d. 1763 m1. 1743 Marie Joseph Forest m2. 1760 M. Doucet [AMC].

Pierre b. 1726 m. Théotiste Dupuis, 1751 [Sch. 208, PQ., Acadian]

Pierre b. 1727 m. Cécile Detcheverry dit Jonis, 1751 [Sch. 163 & 164, Isle Madame. NS.]

Pierre b. 1741 m1. Louise Fournier, m2. Ann Gamaché [Sch. 213, PQ. Acadian]

Pierre b. 1754 d. 1757 [Sch. 217 & 218, PQ., Acadian]

Pierre b. 1768 m. Anne Jenet 1802 [Sch. 216, PQ., Acadian]

Pierre b. 1769 m. Charlotte Duhamel [Sch. 207, PQ., Acadian]

Pierre b. 1771 m. Archange Senet 1802 L'Assomption [Sch. 216, PQ., Acadian]

Pierre b. 1776 m. Madeleine Thibodeaux 1803 [Sch. 162.1, La.]

Pierre b. 1778 [Sch. 162.6, La.]

Pierre b. 1782 [Sch. 400, France]

Pierre b. 1794 [Sch.218, PQ. Acadian]

Pierre b. 1797 d. 1825 m. Marie Allain, 1822 [Sch. 500 & 542 NB.]

Pierre b. 1817 m1. Eliz. Webb, m2. Marie Pettipas [Sch. 0,1,4,8] Tracadie, Ant. Co., NS.]

Pierre b. 1830 m. Marie White 1854 [Sch.500, NB.]

Pierre b. 1834 d. 1840 [Sch. 523, NB.]

Pierre b. 1856 m. Marie Begeant [Sch. 1 Tracadie, Ant. Co., NS.]

Pierre b. 1865 d. 1944 m1. Henriette Jaillet, m2. Marie Wedge [Sch. 527, NB.]

Pierre b. 1873 d. 1940 m. Marguerite Arsenault [Sch. 500, NB.]

Pierre b. 1875 m1. Henriette LeBlanc, m2. Macrine Breau [Sch. 514, NB.]

Pierre b. 1907 d. 1978 m. Aurore Tanguay, 1932 [Sch. 717, NB.]

Pierre b. 1943 m1. Marylyn Hynes (no ch.), m2. Jane K. Taransky McKenzie [Sch. 717, NB.]

Pierre Louis b. 1858 [Sch. 163, La.]

Pierre m. Bibienne Poirier [Sch. 163& 164. Isle Madame. NS.]

Pierre m. Francoise Catudal, 1762 [Sch.3006, Belgium Branch, Québec]

Pierre m. Louise Girard, 1835 [Sch. 208, PQ., Acadian]

Pierre m. Marie Burel, 1720 m2. Francoise Périer [FCMC, PQ.]

Pierre m. Marie Rainaud [Sch. 3006, Belgium Branch, Québec]

Pierre m. Scholastique Leblanc [Sch. 208, PQ., Acadian]

Pierre m. Marguerite Fontaine 1847 [Sch. 213 PQ. Acadien]

Pierre m1. Marie Wade m2. Marie Caissie [Sch. 309, NB.]

Pierre Napoléon b. 1883 [Sch. 208, PQ., Acadian]

Pierre Paul b. 1775 d. 1819 m. Marie-Rose Cormier ca. 1796 [Sch. 300, 500, 600,& 700 NB.; 162.1 La; 514, 523, 527, 542]

Pierre Raymond b. 1808 d. 1861 m. Adéline Melanson, 1830 [Sch. 162.1, La.]

Pierre Raymond b. 1909 d. 1992 [Sch. 163 &164 Isle Madame]

Pierre Réalh m. Marguerite Dupuis, Waremme, Liège, [Sch.3006, Belgium Branch, Québec]

Pierre* b. 1719 d. 1763 m. Marguerite Gaudet, 1740 [Sch. 213, 217 & 218, PQ., Acadian]

Pierre* m. Natalie Decelles Duclos, 1856 [Sch. 213, PQ. Acadian]

Pius Girouard/Green b. 1887 d.1968 m. Edna Cormier, 1913 [Sch. 309, NB.]

Appendices

Placide b. 1870 d. 1944 m. Elizabeth Boucher, 1882 *[Sch. 706, NB.]*
Polycarpe b. 1814 d. 1883 m. Sophie Deslauriers *[Sch. 163, Isle Madame, NS.]*
Priscille b. 1857 m. Ferdinand Belliveau *[Sch. 737, NB.]*
Prosper Honoré Giroir b. 1744 d. ca. 1791 m. Marie Dugas 1764 *[Sch. 162.6, La.]*
Prospère b. 1906 d. 1973 m1. Elodie Cormier, m2. Irène LeBlanc *[Sch. 729, NB.]*
Rachael b. 1940 m. Roger Bisson *[Sch. 717, NB.]*
Rachel *[Sch. 514, NB.]*
Rachel b. 1827 m. Joseph Laberge, 1845 *[FCMC, PQ.]*
Radegonde *[Sch. 400, France]*
Raoul b. 1865 m. Maud Patterson *[Sch. 217, PQ. Acadian]*
Raphael m. Pearl Anne Johnson *[Sch. 5, Ant. Co., NS.]*
Raymond *[Sch. 400, France]*
Raymond *[Sch. 724, NB.]*
Raymond 1872 d. 1953 m. Azélie Richard *[Sch. 500, NB.]*
Raymond *[Sch. 300, NB.]*
Raymond b. 1909 d. 1992 *[Sch. 163 & 164 La]*
Raymond b.1931 d. 1980 m. Juliette Losier *[Sch. 700, NB.]*
Raymond b. 1915 m. Estelle Godinl, 1939 *[Sch. 711, NB.]*
Raymond Jeffrey m. Patricia D. Loughead *[Sch. 48, Guys. Co., NS.]*
Raymond Joseph m. Rosemae Domingue *[Sch. 162.1, La.]*
Raymond m. Nancy Poirier *[Sch. 729, NB.]*
Raymond P. *[Sch. 527, NB.]*
Rebecca m. Paul LaFrance *[Sch. 34, Ant. Co., NS.]*
Reginald b. 28/03/43 m1. Elvira Kirk m2. Barbara Freer *[AMC]*
Regina b. 1884 m. Alyre Cormier *[Sch. 523, NB.]*
Regina b. 1893 *[Sch. 514, NB.]*
Regina Girouard/Green b. 1885 m. Isaie Léger *[Sch. 309, NB.]*
Remi b. 1830 d. 1866 m. Marie Pettipas, 1854 *[Sch. 0,1, 4, & 8, Tracadie, Ant. Co., NS.]*
René Alexandre m. Josephe Morin b. 1840, of Tallud *[Sch. 400, France]*
René Clément b. 1834 *[Sch. 420, France]*
René m. Yvette LeBlanc *[Sch. 729, NB.]*
René de la Bruère b. 1882 d. 1941 m. Katherine Grant *[Sch. 217, PQ. Acadian]*
René Pierre Bouchet b. 1911 m. Edith MacNeil *[Sch. 217, PQ., Acadian]*
Rev. Emedée Thomas Girroir *[Sch. 163 & 164 Isle Madame, NS.]*
Rhéal m. Nancy Cormier *[Sch. 600, NB.]*
Richard b. 1899 d.1918, *[Sch. 600, NB.]*
Richard Désiré b. 1905 d. 1989 m. Lady Blanche Berisford *[FCMC, PQ.]*
Rita m. John Louis *[Sch. 36, Guys. Co., NS.]*
Rita m. Leslie Kay, 1946 *[Sch. 700, NB.]*
Rita Milina m. Lawrence Landry *[Sch. 5, Ant. Co., NS.]*
Robert *[Sch. 208, PQ., Acadian]*
Robert (Albert) b. 1892 m. Laura Mcaffrey, 1917 *[Sch. 705, NB.]*
Robert (Bo) Louis b. 1941 d. 1982 m. Nancy Howe *[Sch. 208, PQ., Acadian]*
Robert *[Sch. 527, NB.]*
Robert b. 1920 d. 1981 *[Sch. 420, France]*

Robert Burns Gerrior m1. Cathy O'Laney m2. Tracy Sewell *[Sch. 162, P.E.I.]*
Robert David m. Merla Way *[Sch. 48, Guys. Co., NS.]*
Robert Edward *[Sch. 35, Guys. Co., NS.]*
Robert Girouard *[Sch.3006, Belgium Branch, Québec]*
Ronald *[Sch. 527, NB.]*
Ronald m. Marie Oda, 1957 *[Sch. 711, NB.]*
Rosalie b. 1742 d. 1757 *[Sch. 213, PQ. Acadian]*
Rosalie b. 1775 d. 1823 m. François Allard, 1796 *[FCMC, PQ.]*
Rosalie* b. 1751 m. Pierre Chesney *[Sch. 217 & 218 PQ., Acadian]*
Rosalie Isabel b. 1797 d.1862 m. Simeon Landry, 1821 *[Sch. 162.6, La]*
Rosalie m. Charles Larivière, 1846 *[Sch. 208, PQ., Acadian]*
Rosalie m. Joseph Boudrot *[Sch. 163 & 164 Isle Madame, NS.]*
Rose Alma m. Vital Carrière, 1919 *[Sch.3001, Rodier Branch, Québec]*
Rose Angélica b. 1873 d. 1924, not married *[Sch. 8, Ant. Co]*
Rose b. 1813 d. 1905 m. Antoine Quevillon 1829 *[FCMC, PQ.]*
Rose De Lima b. 1848 m. Philias Paquin, 1867 *[Sch. 2000, and Block N-5, FCMC]*
Rose Mai m. Richard Roy *[Sch. 315, NB.]*
Rose Mai m. James Carroll 1956 *[Sch. 523, NB.]*
Rose Marie m. Pierre Larivière *[Sch. 600, NB.]*
Rosée m. Willi Léger *[Sch. 737, NB.]*
Rose May m. Freddie Robichaud *[Sch. 514, NB.]*
Robert Northfield *[Sch. 208, PQ. Acadian]*
Roy m. Joan MacNamara *[Sch. 31,Guys. Co. NS.]*
Russel Matthew m. Cindy Brooks *[Sch. 162, P.E.I.]*
Russell m. Barbara Gerrior 1953 *[Sch. 31,Guys. Co. NS.]*
Samuel b. 1864 d. 1864 *[FCMC, PQ.]*
Samuel m. *[Sch. 717, NB.]*
Samuel m1. Barbara Bush. m2. Paula Jo Campbell *[Sch. 717, NB.]*
Sandra *[Sch.3001, Rodier Branch, Québec]*
Sandrine Laetitia *[Sch. 900, France]*
Sarah b. 1862 m. Simon Bastarache *[Sch. 527, NB.]*
Sara b. 1877 m. Pierre Cormier *[Sch. 737, NB.]*
Sara b. 1896 m. Jean Baptiste Cormier, 1919 *[Sch. 705, NB.]*
Sara m. Olivier Allain *[Sch. 729, NB.]*
Sarah b. 1876 (21 months) *[Sch. 705, NB.]*
Sarah *[Sch. 420, France]*
Sarah (Dolly) b. 1913 d. 1977 m. Ambrose Hines *[Sch. 162, P.E.I]*
Scholastique m. Charles Légere, 1809 *[Sch. 300,500,600 & 700, NB.]*
Scholastique b. 1771 d. 1828 m. Alexis Danis, 1791 *[FCMC, PQ.]*
Scholastique m1. Laurent Cormier, m2. Anselme Robichaud *[Sch. 523, NB.]*
Scholastique* b. 1783 m. Jean Bernard 1803 *[Sch. 162.1, La.]*
Scholastique b. 1810 d. 1850 m. Simon Allain ca. 1830 *[Sch. 500 & 514, NB.]*
Scholastique b. 1832 m1. Laurent Cormier m2. Anselme Robichaud *[Sch. 523, NB.]*
Senator Edward Lavin 1871 d. 1932 m1. Loretta Maude Corbin m2. Mary Frances Howard *[Sch. 8, Ant. Co., NS.]*

Severine Marie b. 1839 [Sch. 162.6, La]
Servine Cedric [Sch. 900, France]
Shirley m. Salvadore Branco [Sch. 95, Guys. Co., NS.]
Siffoi b. 1854 d. 1933 m. Marie Thibodeau [Sch. 315, NB.]
Siffoi b.1817 [Sch. 300, NB.]
Siméon b. 1805 d. 1805 [FCMC, PQ.]
Simon à Mon b. 1846 m. Millie Avery [Sch. 48, Guys. Co., NS.]
Simon b. 1804 [Sch. 162.1, La.]
Simon b. 1826 d. 1910 m. Frosine Delorier 1848 [Sch. 0,1, 4, 8, Tracadie, Ant. Co., NS.]
Simon b. 1848 m. Belérane Richard [Sch. 315, NB.]
Simon b. 1872 d. 1955 m. Adèle Bastarache [Sch. 527, NB.]
Simon b. 1874 m. Mary Coleman, [Sch. 72 &76, Guys. Co., NS.]
Simon b. 1875 [Sch. 162, P.E.I.]
Simon b. 1884 d. 1945 m1. Angel Pellerin m2. Susan Jane Pellerin, m3. Madeleine Surette [AMC]
Simon m. b. 1792 d. 1851 Angélique LeBlanc [Sch. 163, 164 Isle Madame, NS.]
Simone m. Roger Cormier [Sch. 315, NB.]
Sister Lola (C.N.D.) [Sch. 34, Ant. Co., NS.]
Sophia b. 1880 census of 1891 [AMC]
Sophia b. 1908 d. 1961 m. Fred LaMont [Sch. 162, P.E.I.]
Sophie b. 1808 d. 1856 m. François Dugas dit La Brèche 1832 [FCMC, PQ.]
Sophie d. 1966 m. Alban LeBlanc [Sch. 514, NB.]
Sophie b. 1923 d. 1927 [Sch.163 & 164 Isle Madame, NS.]
Sophia Camilla b. 1854 [Sch. 162.6, La]
Sophie Girouard/Green [Sch. 309, NB.]
Sophie Joséphine b. 1860 m. Charles LeBlanc [Sch. 163, Isle Madame, NS.]
Sophie m. John Samson [Sch. 163, 164 Isle Madame, NS.]
Susan m. Thomas Cleary [Sch. 32,Guys. Co., NS.]
Stacie [Sch. 724, NB.]
Stanislas m. Régina Valède La Boissière [Sch.3001, Rodier Branch, Québec]
Stephen William m. Karla Sawler [AMC]
Susan m.Thomas Cleary, Taunton, Mass [Sch. 32, Guys Co.]
Steven m. Linda Soars [Sch. 95, Guys. Co., NS.]
Suzanne m. Steven Williams [AMC]
Suzanne b. 1822 [Sch. 542, NB.]
Suzanne b. 1856 m. __Bell [Sch. 163, Isle Madame, NS.]
Suzanne b. 1861 [Sch. 527, NB.]
Suzanne b. 1864 m. Adolphe Daigle [Sch. 724, NB.]
Suzanne b. 1866 d. 1874 [Sch. 729, NB.]
Suzanne m. Constance Pettipas [Sch. 163, Isle Madame, NS.]
Suzanne m. Simon LeBlanc [Sch. 163 & 164 Isle Madame, NS.]
Sydney b. 1899 d. 1973 m. Alma Guilbeaux [Sch. 162.1, La.]
Sydney Patrick b. 1937 m. Janell Duhon [Sch. 162.1, La.]
Sylvain b. 1738 [Sch. 163 & 164 Isle Madame, NS.]
Sylvain b. 1840 d. 1885 m1. Blanche Allain, 1861 m2. Bibianne Caissie [Sch. 705, NB.]
Sylvestre (Calixte) b. 1870 d. 1958 m. Suzanne Robichaud [Sch. 315, NB.]

Sylvie m. Eldon Seaward [Sch. 600, NB.]
Sylvio b. 1920 d. 1979 m. Patricia Krohe, 1942 [Sch. 2000, and Block N-5 FCMC]
Télesphore b. 1854 d. 1932 m. Marie Rose Cormier [Sch. 729, NB.]
Télex b. 1897 d. 1957, not married [Sch. 514, NB.]
Telena m. Frank Frost [Sch. 48, Guys. Co., NS.]
Tena [Sch. 0 Tracadie, Ant. Co., NS.]
Thaddé [Sch. 737, NB.]
Thaddie b. 1865 d. 1931 m. Olive Cormier [Sch. 737, NB.]
Thelisa Elisa b. 1859, d. 1897m. Etienne Ulyssa Pennison [Sch. 162.6, La]
Théophile b. 1826 d. 1897 m. Alexina Pacaud, 1861 [Sch. 217, PQ., Acadian]
Théophile b. 1858 d.1894 m. Marie Bastarache [Sch. 706, NB.]
Théotiste Romaine b. 1765 m1. J.B. Blanchette, 1792, m2. L. Dusseau [Sch. 213, PQ. Acadian]
Theresa [Sch. 72, Guys. Co., NS.]
Thérèsa b. 1873 m. Charles Pellerine, 1893 [Sch. 48, Guys. Co., NS.]
Theresa b. 1903 d. 1990 m. Charles Martin [Sch. 208, PQ., Acadian]
Theresa b. 1929 d. 1963 m. M.A. Shirk [Sch. 162, P.E.I.]
Theresa b. 24/02/1955 m. Don Adams [AMC]
Theresa m. Butch Hughes [Sch. 48, Guys. Co., NS.]
Thérèse m. J. Chapdelaine, 1806 [Sch. 208, PQ., Acadian]
Thomas [Sch. 542, NB.]
Thomas b. 1879 d. 1933, not married [Sch. 523, NB.]
Thomas George Henry b. 1884 m. Charlotte Margaret Kinny 1907 [Sch. 34, Ant. Co]
Thomas Girroir (Rev.) [Sch. 164. Isle Madame, NS.]
Thomas [Sch. 163, Isle Madame, NS.]
Thomas m. Elaine Reid [Sch. 34, Ant. Co., NS.]
Thomas Patrick b. 1889 d. 1890 [Sch. 8, Ant. Co]
Tilmon b. 1888 d. 1889 [Sch. 705, NB.]
Tilmon b. 1900 d. 1967 m. Corinne Nowlan, 1926 [Sch. 705, NB.]
Timothée m. Adéline Brodeur, 1868 [Sch. 213, PQ. Acadian]
Thomas (Tom) b. 04/07/52 m. Stella Herring [AMC]
Tom b. 1874 (d) young [AMC]
Thomas (Tom) Daniel b. 1903 d.1991 m. Ella Muise [AMC]
Tom Gerard b. 1951 (d) infant [AMC]
Tom Vincent b. 1908 d. 1985 m. Edna Richard [Sch. 31,Guys. Co. NS.]
Tossi Mae b. 1912 d. 1979 m. Willi Richard [Sch. 31,Guys. Co. NS.]
Tranquille François b. 1825 m. Charlotte Cheverry [Sch. 162, P.E.I.]
Tranquille Auguste b. 1879 [Sch. 162, P.E.I.]
Tranquille b. 1875 [Sch. 717, NB.]
Ulysse m. Stella Leblanc [Sch. 514, NB.]
Urbain b. 1786 d. 1879 m. Josephte L. Rivard, 1809 [Sch. 217 & 218 PQ., Acadian]
Urbain m. Rosalie Beaufort (Brunelle) 1836 [Sch. 217 & 218, PQ., Acadian]
Valentine b. 1897 d. 1976 m. Gertrude Donovan [Sch. 527, NB.]
Velma Leona m1. Bernard MacMillan m2 Billy Bond [Sch. 76, Guys. Co., NS.]
Vénérande b. 1789 d. 1805 m. 1805, François Boucher [Sch. 300,500,600,700 NB.]
Vénérande b. 1816 m. 1833 Dennis Linden [AMC]

Appendices

Vénérande (Vini à Mon) b. 1862 *[Sch. 48, Guys. Co., NS.]*
Verna b. 19/04/47 m. Alcide Gionet *[AMC]*
Verna Jeanette m. George Franklin Bates *[Sch. 162, P.E.I.]*
Véronique b. 1712 d. May, 1768 in France m. Pierre Barillot (Barrieau) 1730 *[162.1&162.6, La; 163& 164 Isle Madame; Sch. 300, 500,600 & 700 NB.]*
Victoire b. 1760 d. 1843 m. Michel Pettipas, 1787 *[Sch. 163, 164 Isle Madame, NS.]*
Victoire b. 1847 *[Sch. 34, Ant. Co., NS.]*
Victoire b. 1881 m. Françoise Jacques Marmand *[Sch. 164. Isle Madame. NS.]*
Victor b. 1748 m1. Etienne Brasseau, 1797 m2. Françoise Archambault *[Sch. 213, PQ. Acadian]*
Victor b. 1846 m1. Melina Auger, 1873 m2. Nathalie Daigle 1890 *[Sch. 218, PQ., Acadian]*
Victor b. 1820 m1. Caroline Houle, 1847, m2. Eleanor Pellitier *[Sch. 217 & 218, PQ., Acadian]*
Victor m. Bonni_____ *[Sch. 514, NB.]*
Victor m. Marguerite Lacoste, 1795 *[Sch. 213, PQ. Acadian]*
Victoria (Tory) b. 1881 m. Joe Millard Boudreau *[Sch. 164. Isle Madame. NS.]*
Vincent b. 1771 d. 1803 m. Anne Maison,1793 *[Sch. 900, France]*
Vincent b. 1796 d. 1800 m. Marie ____ *[Sch. 900, France]*
Vincent b. 1801 d. 1857 m. Marie Raguit, 1828 *[Sch. 900, France]*
Vincent b. 1738 d. 1805 m. Vincente Maison *[Sch. 900, France]*
Vincent m. Mary Howard *[Sch. 724, NB.]*
Violette Régionald Beaulieu *[Sch. 711, NB.]*
Virginia m. Kevin T. Byrne *[Sch. 1 Tracadie, Ant. Co., NS.]*
Virginie b. 1849 d. 1935 m. Thomas Allain 1867 *[Sch. 300, NB.]*
Virginie b. 1856 m. Théophile Caissie, 1882 *[Sch. 315, NB.]*
Vital b. 1814 d. 1891 m. Marguerite Arsenault,1856 *[Sch. 600, NB.]*
Vital b. 1823 m. Marguerite Coste, 1845 *[Sch. 162, P.E.I.]*
Vitaline b. 1845 m. Odilon Daoust, 1866 *[Sch. 2000, and Block N-5 FCMC]*
Vitaline b. 1871 m. Amédée Cormier, 1890 *[Sch. 705, NB.]*
Wally (d) m. Martha Boyd *[Sch. 95, Guys. Co., NS.]*
Walton Lee m. Julie Domingue *[Sch. 162.1, La.]*
Warren, no children *[Sch. 1 Tracadie, Ant. Co., NS.]*
Wilfred b. 1882 m. Rose Bona *[Sch. 163, Isle Madame, NS.]*
Wilfred b. 1890 d. 1953 m. Prudence Coleman *[Sch. 72 &76 Guys. Co., NS.]*
Wilfred b. 1891 d. 1980 m. Theresa Marcel, 1923 *[Sch. 218, PQ., Acadian]*
Wilfred J. *[Sch. 34, Ant. Co., NS.]*
William b. 1868 d. 1868 *[AMC]*
William b.1873 (d) *[AMC]*
William (Squire) b. 1832 d. 1914 m. Anne Lavin *[Sch.0,1,4 & 8, Ant. Co]*
William (twin to Edward) b. 1911 d. 1911*[Sch. 163 & 164. Isle Madame. NS.]*
William A. (J.P.) b. 1847 d. 1942 m. 1868 Sophie Pellerin *[AMC]*
William Augustine b. 1906 d. 1931 *[AMC]*
William b. 1845, not married *[Sch. 1 Tracadie, Ant. Co., NS.]*
William b. 1868 d. 1945 m1. Suzanne Bourque, m2. Marie Bastarache *[Sch. 523, NB.]*
William b. 1911 d. 1985 m. Mary Fougère *[Sch. 162, P.E.I.]*
William b. ca. 1852 *[Sch. # 0 Tracadie, Ant. Co., NS.]*
William b. ca. 1854 d. 1925 m1. Eliz. Poirier m2. Eliz. LeBlanc *[Sch. 163, Isle Madame, NS.]*

William D. (Bill), *author of this book* b. August 6, 1944 m. Audrey Gray 1969, [AMC].
William Desiré b. 1912 [Sch.163,164, Isle Madame NS.]
William Henry II b. 1915 [Sch. 36, Guys. Co., NS.]
William J. Anne Bonvie [Sch. 5, Ant. Co., NS.]
William P. b. 1868 m. Emma Macdonald [Sch. 1 Tracadie, Ant. Co., NS.]
William Luc b. 1889 d. 1891 [Sch. 33, Guys. Co., NS.]
William m1. Pélagie Manet 1874, m2. Charlotte Laura Pettipas, 1887 [Sch. 35& 36, Guys. Co., NS.]
William Major b. 1850 m1. Agnes McKinnon (d) 1874 m2. Cathy Boyle [Sch. 4 & 5, Ant. Co., NS.]
Wilson [Sch. 31,Guys. Co. NS.]
Winifred b. 1892 [Sch. 4, Ant. Co., NS.]
Xavier m1. Margaret Wright m2. Eva M. Scribner [Sch. 1 Tracadie, Ant. Co., NS.]
Yvette b. 1928 [Sch. 420, France]
Yvon [Sch. 500, NB.]
Yvon b, 1947 d. 1947 [Sch. 600, NB.]
Yvon b. 1927 d. 1927 [Sch.315 NB.]
Yvonne b. 1907 d. 1994 [Sch. 315, NB.]
Yvonne m. Edgar St. Pierre [Sch. 724, NB.]
Yvonne Girouard/Green [Sch. 309, NB.]
Yvonne b. 1904 d. 1993 m. Russel Teed [Sch. 514, NB.]
Yvonne m. Edgar St-Pierre [Sch. 724, NB.]
Zoé m. Vincent Meralis, 1875 [Sch. 213, PQ. Acadian]
Zoël b. 1906 d. 1973 m. Marie Girouard à Hilaire [Sch. 737, NB.]
Zoël b. 1910 d. 1986,n.m [Sch. 500, NB.]